AF576604

Praise for *Under Beijing's Shadow*

"... Hiebert has done a great deal of research for this book that widens, deepens and updates his already extensive knowledge of China's activities in Southeast Asia. The book is essential reading for anyone who wants to understand the successes and shortcomings of China's attempt to dominate its neighborhood to the south."

—Dennis Blair, former U.S. Director of National Intelligence and former Commander of U.S. Forces in the Pacific

"... [This book] provide(s) valuable insight into the balancing acts by regional governments seeking both benefits and protection from their powerful northern neighbor. [It] is an indispensable and enlightening read for anyone who seeks to understand this important region at a moment when major powers are increasingly vying for influence and access."

—Danny Russel, former U.S. Assistant Secretary of State for East Asia and the Pacific

"This book is an extensive take on the geopolitical milieu of Southeast Asia in the face of China's aggressive expansion. It is an engaging take on the existing balance of power in Southeast Asia and is an essential read for those who want to dive deeper into the region's political narrative."

—Albert del Rosario, former Philippine Secretary of Foreign Affairs

"This fine book illuminates the ... challenges facing Southeast Asia, as China's bilateral preferences increasingly influence each nation's domestic and foreign policies, undermining a concerted regional response, and United States positioning inspires little long-term confidence. The most economically dynamic part of the world hangs in the balance."

—Charlene Barshevsky, former U.S. Trade Representative

"A significant and valuable work on a complex subject matter with resonance far beyond the region. Illuminating."

—*Marty Natalegawa, former Indonesian Foreign Minister*

". . . (A) fascinating analysis of how differences in history, religion, economics, and geographic proximity to China have shaped the diverse views that the 10 nations comprising [Southeast Asia] have of China today. . . . [It] is an invaluable roadmap for policy makers and business leader to understand . . . the opportunities and risks that confront the region."

—*Carla Hills, former U.S. Trade Representative*

Under Beijing's Shadow

Southeast Asia's China Challenge

Murray Hiebert

CSIS | CENTER FOR STRATEGIC & INTERNATIONAL STUDIES

ROWMAN & LITTLEFIELD
Lanham • Boulder • New York • London

Center for Strategic & International Studies
1616 Rhode Island Avenue, NW
Washington, DC 20036
202-887-0200 | www.csis.org

Published by Rowman & Littlefield
An imprint of The Rowman & Littlefield Publishing Group, Inc.
4501 Forbes Boulevard, Lanham, MD 20706
www.rowman.com

6 Tinworth Street, London SE11 5AL, United Kingdom

ISBN 978-1-4422-8138-7 (hb)
ISBN 978-1-4422-8140-0 (electronic)

For Nik, Sam, Logan, and Sophie

Contents

LIST OF MAPS

ACKNOWLEDGMENTS

This book would not have been possible without the insights of hundreds of officials, diplomats, think tankers, country experts, businesspersons, economists, journalists, and civil society leaders from Southeast Asia, China, and the United States. Many of them did not want to be acknowledged publicly, but without their insights this book would not have been possible.

In alphabetical order, I would like to recognize especially Craig Allen, Ian Baird, Keith Barney, Jay Batongbacal, Aileen Baviera, Endy Bayuni, Dan Biers, John Blaxland, Thomas Bouchillon, Ernie Bower, Jake Brunner, Mary Callahan, Alvin Camba, Chang Tech Peng, Pramit Pal Chaudhuri, Vannarith Cheang, Ian Chong, Aaron Connelly, Malcolm Cook, Shawn Crispin, Yose Rizal Damuri, Andrew Davenport, Rene de Castro, Le Dang Doanh, Ben Dolven, Sophal Ear, Brian Eyler, Bill Flens, Kim Gehab, Bonnie Glaser, Matt Goodman, Denis Gray, Thao Griffiths, Brian Harding, Paul Heer, Johanes Herlijanto, Richard Heydarian, Jon Hillman, Kavi Chongkittavorn, Ken Jimbo, Bilahari Kausikan, Tom Kean, Judy Ko, Kei Koga, Cheng-Chwee Kuik, Peter Lavoy, Collin Koh, Bertil Lintner, Joseph Liow, Shahriman Lockman, Evan Locksmana, Rupert Paul Manhit, Victor Andres Manhit, John McBeth, Evan Medeiros, Derek Mitchell, Mike Montesano, Shafiah Muhibat, Joe Narus, Marty Natalegawa, Ng Shui Meng, Ngeow Chow Bing, Elina Noor, Aparna Pande, Panitan Wattanayagorn, Tom Parks, Greg Poling, Serge Pun, Doug Ramage, Greg Raymond, Amy Searight, David Shear, Machut Shishak, Jatswan Singh, Pou Sothirak, David Steinberg, Ian Storey, Tran Viet Thai, Pham Sy Thanh, Nguyen Huu Thien, Christine Susanna Tijhin, Le Tinh, Thitinan Pongsudhirak, Ngugen Trung Truc, Sean Turnell, Dan Twining, David Van, Alex Vuving, Barbara Weisel, Colin Willette, Yun Sun, Min Zaw Oo, and Min Zin.

Some of these friends and colleagues read my draft chapters and helped me improve the accuracy and analysis of the book—and, to be sure, saved me from some embarrassing mistakes.

Some of my colleagues and interns from the Southeast Asia Program at the Center for Strategic and International Studies (CSIS) helped with researching specific issues, formatting footnotes, and organizing meeting in the region. These included Adrian Chorn, Ben Contreras, Alden Hartopo, Shannon Hayden, Vu Minh, Andreyka Natalegawa, Vu Minh, Monica Sato, and Natalie Tantisirirat,

I thank Jon Sisk and his colleagues at Roman & Littlefield and Rebecka Shirazi and Jeeah Lee at CSIS for their talents in facilitating the publication process. Thanks to Emily Tiemeyer for her skill in designing maps that depict locations in individual Southeast Asian countries where China is involved and the dispute between China and some of its neighbors in the South China Sea. I thank Kate Gibson at Westchester Publishing Services and Karen Brogno for their admirable editing of my manuscript.

A special thanks to Amy Searight and Mike Green of CSIS for nudging me to write this book. I am appreciative to Ernie Bower for bringing me to the Southeast Asia Program at CSIS in the first place.

I am grateful to the Smith Richardson Foundation, and especially Allan Song, for the grant to support my travel, research, and writing of this book.

This book is the product of several decades of watching and researching developments in Southeast Asia. I am forever grateful to the editors of the *Far Eastern Economic Review* and the *Wall Street Journal* who sent me to work in Thailand, Vietnam, Malaysia, Singapore, and China, where I deepened my understanding of the region. They include Philip Bowring, John Bussey, Nayan Chanda, Gordon Crovitz, David Plott, and Michael Vatikiotis.

I am grateful to my family, especially my wife Linda for her patience, support, and inspiration while I researched and wrote this book.

In the end, I alone am responsible for the contents of this book and, despite the valiant help of many, the remaining errors are mine.

Murray Hiebert
Washington, DC
September 2019

INTRODUCTION

It was shortly after dawn one morning in May 1979 when my rattling Soviet-made black Volga passed through the mist-covered mountains of northern Vietnam and descended into Lang Son, near the border with China. A key bridge south of the town had collapsed and lay buckled on its side as a makeshift bamboo raft ferried people across the river. The ruins of the former brick hospital could be recognized by a few twisted bed frames and a toppled autoclave. Piles of rubble were all that was left of a power plant, the railway station, and an ancient pagoda. A handful of merchants were selling a few bundles of green leafy vegetables and small pieces of fatty pork on the buckled cement floor of what once had been the market.

The destruction inflicted on Lang Son had not come from American bombers backing the former South Vietnamese government that had collapsed four years earlier. Nor had it occurred decades earlier when French colonial forces were driven out of Vietnam in 1954. Lang Son was devastated by tens of thousands of Chinese troops invading across the rugged, tree-covered hills and narrow passes of the China-Vietnam border in February 1979. They came to punish Vietnam for toppling the Khmer Rouge regime in neighboring Cambodia a month earlier.

Lang Son residents who were slowly drifting back from temporary camps along the highway south of town said the attack began with a fierce artillery bombardment from the hills above the town, followed by a several day lull in fighting and then waves of Chinese troops sweeping in on roads from the north, east, and south. The combat was fierce for several days before Chinese soldiers overwhelmed the Vietnamese troops defending Lang Son on March 5. Thousands of Vietnamese civilians and soldiers on both sides had died.

People in Lang Son said they were expecting China to inflict another installment in fighting when the rains ended in a few months.

But Beijing declared that it had achieved its military goals—even though Vietnamese troops remained in Cambodia another decade—and began withdrawing its troops. Most of the destruction in Lang Son occurred when the retreating troops used explosives to blow up the main bridge into town, government offices, and schools as they left town. The crops on the terraced hills surrounding the town had been burned.

The 1979 attack was not China's first invasion of its smaller neighbor. Vietnamese often say it was the seventeenth or eighteenth attack in their over 2,000-year history. But it was the first time that China attacked Vietnam when both countries were ruled by fellow Communist parties. Beijing had helped Vietnamese revolutionaries first in their battle to expel the French colonial power and then to topple the U.S.-backed regime in southern Vietnam.

The withdrawal of the United States from Vietnam in 1975 set up a new dynamic in the relations between China and the countries of mainland Southeast Asia. *Brother Enemy* encapsulates the concept of rapidly crumbling alliances between former comrades that swept across the region and is the title of the extraordinary book by my former colleague Nayan Chanda, who chronicles the geopolitical twists and turns.[1]

As one of the earliest foreigners to witness the destruction of Lang Son after the Chinese withdrawal, I wrote my maiden news story for the now-defunct *Far Eastern Economic Review*, a Dow Jones newsweekly published in Hong Kong.[2] I had worked in southern Vietnam as an aid worker with a private relief agency in the closing days of the war and was there when China seized the Paracel Islands in the northern part of the South China Sea from the South Vietnamese government in 1974.

It was clear early on that Vietnam's invasion of Cambodia and China's attack on Vietnam marked a decisive tipping point in regional affairs. China's pedagogical incursion into Vietnam came some months after China's paramount leader Deng Xiaoping had launched economic reforms that ushered in the country's stunning economic growth. It came six weeks after China and the United States had normalized diplomatic ties and two weeks after Deng had visited Washington.

---

1. Nayan Chanda, *Brother Enemy: The War after the War, A History of Indochina since the Fall of Saigon* (New York: Harcourt Brace Jovanovich, 1986).
2. Murray Hiebert, "Waiting in the Ruins for the Next Installment," *Far Eastern Economic Review*, June 15, 1979, 12–13.

Hanoi's invasion of Cambodia created anxiety in Thailand about a Vietnamese military juggernaut rolling across the region. A week after Vietnam toppled Cambodia's Pol Pot regime, two senior Chinese officials flew secretly to a Thai air base and offered the prime minister millions of dollars of aid to help the Thai military rebuild and arm the Khmer Rouge and non-communist resistance forces to disrupt Vietnam's occupation of Cambodia. Beijing capitalized on this opportunity to build trust in several Southeast Asia's non-communist countries in which China had been or still was supporting local communist opposition to the government.

I began working for the *Far Eastern Economic Review* in 1986 to cover Vietnam. That year a critical Communist Party congress decided to abandon hard-line socialist economic policies which were faltering in the face of Chinese and American sanctions. I reported on China's attack on Johnson South Reef in the South China Sea in 1988, during which 64 unarmed Vietnamese sailors were gunned down by the Chinese Navy. With that attack, Beijing signaled that it intended to become more assertive in staking its claims in the disputed South China Sea.

I accompanied about a half dozen ragtag Vietnamese troop withdrawals from Cambodia in the late 1980s as Hanoi realized it could not escape sanctions and normalize relations with the United States and China until Vietnam abandoned its ambitions in Cambodia. Although Chinese troops mostly withdrew from northern Vietnam in 1979, border skirmishes and shelling continued until 1991, when the Vietnamese Communist Party chief led a delegation to make peace with his counterpart in Chengdu in southern China.

One of the casualties of Vietnam's effort to sue for peace was Beijing's pressure on the Vietnamese party to oust politburo member and foreign minister Nguyen Co Thach, who was one of Hanoi's most vocal critics of Beijing. He was also the first senior Vietnamese official to press hard to normalize relations with Washington as a hedge against China.

Vietnamese and Chinese leaders soon visited each other's capitals and life normalized along the border. Returning to Lang Son, then as a journalist based in Hanoi, I witnessed lines of porters wending their way down mountain trails on both sides of the border, nearly buckling under the weight of bags of everything from dried fish and squealing pigs to porcelain toilets and small water pumps. For the first time since the fighting, the people of Lang Son began investing in bricks and mortar to build new houses.

People in Lang Son constructed several carefully manicured "martyr" cemeteries to formally bury fighters who died in the battle against China. Families say they can burn incense at the graves of those who died, but four decades later they still are not allowed to organize public commemorative events lest China take offense.

Memories of past battles continue to influence the thinking of Vietnamese people about China. When the Vietnamese government in 2018 sought to pass legislation to establish special economic zones to entice foreign investors, protests erupted across the county as people became convinced that their leaders were going to sell Vietnamese assets to China. Vietnam must constantly calculate how far it can go in pushing back against China and when it must back off to avoid Beijing's wrath and still maintain beneficial economic ties.

My interest in China's interactions with Southeast Asia began in Lang Son but deepened as I worked as a journalist in the region for nearly two decades, living in Vietnam, Laos, Thailand, Malaysia, Singapore, and briefly in China. Beijing's shadow over Southeast Asia has loomed increasingly large since 1949 and even more so since China sparked an economic miracle that helped to propel growth in the countries to its south.

This book attempts to provide a snapshot of how Southeast Asia experiences and perceives China today. Because each country's history with and proximity to China is different, many of the stories and experiences are dissimilar from each other. The focus of this book is on how Southeast Asians view and respond to China, although it also tries to pay attention to Beijing interests in and thinking about its southern neighbors.

As a region, Southeast Asia is determined never to let itself be dominated by China. With nine of the region's 10 countries having been colonized until after World War II, they are resolved to avoid again falling under the sway of a large external power. None of them have forgotten that China supported communist insurgents in their countries until the late 1970s, although revolutionaries in Vietnam, Cambodia, and Laos mostly welcomed that support at the time.

The countries of Myanmar, Cambodia, and Thailand have swung closer to China when they have faced American isolation and sanctions for human rights abuses or when their militaries toppled an elected government. And the Philippines pivoted toward Beijing when its leader was looking for capital to upgrade the country's long-neglected infrastructure and to exhibit his historical resentment toward the United States.

The "China model," under which an authoritarian state apparatus is backed by a controlled market economy, has some attraction for the Communist Party in Vietnam and perhaps for Thailand when it has fallen under military rule. Yet, Vietnam's millennia of history living under China's shadow has turned its population fiercely anti-Beijing, and the independent-minded Thais are determined to avoid falling under China's grip.

Beijing can sometimes use its buckets of cash and growing military might to get its southern neighbors to do what they do not necessarily want to do. It has rewarded Cambodia with aid for blocking the Association of Southeast Asian Nations (ASEAN) from issuing statements condemning Beijing for its aggressive actions in the South China Sea. China has been able to use its naval clout to threaten Vietnam and force it to abandon oil and gas exploration off its southern coast and the Philippines to drop plans to exploit desperately needed gas resources on Reed Bank.

All countries in Southeast Asia view China with some mixture of expectation and fear, aspiration and frustration. China has pulled up each nation's economy with its stunning growth. Each country hopes that economic growth continues through China's signature infrastructure-building scheme, the Belt and Road Initiative (BRI). Thailand, Malaysia, Singapore, and more recently Vietnam have profited enormously by being drawn into the electronics supply chain that runs through China (something the U.S. administration of Donald Trump seems determined to disrupt). Ethnic Chinese companies from Thailand, Malaysia, Singapore, and the Philippines played big roles as early foreign investors in helping China build its economic juggernaut.

At the same time, Southeast Asian countries are anxious about how China—whose population, land mass, economy, and military strength are multiples larger than the total of all Southeast Asian countries combined—will use its growing heft. They are concerned that Beijing's infrastructure projects in their countries are often too big, too costly, may never be able to pay for themselves, and are geared toward benefiting China most.

Beijing's increasing militarization of the South China Sea has neighbors like Vietnam, the Philippines, Malaysia, Singapore, and Indonesia worried about Beijing's long-term ambitions. Some countries along the Mekong River are anxious that the dams China is building at home and in Laos and Cambodia will give China increasing access and political weight along the river and have huge long-term environmental costs downstream.

China is stepping up military cooperation with its neighbors, including through low-level joint exercises, but much of the engagement is little more than set-piece dialogues and still lags far behind that of the United States. Young people in Southeast Asia appreciate the scholarships they get to study in China, even if many wish they were going to the United States or other Western countries instead.

China's southern neighbors welcome the income generated by the recent deluge of Chinese tourists but are worried the onslaught will destroy fragile ancient temples like Angkor Wat, devastate the pristine beaches of southern Thailand, and turn the resort town of Sihanoukville into one colossal Chinese casino. The rush of seemingly spontaneous Chinese migrants into the northern areas of Myanmar and Laos and parts of Manila, Bangkok, Vientiane, and Phnom Penh could have long-term implications for the demographics and cultural makeup of these countries.

All Southeast Asian nations hope to benefit from China's BRI to help them build railroads, ports, and power stations. But it is stunning how challenging it has been for Beijing to use its growing economic muscle to get these projects off the ground. Even the poorest and weakest countries have been negotiating for years to shrink down China's outsized ambitions, reduce the costs, and keep the numbers of Chinese workers in check.

Because China snares so many of the region's headlines, it is easy to exaggerate Beijing's influence in the region. As China expert David Shambaugh has observed, "Beijing is quite capable of overplaying its hand, becoming too demanding and even dictatorial toward Southeast Asian states," behavior that could "contribute to a distancing of Southeast Asian states from China in the future," even if they are geographically located right next door.[3]

To varying degrees, each nation looks to the United States as a hedge against China, but most fear Washington's attention span is too short, its focus too distracted, and its resources too limited to be very reliable, outside perhaps of the Pentagon. Southeast Asian countries are hell-bent on avoiding having to choose between Beijing and Washington, but their uncertainties about the United States impact their longer-term strategic

3. David Shambaugh, "U.S.-China Rivalry in Southeast Asia: Power Shift or Competitive Coexistence?," *International Security* 42, no. 4 (Spring 2018): 99.

calculations. These doubts drive these countries to work overtime to boost the influence of their ASEAN grouping and bolster their ties with Japan, India, South Korea, Australia, and the European Union to at least partially balance China.

The 10 countries have important differences between themselves on how they respond to China and varying levels of trust and confidence in each other in mounting joint responses to Beijing. Key dynamics that impact individual countries' relations with Beijing include their physical proximity to China, their economic and geographic size, their history, their government type, and their relations with other countries such as the United States.[4] Internationally sanctioned or shunned states like Cambodia and Myanmar seem more inclined to become client or near-client states of China.

This book explores the diverse experiences that the countries of Southeast Asia have with China and how this impacts their perceptions of Beijing's actions and goals in the political, economic, military, and "soft power" spheres. For convenience, this book divides Southeast Asian countries into three main clusters of nations with subgroupings.

The first grouping is China's near abroad, including Myanmar, Cambodia, and Laos. It could be assumed that these countries are more likely to support Beijing's policies because they benefit more from Chinese economic "carrots," including projects on infrastructure and connectivity. They have less confidence in their ability to resist China because of their size, proximity, weak economies, and limited outside support. They also have no stake in the disputes in the South China Sea, which gives them less incentive than some of their neighbors to cooperate with United States on strategic challenges.

Cambodia under Prime Minister Hun Sen is without a doubt the most beholden to and aligned with China. Phnom Penh is the closest thing to a Chinese client state and a "Beijing bandwagoner" in Southeast Asia.

Landlocked Laos often seems to have "frustrated dependence" on Beijing. As one of the region's poorest countries, Laos has few options but to rely on Chinese aid and investment to develop its economy. Laos can

4. Joshua Eisenman and Eric Heginbotham, "China and the Developing World," in *China Steps Out: Beijing's Major Power Engagement with the Developing World*, ed. Joshua Eisenman and Eric Heginbotham (New York: Routledge, 2018), 17.

balance its relations somewhat through its close and long-standing political ties with Vietnam.

Myanmar has a "bristling dependence" on China and its population demonstrates considerable anti-China sentiment, but the weaknesses of and divisions within the government seem regularly to propel the country closer to Beijing. Myanmar sought to hedge by moving nearer to the United States when it launched political reforms in 2011. But in the wake of the military's crackdown against the Muslim Rohingya minority in 2017 and the ensuing isolation by the West, the country's leaders are again looking to China for political and economic support and infrastructure development. But they insist on projects they want, not necessarily the ones Beijing is trying to press on them.

The second grouping includes the two largest countries on mainland Southeast Asia: Vietnam and Thailand. Thailand might be called a "partial hedger" or "soft balancer" and Vietnam a "hard balancer." These characteristics make them interesting case studies for their ability to woo Beijing as a balance against the United States, when Washington overturns long-standing strategic alignments to punish the military for toppling an elected government (Thailand), or to court the United States when China's rising military capability pushes the country into seemingly costly strategic competition (Vietnam).

Vietnam butts onto southern China but has walked a fine line between Beijing and Washington for the past quarter century to retain its independence. Hanoi tilted toward the United States as China ramped up its aggressive behavior in the South China Sea around 2009, but Vietnam has worked religiously to maintain correct relations with Beijing since before Trump became the U.S. president.

China is Vietnam's largest import market, while the United States buys the largest share of its exports. Fearing overdependence, Hanoi has been very reluctant to accept Chinese infrastructure projects. Massive anti-China protests that erupted in Vietnam in 2014 and 2018 demonstrated that for Hanoi, the Beijing challenge is a nettlesome domestic political issue. Hanoi is determined not to side either with China, because it is right next door, or the United States, because it considers Washington not to be reliable.

Thailand, although a U.S. treaty ally, long tried to have strong ties with both major powers, but after Washington condemned the military's 2014 ouster of a democratically elected government Bangkok shifted closer to

Beijing. Thailand seemed to rebalance its relations with China and the United States after Trump invited junta leader Prayuth Chan-ocha to Washington in 2017. Thailand has purchased some military equipment, including three submarines, from China. Although economically close to Beijing, Bangkok has been very reluctant to accept Chinese loans for building a high-speed rail link.

The third grouping consists of China's maritime periphery, including the Philippines, Indonesia, Malaysia, Singapore, and Brunei. These countries, at least in principle, have more space for balancing Beijing's influence than nations bordering China. They need to take China's policies into account but are not as impacted by them because they are further away.

The Philippines today, of course, may be an exception and might be considered somewhat schizophrenic toward Beijing and Washington. As a formal U.S. ally, it stood up to China in 2012 after its seizure of Scarborough Shoal in the South China Sea and paid dearly when Beijing punished Manila by curtailing trade links. After Rodrigo Duterte became president in 2016, he "bandwagoned" hard toward China, but he still gets irritated by Beijing's aggressive actions around Philippine features in the disputed sea.

Duterte allows his armed forces to continue much of their traditional cooperation with the U.S. military, and the Philippine army looked to Washington for support after fighters aligned to the Islamic State seized the southern city of Marawi in 2017. The armed forces might be considered a "soft balancer" toward the two major powers. China is moving surprisingly slowly to implement the billions of dollars in project agreements it signed with Duterte in 2016, perhaps thwarted by the Philippine bureaucracy but also raising questions about whether Beijing doubts that Manila's pivot toward Beijing will outlast the current president.

Malaysia might be a "partial hedger" or "soft balancer." It has long had close economic ties with Beijing and strong security links with Washington. Prime Minister Najib Razak moved closer to the United States under President Barack Obama's rebalance to Asia, but he drifted back toward China when he needed an enormous infusion of funds to bail out his troubled state investment fund, 1 Malaysia Development Berhad (1MDB).

Massive corruption linked to 1MDB and Najib's agreement to accept grossly overpriced Chinese infrastructure projects prompted Malaysian voters to oust Najib in the 2018 elections. Incoming Prime Minister

Mahathir Mohamad immediately postponed several expensive Chinese infrastructure projects and warned China against practicing a "new form of colonialism." But in early 2019 Mahathir decided to resume work on a giant rail project after China agreed to sharply slash its original inflated price. Still Mahathir has not warmed to Washington since he returned to office.

Singapore, like Vietnam, is a "hard balancer." It has worked to hedge between the two major powers but has faced the ire of Beijing for calling out China, according to international maritime laws, in its actions in the South China Sea and allowing the American military to use bases in Singapore. As the only majority ethnic Chinese nation in Southeast Asia, Singapore comes under tremendous pressure to align its interests with those of Beijing. Singapore plays a key role in China's infrastructure projects in Southeast Asia by structuring and financing some of them through Singapore's highly developed financial institutions.

Singapore's Prime Minister Lee Hsien Loong has been outspoken in calling on the United States and China to resolve their trade dispute to avoid plunging the regional economy into a critical downturn. Lee has urged the two major powers to reconcile their differences to avoid "a more divided and troubled world" for decades to come.

Brunei has long been the quietest of the South China Sea claimants, but in recent years has tilted increasingly to Beijing for investment as the sultanate prepares for a sharp reduction in its hydrocarbon output. The tiny nation might be viewed as "bandwagoning" to China but still maintaining a very "soft balance" with Washington.

The most "fiercely independent" stance in Southeast Asia is demonstrated by Indonesia, the region's most populous country. Indonesia is not in either Beijing's or Washington's camp. Although Jakarta has good relations and cooperates with both China and the United States, it also holds both at arm's length. Indonesia has enough strategic heft to do this because it a Group of 20 (G20) member that controls almost half of Southeast Asia's economy.

The ghosts of history dating back to China's alleged role in the 1965 coup prompt many Indonesians to remain suspicious of Beijing. There is also popular suspicion that Chinese infrastructure projects will bring a flood of Chinese migrants. Despite these concerns, President Joko Widodo is looking to China for help in overcoming the giant infrastructure gap hobbling Southeast Asia's largest economy.

To be sure, these categories are fluid, often in flux, and depend to a considerable extent on domestic politics and how these countries are treated and courted by China and the United States at any given time.

A number of first-rate studies of China's relations with Southeast Asia have been published over the years, from Joshua Kurlantzick's *Charm Offensive: How China's Soft Power Is Transforming the World* (2007) to Ian Storey's *Southeast Asia and the Rise of China: The Search for Security* (2011) and Evelyn Goh's *Rising China's Influence in Developing Asia* (2016). China scholar David Shambaugh has written quite a bit about China's relations with its neighbors, particularly in *China Goes Global: The Partial Power* (2013), but his focus is largely through the lens of Beijing rather than Southeast Asia.

But these books focus their coverage on before Xi Jinping took power in 2013 and China became more activist and assertive in its dealings with its neighbors. Some analysts attribute China's more forceful policies pushing south to the rise of Xi, while others see it as more normal evolution in response to China's growing economic and military heft.

This book is a snapshot of China's relations with Southeast Asia in late 2019 to early 2020. Its strength is that it reflects how China is using a policy mix of economic and military pressure to challenge the Western-led global order, starting with its immediate neighbors to the south. This book reports on the impact of China's ambitious BRI, as the country seeks to invest billions of dollars in infrastructure projects across the region, and explores how China is using its new military might to aggressively press Beijing's claims in the South China Sea and its capital and engineers to push its influence down the Mekong River—and how this action is perceived in individual countries.

The first chapter gives a broad overview of what Beijing is up to and how China's southern neighbors view Beijing's largesse with a sense of hope and anticipation, even as China's economic assertiveness and its forceful actions in the South China Sea and along the Mekong create anxiety and even some trepidation among its neighbors.

The chapters that follow explore China's tool kit for pressing its influence in each of the individual countries: the economic ties in the form of trade, investment, the BRI, development aid, and tourism; its political and defense relations, including military sales and exercises; and its cultural and people-to-people ties, such as Confucius Institutes and scholarships for students. The function of history in shaping relations today and the role played by ethnic Chinese are also explored.

The chapters begin with Myanmar on the mainland and move through the maritime nations of Indonesia and the Philippines.

The final chapter explores how the countries of the region are seeking to hedge against China by deepening ties with a variety of players, ranging from the United States to regional nations including Japan, India, and Australia. It ends with some thoughts on what these countries and their opinion shapers would like to see from Washington.

Much of this book relies on interviews conducted between September 2017 and June 2019 with senior government officials, foreign policy experts, businesspersons, economists, journalists, educators, and civil society representatives in each of the countries represented here. In addition, this book also relies on a review of recent press reporting and scholarly articles, which are footnoted when cited.

1. CHINA'S MARCH SOUTH GREETED BY HOPE AND ANXIETY

> When trade routes open up
> that's when the sharing starts
> Resources changing hands
> and shipping auto parts.
> Ideas start to flow
> and friendships start to form.
> Then things impossible
> all become the norm.
> The future's starting now
> the Belt and Road is how.[1]
>
> —*Chinese music video performed by children touting the Belt and Road*

Eight snapshots capture the complex cocktail of hope and anxiety prompted by China's rise among the smaller neighbors along its southern frontier. These glimpses also highlight the patchwork of expectations and pitfalls Beijing faces in dealing with the eclectic nations of Southeast Asia.

In Malaysia, China's full-court press to boast engagement in Southeast Asia has already claimed its first casualty: former prime minister Najib Razak. He was toppled in elections in 2018 because of mounting frustration with his multibillion-dollar scandal at a state investment fund and the fact that he was saddling the country with massive debts through

1. "Xi Jinping: Last Week Tonight with John Oliver," HBO, 7:30, June 17, 2018, https://www.youtube.com/watch?reload=9&v=OubM8bD9kck. This excerpt from an English language music video, produced by China to tout the Belt and Road Initiative and sung (and rapped) by children, begins 7 minutes 30 seconds into the program.

highly inflated Chinese infrastructure contracts from which he and his allies were benefiting.

The new prime minister, Mahathir Mohamad, said after taking office that he wanted to cancel or renegotiate the "unfair" $15.7 billion high-speed rail project Najib had negotiated with China to avoid Malaysia becoming a "bankrupt country."[2] On his first visit to Beijing, Mahathir, who had previously served as prime minister for 22 years, warned against a "new version of colonialism."[3]

Eleven months later Mahathir agreed to resume the project after China slashed the cost by a third and the 94-year-old leader was invited to give a keynote address at China's second conference on its signature Belt and Road Initiative (BRI).[4]

Further east, in the Philippines, President Rodrigo Duterte faces the opposite problem: getting China to start implementing projects. Three years after Duterte visited Beijing in late 2016, pledged not to press China on its claims in their South China Sea dispute, and signed $24 billion in agreements for help on infrastructure projects, almost none of these pledges have been implemented. By late 2019, only three small schemes worth less than $200 million had been started.[5]

Despite Duterte's efforts to make nice with Beijing and reconsider Manila's longtime links with the United States, China continues to block Manila's efforts to develop a gas field at Reed Bank, some 75 nautical miles off the coast of the Philippines's Palawan Island. Instead, China presses to negotiate an agreement under which the two countries would share development of the gas field, a move that legal experts fear could legitimize Beijing's claims to vast swaths of the South China Sea.

---

2. "Malaysia's Mahathir Cancels China-Backed Rail, Pipeline Projects," *Reuters*, August 21, 2018, https://www.reuters.com/article/us-china-malaysia/malaysias-mahathir-cancels-china-backed-rail-pipeline-projects-idUSKCN1L60DQ.
3. Lucy Hornby, "Mahathir Mohamad Warns against 'New Colonialism' during China Visit," *Financial Times*, August 20, 2018, https://www.ft.com/content/7566599e-a443-11e8-8ecf-a7ae1beff35b.
4. Anisah Shukry, "China, Malaysia to Resume East Coast Rail for $11 Billion," *Bloomberg*, April 12, 2019, https://www.bloomberg.com/news/articles/2019-04-12/china-agrees-to-resume-malaysian-east-coast-rail-for-11-billion.
5. Karen Lema and Martin Perry, "Two Years after Philippines' Pivot, Duterte Still Waiting on China Dividend," *Reuters*, November 18, 2018, https://www.reuters.com/article/us-philippines-china-analysis/two-years-after-philippines-pivot-duterte-still-waiting-on-china-dividend-idUSKCN1NN0UO.

Map 1. Overview map

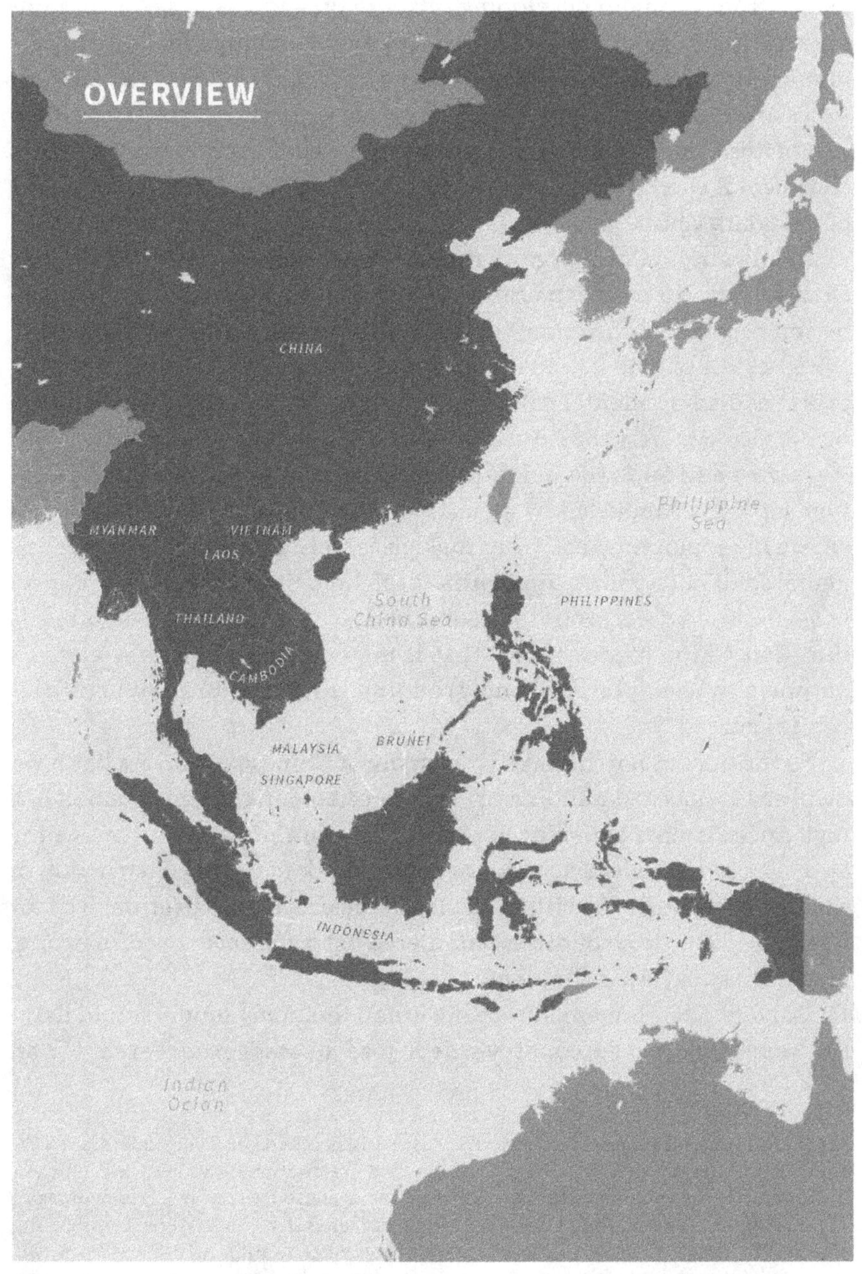

To the southwest, energy-hungry Vietnam has faced similar challenges from China in developing offshore oil and gas projects. In mid-June 2019, a large Chinese Coast Guard vessel accompanied by a gaggle of maritime militia boats showed up near Vanguard Bank, 190 nautical miles off the coast of southern Vietnam, where a rig contracted by Rosneft of Russia was drilling a new production well. The area is on Vietnam's continental shelf but within China's nine-dash-line claim to four-fifths of the South China Sea.

In July 2019, a Chinese government-owned survey vessel, the *Haiyang Dizhi* 8, began its own exploration activities nearby. Vietnam responded by sending law-enforcement ships to shadow the Chinese survey ship. With vessels of both countries operating near each other, analysts were concerned an accidental collision could prompt an escalation.[6] Finally, in late October after the Rosneft rig left, the Chinese vessels pulled out.[7]

In 2017 and 2018, Hanoi had abruptly suspended oil and gas exploration activities conducted by Spanish oil firm Repsol nearby. The blocks where the exploration activities took place were also on Vietnam's continental shelf but within China's nine-dash line. Neither Hanoi nor Repsol have disclosed the reasons for their withdrawal, but Vietnamese officials hint that China made it clear that it might attack some of Vietnam's outposts in the Spratly Island grouping if the exploration activities continued.

To the west in northern Laos, an army of Chinese engineers has been drilling tunnels and building bridges since 2016 in the construction of a high-speed train that Beijing hopes will link Kunming in southern China with Thailand, Malaysia, and Singapore. Work to begin construction of the 260-mile, nearly $6 billion Lao leg of the project had been delayed for five years as the two countries hammered out differences over financing, land rights, and other concerns.

Lao officials were anxious that China's financing model would drive the small landlocked country's debt load to staggering levels for an

---

6. Asia Maritime Transparency Initiative, "China Risks Flare-Up over Malaysian, Vietnamese Gas Resources," Center for Strategic and International Studies, July 16, 2019, https://amti.csis.org/china-risks-flare-up-over-malaysian-vietnamese-gas-resources/.

7. Niharika Mandhana, "Vietnam Told China to Get Out of Its Waters: Beijing's Response: No You Get Out," *Wall Street Journal*, November 1, 2019, https://www.wsj.com/articles/vietnam-told-china-to-get-out-of-its-waters-beijings-response-no-you-get-out-11572625722.

economy with an annual economic output less than three times the estimated cost of the railroad. More recently, Laos has learned that neighboring Thailand to the south has no plans to join the high-speed train any time soon, further challenging the economic viability of the relatively short leg from Kunming to Vientiane.

After Thai generals toppled the elected government in Bangkok in 2014, the junta looked to China for diplomatic cover as the United States condemned the coup and introduced a few sanctions. The military rulers exchanged delegations with Beijing, signed deals for rice and three Chinese submarines, and inked a memorandum to build a high-speed train that would connect Laos to Malaysia along the route from Kunming to Singapore.

But talks with China for the high-speed train have languished for years over how much interest Thailand would have to pay for loans to build the railway. China wanted to supply Chinese equipment and bring in Chinese engineers and workers. Thailand insisted on more options for procuring equipment and demanded a greater role for its own engineers. In the end, the Thais agreed to a short joint pilot project with China but decided to spend their own funds to upgrade an existing railroad rather than invest in the costly Chinese high-speed link.

An El Nino–created drought along the Mekong River in 2019 was a harbinger of possible environmental challenges to come. The severe drought caused water levels in the Mekong to drop to their lowest level in at least a decade, creating devastating problems for rice farmers along the river and for the fish population in Laos, Thailand, Cambodia, and southern Vietnam. The critical monsoon rains, which normally start in late May, were delayed by two months.

The impact of the drought was exacerbated when some of the 11 hydropower dams on the upper reaches of the Mekong inside China and a new dam opened in Laos in late 2019 held back water for their own needs. The lack of water caused farmers to delay planting rice, threatening the food supplies of millions. With less water in the river, the fish reproduction cycle was disrupted because it is the rising water levels that prompt fish to spawn and send out their young.[8]

8. Stefan Lovgren, "Mekong River at Its Lowest in 100 Years, Threatening Food Supply," *National Geographic*, July 31, 2019, https://www.nationalgeographic.com/environment/2019/07/mekong-river-lowest-levels-100-years-food-shortages/.

To the northwest in Mandalay, Myanmar's former royal capital, an influx of Chinese migrants is transforming the city, about 185 miles from the China's Yunnan Province. The wave of migrants is following Chinese enterprises as they expand abroad and Chinese engineers as they come to build infrastructure to connect Southeast Asian countries to China. Some of the Chinese migrants create irritation and exasperation with their assertiveness, cultural condescension, and limited concern about the environment.

In the heart of Mandalay, Chinese merchants are buying swathes of land and shophouses, prompting complaints that locals are being driven out of the city center where it is easier to make a living. One popular song, "The Death of Mandalay," mourns that "The city where I was born is no longer there/Who are these people in the city?"[9] Chinese migrants are causing similar transformations in Vientiane and the northern provinces of Laos, the seaside resort of Sihanoukville in Cambodia, and sections of Bangkok and Manila.

To the south in the beach town of Sihanoukville along Cambodia's coast, over 100 Chinese casinos have sprung into action over the past three years to cater to a flood of Chinese tourists arriving each week. Cambodians complain that they no longer feel at home in their hometown.

In a letter to his bosses in the Ministry of Interior in 2018, the Sihanoukville governor described dissatisfaction among Cambodians displaced by Chinese construction projects and whose shops are languishing in the face of competition from Chinese stores bearing only Chinese signs. "Some foreigners do not respect the traffic laws; they drink alcohol, get drunk, yell, have arguments, and are fighting each other at restaurants and in public places," the governor wrote.[10]

China has reportedly signed a secret agreement allowing its military to use the Cambodian base of Ream near Sihanoukville in exchange for China's billions in soft loans and infrastructure projects. Use of the base would give China easy access to the Gulf of Thailand and the southern reaches of the South China Sea and create heartburn among its neighbors,

---

9. Denis D. Gray, "Chinese Influx Transforming Myanmar's Quintessential City," *AP News*, May 1, 2018, https://www.apnews.com/d2d6b21f61f64178aa5b017633b4f83e.

10. Sheridan Prasso, "Chinese Influx Stirs Resentment in Once-Sleepy Cambodian Resort," *Bloomberg*, June 20, 2018, https://www.bloomberg.com/news/features/2018-06-20/chinese-casinos-stir-resentment-on-cambodia-s-coast-of-dystopia.

particularly Thailand and Vietnam. Cambodian officials have repeatedly denied reports about these plans.[11]

So, what is motivating China's drive south? Paul Heer, who earlier served as the U.S. National Intelligence Officer for East Asia until 2015, is skeptical that it is driven by an inherent Chinese expansionism or communist ideology. One factor is that China has become rich and powerful and sees economic opportunities in the nations to its south, Heer says. Another is no doubt Beijing's response to some of its neighbors' increased activities in the disputed South China Sea, which Beijing interprets as challenging its views of its sovereignty and security.

"My own view is that it is probably an equal measure of opportunity and perceived needs—including the need to defend China's sovereignty and bolster its economic security," says Heer. "And although it is true that China is engaged in mercenary and opportunistic economic activities, in some respects it replicates how other great powers have routinely behaved in the developing world."

China's growing involvement in Southeast Asia prompts a blend of anticipation and uneasiness among its smaller neighbors as Beijing mounts its drive south with an assortment of tools. China's toolbox is loaded with diverse instruments from "soft power"—economic, cultural, and education diplomacy—to "hard power," ranging from threats of military force in the South China Sea to arms sales and military exchanges. Some of Beijing's tactics verge on "sharp power" when it aims at distraction and manipulation in the political and information space.[12]

The experiences of Southeast Asia are important beyond the region itself. For other countries, they are a microcosm of China's ambitions and give signals about how the country, its companies, and its military operate when they move outside China's borders.

Southeast Asians expect that China's soaring growth in recent decades will help propel them out of poverty, fire up their middle-income econo-

11. Jeremy Page, Gordon Lubold, and Rob Taylor, "Deal for Naval Outpost in Cambodia Furthers China's Quest for Military Network," *Wall Street Journal*, July 22, 2019, https://www.wsj.com/articles/secret-deal-for-chinese-naval-outpost-in-cambodia-raises-u-s-fears-of-beijings-ambitions-11563732482.

12. Juan Pablo Cardenal, Jacek Kucharczyk, Grigorij Meseznikov, and Gabriela Poeschova, "Sharp Power: Rising Authoritarian Influence," National Endowment for Democracy, December 2017, https://www.ned.org/wp-content/uploads/2017/12/Sharp-Power-Rising-Authoritarian-Influence-Full-Report.pdf.

mies, and finance infrastructure desperately needed to connect the region's neighbors to each other and to the powerhouse to the north. Myanmar and Cambodia look to Beijing to help them withstand the pressures from Western countries on human rights and democracy.

Countries like Malaysia recognize that mountains of Chinese loans could create a "debt trap" like that facing Sri Lanka, which had to turn over a port to China for 99 years when its loans fell into arrears. Vietnam and the Philippines worry that China will use its growing military might and militarized islands in the South China Sea to bully them into either abandoning oil and gas development off their coasts or force them into joint ventures with Chinese firms.

Singapore's leaders have been shunned by Beijing when they reminded China about the need to respect the rule of law after a 2016 international tribunal rejected most of China's outsized claims in the disputed South China Sea. The mainland Southeast Asian countries are nervous that China may use its dams along the Mekong River and those it is building or funding in Laos and Cambodia to starve those downstream of water, fish, and the silt needed for farming.

Some in Myanmar, Laos, and Cambodia worry that a flood of Chinese immigrants seeking economic opportunity are displacing locals and reshaping swaths of their countries. In Indonesia in 2017, the reelection bid of a Chinese Indonesian Christian for governor of Jakarta was derailed by massive protests organized by conservative Islamic groups charging him with blasphemy to ensure that the political and economic role of non-Muslims would be kept in check.

China has stepped up a "soft power" offensive in which it has bolstered the numbers of students from Southeast Asia granted scholarships to study in China. Growing battalions of academics, journalists, religious leaders, businesspersons, and civil society representatives are being invited to visit provinces across China.

In Singapore, China urged businesspersons to let the city-state's leaders know that standing up to Beijing on the South China Sea could hobble new business opportunities. In Malaysia, the Chinese ambassador visited constituencies of ruling party candidates in the run-up to the 2018 elections in which an opposition coalition toppled the incumbent prime minister.

In most of these countries, Chinese companies pay hefty kickbacks to officials whose approvals they need for launching an infrastructure project or commercial venture. Rumors abound in the Philippines that China injected funds into Duterte's election bid in 2016, perhaps through ethnic Chinese companies. There are fewer doubts in Phnom Penh that Beijing supported Prime Minister Hun Sen's effort to decimate the opposition in Cambodia's 2018 parliamentary elections.

China's size, proximity, and remarkable economic heft have long been both an opportunity and a challenge for Southeast Asia. China's emergence as a commercial powerhouse has become an important force in Southeast Asia's economic growth. The world's second largest economy has displaced the United States and Japan as the region's largest trading partner. Although China is still not the region's largest foreign investor, it has started to become a critical driver in financing and building badly needed infrastructure.

At the same time, China, with a more modernized military and armed with two aircraft carriers, has become more assertive in its dealings with some Southeast Asian neighbors. Vietnam, the Philippines, and, to some extent, Malaysia and Indonesia have borne the brunt of Beijing's increased pressure since 2009 in pressing its claims in the South China Sea.

Southeast Asians have carefully watched the resurgent and assertive China. Some observers attribute China's more activist foreign policy to the election of Xi Jinping, who took over as Communist Party chief in 2012 and became president in 2013. Heer, the former intelligence analyst, says these trends started before the election of Xi. Among other factors, Heer attributes Beijing's increased assertiveness in the region to the global financial crisis of 2008, escalating tensions in the East and South China Seas in 2009, and the U.S. rebalance to Asia mounted by President Barack Obama around 2011.

But Bonnie Glaser, director of the China Power Project at the Center for Strategic and International Studies (CSIS), is convinced that Xi has demonstrated a tougher policy toward China's neighbors than his predecessors had. "After Xi came to power there was a push to intimidate China's neighbors, which resulted in decisions like the [Air Defense Identification Zone] in the East China Sea and the Haiyang Shiyou [oil rig] in Vietnam's [exclusive economic zone], and the island building in the South China Sea."

Ryan Haas, a China expert at the Brookings Institution in Washington and former director for China in the National Security Council, adds: "China's strategy is premised on the assumption that as countries in the region become more economically dependent and militarily inferior to China, they will become more deferential to Chinese interests. . . . Beijing would like over time to compel countries to side with them and not the U.S. in instances when Chinese and U.S. interests are in tension," Haas continues. "China wants a hierarchical relationship in Asia where they are on top."

Most Southeast Asian nations have long felt somewhat secure relying on the United States for a security hedge while turning increasing to Beijing for trade, loans, and investment. But the confidence of the region began slipping under the Obama administration, and these concerns were reinforced after President Donald Trump openly questioned the usefulness of U.S. alliances.

Since Trump pulled out of the Trans-Pacific Partnership trade deal a few days after taking office in 2017, Southeast Asians see Washington mostly focused on North Korea and the trade spat with China and only sporadically attentive to Southeast Asia. In his speech at an Asia-Pacific economic summit in Vietnam later that year, Trump stridently rejected the United States' long-standing commitment to free trade, which had anchored America to the region for decades.

The Trump administration has since announced a "free and open Indo-Pacific" strategy aimed at deepening U.S. partnerships in the region, improving the existing system of alliances, and preparing to deter possible aggression from China.[13] Many Southeast Asian nations were skeptical about the sustainability of the Obama rebalance and they are convinced that Trump's Indo-Pacific strategy has even less substance.

The biggest gap in the wake of Trump's withdrawal from the Pacific trade agreement is in economic engagement. The administration was slated in the autumn of 2019 to launch a new U.S. International Development Finance Corporation (DFC) to provide financing, risk insurance, and equity support for infrastructure and energy projects overseas. But the actual opening was delayed by the U.S. Congress's difficulties in passing the 2020 government budget. The DFC was hoping to start with the $60

13. "Indo-Pacific Strategy Report," Department of Defense, June 1, 2019, https://media.defense.gov/2019/Jul/01/2002152311/-1/-1/1/DEPARTMENT-OF-DEFENSE-INDO-PACIFIC-STRATEGY-REPORT-2019.PDF.

billion provided under the Build Act passed earlier by Congress to help stimulate private-sector investment in infrastructure projects.[14]

Trump's National Security Strategy released in 2017 took a harder line on China than previous administrations. It called out growing threats created by China, stating that China is "using economic inducements and penalties, influence operations, and implied military threats to persuade other states to heed its political and security agenda." The strategy said Beijing's "efforts to build and militarize outposts in the South China Sea endanger the free flow of trade, threaten the sovereignty of other nations, and undermine regional stability."[15]

Some analysts say the U.S. strategy paper went too far when it warned that China's actions in the South China Sea threatened the "free flow of trade." There is no evidence that China has tried or has plans to interfere with commercial trade.

To be sure, China has engaged with much of Southeast Asia, especially the mainland countries, for hundreds of years (and in Vietnam's case, thousands of years) and is not a newcomer to the region. Although most Southeast Asian nations laud U.S. military engagement in the region, many of them doubt that a free and open Indo-Pacific strategy and the new DFC will be big enough and early enough to make much of a dent in China's drive into the region.

Southeast Asians have been anxious that frictions between China and the United States will escalate beyond trade after Vice President Mike Pence's late-2018 speech in which he leveled a litany of charges against China, citing transgressions toward the United States and Beijing's dealings abroad.[16] Although they might agree with a number of Pence's criticisms, particularly on how China does business in their countries, Southeast Asians are wary that they could get caught in a new Cold War that could veer out of control.

14. "The Build Act," Overseas Private Investment Corporation, https://www.opic.gov/build-act/overview (accessed August 26, 2019).

15. White House, *National Security Strategy of the United States of America: December 2017*, 46, https://www.whitehouse.gov/wp-content/uploads/2017/12/NSS-Final-12-18-2017-0905.pdf.

16. Mike Pence, "Remarks by Vice President Pence on the Administration's Policy Toward China," White House, Office of the Press Secretary, speech, The Hudson Institute, Washington, DC, October 4, 2018, https://www.whitehouse.gov/briefings-statements/remarks-vice-president-pence-administrations-policy-toward-china/.

As the nasty trade fight between the United States and China heated up in 2019, countries in Southeast Asia became more anxious about the impact on them. Some companies from the United States and other countries began to move some of their manufacturing to Vietnam and other Southeast Asian destinations. But the biggest concern was that the spat would create an export slump and lead to a sharp economic slowdown in countries like Singapore and Malaysia.

"How the competitive dynamics between the United States and China play out in trade, in technology, or security will impact all of us disproportionately," Singapore's foreign minister Vivian Balakrishnan said in a May 2019 speech at CSIS in Washington. "And Southeast Asia, which stands at the intersection of major power interests, is viewing this duet with great concern, maybe even grave concern," the minister said, reflecting the anxieties of many in the region. "We do not wish to be forced into making invidious choices."[17]

Southeast Asians have also been paying close attention as China's economic growth by mid-2019 had slipped to its slowest pace in nearly three decades.[18] They pondered what would happen to foreign investment by Chinese companies or infrastructure projects under the BRI if China had to pour hundreds of billions of dollars into its domestic economy to prevent it from slipping into a funk.

The year 2017 marked a pretty dramatic shift in the roles of the United States and China in Southeast Asia. Even before Trump pulled out of the Pacific trade deal and the Paris Accord on climate change, Southeast Asians began recognizing that the United States would likely reduce its interest in Asia and that China would increasingly use its economic, military, and diplomatic clout to press its neighbors to recognize and accommodate Beijing's interests.

A late-2018 survey of Southeast Asian regional experts and business, media, and civil society leaders conducted by the ASEAN Studies Centre at the ISEAS-Yusof Ishak Institute in Singapore highlighted the anxieties

---

17. Singapore Ministry of Foreign Affairs, "Edited Transcript of Minister for Foreign Affairs Dr. Vivian Balakrishnan's Remarks on Seeking Opportunities Amidst Disruption—A View from Singapore," speech, Center for Strategic and International Studies, Washington, DC, May 15, 2019, https://www.mfa.gov.sg/Newsroom/Press-Statements-Transcripts-and-Photos/2019/05/20190516_FMV-Washington---CSIS-Speech.

18. Lucy Hornby and Xinning Liu, "China's Economy Grows at Slowest Rate in Nearly 30 Years," *Financial Times*, July 15, 2019, https://www.ft.com/content/73f06b8a-a696-11e9-984c-fac8325aaa04.

in a region trying to forge its way in the face of China's rise and a perceived decline of U.S. influence.[19] The report's authors said the people they surveyed were those whose views could "could inform or influence policy on regional political, economic, and social issues." (ASEAN refers to the 10-nation Association of Southeast Asian Nations.)

Among the key findings:

- Over 45 percent said that "China will become a revisionist power with an intent to turn Southeast Asia into a sphere of influence." Less than 9 percent saw China as a "benign and benevolent power."
- Roughly half of the respondents said China's BRI would draw regional countries into "China's orbit," while the other half thought it would provide "much-needed infrastructure funding" for the region's nations.
- A hefty 70 percent said their government "should be cautious in negotiating BRI projects to avoid getting into unsustainable financial debts with China."
- Nearly three-quarters said that China's "economic influence reigns supreme" in the region, but less than 8 percent thought that about the United States. These numbers may be interpreted to suggest that the region is already within China's sphere of influence.
- The survey found that a little more than 45 percent of regional experts and leaders think China has most influence in political and strategic matters, compared to almost 31 percent who have this view about the United States.
- About 68 percent believe that the level of U.S. engagement with Southeast Asia under Trump has decreased or decreased substantially.
- Almost 69 percent said the China and the United States are on a "collision course" in Southeast Asia.

"Concerns about China's growing assertiveness have been simmering in the past decade, and [are] now coming to a boil," Tang Siew Mun, one of the authors of the study, told the *South China Morning Post*. "However,

19. Tang Siew Mun, Moe Thuzar, Hoang Thi Ha, Termsak Chalermpalanupap, Pham Thi Phuong Thao, and Anuthida Saelaow Qian, *The State of Southeast Asia: 2019 Survey Report* (Singapore: ISEAS-Yusof Ishak Institute, 2019), https://www.iseas.edu.sg/images/pdf/TheStateofSEASurveyReport_2019.pdf.

we should be careful not to interpret these findings as 'anti-China,' but as a wake-up call that China's strong-arm tactics and attempts to mold the region in its image will face considerable pushback."[20]

Most Southeast Asians would prefer a scenario in which they are not beholden to either Beijing or Washington, even if the regional power balance is shifting and China is gaining at the expense of the United States.

To be sure, the situation in Southeast Asia and the dynamics of its relations with Beijing are fluid and have many moving parts. China's slowdown beginning in 2018 raised questions about whether the Chinese economy will keep up its torrid pace of growth, and it is still too early to predict how much China's investment in infrastructure will benefit the region. It is also possible that an overconfident Beijing could overstep the bounds of its southern neighbors, leading to political and trade conflict.

Beyond that, other key players active in Southeast Asia, including Japan, South Korea, the European Union, India, and Australia, can provide at least a partial hedge against China. These dynamics make it difficult to forecast the future of the region with certainty.

Southeast Asia faces a "perennial challenge" of navigating between the two major powers, long a "defining feature of Southeast Asian diplomacy," says Joseph Chinyong Liow, who teaches international politics at the S. Rajaratnam School of International Studies (RSIS) in Singapore. "Southeast Asian states are happy to work closely with China for reasons of trade and economic investments, and indeed, China will slowly become more and more influential in the region."

But "this should not be conflated with abrogation of the region defining 'rights' to China," argues Liow, author of *Ambivalent Engagement: The United States and Regional Security in Southeast Asia after the Cold War.* "Southeast Asia, primarily through ASEAN, remains intent on being central to the regional order, and this has not changed even as China's stakes and investments in the region have increased."

China's rise and its recent policy mix of carrot-and-stick initiatives toward Southeast Asia raise several important questions for the region and for Washington: How do Southeast Asian countries calculate the risks

---

20. Charles McDermid, "Southeast Asia Has Major Doubts about U.S. Reliability in the Region, but Still Wary of China: Survey," *South China Morning Post*, January 7, 2019, https://www.scmp.com/news/asia/southeast-asia/article/2180924/southeast-asia-has-major-doubts-about-us-reliability-region.

of increased dependence on China? Are they concerned about the role of China if the United States is less engaged in the Asia Pacific under the Trump administration? Where are the opportunities for the United States in Southeast Asia considering China's moves?

"PREFER A CHINA THAT'S A LITTLE DISTRACTED"

Southeast Asia lies smack in the middle of the dynamic Asia-Pacific region and serves as the critical link between the Pacific and Indian Oceans. Three Southeast Asian countries border on southern China and one, Myanmar, lies at the crossroad between southwestern China and eastern India. The 10 countries of Southeast Asia have a combined population of 650 million, an economy of $2.8 trillion, and cover an area of 1.7 million square miles.[21]

These countries vary vastly in size, culture, religion, economics, form of government, and history. Thailand and Myanmar follow Buddhism, while Indonesia and Malaysia are majority Muslim. Indonesia and the Philippines are fairly vibrant democracies while Vietnam and Laos are run by Communist parties and Cambodia by one-man authoritarian rule. Singapore has income per person of over $57,000 a year, but in Myanmar and Cambodia personal income is less than $1,400.[22]

Chinese trade with the nations on its southern periphery dates back to the third century when delegations were dispatched to these countries. These missions were later followed by Buddhist pilgrims and then by traders who arrived as early as the Song dynasty, which began in the tenth century. Then came the overseas Chinese who settled in these countries and began developing an informal business network by about the 1500s.[23]

Outside nations have long recognized Southeast Asia's potential for significant wealth and resources. Merchants from China by the year AD 200 realized that access to the South China Sea from what today is

---

21. East-West Center, US-ASEAN Business Council, and ISEAS-Yusof Ishak Institute, *ASEAN Matters for America, America Matters for ASEAN* (Honolulu: East-West Center, 2019), 2, https://asiamattersforamerica.org/uploads/publications/2019-ASEAN-Matters-for-America.pdf.
22. Ibid., 8.
23. Vannarith Chheang, *Trends in Southeast Asia: The Political Economy of Chinese Investment in Cambodia* (Singapore: ISEAS-Yusof Ishak Institute, 2017), 3, https://www.iseas.edu.sg/images/pdf/TRS16_17.pdf.

northern Vietnam provided ideal opportunities for trading with the rest of Southeast Asia and the Indian subcontinent.[24]

Beginning around the same time, Indian traders and religious teachers held sway in Cambodia, Thailand, and the Malay Peninsula, bringing with them Hinduism and Buddhism. By the 1500s, Europeans arrived from Portugal and Spain, and later the Dutch, French, and British colonized most of the region.

As the war in the Pacific ended in 1945, Myanmar, the Philippines, Indonesia, Malaysia, and Singapore moved toward independence, but that did not end big power competition in the region. The Cold War in Southeast Asia between the United States and the Soviet Union (and China) spawned two decades of brutal war in Vietnam, Cambodia, and Laos.

Anxious to hold the major powers at bay and to ensure the war would not spread, five Southeast Asian countries established ASEAN in 1967. Nearly three decades later the grouping established the ASEAN Regional Forum and since then has set up a raft of other groupings, including the East Asia Summit and the ASEAN Defense Ministers Meeting-Plus, to promote regional security cooperation and economic growth and bind foreign powers like the United States and China to the region.

The end of hostilities on the Indochina Peninsula in 1975 laid the groundwork for rapid economic development in Southeast Asia brought about by investment in manufacturing by U.S. and Japanese companies seeking to take advantage of the region's abundant workforce and plentiful natural resources. Today, Southeast Asia as a group has the world's fifth largest economy and engages in two-way trade totaling $5.3 trillion a year.

Southeast Asia is the United States' fourth largest trading partner with American exports of goods and services totaling $105 billion a year, creating over half a million jobs in the U.S. economy. The region is the top destination of U.S. investment in Asia with a cumulative total of $329 billion, more than American companies have invested in China, Japan, South Korea, and India combined. Some 4,200 U.S. companies operate in

24. Christopher Goscha, *Vietnam: A New History* (New York: Basic Books, 2016), 16–17.

Southeast Asia, often as part of a global supply chain that exports to other parts of the world.[25]

In the early years after the communist victory in China in 1949, Beijing adopted a two-pronged policy toward its southern neighbors. On one hand, it sought to nurture friendly regimes along its periphery, while at the same time promoting communist insurgencies in Myanmar, Thailand, Malaysia, and Indonesia. Beginning in the 1980s, as China launched its economic reforms, Beijing started to look to its neighbors as export markets for its manufactured products and for access to the region's natural resources and commodities to fuel its industries and food to feed its increasingly affluent population. It also sought foreign investment from Southeast Asian conglomerates, many of which were owned by ethnic Chinese.

China's efforts to cooperate with Southeast Asia follow a long-standing historical pattern. In the two millennia up to the second half of the nineteenth century, the countries of mainland Southeast Asia (Burma/Myanmar, Cambodia, Laos, Thailand, and Vietnam) at different times were Chinese tributary states, which often meant that they were part of China's network of trade and close foreign and cultural relations.

China's deep historical, cultural, and economic ties in Southeast Asia long predate Beijing's "soft power" push starting in the 1980s. Beginning in the late 1700s and continuing for the next 200 years, thousands of often-landless peasants from southern China began migrating to Southeast Asia. Many of the ethnic Chinese thrived under colonial rule and over time came to play dominant roles in the economies of Indonesia, Malaysia, the Philippines, and Thailand.

Today they total around 32 million, although their exact numbers are difficult to determine because many of them have assimilated into their local cultures. Many have lived in Southeast Asia for generations, play critical roles in the domestic economies, and are fully integrated into the business structure of the countries in which they live.

Sources in Myanmar estimate that 1 million to 2 million Chinese, often from nearby Yunnan Province, have in recent years migrated to Myanmar, particularly in and around the northern city of Mandalay. Many are said

25. East-West Center, *ASEAN Matters for America*, 23.

to have purchased citizenship cards, even though this is technically illegal. Significant numbers of Chinese farmers have also moved to northern Laos.

This migration seems to be largely motivated by personal and economic reasons and does not appear to be sponsored or encouraged by the government. "Those that move typically have access to some capital, marketing contacts, and business savvy," said David Dapice of Harvard University's Kennedy School, who has long worked on the economies of Indonesia, Myanmar, and Vietnam. "They end up controlling much retail and wholesale trade and often buy up urban land and real estate."[26]

In recent years, Beijing has stepped up its efforts to more actively engage ethnic Chinese overseas. At a conference of overseas Chinese organizations in 2014, Xi Jinping said that "rejuvenation of the Chinese nation" is a "common dream" of the "sons and daughters of China within and outside China."[27] In recent years China has placed more emphasis globally on the ethnic Chinese in its Communist Party's United Front influence operations.

In Malaysia in 2015, at a time of heightened political tension just ahead of a pro-Malay demonstration, the Chinese ambassador visited Kuala Lumpur's Chinatown and warned that Beijing would not "sit idly by" if people "infringe upon the legal rights of Chinese citizens."[28] His comments prompted concerns among Malaysians that the ambassador was interfering in the internal affairs of the country.[29]

China in recent decades began using a raft of "soft power" tools such as business networks, foreign assistance, tourism, increased diplomatic interactions, cultural and educational exchanges, and the establishment of Chinese-language and cultural promotion centers to transform relations with its neighbors to the south.[30] But China's focus on mainly charm

---

26. David Dapice, *China's Relations with ASEAN Economies* (Harvard Ash Center, 2015), 5, https://www.uscc.gov/sites/default/files/Dapice_Written%20Testimony_5.13.2015%20Hearing.pdf.
27. Leo Suryadinata, *The Rise of China and the Chinese Overseas* (Singapore: ISEAS-Yusof Ishak Institute, 2017), 19.
28. Ibid., 112–114; "China's Envoy to Malaysia Visits Petaling Street Day before Rally," *The Malay Mail*, September 25, 2015, https://www.malaymail.com/news/malaysia/2015/09/25/chinas-envoy-to-malaysia-visits-petaling-street-day-before-rally/976463.
29. Suryadinata, *The Rise of China*, 117–119.
30. Josh Kurlantzick, *Charm Offensive: How China's Soft Power Is Changing the World* (New Haven, CT: Yale University Press, 2007), 61, 65, 67, 84, 97.

and a relatively passive foreign policy did not last. Beijing became more assertive in enforcing its nine-dash-line claim to about four-fifths of the South China Sea and began turning rocks and reefs into artificial islands, complicating its ties with other claimant countries, particularly Vietnam, the Philippines, and Malaysia.

China also stepped up its ambitious plans to build railroads, roads, power plants, ports, and pipelines to draw its smaller southern neighbors into its economic juggernaut through its massive BRI infrastructure program. When the United States and European countries complained in 2017 that Cambodia had abandoned the democratic path and Myanmar grossly violated the rights of its Muslim Rohingya minority, China was ready with diplomatic support and offers of aid and investment.

Speaking at the 2017 Chinese Communist Party congress, Xi made clear that China planned to play a more active role in international politics, declaring "it is time for us to take center stage in the world and to make a greater contribution to humankind." Clearly convinced that the United States would step back from a key leadership role in Asia under Trump, the Chinese leader added that China is "standing tall and firm in the East."[31]

An editorial in Thailand's *The Nation* newspaper shortly after Xi spoke summed up the sentiments of many Southeast Asians. "While China's economic assistance to countries in Southeast Asia is most welcome, territorial disputes with Beijing in the South China Sea have cast our giant neighbor as an arrogant bully." The paper continued: "Xi's 'One Belt One Road' initiative is set to create a multitude of opportunities for economic development spanning much of the world, but building physical links over land and sea will also give China the wherewithal to expand its influence into every connected nation."[32]

Malaysian writer Karim Raslan added to these concerns. "We prefer a China that's strong but a little distracted by its internal affairs. That way, we in the region can play the Great Powers against one another. We want

31. Charles Clover, "Xi Jinping Signals Departure from Low-Profile Policy," *Financial Times*, October 20, 2017, https://www.ft.com/content/05cd86a6-b552-11e7-a398-73d59db9e399?sharetype=share.

32. The Nation/Asia News Network, "What Xi Jinping's Second Term Can Bring ASEAN," *Philippine Daily Inquirer*, October 19, 2017, https://opinion.inquirer.net/108020/xi-jinpings-second-term-can-bring-asean.

them to vie for our support and attention, not the other way around," he wrote for the website of a Philippine television cable network.

"An all-powerful Xi Jinping and an emboldened China is not in Southeast Asia's interest," Karim continued. "So while China seems to be on an upswing now, another stumble could well be in the offing—especially if the looming debt crisis and growing domestic income equities are not resolved. Looking at history, maybe that's not such a bad thing for Southeast Asia after all. . . ."[33]

China has dramatically stepped up its tempo of engagement with its Southeast Asian neighbors in recent years. There has been a flurry of high-level diplomatic, economic, and military engagement between China and most Southeast Asian nations. One goal no doubt has been to dissipate some of the anxiety in the region about China's increasing economic heft, military might, and assertiveness in the South China Sea.

But this diplomatic blitz has the effect of drawing individual countries closer to Beijing and causes countries to focus more on their bilateral ties with China rather than on ties between Beijing and the 10 countries of the ASEAN grouping. Cambodia has demonstrated that on core issues like the South China Sea it is more concerned about getting aid from China than about solidarity with its ASEAN neighbors.

The Philippines, when it chaired the ASEAN grouping in 2017, also began to show signs of focusing more on its bilateral ties with China than its ASEAN partners by keeping any mention of China's militarization of the South China Sea out of the bloc's official statements. This had the added benefit for Beijing of prompting countries to deal with China bilaterally on the maritime dispute rather than through ASEAN as a group, which has long been China's goal.[34]

CHINA'S ECONOMIC DIPLOMACY

Southeast Asian nations have grown to appreciate but simultaneously worry about the longer-term impact of China's strengthening economic

33. Karim Raslan, "What Xi Jinping Means for Southeast Asia," *ABS-CBN*, December 2, 2017, https://news.abs-cbn.com/blogs/opinions/12/02/17/opinion-what-xi-jinping-means-for-southeast-asia.

34. Laura Zhou, "Is China Chipping Away at the ASEAN Bloc?," *South China Morning Post*, December 2, 2017, https://www.scmp.com/news/china/diplomacy-defence/article/2122587/china-chipping-away-asean-bloc.

clout. China has emerged as both a critical trading partner and a daunting competitor for global market share and foreign investment. For the countries of Southeast Asia, China's growth into the world's second largest economy and its increasing role in the global manufacturing supply chain provide a hefty boost to their own economic development.

For all Southeast Asian countries, China today is their largest trading partner, replacing Japan and the United States. In 2018, the Southeast Asian countries (except Laos, Malaysia, and Thailand) had trade deficits with China as they rely increasingly on the Chinese market for imports, some of which, like in the case of Vietnam, drive their exports. Increasing trade deficits with China prompt concerns in some countries about overdependence on one market.

China was attracted to Southeast Asia by the region's relatively low wage rates, its market size of over 650 million people, and the efforts at regional economic integration between countries through building the ASEAN Economic Community. The community aimed at developing a single market between the 10 members, including a single production network with the free flow of capital and skilled labor, notionally by 2015.

Even earlier China and Southeast Asia had negotiated the ASEAN–China Free Trade Area, which went into effect in 2010. Under this agreement, the participants liberalized their trade and investment systems. Beijing also granted a preferential tax agreement to the poorer mainland countries of Cambodia, Laos, Myanmar, and Vietnam, which made it easier notionally for them to export agricultural products to China, although they still face nontariff barriers such as health and safety standards.[35]

Policymakers in Southeast Asia increasingly see their economic destinies hitched to China's. The larger Southeast Asian nations began around 1990 to plug into the opportunities provided by China's rapid economic growth, including into its global production network. By 2018, Southeast Asia's two-way trade with China reached $591.3 billion—just over two times that of the United States and up from just $8 billion in 1980.[36]

Overall, Southeast Asia's exports to China are mainly raw materials (coal, copper, iron, and rubber) and food products (vegetables and fruit),

35. Chheang, *Trends in Southeast Asia*, 5–6.
36. International Monetary Fund, "Exports, FOB to Partner Countries; Imports, CIF from Partner Countries," *IMF Data*, 2014–2018, https://data.imf.org/regular.aspx?key=61013712.

although some countries also export electronics components. Southeast Asia's main imports from China are manufactured products, consumer goods, and machinery and equipment.

China's trade volume with Southeast Asia has been growing over 13 percent per year since 2005 while the share of the region's trade with more developed economies in the United States, the European Union, Japan, and South Korea has fallen.[37] At least part of the reason for this is that global multinationals have increasingly set up regional production networks that link Southeast Asian suppliers with Chinese manufacturers.

In reality, China's dominant economic position in Southeast Asia is somewhat less than the macro numbers suggest. More than half of China's foreign trade is controlled by foreign-invested companies in China and some 60 percent of the goods China exports are dependent on other markets, especially in the United States and Europe.[38]

For some Southeast Asian economies, China's export of cheap consumer goods has also resulted in serious dislocation to their domestic light industry, particularly in Indonesia and Vietnam. The ASEAN–China Free Trade Area, which came into effect in 2010, ravaged onion and garlic production in Thailand, for example, because Chinese farmers were able to produce and export these farm products more cheaply than their Thai counterparts could grow them.

But China is still much more of a trading heavy weight than an investment powerhouse in Southeast Asia. China's cumulative greenfield foreign direct investment into Southeast Asia between 2003 and 2017 reached $123 billion, roughly half that of Japan's ($220 billion) and well behind that of the United States ($182 billion), according to analysis by the *Financial Times*.[39]

Still, China's investment today in many Southeast Asian countries is growing more rapidly than that of either Japan or the United States.

37. Sanchita Basu Das, "Southeast Asia Worries over Growing Economic Dependence on China," *ISEAS Perspective*, no. 81 (2017): 2, https://www.iseas.edu.sg/images/pdf/ISEAS_Perspective_2017_81.pdf.

38. Robert Sutter, *China's Relations with Southeast Asia: Hearing before the U.S.-China Economic and Security Review Commission*, 114th Cong. (Washington, DC: U.S.–China Economic and Security Review Commission, 2015), 9, https://www.uscc.gov/sites/default/files/transcripts/May%2013%2C%202015%20Hearing%20Transcript.pdf.

39. John Reed and Valentina Romei, "Who Dominates the Economies of South-East Asia?," *Financial Times*, April 30, 2018, https://www.ft.com/content/898fa38e-4882-11e8-8ee8-cae73aab7ccb.

Analysts believe it is only a matter of time until China becomes one of the region's largest investors as it looks to invest its overcapacity of steel and cement and increases its financing for badly needed infrastructure.

There are significant differences between investment by companies from China and the United States. Much of China's investment to this point has been in low-end manufacturing (and real estate in countries like Malaysia and Cambodia), while U.S. investment is more in high tech and in services.

The two countries' companies have distinctly different operating ethos. U.S. firms know they are under scrutiny by the Foreign Corrupt Practices Act and are monitored by shareholders for their dealings on the environment and labor. In contrast, a Vietnamese economist trained in China says, "Chinese investment equals corruption." He says both Chinese and Vietnamese officials benefit from kickbacks in projects, resulting in long delays and huge cost overruns.

"Southeast Asian countries welcome Chinese presence in their economies, but there is a certain degree of fear and caution," Cambodia political scientist Vannarith Chheang said. "Power differences and asymmetry with China pose great challenges for regional countries to be economically competitive and politically independent."[40]

Heavy dependence on China economically at a time when Washington is focused on a trade war with Beijing will make it more complicated for some Southeast Asian countries to stand up to China, particularly in the South China Sea. Witness Hanoi's decision to ask a Spanish oil company to abandon its exploration activities on Vietnam's continental shelf. Beijing abruptly halted lucrative pork exports from Vietnam to China shortly before Hanoi abandoned the oil project.

Or take the decision by Duterte of the Philippines to pocket the arbitral tribunal ruling against Beijing to get China to restore banana imports, promote tourist arrivals, and pledge investment in Philippine infrastructure projects. In 2016, China promised Cambodia $600 million in loans and aid after Phnom Penh forced the ASEAN grouping to retract a strongly worded statement on China's activities in the South China Sea.[41]

---

40. Chheang, *Trends in Southeast Asia*, 9.
41. China Power Project, "Does China Dominate Global Investment?," Center for Strategic and International Studies, https://chinapower.csis.org/china-foreign-direct-investment/ (accessed October 19, 2019).

"As China increases its outbound investments and completes more infrastructure projects, its geopolitical influence in the region will definitely increase," said Sanchita Basu Das, an economist at Singapore's ISEAS-Yusof Ishak Institute. "There is mounting concern among Southeast Asian countries . . . that China's fast-spreading geo-economic influence will see Beijing resorting to economic retribution to settle its political differences with neighboring countries."[42]

To balance China's growing economic weight in Southeast Asia, the 10-nation grouping has taken tentative steps toward greater regional economic integration to knock down intra-regional trade barriers and attract more diverse investment. The group has begun work on an ASEAN–European Union free-trade agreement, but these talks are progressing slowly.

Negotiations on the Regional Comprehensive Economic Partnership (RCEP) were virtually completed in late 2019, seeking to harmonize the various trade agreements the grouping has with five regional powers, including China and Japan, after often-protectionist India pulled out of the talks. Countries like Vietnam and Malaysia had looked to the 12-nation Pacific partnership agreement, including the United States and Japan, to provide economic balance to China, before Trump jettisoned that deal.

BELT AND ROAD: "PROJECT OF THE CENTURY"

China made an ambitious pledge—touted by Xi as the "project of the century" and intended to "create a family of harmonious co-existence"[43]—to plow $1 trillion[44] in investment into the development of much-needed railroads, roads, bridges, ports, and power plants. The BRI scheme

42. Das, *Southeast Asia Worries*, 2.
43. Xi Jinping, "Full Text of President Xi's Speech at Opening of Belt and Road Forum," *Xinhua*, May 14, 2017, https://www.xinhuanet.com/english/2017-05/14/c_136282982.htm.
44. For an analysis of some of the numbers being bandied about for the BRI and for what projects it might include, see Jonathan Hillman, "How Big Is China's Belt and Road?," Center for Strategic and International Studies, April 3, 2018, https://www.csis.org/analysis/how-big-chinas-belt-and-road. "The Chinese Global Investment Tracker," compiled by the American Enterprise Institute (AEI) and Heritage Foundation, estimated that China's construction and investment across all sectors totaled about $340 million between 2014 and 2017. AEI estimates that it would take six to seven years for the BRI to reach $1 trillion. See Cecilia Joy-Perez and Derek Scissors, "The Chinese State Funds Belt and Road but Does Not Have Trillions to Spare," American Enterprise Institute, March 2018, https://www.aei.org/wp-content/uploads/2018/03/BRI.pdf.

highlights China's outsized ambition in its neighboring countries. These projects will use bucketloads of Chinese financing, cement, steel, technology, expertise, and workers to expand Beijing's geopolitical influence and bind other nations more tightly into its fold.

Hard infrastructure will be accompanied by trade agreements, cultural programs, and student scholarships. "When much of the West is looking inward, China is connecting with the world," Jonathan Hillman of the CSIS Reconnecting Asia Project told a congressionally appointed commission.[45]

The BRI is complemented by the Beijing-initiated Asia Infrastructure Investment Bank (AIIB), which began operating in 2016 with $100 billion of initial capital, almost $30 billion of which came from China. Beijing has also injected massive amounts of capital into Chinese financial institutions such as the China Development Bank and the Export-Import Bank of China. These state-owned banks benefit from low borrowing costs because their bonds are treated like government debt. This makes it possible for Chinese state-owned firms to offer highly competitive bids against other competitors.[46]

By the end of 2018, the AIIB had invested only $7.5 billion in contrast to the China Development Bank, a bilateral lender, that had already loaned $110 billion for BRI infrastructure projects and pledged to invest another $150 billion over the next five years.[47] The AIIB has partnered with the World Bank and other multilateral development banks and generally uses their lending standards. The China Development Bank and other Chinese bilateral banks are less transparent and do not seem to subscribe to the approach of multilateral development banks.

Haas of Brookings calls the BRI China's "economic vehicle" for the region. "They want Southeast Asian countries to depend on China for their economic growth," he says. "This places Beijing's vision in tension with

45. Jonathan Hillman, "China's Belt and Road Initiative: Five Years Later: Statement before the U.S.-China Economic and Security Review Commission," Center for Strategic and International Studies, 2018, 2, https://csis-prod.s3.amazonaws.com/s3fs-public/publication/ts180125_hillman_testimony.pdf.

46. Shu Zhang and Matthew Miller, "Behind China's Silk Road Vision: Cheap Funds, Heavy Debt, Growing Risk," *Reuters*, May 15, 2017, https://www.reuters.com/article/us-china-silkroad-finance/behind-chinas-silk-road-vision-cheap-funds-heavy-debt-growing-risk-idUSKCN18B0YS.

47. Nikki Sun, "China Development Bank Commits $250bn to Belt and Road," *Nikkei Asian Review*, January 15, 2018, https://asia.nikkei.com/Economy/China-Development-Bank-commits-250bn-to-Belt-and-Road.

America's desire to forge a more integrated and diversified trade architecture in the region." Haas adds, "The more the countries are dependent on China for their future economic prosperity, the more Beijing believes it will gain leverage over countries in the region."

Neither Beijing nor the Southeast Asian countries have released figures on the total value of the BRI projects in the region. RWR Advisory Group, a Washington company that monitors Chinese investment, estimates China invested some $200.5 billion in BRI projects in Southeast Asia between 2013 and 2018.

The biggest year was 2015, with BRI projects in the region totaling $92.4 billion, according to RWR. The numbers have dropped each year since then, reaching only $12.8 billion in 2018. Indonesia has the largest value of projects amounting to $84.4 billion and Vietnam the lowest at $4.5 billion.

RWR gathers its figures from news reports and press releases from China and the recipient country of a project and only counts "deals that we believe have become real and official." It does not count the many projects that are "announced but not finalized." Nonetheless, these figures seem quite a bit too high to a recent visitor who has traveled to all these countries.

Beijing is stepping up its ties with Southeast Asia across the board from political to cultural relations, but its growing economic diplomacy—and especially its credit for infrastructure projects—is Beijing's strongest attraction for most Southeast Asian nations.

At a summit celebrating the BRI with leaders from Central and Southeast Asia in 2017, Xi described the plan "as economic globalization that is open, inclusive, balanced, and beneficial to all." Beijing's commitment to invest massive sums in infrastructure projects to boost connectivity and trade may be risky for China's economy, but it is broadly welcomed in Southeast Asia.

The BRI will help fill a desperately large gap. The Asian Development Bank projects Southeast Asia will need some $2.8 trillion in infrastructure investment over the 15 years ending in 2030. The region now invests about $55 billion a year, roughly one-third of the $147 billion the bank estimates it needs.[48]

48. Asian Development Bank, *Meeting Asia's Infrastructure Needs* (Manila: Asian Development Bank, 2017), 40, 50, https://www.adb.org/sites/default/files/publication/227496/special-report-infrastructure.pdf.

Analysts offer different interpretations about China's objectives. Some argue that Beijing's overarching goals appear to be to boost economic development at home. Two academics that have focused on China's high-speed train projects say the government is seeking to promote economic restructuring in China (including increased development in remote regions in the west) and reduce overcapacity in such sectors as steel and cement. They add that Chinese leaders are working to open neighboring markets to Chinese products and companies and "project to the world the image of Beijing as a technologically capable economic power."[49]

China is also seeking to build alternative trade routes that allow it to avoid the Strait of Malacca, which in a time of hostilities could be a potential bottleneck blocking traffic between Indonesia and Malaysia leading to the South China Sea. Some 60 percent of Chinese traded goods and 80 percent of its imported oil passes through the strait.[50]

Others recognize Beijing's economic motivations but argue the BRI also is driven by military and geostrategic ambitions as China seeks to boost its global role to compete for influence with the United States and Japan. Ely Ratner, at the time with the Council on Foreign Relations, told a congressionally appointed commission that the BRI "bears on military and security affairs because it demonstrates Xi's willingness and desire to pursue big, bold ideas that put China at the center of international politics in ways it has strongly resisted for decades."[51]

Still, there are worries in Southeast Asia that these investments will be accompanied by heavy debt burdens in recipient countries and slim

49. Agatha Kratz and Dragan Pavlicevic, "Chinese High-Speed Rail in Southeast Asia: Fast-Tracking China's Regional Rise?," Center for Strategic and International Studies—Reconnecting Asia, September 18, 2017, https://reconnectingasia.csis.org/analysis/entries/chinese-high-speed-rail-southeast-asia/?utm_source=Members&utm_campaign=45352d1bed-EMAIL_CAMPAIGN_2017_09_27&utm_medium=email&utm_term=0_e842221dc2-45352d1bed-137665349; see also, Peter Cai, *Understanding China's Belt and Road Initiative* (Sydney: Lowy Institute, 2017), https://www.lowyinstitute.org/sites/default/files/documents/Understanding%20China%E2%80%99s%20Belt%20and%20Road%20Initiative_WEB_1.pdf.

50. Truong Minh Vu, "The Geopolitics of Infrastructure: ASEAN's China Challenge," Center for Strategic and International Studies—Asia Maritime Transparency Initiative, February 13, 2017, https://amti.csis.org/geopolitics-infrastructure-asean-china/.

51. Ely Ratner, "Geostrategic and Military Drivers and Implications of the Belt and Road Initiative: U.S.-China Economic and Security Review Commission, Hearing on China's Belt and Road Initiative," 115th Cong. (prepared statement by Council on Foreign Relations, 2018), https://www.uscc.gov/sites/default/files/Ratner_USCC%20Testimony%20CORRECTED.pdf.

prospects of turning profits to help repay loans to Chinese banks anytime soon. Southeast Asian capitals are also anxious about Beijing's insistence on the use of Chinese contractors, technology from China, and thousands of imported Chinese construction workers.[52]

On some 34 China-funded infrastructure projects in Asia and Europe, 89 percent of the contractors were Chinese, with the remaining 11 percent from other countries, according to a study by the Reconnecting Asia project at CSIS. In contrast, in 178 infrastructure projects in Eurasia funded by the multilateral development banks, 41 percent of the contractors were from the country where the infrastructure was being built, 29 percent were from China, and 30 percent were from third countries.[53]

To be sure, roads and railroads carrying goods and commodities could just as easily be used to move military equipment and troops across the region. These concerns are prompting anxiety among some Southeast Asians that Beijing may seek to extract economic or political concessions down the road, said China expert David Shambaugh of George Washington University.[54]

One possible example is the Chinese-built resort in Koh Kong, on the Gulf of Thailand in southwestern Cambodia, where satellite images have revealed a 3,700-yard runway, longer than that required for civilian airplanes serving primarily one beachside resort. The runway coupled with a deepwater port capable of berthing four container ships at once has prompted speculation that China wants to use the facilities to gain a military foothold on the Gulf of Thailand. Cambodia has vigorously denied this claim.[55]

Sri Lanka off the coast of southern India is a poster child of some potential problems facing BRI recipient countries. In 2017, Sri Lanka formally handed over the $1.3 billion Hambantota Port in the south in a 99-year lease to China Merchants Port Holdings, which led critics to charge that the country was giving up its sovereignty. The port, which

52. James Kynge, "China's Contractors Grab Lion's Share of Silk Road Projects," *Financial Times*, January 24, 2018, https://www.ft.com/content/76b1be0c-0113-11e8-9650-9c0ad2d7c5b5.

53. Ibid.

54. David Shambaugh, *China's Future* (Madden, MA: Polity, 2016), 141.

55. Andrew Nachemson, "Is Cambodia's Koh Kong Project for Chinese Tourists—or China's Military?," *South China Morning Post*, March 5, 2019, https://www.scmp.com/week-asia/geopolitics/article/2188558/cambodias-koh-kong-project-chinese-tourists-or-chinas-military.

was built using debt from Chinese state-owned companies, had faced heavy losses since it opened in 2009 and had trouble repaying its loans.[56]

Corruption is another challenge facing regional infrastructure projects, including those financed and built by China. After elections toppled the prime minister in Malaysia in 2018, his successor suspended and mounted investigations into several projects, including a $16 billion high-speed train project, suspected of receiving inflated loans from a Chinese state-owned bank that were siphoned off to cover the debts of a scandal-plagued state investment fund.[57]

Beyond financial challenges, BRI projects confront land acquisition headaches, implementation delays, and environmental challenges, particularly on hydropower projects on the Mekong River. For some Southeast Asians, China's infrastructure charm offensive is viewed with suspicion because it takes place in tandem with Beijing's more assertive behavior in the South China Sea. China's larger geopolitical intentions are never far from the minds of Southeast Asian leaders owing to their geographical proximity.

The Digital Silk Road is a subgrouping of the BRI under which Chinese firms install telecom, broadcasting, and surveillance technology. Some of the "frontier areas" the Digital Silk Road will focus on are the digital economy, artificial intelligence, nanotechnology, quantum computing, cloud computing, and "smart cities."[58] Critics charge that this infrastructure provides an easy target for intelligence gathering. Global projects and those in Southeast Asia involving Chinese firms such as telecom companies Huawei, ZTE, and others now total around $79 billion, according to the RWR Advisory Group.[59]

---

56. Kiran Stacey, "China Signs 99-year lease on Sri Lanka's Hambantota Port: Critics Denounce Move as an Erosion of Country's Sovereignty," *Financial Times*, December 11, 2017, https://www.ft.com/content/e150ef0c-de37-11e.

57. Stefania Palma, "Malaysia Suspends $22bn China-Backed Projects," *Financial Times*, July 4, 2018, https://www.ft.com/content/409942a4-7f80-11e8-bc55-50daf11b720d; Jonathan E. Hillman, "Corruption Flows along China's Belt and Road," Center for Strategic and International Studies—Reconnecting Asia, January 18, 2019, https://reconnectingasia.csis.org/analysis/entries/corruption-flows-along-chinas-belt-and-road/.

58. Shi Jiangtao, "Pentagon Warns of Global Power Play behind Chinese Projects such as Belt and Road Initiative," *South China Morning Post*, January 16, 2019, https://www.scmp.com/news/china/diplomacy/article/2182380/pentagon-warns-global-power-play-behind-chinese-projects-such.

59. Sheridan Prasso, "China's Digital Silk Road Is Looking More Like an Iron Curtain," *Bloomberg*, January 10, 2019, https://www.bloomberg.com/news/features/2019-01-10/china-s-digital-silk-road-is-looking-more-like-an-iron-curtain.

Concern that Chinese security services would be able to intercept government, military, and business communications has prompted the United States to block Chinese firms from telecom and computing networks, including the new 5G network many countries are installing. Japan, Australia, and New Zealand have joined the United States in blocking Huawei from rolling out 5G equipment and are pressing others to join.[60]

Because Chinese digital companies are facing a lot of distrust and security concerns in more developed markets, they are working overtime to gain market share in third markets, including in Southeast Asia, says Robert Atkinson, head of the Information Technology Foundation in Washington. China's goal is to give "pretty good technology at a discount" to help these countries but to "tie that help to selling from Chinese digital companies—Huawei, ZTE, Alibaba, and the like," Atkinson says.[61]

China's Digital Silk Road projects in Southeast Asia are valued at almost $4 billion in Malaysia, over $2 billion in the Philippines, nearly $2 billion in Cambodia, and more than $1 billion in Thailand, according to RWR.[62] No Southeast Asian nation so far has banned Chinese telecom and computer networks, although Vietnam has avoided using Chinese digital technology and is working to build its own 5G network.

Chinese companies are providing a raft of telecom equipment, facial recognition technology, and data-analytics tools to the region. Some of this Chinese technology is going to countries like Myanmar and Cambodia with poor human rights records. "Digital authoritarianism is being promoted as a way for governments to control their citizens through technology, inverting the concept of the internet as an engine of human liberation," Freedom House said in a 2018 report.[63]

In a 2017 speech, Xi outlined a plan to transform China into a "cyber superpower." He said China could offer its management of the Internet

60. David E. Sanger, Julian E. Barnes, Raymond Zhong, and Marc Santora, "In 5G Race with China, U.S. Pushes Allies to Fight Huawei," *New York Times*, January 26, 2019, https://www.nytimes.com/2019/01/26/us/politics/huawei-china-us-5g-technology.html?module=inline.
61. "China's Digital Silk Road" (transcript), Center for Strategic and International Studies—Simon Chair in Political Economy, Washington, DC, February 5, 2019, https://csis-prod.s3.amazonaws.com/s3fs-public/event/190211_Chinas_Digital_Silk_Road.pdf.
62. Prasso, "China's Digital Silk Road."
63. Adrian Shahbaz, *Freedom on the Net 2018: The Rise of Digital Authoritarianism* (Washington, DC: Freedom House, 2018), https://freedomhouse.org/report/freedom-net/freedom-net-2018/rise-digital-authoritarianism.

at home as "a new option for other countries and nations that want to speed up their development while preserving their independence." China in recent years has hosted seminars on "cyberspace management" for foreign officials, including from the Philippines and Vietnam.[64]

China's foreign assistance overseas cannot be neatly distinguished from investment because China has developed a hybrid development model that includes some foreign assistance grants, state-owned bank and company loans requiring interest payments of about 4 percent or more, and business deals for Chinese companies. Researchers at AidData, a research lab at the College of William and Mary in Williamsburg, Virginia, analyzed nearly 4,400 Chinese government-aided projects between 2000 and 2014 worth a total of $354.4 billion.[65]

Of this funding, AidData found that about one-fifth was government grants or other assistance while another 20 percent was not clearly identified to determine whether it was development aid or a business deal. The remaining three-fifths of the projects were primarily commercial ventures, highlighting that for Beijing foreign assistance is also intended to snare business deals for Chinese firms and make money for its banks.

In Southeast Asia, the AidData researchers estimated that Cambodia had received $3 billion in official development aid in the years reviewed, meaning that more than 25 percent of the aid had concessional terms. Laos was given $11 billion, presumably including for construction of its high-speed rail, in "other official flows," meaning that less than 25 percent had non-concessional terms and was intended for commercial purposes.

For comparison, AidData found that China provided foreign aid of just over $350 billion globally between 2000 and 2014, not far behind the United States, which delivered almost $395 billion. But the two countries differ sharply in the types of aid provided. Just over one-fifth of Chinese aid is purely for economic development and welfare improvement with the remainder given in the form of commercial loans that need to be repaid with interest. This means that Beijing seeks economic returns on much of its aid financing. In contrast, over 90 percent of the U.S. aid was

---

64. Ibid.

65. "China's Global Development Footprint," AidData, https://www.aiddata.org/china-official-finance (accessed October 20, 2019).

for economic development and improving welfare and at least a quarter was in direct grant aid.[66]

China presents itself as a reliable, empathetic, and alternative source of international aid and one that provides assistance "without strings" attached. But at least some Chinese projects have faced significant criticism and protest, especially in Myanmar, Thailand, and Vietnam. In at least some instances, these complaints could have been overcome if the Chinese entities involved had been committed to more transparency, accountability, and corporate social responsibility and had developed closer working relations with host communities and civil society.[67]

Some Chinese projects have faced significant domestic opposition. The Chinese company building the Lower Sesan 2 Dam in Cambodia faced protests in 2013 and 2014 for alleged forced resettlement of villagers without consultation, illegal logging, practicing poor labor practices, and causing deteriorating water quality downstream.

Similar protests erupted in Myanmar against land expropriation, corruption, and ecological damage to rivers and forests when China began building its oil and gas pipelines from Kunming to Kyaukphyu on the Indian Ocean.[68]

Although China signs many memorandums of understanding—often before working out the details of a project, including even the interest rates its banks will charge for credit—Southeast Asian officials sometimes wonder just how many of China's giant aid pledges, often announced with considerable fanfare, will actually be delivered in the end. Of the $30 billion China promised Indonesia between 2005 and 2014, only about 7 percent has been implemented.[69]

More than three years after China snagged a deal from Japan to build Indonesia's first high-speed train from Jakarta to Bandung, work has barely begun. One of the project's problems is that some farmers refuse to give up their land along the proposed route.

---

66. Celia Hattan, "China's Secret Aid Empire Uncovered," *BBC News*, October 11, 2017, https://www.bbc.com/news/world-asia-china-41564841.
67. Neil Renwick, "China's Approach to International Development: A Study of Southeast Asia," *Journal of China and International Relations* 3, no. 1 (2015): 108, https://journals.aau.dk/index.php/jcir/article/view/1148/969.
68. Ibid., 119–120.
69. Gatra Priyandita and Trissa Wijaya, "China's Southeast Asia Gambit: China Paradoxically Presents Both Threats and Opportunities to Southeast Asia," *The Diplomat*, May 31, 2017, https://thediplomat.com/2017/05/chinas-southeast-asia-gambit/.

In reality, China's memorandums of understanding for megaprojects far outpace the delays, the red tape, the difficulties getting land-use rights, the rounds of renegotiations, and the protests by disgruntled villagers that many projects face.

And not all Chinese projects are successful. Chinese commentators complain that half of China's investment projects overseas are unprofitable and that fully 80 percent of China's mining projects have failed.[70] RWR Advisory Group has determined that projects worth nearly $420 billion, about a third of the total invested in BRI countries since 2013, have faced "trouble" such as performance delays, public opposition, or national security disagreements.[71]

Southeast Asian officials often complain that they find a lack of transparency about the terms and objectives of individual projects. China's infrastructure push has been a "bumpy one, marked with as many challenges and concessions as achievements," wrote Agatha Kratz and Dragan Pavlicevic, two experts on China's railway investments.

"Rather than being symbols of China's growing strength, [high-speed rail] projects have drawn divisions between China and host countries. Protracted, complex, and difficult negotiations have generated bad press, nurturing resentment and the perception of China as an incompetent or ill-meaning aspiring hegemon," Kratz and Pavlicevic said.[72]

Despite some of the anxieties in Southeast Asia, China has so far demonstrated flexibility and a willingness to compromise, at least on rail projects. For example, on the rail projects in Thailand and Laos, Beijing has dropped most of its earlier claims for sizable chunks of land along the railroad and around its stations. China was also willing to negotiate more concessional financing packages and ownership models and dropped demands for resource collateral for loans, such as the earlier proposal for a rice-for-rail arrangement with Thailand.

For now, money for infrastructure development is the biggest prize China has to offer its Southeast Asian neighbors. In the early days of the BRI, it is still too soon to tell whether all of these mammoth infrastructure plans will benefit the region or be hobbled by inefficiencies and

70. Sutter, *China's Relations with Southeast Asia*, 13.

71. The FT View, "China's Belt and Road Initiative Is Falling Short," *Financial Times*, July 29, 2018, https://www.ft.com/content/47d63fec-9185-11e8-b639-7680cedcc421.

72. Kratz and Pavlicevic, "Chinese High-Speed Rail in Southeast Asia."

massive debt overhangs that it will make it difficult for the beneficiary countries to boost economic growth and garner profits for their own companies.

With the slowing of the Chinese economy and the trade dispute with the United States, spending on the BRI appears to have fallen in 2018. According to Chinese Commerce Ministry figures, the value of newly signed projects was down just over 20 percent in the first 11 months of 2018 compared to the same period a year earlier.[73]

"Pushback to the BRI is becoming evident internationally, including in Southeast Asia," Bilahari Kausikan, a former senior Singapore Foreign Ministry official, said in a speech at a conference in Singapore in late 2018. "No one is going to shun working with China. That would be foolish. But the implementation of the BRI is going to be problematic," said the foreign policy expert. "Some projects will work better than others, some will stall."[74]

Even in China, resentment against the BRI seems to be growing on social media, reflecting concerns about Beijing spending money abroad that might be better spent at home as China's economy slows. Tsinghua University professor Xu Zhangrun called in 2018 for an end to "empty grand gestures and wasteful international largesse" in a long critique published online. State censors moved quickly to remove his essay from social media platforms.[75]

Beijing's official information network seems to have cut back its reporting on the BRI. In January 2018, *The People's Daily*, the Communist Party's mouthpiece, ran 20 articles about BRI's accomplishments, according to Minxin Pei, a China expert at Claremont McKenna College in California. In the same month a year later, the paper only carried seven BRI stories.[76]

---

73. Keith Bradsher, "China Proceeds with Belt and Road Push, but Does It More Quietly," *New York Times*, January 22, 2019, https://www.nytimes.com/2019/01/22/business/china-foreign-policy.html.
74. Bilahari Kausikan, speech delivered at editors roundtable organized by the Economic Research Institute for ASEAN and East Asia in Singapore, 2018. The text of this speech was sent to the author by Kausikan.
75. Tom Mitchel, "Beijing Insists BRI Is No Marshall Plan," *Financial Times*, September 25, 2018, https://www.ft.com/content/48f21df8-9c9b-11e8-88de-49c908b1f264?shareType=nongift.
76. Minxin Pei, "Will China Let Belt and Road Die Quietly?," *Nikkei Asian Review*, February 15, 2019, https://asia.nikkei.com/Opinion/Will-China-let-Belt-and-Road-die-quietly.

China's leaders appear to have heard at least some of the criticisms against the BRI and have begun fine-tuning the scheme. In a speech to the second conference celebrating the BRI in Beijing in April 2019, Xi backed off the triumphant tone he had long used to promote the initiative. He pledged to rein in corruption, boost transparency, and avoid heaping loads of debt on BRI recipient countries.

"Everything should be done in a transparent way, and we should have zero tolerance for corruption," Xi said. He vowed to safeguard the financial sustainability of infrastructure projects and to support compliance with international standards when issuing contracts for infrastructure projects.[77]

To be sure, the BRI has brought China significant benefits in Southeast Asia, even though it has "not managed its risks and public relations well," argues a diplomat from the region posted in Beijing. "On the political side, the BRI has got China a lot of influence. The Philippines has gone quiet [about its South China Sea dispute] and Vietnam has more balanced relations [with China]," the envoy said.

HARD POWER IN THE DISPUTED SEA

Chinese Coast Guard and maritime militia vessels launched several months of harassment against drilling rigs contracted for oil and gas exploration off the coasts of Malaysia and Vietnam beginning in May 2019. The operation started May 21, when the *Haijing 35111*, a coast guard ship, circled two vessels contracted by a subsidiary of Royal Dutch Shell to drill for oil and gas off the coast of Sarawak, Malaysia, and at one point approached within 80 meters of the contracted vessels.

In late May, the *Haijing 35111* returned to its port in Hainan Province, but on June 16 it reappeared off the coast of southern Vietnam where Russia's Rosneft had contracted a Japanese rig to drill a well and, at one point, darted between the rig and two service vessels. Then on July 3, a Chinese survey ship, the *Haiyang Dizhi* 8, accompanied by coast guard and maritime militia vessels, began its own oil and gas surveying activities.

77. Chun Han Wong and James T. Areddy, "China's Xi Vows New Direction for 'Belt and Road' after Criticism," *Wall Street Journal*, April 26, 2019, https://www.wsj.com/articles/chinas-xi-vows-new-direction-for-belt-and-road-after-criticism-11556249652.

Vietnam sent its own coast guard vessels to protect the rig working for Rosneft.[78]

Soon another Chinese survey vessel returned to the waters off Malaysia and began surveying near the rig contracted by Shell. Then on August 14, a separate Chinese survey vessel began surveying in an area of the continental shelf claimed by both Malaysia and Vietnam.

Beijing did not spell out its objectives in this multi-front, multi-month harassment operation. Collin Koh Swee Lean, a research fellow of defense and strategic studies at RSIS in Singapore, says China has long perceived its "relative weakness . . . related to offshore energy work in the South China Sea." In response, Beijing has embarked on a "multi-prong effort" to "prevent or forestall other South China Sea littoral states, either unilaterally or with foreign partners, from undertaking such activities."

For several countries in Southeast Asia, China's apparent long-term strategy to control the maritime domain has been a major irritant in their relations. Beijing said in its 2009 note to the United Nations that it has "indisputable sovereignty over the islands in the South China Sea and the adjacent waters, and enjoys sovereign rights and jurisdiction over the relevant waters as well as the seabed and subsoil thereof."[79] But beyond that, Beijing has remained vague about the exact scope of its claims in the sea.

By claiming four-fifths of the South China Sea, China has overlapping claims with Brunei, Malaysia, the Philippines, and Vietnam. These nations, plus Indonesia and Singapore, are troubled that China rejects the principles they all agreed to under the UN Convention on the Law of the Sea (UNCLOS) and refuses to negotiate differences multilaterally with other disputing countries.

The South China Sea encompasses about 1.4 million square miles and links the Pacific Ocean to the Indian Ocean through the Strait of Malacca.

78. Asia Maritime Transparency Initiative, "China Risks Flare-Up"; Greg B. Poling and Murray Hiebert, "Stop the Bullying in the South China Sea," *Wall Street Journal*, August 29, 2019, https://www.wsj.com/articles/stop-the-bully-in-the-south-china-sea-11567033378?shareToken=st99a85f3973b3443487a4ecbae90aa081&reflink=article_email_share.

79. Permanent Mission of the People's Republic of China, "Notes Verbale CML/17/2009," May 7, 2009, https://www.un.org/depts/los/clcs_new/submissions_files/mysvnm33_09/chn_2009re_mys_vnm_e.pdf.

Map 2. China's nine-dash-line claim in the South China Sea

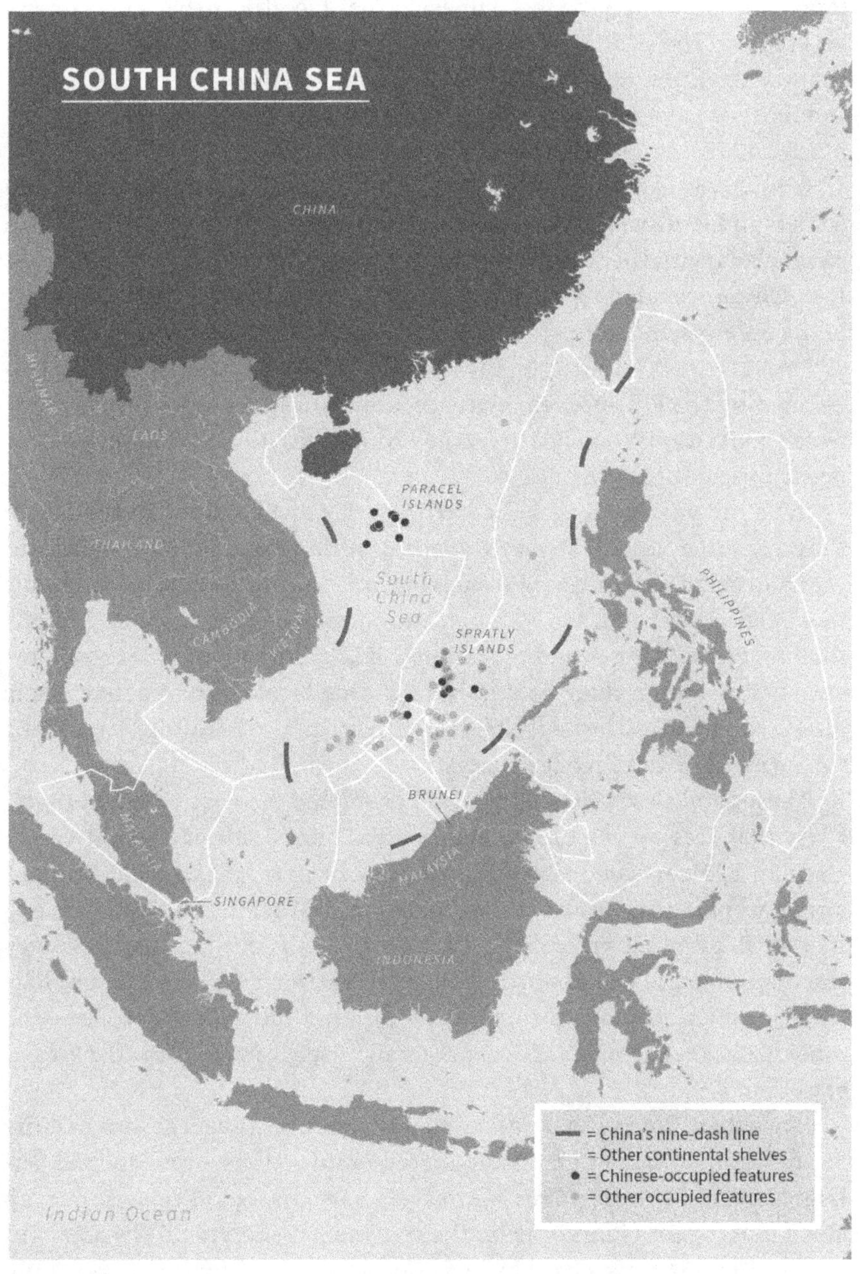

Each year some $3.4 trillion worth of trade, about one-third of the global total, passes through the sea, which also has lucrative fisheries (although less than in the past) and significant hydrocarbon reserves (albeit less than is often touted). The sea contains hundreds of rocks, islets, and shoals, most of which are uninhabited but are nonetheless subject to a patch quilt of competing sovereignty claims.

China is a relative latecomer in the effort to occupy the South China Sea's land features. In 1974, it snatched the western Paracel Islands in a naval clash with the former U.S.-back government of South Vietnam. In 1988, China occupied six submerged or partially submerged isles and reefs in the Spratlys, including Johnson South Reef, which resulted in a bloody skirmish with Vietnam. In 1995, China occupied Mischief Reef also claimed by the Philippines, Vietnam, and Taiwan. Today, Vietnam controls about twenty-one features, the Philippines nine, China seven, Malaysia five, and Taiwan one.

What ultimately set off the current round of tensions in the South China Sea in 2009? That year was the deadline for countries wishing to claim an extended continental shelf beyond 200 nautical miles to submit those claims to the United Nations Commission on the Limits of the Continental Shelf. "This prompted a range of activities among all the claimants to strengthen their positions, including legal steps to bolster their jurisdiction, patrolling activity, and infrastructure building," says Heer, the former U.S. intelligence analyst.

These activities in the disputed sea prompted increased diplomatic activity that drew in the United States, often on the side of the non-China claimants, Heer says. "Beijing saw this as part of U.S. containment strategy," particularly after it was followed by Washington's rebalance to Asia strategy a year or two later. Many of China's South China Sea moves since then have been seen by Beijing as a "reaction to this perceived challenge, and an attempt to catch up with—and ultimately surpass—the other claimants in terms of occupational presence in the disputed areas," says Heer.

Since then, China has sought to step up its control over the South China Sea by using relatively small and incremental actions, often dubbed "salami slicing" by critics. Chinese vessels have disrupted seismic survey ships looking for oil and gas on the continental shelves of Vietnam and the Philippines. China has blocked efforts by the Philippines to resupply a small crew on a rusting ship stranded for years on a tiny reef claimed by Manila called Second Thomas Shoal.[80]

Since 2013, China has built seven artificial islands in the Spratlys and equipped three of them with airfields that can handle military aircraft, radar installations, and missile shelters. Beijing imposes an annual commercial fishing ban in areas of the South China Sea, often fining violators and ramming their boats with law-enforcement ships.

"Sensing Obama's 'rebalance' rhetoric was hollow, China stuck to its creeping conquest of the South China Sea," said Thitinan Pongsudhirak, a political scientist at Thailand's Chulalongkorn University. He added, "China has been gaining ground in Southeast Asia by picking off ASEAN member states one by one. No Southeast Asian state can afford to stand up to Beijing on its own."[81]

Beijing's more assertive moves in the South China Sea and uncertainty about its long-term goals have prompted most countries around the rim of the disputed sea to pursue closer military relations with United States, Japan, India, and others.

In 2018, the Philippines began constructing a new beaching ramp at Thitu Island, the largest of the nine features occupied by the country in the Spratlys, and reclaiming land to construct a fish port and a marine research facility. China responded by deploying a fleet of ships from Subi Reef, 12 nautical miles southwest of Thitu, and by late that year, 95 Chinese Navy, Coast Guard, and fishing vessels were operating around Thitu, according to satellite imagery obtained by the CSIS Asia Maritime Transparency Initiative (AMTI). Their numbers had dropped to 42 a month later.[82]

China has not spelled out what its ultimate strategic objectives are in the South China Sea. One clearly appears to be for Beijing to assert

80. Jane Perlez, "Philippines and China in Dispute over Reef," *New York Times*, March 31, 2014, https://www.nytimes.com/2014/04/01/world/asia/beijing-and-manila-in-dispute-over-reef.html.

81. Thitinan Pongsudhirak, "A Sino-American Showdown in Southeast Asia?," *Nikkei Asian Review*, January 15, 2017, https://asia.nikkei.com/Viewpoints/Thitinan-Pongsudhirak/A-Sino-American-showdown-in-Southeast-Asia.

82. Asia Maritime Transparency Initiative, "Under Pressure: Philippine Construction Provokes a Paramilitary Response," Center for Strategic and International Studies, February 6, 2019, https://amti.csis.org/under-pressure-philippine-construction-paramilitary-response/.

sovereignty and control over much of the disputed sea. A second seems to be for China to exercise control over the sea's water and airspace so that it will be able to better defend its lines of communication and raise the risks to foreign navies, including that of the United States, operating in the South China Sea.[83]

A third Chinese objective is undoubtedly control over natural resources, especially hydrocarbons and fish. Beyond Chinese vessels harassing oil and gas exploration ships looking for hydrocarbons off the coasts of Vietnam and the Philippines, Beijing more recently has pressed Hanoi and Manila to join with Chinese firms in joint development of oil and gas. Both Southeast Asian countries are unenthusiastic about joint ventures with China because of the possible implications for Philippine and Vietnamese sovereignty.

The South China Sea in 2015 still accounted for 12 percent of the global fish catch, but the sea is increasingly overfished by countries on its rim and on the "brink of collapse," Gregory Poling of AMTI said in a 2019 report. The disputes over islands and water in the sea make fisheries management almost impossible "even as a calamitous stock collapse threatens livelihoods," he said.

Using different technologies and optical satellite imagery, Poling found that the numbers of fishing fleets operating around the Spratlys is "exponentially higher" than commonly thought and that the largest number of ships operating in the area are militia vessels rather than fishing boats.[84]

In July 2016 an international tribunal in The Hague ruled on a case brought by the Philippines that Beijing's vast claims to maritime rights and resources were not in compliance with international law and rejected China's claim that it had historically controlled the disputed waters. Beijing, which refused to participate in the proceedings, angrily rejected the ruling, and the international community, including the United States, did little to press China on the verdict after the Philippines, which brought the case, decided to shelve it.

83. Carlyle A. Thayer, "South China Sea: Assessing China's Land Reclamation Activities," Chennai Centre for China Studies, March 16, 2015, https://www.c3sindia.org/archives/south-china-sea-assessing-chinas-land-reclamation-activities-by-carlyle-a-thayer/.

84. Gregory B. Poling, "Illuminating the South China Sea's Dark Fishing Fleets," Center for Strategic and International Studies—Stephenson Ocean Security Project, January 9, 2019, https://ocean.csis.org/spotlights/illuminating-the-south-china-seas-dark-fishing-fleets/.

Senior Chinese officials have told Southeast Asian leaders that their dredging and island building stopped in 2015, but upgrading the island bases with missile installations, high-frequency radar facilities, and aircraft hangars was continuing in 2018, according to satellite imagery released by AMTI.[85] China has built large underground tunnels apparently to serve as storage depots, perhaps for arms stockpiles, on the three largest Spratly Islands.

In the Paracels, particularly on Tree Island, construction continued of helipads, wind turbines, solar energy production equipment, and administration buildings. In mid- 2018, China announced for the first time that one of its H-6K strategic bombers had landed on Woody Island in the Paracels.[86]

With the modernization of its armed forces, construction of artificial islands, and placement of military hardware in the South China Sea, China has created nearly uncontested domination over its neighbors in the disputed sea. The Chinese military "will be able to use these bases to challenge [the] U.S. presence in the region, and any forces deployed to the islands would easily overwhelm the military forces of any other South China Sea-claimants," Admiral Philip Davidson said in comments to the U.S. Senate in 2018 during his confirmation hearing to be commander of the U.S. Indo-Pacific Command.

"In short, China is now capable of controlling the South China Sea in all scenarios short of war with the United States," Davidson said.[87] By upgrading its capabilities in such areas as submarine warfare and anti-ship ballistic missiles, Davidson said "there is no guarantee that the United States would win a future conflict with China."[88]

Even though Beijing exercises more control over the sea, it does not interfere with routine commercial traffic. In part, this is probably the case

---

85. Jeremy Page, "As China Courts Neighbors, New Images Show More Building in Disputed Waters," *Wall Street Journal*, December 14, 2017, https://www.wsj.com/articles/as-china-courts-neighbors-new-images-show-more-building-in-disputed-waters-1513270862.
86. Steven Lee Meyers, "China Warns 2 American Warships in South China Sea," *New York Times*, May 27, 2018, https://www.nytimes.com/2018/05/27/world/asia/china-us-navy-paracel-islands.html.
87. U.S. Senate Committee on Armed Services, "Advance Policy Questions for Admiral Philip Davidson, USN Expected Nominee for Commander, U.S. Pacific Command," 17, https://www.armed-services.senate.gov/imo/media/doc/Davidson_APQs_04-17-18.pdf (accessed October 20, 2019).
88. Ibid., 11.

because China itself is as dependent on the free passage of its goods and energy supplies as the other countries in the region.

The United States does not take a position on the various countries' maritime claims but calls for freedom of navigation and open shipping lanes for trade. Where Beijing takes exception is on the rights of "innocent passage" for military vessels.

Because of their proximity to China and their dependence on its mammoth economy, no country in Southeast Asia would back a U.S. effort to try to push China off its recently constructed outposts in the South China Sea. Many regional countries also have lingering doubt over the U.S. long-term security commitment to the region.

But the United States under Trump has stepped up the frequency of so-called freedom of navigation operations (FONOPS) and flying military aircraft over disputed waters, which prompts Beijing to charge that Washington is militarizing the disputed sea. Recently Beijing's military has sent warships to challenge U.S. naval vessels operating in South China Sea waters and often orders them to leave.

On September 30, 2018, a Chinese warship warned a U.S. destroyer, the *Decatur*, that it was on a "dangerous course" in the South China Sea and raced up beside the American vessel. A collision was avoided when the *Decatur* took a sharp turn to avoid an accident, but the vessels came within less than 50 yards of each other. U.S. officials report some 18 unsafe incidents between Chinese and U.S. planes and ships in the Pacific between 2016 and late 2018.[89]

In a speech to the Chinese Communist Party congress in 2017 that re-elected him as party chief, Xi talked about "steady progress" in the construction of islands in the South China Sea as a major accomplishment. China watchers interpreted that to forecast that Beijing will continue its forceful policies in the coming years.

Observers expect Beijing to keep pushing its claims in the sea. One target could be construction on Scarborough Shoal, which China seized from the Philippines in 2012, although this would create major heartburn in Manila and likely derail Duterte's efforts at rapprochement with China.

89. Jane Perlez and Steven Lee Myers, "U.S. and China Are Playing 'Game of Chicken' in South China Sea," *New York Times*, November 8, 2018, https://www.nytimes.com/2018/11/08/world/asia/south-china-sea-risks.html.

Another possibility is that China could declare baselines around the Spratlys as it already has done with the Paracels. Then Beijing could treat the islands as a single grouping with internal waters complete with a continental shelf in which no one else can sail. China could use the baselines to declare an Air Defense Identification Zone, an airspace in which the government would require the identification and location of outside aircraft for the purpose of maintaining national security.

China and Southeast Asia agreed in 2002 to begin negotiating a code of conduct to prevent conflict in the South China Sea, but progress has been slow. Still some headway was made in August 2018 when the parties agreed on a single negotiating text. The code was never intended to resolve the South China Sea dispute; instead, it is envisioned as a mechanism to manage the various disputes until a resolution is negotiated, said Poling of AMTI.

Given the differences between the disputing parties, agreement on a code of conduct should not be expected soon, even though Chinese leaders have said they are committed to a three-year timeline to get the code completed.[90] Beijing can give lip service to this schedule for completing the code because it knows that the ASEAN claimants themselves cannot agree on terms that would make the code strong or binding.

Unless China resorts to force, resolution between claimants to the South China Sea dispute will be difficult. "Xi will never give up an inch of territory," says Haas of Brookings. "That's Xi's version of the Trump wall."

Still, there might be ways to tamp down U.S.-China hostilities over the South China Sea. The "prevailing narrative" is one of "China winning and the U.S. losing," Haas says. Both sides find themselves in a stalemate in which neither Washington nor Beijing can oust the other from the disputed sea without instigating armed conflict. In the end, Hass argues, "both sides will have to live with each other's presence there and will need to find ways to mitigate risk of unplanned incidents" as they operate near each other.

The South China Sea ultimately is a diplomatic and legal problem, not a military one. The more the different parties "militarize" it, the harder any resolution gets.

90. Gregory B. Poling, "South China Sea Code of Conduct Still a Speck on the Horizon," *East Asia Forum*, September 6, 2018, https://www.eastasiaforum.org/2018/09/06/south-china-sea-code-of-conduct-still-a-speck-on-the-horizon/.

CHINESE DAMS IMPERIL THE MEKONG

Stretching some 2,700 miles, the Mekong is the world's 12th longest river, beginning in the snowy mountains of Tibet in China, where it is known as the Lancang, and runs through Myanmar, Thailand, Laos, Cambodia, and Vietnam on its way to the South China Sea. Roughly 60 million farmers and fishers live along the banks and on the watershed of the Mekong, depending on its water, silt, fish, and transport for their livelihoods.

China has built 11 hydropower dams—and plans nine more—in China to produce electricity, and Chinese companies are planning to finance and/or build about half of the 11 other dams planned for the mainstream of the Mekong in Laos and Cambodia. These projects are creating anxiety and controversy downstream because the dams will impact the flow of water, curtail the movement of fish, and reduce the flow of sediment to farmers and fishers making their livelihoods from the Mekong.

By the time all of China's planned dams are built their reservoirs will hold enough water to fill the Chesapeake Bay twice over, according to Brian Eyler, author of *Last Days of the Mighty Mekong*, referring to the giant bay near Washington, DC.[91] "During the dry season, more than 40 percent of the water in the whole Mekong system comes from melting glaciers and groundwater runoff in China's portion of the [Mekong] basin," says Eyler, a Mekong expert at the Stimson Center in Washington.

This water is critical for farm production in the downstream countries of Laos, Thailand, Cambodia, and Vietnam. When drought hits, which is anticipated to happen more often with the impact of climate change, water from China is especially critical. In the Mekong Delta of southern Vietnam, the country's fertile rice basket, freshwater from China helps protect against the intrusion of saltwater from the South China Sea.

In normal years, sediment carried by the river is vital for reinforcing riverbanks in Thailand and Cambodia and protecting the "geological integrity" of the delta in Vietnam. More than half the sediment carried by the Mekong comes from China, but much of this sediment is now blocked by China's dams, which do not have effective sediment flushing systems in their designs, Eyler says.

91. Brian Eyler, *Last Days of the Mighty Mekong* (London: Zed Books, 2019), 51.

In Chiang Saen in northern Thailand nearest China's dams, the volume of suspended sediment dropped to 10 metric tons in 2009 from 60 metric tons in 2003, according to a UNESCO study.[92] The authors found that if all the dams proposed on the lower Mekong were built, they would trap fully 96 percent of the sediment load carried by the river. They estimated that this would reduce the farm output downstream by between 12 and 27 percent.[93]

The upper Mekong nearest China gets the "most nutrient rich" sediment from the Himalayas and the mountains of Yunnan Province in southern China, Eyler points out. Today the loss of sediment is "starving" the floodplain and delta downstream of nutrients, which is causing losses totaling billions of dollars.[94]

In Vietnam, agronomists and environmentalists are concerned that during times of heavy rains and floods, China and Laos will need to release water that could cause two waves of flooding downstream. In times of drought in China, water could be stored in the reservoirs of the dams, worsening the drought downstream.

Reduced sediment and water flow in the low-lying, fertile Mekong Delta in southern Vietnam has already contributed to increased saltwater incursion and drought in recent years. China's dams have decreased fish migration between the upper and lower Mekong, denting fish supplies in downstream countries. A 2018 study by the intergovernmental Mekong River Commission estimated that the decline of fish migration down the river could cost countries south of China over $16 billion in the years until 2042.[95]

But, in the end, the dams in China are likely to have less impact in Southeast Asia than the dams built or planned in Laos and Cambodia, which account for as much as 80 percent of the water flow and sediment

---

92. Thanapon Piman and Manish Shrestha, *Case Study on the Sediment in the Mekong River Basin: Current State and Future Trends* (Stockholm: Stockholm Environment Institute, 2017), 5.
93. Mekong River Commission, *The Council Study: The Study on the Sustainable Management and Development of the Mekong River Basin, including Impacts of Mainstream Hydropower Projects* (Phnom Penh: Mekong River Commission, 2017), 7, https://www.mrcmekong.org/assets/Publications/Council-Study/Council-study-Reports-discipline/180207-Macroeconomic-Assessment-Report-final-5-MG-2.pdf.
94. "Flood and Drought," Mekong River Commission, https://www.mrcmekong.org/topics/flood-and-drought/ (accessed August 20, 2019).
95. Mekong River Commission, *The Council Study*, 7.

in the Mekong. Roughly half of these dams will be built or financed by Chinese companies.

To help fund its economic development, Laos has already built scores of hydropower dams on the tributaries of the Mekong and two completed dams on the river's mainstream. Laos is planning the construction of up to six more. Much of the electricity from these dams is being exported to neighboring Thailand. Countries downstream are anxious that these dams will block the migration of fish and the flow of nutrient-rich sediment that boosts crops in Vietnam's low-lying delta and helps prevents intrusion of saltwater from the South China Sea.

China is a major investor in hydropower dams in Cambodia. The Lower Sesan 2, in which a Chinese firm holds a majority stake and which was inaugurated in late 2018, is also projected to have a major environmental impact. A study undertaken by a U.S. environmental group for the Cambodian government said the Lower Sesan 2 is "probably the largest and most destructive dam in the Mekong River Basin."[96]

As in Laos, Lower Sesan 2—and the second Sambor Dam in the pipeline—will ravage the migration of fish, on which millions of people depend for protein. These dams will also block the flow of sediment on which Vietnam's delta depends.

Because the Mekong and its water are so critical to the economies of southwestern China and mainland Southeast Asia, analysts often describe the river as a potential flashpoint between China and its neighbors, much like the South China Sea has become. In some countries, particularly in Myanmar and Vietnam, nongovernmental organizations and concerned citizens have started to push back against Chinese infrastructure projects because of their environmental impact.

At the height of a serious drought on the Mekong, U.S. Secretary of State Mike Pompeo, speaking at an ASEAN summit in Thailand in August 2019, called China's dam building and dredging on the Mekong "troubling trends." "We see a spree of upstream dam building which concentrates control over downstream flows," he said. "The river is at its lowest levels in a decade—a problem linked to China's decision to shut off water upstream."

---

96. "Cambodia: Samor," Natural Heritage Institute, https://n-h-i.org/programs/restoring-natural-functions-in-developed-river-basins/mekong-river-basin/cambodia-sambor/ (accessed October 20, 2019).

Pompeo also called Chinese policing activities on the Mekong "extra-territorial river patrols." Since the death of 13 Chinese sailors on the Mekong in 2011, China has been sending monthly gunboat patrols down the river into waters flowing through Myanmar and Laos. When they approach Thai waters, the boats blast their horns and turn back toward China. For years China has been pressing the Thais to allow the boats to continue downstream, but Bangkok has resisted Beijing's overtures.[97]

The U.S. secretary also warned in his speech that a new Mekong organization China is setting up would "push to craft new Beijing directed rules to govern the river" and sideline an existing institution.[98] China set up the Lancang-Mekong Cooperation (LMC) organization in 2015 to serve as a vehicle to boost aid and cooperation between China and the lower Mekong countries. In recent years, China has committed billions of dollars to support dozens of projects, ranging from poverty alleviation to connectivity projects and water resource research centers.[99] Some see the LMC as a competitor with the six-decade-old Mekong River Commission, which includes Laos, Thailand, Cambodia, and Vietnam but excludes China and Myanmar.[100]

The Mekong River Commission was established to provide a platform through which member countries can discuss dam projects before construction is begun. Because China is not a member, it did not have to inform the lower Mekong countries about its plans to build dams on the river's upper reaches. Some observers see Beijing's formation of the LMC as a recognition that it needs to pay heed about the impact of its projects in the downstream countries.

But not all Southeast Asians are convinced that Beijing's establishment of the LMC will result in increased Chinese coordination with Southeast Asia on the Mekong. "The LMC is a way of showing that China only plays

97. Michael Sullivan, "China Reshapes the Vital Mekong River To Power Its Expansion," *National Public Radio*, October 6, 2018, https://www.npr.org/2018/10/06/639280566/china-reshapes-the-vital-mekong-river-to-power-its-expansion.

98. Associated Press, "U.S. Decries Chinese Dams, Disruption of Mekong River," *Waco Tribune-Herald*, August 1, 2019, https://www.wacotrib.com/news/ap_nation/headlines/us-decries-chinese-disruption-of-mekong-river/article_0ad0f7e2-e6e3-50bf-9b59-2856e0ff55a1.html.

99. Catherine Wong, "Is Mekong River Set to Become the New South China Sea for Regional Disputes?," *South China Morning Post*, January 2, 2018, https://www.scmp.com/news/china/diplomacy-defence/article/2126528/mekong-river-set-become-new-south-china-sea-regional.

100. Chheang, *Trends in Southeast Asia*, 6.

by its own rules," says political scientist Thitinan of Chulalongkorn University. "It creates [a] fait accompli by building dams upstream to the detriment of downstream countries and then sets up its own governing body as a rejection of the [Mekong River Commission]." Thitinan adds that "China has dealt with Mekong countries bilaterally so that these countries are not able to unite and stand up to China as a regional grouping."[101]

STEPPED-UP MILITARY DIPLOMACY

In addition to bolstering its diplomatic and economic relations with Southeast Asia, China has also sharply increased its military engagement with the region in recent years. Indonesia, Myanmar, the Philippines, and Thailand—countries that have been sanctioned for various political reasons by Washington over the years—have been particularly happy to have another source of weapons.

In 2017, China provided its second shipment of assault rifles to the Philippines valued at $4.3 million for the country's police after the U.S. Congress blocked the sale of M4 rifles to protest the extrajudicial killing of thousands in Duterte's war on drugs. Thailand meanwhile was preparing to take delivery of its first batch of 28 VT4 tanks purchased for $147 million from China North Industries Corporation. Bangkok also put in an order in 2016 for three Chinese Type 039A Yuan-class diesel-electric attack submarines.[102]

Neighboring Malaysia agreed the same year to buy four Chinese coastal patrol vessels in a deal worth $277 million. Two of these littoral ships will be built in China and two in Malaysia. Indonesia in 2016 ordered a Chinese Type 730 radar-guided weapons system for installing on frigates to defend against anti-ship missiles and precision-guided munitions. While Myanmar faced several decades of sanctions from the United States and Europe until 2015, China was the main supplier of fighter aircraft, armored vehicles, naval ships, and guns.[103]

---

101. Wong, "Is Mekong River Set to Become the New South China Sea."
102. Kristin Huang, "The Weapons Sales Making China a Big Gun in Southeast Asia," *South China Morning Post*, October 5, 2017, https://www.scmp.com/news/china/diplomacy-defence/article/2114172/weapons-sales-making-china-big-gun-southeast-asia.
103. Ibid.

Globally, China accounted for 6.2 percent of the worldwide arms trade between 2012 and 2016, making China the world's third largest arms exporter behind the United States and Russia. China's arms exports rose 74 percent over the years from 2007 to 2011 and 2012 to 2016.[104] In 2016, China's arms sales reached $2.1 billion. In the five-year period before 2016, the lion's share went to only three countries: Pakistan, Bangladesh, and Myanmar.

China is quickly moving up the technology ladder from old Soviet platforms to more "indigenous" models. Today its exports include Type-99 MBT tanks, J-10 fighter planes, and Yuan-class submarines.

Export earnings are not China's primary goal for military sales. Rather, "Beijing's end-game is longer-term geopolitical and strategic influence," argued Ron Matthews of the Centre for Defense Management and Leadership in the United Kingdom and Xiaojuan Ping of the National University of Singapore. "The search for regional and global influence is the critical aim of Chinese economic diplomacy."[105]

China's arms philosophy often faces criticism from Western countries, but it does win contracts and influence. "Beijing's long-standing approach of linking non-interference to arms sales rests on the view that the customer's political, military, and human rights record lies outside the contractual arrangements," Matthews and Ping said. "Chinese arms offer poorer states the opportunity to diversify arms sources, regain a degree of sovereignty over military capability, and reduce strategic vulnerability to arms embargoes."[106]

In addition to weapon's sales, China's military has also significantly stepped up military diplomacy in recent years. But senior-level military meetings rather than joint military exercises accounted for 83 percent of the Chinese military's global engagements, China military experts Kenneth Allen, Phillip Saunders, and John Chen pointed out in a 2017 study

---

104. Aude Fleurant, Pieter D. Wezeman, Siemon T. Wezeman, and Nan Tian, *Trends in International Arms Transfers, 2016* (Stockholm: Stockholm International Peace Research Institute, 2017), https://www.sipri.org/sites/default/files/Trends-in-international-arms-transfers-2016.pdf.

105. Ron Matthews and Xiaojuan Ping, "The End Game of China's Arms Export Strategy," *East Asia Forum*, September 27, 2017, https://www.eastasiaforum.org/2017/09/27/the-end-game-of-chinas-arms-export-strategy/.

106. Ibid.

published by the U.S. National Defense University.[107] They argued, however, that this level of interaction does not necessarily translate into influence because "much of China's military activity consists of formal exchanges of scripted talking points."[108]

Still, the actual number of Chinese joint exercises globally increased dramatically in 2016 to 124, almost equal to the total of 130 from 2003 to 2016.

Almost a quarter of China's total military interactions between 2003 and 2016 were with militaries in Southeast Asia. The largest number, 84, were with Thailand, which included 21 actual military exercises. The second largest was with Vietnam, but these interactions consisted of 54 senior-level meetings and only two exercises, presumably because of tensions between the two countries in the South China Sea. Even among China's closest friends in the region, meetings far outstripped exercises. Cambodia had two exercises during this period, while Myanmar and Laos each only had one.[109]

In October 2019, China and ASEAN conducted their first maritime training exercise in southern China, including helicopter cross-deck landings and joint search-and-rescue operation.[110]

China's goals for engaging in military diplomacy are to create a favorable international image for Beijing, shape China's security environment, gather intelligence, and learn from more advanced foreign militaries, Allen, Saunders, and Chen said.[111] Another Chinese military objective is to "make sure the U.S. posture continues to decline" in the region, says Tai Ming Cheung, director of the University of California's Institute on Global Conflict and Cooperation and an analyst of Chinese defense affairs.

107. Kenneth Allen, Phillip Saunders, and John Chen, *Chinese Military Diplomacy, 2003–2016: Trends and Implications* (Washington, DC: National Defense University Press, 2017), 2, https://ndupress.ndu.edu/Portals/68/Documents/stratperspective/china/ChinaPerspectives-11.pdf?ver=2017-07-17-153301-093.

108. Ibid., 4.

109. Ibid., 62–63.

110. Lim Min Zhang, "China, ASEAN Kick Off Inaugural Maritime Field Training Exercise in Zhanjiang, Guangdong," *Straits Times*, October 22, 2018, https://www.straitstimes.com/asia/east-asia/china-asean-kick-off-inaugural-maritime-field-training-exercise-in-zhanjiang?&utm_source=email&utm_medium=social-media&utm_campaign=addtoany.

111. Allen, Saunders, and Chen, *Chinese Military Diplomacy*, 1.

Cheung points out that Chinese military engagements with Thailand, Cambodia, Malaysia, and even Indonesia have "developed much closer relations" in recent years while "some friction with traditional friends in Singapore and Myanmar" has emerged. China is exploring joint arms production and defense industrial production with Thailand, Indonesia, and Malaysia, he says.

The "big question" is whether China will try to gain access to any military bases in Southeast Asia like the one it established in Djibouti in Africa, Cheung says. Some analysts speculate that China might explore gaining military access to Kyaukphyu in western Myanmar on the Bay of Bengal, where Chinese companies have negotiated an agreement to build a commercial seaport. But so far there is no indication that the Myanmar government is considering allowing the Chinese military access to the yet-to-be-built port.

"China's peripheral diplomacy, especially under Xi, is to make sure surrounding countries are more closely tied with China," Cheung argues. "China was worried that with the island building [in the South China Sea], the U.S. presence [in the region] would be reinforced." But the fact that Southeast Asia has downplayed the island building since Duterte took over in the Philippines in 2016 "represents an important opportunity for China to repair the damage," Cheung says.

SOFT POWER TO SHARP POWER

Beijing has also mounted a "charm offensive" in Southeast Asia to bolster the popular image of China and launched various initiatives to expand its cultural influence and knowledge of Mandarin. It has established a raft of Confucius Institutes in the region with 15 in Thailand, six in Indonesia, four in the Philippines, two in Malaysia, but only one in Vietnam.[112]

Thanks to several decades of economic growth, China has turned its education system into an attractive hub for foreign students. Earlier international students went to China mainly for language study, but more recently they have also been attracted to professional degree programs and technical courses. In 2016, China drew over 442,000 foreign students, about 68,000 of which were from Southeast Asia.

---

112. Confucius Institute/Classroom, https://english.hanban.org/node_10971.htm (accessed December 18, 2017).

The Southeast Asians included more than 23,000 from Thailand, nearly 15,000 from Indonesia, and almost 11,000 from Vietnam. Roughly 40 percent of foreign students went on Chinese government scholarships.[113] To boost the numbers of Southeast Asians who benefit from a Chinese education, China has also established satellite university campuses in three Southeast Asian countries: Laos, Malaysia, and Thailand.[114]

Yang Xiping, secretary-general of ASEAN–China Center, says "students from Southeast Asia are the bridge and future of the relationship between ASEAN [countries] and China."[115]

Chinese tourist numbers have exploded in recent years, boosting regional economies and giving China geopolitical leverage over its southern neighbors. Southeast Asia is one of the top destinations for Chinese tourists, with 19.8 million visiting in 2016, up 6.4 percent from the previous year. Some 10.3 million Southeast Asians visited China in 2016, an increase of nearly 60 percent.[116]

Thailand, Singapore, Vietnam, Malaysia, Indonesia, and the Philippines are among the most popular Southeast Asian destinations for Chinese tourists. About 2,700 flights connect Southeast Asian countries with China every week and most Southeast Asian countries offer visa-free or visa-on-arrival entry for Chinese visitors.[117]

Globally, the Chinese are the biggest group of international travelers, making 142 million international trips in 2017 and spending $258 billion,

113. China Power Project, "Is China Both a Source and a Hub for International Students?," Center for Strategic and International Studies, October 31, 2017, https://chinapower.csis.org/china-international-students/?utm_source=CSIS+All&utm_campaign=09495c40e2-EMAIL_CAMPAIGN_2017_10_04&utm_medium=email&utm_term=0_f326fc46b6-09495c40e2-138494157; "China Seeks More Students from Southeast Asian Countries," *Jakarta Post*, October 25, 2016, https://www.thejakartapost.com/youth/2016/10/25/china-seeks-more-students-from-southeast-asian-countries.html.

114. Coco Liu and Tashny Sukumaran, "Belt and Read: How China Is Exporting Education and Influence to Malaysia and Other ASEAN Countries," *South China Morning Post*, July 30, 2017, https://www.scmp.com/week-asia/politics/article/2097965/belt-road-and-books-how-chinas-trying-soft-power-outreach.

115. "China Seeks More Students."

116. Stanley Loh, "Taking ASEAN–China Ties to the Next Level," *The Straits Times*, September 15, 2017, https://www.straitstimes.com/opinion/taking-asean-china-ties-to-the-next-level.

117. Xinhua, "Southeast Top Choice for Chinese Outbound Tourists during Holiday," *China Daily*, October 8, 2017, https://www.chinadaily.com.cn/travel/2017-10/08/content_32990192.htm.

according to Elizabeth Becker, author of *Overbooked: The Exploding Business of Travel and Tourism*. China's heft in international tourism is expected to grow because Beijing has established its own global tourist organization, the World Travel Alliance, and linked it to its giant BRI infrastructure scheme.[118]

Southeast Asian tour operators complain, however, that they often do not make money from Chinese travelers because of what they call "zero cost" tourism. This means that a Chinese tourist books and pays for her flight, hotel stays, and restaurant meals with a travel agent in China. Even the hotels where Chinese stay and restaurants where they eat are owned by Chinese companies, giving Southeast Asian firms little opportunity to make money from Chinese tourists.

But like other tourist destinations, Southeast Asia is also starting to welcome more Chinese tourists from the "middle, rich, and very rich classes," Becker said. "Fewer travel in groups."[119]

Beijing takes advantage of its heft in tourism to punish countries whose governments Chinese officials perceive to be stepping out of line. In 2012, at the height of the standoff with the Philippines in the South China Sea after China seized Scarborough Shoal, long controlled by the Philippines, Chinese travel agencies suspended tour groups to the country.[120]

Chinese tourist confidence is also highly dependent on local and regional developments. Tourists from China reduced their travel to Malaysia after a Malaysian Airlines plane disappeared on its flight to Beijing in 2014. They also canceled trips to Thailand after a pleasure boat sank off the coast of Phuket in southern Thailand in 2018, killing nearly 50 Chinese tourists.[121]

So far, little is publicly known about the extent of Chinese efforts using cultural projects or informational tactics to influence politics in Southeast Asian countries. Beijing helped fund the election commission in

---

118. Meagan Drillinger, "Breathtaking Bliss at the Banyan Tree Samui," *Travel Weekly*, January 31, 2019, https://www.travelweekly.com/Asia-Travel/Breathtaking-bliss-Banyan-Tree-Samui.
119. Ibid.
120. "Philippines Seeks New Markets Amid Sea Dispute with China," *Reuters*, May 17, 2012, https://www.reuters.com/article/uk-philippines-china-idUSLNE84G02520120517.
121. Ben Bland, "Chinese Tourists Spurn SE Asia Holidays," *Financial Times*, July 26, 2015, https://www.ft.com/content/348c0486-335e-11e5-bdbb-35e55cbae175.

Cambodia ahead of the 2018 elections and it was widely assumed Chinese companies, if not the government as well, were providing funds to Hun Sen's Cambodia People's Party. Many Filipinos assume that Chinese companies, possibly working through ethnic Chinese companies in the Philippines, provided at least some funding for the election of Duterte as president in 2016.

China's influence operations in Southeast Asia are nowhere as clear as in Singapore, a city-state where three-quarters of its population is of Chinese descent. In a 2018 speech (one that sparked a sharp response from the Chinese ambassador), Bilahari Kausikan, the straight-talking former senior Foreign Ministry official, warned Singaporeans that Beijing not only wants them "to comply with its wishes" but it wants them to "do [what] it wants without having to be told."[122]

Beijing has been particularly irritated about Singapore's harping on the rule of law in dealing with the South China Sea and the fact that the city-state allows U.S. naval vessels and military aircraft to use Singapore facilities. China took several steps to ding Singapore for several months beginning in late 2016, including seizing nine armored vehicles in Hong Kong in transit from Taiwan to Singapore. The city-state's misdeed? Prime Minister Lee Hsien Loong called on all parties involved in the dispute to follow the "rules-based international order" in implementing the 2016 arbitral tribunal ruling against China's claims in the South China Sea.

Increased interest in China's possible role in politics in Southeast Asia has emerged against a backdrop of rising Chinese political involvement in Australia, New Zealand, and Western countries. News outlets in Australia have stepped up reporting about prominent ethnic Chinese businesspersons donating millions of dollars to parliamentary election campaigns. Property developer Huang Xiaomo, an Australian resident who has applied for citizenship, withdrew a $300,000 pledge to the Labor Party in 2016 because of its position critical of Beijing on the South China Sea dispute.[123]

---

122. Charissa Yong, "S'poreans Should Be Aware of Chinese Influence Ops: Bilahari," *Straits Times*, June 28, 2018, https://www.straitstimes.com/singapore/sporeans-should-be-aware-of-chinas-influence-ops-bilahari.

123. Damien Cave and Jacqueline Williams, "Australian Politics Is Open to Foreign Cash, and China Has Much to Gain," *New York Times*, June 6, 2017, https://www.nytimes.com/2017/06/06/world/australia/china-political-influence-campaign-finance.html.

In late 2019, Australian officials confirmed that they were investigating accusations that a Melbourne-based luxury car dealer, Bo "Nick" Zhao, was part of a plot to install him as a Chinese agent in the country's Parliament. Zhao, who was a member of Australian Liberal Party, told the country's intelligence agency that another businessman linked to the Chinese government had offered him nearly $700,000 to fund his election campaign. Not long after, Zhao was found dead in a hotel room. The cause of death is still being investigated. A Chinese spokesman rejected the accusations as "nothing but lies."[124]

In New Zealand, the national intelligence agency has investigated a Chinese-born member of Parliament who earlier spent more than a decade teaching at a linguistics academy for military intelligence officers in China. Since his election in 2011, Jian Yang, had pushed for closer New Zealand relations with Beijing, including while serving on a parliamentary committee for foreign affairs, defense, and trade from 2014 to 2016.[125]

New Zealand police in late 2018 were investigating the case of a professor at the University of Canterbury, Anne-Marie Brady, who had been the focus of a harassment effort that included break-ins of her house, office, and car. Brady, who published a report in 2017 called "Magic Weapons" that outlined China's efforts to establish more political sway in Western countries, said the only items stolen were technology used in her China research.[126]

China's influence-buying activities, which are separate from traditional spying, are guided by the United Front Work Department of the ruling Communist Party. The original goal of the department was primarily to influence the activities of overseas Chinese, including neutralizing criticisms from Chinese dissidents, democracy activists, and supporters of Taiwan and Tibet independence. But in recent years the United Front has also sought to influence a range of players from

---

124. Jamie Smyth, "Chinese Spy Tales Fuel Australian Fears," *Financial Times*, November 28, 2019, https://www.ft.com/content/83e322d6-118e-11ea-a7e6-62bf4f9e548a?shareType=nongift.

125. Charlotte Graham-McLay, "A New Zealand Lawmaker's Spy-Linked Past Raises Alarms on China's Reach," *New York Times*, October 4, 2017, https://www.nytimes.com/2017/10/04/world/asia/new-zealand-china-spy.html.

126. Charlotte Graham-McLay, "China Watchers Demand Action on Harassment of New Zealand Professor," *New York Times*, December 7, 2018, https://www.nytimes.com/2018/12/07/world/asia/new-zealand-academic-harassment-china.html.

politicians to news organizations and academics in foreign countries about the legitimacy of China's party.[127]

Western publishers have faced pressure from Beijing to block access to articles critical of China. Springer Nature of Germany, which owns *Nature* magazine, prevented access in China in 2017 to more than 1,000 articles after it faced censorship demands from Beijing over keywords such as "Tibet" and "Cultural Revolution." A few months earlier, Cambridge University Press gave way to similar pressure from China, but it later reversed its action after public protests.[128]

In October 2019, the Houston Rockets general manager apologized for tweeting support two days earlier for the months-long pro-democracy protests in Hong Kong. The tweet prompted the Chinese Basketball Association and some Chinese companies to suspend ties with the National Basketball Association's most popular teams in China.[129]

A 2018 report by a working group on Chinese influence activities organized by the U.S.-based Hoover Institution concluded that many people outside China are not fully "aware of the myriad ways Beijing has recently been seeking cultural and informational influence, some which could undermine our democracy." The report said that some of China's efforts fall into the category of "normal public diplomacy" pursued by other countries, but "others involved the use of coercive or corrupting methods to pressure individuals and groups and thereby interfere in the functioning of American civil and political life."[130]

China has invested giant sums on media platforms abroad, including in Southeast Asia, which Beijing uses to influence views about China and boost Beijing's image. In Singapore, the two largest cable providers each offer about half a dozen Chinese-language news and documentary channels from Hong Kong and Taiwan, several of which take funding

---

127. Jamil Anderlini and Jamie Smyth, "West Grows Wary of China's Influence Game," *Financial Times*, December 19, 2017, https://www.ft.com/content/d3ac306a-e188-11e7-8f9f-de1c2175f5ce?sharetype=share.
128. Ben Bland, "Outcry as Latest Global Publisher Bows to China Censors," *Financial Times*, November 1, 2017, https://www.ft.com/content/2d195ffc-be2e-11e7-b8a3-38a6e068f464.
129. Scott Neuman, "Houston Rockets GM Apologizes for Tweet Supporting Hong Kong Protestors," *National Public Radio*, October 7, 2019, https://www.npr.org/2019/10/07/767805936/houston-rockets-gm-apologizes-for-tweet-supporting-hong-kong-protesters.
130. Working Group on Chinese Influence Activities in the United States, *Chinese Influence and American Interests: Promoting Constructive Vigilance*, rev. ed. (Stanford, CA: Hoover Institution Press, 2018), 1, https://www.hoover.org/sites/default/files/research/docs/00_diamond-schell_fullreport_2ndprinting_web-compressed.pdf.

from China and actively push Beijing's perspectives to their Singapore audience.

Initially when the cable providers began including channels from Taiwan and Hong Kong in the 1990s and 2000s, they were less "Beijing-leaning," says political scientist Ian Chong of the National University of Singapore. Chong says these tendencies only increased later as China began kicking in more capital. For example, he says on "contentious issues" such as coverage of the South China Sea, they make clear Singapore should not "resist China's position."

In neighboring Malaysia, a China-friendly ethnic Chinese timber tycoon played a critical role in helping Beijing gain influence over some newspapers often critical of the Chinese government. In the mid-1990s, he bought the Ming Pao group in Hong Kong with the goal of turning its flagship paper into a "pro-mainland paper," says a Chinese-Malaysian editor who worked on the newspaper. An academic who monitored the paper carefully says the paper, which was formerly "critical" of China, became "significantly pro-China" under the new management.

Southeast Asian governments do not talk much about Chinese attempts to intervene in their governments or societies, including about cyberattacks. But the U.S. cybersecurity firm FireEye Inc. reported in 2015 that hackers, likely from China, had been spying on governments, businesses, and journalists in Southeast Asia uninterrupted since 2005, apparently without being detected. The company said the attacks were intended to gather intelligence from classified government networks and other sources related to military and political issues, including the South China Sea dispute.

FireEye said some of the attacks came in the form of phishing e-mails, crafted in the recipients' native language and accompanied by legitimate-looking documents containing malware. In other cases, the hackers penetrated secure networks by tricking administrators into downloading malware to their computers that was then implanted on their portable drives, which were later plugged into a secure network, infecting it.

In cases dating back to 2011, FireEye reported that hackers had infiltrated the computer systems of Southeast Asian governments to gain understanding of the dynamics between them and their key discussion points ahead of the meetings with the ASEAN grouping, which often include discussion of China's activities in the South China Sea. In another case in 2014, the company said the hacking group, known as APT30, launched an attack in the defense and financial services sectors of a Southeast Asian nation in the midst of a "significant political transition."[131]

Beijing has long denied that it uses the Internet to spy on foreign governments and businesses. But the U.S. Justice Department in 2018 unsealed criminal charges against two Chinese nationals who were allegedly linked to a government-supported effort to pilfer sensitive information from U.S. companies and government bodies. U.S. officials said a cross-section of different businesses in at least 12 nations had been targets of cyber campaigns carried out by APT30. A few months earlier, U.S. prosecutors had unsealed charges against 10 Chinese agents with the Ministry of Public Security who had allegedly hacked into U.S. aviation firms.[132]

Separately, FireEye reported in mid-2017 during a time of heightened tensions in the South China Sea that cyber spies working on behalf of the Chinese government had launched attacks against the Vietnamese government and business targets. The cybersecurity firm said the attacks involved sending users documents in Vietnamese requesting financial information. When the user opened the documents, the attackers delivered malware that infected a computer, sent back information, and allowed them access to the computer network.[133]

In 2018, in the most serious cyberattack in Singapore, hackers broke into the computers of SingHealth, the city-state's largest health care provider, and stole the personal information of 1.5 million people. Some 160,000, including Prime Minister Lee, had their drug prescription information taken.[134] The government has not identified the hackers, but they are widely assumed to be affiliated with a Chinese group.

---

131. Newley Purnell, "China's Hackers Run 10-Year Spy Campaign in Asia, Report Finds," *Wall Street Journal*, April 12, 2015, https://www.wsj.com/articles/chinas-hackers-run-10-year-spy-campaign-in-asia-report-finds-1428854482.

132. Dustin Volz, Kate O'Keeffe, and Bob Davis, "U.S. Charges China Intelligence Officers over Hacking Companies and Agencies," *Wall Street Journal*, December 20, 2018, https://www.wsj.com/articles/u-s-to-unseal-criminal-charges-against-chinese-intelligence-officers-11545316450.

133. Matthew Tostevin, "Chinese Cyber Spies Broaden Attacks in Vietnam, Security Firm Says," *Reuters*, August 31, 2017, https://www.reuters.com/article/us-vietnam-china-cyber-idUSKCN1BB0I5?lipi=urn%3Ali%3Apage%3Ad_flagship3_feed%3BZehLHI9oRculvg09i4F%2B7Q%3D%3D.

134. Irene Tham, "Personal Info of 1.5m SingHealth Patients, Including PM Lee, Stolen in Singapore's Worst Cyber Attack," *The Straits Times*, July 20, 2018, https://www.straitstimes

Growing trade, tourism, and other exchanges between China and Southeast Asia have also resulted in the expansion of Chinese involved in crime in the region. Goods smuggling, illicit drug flows, and human trafficking, including brides for Chinese men, have long been problems along the border. In recent years, new scams have emerged.

Scores of Chinese nationals were deported from Cambodia in 2017 after they were arrested for extorting money from people over the Internet and by telephone.[135] Singapore announced that in the first 11 months of 2017 at least 158 people had been duped out of about $9 million by bogus Chinese officials pretending to be from the Ministry of Public Security.[136]

China has made enormous strides in Southeast Asia in recent years, particularly on the economic front. In achieving its goals, China's has important assets in dealing with Southeast Asia, including its physical proximity, its mountains of cash, and the fact that it does not hector countries on democracy and human rights.

But Beijing also carries significant liabilities. "China's greatest drawback is its inability to view itself as others view it" and the tendency of the Chinese to "believe their government's propaganda about its benign intentions and behavior," said Shambaugh of George Washington University. "Beijing is not self-critical, never admits fault or error, and routinely blames others when strains emerge in its foreign relations."[137]

Another liability is Beijing's assertiveness in the South China Sea and its use of its near-client in Cambodia to block criticisms of its actions by ASEAN. It also uses hardball tactics such as economic and political isolation of governments like the Philippines and Singapore when they press China to follow the principles of international law in the disputed sea.

.com/singapore/personal-info-of-15m-singhealth-patients-including-pm-lee-stolen-in-singapores-most.

135. "Cambodia Deports 74 Chinese Arrested for Telecom Extortion Scams," *Reuters*, October 12, 2017, https://www.reuters.com/article/us-cambodia-china/cambodia-deports-74-chinese-arrested-for-telecom-extortion-scams-idUSKBN1CH12G.

136. Ng Huiwen, "158 Victims Lost $12m to Scams Involving Bogus Chinese Officials between January and November," *The Straits Times*, December 28, 2017, https://www.straitstimes.com/singapore/158-victims-fall-prey-to-chinese-officials-impersonation-scams-between-january-and.

137. David Shambaugh, "U.S.-China Rivalry in Southeast Asia: Power Shift or Competitive Coexistence?," *International Security* 42, no. 4 (Spring 2018): 125.

Another challenge is the lack of transparency and corruption in its infrastructure projects, and its willingness (as in the case of Malaysia and Laos) to provide unsustainable levels of debt. A potential problem down the road is the flood of ethnic Chinese into places like northern Myanmar, northern Laos, and Sihanoukville in Cambodia, displacing locals and raising concerns in some countries about whether China might use the ethnic Chinese for political purposes in the future.

2. MYANMAR: MARRIAGE OF CONVENIENCE, NOT A MATCH MADE IN HEAVEN

> I live by the river's head, You live by its tail.
> Limitlessly, we love each other, We drink the same river's water.
> I drink from the upper flows, You drink from below.
> Endlessly the river flows, We share everlasting happiness.
> We are neighbors, Our friendship lasts.
> Like the ageless evergreen, The waters flow forever.
> Our lands are connected, We rely on the same mountains
> and water . . .
> We are united and help each other, Peace is powerful.[1]
>
> —*General Chenyi, December 14, 1956*

In November 2017, after weeks of criticism by Washington and United Nations officials about the brutal treatment of Myanmar's Rohingya population, the country's nominal leader Aung San Suu Kyi visited Beijing for the second time in six months. Less than a week earlier, Senior General Min Aung Hlaing—Myanmar's military commander and in many ways the country's de facto leader, who oversaw the attacks that prompted hundreds of thousands of Rohingya to flee the country—had received a red-carpet welcome from Chinese president Xi Jinping and his generals in Beijing.

---

1. The poem, *For Friends in Burma,* was written by General Chenyi, who was close to Chairman Mao Zedong. An adaption of a love poem by Li Qingzhao, it was intended to capture the official friendship between China and Myanmar. See David I. Steinberg and Hongwei Fan, *Modern China-Myanmar Relations: Dilemmas of Mutual Dependence* (Copenhagen: Nordic Institute of Asian Studies, 2012), 41.

The exodus of over 700,000 Rohingya Muslims from Myanmar was in response to a military crackdown following attacks by militants against some border posts. The resulting flood of condemnation about the government's handling of the crisis was a bonanza for Beijing. The crisis handed China a strategic opening to regain its influence with its neighbor and helped reestablish some semblance of stability not far from China's border.

"The Rakhine crisis will push [Aung San Suu Kyi] closer to China," Min Zin, a U.S.-educated political scientist in Yangon, observed shortly after the Rohingya exodus erupted. "The economy is slowing down and no international aid and investment is coming." Min Zin, who heads the Institute for Strategy and Policy in Yangon, adds, "Myanmar was looking to the United States . . . [Aung San Suu Kyi] will [now] rely on China for economic and diplomatic support."

But Thant Myint-U, a Myanmar historian and writer, argues the country's leaders did not jump completely into Beijing's camp. In late 2019 during a talk in Washington to promote his latest book, *The Hidden History of Burma: Race, Capitalism, and the Crisis of Democracy in the 21st Century*, Thant said they sought to balance their ties with China with much closer relations with Japan, Korea, and their Southeast Asian neighbors.[2]

At the highest political levels, diplomatic relations between Myanmar and China have once again become highly cordial. But on the ground, decades of often complicated and fraught ties mean that China faces considerable negative sentiment in its southern neighbor, despite Beijing's recent public diplomacy offensive. Beijing's plans for enormous infrastructure projects in Myanmar under its colossal Belt and Road Initiative (BRI) have barely been hobbling along in recent years.

Military ties are still quite tentative. Myanmar's nationalistic officers often wonder about China's intentions in backing the armed ethnic groups along the countries' borders fighting the central government. The migration of hundreds of thousands of ethnic Chinese creates considerable anxiety in cities like Mandalay about the cultural and economic transformation they are bringing to the northern reaches of Myanmar.

2. Thant Myint-U, "The Hidden History of Burma: Race, Capitalism, and the Crisis of Democracy," Banyan Tree Leadership Forum, Center for Strategic and International Studies, November 20, 2019, https://www.csis.org/events/hidden-history-burma-race-capitalism-and-crisis-democracy-21st-century.

Map 3. Myanmar

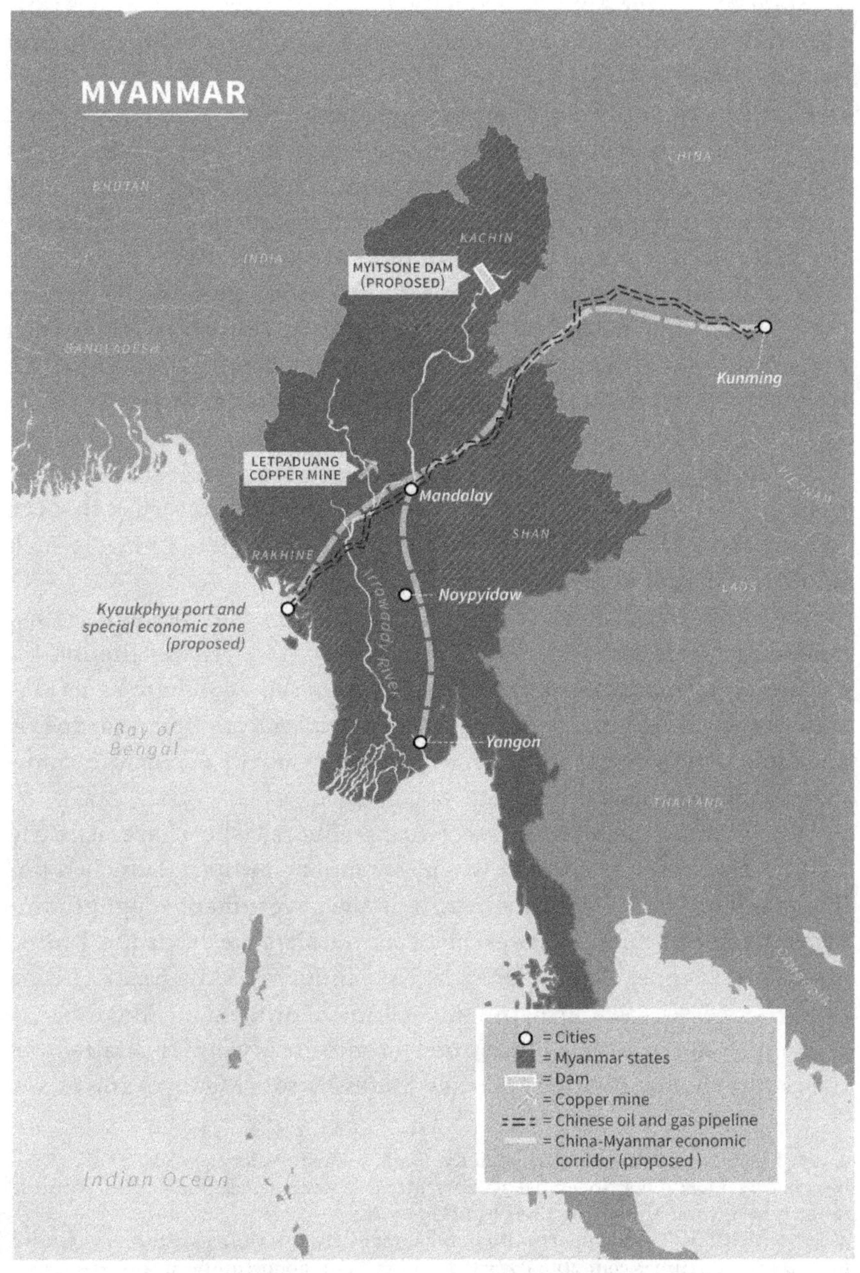

During a 2017 visit to Myanmar by Chinese foreign minister Wang Yi, State Counselor Aung San Suu Kyi told him: "Myanmar values China's understanding of the Rakhine issue, which is complicated and delicate."[3]

China's sympathy for Myanmar on the Rohingya may have been prompted at least in part by the fact that Beijing has also faced challenges from its own Muslim Uyghur minority in the Xinjiang region of China's northwest. Beijing may want to ensure that any possibility of links between the Rohingya and Uyghur militants are minimized.[4]

In addition, China may be concerned about a possible "Rohingya problem" of its own, says Yun Sun, an expert on China's relations with Myanmar at the Stimson Center in Washington. Some 10,000 Rohingya have settled in Ruili, not far from China's border with Myanmar. Many arrived as businesspeople who overstayed their visas. Beijing has deported many of them, but quite a few have come back and established an Islamic "congregation" in the city. Yun says China is concerned that the Rohingya could eventually try to mount a "migration to China," which would be difficult for Beijing to control.

For two decades after Myanmar's brutal military crackdown against democracy protestors in 1988, China served as a critical lifeline for Myanmar as many Western countries imposed economic sanctions against the ruling junta. Beijing provided aid, trade, military hardware, and diplomatic support at the United Nations as many democratic countries sought to isolate the regime.

But relations between these two neighbors, who share a nearly 1,400-mile border, weakened when Myanmar's military launched political and economic reforms in 2011 as the government sought to improve ties with and get investment and assistance from the United States and Europe. "The factors that have influenced Myanmar's China policy since 2011 are growing anti-China sentiment in Myanmar, a growing concern over China's interference in Myanmar affairs, and the rapprochement with the United States," wrote Maung Aung Myoe,

3. Jane Perlez, "In China, Aung San Suu Kyi Finds a Warm Welcome (and No Talk of Rohingya)," *New York Times*, November 30, 2017, https://www.nytimes.com/2017/11/30/world/asia/china-myanmar-aid-sanctions.html?emc=eta1.

4. Yun Sun, "China Finds Opportunity in Myanmar Crisis," *Asia Times*, February 13, 2018, https://www.asiatimes.com/2018/02/article/china-finds-opportunity-myanmar-crisis/.

a Myanmar expert at International University of Japan, before the Rohingya crisis erupted.[5]

As political prisoners were freed in 2012, more space was opened for the media, the economy was liberalized, and foreign investors from the West were courted. The Myanmar government in Naypyidaw put a freeze on China's largest and most prestigious project, the Myitsone hydropower dam in Kachin State at the confluence of two rivers that join to become the Irrawaddy River. Beijing's interests in Myanmar were constrained by these efforts at rapprochement with Washington.

Fierce nationalism and considerable anti-China sentiment within the population has long made Myanmar a tough target for Beijing. The view in Myanmar of China's role during the rule of the military junta was exacerbated by the exploitative nature of some Chinese investments, which did not pay much heed to the environmental impact of some projects and did not adequately reimburse farmers for their land.

China's ties with the Myanmar military had worn a bit thinner as its generals became frustrated that China was supporting armed ethnic groups fighting the central government in Myanmar's northern states of Kachin and Shan. One of these groups, the United Wa State Army, also buys weapons from China and supplies about four of these groups with Chinese-made weapons.

China's sale of less-than-stellar fighter planes two decades ago frustrated Myanmar and prompted the military to buy equipment from Russia and Israel.[6] The Myanmar military commander's visit to Beijing in late 2017, as the United States and European countries considered sanctions against military officers for their actions against the Rohingya, helped at least partially to restore military relations between these neighbors.

China, for its part, has three strategic interests in Myanmar, according to a 2018 study group report prepared for the U.S. Institute of Peace. One

5. Maung Aung Myoe, "Myanmar's China Policy since 2011: Determinants and Directions," *Journal of Current Southeast Asian Affairs* 34, no. 2 (August 2015): 23, https://www.researchgate.net/publication/281565360_Maung_Aung_Myoe_Myanmar's_China_Policy_since_2011_Determinants_and_Directions_Journal_of_Current_Southeast_Asian_Affairs_Vol_34_No_2_August_2015_pp_21-54.

6. Perlez, "In China, Aung San Suu Kyi Finds a Warm Welcome."

interest is stability along their joint border. Access to the Indian Ocean is a second interest, and a third is a variety of economic benefits.[7]

Beijing is concerned about maintaining peace and security along its southern border with Myanmar and ensuring that fighting between armed ethnic groups and the military in Myanmar does not spill across the frontier or drive refugees into China. "Political stability in Myanmar is necessary for China's security," Maung Aung Myoe said. "Any armed conflict on the China–Myanmar border regions is detrimental to China's border security and stability."[8]

In 2011 Beijing was anxious when the Myanmar government launched peace talks with the armed ethnic groups on the Chinese border because the initiative was funded by the European Union, Japan, and Norway, said Thant Myint-U. China saw the talks as "fundamentally threating to them because it opened up a degree of uncertainty on its border where there had been fighting."[9]

Myanmar, with its long coast on the Bay of Bengal, can provide the landlocked provinces in southwestern China with their only access to the Indian Ocean and direct trade routes with the Middle East and Europe. Beijing has long hankered to build a deepwater port in Kyaukphyu to cut shipping costs and reduce China's dependence on shipments through the congested Malacca Strait.[10] "If China wants to go to the Indian Ocean, then we need to grasp Myanmar's hand tightly," Chinese military affairs analyst Qiu Yongzheng told the official *People's Daily*.[11]

China also has important economic interests in Myanmar, especially access to its vast natural resources in the north. Trade with Myanmar is particularly important for China's southern Yunnan Province, which is one of the country's poorest. China is also a key market for illicit cross-border trade of jade, drugs, forestry products, and wildlife from Myanmar.

---

7. USIP Senior Study Group Final Report, *China's Role in Myanmar's Internal Conflicts* (Washington, DC: United States Institute of Peace, 2018), 16.
8. Maung Aung Myoe, "Myanmar's China Policy since 2011," 27.
9. Thant Myint-U.
10. One of the first news reports on China's push to the Indian Ocean was published by my former colleague Bertil Lintner and dates to 1994. Bertil Lintner, "Enter the Dragon," *Far Eastern Economic Review*, December 22, 1994, 23.
11. James Hookway and Josh Chin, "Myanmar's Rohingya Crisis Opens Door for China to Regain Influence," *Wall Street Journal*, November 28, 2017, https://www.wsj.com/articles/china-senses-opportunity-to-regain-influence-in-myanmar-1511865000?shareToken=st350366fbda94438db080c49047f2294b&reflink=article_email_share.

Myanmar is a critical piece in China's BRI as Beijing seeks to build ports, railroads, roads, economic corridors, and oil and gas pipelines to link landlocked southwestern China to the outside world. For Myanmar, China is a key source of funding for developing the country's dilapidated infrastructure and an increasingly important supplier of foreign investment.

But largely Buddhist and deeply nationalist Myanmar has long been suspicious about Beijing's intentions, creating less than full-throated enthusiasm for Chinese infrastructure and investment projects. Many of these projects are perceived in Myanmar as benefiting China's economy more than the people of Myanmar.

Beijing today is trying to demonstrate that it is a strong friend of Myanmar at a time when the West is again shunning the country's government. China seems convinced that Myanmar should reciprocate for Beijing's intervention to block condemnation of the country at the United Nations and its help in facilitating a deal with Bangladesh that could eventually make it possible for at least some of the Rohingya refugees to return to Myanmar. In 2017, even before Beijing began supporting Myanmar on the Rohingya crisis, China helped deliver the armed ethnic groups from Myanmar's northern states to peace talks in Naypyidaw with the government.

But the battle inside the Myanmar government over ties to China seems far from settled. "There's one group that says, 'Let's regard China with caution,'" says a Yangon-based diplomat. "Then there are those who want to throw in their lot with China, convinced that this will give the country its biggest boost. But the Lady is attuned to the risks of throwing in the country's lot with China," he says, referring to Aung San Suu Kyi and implying that she is still trying to hedge the country's bets.

Despite widespread skepticism a visitor hears about China in Yangon and Mandalay, only 23 percent of elite opinion makers in the country consider China "a revisionist power with an intent to turn Southeast Asia into its sphere of influence." This finding is according to a survey of foreign policy experts, researchers, business leaders, civil society representatives, and media persons conducted by Singapore's ISEAS-Yusof Ishak Institute in late 2018. This is the lowest figure among the 10 Southeast Asian countries. Fully 50 percent in Cambodia and 45 percent in Thailand saw China as a "revisionist power."

The survey showed more skepticism about China's infrastructure projects. Some 32 percent of those surveyed in Myanmar said China's BRI would provide "needed infrastructure funding for countries in the region." But fully 63 percent said, "My government should be cautious in negotiating BRI projects to avoid getting into unsustainable financial debts with China."

In the same survey, 73 percent said China has "the most influence economically in Southeast Asia" (compared to only 7 percent who thought this about the United States). About 48 percent said China has "the most influence politically and strategically in Southeast Asia" (compared to 22 percent who thought this about the United States).

Some 38 percent had "no confidence" or "little confidence" that China would "do the right thing" in contributing to global peace, security, prosperity, and governance (compared to 21 percent who were "confident" or "very confident" that China would do the right thing). Forty-five percent had "no confidence" or "little confidence" about the United States doing the right thing.[12]

INFRASTRUCTURE PROJECTS SLOWLY SPUTTER TO LIFE

On the surface, it seems counterintuitive that China's infrastructure projects in Myanmar under the BRI have been so slow to get off the ground, despite the warming of bilateral political ties since late 2017. Myanmar desperately needs all types of infrastructure, from roads to ports and railroads to electricity, and Beijing is ready with bucketloads of cash to launch an infrastructure-spending spree on its neighbor. But when you scratch beneath the surface, it quickly becomes clear that both sides carry hefty doses of emotional baggage about their past economic relations.

In August 2018, more than two years after Aung San Suu Kyi's government took office, the two sides finally agreed on a scaled-back Chinese port project in Kyaukphyu on the Indian Ocean in Rakhine State on Myanmar's western coast. The new cost is about $1.3 billion, down from a whopping $7 billion-plus in the memorandum of understanding signed by the previous military-backed government in 2015.

12. Tang Siew Mun, Moe Thuzar, Hoang Thi Ha, Termsak Chalermpalanupap, Pham Thi Phuong Thao, and Anuthida Saelaow Qian, *The State of Southeast Asia: 2019 Survey Report* (Singapore: ASEAN Studies Centre at ISEAS-Yusof Ishak Institute, 2019), 18, https://www.iseas.edu.sg/images/pdf/TheStateofSEASurveyReport_2019.pdf.

A Chinese consortium spearheaded by investment conglomerate CITIC Group will hold a 70 percent stake in the project, the Myanmar government will have a 15 percent share, and a grouping of about half a dozen domestic companies will holding the remaining 15 percent. "The companies will hold the debt" with funding "from a Chinese bank," says Sean Turnell, economic adviser to State Counselor Aung San Suu Kyi.

Few details about the project financing have been revealed, but Turnell says the loan will not have a Myanmar government guarantee and "the port will not revert to China if it fails," a reference to the failed Hambantota port in Sri Lanka.

Myanmar officials pushed to scale back the project to avoid saddling the government with unsustainable debt. The port will have one wharf capable of receiving two ships at a time, down from the earlier plan that was intended to berth up to 10 ships at once. Two 480-mile pipelines—one for oil, the other for gas—already run from Kunming in southwestern China to Kyuakphyu, and the existing port can dock large oil tankers. This provides China a supplementary route around the crowded Malacca Strait for fossil fuel imports from the Middle East.

The two sides have agreed that additional investment to expand the port is possible in a second stage if the remotely placed facility proves viable. Separately, CITIC has organized another group to develop an industrial park next to the port, but Turnell says its future depends on the economic viability of the port.[13] (No work had begun on the port project by late 2019.)

To win the hearts and minds of locals in Rakhine State in support of the Kyaukphyu project, China has put up billboards in major towns in Rakhine touting the benefits of the port for the state, according to diplomats who recently visited. Even in offices of the Arakan Army, an insurgent group fighting the central government, diplomats report seeing posters promoting the BRI.

---

13. Kanupriya Kapoor and Aye Min Thant, "Myanmar Scales Back Chinese-Backed Port Project due to Debt Fears—Official," *Reuters*, August 2, 2018, https://www.reuters.com/article/us-myanmar-china-port-exclusive/exclusive-myanmar-scales-back-chinese-backed-port-project-due-to-debt-fears-official-idUSKBN1KN106; Yuichi Nitta, "Myanmar Cuts Cost of China-Funded Port Project by 80%," *Nikkei Asian Review*, September 28, 2018, https://asia.nikkei.com/Spotlight/Belt-and-Road/Myanmar-cuts-cost-of-China-funded-port-project-by-80.

In September 2018, Myanmar and China signed a separate memorandum of understanding to establish the China–Myanmar Economic Corridor (CMEC), according to a project announcement by the Chinese side. The roughly 1,060-mile corridor is slated to provide roads and railroads that will connect Kunming in southern China with Mandalay in central Myanmar before heading east to Yangon and west to Kyaukphyu. A feasibility study for the proposed $9 billion rail linking Muse on the Chinese border to Kyaukphyu was under way in early 2019.[14]

In the face of warnings by economists that the economic corridor project could burden Myanmar with unsustainable levels of debt, the government has raised three key points with China that Myanmar wants to see included in a memorandum of understanding, according to the *Irrawaddy* website. First, Myanmar must be allowed to seek financing from international financial institutions in implementing projects. Second, Myanmar must be permitted to invite international tenders to ensure international participation in the projects. Third, projects implemented must be selected by Myanmar while ensuring benefits for both China and Myanmar.[15] These concessions appear considerably more generous to Myanmar than those offered other Southeast Asian countries under the BRI.

Under the economic corridor project, the two sides agreed to cooperate in about two dozen areas ranging from infrastructure to manufacturing and agriculture to transport, finance, human resources development, and telecommunications.[16] The initial stages are estimated to cost about $2 billion, but no information about the project breakdown between the two sides has been released. Turnell says the project will incur "no government debt" and provide "no government guarantees."

These initial early-stage agreements on the port and the economic corridor suggest that China and Myanmar may have begun to resume work on infrastructure projects after a very difficult patch that dates back to

14. Chan Mya Htwe, "Survey Starts for Major Railway Project," *Myanmar Times*, February 1, 2019, https://www.mmtimes.com/news/survey-starts-major-railway-project.html.
15. Nan Lwin, "Gov't Spells Out Conditions for Signing BRI Deals with China," *Irrawaddy*, May 30, 2019, https://www.irrawaddy.com/business/govt-spells-conditions-signing-bri-deals-china.html.
16. Nan Lwin, "Gov't Signs MoU with Beijing to Build China–Myanmar Economic Corridor," *Irrawaddy*, September 13, 2018, https://www.irrawaddy.com/news/burma/govt-signs-mou-beijing-build-china-myanmar-economic-corridor.html.

2011, when the previous Myanmar president canceled a hydropower project in the face of large-scale public protests.

To get some Chinese infrastructure projects back online, the government set up a Project Bank in line with models established by the World Bank to evaluate proposed development schemes. "It will evaluate all projects for socio-economic returns," says Turnell. "It will be used on all Chinese projects and China has agreed."

Advisers to the Project Bank include some of the best and brightest of Myanmar's tiny economic and financial elite. A key anchor is Soe Win, the minister of planning and finance who served earlier as a managing partner at Deloitte, the international audit and consulting firm. Another adviser is Set Aung, the deputy minister for planning and finance, who holds a PhD from Keio University in Japan and negotiated the final stages of the Kyaukphyu port project with China. A third key player is Min Ye Paing Hein, director of the Myanmar Development Institute who has served as an economist and poverty specialist at the World Bank and has a doctorate in political economy from the University of Wisconsin.

Myanmar economists also got some advice from a handful of foreign consultants, including a few Americans, in figuring out how to respond to China's proposed projects. "We reached out for help to understand [China's] complex legal documents," says an economist in Naypyidaw. "They helped very quietly. The help was modest with only one or two people."

Some months after the Kyaukphyu port project had been renegotiated, a *Wall Street Journal* report stated that "a team of U.S. economists, diplomats and lawyers had been dispatched to the country on a pilot program to scrutinize contracts, flag bad deals and empower the country to push for better terms with Chinese agencies and companies."[17] The officials involved in the port negotiations "took some flak" from the Chinese as well as their Myanmar colleagues, according to a diplomat in Yangon.

In the run-up to Chinese president Xi's second Belt and Road summit in Beijing in April 2019, Beijing's ambassador Hong Liang, who left Myanmar a few months later, repeatedly charged publicly that "some forces backed by foreign countries" had promoted opposition to the controversial

17. Ben Kesling and Jon Emont, "U.S. Goes on the Offensive against China's Empire-Building Funding Plan," *Wall Street Journal*, April 9, 2019, https://www.wsj.com/articles/u-s-goes-on-the-offensive-against-chinas-empire-building-megaplan-11554809402.

Myitsone Dam eight years earlier to derail China–Myanmar relations. "Their goal is to create misunderstanding about the project."[18]

During a late 2018 visit to Kachin State where the dam was to be located, the ambassador warned Kachin leaders not to develop close friendships with Western diplomats otherwise they "would face serious consequences." The threat came one week after both the U.S. and U.K. ambassadors had visited the state and met with the same leaders.[19]

The Chinese ambassador's ham-fisted and tone-deaf lobbying prompted renewed protests against the dam in cities across the country. Civil society leaders and environmentalists set up a "One Dollar" campaign calling on each person to contribute a U.S. dollar to compensate China for Myanmar scrapping the dam.[20]

Many observers in Yangon believe that the Chinese ambassador kept raising Myitsone in early 2019, fully seven years after it was suspended, to use as "leverage to get other projects," in the words of one diplomat. Journalist and Myanmar expert Bertil Lintner added: "But China's new push for the Myitsone Dam represents a gamble, one that could reignite the popular anti-China movement that swept the country in 2011, and one that even [Aung San] Suu Kyi would be hard-pressed to stop once started."[21]

The Chinese ambassador was still smarting from 2011, when military-backed President Thein Sein, who launched the junta's tentative reform policies the previous year, abruptly canceled construction of the $3.6 billion dam following widespread public protests. The dam had been under construction by a consortium including China Power International, a Myanmar government ministry, and Myanmar's Asia World Company.

The protests were sparked by the fact that it was being built on land sacred to the local Kachin people and on the Irrawaddy River, often

18. Nan Lwin, "Foreign Countries behind Myitsone Dam Opposition: Chinese Ambassador," *Irrawaddy*, May 22, 2019, https://www.irrawaddy.com/news/burma/foreign-countries-behind-myitsone-dam-opposition-chinese-ambassador.html.

19. Nan Lwin, "Analysis: Behind the Threats and Warnings of Chinese Ambassador's Kachin Visit," *Irrawaddy*, January 9, 2019, https://www.irrawaddy.com/news/burma/analysis-behind-threats-warnings-chinese-ambassadors-kachin-visit.html.

20. Lwin, "Foreign Countries behind Myitsone Dam Opposition."

21. Bertil Lintner, "China Seeks Big-Ticket Payback from Myanmar," *Asia Times*, January 16, 2019, https://www.asiatimes.com/2019/01/article/china-seeks-big-ticket-payback-from-myanmar/.

dubbed the "mother river" by the people of Myanmar. In addition, there was concern that construction and flooding would displace several thousand villagers, interrupt fish migration and sediment flows, and disrupt the livelihoods of people hundreds of miles downstream. As the government freed up the political environment, protests against the dam led Thein Sein to suspend work on the project, creating a period of tension in bilateral relations with China. For many in Myanmar, the suspension of the project became a symbol of the country's democratization because it took place amid other political reforms launched by the government.

Beijing read the Myitsone suspension as "an act of profound disrespect" and was concerned what it would mean for "China's standing as a great and rising power," Thant Myint-U said. But the suspension of the project was made in response to domestic political considerations and had nothing to with the government's desire to "shift away from China" and "pivot toward the West."[22]

It is far from certain that the Myitsone project can ever be resurrected. China Power officials say if it is canceled, Myanmar will owe some $800 million for money already spent on the project, although they also say they would be ready to scrap the project in exchange for other smaller hydropower projects.[23] Chinese sources also say that the dam, once intended to export most of its electricity to Yunnan, has become redundant because the Chinese province has achieved a surplus of electricity since the original contract was signed.

A second project, the Letpadaung copper mine, located just north of Mandalay, stopped operating in November 2011 following demonstrations against alleged land grabbing by the operators and environmental damage. The $1.1 billion project was a joint venture between a subsidiary of state-owned China North Industries Corporation and the Myanmar military's Union of Myanmar Economic Holdings Limited. Work at the mine started in early 2011 and was shut down that November after police brutally suppressed protests against the mine.

The government responded by setting up an investigation headed by then opposition leader Aung San Suu Kyi. It concluded that the compensation of farmers displaced by the project was "improper," that the mine

22. Thant Myint-U.

23. Yimou Lee and Shwee Yee Saw Myint, "RPT-China May Scrap Divisive Dam in Myanmar to Advance Other Interests—Sources," *Reuters*, April 5, 2017, https://uk.reuters.com/article/china-silkroad-myanmar-dam-idUKL3N1HD3M9.

"lacked environmental protection measures," and that profit-sharing between the parties was unfair.[24]

Following months of negotiations, a new contract was hammered out between the various parties that agreed to sharply reduce the stakes of the Chinese and Myanmar companies in the mine and give the Myanmar government 51 percent of the shares. The new contract required the mine to boost compensation for the land taken from local farmers, while also providing $1 million a year in social responsibility funds for the area around the mine and another $2 million for environmental protection.[25]

Beijing was thoroughly displeased by the disruption at the dam and the mine, especially because Myanmar officials who had earlier supported these projects now suddenly opposed them. But in the case of the mine, Beijing was willing to renegotiate the contract recognizing that the original terms included an unfair profit-sharing arrangement with local partners, did not do enough to protect the environment, and provided few benefits for the villagers impacted by the project.[26]

The protests over environmental and social issues related to these large infrastructure projects and the course corrections they forced on the Chinese companies prompted them to stop launching new infrastructure projects in Myanmar for some six years.

The massive investments China launched in Myanmar in 2010 and 2011 caused anxiety about Beijing's potential overwhelming influence on the country's economy. "There's a great fear about being swallowed up," says Turnell. "Still China is understood to be indispensable even if it isn't particularly liked."

Predatory lending for projects is a major concern among Myanmar's economists. Officials have many stories about the less-than-generous terms of Chinese financing for some projects during the military government. Aung San Suu Kyi set up a team of economists to study the terms of earlier Chinese projects after she took office in 2016. Members of the team tell the story of a $300 million loan provided through the Ministry of Cooperatives shortly before the 2015 elections.

---

24. "Complete Final Report of Investigation Commission into Letpadaung Taung Copper Mining Project," quoted in Yun Sun, *Chinese Investment in Myanmar: What Lies Ahead?* (Washington, DC: Stimson Center, 2013), 6, https://www.stimson.org/sites/default/files/file-attachments/Yun_Issue_Brief1_1.pdf.
25. Yun Sun, *Chinese Investment in Myanmar*, 6.
26. Ibid., 6.

Under the terms of the loan, China supplied agricultural goods including fertilizer, seeds, and water pumps in kind to the ministry, which it could either sell to farmers to earn income for the then-ruling, pro-military Union Solidarity and Development Party or distribute to villagers to create goodwill for the party ahead of the elections. China valued the inputs it provided at $300 million, which the government is expected to repay in 10 years in hard currency at a hefty 4.5 percent interest.

"It leaves a bad taste in the mouth," one of the economists involved in reviewing the project said. "We badly need infrastructure," he says, "but we also need good loans."

In early 2019, some members of Myanmar's Parliament urged the government to repay loans from China as quickly as possible because of the high interest rates China charges Myanmar for its loans. According to a government debt report released at the time, Myanmar owes $10 billion to international lenders, of which $4 billion is owed China. The lion's share of this debt was accrued between 1988 and 2011, when Myanmar faced international sanctions. Lawmakers said China's rates are the highest at 4.5 percent.[27]

Aung San Suu Kyi's economic advisers had a raft of concerns about the Kyaukphyu port project before its scale and terms were revised. Many of them thought it was too big and too expensive. Before the project was scaled back, "a port there would not be beneficial to Myanmar," Turnell says. "It doesn't make sense," he adds, alluding to the fact that most of Myanmar's industrial activity is around Yangon and Mandalay and most companies use the Yangon port for their overseas trade.

Myanmar's deeply nationalist officials also raise concerns about what China's real long-term goals are for the deep-sea port. Does Beijing hope down the road that the port can be turned into a dual-use facility that can be used by the Chinese Navy as part of its strategy to gain more access to the Indian Ocean? This anxiety has been heightened by reports that Pakistan has agreed to allow China to build another port near an existing one in Gwadar on the Arabian Sea for use by the Chinese Navy to dock and maintain naval vessels.[28]

---

27. Moe Moe, "Loans from China Must Be Repaid 'As Early as Possible,'" *Irrawaddy*, January 25, 2019, https://www.irrawaddy.com/news/burma/loans-china-must-repaid-early-possible.html.

28. Minnie Chan, "First Djibouti . . . Now Pakistan Port Earmarked for a Chinese Overseas Naval Base, Sources Say," *South China Morning Post*, January 5, 2018, http://www.scmp

Officials were also concerned that taking loans for this project from China would add to Myanmar's growing public debt burden. "If we take a loan from the China Development Bank the interest rate is not good, but we get a lot of flexibility," says another economist. "The nature of the loan is that we'll have to buy Chinese products and [pay for Chinese] labor. The agreement is that we'll have to spend 50 percent of the loan or more in China. This raises the question of the valuation of Chinese products versus quality," the economist asks. "Is this value for money?"

China has its own share of separate frustrations. Beijing feels offended at how it was treated when the government launched reforms. "With Myanmar's democratic reform and foreign policy calibration since 2011, China sees itself, its investment, and its influence as the largest victims of Myanmar's political process," Yun Sun of the Stimson Center observed.[29]

In addition, China is put off by what it perceives to be Myanmar's inflated self-confidence and arrogance, Yun said, based on its strategic geographic location and its hopes that the country's reforms would open the door to a flood of investors falling all over themselves to get projects. "Even though China is keen on pushing forward with the [BRI], there is little appetite from the Chinese to let Myanmar endlessly exploit Chinese enthusiasm based on their unrealistically high demands and expectations."[30]

In the end, it appears that the Myanmar government has used the public's substantial anti-Chinese feeling and the concerns of economists about the viability of the proposed massive port project to press Beijing to rejig and reconfigure the size, costs, and financing for the project. It remains to be seen whether the revised port project is a one-off or whether Beijing has come to the longer-term realization that it has to take local sentiments into account when formulating and proposing infrastructure projects.

.com/news/china/diplomacy-defence/article/2127040/first-djibouti-now-pakistan-port-earmarked-chinese.

29. Yun Sun, "China and Myanmar's Peace Process," United States Institute of Peace, March 2017, https://www.usip.org/sites/default/files/SR401-China-and-Myanmar-Peace-Process.pdf, 13.

30. Ibid.

CONTROVERSIAL CHINESE FIRM LOOKS TO DEVELOP NEW YANGON

With a few large infrastructure projects haltingly getting back on track, Chinese property developers are starting to explore giving the crumbling colonial-era city of Yangon a makeover. In the rice fields across the river to the west of the former capital, a local company working with Chinese firms armed with mountains of cash is looking to build an ultramodern enclave known as the Yangon New City.

The roughly 20,000-acre project is the brainchild of Yangon chief minister Phyo Min Thein working with ethnic Chinese tycoon Serge Pun, who was born in Myanmar but moved to China after the 1962 coup in Myanmar shut down many ethnic Chinese businesses. (Interestingly, most other ethnic Chinese who fled Myanmar in the 1960s went to Thailand, Singapore, and Taiwan.) After returning to Myanmar in the early 1990s, Pun made his fortune in real estate, banking, and manufacturing.

The mammoth development project will be spearheaded by the New Yangon Development Company Limited, established in 2018 and wholly owned by the regional government of Yangon. Its board has three independent directors: Pun, who was named executive director; George Yeo, former Singapore foreign minister; and Tun Myat, a former senior United Nations official.

The New Yangon project will not come cheap. The cost alone for the infrastructure for the city, including water, power, telecommunications, roads, bridges, schools, hospitals, and so on, is estimated at between $5 billion and $11 billion, according to an unpublished report prepared by McKinsey and Company, the U.S. consulting firm.

The project has run into a buzz saw of complaints, which the company has sought to address by holding public town hall meetings, several of which turned highly contentious. One common question raised by Yangon residents was why colossal state-owned China Communications Construction Company (CCCC) was chosen to implement the project without conducting a public tender. These concerns focused particularly on CCCC's role in the Hambantota deep-sea port in Sri Lanka, which got saddled with debt and had to lease the port back to the company for over 90 years.

CCCC is one of the biggest Chinese conglomerates involved in the BRI, claiming to have some 700 projects in more than 100 countries valued at over $100 billion, according to Bloomberg.[31]

But Pun insists that CCCC, in fact, has not yet won the contract to implement the project but only the right to prepare the documents for the first stage of the infrastructure work, including roads and power plants, according to an agreement signed in May 2019. Once these documents are completed by CCCC, the proposal will be open to bids using a vehicle known as the "Swiss challenge," Pun says. (This is a style of government procurement under which officials who have received a bid for a public project invite other firms to match or better the original bid.)

Pun acknowledges that the project may be too large and Myanmar's investment environment too risky for any companies other than a deep-pocketed firm with Beijing's backing. "The inherent risks for this undertaking [are] quite onerous and not many [companies] have the risk appetite to undertake it," he says. "It is easy to allege that CCCC is given the advantage to undertake this [project] but in all honesty, we will be very glad to see other companies, especially non-Chinese entities, compete for these work streams but I am highly doubtful that there would be many coming forward."

Just the first stage of the project, including two bridges, 16 miles of roads, infrastructure for five resettlement villages for farmers displaced by the project, a water plant, waste treatment plants, and nearly nine square miles of industrial estate, is estimated to cost $1.65 billion.

Pun rejects the notion that Myanmar might be at risk of losing the project land as happened in Sri Lanka because the government will not take on any debt to implement the scheme. The financing for the first stage and the one that follows will be private equity raised by the joint venture company that will include the winning bidder and the Yangon regional government, the executive director says. "The government is not providing any guarantees for any loans . . . and thus shall not be liable for the project's debts."

Because "the return on investment will be too low to make the project bankable," the joint venture, which could include CCCC if its bid is suc-

31. Sheridan Prasso, "A Chinese Company Reshaping the World Leaves a Troubled Trail," *Bloomberg*, September 18, 2018, https://www.bloombergquint.com/businessweek/a-chinese-company-reshaping-the-world-leaves-a-troubled-trail.

cessful, will be provided 4.2 square miles to develop to recoup its investment in Yangon New City's infrastructure, Pun says.

The people most anxious to see the project get started as soon as possible are the farmers and landowners who currently live on the land to be developed and want to exchange their farmland for land in one of the resettlement villages, Pun says. In exchange for their farmland, much of which was damaged by saltwater during devastating Cyclone Nargis in 2008, sellers will get two acres of land for development for every 10 acres of farmland. Pun estimates that the value of the land for development is "easily in excess of 10 times" that of farmland, so he reckons that "many of them will sell their land to developers."

In press reports on the town hall meetings, others oppose the project because they feel the funds used on the new project should be used to upgrade the existing city of Yangon first. Some criticize the fact that a chunk of the project will be turned over to foreign investors who will gain the largest benefit and provide few jobs for locals. Still others do not trust China as a reliable partner in developing Myanmar or fret that Yangon New City will be populated by thousands of immigrants from China.

More than a few foreign observers in Yangon fear the project will turn into a white elephant. "The project smells bad," says a diplomat in Yangon. "The chief minister seems bent on making Yangon New City part of his legacy." Adds a government economist: "Naypyidaw has reservations about the project."

The McKinsey report prepared for the company, while largely very optimistic, raised several concerns about the risks and challenges in building greenfield cities, issues that are based on the experience in other countries, including in China. The authors say that fully 50 percent of these new city projects underperform their original economic expectations. According to an unpublished McKinsey report these cities faced 30 to 40 percent underutilization of the built infrastructure and 86 percent face sizable cost overruns.

The project also faces multiple notional risks in its implementation, McKinsey said. These include possible flooding on the project site and delays in resettling people now living on the land to be developed; in addition, the incentives may prove unattractive to investors or the global economy may face a slowdown. Among other risks are possible insufficient funding or a new central or regional government that does not support the project (elections are slated for 2020).

Most of the criticisms raised about CCCC's likely involvement focus on its role in the Sri Lanka port project, but the conglomerate has been enmeshed in numerous other controversial projects in the region. In the South China Sea, CCCC's subsidiaries operated most of the giant barges digging sand from the seabed and piled it on seven disputed coral reefs such as Fiery Cross Reef on which Beijing has built runways for military aircraft and placed weapon's systems.[32]

CCCC and its subsidiaries have struggled to implement projects in neighboring Southeast Asian countries and several of their agreements have unraveled or been canceled by host governments. In the Philippines, CCCC Dredging signed an agreement in 2016 to reclaim some 500 acres of land in the Davao City harbor to build new government offices, port terminals, factories, and houses.[33] Mayor Sara Duterte-Carpio terminated the project signed by her father President Rodrigo Duterte after reviewing the project's social and environmental impact.[34]

Another CCCC-linked firm, China Road and Bridge Corporation, signed an agreement with a Philippine firm to develop a segment of the Metro Manila Bus Rapid Transit project.[35] The Chinese firm withdrew after the Philippine government released its guidelines for the project.[36]

Separately, CCCC was blacklisted by the World Bank in 2009 for alleged graft in its bidding practices on a highway construction project in the Philippines.[37]

But Pun says he is convinced that China and its companies have reformed. "I can only give them the benefit of the doubt that under the current regime, a lot of things in China [have] changed," he says, referring

32. Laura Zhou, "Chinese Island-Building Firm Wins Contract with South China Sea Rival Claimant, the Philippines," *South China Morning Post*, October 26, 2016, https://www.scmp.com/news/china/diplomacy-defence/article/2040256/chinese-firm-helped-build-islands-disputed-area-south.

33. Global Construction Review, "China's CCCC to Build Artificial Islands for Duterte-Backed Scheme in Philippines," *Global Construction Review*, October 27, 2016, http://www.globalconstructionreview.com/news/chinas-cccc-build-artifi7cial-isla7nds-dut7erte/.

34. Ace June Rell S. Perez, "Davao City Backs Out of Mega Harbour Project," *SunStar*, July 25, 2017, https://www.sunstar.com.ph/article/155127.

35. Nikko Dizon, "Chinese Company Banned by World Bank Bags PH Infrastructure Project," *Philippine Inquirer*, October 26, 2016, https://business.inquirer.net/217467/chinese-company-banned-by-world-bank-bags-ph-infrastructure-project.

36. "Are 'Blacklisted' Chinese Firms on Board Duterte's Infra Projects?," *ABS-CBN*, April 24, 2017, https://news.abs-cbn.com/business/04/24/17/are-blacklisted-chinese-firms-on-board-dutertes-infra-projects.

37. Prasso, "A Chinese Company Reshaping the World Leaves a Troubled Trail."

to President Xi's pledge during the BRI summit in Beijing in April 2019 to address some of the most egregious abuses of BRI projects.

In the end, Pun believes it is up to Myanmar to police the project against corruption and other problems: "I think it is more important for us to maintain our strict standards of proper governance as this will be the ultimate factor of how [the Chinese companies] behave in their undertaking with us." Considering Myanmar's weak legal system, inefficient policing system, and poorly trained civil service, controlling a wily and experienced Chinese conglomerate may prove more challenging than the executive director wants to acknowledge.

The Chinese government has not commented publicly about the Yangon New City project. But academics who have talked to officials say they express reservations about whether plowing giant sums of money into this project would bring many returns. They would much rather invest in the China–Myanmar Economic Corridor, which they think has the potential to benefit both countries.

JUMP-STARTING ECONOMIC LINKS

The arrival of CITIC and CCCC in Myanmar in recent years marks a "second coming" of sorts for Chinese companies. As the United States and European nations began sanctioning Myanmar after the military crushed the 1988 democracy protests, China emerged as a dominant player in its southern neighbor's underdeveloped economy. But when the military mounted reforms in 2011, giant protests erupted opposing China's plans for infrastructure projects that threatened the environment and poorly compensated farmers for confiscated land.

In the 1980s, with a rapidly growing economy, China was attracted to Myanmar's array of mineral resources and forests, energy resources, vast agricultural land, and access to the Indian Ocean. Myanmar became a market for Chinese products, and China emerged as an important aid donor, concessional loan provider, investor in the Myanmar economy, and supplier of military hardware during the tough times after the West imposed sanctions in the late 1980s following the military's crushing of pro-democracy protests.

Myanmar, which today has a population of about 54 million, was one of the richest nations in Asia at the end of World War II, serving as a major rice exporter and having some of the best medical facilities and universities in Asia. But the economy slipped badly during the years of Ne Win's "Burmese Road to Socialism," the military government's misrule, the rise of a crony business culture, and years of economic sanctions imposed by Western countries.

Myanmar's gross domestic product in 2018 reached $1,326, less than one-fifth that of neighboring Thailand.[38] Farmers today still make up half of the country's workforce,[39] have some of the lowest output in the region,[40] and are enormously poor. Only about 30 percent of the population has access to electricity and the country's roads, ports, and railroads are badly rundown.

In recent decades, China became Myanmar's most dominant trading partner, snaring 44 percent of its imports and 31 percent of its exports in 2018.[41] Myanmar exports minerals and agricultural products to China while importing machinery, electronics, and consumer goods. China only began stepping up its investment in infrastructure projects in 2008, near the end of the military's hardline rule, and this continued until 2011, when some of its projects encountered public protests.

In the early 2000s, much of China's interest in Myanmar focused on the oil and gas sector. Over the next decade, China's state-owned energy firms snared many of the exploration and production contracts for onshore and offshore oil and gas blocks with Myanmar Oil and Gas Enterprise.[42]

Myanmar produces some 90 percent of the world's jade and is a key source of rubies, sapphires, and other colored gemstones. But because Myanmar's jade and gemstone industry is largely unregulated, up to two-thirds of the country's output is not taxed, according to report by the Natural Resource Governance Institute in early 2019.[43]

---

38. "GDP per Capita (Current US$), Myanmar and Thailand," The World Bank, https://data.worldbank.org/indicator/NY.GDP.PCAP.CD (accessed November 21, 2019).

39. "Employment in Agriculture (% of Total Employment)," The World Bank, https://data.worldbank.org/indicator/sl.agr.empl.zs (accessed October 22, 2019).

40. "Myanmar: Analysis of Farm Production Economics," The World Bank, http://www.worldbank.org/en/country/myanmar/publication/myanmar-analysis-of-farm-production-economics (accessed October 22, 2019).

41. "Trade Map—Trade Competitiveness Map: Bilateral Trade between Myanmar and China in 2018," International Trade Centre, https://www.trademap.org/countrymap/Bilateral.aspx?nvpm=1%7c104%7c%7c156%7c%7cTOTAL%7c%7c%7c2%7c1%7c2%7c2%7c1%7c1%7c1%7c1%7c1 (accessed October 22, 2019).

42. Ian Storey, *Southeast Asia and the Rise of China: The Search for Security* (New York: Routledge, 2011), 161–162.

43. Paul Shortell, *Losing Luster: Addressing Tax Evasion in Myanmar's Jade and Gemstone Industry* (New York: Natural Resource Governance Institute, 2019), 3, https://resource

Chinese companies finance many of these mining operations and the output is smuggled to China, which means the Myanmar government loses billions of dollars in tax revenue.[44] A 2018 Asia Foundation report found that Myanmar's tax receipts in the 2016–2017 period totaled only 6 to 7 percent of its gross domestic product, the lowest rate among Southeast Asian countries.[45]

China's investment spending in Myanmar has been surprisingly erratic in recent years, apparently depending largely on domestic politics in Naypyidaw and popular attitudes toward Chinese infrastructure projects. It hit an all-time high in 2010–2011 (ending in March), reaching $8.3 billion. By 2012–2013 (ending in March), when the reform government of President Thein Sein had taken office and the Myitsone Dam was suspended, China's investment fell to $231.8 million and, the following year, it dropped to $56.2 million. In 2015–2016 (ending in March), the last year Thein Sein was in office, Chinese investment rose to $3.3 billion as the outgoing government signed several deals.

Aung San Suu Kyi's first year in office was 2016–2017 (ending in March), and during this period investment from China reached only $482.6 million. Government economists say part of slowdown resulted from the new administration's efforts to tamp down the go-go real estate construction boom that erupted when the reforms began. During this time the United States also started easing sanctions. Investment from Chinese companies rose to $1.4 billion in 2017–2018 (ending in March) before the memorandums of understanding with China were signed for construction of the Kyaukphyu port project and the China–Myanmar Economic Corridor.[46]

---

governance.org/sites/default/files/documents/losing-luster-addressing-myanmar-tax-evasion.pdf.

44. Gabriel Walker, "China's Role in Myanmar's Dangerous Jade Trade," *Council on Foreign Relations*, November 2, 2015, https://www.cfr.org/blog/chinas-role-myanmars-dangerous-jade-trade.

45. James Owen and Hay Mahn Htun, *Attitudes towards Taxation in Myanmar: Insights from Urban Citizens* (San Francisco: The Asia Foundation, 2018), 2, https://asiafoundation.org/wp-content/uploads/2018/03/Tax-Attitude-Summary-12-page_English.pdf.

46. Figures from the Directorate of Investment and Company Administration are quoted in Nan Lwin, "Infographic: 30 Years of Chinese Investment in Myanmar," *Irrawaddy*, January 25, 2019, https://www.irrawaddy.com/specials/infographic-30-years-chinese-investment-myanmar.html; "China's First Foreign Direct Investment in Myanmar's 'One Belt, One Road' to Bring Dividends," *Guangming Daily*, April 18, 2018, https://www.imsilkroad.com/news/p/92293.html.

Total cumulative foreign investment in Myanmar by 2018–2019 (ending in March) reached $80.2 billion. China's investment (if Hong Kong is included) totaled $24.9 billion, ahead of Singapore with $21.3 billion.[47]

China's relatively low investment totals in recent years suggests that "Chinese investment interest in Myanmar is not in line with the rhetoric that Myanmar is a key country for China's BRI," says Yun Sun. But China's investment is expected to begin rising again when work on the Kyaukphyu port project and the China–Myanmar Economic Corridor begins in earnest.

A survey of business attitudes among both domestic and foreign firms in December 2017, shortly after the massive outflow of Rohingya refugees, found that only 49 percent expected the business environment to improve, down from 73 percent the previous year. The survey by a German consulting firm and the Myanmar Chamber of Commerce said that the two biggest issues cited by companies as factors holding them back were the shortage of trained staff and the lack of clear government policies.[48]

The trade dispute between China and the United States can be expected to push some Chinese companies to invest in Myanmar to escape U.S. tariffs. After Washington imposed additional tariffs on $200 billion of Chinese products in September 2018, Yakeda Tactical Gear Company, which supplies bulletproof vests, rifle bags, and other gear to the United States, decided to shift operations from Guangzhou to Myanmar.[49]

Some Chinese firms are also starting to invest in small-scale electricity projects. In June 2019, state-owned Sinohydro signed an agreement with Myanmar's Supreme Group to invest $180 million to use gas from Myanmar's Shwe field to generate 135-megawatts of power in Kyaukphyu for Rakhine State. The project had floundered for months as the

---

47. Republic of the Union of Myanmar, Directorate of Investment and Company Administration, "Foreign Investment of Permitted Enterprises as of 31/5/2019," https://www.dica.gov.mm/sites/dica.gov.mm/files/document-files/bycountry_1.pdf.

48. Murray Hiebert, "Whither U.S. Myanmar Policy after the Rohingya Crisis?," Center for Strategic and International Studies—Southeast Asia Program, April 2018, https://csis-prod.s3.amazonaws.com/s3fs-public/publication/180502_Hiebert_USMyanmarPolicy_Web.pdf?SHWlvHj1h72NkfAQlmKu7yKyM5sRbkom.

49. Joyce Zhou, "To Dodge Trade War, Chinese Exporters Shift Production to Low-Cost Nations," *Reuters*, June 26, 2019, https://www.reuters.com/article/us-usa-trade-china-manufacturing/to-dodge-trade-war-chinese-exporters-shift-production-to-low-cost-nations-idUSKCN1TS01L.

two sides tried to hammer out a power purchasing agreement. *Frontier Myanmar* called the agreement "an important milestone" for the government, which has struggled to agree on the terms of power purchasing agreements to entice long-term investors to build smaller power stations to meet the country's major power shortfalls.[50]

Chinese companies have actively invested in Myanmar's Digital Silk Road. In 2019, Chinese telecommunications giant Huawei Technologies announced that it would help transform Mandalay into a "smart city." The firm said that it would spend $1.2 million to install Huawei CCTV monitoring systems equipped with artificial intelligence and facial-recognition technology in three crime-ridden townships. Mandalay officials say Huawei's plan for the city will help them reduce crime and increase police efficiency.[51]

Separately, China's ZTE Corporation signed an agreement in 2019 with Ooredoo Myanmar, a subsidiary of Qatari Ooredoo Group, to develop the next generation of 5G technology in the country.[52] In 2014, Myanmar Posts and Telecommunications along with several mobile phone carriers chose Huawei to develop a wireless network across the country. Huawei pledged to spend at least $34 million, according to estimates by the RWR Advisory Group.

The same year, China United Network Communications Group Company Limited (China Unicom) completed a $50 million, 940-mile fiber optic link from Myanmar's northwest to the far south in a project with Myanmar Posts and Telecommunications, according to RWR Advisory Group. China Unicom provided a fiber optic link to China and the international submarine communication network designed with 100-gigabits-per-second technology.

Much like in northern Laos, Chinese farmers are increasingly setting up plantations in Shan and Kachin States in northern Myanmar to grow crops—everything from bananas to watermelon and rubber—to send back to China. Recent visitors to Kachin report seeing wide unbroken

---

50. Thomas Kean and Kyaw Ye Lynn, "Kyaukphyu Power Deal Expected 'Within Weeks': Supreme Group," *Frontier Myanmar*, June 13, 2019, https://frontiermyanmar.net/en/kyaukphyu-power-deal-expected-within-weeks-supreme-group-0.

51. Nan Lwin, "Amid Int'l Espionage Concerns, Mandalay to Embrace Huawei for 'Safe City' Project," *Irrawaddy*, June 19, 2019, https://www.irrawaddy.com/opinion/analysis/amid-intl-espionage-concerns-mandalay-embrace-huawei-safe-city-project.html.

52. Khine Kyaw, "Ooredoo Myanmar Joins China's ZTE in 5G push," *The Nation*, May 17, 2019, http://www.nationthailand.com/breakingnews/30369575.

swaths of identical bright green banana plants along key roads, thanks to a controversial revolution in plantation farming brought from China.

The plants are "tissue culture" bananas that begin in laboratories where "suckers" are snipped from prime plants, sterilized, and cloned into saplings that develop in a "soup" of nutrients and plant hormones. From there they are moved to commercial nurseries before being planted in fields. Using this technology, the plants produce almost uniform crops that can be harvested within a year and, at least in theory, are free of disease.

According to *Frontier Myanmar* journalists who researched this banana industry, the plantations are operated by a combination of Chinese investors, armed ethnic groups, local officials, and Kachin-based companies. Much of the land on which these tissue-culture bananas are grown was confiscated earlier from farmers or was formerly occupied by people displaced by the fighting between the Myanmar military and the Kachin Independence Army that resumed in 2011 after the collapse of a 17-year cease-fire. Some of the plantations are operated by the Myanmar military, *Frontier Myanmar* determined.[53]

A December 2018 survey by the agriculture minister of Kachin State found that some 36 companies had established illegal banana plantations on over 140,000 acres without local state permission and with investment from China. People living around the plantations complain about the diversion of water from streams for the thirsty banana plants and the contamination of surrounding land and water by the spraying of pesticides on the banana plants.[54]

A separate *Frontier Myanmar* article in early 2019 learned that fish were dying in streams near banana plantations. The newspaper reported a study by a coalition of 11 civil society groups that found incidents of "cows dying after drinking water downstream from plantations, pigs dying after eating banana flowers and villagers developing respiratory problems seemingly because of prolonged exposure to chemicals."[55]

---

53. Hein Ko Soe, "Kachin's Plantation Curse," *Frontier Myanmar*, January 17, 2019, https://frontiermyanmar.net/en/kachins-plantation-curse.

54. Nan Lwin, "Growing a Controversy: A Kachin Banana Plantation in Pictures," *Irrawaddy*, March 25, 2019, https://www.irrawaddy.com/photo-essay/growing-controversy-kachin-banana-plantation-pictures.html.

55. Emily Fishbein, "'All the Fish Died': Kachin Communities Alarmed at Impact of Banana Plantation," *Frontier Myanmar*, https://frontiermyanmar.net/en/all-the-fish-died

Because of the harmful environmental impact of tissue-culture bananas, neighboring Thailand and Laos have banned the practice. But in Kachin the farming practice remains widespread, although the state agriculture minister said in March 2019 that he would investigate the controversial practice and tighten regulations.[56]

A considerable number of the workers appear to be Chinese working illegally on the banana plantations. In May 2019, for example, 10 Chinese nationals were deported from Kachin State for working in Myanmar illegally, while another 13 had been detained on similar charges.[57]

Shan State has long been a hub for illicit drug production—earlier heroin and more recently methamphetamine tablets. As the International Crisis Group spelled out in a report in early 2019, the area has advantageous infrastructure, easy access to precursors from China, and a safe haven provided by rebel groups and pro-government militias. Profits from billions of dollars of crystal methamphetamines sales now outstrip Shan's formal economy and make efforts to resolve the ethnic conflicts in the area much harder.[58]

Separately, Chinese nationals are now the largest group of tourists visiting Myanmar, with just under 300,000 arriving in 2018, an increase of almost 40 percent over the previous year but still many less than the 10 million that visited Thailand. A total of some 3.6 million tourists arrived in the country in 2018, with just over 290,000 from Thailand, making the Thais the second largest group of tourists after the Chinese.[59]

-kachin-communities-alarmed-at-impact-of-banana-plantations (accessed October 22, 2019).

56. Nan Lwin, "Kachin Gov't Vows to Crack Down on China-Backed Banana Plantations," *Irrawaddy*, March 14, 2019, https://www.irrawaddy.com/news/burma/kachin-govt-vows-crack-china-backed-banana-plantations.html.

57. "Twenty-Three Chinese Banana Plantation Workers Deported from Myanmar," *Radio Free Asia*, June 13, 2019, https://www.rfa.org/english/news/myanmar/myanmar-chinese-banana-06132019164049.html.

58. "Fire and Ice: Conflict and Drugs in Myanmar's Shan State," International Crisis Group, January 8, 2019, https://www.crisisgroup.org/asia/south-east-asia/myanmar/299-fire-and-ice-conflict-and-drugs-myanmars-shan-state.

59. Myo Pa Pa San, "2018 Tourist Numbers Rise Slightly, Chinese up 38%," *Irrawaddy*, January 28, 2019, https://www.irrawaddy.com/news/burma/2018-tourist-numbers-rise-slightly-chinese-38.html; Tourism Authority of Thailand Newsroom, "Chinese Visitors to Thailand Hit 10 Million for First Time in December 2018," *TAT News*, December 19, 2018, https://www.tatnews.org/2018/12/chinese-visitors-to-thailand-hit-10-million-for-the-first-time-in-december-2018/.

After the Rohingya crisis in late 2017 prompted many American and European tourists to cancel their plans to visit Myanmar, the government launched a promotion campaign targeting China by granting to Chinese visitors visa-on-arrival privileges. Some officials argue that to increase the country's attractiveness to China, Myanmar ought to legalize gambling like Cambodia has. Many of Myanmar's border regions have already set up casinos to take advantage of tourists from China and Thailand.

Tour operators and hotel companies in Myanmar complain that they make little money from Chinese tourists because many of them buy cheap tour packages from companies in China that cover the Chinese-owned hotels, restaurants, and retail shops frequented by tourists from China. This means that the local economy benefits little and governments lose tax revenue.

When Chinese tourists use the Chinese digital payment platforms Alipay and WeChatPay, the benefits to Myanmar's economy from Chinese tourists is further reduced. "Mandalay is effectively becoming part of the Chinese monetary system," adviser Turnell says, referring to much of northern Myanmar near the border with China.

In one of the more bizarre projects proposed by Chinese companies in Myanmar, the Shanghai Shellpay Internet Technology Company announced plans in early 2019 to establish the Yongbang Blockchain Special Economic Zone (SEZ) in Mongla Special Administrative Region in Shan State on Myanmar's northern border with China. In a video broadcast by Channel News Agency, *Inside the Crypto Kingdom*, the company chief executive officer is quoted as saying that the SEZ would have an experimental digital economy and have a high degree of autonomy.

The Chinese company executive said the SEZ would use an "e-citizen" system open to all and a cryptocurrency called the Yongbang coin. The SEZ was said to be part of the BRI and would cover some 85 square miles.

"It's impossible," the chief executive of Mongla Special Administrative Region told the *Irrawaddy*. "We don't know what they're talking about." Mongla is controlled by the former rebel army called the National Democratic Alliance Army–Eastern Shan State (NDAA). The group was set up in 1989 after splitting with the former Communist Party of Burma and signed a cease-fire agreement with the government in 2011.[60]

60. "Inside the Crypto Kingdom," *Channel News Asia*, video, 47:34, https://www.channelnewsasia.com/news/video-on-demand/inside-the-cryptokingdom (accessed September 15,

A LONG AND COMPLICATED HISTORY

Myanmar and China are closely connected through geography, a shared history, ethnic links, and economic ties. The earliest Bama people came from Tibet and from among them came the kings who first united and created the kingdom of Bama in the twelfth century. Similar ethnic groups populate both sides of their land border, especially across from the northeastern states of Kachin and Shan.[61]

Access to the sea for the landlocked western provinces of China through Myanmar, long known as Burma,[62] has been a goal of Beijing since at least the eighteenth century. Chinese emperors often viewed Burma as a vassal state and expected its kings to send tribute to the emperor in the precolonial period. China's Qing dynasty in the 1760s launched several military incursions into Burma, but they were driven back by the country's armed forces. Burma managed to survive as an independent country until the British arrived and colonized the country in the nineteenth century.[63]

Burma's perceptions of China have long been driven by a sense of insecurity prompted by its long and extensive history of relations. This past, especially since the late 1940s, continues to play a key role in bilateral ties.

Relations between Burma and China entered a new period when Burma was granted independence by the British in 1948 and communist forces loyal to Mao Zedong seized control of China the following year. Since then, bilateral ties have gone through several distinct phases.[64]

2019); Nan Lwin, "Mongla Official Denies Chinese Firm Permitted to Set Up Autonomous Digital Economic Zone," *Irrawaddy*, February 20, 2019, https://www.irrawaddy.com/news/burma/mongla-official-denies-chinese-firm-permitted-set-autonomous-digital-economic-zone.html.

61. Priscilla A. Clapp, "China's Relations with Burma: Testimony before the U.S.-China Economic and Security Review Commission China's Relations with Southeast Asia," May 13, 2015, https://www.uscc.gov/sites/default/files/Clapp_Written%20Testimony_5.13.2015%20Hearing.pdf.

62. I will generally use Burma as the name of the country before 1989 and Myanmar for the period after that.

63. Bertil Lintner, "The People's Republic of China and Burma: Not Only Pauk-Phaw," Project 2049 Institute, May 9, 2017, https://project2049.net/2017/05/09/the-peoples-republic-of-china-and-burma-not-only-pauk-phaw/, 3–5.

64. This differentiation of five periods in China–Myanmar relations borrows from Lintner, "The People's Republic of China and Burma," 3–5.

In the early years of independence, Burma's nonaligned, democratic government had relatively friendly ties with Beijing, despite differences over their border that was not demarcated until 1960. Large numbers of Chinese workers, farmers, and businesspersons migrated into Burma during this period in search of economic opportunities.

A complicating development was the arrival of Kuomintang troops in northern Shan State at the end of China's civil war. These troops backed by Taiwan, Thailand, and U.S. intelligence agencies often launched raids into China, creating concern in Burma that Chinese communist soldiers would mount an attack to destroy the Kuomintang forces. Burma in the early 1950s brought the issue of the Kuomintang troops in the country to the United Nations, but this problem did not really get resolved until the late 1980s.[65]

Bilateral relations entered a second period in 1962, when General Ne Win and his military staged a coup that toppled Burma's nascent civilian government. Many ethnic Chinese businesses were nationalized under Ne Win's "Burmese road to socialism."

As the Cultural Revolution gripped China, Beijing began supporting and arming the Communist Party of Burma (CPB)—as well as similar movements in Thailand, Malaysia, and Indonesia—which sought to overthrow the military government. A Burmese communist radio station began broadcasting from southern China in 1971 and thousands of Chinese "volunteer" soldiers arrived in Burma to fight alongside the communist guerrillas, who seized control of a sizable swath of land along the China border.[66]

At the height of the Cultural Revolution in 1967, some riots erupted against ethnic Chinese living in Yangon, leading to some deaths and the destruction of property, says Myanmar expert David Steinberg, who long taught at Georgetown University in Washington. Some ethnic Chinese fled back to China.

A third era in bilateral ties began after Deng Xiaoping returned to power in China in 1978 following the death of Mao and sought to restore normal relations with Burma. Deng continued but substantially reduced the level of Chinese support for the communists in Burma.

65. Lintner, "The People's Republic of China and Burma," 5–7, 12–13.
66. Ibid., 12.

A fourth stage was launched after Myanmar's military brutally cracked down on pro-democracy protests in 1988. The United States and other Western nations responded by imposing sanctions against the ruling junta, which prompted Beijing to deepen its economic and political ties and take steps to protect the government against international condemnation in forums like the United Nations.

In 1989, not long after the harsh suppression of protestors at Tiananmen Square in Beijing, China committed to delivering to Myanmar tanks, transport vehicles, rifles, F-7 jet fighters, helicopters, and naval vessels, which were badly needed to ensure the regime's survival.[67] The two countries became close economic partners with China providing assistance, granting loans, and sending consumer goods while Myanmar exported forestry products, minerals, and agricultural products.

China also began upgrading Myanmar's rundown roads and railroads and sending military advisers. In 2008, the two countries agreed to build pipelines for oil and gas costing over $2.5 billion from Kyaukphyu on Myanmar's Bay of Bengal coast to Kunming in southern China to make it possible for China's hydrocarbon imports to avoid the congested Malacca Strait. Then, in 2010, Beijing agreed to provide Myanmar with a $4.2 billion interest-free loan for the construction of hydropower projects, roads, and a railroad. During this period, Myanmar had very little leeway in its foreign relations.[68]

The reforms launched by the quasi-civilian government of President Thein Sein in 2011 marked the beginning of a fifth distinct period in bilateral relations. The Myanmar government began to take steps to improve ties with the United States and Europe and reduce the country's heavy dependence on China. One of the military's goals was ending the decades of crippling economic sanctions that blocked most foreign investment and aid from international financial institutions.

Another objective was to diversify ties beyond overwhelming reliance on Beijing, which had begun to concern many Myanmar nationalists, including in the military. A 2004 document prepared by the military that provided a strategic roadmap for improving ties with the United States

---

67. Storey, *Southeast Asia and the Rise of China*, 152.

68. Lintner, "The People's Republic of China and Burma," 20–21; Enze Han, "Geopolitics, Ethnic Conflicts along the Border, and Chinese Foreign Policy Changes toward Myanmar," *Asian Security* 13, no. 1 (2017): 59, https://www.enzehan.com/uploads/1/2/1/8/121872033/han_asian_security.pdf.

referred to Myanmar's diplomatic and economic dependence on China as a "national emergency" that endangered the nation's independence.[69]

One clear sign that times were changing was Thein Sein's suspension of the domestically controversial Myitsone Dam that China was building in the far north. Another signal was that Senior General Min Aung Hlaing, who was named military commander in March 2011, took his first foreign trip not to Beijing but to Vietnam, which shares with Myanmar deep anxiety about their mighty northern neighbor.[70]

"China's relations with Myanmar . . . ebbed under President Thein Sein, down to levels not seen since the Cultural Revolution in the late 1960s," Myanmar academic Min Zin wrote.[71] China's support for communist rebels in Myanmar at the time caused anti-Chinese riots to break out.

Beijing maintained its generally cordial relations with the Myanmar government, on one hand, while on the other continuing to arm ethnic insurgent armies fighting the government along the northern Myanmar border.

Enze Han, an expert on China's foreign policy at the School of Oriental and African Studies in London, has argued that by broadening its foreign ties Myanmar "significantly improved its bargaining position toward China" and was able to "push back against China's economic and strategic penetration into the country." Han says the fact that this happened at the same time President Barack Obama was mounting the United States' rebalance to Asia created for China "substantial competition" and "tremendous uncertainty" in its dealings with Myanmar.[72]

Budding ties between Myanmar and the United States prompted some "who lost Myanmar" soul-searching in China. Beijing mounted a public relations campaign in Myanmar to enhance China's image and began courting Aung San Suu Kyi, who had recently been freed after spending roughly 15 years under house arrest. China invited members of her op-

69. Lintner, "The People's Republic of China and Burma," 25.
70. "Vietnam, Myanmar Boost Military Ties," *VietNamNet*, March 7, 2017, http://english.vietnamnet.vn/fms/government/173938/vietnam--myanmar-boost-military-ties.html.
71. Min Zin, "Aung San Suu Kyi, the Dragon's Lady," *New York Times*, January 21, 2016, https://www.nytimes.com/2016/01/22/opinion/aung-san-suu-kyi-the-dragons-lady.html?emc=eta12016.
72. Han, "Geopolitics," 59.

position party, along with representatives from nongovernment organizations, academics, and journalists, to visit China as part of a public diplomacy campaign.[73]

China wanted, on one hand, to protect its interests in Myanmar from "further erosion," given it had major investments in northern Myanmar such as the oil and gas pipelines, Han says. On the other hand, China also wanted to remind Myanmar of the "great leverage" the northern neighbor holds over armed ethnic groups operating along the border of the two countries.[74] China's links with these groups complicated the peace process begun by Thein Sein and continued by Aung San Suu Kyi, the daughter of revered nationalist Aung San, who spearheaded Myanmar's independence from British colonial rule.

In 2012, China provided the United Wa State Army, the most powerful of the ethnic armies along the China border, with "tank destroyers," an armored combat vehicle, portable air defense systems, and a surface-to-air missile system, according to *Jane's Defence Weekly*. In early 2013, the Wa army also reportedly received armed transport helicopters.[75] Myanmar officials sometimes complain privately that the armed groups allied with China have better weapons than their own military has and that their troops suffer many casualties from these sophisticated weapons when trying to confront these groups.

China seems convinced that a strong Wa army gives Beijing a bargaining chip with Naypyidaw. "Beijing's policies are no doubt a way of putting pressure on Burma at a time when its relations with the United States are improving," said Lintner. "China feels it cannot afford to 'lose' Burma to the West, and seems to define Burma's foreign relations with other regional actors in zero sum terms."[76]

To demonstrate its determination to protect China's interests against the reform government in Naypyidaw, Beijing used the rise of "domestic nationalism" against Myanmar to signal its resolve regarding security along the border, Han said. China exhibited this by the way it handled fighting that erupted in 2015 between the Myanmar military and the Myanmar Nationalities Democratic Alliance Army, which had been

73. Lintner, "The People's Republic of China and Burma," 25, 27.
74. Han, "Geopolitics," 60.
75. Lintner, "The People's Republic of China and Burma," 25, 28.
76. Ibid., 25, 28–29.

expelled from its region in Shan State in 2009. In February 2015, the group, also known as the Kokang Army, attacked government positions around the Kokang capital of Laojie; the fighting that followed caused between 40,000 and 50,000 refugees to flee to China.

A few days after the fighting erupted, an open letter written in Chinese and allegedly drafted by Kokang leader Peng Jiasheng began circulating on the Internet. The letter detailed the tragedy inflicted on the Kokang people and appealed for support from the Chinese people. It stressed that the Kokang are Han Chinese and used to be part of China until the British encroached on the country during the Opium War and ceded the Kokang area to British Burma in 1897.

The letter prompted Chinese nationalists to complain about Beijing being weak and calling on the government to act against Myanmar. Chinese media picked up the letter and published interviews with Peng and stories about the years of conflict between the Kokang group and the Myanmar military. On March 13, 2015, Chinese media reported that bombs from a Myanmar air strike had killed five Chinese on China's side of the border and injured nine.

The incident fired up Chinese citizens, who called on Beijing to take punitive action against its southern neighbor. China's ambassador to Myanmar lodged an official protest and the vice chairman of the Chinese Central Military Commission, Fan Changlong, called on Myanmar's military commander to investigate the incident, apologize, and compensate the victims. Myanmar's foreign minister quickly offered an official apology on behalf of the Myanmar government and military.[77]

Beijing found the Kokang conflict a useful tool to remind Myanmar's leaders of China's interests in the country, Han said. Another factor, of course, could have been the leadership change in China in 2012 which brought Xi Jinping to power. Under Xi, China has become more assertive in its relations with its neighbors, especially those that had overlapping claims with Beijing in the South China Sea.[78]

Sino-Myanmar relations entered a sixth phase as China began courting Aung San Suu Kyi even before she took office in early 2016 and the Rohingya crisis erupted the following year. Beijing began to woo the democracy icon and opposition leader as "a consummate pragmatist" at a time

77. Han, "Geopolitics," 66–67.
78. Ibid., 70.

when the previous military-backed government was actively pursuing the United States and the West.[79]

Even though diplomatic relations have improved between the China and Myanmar, several outstanding issues with roots in the two countries' earlier history could still create problems down the road.

One issue is the fact Beijing maintains its support for weapons shipments to the Wa and the Kokang militaries, both descendants of the former Burmese communists in northern Shan State. The Wa army "serves as a 'stick' in China's relationship with Burma while diplomacy and promises of aid, trade, and investment are the 'carrot,'" said Lintner. "As China sees it, it cannot simply hand over Burma to the West. The country is far too important strategically and economically to [China] for that to happen."[80]

SURGE OF CHINESE MIGRANTS INTO THE NORTH

Chinese migrants in the last few decades have bought up most shops and houses in the center of Mandalay, transforming the character of the one-time royal capital of Myanmar and prompting many of the original residents to move to the outskirts of the city. As many as half of the city's estimated 1.2 million people are often said to be Chinese. A senior Chamber of Commerce official told a visiting journalist that seven of the top-10 entrepreneurs in Mandalay are Chinese and that fully 60 percent of the economy is now in Chinese hands.[81]

Mandalay, some 185 miles from Yunnan Province, lies at "the crossroads of trade, transport and smuggling routes" from southern China to Myanmar and mainland Southeast Asia, in the words of Denis Gray of the Associated Press. The "makeover of Mandalay . . . reflects a Chinese footprint across Southeast Asia that has grown alongside Beijing's economic and military clout," Gray said.

The spontaneous flow of hundreds of thousands of migrants from China into northern Myanmar is an issue that could create challenges between Beijing and Naypyidaw down the road.

79. Min Zin, "Aung San Suu Kyi, the Dragon's Lady."

80. Lintner, "The People's Republic of China and Burma," 5, 25.

81. Denis D. Gray, "Chinese Influx Transforming Myanmar's Quintessential City," *Associated Press*, May 1, 2018, https://www.apnews.com/d2d6b21f61f64178aa5b017633b4f83e.

Chinese migrants have arrived in droves in other towns and cities across Myanmar's north, such as Lashio, Muse, and Taunggyi. Many of the new arrivals have illegally purchased residency cards from corrupt immigration officials, creating anxiety among those displaced and concern among officials uncertain about the implications of the continuing migration. The numbers of Chinese in Myanmar today are often estimated at over 2 million.[82] The migration is continuing without an end in sight and no one seems to have ideas about how to stem the flow.

China's Qing dynasty had considered people of Chinese ethnicity, regardless of where they lived, to be Chinese citizens. But after the Communist Party seized control of China and Burma had been granted independence from the British, Beijing agreed to the Burmese government's plan to give citizenship to Chinese who were eligible. Beijing also agreed that it would not use the Chinese diaspora to interfere in Burma's internal affairs, Steinberg says.

The situation of ethnic Chinese in Myanmar today is dramatically different from the years after General Ne Win seized power in the early 1960s. He introduced Burmanization polices under which ethnic Chinese were banned from professions such as banking and Chinese medium schools; Chinese-language newspapers and Chinese voluntary organizations were closed. Chinese were forced to take Burmese names and, after the 1967 riots, they adopted Burmese dress and many refrained from speaking Chinese even at home.[83]

Following the 1988 crackdown against pro-democracy demonstrators, the junta allowed the reopening of Chinese newspapers and Chinese-language after-school programs, as it looked to China to provide goods and foreign capital to jump-start the economy.[84]

The current surge of ethnic Chinese into Myanmar began in the late 1980s at a time when Beijing made it easier for Chinese to migrate abroad and when much of the rest of the world was shunning Myanmar in the wake of military's crackdown on democracy activists, according to academics Nicholas Farrelly and Stephanie Olinga-Shannon. These changes

---

82. Nicholas Farrelly and Stephanie Olinga-Shannon, "Establishing Contemporary Chinese Life in Myanmar," *Trends in Southeast Asia 2015*, no. 15 (2015): 2, https://www.iseas.edu.sg/images/pdf/TRS15_15.pdf.
83. Farrelly and Olinga-Shannon, "Establishing Contemporary Chinese Life in Myanmar," 18.
84. Ibid., 18.

were also accompanied by Myanmar's decision to jettison the country's earlier socialist economic dogma, which opened new business opportunities for migrants from China, Farrelly and Olinga-Shannon said.

In earlier years, the government in Myanmar had resented China's support for the Communist Party of Burma, which had inflicted heavy casualties on the military. Beijing finally cut this support in 1985. As cease-fires were negotiated between the local ethnic armies and the Myanmar government, the border area became safer and more accessible, making trade and movement across the frontier easier.[85]

The presence of Chinese in Myanmar increased dramatically as the government looked for support and investment to kick-start the country's failing economy. After decades of socialism, the population of Myanmar was increasingly looking for consumer products, which were being produced in China in growing quantities.[86]

Chinese migration from the late 1980s through the 1990s transformed Myanmar's demographics as border towns in the north and northeast became dominated by Chinese language, currency, and culture, Farrelly and Olinga-Shannon observed. While other foreigners enter Myanmar mostly through ports and airports, Chinese traders and migrants enter the Irrawaddy River basin overland, through the "back door." The remoteness of the "wild frontier" offers natural hiding places for opium and methamphetamines, the smuggling of goods and people, and tourist towns for gambling and prostitution. And Myanmar's coast provides Yunnan greater access to global markets than do China's ports further away.[87]

Chinese in Myanmar today are involved in supporting China's giant infrastructure projects and running small noodle shops across towns in northern Myanmar. When Myanmar embraced state-led capitalism, Chinese migrants provided the country with skills, goods, and capital in the midst of economic and political chaos with limited rule of law. As many refugees fled the confusion in Myanmar after 1988 for Thailand, thousands of Chinese were coming into the country, viewing it as a land of opportunity. Many Chinese became enormously wealthy in the process.[88]

85. Ibid., 5, 6.
86. Ibid., 7, 8.
87. Ibid., 9, 10, 12.
88. Ibid., 13–15.

Writer Thant Myint-U said "the thousands of small and medium businesses and investors" coming to Myanmar are more important to Beijing than the giant BRI infrastructure projects. The entrepreneurs crossing the border are "doing some good things and creating jobs and everything else but will almost certainly lead to a much bigger Chinese footprint in the country, at least in the medium term," Thant Myint-U said.[89]

Still, Chinese people living in Myanmar are "permanent outsiders" in the country's society, even if their families have lived there for generations. "The dichotomy between 'Chinese' and 'locals' . . . persists and is reinforced through discriminatory laws, media and popular culture," Farrelly and Olinga-Shannon said. "Chinese in Myanmar face discrimination as they interact with state institutions and in daily life." Although Chinese relations with other ethnic groups remain uneasy, they do not encounter the "hatred and vitriol" facing the Muslim population.[90]

The "flexible cultural orientation" of the Chinese has eased their efforts to integrate with the different societies in Myanmar, Farrelly and Olinga-Shannon argued. Most of those who have come since 1988 have adapted to Myanmar culture while also maintaining their "Chinese-ness." They recognize that they must learn the local language to trade and communicate with customers and local officials. Religious flexibility in adopting Buddhism also helps Chinese integrate into Myanmar's society and enhances local tolerance of their presence in the country.[91]

"Yet the implications of the growing number of Chinese living in Myanmar have yet to be fully appreciated," Farrelly and Olinga-Shannon concluded. "Their long-term situation in the country remains profoundly unclear."[92]

"We're overwhelmed," admits a government official. "We don't know what to do." Many in Myanmar continue to have suspicions that Beijing might use the ethnic Chinese to try to influence events in the country in the future.

"The government can't tell who is a citizen among the ethnic Chinese," says a diplomat in Yangon. "There's so much fluidity, so much movement

89. Thant Myint-U.
90. Ibid., 15, 16.
91. Ibid., 19, 20.
92. Ibid., 17, 23.

across the border. As more Chinese come, the anti-China sentiment will only increase."

Opinion polling in Myanmar, of course, would have been politically too sensitive during the days of military rule, and even now under the reforms it is still at a very nascent stage, so little is known about broader views toward China and ethnic Chinese among the population. But to get at this question, political scientist Min Zin did a study on the attitudes expressed in Myanmar's literature from 1988, the year the military crushed the pro-democracy movement, until 2011, when the military launched reforms and reached out to the West.

Min Zin focused on writings such as poems, short stories, cartoons, jokes, and songs written by artists, writers, and social critics and used only works legally published through the junta's official censorship process rather than those circulated illegally to capture mainstream attitudes.[93] Myanmar, like Vietnam, has a long literary tradition dating back hundreds of years that played an important role in championing ideas like nationalism and independence during the colonial period that ended in 1948.

Min Zin reviewed a dozen memoirs by former generals to explore the views of officials about China and its policies toward Myanmar. The generals describe their battles against Communist Party of Burma fighters from the 1960s to the 1980s as "a struggle against foreign invasion by proxy." A top general complained about the communist forces possessing "new weaponry" superior to that of the Myanmar military and receiving "strong military and logistics support."

Min Zin concluded that the many military writers "don't trust the Chinese." Because the memoirs were published under the strict censorship rules of the junta, he argues they could not have been published without "tacit agreement from their fellow incumbent generals."[94]

Much of the literature after the 1988 democracy protests focused on attitudes toward ethnic Chinese migrants. Min Zin found that popular short stories reflected "intense public outrage" against "massive Chinese migration and purchases of real estate, [the] take-over of businesses,

93. Min Zin, "Burmese Attitudes toward Chinese: Portrayal of the Chinese in Contemporary Culture and Media Works," *Journal of Current Southeast Asian Affairs* 31, no. 1 (March 2012): 119, https://journals.sagepub.com/doi/full/10.1177/186810341203100107.
94. Ibid., 119–120.

and sensational incidents of abuses against local people" in northern Myanmar.

In a collection of seven short stories by popular novelists, *The Python* by Nyi Pu Lay is probably best known. It is a satire about Chinese migrants arriving in the ancient capital of Mandalay and, like "a python slowly swallowing his prey," pushing out the original residents, says Nyi Pu Lay, who in 1990 was sentenced to 10 years in prison for his opposition activities against the government.

The translator of *The Python* describes the Chinese migrants as "laundering their illegal profits by investing in property, they are seen driving up house prices to the point where the Burmese, who are struggling to make an honest living, are forced to sell . . . and move out of their old family houses, in prime downtown sites, to the outer suburbs."[95]

One of the most prolific writers from 1994–2007 was the female journalist Ludu Daw Amar,[96] whose works were published in three volumes. In her preface, she says her writings about "foreigners" are "intended not to trigger social hostility but to encourage cultural preservation." She complains that women in Myanmar are abandoning the traditional sarong for pants in the era of "rich Chinese businessman." Ludu Daw Amar blames the "superhuman" (generals and their children) and "rich Chinese businessmen" for Myanmar's social disintegration and cultural decline and urges the public to resist their "decadent role model."[97]

One of the most popular stories, *Karaoke Evening* by Wun Sithu, is about the moat around the Mandalay royal palace—which symbolizes the last kingdom of Myanmar, independence, and cultural pride—being turned into the venue for a karaoke bar. Female singers dressed in miniskirts perform Chinese songs for Chinese clients and, in the end, a drunk Chinese man throws up into the highly symbolic moat.[98]

Comedians touched on similar themes. A 2009 play, *I Am a Real Mandalay Native!*, performed by a famous comedian group, has the lead character taking rural villagers on a tour of the major sites in Mandalay. When

95. Ibid., 121.

96. Ludu Daw Amar is the mother of Nyi Pu Lay and two of her other sons joined the Communist Party of Burma, according to Lintner. One of them was killed during a purge within the party, while the other now lives in Tengchong, China.

97. Min Zin, "Burmese Attitudes toward Chinese," 122–123.

98. Ibid., 123.

the villagers ask if the giant (stone) snakes at the top of the city's famous hill are alive, he answers: "Of course, they are not alive. If they were alive, they would have already [been] sold to the other side" of the border with China. In another scene, he counts the names of the rich people in Mandalay, all whom are Chinese and have the same family name.[99]

Min Zin concludes from his review of this literature that China confronts a "soft power" deficit in Myanmar and faces a major task in generating "goodwill among Burmese toward Chinese interests in Burma."[100]

FRAUGHT MILITARY TIES

During Myanmar's years under sanctions, the military was dependent on China for hardware and training. As the country began liberalizing in 2011, the military began diversifying its arms and training relations. Following the expulsion of the Rohingya in 2017, the military was again isolated by Western countries, but its leaders were reluctant to jump fully back into China's camp. Mistrust continued at least in part due to Beijing's support for the ethnic armed groups fighting the Naypyidaw government along Myanmar's northern border.

Most foreign governments have focused their relations in recent years on the country's quasi-civilian government under Aung San Suu Kyi. But China has worked hard to develop strong ties with both the new civilian leadership while also working on connections with the military, which have often been prickly over the years. Because of the continuing border fighting with ethnic armed groups, the Rohingya crisis, and the inability of the civilian government to wrestle a bigger political role from the military, China has determined that the military will continue to play a critical political role in Myanmar for the foreseeable future.

"China has concluded that the authority and control the military enjoys in Myanmar will likely persist for the foreseeable future given Aung San Suu Kyi's inability to craft sound polices to assert effective control over the military," notes Yun Sun of the Stimson Center.

From 2013 through 2017, China provided an estimated 68 percent of Myanmar's weapons purchases, while Russia supplied 15 percent. In 2017,

99. Ibid., 124.
100. Ibid., 128.

Myanmar's main arms deals centered on the procurement of combat aircraft from China and Russia.[101] In early 2019, Russia began assembling the six Su-30SM fighters the Myanmar military had ordered from Moscow.[102]

Over the years, China has supplied Myanmar's military with helicopters, jet trainers, tanks, armored personnel carriers, and other equipment. "China provided the equipment at a 'friendship price,'" says a former military officer who now works as a military-security analyst in Yangon. "Nothing was free."

India, as part of its Look East policy and to counter China's strong influence, in 2013 offered to supply the Myanmar military with artillery guns, radar, and night-vision glasses.[103] In 2015, Germany delivered 10 G120TP turboprop training planes to Myanmar.[104] More recently, Myanmar ordered JF-17 single-engine combat aircraft, jointly developed by Pakistan and China, which can be used for reconnaissance and ground attacks.

In 2019, the Myanmar military also stepped up its cooperation with India on the ground. In January, the Myanmar army helped rout out an ethnic Naga rebel camp on its territory, which pleased India and deprived the insurgents of a sanctuary inside Myanmar. Journalist Lintner sees this as part of the military's wider strategy to balance China in the wake of the Rohingya crackdown.

In 2017, when Britain suspended its training of Myanmar soldiers, Indian offered to train them at its elite defense institutes. In November that year, the two countries held their first-ever military exercises

101. Pieter D. Wezeman, Aude Fleurant, Alexandra Kuimova, Nan Tian, and Siemon T. Wezeman, "Trends in International Arms Transfers, 2017," SIPRI Fact Sheet, Stockholm International Peace Research Institute, March 2018, 9–10, https://www.sipri.org/sites/default/files/2018-03/fssipri_at2017_0.pdf.

102. "Russia Begins Assembly of Su-30SMs Meant for Myanmar," *DefenseWorld.Net*, April 24, 2019, https://www.defenseworld.net/news/24658/Russia_Begins_Assembly_Of_Su_30SMs_Meant_For_Myanmar#.XR_Al-hKhhE.

103. Sanjeev Miglani, "India Presses On with Myanmar Defense Supplies in Show of Support," *Reuters*, September 21, 2017, https://www.reuters.com/article/us-myanmar-rohingya-india/india-presses-on-with-myanmar-defense-supplies-in-show-of-support-idUSKCN1BW1UU.

104. Craig Hoyle, "Grob Aircraft Begins G120TP Deliveries to Myanmar," *FlightGlobal*, July 14, 2015, https://www.flightglobal.com/news/articles/grob-aircraft-begins-g120tp-deliveries-to-myanmar-414605/.

focused on peacekeeping operations. In March 2018, the two navies conducted their first joint exercise in the Bay of Bengal.[105]

Despite the Myanmar military's financial challenges, it ranked 31st in the 2017 Global Firepower Index, which seeks to measure the military might of 133 countries based on 50 indicators, including budget, manpower, and equipment. In Southeast Asia, Myanmar's military ranks fourth behind Indonesia (ranked 14th), Vietnam (16th), and Thailand (20th).[106]

The Myanmar military has often been dissatisfied with the quality of the weapons it got from China and the lack of spare parts and after-purchase service. One example often cited by military officials are the Y-8 transport planes China provided which had to be grounded for a year because Myanmar did not have the spare parts it needed.

And in the fighter aircraft delivered in the 1990s, the head-up display units had been removed, said Maung Aung Myoe, an expert on the Myanmar military teaching in Japan. He said that China usually did not provide technical training for use of the equipment it provided which meant that pilots had to learn supersonic flying technics on their own in Myanmar.[107] Often China did not even provide technical manuals, even in Chinese.

Despite decades of engagement between the two militaries, suspicion, resentments, and distrust hobble their relations, because the Myanmar armed forces not been able to diversify their ties with other militaries. "The army is fed up with China," says Mary Callahan, a Myanmar expert at the University of Washington who has been living in Yangon in recent years. "They don't want to depend on China as the main provider [of military hardware]. They feel like they are treated as a third-class market for old [gear]." When the equipment breaks down, they are "still stuck repaying for flawed equipment."

Prior to the Rohingya crisis in late 2017, military commander Min Aung Hlaing traveled to Belgium, Germany, Austria, Japan, and India in

---

105. Bertil Lintner, "Myanmar and India Becoming Brothers in Arms," *Asia Times*, June 12, 2019, https://www.asiatimes.com/2019/06/article/myanmar-and-india-becoming-brothers-in-arms/.

106. John Grafilo, "Index Ranks Myanmar Fourth in Military Power in Southeast Asia," *Myanmar Times*, March 14, 2018, https://www.mmtimes.com/news/index-ranks-myanmar-fourth-military-power-southeast-asia.html.

107. Maung Aung Myoe, "Myanmar's China Policy since 2011," 30.

search of alternative sources for weapons and explored buying military equipment from Russia, Israel, and the Ukraine. In the wake of the international condemnation of the treatment of the Rohingya, European countries have joined the United States in barring arms sales.[108]

China also provides training for officers. "Some officers still study in China, but the numbers are less than before," Min Zin says, adding that there are currently about 3,000 officers studying in Russia. Since 2012, more officers are also going to India. Under an agreement with Tokyo, the Myanmar military began in 2015 sending two officers a year to study in Japan's defense academy and a Japanese foundation provided 10 scholarships for officers to study international relations in Japan.[109] A handful of officers also have attended short courses at the Asia-Pacific Center for Security Studies in Hawaii in recent years.

Despite the intense interaction between the two armed forces over the years, China's military diplomacy with Myanmar between 2003 and 2016 included only one military exercise (compared to 21 exercises with Thailand), four naval port calls (in contrast to nine with Thailand), and 34 senior-level meetings (compared to 54 with Thailand), according to a recent National Defense University study on Chinese Military Diplomacy.[110]

In May 2017, China and Myanmar conducted their first naval exercise in the Bay of Bengal, involving a Chinese guided-missile destroyer, a guided-missile frigate, and a supply ship. According to a Chinese military spokesman, the exercise focused on formation maneuvers, fleet communication, and joint search-and-rescue operations.[111] Interestingly, although the Myanmar army does very few joint exercises, the navy has done low-level exchanges with India, Singapore, and New Zealand, says a former military officer who now works as a security analyst.

---

108. Wezeman et al., "Trends in International Arms Transfers, 2017," 9–10.
109. Nikkei Asian Review, "Maung Aung Myoe—Tokyo Revives Military Ties with Myanmar," *Nikkei Asian Review*, July 27, 2016, https://asia.nikkei.com/Politics/Maung-Aung-Myoe-Tokyo-revives-military-ties-with-Myanmar.
110. Kenneth Allen, Phillip C. Saunders, and John Chen, *Chinese Military Diplomacy 2003–2016: Trends and Implications* (Washington, DC: National Defense University Press, 2017), 62, https://ndupress.ndu.edu/Portals/68/Documents/stratperspective/china/ChinaPerspectives-11.pdf?ver=2017-07-17-153301-093.
111. Prashanth Parameswaran, "China Holds First Naval Exercise with Myanmar," *The Diplomat*, May 25, 2017, https://thediplomat.com/2017/05/china-holds-first-naval-exercise-with-myanmar/.

Despite the ongoing low-grade conflict between the Myanmar military and the ethnic armed groups along the border, the 34 high-level meetings between the two militaries lag countries such as Thailand, Singapore, and Indonesia, which are further away and do not share a border with China. The authors of the National Defense University study found that these meetings are often "formal exchanges of scripted talking points" and emphasize "form over substance."[112]

China and Myanmar also had two plus two consultations (in November 2016, February 2017, and January 2018) between the ministers of defense and foreign affairs from the two countries that focused on the peace process and border security, Chinese sources told Yun Sun. Myanmar also has bilateral defense talks with India, Bangladesh, and Thailand.

In addition, some Myanmar police officers along with a few counterparts from Laos have joined Chinese patrols on the Mekong since 2012, after a drug-trafficking ring killed 13 Chinese soldiers in the Golden Triangle area of the river the previous year.[113]

Despite years of frequent interaction, relations between the two militaries are often strained. Myanmar generals have had questions about Beijing's intentions toward its smaller neighbor, dating back to the days of China's support for the Communist Party of Burma. These concerns have been exacerbated by China's continued arming of the ethnic groups in Kachin and Shan States.

On the Chinese side there is reportedly also growing irritation within the military toward its Myanmar counterparts. Yun describes a "sense of rising frustration, distrust, and even resentment from China toward the *tatmadaw*," the Burmese word for the Myanmar military. She says Beijing has concluded that the Myanmar "military has been keen on stirring up domestic security crises to justify and protect its existing political authority and economic privilege in the country."

China believes that the Myanmar military is trying to demonstrate to the people that it is the "ultimate guardian of Myanmar's national security" by "escalating the ethnic conflict" and "persecuting the Rohingya" to increase its "special status" in the country, Yun says.

112. Allen, Saunders, and Chen, *Chinese Military Diplomacy 2003–2016*, 4, 45.

113. China Military Online, "68th China-Laos-Myanmar-Thailand Joint Patrol on Mekong River Starts," *China Military Online*, March 21, 2018, http://eng.chinamil.com.cn/view/2018-03/21/content_7979908.htm.

Some Chinese officials are convinced that some of the Myanmar military's actions have damaged China's interests along the border and are hampering Beijing's efforts to build some key infrastructure projects in Myanmar. Yun says this has prompted some discussion among Chinese Myanmar experts about "how China could help to curtail the influence of the [Myanmar] military" and work more closely with the civilian government which appears to be more interested in improving bilateral relations.

STALLED PEACE TALKS WITH ARMED ETHNIC GROUPS

Aung San Suu Kyi declared that negotiating a peace deal with Myanmar's ethnic armed groups was one of her top priorities when she took control of the civilian side of the government in 2016. But after several rounds of talks under an initiative called the Twenty-first Century Panglong Conference, the negotiations seem dead in the water.

Efforts at hammering out a settlement after six decades of fighting are stalled roughly where they were when the previous government left office after having signed a nationwide cease-fire agreement in late 2015 with eight groups located mostly along Myanmar's border with Thailand. Two more groups signed the cease-fire agreement in 2018.[114]

But only two of the 10 groups that signed the cease-fire have actual armies: the Karen National Union and the Restoration Council of Shan State.

"The national cease-fire [is] a nonstarter," says Lintner, echoing the concerns of many observers. "You don't sign a cease-fire agreement before you have reached a political agreement. That's putting the cart before the horse and that's why it's not working." Another problem is the differences between the civilian and military side of the Myanmar government. The military has launched a series of offensives against the armed groups particularly in Kachin and Shan States, including in late 2017 and early 2018, which were led by the army's 33rd Light Infantry Division, the same unit that was involved in the operations against the Rohingya in Rakhine State in 2017.

114. Antoni Slodkowski, "Myanmar Signs Ceasefire with Two Rebel Groups Amid Decades of Conflict," *Reuters*, February 13, 2018, https://www.reuters.com/article/us-myanmar-military/myanmar-signs-ceasefire-with-two-rebel-groups-amid-decades-of-conflict-idUSKBN1FX19M.

One of the military's goals for the offensives was to press the ethnic armed groups back to the negotiating table. Thousands have been displaced, but those that flee across the China border are regularly pushed back into Myanmar. China repeatedly called for an end to the conflict and warned that its forces would take steps to protect the border and defend the country's sovereignty after three Chinese nationals were killed in a battle that spilled across the frontier in May 2018.[115]

Another objective of the Myanmar military appeared to be to seize the mining operations from the Kachin Independence Army (KIA) along the border with China, particularly the lucrative jade, gold, amber, and rare earth mines, says a Kachin journalist who visited the area in late 2018. She says the operations of many of these mines has been taken over by the Myanmar military with investment and know-how provided by Chinese companies, which export the mines' output to China.

China has had a complicated role in the Myanmar's civil war for decades. While working to improve its relations with the Aung San Suu Kyi government and to support the peace process, China is also looking to maintain its influence with the armed ethnic groups along its border. On one hand, Beijing at the request of Aung San Suu Kyi, delivered seven holdout groups to peace talks in Naypyidaw in May 2017 after she asked for help from President Xi during a trip to Beijing.

On the other hand, China also coordinates closely with the seven armed ethnic groups. In early 2017 these groups formed an umbrella organization called the Federal Political Negotiating and Consultative Committee (FPNCC) that operates along China's border. The grouping is led by the United Wa State Army (UWSA), which has around 30,000 fighters, making it the largest militia in the northern states.

The UWSA provides some other ethnic armies with Chinese-made weapons, among them the Myanmar National Democratic Alliance Army (Kokong), the Ta'ang National Liberation Army (Palaung), and Arakan Army, says Lintner. "Contrary to popular belief, the KIA is not getting any weapons from China, and only a few from the UWSA," he says.

"The Chinese have close relations with the KIA, but they don't trust the Kachin," Lintner adds. He says China was "infuriated" when the

115. Anthony Davis, "Chinese Military Issues Warning over Myanmar Border Fighting," *Jane's 360*, May 21, 2018, http://www.janes.com/article/80212/chinese-military-issues-warning-over-myanmar-border-fighting.

group's deputy commander in chief, General Gwan Maw, visited the United States in 2014 and pressed for him to be replaced.

What are Beijing's views about the FPNCC umbrella grouping? "While the Chinese government did not express any preference or objection to the creation of the FPNCC, the move was privately regarded as a positive development by many in China," says Yun. She says the formation of the grouping makes it easier to "harmonize the positions among the seven members" and "China expects to be able to better manage the peace process and shape its outcome given China's traditional ties and influence with the UWSA."

Yet, Yun points out that the Wa army and China disagree on key aspects of the peace process. For starters, they disagree over whether the FPNCC should sign the cease-fire agreement signed by the other groups in 2015, which China supported. The Wa army, however, has no interest in signing the cease-fire agreement because it is convinced that the FPNCC, with its "superior armed forces, deserves a better political deal" than that offered to the eight earlier signatories.

In the "general principles and specific demands" spelled out by the UWSA, the Wa demand a federal state with equality among all ethnic groups, autonomy in ethnic areas over resources and taxes, and the right to manage security and maintain ethnic armies.[116] These demands will probably be impossible for the Naypyidaw government to accept and they add new complications to the already-fraught peace process.

China recognizes it is "an indispensable link" in the Myanmar peace process, but Beijing's interest in pressing the FPNCC to the negotiating table "remains weak," says Yun. She says that Beijing believes the "lack of strategic thinking" by the National League for Democracy (NLD) makes it doubtful the group would get "a fair deal" and that "the military is unlikely to honor deals reached with the NLD government."

Second, Yun says, "China has to secure sufficient payback from Myanmar to justify the abandonment of the ethnic groups in northern Myanmar, which have traditionally been perceived as China's strategic leverage vis-à-vis the Burmese government." In recent years, Beijing has seen little interest by the previous or current governments in helping China achieve its infrastructure development goals in Myanmar.

---

116. Yun Sun summarized these conditions from the Chinese version of the "General Principles and Specific Demands by the Wa State on Political Negotiations."

"China may well want to prolong the status quo" along Myanmar's northern border. "It now controls resources coming in and out of the Wa area" of Shan State. That dynamic might change if the peace process expanded, Yun says.

China's Foreign Ministry may well support the peace process, but in a strategically located neighbor like Myanmar the multiple layers of different Chinese government and Communist Party departments and organizations often have different, and even conflicting, priorities. The International Liaison Department of the Communist Party's Central Committee, which earlier had ties to the Burmese communists, today is developing close ties with the ruling NLD, the opposition Union Solidarity and Development Party, as well as the Wa army, to promote China's longer-term strategic and economic interests, said Lintner.[117]

The Chinese army has separate ties to the Myanmar military, which are often strained, and the Wa army, which gets weapons from the Chinese military and its companies and which the Wa share with their Northern Alliance allies.[118] Another layer is the local government, the companies, and the ethnic groups in Yunnan, which have deep economic, cultural, social, and political ties across the border and to members of the FPNCC, Yun says.

These different Chinese players have varying goals, including engaging in the lucrative mining industry in Kachin and Shan States and ensuring that fighting and displaced people do not spill across the border. But in Naypyidaw, many officials and economists believe that one of the top Chinese interests in recent years has been to get approval to build the proposed deep-sea port in Kyaukphyu and the China–Myanmar Economic Corridor to boost trade and economic cooperation between the two neighbors.

Andrew Ong, a fellow in the Asia Research Institute of the National University of Singapore, who spent 18 months working for the World Food Program in the Wa region until 2015, has challenged common assumptions about how much influence China has over the USWA in Myanmar's peace process. "While China can put significant pressure on the UWSA, it remains wary of ruining the relationship," Ong said. "Ultimately China

117. Shawn Crispin, "China Uses Carrot and Stick in Myanmar," *Asia Times*, February 28, 2017, https://cms.ati.ms/2017/02/china-uses-carrot-stick-myanmar/.
118. Ibid.

cannot coerce" the Wa to sign the national cease-fire agreement with the Myanmar government or compel it attend the peace talks.

For Ong, the peace process must start by trying to integrate the ethnic armed groups, including the Wa, into the larger political "fold" with the help of China and the international community. He says this could start with development assistance that might include expanding the networks of the ministries of education and health in the Wa region. Ong says that gestures like providing identification cards could be "a starting point for integration that [would] demonstrate the goodwill and generosity of the Myanmar state."

"Meaningful relationships are not built by merely facilitating visits and talks, as China . . . has tried" because the Myanmar military and UWSA "do not lack these ties," Ong said. "It is the institutional constraints and incompatibilities of political culture that have held up peace" between the government and armed ethnic groups such as the Wa.[119]

CHINA LAUNCHES SOFT POWER CAMPAIGN

Beijing confronts serious headwinds in Myanmar at both the social and government level in deepening its ties. From the point of view of many in Myanmar, China's support long kept the military government in power and made moves toward greater democracy difficult, and the weapons China provided were used to suppress the armed ethnic groups along the border, says Maung Aung Myoe, the academic in Japan. The Myitsone Dam and the Letpadaung mine convinced many that Chinese firms did not care much about the social and environmental impact of their projects.[120]

Consumers complain that too often the goods and equipment China exports to Myanmar are of poor quality and break down easily, the food lacks sanitation and hygiene, and many medicines and pesticides exported to the country are fake. An economist said in late 2017 that Mandalay had started sending food products from China, especially vegetables, to Yangon laboratories for testing for dangerous chemical residue.

---

119. Andrew Ong, "Producing Intransigence: (Mis)understanding the United Wa State Army in Myanmar," *Contemporary Southeast Asia* 40, no. 3 (2018): 465–467.
120. Maung Aung Myoe, "Myanmar's China Policy since 2011," 29–30.

Soon after the protests erupted against the Myitsone Dam, China launched a public outreach blitz to try to reshape the thinking in Myanmar about China's economic and geopolitical interests. Beijing began inviting thousands of political and civil society leaders, journalists, teachers, monks, and other opinion shapers from Yangon and other parts of Myanmar to visit China. From Mandalay, these visits are organized by the Mandalay China Friendship Association and the Chinese consulate general.

"These trips are very important," Khin Saw Oo, the head of the friendship association, a restaurant owner, and second-generation ethnic Chinese, told *The Straits Times*. "The people over here who misunderstand China, when they go over there, they will understand."[121]

In 2013, China also started hosting hundreds of political party leaders, including from the then-ruling Union Solidarity and Development Party, ethnic parties such as the Shan Democracy Party, as well as the NLD, which was the opposition party at the time.[122] "China began to recognize that it had to do something to prepare for the possible election of the NLD government," says Min Zin. The outreach included Aung San Suu Kyi, who made her first visit to China in June 2015. Beijing had watched how she handled the Letpadaung commission, which Aung San Suu Kyi chaired, and noticed she was "conciliatory" and "cautious," even when police launched a violent crackdown against the protestors.

As the NLD government took office in 2016, Chinese companies operating in Myanmar mounted fresh public relations campaigns to change their often-negative public image. Wanbao Mining, a joint operator of the Letpadaung mine, released a 10-minute video in which the deputy general manager explained the company's philosophy in terms not heard during military rule: "If we do not take social risk into account, if we don't serve the local community well, and ensure stability, then without the support of the local people, no matter how much money we have, or how good our technology is, the project will not succeed."[123]

121. "Beijing Turns to 'Soft power' to Win over the People," *Straits Times*, May 16, 2017, https://www.straitstimes.com/world/beijing-turns-to-soft-power-to-win-over-the-people.
122. Maung Aung Myoe, "Myanmar's China Policy since 2011," 46.
123. Clare Hammond, "China Launches Local Charm Offensive," *Myanmar Times*, May 11, 2016, https://www.mmtimes.com/business/20232-china-launches-local-charm-offensive.html.

That April, *China Daily* ran a six-page special report on Myanmar. A front-page headline read: "Lending a hand: Chinese firms realise the value of helping local communities as they focus on building a long-term presence in Myanmar."[124]

Most significantly, Beijing has begun trying to win the hearts and minds of young people by inviting more students from Myanmar to study in China. Some 80,000 students from Southeast Asia were studying in China in 2016, up 15 percent from two years earlier, according to the China University and College Admission System, an online student application portal tied to China's Education Ministry. Students from Southeast Asia are now the largest grouping of foreign students, having overtaken South Korea.

One key reason students are choosing China is because the government has a generous scholarship program launched as part of the Beijing's BRI. In 2016, China provided some 50,400 scholarships covering tuition, housing, and living expenses, according to Zhou Dong, who heads the China University and College Admission System.[125]

China today has 45 universities that offer slots to international students, with many offering degrees entirely in English. One advantage for students from Southeast Asia is that China's schools are cheaper than those in the United States, Britain, or Australia. Another is job prospects back home.

"China and Myanmar have many joint ventures, providing more job opportunities," Ko Ko Kyaw, a 22-year-old Myanmar accounting student at Shanghai's Jiaotong University told *Channel News Asia*. "My experience in China will give me an advantage when applying for a job back home."[126]

Ko Ko Kyaw and other Southeast Asians say they find the academic environment in China to be quite competitive. "It's highly stressful. From when they are young until the national entrance [level], [Chinese students] have been studying and studying," Ko Ko Kyaw said. "They're always studying even at university."[127]

---

124. Ibid.
125. Valerie Tan, "Why More Southeast Asian Students Are Choosing China for Higher Education," *Channel News Asia*, March 18, 2018, https://www.channelnewsasia.com/news/asia/why-more-southeast-asian-students-are-choosing-china-for-higher-10042118.
126. Ibid.
127. Ibid.

Beijing sees foreign students studying in China as creating significant goodwill back home. "For China to be more accepted in the global community in terms of its rise as a new superpower, it starts with people," Lucian Koh, the managing director of Singapore Success Stories, a consulting company that designs education programs for students, told *Channel News Asia*. "In Chinese, they call them 'zhihua youhua' students, which means [students] who know China and are friendly to China—these graduates will be the best ambassadors for the country."[128]

Exchanges between academics from universities and think tanks in Myanmar are also increasing, especially with Yunnan Province. Professors from Yunnan have proposed that academics from the two countries write a joint history of relations between China and Myanmar. "They want to start thousands of years ago to show that Myanmar people migrated from northeast China," says an academic who teaches international relations in Yangon and is participating in the project. "They want to say we are people from China, but we can't write that."

"We want to start in 1949," after Myanmar got independence and the victory of the Communist Party in China, the academic says. "We want to write the negative and the positive," she says, referring particularly to China's years of support for the Burmese communists. "The Chinese side wants to only write the positive things." How are the two sides resolving the difference? "We are proposing to put the history into a longer introduction."

Despite its proximity to China, Mary Callahan, the Myanmar expert at the University of Washington, points out that Myanmar has no China experts in the country and no China studies program in a university or think tank. "Who is advising [Aung San Suu Kyi] on China?" Callahan asks. In contrast, Yunnan University in southern China has about a dozen Myanmar experts, many of whom have lived and worked in Myanmar and are fluent in the Burmese language.

China also provides short-term training for Myanmar journalists at the China-ASEAN Center of Training at the Communication University of China. The program is supported by China's ministries of Foreign Affairs and Education. Some of the training involves teaching how to set up a digital recording studio, for example. "Training foreign journalists in China allows them to experience the country's full complexity, thus

128. Ibid.

ensuring objectivity and consideration when they portray China to their audience," Hu Zhengrong, a lecturer in the program for Southeast Asian journalists, told the *China Daily*. Hu added that "I avoid using Western concepts like liberal or conservative because they are loaded with implications that may not reflect China's true conditions."[129]

China also offers capacity-building training programs for government officials as part of its foreign aid program. Most of these programs are run by the Ministry of Commerce and involve bringing officials to China to visit the Great Wall and the Peking opera. For some countries, training programs are run for party officials by the Chinese Communist Party with the goal of "strengthening the legitimacy of the party," "promoting China's development experience," and "promoting bilateral cooperation and the value of the BRI," says Yun Sun.

The Chinese Embassy in 2017 provided six months of Chinese-language training to over 100 Union Solidarity and Development Party officials. Yunnan University initiated two training programs for young NLD officials on running foreign aid projects. The goal of the program was to teach the officials about China's experience in governance and development, Yun says, citing Chinese sources.

Judging by attitudes in Myanmar, China's public diplomacy and soft power efforts still face considerable work in changing widespread and long-standing negative sentiment about China on the ground.

Myanmar in many ways is a case study in the challenges China faces in gaining influence and cooperation among the neighbors in its backyard. Myanmar stands almost at the opposite end of the continuum from Cambodia and Laos, which often seem ready to let China build giant infrastructure projects, casinos, and special economic zones even though they do little for the host country and seem to benefit China and its companies most.

Despite decades of dependence on China for aid, trade, and investment when the West isolated and sanctioned Myanmar, the country remains wary and distrustful of Beijing's intentions. Myanmar desperately needs roads, ports, and hydropower, but the fiercely nationalist population fears

---

129. Yuan Zhou and Zhang Zhihao, "China boosts soft power by training foreign journalists," *China Daily*, October 17, 2016, http://www.chinadaily.com.cn/beijing/2016-10/17/content_27097626.htm.

that China has mainly its own interests at heart and will take advantage of its weaker, smaller neighbor.

Many in Myanmar wonder which side China is on in Naypyidaw's low-grade conflict with a raft of ethnic minority groups along the border between the two countries. Does Beijing want to end the fighting to bolster economic development along their resource-rich border area or is it accommodating the Chinese provinces and businesspeople who benefit from access to gems, gold, and rare earth without having to pay any royalties to the central government?

As the numbers of Chinese migrants in northern Myanmar soars, locals wonder why China does not do more to stem the flow and are anxious that the growing Chinese population will transform the country's ethnic makeup and social dynamics in the decades to come. In Myanmar (like in Vietnam), China has its work cut out in overcoming the deep anti-China sentiment and distrust of Beijing.

3. CAMBODIA: CHINA'S PROXY IN SOUTHEAST ASIA

> China is "the root of everything that is evil" in Cambodia.
>
> —*Hun Sen, 1988*

> China is Cambodia's "most trusted friend."[1]
>
> —*Hun Sen, 2006*

Cambodia's coastal city of Sihanoukville, named after the former king, has emerged as a poster child of the transformation that a flood of Chinese investment can bring to an area when China decides to unleash its mountain of cash. The once sleepy backwater port city in recent years has been transformed into a boomtown as Chinese companies have arrived in droves to build hotels, casinos, and apartments. The city has developed into an economic hub along Cambodia's southern coast and become a symbol of the increasingly close cooperation between China and this longtime war-ravaged Southeast Asian nation.

In a surprising occurrence in a country where public criticism of China is rare, Sihanoukville governor Yun Min, who is a government appointee, sent a letter in January 2018 to Cambodia's Interior Ministry complaining that the surge of Chinese investment had "created opportunities for Chinese mafia to come in and commit various crimes and kidnap Chinese investors, causing insecurity in the province." In the letter obtained by Reuters, the governor went on to say that Chinese were getting drunk and getting into fights.[2]

1. "Why Cambodia Has Cosied Up to China," *The Economist*, January 21, 2017, https://www.economist.com/asia/2017/01/21/why-cambodia-has-cosied-up-to-china.
2. Prak Chan Thul, "Chinese Investment in Cambodian Province Pushes Up Crime Rate, Says Governor," *Reuters*, January 26, 2018, https://www.reuters.com/article/us

Map 4. Cambodia

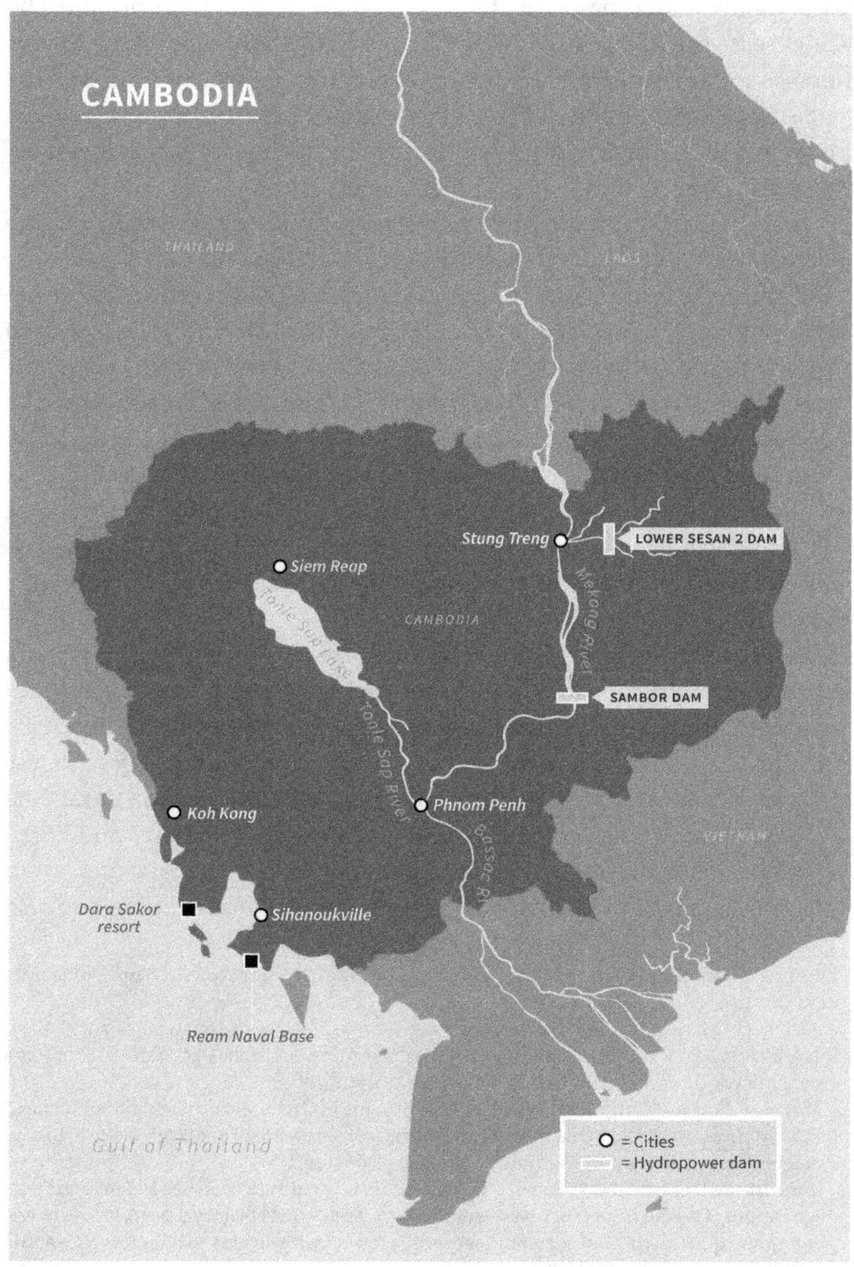

In this city of 160,000 where 88 casinos[3] have opened in recent years, local Cambodians complain about being evicted from their property by Chinese investors and soaring land prices. Police have reported problems such as money laundering, human trafficking, Internet scams, and the opening of illegal casinos.[4] To be sure, the Sihanoukville governor had some positive things to say as well: jobs were being created and real estate prices were rising thanks to Chinese investment.

In an almost-unprecedented move, the Chinese ambassador to Cambodia hosted a two-hour press conference to address the unruly behavior of Chinese citizens in Sihanoukville soon after the governor's letter became public. "The Chinese government has been informing Chinese who go overseas to countries like Cambodia that they need to strictly obey the laws of Cambodia, respect their traditions, and communicate with the people peacefully," Ambassador Xiong Bo told reporters.

"While the majority of Chinese people can follow this order . . . , a small amount of low-educated people break the law in Cambodia," he said. The ambassador called on Cambodian officials to stamp out illegal activities and said China was working with the country to "build Cambodia's rule of law."[5]

Strengthening cooperation between the two countries in recent years allowed strongman ruler Hun Sen to crack down on his opponents and dissolve the main opposition party ahead of the July 2018 parliamentary elections, in which he could have assured victory for his party with less draconian measures. Hun Sen threw the head of the opposition Cambodia National Rescue Party in prison, and when the United States and European countries protested, the long-serving prime minister moved to loosen diplomatic relations with nations critical of his actions. He also

-cambodia-china/chinese-investment-in-cambodian-province-pushes-up-crime-rate-says-governor-idUSKBN1FF0XP.

3. Andrew O'Malley, "Cambodia Casinos Have Increased from 98 to 150 since 2017," *Vegas Slots Online*, January 3, 2019, https://www.vegasslotsonline.com/news/2019/01/03/cambodia-casinos-have-increased-from-98-to-150-since-2017/.

4. Sheridan Prasso, "Chinese Influx Stirs Resentment in Once-Sleepy Cambodian Resort," *Bloomberg*, June 20, 2018, https://www.bloomberg.com/news/features/2018-06-20/chinese-casinos-stir-resentment-on-cambodia-s-coast-of-dystopia.

5. Hor Kimsay and Brendan O'Byrne, "Chinese Embassy Admits to Issues in Sihanoukville while Lauding Overall Impact of Investment," *Phnom Penh Post*, February 8, 2018, https://www.phnompenhpost.com/business/chinese-embassy-admits-issues-sihanoukville-while-lauding-overall-impact-investment.

cracked down on civil society organizations and shut down the remaining vestiges of an independent media.

Hun Sen—whose full honorific title is "lord prime minister, supreme military commander"—revealed his sentiments toward China when he opened a nearly $60 million Chinese-built bridge across the Mekong River in Stung Treng in March 2018. "The Chinese leaders respect me highly and treat me as an equal," Hun Sen declared while holding the hand of the Chinese ambassador. "Let me ask those of you who have accused me of being too close to China: What have you offered me besides cursing and disciplining me and threatening to put sanctions on me?"[6]

In recent years, Hun Sen's Cambodia has emerged has China's most reliable ally in Southeast Asia, and the 67-year-old leader is not shy about touting that pedigree. "Some people questioned why there are so many Chinese?" he noted in a speech marking the inauguration of a Chinese-supported road project in May 2018, referring to the concern among Cambodians that many Chinese workers are arriving in Cambodia. "There are numerous [Chinese] investment projects, so how could there be no Chinese?" Still Hun Sen insisted that Cambodia is no junior Chinese partner, saying the two nations "maintain a status of equal partnership and footing."[7]

In exchange for China's robust support, Phnom Penh has done Beijing's bidding on several occasions by blocking consensus statements in meetings of the 10 countries in the Association of Southeast Asian Nations (ASEAN), particularly on the matter of the South China Sea, in which China has overlapping claims with four of Cambodia's neighbors.

"The benefit Cambodia offers China is a seat at the ASEAN table where China has no direct influence," says Sophal Ear, a Cambodian-American political scientist teaching at Occidental College in California. "What China offers Cambodia are resources" for developing its economy and lining the pockets of corrupt officials.

---

6. Hannah Beech, "Embracing China, Facebook and Himself, Cambodia's Ruler Digs In," *New York Times*, March 17, 2018, https://www.nytimes.com/2018/03/17/world/asia/hun-sen-cambodia-china.html.

7. Marwaan Macan-Markar, "China Emerges as Wild Card in Elections across Asia," *Nikkei Asian Review*, June 5, 2018, https://asia.nikkei.com/Spotlight/Asia-Insight/China-emerges-as-wild-card-in-elections-across-Asia.

And the strategic benefits for Cambodia? "China has offered significant economic and diplomatic support to Cambodia to counter mounting pressures from the West," says Vannarith Chheang, a Cambodian visiting fellow at the ISEAS-Yusof Ishak Institute in Singapore. He is referring to threats from the European Union to suspend Cambodia's duty-free trade access after Hun Sen cracked down on the opposition. Chheang adds that "the perceived lack of commitment from the U.S. in Southeast Asia" is providing "an opportunity for China [to] accelerate its presence and influence in the region."

And in 2019, the "opportunity" for China to boost its influence in the region seems to have scored big, with China landing access to a military base in Cambodia. *The Wall Street Journal* reported in July that Beijing signed a secret agreement with Phnom Penh that would grant China exclusive use of part of the Cambodian navy base at Ream, near Sihanoukville, on the Gulf of Thailand. The base would allow China to post military staff, stock weapons, and dock warships, and gives China its first dedicated naval facility in Southeast Asia from which to press its military claims in the South China Sea.[8]

Despite the enthusiasm of Hun Sen for China's partnership with Cambodia, the views of some of his compatriots are considerably less trusting. A poll of Southeast Asian experts and business and civil society leaders conducted by ISEAS-Yusof Ishak Institute in late 2018 found that over 58 percent of Cambodians interviewed have little or no trust that China will "do the right thing" in contributing to global peace, security, prosperity, and governance.

Fully half of the Cambodians surveyed thought that "China will become a revisionist power with an intent to turn Southeast Asia into its sphere of influence." Just 12 percent viewed China as "a benign and benevolent power."

On the economic side, the survey found that nearly 71 percent of Cambodians are optimistic that China's signature Belt and Road Initiative (BRI) will provide funding for "much needed infrastructure" for Southeast Asian countries. But an equal number believe that regional govern-

8. Jeremy Page, Gordon Lubold, and Rob Taylor, "Deal for Naval Outpost in Cambodia Furthers China's Quest for Military Network," *Wall Street Journal*, July 22, 2019, https://www.wsj.com/articles/secret-deal-for-chinese-naval-outpost-in-cambodia-raises-u-s-fears-of-beijings-ambitions-11563732482.

ments should be "cautious in negotiating BRI projects to avoid getting into unsustainable financial debts with China."[9]

These poll findings should signal to Beijing that it might not want to be too complacent about relying exclusively on Hun Sen for the long term. Clearly Beijing has work to do to boost its image among key opinion shapers in Cambodia if it hopes to hang onto its dominant position in Phnom Penh after the long-serving prime minister leaves the stage.

CHINA STANDS BY ITS MAN

Cambodia's relations with China in recent decades have not always been as cozy as they are today. The earliest encounter between the countries dates to 1296, when Chinese emissary Zhou Daguan visited the Kingdom of Angor for a year. Between 1371 and 1419, Cambodian rulers sent more than a dozen tributary missions to China as Cambodia's elite explored trade ties with their neighbor to the north.[10] From the end of the Angor period in the fifteenth century until the arrival of the French in the nineteenth century, Cambodia was often buffeted by rivalry between its two larger neighbors, Thailand and Vietnam.[11]

After Cambodia gained independence from France in 1953, its relations with China were caught in the turbulence of the Cold War. King Norodom Sihanouk, who France put on the throne in 1941 but who abdicated in 1955, formally established diplomatic relations with China in 1958, three years after he had met then Chinese premier Zhou Enlai at a nonaligned summit in Indonesia. Sihanouk was serving as Cambodia's prime minister after his abdication. China began providing some aid to Cambodia as the country tried to maintain a policy of neutrality between the United States and the Soviet Union, which were vying for influence in neighboring Vietnam.

Sihanouk's relations with China were severely strained in 1967 when he discovered that Beijing was supporting and arming the Communist Khmer Rouge in its effort to topple his government. But Sihanouk mended

9. Tang Siew Mun, Moe Thuzar, Hoang Thi Ha, Termsak Chalermpalanupap, Pham Thi Phuong Thao, and Anuthida Saelaow Qian, *The State of Southeast Asia: 2019 Survey Report* (Singapore: ASEAN Studies Centre at ISEAS-Yusof Ishak Institute, 2019), https://www.iseas.edu.sg/images/pdf/TheStateofSEASurveyReport_2019.pdf.
10. David P. Chandler, *A History of Cambodia* (Boulder, CO: Westview Press, 1983), 77.
11. Ibid., 113.

his ties with China after a coup by General Lon Nol overthrew his government in 1970. Sihanouk moved to Beijing, set up a government in exile, and became the public face of the Khmer Rouge. The Maoist Communist movement, with backing from China, seized control of Cambodia in 1975 and quickly mounted a brutal revolution that resulted in the deaths of an estimated 1.7 million people.

Following several years of Khmer Rouge border attacks across the Vietnam border, Hanoi launched an invasion of Cambodia in late 1978 that toppled the Khmer Rouge regime and installed a pro-Vietnamese government over which Hun Sen seized control in 1985. Because Vietnam was viewed as a proxy of the Soviet Union, China, the United States, and Cambodia's non-Communist ASEAN neighbors, including Thailand and Singapore, moved to support the Khmer Rouge government in exile and its two non-communist allies. Beijing retaliated against Hanoi's invasion by attacking northern Vietnam and later providing most of the weapons to the rebels fighting against the Hanoi-backed government in Phnom Penh.

Vietnam finally withdrew its troops from Cambodia in 1989; two years later, the warring Cambodia factions negotiated a deal in Paris to end the fighting. The United Nations organized elections in 1993. The party led by Sihanouk's son, Norodom Ranariddh, won the largest number of seats, but Hun Sen protested, resulting in a brokered arrangement under which the two men shared power as co-prime ministers.

In July 1996, China invited Hun Sen, who was widely viewed as a Vietnam protégé, to visit Beijing. While his co-prime minister was left behind in Phnom Penh, Hun Sen was flown to Beijing on a Chinese government plane and granted meetings with then president Jiang Zemin and the premier at the time, Li Peng. Chinese leaders signed a new agreement on trade and investment with Hun Sen, clearly betting he was a leader with whom they could do business. The following year Hun Sen toppled his co-prime minister in a coup.

The United States and other Western donors were livid with Hun Sen's power grab and suspended aid to the country, which had become one of the most aid-dependent countries on the planet since the United Nations arrived to implement a peace deal and elections in the early 1990s. Beijing quickly jumped into the void and increased its financial support for Hun Sen's government. These developments convinced Hun Sen that China would stand by its man in Phnom Penh.

A key turning point in Cambodia's close alliance with China began in late 2009, when 22 Muslim Uighurs from Xinjiang Province in western China arrived in Phnom Penh. They had fled a crackdown following protests that erupted in July and made their way overland into Vietnam and over to Cambodia. The United Nations High Commissioner for Refugees provided letters to the refugees declaring them "persons of concern" under the agency's protection.

When the story about the refugees in Cambodia broke in the press, Beijing branded the Uighurs "criminals" and insisted they be returned to China. Cambodia had signed the 1951 UN Refugee Convention, which required Phnom Penh to assess the Uighurs refugee claim and prevent their repatriation to a country where they might face mistreatment or torture.

But the timing of their arrivals in Phnom Penh turned out to be a disaster for the Uighurs. China's then vice president Xi Jinping was due to visit Cambodia in mid-December bringing with him $1.2 billion worth of loan and grant agreements. On December 17, 2009, Hun Sen signed a decree that granted the Interior Ministry the right to deny protection status for a refugee and send asylum seekers home.

The next day a ministry spokesman declared that the Uighurs were "not real refugees" but "criminals escaping from China and involved with a terrorist organization." On December 19, the day before Xi arrived in Phnom Penh to sign Beijing's hefty aid agreement, 20 Uighurs (two had escaped) were forced at gunpoint to board a charter flight to China.[12]

The Uighur incident highlighted the increasing close political and economic ties between China and Cambodia. Today, China is Cambodia's closest political supporter, biggest donor in one of the world's most aid-dependent countries, and largest foreign investor. In fact, China has no closer ally in Southeast Asia than Hun Sen's Cambodia.

After Hun Sen's first visit to Beijing in 1996 and the coup the following year that gave him total control of the government, he moved to shut down the trade office of Taiwan, which had emerged as one of Cambodia's largest foreign investors. China rewarded Hun Sen soon after by delivering almost 200 military trucks and jeeps to offset military aid frozen

12. Sebastian Strangio, *Hun Sen's Cambodia* (New Haven, CT: Yale University Press, 2014), 211–213.

by the United States and other Western governments after Hun Sun toppled his government partner.[13]

Hun Sen's views of China have gone through a dramatic metamorphosis. In 1988, while he was still allied with Vietnam to fight the rebels aligned with China, Hun Sen called China "the root of everything that is evil" in Cambodia. A dozen years later, following a peace agreement, an election, and a coup in which he ousted his former co-prime minister, Hun Sen lauded China as Cambodia's "most trusted friend."[14]

In late 2000, then president Jiang Zemin became the first Chinese leader to visit Cambodia since the early 1960s. Demonstrators who protested China's role in supporting Pol Pot's Khmer Rouge were quickly picked up.[15] Hun Sen told Jiang that China's ties with Cambodia were of "long term and strategic significance for our country."[16]

Hun Sen uses his support from China as a hedge against the traditionally strong sway that Vietnam and Thailand, two larger neighbors on Cambodia's east and west, had in the country since the days before the arrival of French colonial rule. Cambodia with its population of about 16 million and annual per capita income of $1,300 is much smaller than Vietnam with 95 million people and annual per capita income of $2,200. On the other side is Thailand with a population of 68 million and annual per person income of $5,900.

"Cambodia has historically always had problems with Vietnam and Thailand on its border," says Pou Sothirak, who heads up the Cambodian Institute for Cooperation and Peace. "Hun Sen's closeness to China helps Cambodia protect its sovereignty," says Sothirak, who earlier served as minister for industry, mines, and energy and was elected to Parliament in the early 2000s. "Hun Sen is looking to China as an insurance policy."

When it comes to the territorial disputes between China and Vietnam in the South China Sea, Hun Sen in recent years has sided with Beijing against his Southeast Asian neighbors. At a meeting of the ASEAN foreign ministers in Cambodia in July 2012, Cambodia's foreign minister blocked a joint statement criticizing Beijing for its assertive behavior in the disputed sea.

---

13. Ibid., 214.
14. "Why Cambodia Has Cosied Up to China," *The Economist*.
15. Strangio, *Hun Sen's Cambodia*, 215.
16. Ibid., 215.

A Cambodian Foreign Ministry spokesperson said ASEAN leaders "had decided that they will not internationalize the South China Sea from now on," a line straight from Beijing's talking points.[17] Cambodia's move as chair of the grouping marked the first time since the founding of ASEAN in 1967 that its foreign ministers failed to craft a consensus statement following a summit.

Four years later, Cambodia blocked an ASEAN foreign ministers' communiqué from including language proposed by Vietnam and the Philippines supporting an arbitral tribunal ruling against China in a case brought by the Philippine government.[18] China quickly pledged $600 million in aid to support the country's election infrastructure and education and health programs.[19]

In contrast to Cambodia, neighboring Laos, which is also closely aligned with China and a heavy recipient of Beijing largesse, has maintained a more even-handed stance on the South China Sea dispute. When it chaired the ASEAN grouping in 2014, Laos managed to strike a compromise statement on the maritime dispute that balanced the needs of both China and Vietnam, which is the other close patron of Laos.[20]

Hun Sen insisted that it was an insult to Cambodia for observers to insist that he had been bought off: "I will not allow anyone to insult the Khmer nation. I am not supporting any one country." But the then-outgoing Chinese ambassador Bu Jianguo praised Phnom Penh for its "neutral and fair stance over the South China Sea issue."[21]

China has obtained a proxy in ASEAN to ensure that no parties act against Chinese interests. "Today, when debating the South China Sea issue in ASEAN meetings, Cambodian officials and scholars are widely

---

17. Jason Szep and James Pomfret, "Tensions Flare over South China Sea at Asian Summit," *Reuters*, November 19, 2012, https://www.reuters.com/article/us-asia-summit/tensions-flare-over-south-china-sea-at-asian-summit-idUSBRE8AI0BC20121119.

18. Manuel Mogato, Michael Martina, and Ben Blanchard, "ASEAN Deadlocked on South China Sea, Cambodia Blocks Statement," *Reuters*, July 25, 2016, https://www.reuters.com/article/us-southchinasea-ruling-asean-idUSKCN1050F6.

19. Associated Press/Press Trust of India, "China Gives $600 Million Aid to Ally Cambodia," *Business Standard*, July 15, 2016, https://www.business-standard.com/article/international/china-gives-600-million-aid-to-ally-cambodia-116071500303_1.html.

20. Edgar Pang, "'Same-Same but Different': Laos and Cambodia's Political Embrace of China," *ISEAS Perspective*, no. 66 (2017), https://iseas.edu.sg/images/pdf/ISEAS_Perspective_2017_66.pdf.

21. David Hutt, "How China Came to Dominate Cambodia," *The Diplomat*, September 1, 2016, https://thediplomat.com/2016/09/how-china-came-to-dominate-cambodia/.

considered as representatives of the national interests of China," Chinese academic Zhou Shixin of the Shanghai Institute for International Studies is quoted as saying.[22]

Cambodia's disillusionment with ASEAN allegedly also plays into Phnom Penh's calculus. Cambodian officials insist that the South China Sea, even though it involves four Southeast Asian countries, is not an ASEAN issue. Cambodian views reportedly are shaped at least in part by its disappointment that ASEAN did not do much to mediate a dispute with Thailand in 2011 over the Preah Vihear temple, a 900-year-old Hindu complex along the Thai-Cambodia border.

Cambodians complain that ASEAN failed to prevent violent clashes and forced Cambodia to look to the International Court of Justice to resolve the dispute. The court ruled in 2013 that Cambodia has sovereignty over the temple and its immediate surroundings but left unresolved other disputed territory nearby where clashes have erupted in recent years.[23] Cambodian officials say that if ASEAN cannot help resolve a dispute between two ASEAN states, it makes little sense to view the grouping as a platform for resolving the South China Sea dispute that involves six parties, writes Terence Chong, deputy director of the ISEAS-Yusof Ishak Institute in Singapore. One Cambodian told him: "ASEAN has failed Cambodia."[24]

What does Beijing get out of its ties to Cambodia? "Having a strong ally in Cambodia means China [is] occupying a central position on Indochina," writes David Koh Wee Hock, a former researcher at Singapore's ISEAS-Yusof Ishak Institute, referring to an earlier common designation of the Cambodia, Laos, and Vietnam grouping.[25] Cambodia gives China

22. Zhou Shixin, Head of Department of Major-Power Diplomacy, Institute for Foreign Policy Studies, Shanghai Institute for International Studies, quoted in *Indo-Pacific Strategic Review* 10, no. 1 (June 2016): 17, as cited in Terence Chong, "The Politics behind Cambodia's Embrace of China," *ISEAS Perspective*, no. 59 (2017): 6n21, https://www.iseas.edu.sg/images/pdf/ISEAS_Perspective_2017_59.pdf.

23. Thomas Fuller, "U.N. Court Rules for Cambodia in Temple Dispute with Thailand," *New York Times*, November 11, 2013, https://www.nytimes.com/2013/11/12/world/asia/un-court-rules-for-cambodia-in-temple-dispute-with-thailand.html.

24. Chong, *The Politics behind Cambodia's Embrace of China*, 6.

25. David Koh, *Chinese Investments in Cambodia: View of Chinese Soft Power from the Ground Up* (Phnom Penh: Selected CICP Publications, 2016), 79–87, https://www.cicp.org.kh/userfiles/file/Publications/Selected%20CICP%20Publications%202016.pdf, quoted in Vannarith Chheang, *Trends in Southeast Asia: The Political Economy of Chinese Investment in Cambodia* (Singapore: ISEAS-Yusof Ishak Institute, 2017), 2, https://www.iseas.edu.sg/images/pdf/TRS16_17.pdf.

leverage to surround independent-minded Vietnam not only in the north and checkmate it in the South China Sea in the east, but also in the southwest.

Cambodia has an advantage in its dealings with China compared to Myanmar and Laos, which share long land borders with China. Cambodia's distance gives the country "a sense of geographical and psychological distance," says Chong of ISEAS in Singapore.[26]

Fear of Vietnam and Thailand may have been a factor pushing Hun Sen into the arms of Beijing early on, but more recently he appears to be seeking China's help to serve as a counterweight to the West. He is looking to China to prop up his rule and, from his point of view, hopefully keep his family in power for the long term—and with the lifestyle to which they have become accustomed. Hun Sen has long used ruthless tactics to crush his political opposition, journalists, nongovernmental organizations, and protestors, but he seems to have ratcheted up his crackdown since the opposition gave his ruling Cambodia People's Party (CPP) a political scare in recent elections.

In 2013, the opposition snared 55 seats in the National Assembly compared to 68 by the CPP, creating a wake-up call for the ruling party. In local elections in June 2017, the opposition won nearly 44 percent of the vote compared to the ruling party's 51 percent.[27] Sources in Phnom Penh report that an independent poll taken shortly after the communal elections (but not publicly released) showed that the ruling party could actually lose the nationwide elections in July 2018.

Hun Sen sprang into action by arresting the opposition leader and forcing most opposition members to flee the country. In November 2017, Cambodia's Supreme Court issued an order dissolving the country's leading opposition party, which effectively abolished all the seats the opposition had in Parliament and disenfranchised more than 3 million Cambodian voters who had supported the party in recent elections.

By effectively destroying Cambodia's opposition and turning to China for international cover and economic support, Hun Sen has demonstrated that billions of dollars of Western aid dating back to the early 1990s have

26. Chong, *The Politics behind Cambodia's Embrace of China*, 2.

27. Holly Robertson, "Suddenly It's Open Season on the Press in Cambodia," *Washington Post*, August 30, 2017, https://www.washingtonpost.com/news/democracy-post/wp/2017/08/30/suddenly-its-open-season-on-the-press-in-cambodia/?u&utm_term=.bba3a36a6421.

done little to build democracy, improve governance, rein in corruption, and pull the country out of poverty. "Modern Cambodia is a kleptocracy cum thugocracy, and the international community, led by the UN, is its enabler," political scientist Sophal Ear wrote in his book *Aid Dependence in Cambodia: How Foreign Assistance Undermined Democracy in Cambodia*.[28] China's arrival in Cambodia with buckets of cash has made it possible for Hun Sen to topple his opponents and more difficult for Western donors to press for reform.

Hun Sen attacked the opposition as "rebels in the city" determined to stage a "color revolution."[29] By August 2017, the government had shuttered 19 radio stations, citing contract violations in providing slots to broadcasters such as the Voice of America and U.S.-funded Radio Free Asia. In September, the *Cambodia Daily*, one of two independent English-language newspapers published in Cambodia since the 1990s, was forced to close for allegedly failing to pay a $6.3 million tax bill.[30] In May 2018, the other daily, the *Phnom Penh Post*, was sold to a Malaysian public relations firm, which earlier had done work for Hun Sen.[31]

The government also cracked down on civil society groups culminating in late 2017 with the expulsion of the National Democratic Institute, which is funded by the U.S. Democratic Party. Officials also moved against an election watch group called the Situation Room, which allegedly served as base for a possible "color revolution" to topple the government.[32] Hun Sen also ordered the U.S. Peace Corps volunteer agency to leave the country and a woman was arrested for throwing a shoe at a billboard that had a picture of the prime minister.

These moves prompted the United States and European governments to step up their criticism of Hun Sen and reduce their aid, but their leverage had waned in recent years. The Cambodian leader turned in-

28. Quoted in Sebastian Strangio, "Review: 'Aid Dependence in Cambodia,' by Sophal Ear," *Asia Times*, November 1, 2012, http://www.sebastianstrangio.com/2012/11/01/review-aid-dependence-in-cambodia-by-sophal-ear/.

29. "Cambodia's Hun Sen Urges Arrests of Opposition 'Rebels in the City,'" *Reuters*, October 2, 2017, https://www.reuters.com/article/us-cambodia-politics/cambodias-hun-sen-urges-arrests-of-opposition-rebels-in-the-city-idUSKCN1C70HS.

30. Robertson, "Suddenly It's Open Season on the Press in Cambodia."

31. "Cambodian Newspaper Sold to PR Firm Linked to Hun Sen," *Asian Correspondent*, May 7, 2018, https://asiancorrespondent.com/2018/05/cambodian-newspaper-sold-to-pr-firm-linked-to-hun-sen/#zLelHD9kP7focUPJ.97.

32. Human Rights Watch, "Cambodia: Onslaught on Media, Rights Groups," August 25, 2017, https://www.hrw.org/news/2017/08/25/cambodia-onslaught-media-rights-groups.

creasingly to China, which like in its response to the Rohingya crisis in Myanmar, did not criticize the Cambodian ruling elite.

"Beijing provides diplomatic support and strategic space for Cambodia when Phnom Penh is pressured by international bodies on allegations of human rights abuses, oppression, corruption, and misuse of power at high government levels," wrote Chheang, the Cambodian analyst working at a Singapore-based think tank. "In return, diplomatic and political ties help secure approval and protection of Chinese investments."[33]

But not everyone in China was enthusiastic about Hun Sen's latest antics or convinced that they will have no blowback in China. In October 2017, at the height of the Chinese Communist Party's congress, the *Global Times*, a state-owned paper that often reflects what party officials think, ran a headline declaring: "Political turmoil may threaten Cambodia's hard-won economic achievements."[34] Presumably the writer was anxious about idea that the European Union and the U.S. Congress might impose trade sanctions or cut the preference benefits under which the lion's share of Cambodia's exports enter these markets.

Cambodia announced earlier that Beijing had agreed to help "reform" the country's judicial system. In 2017, China said that it would establish a think tank in Cambodia that would study methods to prevent "color revolutions" supported by foreign donors to topple their governments.[35]

In a leaked platform of the ruling party in early 2018 before the elections, party officials said that they planned to move closer to China and to "reform" the country's foreign policy toward "economic diplomacy" from "traditional diplomacy," a reference to Phnom Penh's shift away from Western donors and the United States. The document said Cambodia will continue to "recognize China's dynamic rise and growth as a

---

33. Chheang, *Trends in Southeast Asia*, 22, quoted in Sigfrido Burgos and Sophal Ear, "China's Strategic Interests in Cambodia," *Asian Survey* 50, no. 3 (May/June 2010): 637, https://www.jstor.org/stable/10.1525/as.2010.50.3.615.

34. David Hutt, "Cambodia Clampdown Threatens Chinese Interests," *Asia Times*, October 29, 2017, https://www.asiatimes.com/2017/10/article/cambodia-clampdown-threatens-chinese-interests/.

35. David Hutt, "China's Largesse Abets Cambodia Clampdown," *Asia Times*, September 25, 2017, https://www.asiatimes.com/2017/09/article/chinas-largesse-abets-cambodias-clampdown/.

contribution to the economic prosperity and the strengthening of peace stability in the region."[36]

It was not clear in the run-up to the July 2018 elections exactly what role China would play. But Beijing in late 2017 had offered to provide equipment, including computers, ballot boxes, and voting booths, after the European Union and the United States withdrew their support in response to Hun Sen's crackdown. The previous year, China donated vehicles and other supplies for the elections worth $11 million.[37]

China's economic role in Cambodia also bolsters the country's political leaders. "[The] Chinese economic presence also gives legitimacy [to] the ruling elite and empowers its patronage system," argued Chheang. "These rulers rely on economic performance and development outputs particularly in terms of infrastructure development and employment opportunities to gain popular support and votes."[38]

Officials explain China's substantial role in the country by arguing that without China, Cambodia could not survive. "Without China, there would be no Cambodia today—one must learn to accept that," said Secretary of State Vongsey Vissoth at the Ministry of Economy and Finance. "Why should we go to China for assistance? We don't want to favor China, but if they give us what we need, shouldn't we take it?"[39]

To be sure, China and Cambodia are not natural soulmates. Especially older Cambodians, who remember Beijing's support for the brutal Khmer Rouge, continue to be suspicious of Beijing's goals. Cambodians also complain about Chinese corrupt practices in buying off officials, poor-quality products, and substandard workmanship. "We take the bad and the good from China," one Cambodian told Chong of the Singapore think tank.[40]

Beijing monitors any discussion about China in Cambodia closely, including in the country's think tanks. A Phnom Penh think tank was planning a talk in 2018 about China-Cambodia relations under Sihanouk

---

36. Aun Chhengpor, "Leaked Ruling Party Platform Shows Desire for Closer Relations with China," *Voice of America*, February 13, 2018, https://www.voacambodia.com/a/leaked-ruling-party-platform-shows-desire-for-closer-relations-with-china/4251740.html.
37. "China Pledges Support for Cambodia Election after EU, U.S. Withdraw," *Reuters*, December 28, 2017, https://www.reuters.com/article/us-cambodia-politics/china-pledges-support-for-cambodia-election-after-eu-u-s-withdraw-idUSKBN1EM0JQ.
38. Chheang, *Trends in Southeast Asia*, 22.
39. Quoted in Chheang, *Trends in Southeast Asia*, 23.
40. Chong, *The Politics behind Cambodia's Embrace of China*, 7.

by a prominent scholar who formerly worked for Sihanouk. The Chinese Embassy protested, effectively forcing the think tank to cancel the meeting.

Many Cambodians are "anxious" that the country is "slipping out of their control," says Ear, the political scientist who was born in Cambodia. "They fear they are not masters of their destiny. They feel they are being overrun by Chinese—Chinese tourists, Chinese investors."

To be sure, Beijing has not taken steps to actively undermine democracy in Cambodia and in Southeast Asia generally, but Eric Heginbotham, coauthor of *China Steps Out*, argues "it has exploited economic and political circumstances in weak non-democratic states to build effective patron-client relations."[41]

At the same time, China benefits when Western donors make demands for rigorous and often slow economic, social, and environmental impact studies before approving aid to countries. Beijing's willingness to quickly approve and build hydropower dams to tackle Cambodia's energy shortage and roads and bridges to boost connectivity, without conditions, make China highly attractive as a donor.

China's hefty economic role gives Beijing substantial political leverage over Cambodia and its foreign policy. "The government is at risk of losing its autonomy. If it were to rely solely on China, Cambodia also risks losing face and trust from the international community, and its role in ASEAN might be marginalized if it continues to put China ahead of ASEAN," said Heng Pheakdey of the Enrich Institute, a think tank focused on the implementation of sustainable development goals in Cambodia.[42]

The fact that Beijing's influence is increasing in all aspects of Cambodian life makes it necessary for the government to manage anti-China sentiments on the ground. "Manipulating anti-Vietnamese sentiments has been a traditional and effective ploy" used by the government to balance negative attitudes toward China, said Chong of ISEAS. Anti-Vietnam feeling dates back centuries, including to the French colonial period when the colonial leaders used Vietnamese as administrators and allegedly

41. Eric Heginbotham, "China's Strategy in Southeast Asia," in *China Steps Out: Beijing's Major Power Engagement with the Developing World*, ed. Joshua Eisenman and Eric Heginbotham (New York: Routledge, 2018), 55.
42. Heng Pheakdey, "Chinese Investment and Aid in Cambodia a Controversial Affair," *East Asia Forum*, July 16, 2013, https://www.eastasiaforum.org/2013/07/16/chinese-investment-and-aid-in-cambodia-a-controversial-affair/.

turned over swathes of Cambodian land to Vietnam. These days most anti-Vietnam sentiment is directed at immigrants, many of whom enter Cambodia illegally.

A second way the government keeps anti-China sentiment in check is by regularly praising China for providing Cambodia what it needs economically. Phnom Penh differentiates China's aid and capital flows from "the army of international organizations that harp on human rights and democracy, or international banks that worry about credit ratings," Chong said.[43]

Third, the government provides a safety valve by allowing the press to report from time to time on Chinese businesspeople flouting Cambodian regulations and exploiting workers in Chinese-owned factories by underpaying employees or absconding back to China without paying them.[44] On the other side, Chinese businesspeople blame Cambodia's corrupt culture for the fact that they use bribes to get stuff done. "Chinese businessmen tell Cambodian activists that they are merely following Cambodian norms when they bribe officials or break the rules," Chong wrote.[45]

Cambodian officials, both national and local, work hard to find opportunities to be seen hobnobbing with Chinese officials, diplomats, and businessmen. Many Cambodians today try to tout their Chinese heritage. Even Hun Sen has Chinese heritage. The paternal grandparents of Hun Sen's father, Hun Neang, are identified as having been wealthy landowners of Teochew heritage from Guangdong Province in southern China.

But many ordinary "Cambodians don't think China is their number-one friend," says Sothirak. "Young people look to the United States and Australia. They've been influenced by Western soft power."

DEEPENING MILITARY TIES

Beijing's secret agreement with Cambodia to allow the Chinese military use of the naval port at Ream on the Gulf of Thailand, if confirmed, could

43. Chong, *The Politics behind Cambodia's Embrace of China*, 3.
44. David Eimer, "Cambodia's Textile Workers Hang by a Thread under Chinese Bosses," *South China Morning Post*, July 27, 2013, https://www.scmp.com/news/asia/article/1291466/cambodias-textile-workers-hang-thread-under-chinese-bosses.
45. Chong, *The Politics behind Cambodia's Embrace of China*, 5–6.

be an important game changer in Southeast Asia. Chinese armed forces would have access to the gulf opposite Thailand, making it easier for Beijing to press its territorial claims in the southern reaches of the disputed South China Sea and stretch its influence over the strategic Malacca Strait.

Chinese and Cambodian officials denied the plans reported by *The Wall Street Journal* in mid-2019, but U.S. officials said a deal had been signed that would give Beijing access to a dedicated staging facility, its first in Southeast Asia. The base at Ream occupies some 190 acres and has two facilities built with U.S. assistance for the Cambodian navy. Apparently, China plans to build two new piers, one that would be used by the Chinese, the other by Cambodians.

Use of the port would give China a stronger toehold in Cambodia, whose government has grown more dependent on Beijing for support against Western criticism of Hun Sen's crackdown on his opposition and on Chinese investment and loans to build the country's infrastructure and develop its economy.

In 2018, the United States and its allies became concerned when satellite images showed a two-mile-long runway being built at the Dara Sakor resort in Koh Kong by China's Union Development Company that would be able to land giant passenger planes as well as Chinese long-range bombers and military transport planes. But Cambodian officials quickly denied the report, adding that the Cambodian constitution did not allow foreign military bases on Cambodian soil.

China in 2017 gained access to its first military base overseas in Djibouti in East Africa, which made it easier for China to operate in the Indian Ocean and off Africa. In recent years, China has also built runways capable of handling military planes on three of the seven artificial islands it has created in the South China Sea.

Yun Sun, a China foreign policy expert at the Stimson Center, said perhaps the facilities under construction at Koh Kong could have both a military and civilian purpose, adding that Beijing had developed a "pattern of dual use port development in Djibouti, Sri Lanka, Pakistan, Burma." She said that "China has intentionally [pursued] this type of port to avoid controversies."[46]

46. Andrew Nachemson, "Is Cambodia's Koh Kong Project for Chinese Tourists—or China's Military?," *South China Morning Post*, March 5, 2019, https://www.scmp.com/week-asia/geopolitics/article/2188558/cambodias-koh-kong-project-chinese-tourists-or-chinas-military.

China gained access to the base in Djibouti in its efforts to support the United Nations initiative to tackle piracy. Hun Sen could devise a similar solution to get around Cambodia's constitutional ban on foreign bases. He has already said that an exception to no stationing of foreign troops in Cambodia could be made if they were part of a UN mission.

Phnom Penh has been downgrading its military links with the United States in recent years. Cambodia announced in January 2017, just before Donald Trump was sworn in as U.S. president, that it was postponing its annual Angkor Sentinel exercises with the United States for two years because the armed forces would be busy supporting upcoming elections in June 2017 and July the following year. Speculation was rife that this move was prompted by increasingly close military relations with China, but Cambodian government spokespersons rejected this explanation.

"We haven't stopped cooperating with the U.S.," said General Chum Socheath, the Defense Ministry's spokesman. "It's not about the U.S. and China. We do not side with any country."[47]

Shortly after canceling the exercises, Cambodia also told a U.S. Navy aid unit that had provided humanitarian assistance since 2008 to leave the country. The ouster of the Mobile Construction Battalion, known as the Seabees, resulted in the cancellation of some 20 planned projects, including maternity units and school bathrooms. The decision to end this program suggested a further reduction of military ties with the United States while boosting those with China.[48]

But in March 2018, four months before the national elections, the military was able to hold the Golden Dragon 2018 exercise with China west of Phnom Penh. The 15-day exercise, which involved 280 Cambodian troops and 216 from China, focused on counterterrorism and rescue operations.[49] The first Golden Dragon exercise took place in late 2016 just before the announcement that U.S. exercises had been postponed. China and Cambodia also had their first joint naval exercise in 2016.

---

47. Michael Peel and Robin Harding, "Cambodia Scraps Joint US Military Exercise," *Financial Times*, January 17, 2017, https://www.ft.com/content/ba123ed8-dc8e-11e6-9d7c-be108f1c1dce.
48. Prak Chan Thul, "U.S. Navy Aid Unit Told to Leave Cambodia," *Reuters*, April 4, 2017, https://www.reuters.com/article/us-cambodia-usa-navy-idUSKBN1760TA.
49. Reuters, "Cambodia Begins Military Drills with 'Great Friend' China," *South China Morning Post*, March 17, 2018, https://www.scmp.com/news/china/diplomacy-defence/article/2137636/cambodia-begins-military-drills-great-friend-china.

China's growing role in Cambodia is strengthening the Cambodian military and effectively reducing the U.S. role. Prior to the suspension announcement, U.S. forces had held exercises annually with Cambodia since about 2009.

China today is the largest supplier of military aid, providing Cambodia with tanks and armored personnel vehicles, and it is also building an air defense force training facility in southern Cambodia.[50] Cambodia used a $195 million loan in 2013 to buy 12 Harbin Z-9 helicopters and in 2014 it obtained 26 Chinese military trucks.[51] The following year China supplied some 44 military vehicles, including rocket-launcher-mounted trucks, jeeps, and about a half dozen anti-aircraft guns mounted on wheels.[52] Beijing provides this equipment without looking at human rights abuses as the United States and other Western countries do.

During celebrations in mid-2018 marking the 60th anniversary of diplomatic relations and just before Cambodia's elections, Chinese Defense Minister Wei Fenghe offered Cambodia additional military assistance valued at $130 million, but neither side provided details about what this was for. Cambodia also pledged to host an exchange with the Chinese navy and to hold another round of Golden Dragon exercises in 2019. Cambodian officers asked the Chinese minister for assistance in training special counterterrorism forces.[53]

China is also stepping up its role in military training. It provided aid in 1999 to set up a prestigious Army Institute, the first of its type built by China in Southeast Asia, about 50 miles southwest of Phnom Penh. Some 200 cadets are admitted each year to study in the four-year military training course developed by Chinese advisers at the institute. The

---

50. "China to Donate Tanks, APCs to Cambodia," *War Defense News*, January 30, 2018, https://wardefenseenews.blogspot.com/2018/01/china-to-donate-tanks-apcs-to-cambodia.html; Cheang Sokha, "China to Boost Military Aid," *Khmer Times*, December 6, 2017, https://www.khmertimeskh.com/94161/china-boost-military-aid/.

51. Aubrey Belford and Prak Chan Thul, "Chinese Influence in Cambodia Grows with Army School, Aid," *Reuters*, April 2, 2015, https://www.reuters.com/article/us-cambodia-china-military/chinese-influence-in-cambodia-grows-with-army-school-aid-idUSKBN0MT0SW20150402.

52. Aun Pheap, "China Donates Heavy Weaponry to Military," *Cambodia Daily*, May 25, 2015, https://www.cambodiadaily.com/news/china-donates-heavy-weaponry-to-military-84249/.

53. "China Pledges over $100 Million Military Aid to Cambodia," *Reuters*, June 19, 2018, https://www.reuters.com/article/us-cambodia-china/china-pledges-over-100-million-military-aid-to-cambodia-idUSKBN1JF0KQ.

students spend a compulsory six-month period in a Chinese military school in China.[54]

Separately, the Confucius Institute at the Royal Academy of Cambodia in 2012 opened a special training institute to provide Chinese-language training to military officers.[55]

In 2016 a Mandarin Center was launched at the Ministry of Defense to provide Chinese-language training to military officers. "Most weapons and equipment are imported from China, and the instructions to use them are in Chinese," explained Sok Touch, who heads up the Royal Academy of Cambodia, which collaborates with the Confucius Institute. "Military officers also need to learn Chinese in order to communicate with Chinese military officials within their work."[56]

Even if military ties with the United States are scaled back, the Cambodian military still receives training from diverse sources. "Vietnam still trains more military officers than anyone else," says a foreign military analyst based in Phnom Penh, alluding to the military that toppled the Khmer Rouge in 1979 and that helped build the current military. Other countries involved in providing training are France, Korea, Indonesia, and Thailand.

The United States continues to be active in demining the countryside after the country's wars that lasted from the late 1960s through the late 1990s. Washington had spent $140 million on this program through 2017. Many of the cluster bombs and mines along the Ho Chi Minh trail in the east were planted by the United States. But the mines in the west were of Chinese origin, planted by the Khmer Rouge against the Vietnamese; those of Vietnamese origin were planted by the Vietnamese military.

In addition, the Thai military placed bombs to keep the Khmer Rouge out of Thailand. In 2016, the number of victims killed or injured by land-

54. Belford and Thul, "Chinese Influence in Cambodia Grows with Army School, Aid."

55. Jeffrey Becker, "What Is the PLA's Role in Promoting China-Cambodia Relations?," *The Diplomat*, April 29, 2017, https://thediplomat.com/2017/04/what-is-the-plas-role-in-promoting-china-cambodia-relations/.

56. James Reddick and Cindy Co, "In Cambodia's Chinese-Language Schools, a Hard Push for Soft Power," *Phnom Penh Post*, December 18, 2017, https://www.phnompenhpost.com/national-post-depth/cambodias-chinese-language-schools-hard-push-soft-power.

mines from the country's wars dropped below 100 for the first time since the Khmer Rouge were ousted in 1979.[57]

China's goal is to build military ties with Cambodia and other Southeast Asian countries. "The Cambodian defense sector is less developed and modernized compared with Thailand and Vietnam, so external support . . . is critical for Cambodia to defend itself," says Chheang of ISEAS. "Terrorism, search and rescue, disaster relief, and transnational crimes are the key areas of security cooperation" between China and Cambodia.

Apparently at least some Chinese visitors are already recognizing the army's growing political clout in the government bureaucracy, particularly after 80 new senior army and police commanders were appointed members of the CPP's Central Committee in 2015.[58] "Because the Cambodian military has access to the political elite and decision-makers, Chinese businessmen and entrepreneurs have found it expedient to head straight to the military to bypass the bureaucratic process," Chong of ISEAS said.[59]

NO WORRY ABOUT TOO MANY CASINOS

China seems to face fewer trust deficit issues in Cambodia than in most other Southeast Asian countries. As one of the region's smallest and poorest countries, Cambodia remains highly dependent on foreign aid and investment and demonstrates few of the concerns about overdependence on China that affect its neighbors. Still, private grumbling about Beijing's growing footprint in the country is increasing in cities like Phnom Penh. China is by far Cambodia's biggest benefactor, after replacing Japan several years ago.

Investment from China totaled $14.7 billion between 1994 and 2016 and was concentrated in four key areas: tourism and real estate, infrastructure such as roads and bridges, light industry and garment

57. Zsombor Peter, "Landmine Casualties Dip below 100 for the First Time," *Cambodia Daily*, January 4, 2017, https://www.cambodiadaily.com/editors-choice/landmine-injuries-dip-below-100-for-first-time-122921/.

58. Aun Chhengpot, "Cambodia Joins China for Military Drills as US Relations Cool," *VOA News*, March 18, 2018, https://www.voanews.com/a/cambodia-china-joint-military-drills-us-relations-cool/4302875.html.

59. Chong, *The Politics behind Cambodia's Embrace of China*, 7.

factories, and agriculture such as growing rice, cassava, and other crops for export.[60]

Many of these projects fall under China's ambitious BRI and are contracted out to Chinese state-owned conglomerates. Cambodia's transport minister said 70 percent of the country's roads and bridges were built with concessionary loans from China.[61]

Neither Beijing nor Phnom Penh has released figures on how much investment China has provided Cambodia under the BRI. But RWR Advisory Group in Washington, DC, has calculated this figure at $13.4 billion by monitoring media reports in China and Cambodia and press releases by Chinese companies. The company counts only deals that it believes have become "real and official" and that have start dates after January 1, 2013, says Andrew Davenport, RWR's chief operating officer.

Under the BRI, China is investing in hydropower facilities, roads, and improvements of the deepwater port in Sihanoukville. Chinese loans and investments reached $5 billion by the end of 2017. And more aid is on the way after Premier Li Keqiang signed 19 infrastructure projects in early 2018.[62]

According to some estimates, the China Development Bank and China's Export-Import (EXIM) Bank are financing more than half of the infrastructure projects in Cambodia.[63] Almost no information is available on the size of individual loans, the interest rates charged, the repayment period, and the currency (often in hard currency) in which the loan is to be repaid.

Chinese companies have invested in several coal-fired electricity projects[64] and in a raft of garment factories that have created jobs for about half a million Cambodians and integrated the country into the supply

60. Chheang, *Trends in Southeast Asia*, 12; Pal Nyiri, "Investors, Managers, Brokers, and Culture Workers: How Migrants from China Are Changing the Meaning of Chineseness in Cambodia," in *Chinese Encounters in Southeast Asia: How People, Money, and Ideas from China Are Changing a Region*, ed. Pal Nyiri and Danielle Tan (Seattle: University of Washington Press, 2017), 26.

61. "70 Pct of Roads, Bridges in Cambodia Built under Chinese Support: Transport Minister," *Xinhua*, July 21, 2017, http://www.xinhuanet.com/english/2017-07/21/c_136461623.htm.

62. Macan-Markar, "China Emerges as Wild Card in Elections across Asia."

63. Nyiri, "Investors, Managers, Brokers, and Culture Workers," 30.

64. Chheang, *Trends in Southeast Asia*, 14.

chain that runs through China.[65] Firms from China are operating a number of mines, including in iron and gold, and granite quarries in Kratie Province in the east.[66]

One of China's biggest tourism projects is the $3.8 billion Dara Sakor Beachside Resort in the southwestern province of Koh Kong along the Gulf of Thailand, which is being developed by China's Tianjin Union Development Group, a real estate development firm. The project includes a deepwater port that can handle cruise ships and four 20,000-ton container ships.[67] The resort, which will boast five-star hotels, international schools, and an international airport, has attracted considerable controversy.

Work began on the resort in 2008, when the Cambodian government leased the developers over 111,000 acres, some of it in a national park. When Reuters journalists visited the site in 2018, they found "a sprawl of mostly empty hotel buildings, deserted beach bars, and the unfinished shell of a casino on a remote part of the Cambodian coast." They added: "Beyond the resort, the dusty foundations of a planned investment zone stretch down to a container port—both unfinished and idle." But the reporters found that work was under way on a two-mile runway, long enough to land an Airbus A380 plane.[68]

Some villagers say they were forcibly moved off their land by security forces that destroyed their houses and crops of coconuts, mangoes, and cashews, according to local human rights group Licadho. A report by the U.S. analytical group C4ADS says that Chinese investment in the province "has come at the expense of the local population, the environment and potential future income for Cambodia."[69] In Cambodia, as in other

65. Sophal Ear, "Cambodia's Garment Industry: A Case Study in Governance," *Journal of Southeast Asian Economies* 30, no. 1 (April 2013): 91–105, https://muse.jhu.edu/article/512148/pdf.

66. Chheang, *Trends in Southeast Asia*, 14.

67. James Kynge, Leila Haddou, and Michael Peel, "FT Investigation: How China Bought Its Way into Cambodia," *Financial Times*, September 8, 2016, https://www.ft.com/content/23968248-43a0-11e6-b22f-79eb4891c97d; Brenda Goh and Prak Chan Thul, "In Cambodia, Stalled Chinese Casino Resort Embodies Silk Road Secrecy, Risks," *Reuters*, June 6, 2018, https://www.reuters.com/article/us-china-silkroad-cambodia-insight/in-cambodia-stalled-chinese-casino-resort-embodies-silk-road-secrecy-risks-idUSKCN1J20HA.

68. Goh and Thul, "In Cambodia, Stalled Chinese Casino Resort Embodies Silk Road Secrecy, Risks."

69. Andrew Nachemson, "A Chinese Colony Takes Shape in Cambodia," *Asia Times*, June 5, 2018, https://www.asiatimes.com/2018/06/article/a-chinese-colony-takes-shape-in-cambodia/.

mainland Southeast Asian countries, land disputes can be quite disruptive, can last a long time, and often result in project delays.

Some of the land on which the resort is being built was previously part of the protected Botum Sakor National Park, which was made available to the investors under a royal decree. Critics say the resort is slated to open exclusively for the use of Chinese businesspersons, tourists, and Chinese working in Cambodia.

The slow pace of construction (and the fact that former Chinese vice-premier Zhang Gaoli, who chairs a group with a key role in the BRI, attended the project signing ceremony in 2008) has raised questions about the long-term goal of the project. So has the release of satellite images from the European Space Agency that showed that the runway for the resort's airport was longer than what was needed to land most civilian airplanes. Diplomats and analysts believe the resort could be as much about hosting visits from the Chinese military as it is about welcoming tourists from China.[70]

A second giant $5.7 billion international resort in the neighboring coastal province of Sihanoukville is being developed by a subsidiary of Unite International (Cambodia) Investment Group Co Ltd.[71] This project, which the developers claim will become Cambodia's second largest tourist attraction after the iconic Angkor Wat, will reportedly be built on a whopping 8,150 acres of land, some of which comes from inside the protected Ream National Park and fronts on 18 miles of some of Cambodia's most pristine beaches.[72]

The company is owned by Fu Xianting, a former officer in the Chinese army and one of the most prominent members of Cambodia's Chinese business community who is closely linked to Hun Sen. Fu's company got the giant land concession in 2009 after donating 220 motorbikes to the prime minister's bodyguard unit. Hun Sen waved the restrictions against developing the resort partially inside a protected park and sent Fu a letter, seen by the *Financial Times*, wishing him "complete success" in the project.

70. Nachemson, "Is Cambodia's Koh Kong Project for Chinese Tourists—or China's Military?"

71. Chheang, *Trends in Southeast Asia*, 13.

72. Kali Kotoski and Sor Chandara, "Developer Finds New Partners for Planned Resort in Preah Sihanouk," *Phnom Penh Post*, March 21, 2016, https://www.phnompenhpost.com/business/developer-finds-new-partners-planned-resort-preah-sihanouk.

Hundreds of farm families were kicked off their land to make way for the resort, according to Licadho, the human rights organization. Global Witness of the United Kingdom said in a 2016 report that Hun Sen headed up a "huge network of deal making and nepotism" that made it possible for his family members to snare stakes in leading companies and help the prime minister secure his "political fortress."[73]

Both mammoth tourism projects demonstrate that firms from China at least sometimes get special concessions that allow them to circumvent Cambodia's regulations, making it possible for them to operate in protected national parks or along the country's coastline.

The Cambodian government does not seem worried that it will have too many casinos any time soon as it increasingly starts to compete with Macau. In early 2019, Cambodia had some 150 licensed casinos in Phnom Penh, Sihanoukville, clustered around Poipet on the Thai border and along the eastern border with Vietnam. They generated the government estimated tax revenue of $58 million in 2018.[74] Cambodia, which prohibits locals from participating in gaming activities, hopes to benefit from the fact that neighboring Thailand bans casinos and Vietnam blocks local gamblers from using its casinos.

The lion's share of the gamblers in Cambodia are Chinese who are brought to the casinos with offers of free travel, hotel accommodation, and other perks. Hong Kong–listed Naga World Hotel and Entertainment Complex in Phnom Penh, Cambodia's leading casino, had turnover of $21.1 billion in 2017, an increase of 140 percent from a year earlier, and its revenue reached $625.3 million in 2017, up 39 percent from 2016.[75]

China has also provided capital for giant agriculture projects in Cambodia. Chinese companies have invested in about one-quarter of the 2.5 million acres of so-called economic land concessions set aside by Cambodia since the early 1990s for large-scale agriculture, according to a report prepared by the U.S. Department of Agriculture. Chinese firms have planted such crops as palm oil, fruit trees, acacia (often used for

---

73. Kynge, Haddou, and Peel, "FT Investigation: How China Bought Its Way into Cambodia."

74. Andrew O'Malley, "Cambodia Casinos Have Increased from 98 to 150 since 2017," *Vegas Slots Online*, January 3, 2019, https://www.vegasslotsonline.com/news/2019/01/03/cambodia-casinos-have-increased-from-98-to-150-since-2017/.

75. Ron Corben, "Cambodia Looks to Foreign Investors to Boost Casino Gaming Industry," *Voice of America*, March 13, 2018, https://www.voanews.com/a/cambodia-casinos-gaming-gambling/4296389.html.

medicinal purposes), cashews, rubber, sugarcane, peanuts, rice, corn, and soybeans.[76]

Five companies, all subsidiaries of Hengfa Group Sugar Industry Company Limited of Guangdong Province, pooled their concessions to plant sugarcane to supply a $360 million sugar mill opened in 2016 in Preah Vihear Province in the north to produce sugar for export. But members of the indigenous Huy minority that long populated the area complain that the Chinese companies cleared their ancestral lands and forests without consulting them, destroying their livelihoods and culture. The Huy say when they protested to local officials, they were charged with illegally settling on state land.[77]

A Chinese tropical crop research institute is partnering with a Cambodian company to do research on cassava and rubber tree seed reproduction and the mechanization of cassava cultivation.[78] The U.S. Department of Agriculture report concluded that China's goal with these investments is to "help reshape patterns of agricultural trade and increase China's influence in global markets."[79]

China constructed a special economic zone in Sihanoukville in 2009 jointly operated by the Jiangsu Taihu Cambodia International Economic Investment Company and the Cambodia International Economic Cooperation Investment Group Company. Today there are more than 100 factories engaged in light industry in the zone, 87 of which are owned by Chinese companies. (Others come from the United States, Japan, France, South Korea, Vietnam, and Thailand.) Chinese companies come in search of lower wages than they have to pay back home and to escape the import and export tariffs charged Chinese products in many developed markets. One of the biggest challenges facing companies in Cambodia is finding skilled workers.[80]

---

76. Elizabeth Gooch and Fred Gale, *China's Foreign Agriculture Investments* (Washington, DC: U.S. Department of Agriculture, 2018), 23, https://www.ers.usda.gov/webdocs/publications/88572/eib-192.pdf?v.

77. May Titthara, "Coalition Condemns Land Grabbing," *Khmer Times*, February 6, 2018, https://www.khmertimeskh.com/106701/coalition-condemns-land-grabbing/.

78. Gooch and Gale, *China's Foreign Agriculture Investments*, 23–25.

79. Ibid., 43.

80. "Sihanoukville Special Economic Zone Marks Milestone Thanks to Chinese Pioneers in Cambodia," *Yicai Global*, June 13, 2016, https://www.yicaiglobal.com/news/sihanoukville-special-economic-zone-marks-milestone-thanks-chinese-pioneers-cambodia.

There are now plans to expand this special economic zone to accommodate 300 factories, mostly from China, employing 700,000 workers to produce garments and consumers goods more cheaply than in China. One of the biggest attractions is that they will be able to benefit from Cambodia's tariff-free status within the ASEAN grouping and with the European Union.[81]

Sihanoukville is not the only Cambodian city experiencing a real estate construction boom. So is the capital, Phnom Penh. Until about 10 years ago, the city had no buildings more than six or so stories tall; today, dozens of office buildings and apartment blocks with 10 or more floors have been constructed by Chinese companies and workers. The Prince Central Plaza with over 1,000 condominium units stands a massive 37 stories high.[82]

These new buildings used architectural designs straight from China and often overshadow the pervasive Chinese shophouses, many of which date back to the late-nineteenth century and early-twentieth century French colonial villas. None of the new buildings show any influence of the "new Khmer" architecture of the 1960s as seen in the Chaktomuk Theater and the independence monument.

On 170-acre Koh Pich, or Diamond Island, an artificial island in the Bassac River, Chinese firms have constructed giant high-rise office buildings, condominiums, waterside restaurants, a new National Assembly building, and an international school, transforming the skyline of Phnom Penh's traditional low-rise architecture. Near the bridge that takes visitors to the island stands the Chinese-run NagaWorld casino complex. Many of the completed condos have been sold to Chinese owners who use them as investments rather than places to live. A visit in the evening, after the construction workers have gone home, finds most of the condos to be dark.

Phnom Penh was expected to have nearly 23,000 luxury apartments by the end of 2018, many of them constructed by Chinese investors such as Prince Real Estate Group. This will more than double the nearly 9,000 units at the beginning of that year, real estate consultants told Reuters.

81. Prasso, "Chinese Influx Stirs Resentment in Once-Sleepy Cambodian Resort."

82. Chris Horton, "Cambodia Finds New Target for Real Estate: Chinese Investors," *New York Times*, January 9, 2018, https://www.nytimes.com/2018/01/09/business/cambodia-real-estate.html.

The total is forecast to grow to 30,000 by 2020, likely creating an oversupply.[83]

Most of these units are waiting for Chinese occupants. "We Cambodians prefer to live in a house on the ground," jokes a Cambodian businessperson. "I might buy some units for investment and lease them to Chinese."

Bangkok political risk consultant George McCloud told *The New York Times* that Chinese business owners "with wealth in excess of a few million dollars" are looking for a safe haven to "squirrel cash outside of China's borders and the reach of unpredictable authorities." McCloud added: "Given my experience doing investigations in Cambodia, I am convinced that laundered money from [China] is a substantial portion of property investment in Phnom Penh."[84]

In June 2019, at least 24 workers were killed and some 24 injured when a seven-story Chinese building under construction in Sihanoukville collapsed. Officials said the builders did not have the necessary permits and had continued working despite several orders to stop, underlining the perils of unregulated construction. Three Chinese and one Cambodia were arrested at the site, police told journalists. The Chinese Embassy in Phnom Penh offered condolences to the victims' families and promised to help in the rescue efforts.[85]

Much of Cambodia's strong economic growth in recent years has been based on real estate, prompting concerns about what happens when the bubble bursts. "The coattails of China are great . . . but too much dependence on anyone is bad," Sophal Ear, the Cambodian-American political scientist, said in an interview with Voice of America. "When China sneezes, Cambodia will catch a cold."

Ear also has a warning about Cambodia pocketing too much Chinese debt, saying there needs to be transparency about the terms and amount of the loans Phnom Penh takes on. He cited the example of China building a $157 million stadium but asks what happens if the stadium is only worth

83. Brenda Goh and Prak Chan Thul, "In Cambodia's Capital, Chinese Buyers Pump Luxury Property Bubble," *Reuters*, May 24, 2018, https://www.reuters.com/article/us-china-cambodia-property/in-cambodias-capital-chinese-buyers-pump-luxury-property-bubble-idUSKCN1IP0MU.

84. Horton, "Cambodia Finds New Target for Real Estate: Chinese Investors."

85. Sun Narin and Hannah Beech, "Building Collapses in Cambodian City Kills at Least 24," *New York Times*, June 23, 2019, https://www.nytimes.com/2019/06/23/world/asia/cambodia-building-collapse.html.

$57 million. "Sure, the terms might be very low-interest . . . , but the value of the goods built is inflated." Eventually, Ear said, "you owe a country so much they own you."[86]

China has also invested in telecommunications and broadband in Cambodia. Shenzhen Keybridge Communications in 2014 acquired a 65 percent stake in Cambodian telecom firm EMAXX for about $15 million. Following the acquisition, EMAXX announced it would invest $148 million to expand the company's telecom network, according to RWR Advisory Group. The following year, China's EXIM Bank provided a $50 million loan to the government to finance the construction of a nationwide high-speed broadband network, RWR reports.

During a visit in 2018 by Premier Li, China signed 19 new agreements worth billions of dollars to develop Cambodia's infrastructure, agriculture, and health system. The projects included an agreement to develop the Sihanoukville special economic zone, build a new airport in Phnom Penh, and construct a 125-mile highway from Phnom Penh to Sihanoukville estimated to cost $2 billion.[87]

Cambodia's ruling elite is pleased that Chinese projects are quicker to get off the ground than those proposed by other donors, including Japan. They also appreciate that projects by Chinese investors have generated an estimated 1 million jobs.[88]

But behind China's achievements and impressive aid numbers lie serious political and social repercussions. At a popular level China faces considerable grumbling about its projects. China's megaprojects prompt charges about widespread corruption, environmental damage, human rights abuses, and the elimination of jobs. Another concern is that Chinese investors do minimal technology and knowledge transfer because many of their investments are in labor-intensive industries, such as garment manufacturing or resource extraction.

86. Sok Khemara, "'At Some Point, You Owe a Country So Much That They Own You,'" *Voice of America*, February 16, 2018, https://www.voacambodia.com/a/at-some-point-you-owe-a-country-so-much-that-they-own-you/4256402.html.

87. Laura Zhou and Sarah Zheng, "China Pledges More Investment in Cambodia, but Is Phnom Penh Selling Itself Short?," *South China Morning Post*, January 14, 2018, https://www.scmp.com/news/china/diplomacy-defence/article/2128118/china-pledges-more-investment-cambodia-phnom-penh; Darren Touch, "What Does Chinese Investment Mean for Cambodia?," *The Diplomat*, February 2, 2018, https://thediplomat.com/2018/02/what-does-chinese-investment-mean-for-cambodia/.

88. Chheang, *Trends in Southeast Asia*, 14–15.

The operating culture of Chinese companies also worries many Cambodians. "Many companies are coming without transparency," says Sothirak, the former politician who now heads the Cambodian Institute for Cooperation and Peace. "Often the quality of their work is not good, and we have to do repairs very soon" after a project is completed. "Our economy needs China so there's no problem if China makes money, but Cambodians should receive reliable products," Sothirak says.

In rural areas, farmers are angry about being displaced, often by force, and paid little for the land and livelihoods they have lost. There is frustration that many Chinese projects bring in many workers from China rather than hiring locals. Corruption in projects and kickbacks to senior government officials in exchange for access to pristine national parks and beaches irritates many locals.

In early 2016, land activist Tep Vanny was sentenced to over two years in prison for joining a demonstration protesting a forced eviction order from the Boeung Kak Lake area in Phnom Penh where Chinese companies were developing a real estate project on reclaimed land. Some 63 civil society organizations issued a joint statement criticizing Cambodia's security forces for using violence to quiet down the voices of former residents.[89]

"China's unquestioning approach to how its aid and investment money is distributed and used has exacerbated corruption, deteriorated good governance and human rights, and ruined Cambodia's resources and natural environment," writes Heng Pheakdey of the Enrich Institute. "Human rights activists have often accused Chinese textile factories of abusing workers' rights, while China's hydropower investments have destroyed protected areas, forest biodiversity, and wildlife habitat."[90]

To reduce public resentment among locals, Sothirak of the Cambodian Institute for Cooperation and Peace added, China and Cambodia will need to "work together to improve transparency, promote participatory and sustainable development by involving all relevant stakeholders, and minimize environmental degradation."[91]

---

89. Chheang, *Trends in Southeast Asia*.
90. Pheakdey, "Chinese Investment and Aid in Cambodia a Controversial Affair."
91. Sothirak Pou, Remarks at the Twenty-first Century Maritime Silk Road Conference, China Foreign Affairs University and Peace Boat, August 1–6, 2016, quoted in Chheang, *Trends in Southeast Asia*.

Chinese funding for projects is a mixture of investment, loans, and aid. Often it is difficult for an observer to figure out what form of Chinese funding is involved in a specific project. Little of this aid or investment is free or even cheap, however.

Cambodia's external debt to bilateral sources stood at $7.6 billion by the end of 2018, about a third of the country's 2017 gross domestic product estimated at $22.2 billion. Roughly $2.9 billion, or about 48 percent, is owed to China.[92] Some analysts are worried about the high proportion of Phnom Penh's debt owed to China. "If you have your hand in one man's pocket, you have to walk where he walks," Cambodian-American political scientist Ear says, quoting an African saying. The Washington-based Center for Global Development listed Cambodia among eight countries considered to be facing potential debt distress because of Chinese loans for infrastructure projects.[93]

Ear added to this in an article about Cambodia's garment industry: "Taking the geopolitical interests of China in Southeast Asia into account, Chinese investment does not come free; political and economic strings tie those who benefit to the influence of China."[94]

Although China is Cambodia's biggest trading partner, both the European Union and the United States are bigger export markets for Cambodia. In 2018, Cambodia exported $5.4 billion worth of goods to the European Union and $3.1 billion to the United States, seven times more than exports to China, which reached $1.4 billion.[95]

Cambodia is considering a Chinese proposal to begin using Chinese currency instead of U.S. dollars to calculate bilateral trade, another indicator about deepening ties between the two countries. Bilateral trade was

---

92. Cheng Sokhorng, "Government Plans to Borrow $1.4B for 2018 National Budget," *Phnom Penh Post*, October 30, 2017, https://www.phnompenhpost.com/business/government-plans-borrow-14b-2018-national-budget.

93. Prasso, "Chinese Influx Stirs Resentment in Once-Sleepy Cambodian Resort."

94. Ear, "Cambodia's Garment Industry: A Case Study in Governance," 100.

95. Philip Blenkinsop, "EU Begins Process to Hit Cambodia with Trade Sanctions," *Reuters*, February 11, 2019, https://www.reuters.com/article/us-cambodia-eu/eu-begins-process-to-hit-cambodia-with-trade-sanctions-idUSKCN1Q015D; Office of the United States Trade Representative, "Cambodia: U.S.-Cambodia Trade Facts," https://ustr.gov/countries-regions/southeast-asia-pacific/Cambodia (accessed October 24, 2019); International Monetary Fund, "Exports, FOB to Partner Countries; Imports, CIF from Partner Countries," *IMF Data*, 2014–2018, http://data.imf.org/regular.aspx?key=61013712.

$7.4 billion in 2018 with Chinese exports to Cambodia outpacing imports by roughly five to one.[96]

If the European Union and the United States imposed trade sanctions against Cambodia in response to Hun Sen's political crackdown, as some have urged, it would do little to affect China's investment in tourism, energy, and mining operations. But sanctions could harm manufacturing, especially garments, in which China has invested some $15 billion.[97] The garment industry employs some 700,000 people and mostly in Phnom Penh. But should Washington or Brussels impose sanctions, Hun Sen is confident that China will ride to his rescue.

KILLING THE MEKONG

Soon after passing the cascades of the Khone Falls, the largest waterfall in Southeast Asia in southern Laos, the Mekong crosses into Cambodia where it is soon met by three tributaries: the Sekong, Sesan, and Srepok Rivers. Here the Mekong broadens as it heads toward the capital of Phnom Penh, where it is joined by the Tonle Sap and Bassac Rivers before dividing into four channels that flow into Vietnam.

Fully half of Cambodia's population lives within sight of the mainstream of the Mekong and along or on houseboats in the Tonle Sap, fishing or farming the fertile floodplains created by the rivers.[98] During the annual monsoon rains (beginning around May), as the Mekong swells it sends astonishing volumes of water up the Tonle Sap River, expanding the Tonle Sap Lake to five times its size during the dry season. When the rains end, the Tonle Sap River reverses course (around December), draining the lake's waters back into the Mekong.

As Cambodia has sought to boost electricity output, China has emerged as the largest investor in hydropower dams in the country. The Chinese Embassy in Phnom Penh estimated in 2016 that power projects in Cambodia involving companies from China generated about four-fifths of the electricity produced in the country.[99]

---

96. International Monetary Fund, "Exports, FOB to Partner Countries; Imports, CIF from Partner Countries."
97. Hutt, "Cambodia Clampdown Threatens Chinese Interests."
98. Brian Eyler, *Last Days of the Mighty Mekong* (London: Zed Books, 2019), 220.
99. Chheang, *Trends in Southeast Asia*.

The biggest hydropower project is the $800 million Lower Sesan 2 Dam, a 400-megawatt scheme near the confluence of the Sesan and Srepok Rivers in the north. The four-mile wide dam, apparently Asia's longest, opened in late 2018 and is expected to boost Cambodia's electricity output by 20 percent to over 1,300 megawatts.

Lower Sesan 2, Cambodia's seventh hydropower dam, is projected to flood an area of nearly 74,000 acres of forest and land and force some 5,000 villagers to relocate.[100] About 78,000 people living above the dam are expected to lose access to migratory fish, a critical component of their livelihoods. The government says it has paid compensation in the form of land, houses, and a little over 12 acres to those displaced by the dam, while the joint venture company that constructed the dam reports that it has built roads and schools.[101]

The dam is a three-nation joint venture between China's Hydrolancang International Energy, which has a 51 percent stake, Cambodia's Royal Group (39 percent), and Vietnam's EVN International Joint Stock company (10 percent). The dam, constructed under a build-operate-transfer scheme, will be turned over to the government in 45 years.[102] Once in full operation, the dam will provide power to Phnom Penh and three northern provinces.

The dam will have a devastating impact on the environment. Fisheries, on which many people living along the river depend for protein and their livelihoods, will face a major hit because the dam will block the fish migration route and make it impossible for fish to move between the Sesan and Srepok Rivers and the Tonle Sap to breed, according to Ian Baird, a University of Wisconsin geographer who studies fisheries along the Mekong River.[103]

---

100. "Cambodia's PM Hun Sen Launches Lower Sesan 2 Dam, Blames Foreign 'Incitement' for Opposition," *Radio Free Asia*, December 17, 2018, https://www.rfa.org/english/news/cambodia/incitement-12172018160314.html.
101. Soth Koemsoeun, "Lower Sesan II Dam Opens," *Phnom Penh Post*, December 18, 2018, https://www.phnompenhpost.com/national/lower-sesan-ii-dam-opens; Laura Zhou, "Are Chinese-Funded Dams on the Mekong River Washing Away Cambodian Livelihoods?," *South China Morning Post*, March 31, 2018, https://www.scmp.com/news/china/diplomacy-defence/article/2139751/are-chinese-funded-dams-mekong-river-washing-away.
102. May Kunmakara, "Dam in Sesan Begins Operations," *Khmer Times*, December 18, 2018, https://www.khmertimeskh.com/560364/dam-in-sesan-begins-operations/.
103. Phak Seangly and Daphne Chen, "Sesan Dam Goes Online, While PM Dismisses Environmental Concerns," *Phnom Penh Post*, September 26, 2017, https://www.phnom

Of all the dams under construction or planned on tributaries of the Mekong, Lower Sesan 2 will have the largest impact on fish, cutting the population on the two rivers by some 9.3 percent, according to 2012 study published by the National Academy of Sciences. More than 1 million tons of freshwater fish are caught each year in the floodplains of Cambodia and Vietnam, making fish in this area vital for the area's food security.

The authors of the study found that not only fish production but also their biodiversity would be affected by the dam. They identified nearly 900 species of fish in the Mekong, making it the second most biodiverse river in the world after the Amazon. As many as 103 of these species migrate upstream from the dam and would be affected by Lower Sesan 2.[104]

The Lower Sesan 2 is one of "the worst placed dams" for protecting "environmental flows" in the Mekong River system, says Brian Eyler, a Mekong specialist at the Stimson Center in Washington. At the beginning of each dry season, the "earth's largest freshwater fish migration kicks off" as water begins to drain from the Tonle Sap and fish swim upstream to spawn in the shallow reaches of tributaries along the Mekong.

"After spawning, intense rains during Mekong monsoon season send fish, eggs, and an incredible mass of sediment and organic nutrients back downstream and into the Tonle Sap River, where this mix comes together to create an explosion in the fish population," Eyler says. But now the Lower Sesan 2 Dam will block the migration of fish. "Even if fish can make their way over the fish ladders . . . ," he says, "they will not likely find their way upstream to spawn since they will dump out into a still or slow-moving reservoir" created by the dam.

Another dam, the Sambor, planned on the Mekong about 87 miles south of Lower Sesan 2, is projected to provide 2,600 megawatts of electricity. Designed by China Southern Power Grid Co., the Sambor would be the largest hydropower dam constructed on the Lower Mekong at more than 11 miles wide and with a reservoir over 50 miles long.[105]

---

penhpost.com/national/sesan-dam-goes-online-while-pm-dismisses-environmental-concerns.

104. Guy Ziv, Eric Baran, So Nam, Ignacio Rodriguez-Iturbe, and Simon Levin, "Trading-Off Fish Biodiversity, Food Security, and Hydropower in the Mekong River Basin," *Proceedings of the National Academy of Sciences of the United States of America* 109, no. 15 (April 2012), https://www.pnas.org/content/109/15/5609.

105. Natural Heritage Institute, *Sambor Hydropower Dam Alternatives Assessment: Final Report* (San Francisco: Natural Heritage Institute, 2017), https://n-h-i.org/programs/restoring

In a 2017 report, the National Heritage Institute, a U.S. organization dedicated to preserving river basins and commissioned by the Cambodia government to study the Sambor, concluded that the dam "would create a barrier that would be devastating for the migratory fish stocks that move from the Tonle Sap Great Lake to the spawning grounds upstream." The dam would "disrupt the reproductive cycle because the eggs, larvae, and [fry] would not be able to drift back downstream." Over 80 long-range migratory fish species would become "endangered" by the dam and would place the remaining roughly 80 Irrawaddy River dolphins "at high risk of extinction."

The report added that the dam would "capture all of the bedload and 60 percent of the suspended sediments" needed to lay the food web that is vital to sustaining the productivity of fish in the Tonle Sap and the Mekong River. This sediment also maintains and replenishes Vietnam's Mekong Delta and prevents this fertile rice-producing area from being devastated by saltwater incursion from rising sea levels in the South China Sea.

The dam "would literally kill the Mekong River and devastate Cambodia's economy and food security," the report's authors concluded.[106] Neither the Cambodian government nor its Chinese partners have commented publicly on the report. Nor has the government of Vietnam, which could face a devastating impact from the dam.

Eyler, in his 2019 book *Last Days of the Mighty Mekong*, says Cambodia and its neighbors have an alternative that would protect the river but still allow them to produce the electricity they need: "If the region shifts away from damming the river past the point of no return and generates electricity from other sources like solar and wind, perhaps the Tonle Sap, the beating heart of the Mekong, will continue to thrive."[107]

OVERSEAS CHINESE FACILITATE CHINA'S INVESTMENT

Overseas Chinese have played an important role in attracting investment from China to Cambodia, which stands in sharp contrast to their counterparts in most other Southeast Asian countries. Many overseas Chinese

-natural-functions-in-developed-river-basins/mekong-river-basin/cambodia-sambor/.
106. Ibid.
107. Eyler, *Last Days of the Mighty Mekong*, 283.

arrived in Cambodia in the nineteenth and twentieth centuries, but a new wave arrived in the 1990s to engage in trade or work on Chinese projects. Some of the overseas Chinese have developed strong political ties with Cambodian leaders and have gained access to natural resources.[108]

Cambodians say more recent Chinese migrants are different from those who came earlier. "The new Chinese immigrants do not try to understand or learn [the] local culture and language," says Chheang of the think tank in Singapore. "They usually live and work within their own circle. . . . The presence of Chinese immigrants also creates a sentiment of economic discrimination."

Overseas Chinese migrants, those from the more distant past and those who came more recently, often play a critical role in economic ties between China and Cambodia. Their exact numbers are difficult to estimate, but some scholars believe the numbers that have come since the two countries normalized ties in the late 1990s at between 50,000 and 100,000. Others think the numbers are much higher.

The first major influx of overseas Chinese took place before and during French colonial rule (1863–1953), when traders and workers played a critical role in the country's economy.[109] The Chinese population rose from 170,000 in 1905 to 300,000 when World War II broke out. Most of them were involved in small commercial activities.[110] Many of these arrivals intermarried with the Cambodian population but kept their language (mainly the Teochew dialect) and, to some extent, their separate identity.

This flow of Chinese was interrupted in 1970 by Lon Nol's coup against Sihanouk and did not resume until Vietnamese troops withdrew in 1989, after which the ethnic Chinese recouped their key economic role as importers, wholesalers, and retailers.[111] In 1990, a senior Cambodian official told a group looking to organize a new Cambodia-Chinese organization that "you should unite and liaise with your relatives and friends overseas, attract foreign investment and become a bridge to developing the economy." This deal of "encouraging Chinese Cambodians to pursue wealth in return for support of the ruling party" has been Phnom Penh's policy ever since.[112]

108. Nyiri, "Investors, Managers, Brokers, and Culture Workers," 27–39.
109. Ibid., 27.
110. Chandler, *A History of Cambodia*, 161.
111. Nyiri, "Investors, Managers, Brokers, and Culture Workers," 27.
112. Quoted in Nyiri, "Investors, Managers, Brokers, and Culture Workers," 28.

Increasingly products from China began to dominate the goods for sale in Cambodia's markets and the demand for low-cost goods from China propelled a new wave of migrants from China. These businesspersons, who played an important role in real estate and were familiar with government procedures and patronage networks, became critical conduits in matching investors from China with business opportunities in Cambodia.[113]

Dutch historian and anthropologist Pal Nyiri describes the more recent arrivals from China "as providers of flows of capital, information, and culture from mainland China," adding they also serve as "brokers between these flows and the sizeable Chinese-Cambodian population," which arrived in earlier waves.[114] He says the new migrants act as intermediaries between Chinese capital and the Cambodian government and between Chinese managers and Cambodian workers.

Many of the richest Chinese-Cambodian businesspeople have received the title of "oknha," or lord, granted by the king. This title requires that a recipient provides a gift of at least $200,000 to the government and in exchange the oknha gets tax privileges and other benefits. The elite in this group often appear to receive special links to Hun Sen and other senior leaders. Chinese investors who are looking to acquire land look to the oknha for help when the majority stake in the project is held by a Cambodian company. The oknha also provide contacts with government officials.[115]

Oknha Lau Meng Khin, for example, holds stakes in a timber concession thanks to his ties with a Chinese agricultural company from the city of Wuzhishan on Hainan Island, as well as to the Sihanoukville special economic zone and the controversial Boeung Kak Lake development project in Phnom Penh. These oknha also play a key role as brokers between Chinese companies and banks and Cambodian ministries on infrastructure projects, including as agents for the loans that finance these projects.[116]

Some of these prominent Chinese businesspeople such as Oknha Keth travel using Cambodian official passports. Often the companies belonging to an oknha invest little or almost nothing in the projects. Instead they

113. Nyiri, "Investors, Managers, Brokers, and Culture Workers," 28.
114. Ibid., 26.
115. Ibid., 30.
116. Ibid.

get sizable shares and profits by serving as brokers and intermediaries in finding financing for projects. To be sure, they can also fail and lose favor operating as brokers "straddling the worlds of state power and private capital," Nyiri points out.[117]

The Association of Chinese in Cambodia was established at the encouragement of senior Cambodian officials in 1990. Five years later, a visiting Chinese Communist Party Politburo member told ethnic Chinese that "you should enter local society and make an effort to develop the economy. Cambodia is your second home country."[118] Only 15 years earlier, China had been aiding the Khmer Rouge, who were actively persecuting Chinese Cambodians.

The Association of Chinese in Cambodia maintains close ties with the Chinese Embassy in Phnom Penh and publishes a regular newspaper, the *Jian Hua Daily*. The association celebrates the ethnic Chinese as the "conduits of economic and political ties between two friendly nations, to both of which they owe a certain allegiance," Nyiri writes. This differs from the role of similar associations in neighboring countries that focus on "celebrating ancestral origins or demanding rights in an officially multicultural society."[119] The *Jian Hua Daily* regularly publishes information for new migrants and new investors from China.

Many new migrants from China see themselves as being in Cambodia temporarily, working on a specific investment or project, and they do not bring their children to be raised in Cambodia.[120]

Some of the Chinese who land in Cambodia and other Southeast Asian countries come to participate in telephone fraud schemes in which they pretend to be mainland government or security officials demanding payment. An extortion network will rent an apartment in Cambodia and set up telephone equipment to identify the calls as coming from a Chinese phone number. The callers then call numbers in China and claim they work for the public security service or tax office, frightening the call recipient, who often complies with the fraudster's demands. Sometimes they gain access to bank accounts by telling the persons answering the calls that they are being used to launder money or by terrorists.

117. Ibid., 31.
118. Ibid., 32.
119. Ibid., 34.
120. Ibid., 39.

Beijing often works with the governments where the Chinese scammers are operating to facilitate their arrest. China insists that its citizens and those from Taiwan be extradited to China where they are put on trial and given sentences of up to 15 years in prison.[121]

Cambodia is estimated to have arrested and sent over 1,000 Chinese (and many from Taiwan) back to China for involvement in various defrauding schemes since 2012. About 100 telecom defrauders were arrested in March 2018.[122] Another 89 were deported to China the following month for using social media to contact women in China, tricking them into sending nude or erotic pictures and then extorting money by threatening to spread the images online.[123]

BEIJING RAMPS UP PUBLIC DIPLOMACY

China uses a broad range of public diplomacy tools—from scholarships for students to Confucius Institutes and people-to-people exchanges to official visits and tourism—to strength ties with Cambodia, foster positive exchanges between the two countries, and promote constructive images about China. Cambodia is in a category of countries (the others being Indonesia, Malaysia, and Thailand) that receive the second-highest volume of public diplomacy activities behind the highly developed democracies in Japan, South Korea, and Australia.

Some 51 percent of China's public diplomacy is focused on elite visits, with another 42 percent centered on financial diplomacy, according to a study by AidData, a research lab at the College of William and Mary in Virginia.[124]

---

121. Associated Press, "How Telecom Fraud Is Piling Even More strain on Taiwan-Beijing Ties," *South China Morning Post*, March 8, 2018, https://www.scmp.com/news/china/policies-politics/article/2136304/how-telecom-fraud-piling-even-more-strain-taiwan.
122. "Cambodia Arrests 100 Suspects over China Telecoms Fraud," *Reuters*, December 12, 2018, https://www.reuters.com/article/us-cambodia-china-idUSKCN1GO0Y7.
123. Associated Press, "Cambodia Deports 89 Suspects in Online Scam to China," *Seattle Times*, April 11, 2018, https://www.seattletimes.com/nation-world/cambodia-deports-89-suspects-in-online-scam-to-china/.
124. Samantha Custer, Brooke Russell, Matthew DiLorenzo, Mengfan Cheng, Siddhartha Ghose, Harsh Desai, Jacob Sims, and Jennifer Turner, *Ties That Bing: Quantifying China's Public Diplomacy and Its "Good Neighbor" Effect* (Williamsburg, VA: AidData at William and Mary, 2018), 2, https://docs.aiddata.org/ad4/pdfs/Ties_That_Bind--Full_Report.pdf.

Beijing and Phnom Penh formally became "sister" cities in May 2018 to boost cooperation.[125] Few details have been released about what these cities plan to do together, but often these agreements include commitments to boost trade, sponsor cultural festivals, and build capacity. China also facilitates a broad range of exchanges for national and local party and government officials, senior military officers, academics, students, and journalists.[126]

Chinese tourists play a key role in bolstering Cambodia's tourist industry, which is anchored around Angkor Wat and the country's other famous twelfth-century temples. Some 1.2 million Chinese tourists visited in 2017, an increase of 46 percent from the previous year and accounting for one-fifth of the total of 5.6 million.[127] This increase has been spawned in part by the emergence of budget airlines and the growing availability of visa-on-arrival agreements. Chinese tourists run the gamut from backpackers to high-end individual tourists.[128] The governments have agreed to boost the numbers of Chinese tourists to 2 million by 2020.[129]

As in neighboring countries, some locals are anxious that few of the benefits of Chinese tourists boost domestic business. "The growth of Chinese tourists doesn't mean it will bring [Cambodians] good business and increase profits, because most of Chinese visitors are concentrated in the hands of Chinese companies and business owners," said Ho Vandy, who heads the Cambodia National Tourism Alliance.[130] He is referring to the fact that many Chinese tourists arrive on Chinese chartered planes, are transported by Chinese-owned companies, stay in Chinese-owned hotels, and eat in Chinese-owned restaurants.

In Sihanoukville, where Chinese developers have built bustling new casinos such as New Macau or MGM and where Cambodians are banned from gambling, locals who used to run and work in restaurants, back-

---

125. Xiang Bo, "Cambodia's Phnom Penh, China's Beijing Become 'Sister Cities,'" *Xinhua*, May 21, 2018, https://www.xinhuanet.com/english/2018-05/21/c_137195145.htm.
126. Custer et al., *Ties That Bing*, 2–3.
127. Cheng Sokhorng and Brendan O'Byrne, "Spike in Chinese Visitors Drives Tourism Boom," *Phnom Penh Post*, January 25, 2018, https://www.phnompenhpost.com/business/spike-chinese-visitors-drives-tourism-boom.
128. Pal Nyiri and Danielle Tan, "Introduction: China's 'Rise' in Southeast Asia from Bottom-Up Perspective," in *Chinese Encounters in Southeast Asia: How People, Money, and Ideas from China Are Changing a Region*, ed. Pal Nyiri and Danielle Tan (Seattle: University of Washington Press, 2017), 19.
129. Touch, "What Does Chinese Investment Mean for Cambodia?"
130. Sokhorng and O'Byrne, "Spike in Chinese Visitors Drives Tourism Boom."

packer bars, and cheaper hotels complain that their business is about to die.[131] "We all used to go to Sihanoukville," says Ear, the Cambodian-American. "Now it's a wholly owned subsidiary of China."

Cambodian are particularly anxious about Chinese tourists overwhelming ancient Angkor Wat, the world's largest temple complex built by King Suryavarman II to honor the Hindu god Vishnu in the early twelfth century before it transformed into a Buddhist temple by the end of the century. The temple, which was lost to the jungle and reclaimed by French conservationists in the nineteenth century, has long been threatened by jungle growth, monsoon storms, war, and vandals.

Today Cambodians, who view the temple as a sacred space, are offended by the hordes of Chinese tourists wandering through the complex talking and laughing loudly. Architects are concerned that the onslaught of visitors climbing through the complex will cause irreparable damage to the soft giant sandstone bricks used to construct the temple.

Mandarin-language schools have become wildly popular in Phnom Penh and other Cambodian cities, equaling if not outstripping the numbers of English-language schools. Young Cambodians believe studying Chinese will bolster their chances of getting high-paying jobs. The rapid increase of Chinese-language schools is "sparking fears that Cambodia's own weaker national education system may be overwhelmed or neglected in the longer term," Chong says.[132]

Phnom Penh today sports one of the largest Mandarin-language elementary and junior high schools outside of China. The Tuan Hoa School, which first opened a century ago but was forced to close during the war in the early 1970s before reopening in 1992, receives support and guidance from the Association of Chinese in Cambodia. The association supervises the curriculum and its wealthy, connected members make donations to the school, which today has some 11,000 students. China also provides some assistance in the form of teaching materials and funds to cover the salaries of visiting teachers.[133]

---

131. Anna Fifield, "This Cambodia City Is Turning into a Chinese Enclave, and Not Everyone Is Happy," *Washington Post*, March 29, 2018, https://www.washingtonpost.com/world/asia_pacific/this-cambodian-city-is-turning-into-a-chinese-enclave-and-not-everyone-is-happy/2018/03/28/6c8963b0-2d8e-11e8-911f-ca7f68bff0fc_story.html?utm_term=.03fc02e117c4.

132. Chong, *The Politics behind Cambodia's Embrace of China*, 7.

133. Nyiri, "Investors, Managers, Brokers, and Culture Workers," 34.

"More and more local parents feel that learning Mandarin will help their kids find jobs," said headmaster Loeung Sokmenh. "Even parents with no Chinese background are sending their kids here, including government officials."[134] Cambodians who speak some Chinese find jobs in Chinese-owned garment factories and in construction firms as interpreters, clerks, drivers, and other jobs.[135]

"Managers from China believe that Chinese Cambodians are culturally primed to understand the expectations of management regarding labor discipline and behavior," noted Nyiri. "They are therefore expected to function as cultural brokers of sorts, ensuring that Khmer workers comply with management instructions and do not make trouble."[136]

As part of its public diplomacy efforts, China in 2009 set up a branch of its global Confucius Institute network in Cambodia offering Chinese-language classes. Today the institute has about 80 teachers, three-quarters of whom are volunteers, in Cambodia sent by Hanban, the language promotion wing of the Chinese government. The institute has 27 "teaching classrooms" in the country, teaching in high schools, government ministries, and private companies. In addition to the Ministry of Defense, the Commerce Ministry and the Phnom Penh police department are in the process of setting up Chinese-language classrooms.[137]

China is also providing hundreds if not thousands of scholarships to Cambodian students, particularly those who do well in Mandarin-language schools, to study in China. By early 2018, more than 1,000 Cambodians had graduated with bachelor's and graduate degrees in China. Many of them now hold key positions in government ministries and private companies. Prak Phannara, who heads up an alumni association of Chinese graduates and today serves as a senior official in the Council of Ministers office, says that Cambodians who have studied in China have "acted as a bridge connecting Cambodia and China."[138]

Tes Rukhaphal, who earned a master's degree at Tsinghua University, today works at the Labor Ministry's Committee for the Settlement of

134. Chheang, *Trends in Southeast Asia*, 3.
135. Nyiri, "Investors, Managers, Brokers, and Culture Workers," 29.
136. Ibid.
137. Reddick and Co., "In Cambodia's Chinese-Language Schools, a Hard Push for Soft Power."
138. Mao Pengfei and Nguon Sovan, "Feature: Chinese-Educated Cambodians Play Vital Roles in Helping Develop Nation, Boosting Sino-Cambodian Ties," *Xinhua*, April 28, 2018, https://www.xinhuanet.com/english/2018-04/28/c_137143688.htm.

Strikes and Demonstrations. With Chinese investors owning the lion's share of garment factories in Cambodia, Rukhaphal sees one of his main roles being to "promote labor relations" between Cambodian workers and Chinese employers.[139]

Despite China handing out many scholarships a year to Cambodians, many students would rather study in Western or other Northeast Asian countries. "Cambodian students prefer to study in Australia, the United States, Japan, and Korea," says Sothirak. "They prefer not to go to China."

Five Chinese-language newspapers operate in Cambodia. The oldest paper, *Commercial News*, is owned by an oknha; the *Jian Hua Daily* is owned by the Association of Chinese in Cambodia, the *Sin Chiew Jit Poh* is Malaysian owned, and the *Phnom Penh Evening News* is published by the Cambodian-Chinese Chamber of Commerce. The *Khmer Daily* is owned by a former Chinese official who invested in Cambodian mines and became an adviser to a senior government official.

Some of the editors and journalists of these papers are recruited from China on short-term stints. Visiting Chinese journalists offer training for Cambodian journalists. The papers publish articles about Chinese investment and aid projects in Cambodia and pick up news from mainland Chinese news agencies.

The *Jian Hua Daily*, which is close to the Hun Sen government, has an editorial policy that aims to "strengthen positive propaganda, dampen the effect of negative news." An editor told Nyiri that the paper would refrain from publishing articles "against China's interests."[140]

Shortly after many media outlets were closed in 2017, Cambodia's Interior Ministry announced that it launched its own television station called NICE TV. China's Fujian Zhongya Cultural Media company had said two years earlier that it would back this new station, which the ministry said would cost $30 million to set up. The station said it would cover security issues, police operations, government policies, and legal issues.[141]

Unlike the more rudimentary newsrooms of local television stations and news rooms, NICE has a state-of-the-art building inside the ministry's

139. Pengfei and Sovan, "Feature: Chinese-Educated Cambodians Play Vital Roles in Helping Develop Nation."

140. Nyiri, "Investors, Managers, Brokers, and Culture Workers," 36.

141. Mech Dara and Ananth Baliga, "Interior Ministry Launches Its Own China-Backed TV Station," *Phnom Penh Post*, September 28, 2017, https://www.phnompenhpost.com/national/interior-ministry-launches-its-own-china-backed-tv-station.

compound and a restaurant on the fifth floor with a 360-degree view of Phnom Penh. The station's news fare includes innocuous stories about the annual water festival and citizen complaints about floods and traffic. The reason the station avoids more sensitive political stories has more to do with viewer interests rather than government directive, Jason Liu, NICE TV's chief operations officer, told the Voice of America. "The role of TV is to make people's living better, it is not to make conflict," he said.[142]

No country in Southeast Asia is more beholden to China than Cambodia. Phnom Penh has long irritated other ASEAN members by blocking statements that criticize China's actions in the South China Sea, where four of ASEAN members have overlapping claims with China. If Cambodia moves ahead with its reported plans to allow the Chinese navy to use its naval facilities in Ream on the Gulf of Thailand, Phnom Penh will attract the concern of neighbors who will be anxious that China is extending its strategic influence much deeper into their neighborhood.

Domestically, many Cambodians express concern about China's overwhelming influence in places like Sihanoukville, which has morphed into little more than a giant hodgepodge of Chinese casinos. Recent polling suggests that fully half of Cambodian elites see Beijing's goal as turning Southeast Asia into China's "sphere of influence" and only 12 percent view Beijing as a "benevolent power."

As Cambodia begins to prepare for a transition from Hun Sen, who has ruled the country with an iron fist for over three decades, China might want to consider deepening its ties to a broader swath of stakeholders. Hun Sen is grooming his son Hun Manet to take over, but as a military officer who has studied in the United States and the United Kingdom, Hun Manet may feel he needs to develop closer ties with the Americans, Europeans, and Japanese to overcome domestic anxiety about China having become overbearing.

---

142. David Boyle and Sun Narin, "Cambodia's Nice New TV Channel from China," *VOA News*, April 19, 2018, https://www.voanews.com/a/cambodia-nice-new-tv-channel-from-china/4354124.html.

4. LAOS: FRONTLINE STATE ON CHINA'S BELT AND ROAD

> President Xi Jinping looks far ahead and aims high
> We advance side by side on the silk road
> And make achievements hand in hand
> You and me jointly build the Belt and Road
> Facing problems big and small together
> We keep close communications to better understand each other
> As the Belt and Road enhances connectivity across nations. . . .[1]
>
> —*Lyrics from a Lao rock video produced by a Chinese television network*

Billows of red dust hang in the air like a dense fog as yellow Chinese excavators claw dirt from a hill into giant dump trucks along the road just south of Boten on the Laos border with China. Dozens of lumbering trucks create a traffic jam on the narrow road as they haul soil from a mound on one side of the road to fill in the valley on the opposite side to make way for an expanded highway and a new high-speed rail link with China.

Just up the road, hundreds of Chinese workers are erecting cement buildings and carving the Boten Special Economic Zone (SEZ) out of the hills where local villagers used to farm and raise animals. The 6.3-square-mile SEZ in the remote northern Lao province of Luang Nam Tha is slated to feature an area for international tourists complete with a protected

1. "Lao Rock Song Explains the ABC of Belt and Road Initiative," YouTube video, 2:12, May 3, 2017, https://www.youtube.com/watch?v=UoLbGxo1EIo. This music video by a journalist turned songwriter depicts scenes from Laos of people dancing on the streets, Buddhist monks collecting alms, children playing basketball, people shopping for Chinese Huawei smartphones. The video was produced by China's CGTN television network, which is funded by the Chinese government.

forest area, elephant rides, water sports, golf courses, high-rise condominiums, and exhibitions of Lao and Chinese history. Other parts of the SEZ will have commercial and financial facilities, industrial areas with warehouses, and a section for state-of-the-art medical treatment.

The SEZ now under construction is the second iteration of Chinese investment in Boten. Before 2011, it had been converted into a wild boomtown thriving on casinos (illegal in China), brothels and karaoke bars, and the spending of thousands of Chinese visitors each month. When reports surfaced that the casino operators were detaining people who could not pay off their gambling debts, the Chinese government ordered the casinos shut down and cut the electricity supply to the town. Boten all but collapsed.[2]

The massive new project is being spearheaded by Yunnan Haicheng Industry Group Company and Hong Kong Fuk Hing Travel Entertainment Group, which expect construction of the SEZ to be completed by 2040. The two firms and their dozens of Chinese state-owned enterprise partners have a 50-year lease that is eligible for two 20-year extensions.

A Chinese company representative who introduces the project to visitors on a giant model says, "The goal is to boost the Lao economy, provide jobs and opportunities for local people, and help Laos graduate from its least developed economic status by 2020."

The developers have outsized plans for the SEZ. So far, they claim they have spent a hefty $4.5 billion on clearing land and building infrastructure. They recently told the *Vientiane Times*, a Lao government daily, that they would invest a whopping $1 trillion in the project—no doubt a highly exaggerated amount nearly 60 times the country's gross domestic product (GDP) of just under $17 billion in 2017.[3]

"I was concerned this [SEZ] is not helping Laos, and is not going to help Laos," says Keith Barney, a senior lecturer at the Australian National University who does research in Laos and recently visited Boten. He notes the flood of Chinese workers and entrepreneurs into the area and says he found only one Lao noodle seller left in the town.

---

2. Sebastian Strangio, "The Rise, Fall and Possible Renewal of a Town in Laos on China's Border," *New York Times*, July 6, 2016, https://www.nytimes.com/2016/07/07/world/asia/china-laos-boten-gambling.html.

3. Souksamai Boulom, "US$1 Trillion to Be invested in Luang Namtha SEZ," *Asia News Network*, December 5, 2018, http://annx.asianews.network/content/us1-trillion-be-invested-luang-namtha-sez-87276.

Several dozen families formerly farming in Boten were relocated about 15 miles south along the dusty road leading to the town in 2005, when the casino project was launched. Only a few have recovered. A woman in her 30s said her family had been given a small plot of land, but she was much better off in her old village where she had fields to grow rice, raise animals, and produce salt to feed her family.

"I now sell some vegetables in the market and have to buy most of our food," she says. The few people who are well off are those who got loans from the bank to buy vehicles they use along the road to transport people and goods. "The SEZ only hires Lao who speak Chinese," the market vegetable seller says. "Less than 100 are working there." With more than a tinge of frustration in her voice, she adds, "The government is supposed to take care of its own people, but now it only takes care of foreign investors."

What makes small landlocked Laos with a population of just under 7 million so alluring to its giant northern neighbor? China is attracted by its rich natural resources, abundant fertile land for agriculture, immense hydropower opportunities, and the fact that it can serve as a bridge between Yunnan Province and the much more developed economy in Thailand. Historically China has seen Laos as serving as buffer against potential enemies in its more exposed southwestern border.[4]

Laos carries little of the historical baggage and resentment toward China of, say, Vietnam or Myanmar. Lao officials look to China to help jump-start the country's economic growth. China has become the country's largest source of foreign investment and official development aid and has played a major part in the country's significant economic growth in recent years. Chinese firms are key investors in building hydropower dams—Laos's largest source of export income—transportation networks, shopping malls and hotels, and operating mines and plantations.

Much of what China does in Laos in building dams and infrastructure is not aid or investment by companies but arrives in the form of loans that threaten to hobble the economy for years. The country's debt has risen to roughly two-thirds the size of its economy and much of it is owed to China, prompting concern from international financial institutions. Economists ask whether it makes long-term sense for Laos to continue

4. Ian Storey, *Southeast Asia and the Rise of China: The Search for Security* (New York: Routledge, 2011), 165.

Map 5. Laos

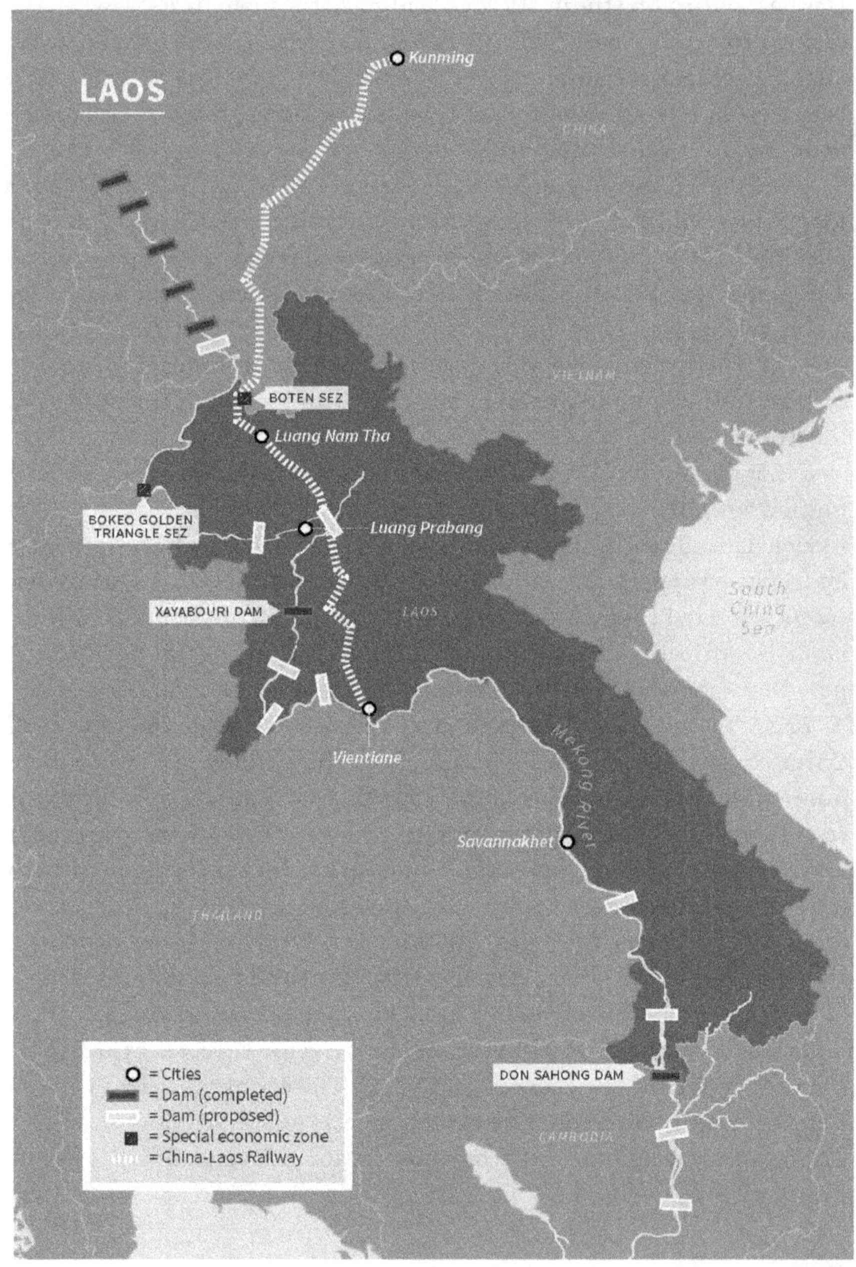

constructing costly hydropower dams on the Mekong River when Thailand, the main export target, is looking increasingly to renewable energy sources.

China's loans to Laos for infrastructure projects have political objectives that go well beyond financial justification. The massive loans and projects build political interdependence that challenges the sensitivities of many Lao, including some officials. "China's economic power could give Beijing a lot of influence in Laos," says Ian Baird, a geographer at the University of Wisconsin-Madison, who does research in Laos.

From time to time, China's economic role sparks friction in Laos. The improper use of pesticides on Chinese-run plantations has caused people to get sick, prompting bans on the use of chemicals. Villagers displaced by Chinese SEZs, hydropower dams, and the high-speed rail project complain about inadequate resettlement packages that often make it hard for them to make a living. But tight political control ensures that any popular resentment will be contained. Three violent attacks against Chinese nationals in Laos a few years ago demonstrated that some local discontent against China's dominant economic role and business practices erupts from time to time.

China's growing heft in the Laos economy has prompted some to speculate that Vientiane is pivoting toward Beijing and away from Vietnam. But most observers in Laos are convinced that its leaders are working overtime to demonstrate that they want to maintain close ties to both of their communist neighbors. "On foreign policy decisions, Vietnam is their closest political brother while China is their economic brother," says a diplomat in Vientiane. "Laos is not yet a vassal state of China."

In early 2019 Singapore's ISEAS-Yusof Ishak Institute surveyed attitudes toward China, the United States, and other issues among Southeast Asian academics, the business community, and representatives of civil society and media. Lao respondents had some of the most positive attitudes toward China among the 10 countries surveyed. Only 24 percent of Lao said China "will become a revisionist power with an intent to turn Southeast Asia into its sphere of influence," compared to fully 50 percent in Cambodia, whose leadership is probably closer to China than any of its regional counterparts. Almost 14 percent of Lao said China will be "a benign and benevolent power" as compared to a Southeast Asia average of 8.9 percent.

Asked about China's signature Belt and Road Initiative (BRI), nearly 76 percent of Lao said the initiative would "benefit regional economic development" compared to just under 42 percent in Cambodia, where many have a closer view of sometimes-excessive Chinese largess. Just over 46 percent of Lao said their government should be "cautious" in negotiating BRI projects in light of the fact that Sri Lanka had to turn over a key port when it could not repay its debt to China, compared to almost 71 percent in Cambodia.

In commenting on the United States, nearly 52 percent of Lao thought American engagement with Southeast Asia had "decreased" or "decreased substantially" under President Donald Trump. Slightly over 26 percent said they "some confidence" or "full confidence" in the United States as a "strategic partner."[5]

HIGH-SPEED TRAIN TO WHERE?

Just south of Boten, a small army of Chinese workers are painstakingly drilling and blasting a tunnel through the first mountain in Laos along the nearly 260-mile high-speed rail that Chinese companies are building to connect Kunming in southern China to Bangkok, Thailand, and on to Singapore. (By normal international standards, the project would be considered a medium-speed rail project.) Chinese engineers said in late 2018 that tunneling through this nearly four-mile-wide mountain will take them more than two years. Some days their progress through the rock is less than 10 feet.

The nearly $5.9 billion project, a centerpiece of China's BRI and costing more than one-third of Laos's annual GDP, includes some 75 tunnels, 167 bridges, and thousands of concrete pillars that will elevate the rail across valleys. Around 40 percent of the work had been completed by the end of 2018. Lao officials tout the project as an effort to turn the landlocked country into a "land-linked" nation.

Like with many Chinese projects, the terms for high-speed train in Laos are not transparent. According to some economists in Vientiane, a joint venture Chinese-Lao rail company will obtain a loan from the

5. Tang Siew Mun, Moe Thuzar, Hoang Thi Ha, Termsak Chalermpalanupap, Pham Thi Phuong Thao, and Anuthida Saelaow Qian, *The State of Southeast Asia: 2019 Survey Report* (Singapore: ISEAS-Yusof Ishak Institute, 2019), https://www.iseas.edu.sg/images/pdf/TheStateofSEASurveyReport_2019.pdf.

Export-Import (EXIM) Bank of China for about $4.1 billion, or 70 percent of the cost. Of the remaining $1.8 billion, China will provide equity of about $1.3 billion.

Laos will kick in the balance of $531 million, of which $480 million will come in the form of a China EXIM Bank loan with interest of 2.3 percent to be repaid over 25 years with a five-year grace period. In addition, the Lao government will provide an additional $50 million a year for five years for a total of $250 million. What is not clear is how much of the compensation costs for resettling people displaced by the project Laos is paying for and whether the government can deduct this cost from the $250 million obligation.

International economists have raised concerns in recent years that Laos's heavy borrowing could snare the country in a "debt trap." Although the Lao economy has grown at about 7 percent in recent years, the country's ratio of public and public guaranteed debt to GDP topped 60 percent in 2017 and was projected to rise to nearly 66 percent in 2019, according to the International Monetary Fund.[6]

The fund in 2017 raised its debt distress level for Laos from "moderate" to "high" after the country's debt jumped above the 40 percent threshold set by the multilateral financial institution.[7] Much of this debt is owed to China as Laos has stepped up lending for building the high-speed rail and hydropower dams. Christine Lagarde, the fund's then managing director, warned that increases in debt could limit other spending as the cost of debt-servicing rises and creates balance of payments challenges.[8]

In addition to these development loans, Laos has received another estimated $11 billion in a category classified as "other official flows." In Asia, Laos is second only to Pakistan, which received some $16.3 billion in other official flows, according to a study by the China Power Project of the Center for Strategic and International Studies. More than three-quarters

6. International Monetary Fund, "IMF Executive Board Completes the 2017 Article IV Consultation with Lao People's Democratic Republic," news release, March 12, 2018, https://www.imf.org/en/News/Articles/2018/03/12/pr1883-lao-peoples-democratic-republic-imf-executive-board-completes-the-2017-article-iv.

7. International Monetary Fund and International Development Association, "Lao People's Democratic Republic: Staff Report for the 2016 Article IV Consultation—Debt Sustainability Analysis," January 6, 2017, https://www.imf.org/external/pubs/ft/dsa/pdf/2017/dsacr1753.pdf.

8. Charles Clover, "IMF's Lagarde Warns China on Belt and Road Debt," *Financial Times*, April 12, 2018, https://www.ft.com/content/8e6d98e2-3ded-11e8-b7e0-52972418fec4.

of China's financing between 2000 and 2014 did not meet the rigorous official development assistance standards set by the Organization for Economic Cooperation and Development (OECD).[9]

Sri Lanka is a poster child of what can happen to a country when it falls behind in debt payments to China. The South Asian country had to turn over its Hambantota port and 15,000 acres of land around it to China for 99 years when Sri Lanka struggled to make loan payments.[10] New governments elected in Malaysia, Pakistan, and the Maldives in 2018 have been concerned about some of the infrastructure deals their predecessors signed with China and have sought to review their loan and project terms.

In 2007, a senior Lao official sought a $100 million loan from the China Development Bank to build a sports stadium and the infrastructure that Laos required to host the Southeast Asian Games in 2009. The bank apparently awarded the loan on the condition that the Chinese contractor, Suzhou Industrial Park Overseas Investment, would be given a 50-year lease to develop a 3,950-acre area in the northeastern part of Vientiane into a "modern town" with business centers, hotels, factories, and facilities for tourists.

The deal was negotiated in almost total secrecy resulting in a spate of rumors, including that Laos had agreed to allow 50,000 Chinese families to move into the area around the gold-leaf-covered That Luang stupa, the most venerated Buddhist monument in Laos. The project also raised environmental hackles because the land offered was part of the That Luang Marsh, one of the largest remaining wetlands in Vientiane municipality.

Members of the National Assembly, the country's parliament, reportedly opposed the plan, prompting the government eventually to launch a public relations campaign that included reducing the development area to just under 500 acres. The balance of the land committed to the Chinese developer was to be located near the stadium complex away from the city center. But in the end, the amount of land provided to the developer at the That Luang Marsh was increased to almost 1,500 acres.[11]

---

9. China Power Project, "Where Is China Targeting Its Development Finance?," Center for Strategic and International Studies, December 8, 2017, https://chinapower.csis.org/china-development-finance/.

10. Maria Abi-Habib, "How China Got Sri Lanka to Cough Up a Port," *New York Times*, June 25, 2018, https://www.nytimes.com/2018/06/25/world/asia/china-sri-lanka-port.html.

11. Miles Kenney-Lazar, *Land Concessions, Land Tenure, and Livelihood Change: Plantation Development in Attapeu Province, Southern Laos* (Vientiane: Faculty of Forestry, National University

The official who negotiated the deal with the Chinese was Somsavat Lengsavad, an ethnic Chinese who ranked tenth in the ruling Lao People's Revolutionary Party at the time. He also served as standing deputy prime minister and chair of the Lao Southeast Asian Games organizing committee. Somsavat was dropped from the politburo during a party congress in 2016. Perhaps in response to some of the problems created by the Southeast Asian Games loan, a plenum meeting of the party central committee in 2018 discussed the issue of how to limit the number of officials allowed to sign foreign loans.

Economists have raised questions about how Laos will begin repaying the loan for the high-speed rail because even an optimistic Chinese feasibility study calculated that the project would lose money for the first 11 years.[12] And that estimate was based on the assumption that Thailand would work with China to build a high-speed rail from Bangkok to Nong Khai, across the Mekong River from Vientiane. Now that link appears far from certain any time soon. Thailand has decided not to accept Chinese financing for a high-speed rail and has launched several projects to upgrade the existing rail lines, including to the Lao border, to boost economic efficiency.

Thai transport experts estimate that it will take at least 10 years before Thailand will build a high-speed rail link to the Lao border. This means that the Laos high-speed rail from Kunming would run only as far as Vientiane, the capital of one of Southeast Asia's least populated and least developed countries. With no easy connection to Thailand, the Laos railroad would likely continue to lose money for years and overstretch the funds available from the Lao government's already strained coffers. In addition, the access of the southwestern provinces of China to the more populated countries of Southeast Asia would also be delayed.

Interestingly, Laos has demonstrated that even small underdeveloped countries can negotiate with China on the terms and scope of a project along China's BRI. Beijing and Vientiane wrangled for five years over the conditions of the project and China relented on several of its initial demands, even though Laos held a relatively weak hand.

---

of Laos, 2010), http://www.laolandissues.org/wp-content/uploads/2012/01/Kenney-Lazar-Land-Concessions-Attapeu.pdf.

12. Jane Perlez and Yufan Huang, "Behind China's $1 Trillion Plan to Shake Up the Economic Order," *New York Times*, May 13, 2017, https://www.nytimes.com/2017/05/13/business/china-railway-one-belt-one-road-1-trillion-plan.html?_r=0.

One issue was the size of Laos's stake in the project. Initially it appeared that Vientiane had agreed to take a loan from China's EXIM Bank for $7.2 billion for the project, roughly three-quarters of Laos's GDP at the time. The government talked about using its potash and bauxite deposits as collateral for the loan. The Asia Development Bank declared the project "unaffordable" and the World Bank called on Laos to do an analysis of debt sustainability and the cost-benefits of the project. Deputies to the country's often rubber-stamped parliament-raised concerns about the implications for Lao sovereignty.[13] In the end, China agreed to take a much larger stake in the project and Laos took a loan of less than $500 million.

Another matter was the interest rate. "China initially offered Laos 3 percent interest, but when they heard that Thailand had been offered 2 percent, the Lao insisted on renegotiating the terms," says a diplomat in Vientiane.

The two sides also haggled over how much land China would get along each side of the railroad where Chinese companies, rather than their Lao counterparts, could set up moneymaking retail shops, restaurants, and guesthouses. Beijing opened its bid by insisting on 55 yards on each side but, in the end, it agreed to just over 16 yards, according to diplomats in Vientiane. Beijing did, however, get more land around train stations, where real money can be made. At the station in Oudomsay south of Boten, China got a 1.2-square-mile tract to develop services for travelers.

So why is the high-speed rail so important for Beijing? "China will benefit the most," argues an Asian diplomat in Vientiane. "Its goal is to get to the sea," he says about Beijing's objective of gaining access to a seaport for goods from southwestern China. If Thailand delays its section of the high-speed rail, the most important benefits for China will be postponed.

What is in it for Vientiane? "Because Laos is landlocked it pays high logistical costs," says a Lao economist who asked not to be identified. "Trade is not diversified" and Laos depends on Thailand to transport the lion's share of goods moving in and out of Laos. "We hope with the high-speed train we can diversify our trade to Europe." The economist lists competitive advantages of Lao agribusiness, including coffee, vegetables,

13. Simon Creak, "Laos in 2013: International Controversies, Economic Concerns, and the Post-Socialist Rhetoric of Rule," *Southeast Asian Affairs* (2014): 161–162.

and tea. Teak furniture built from teak plantations in northern Laos might also benefit from rail links to Europe.

What is not clear is whether exporting these products would cover the high-cost rail's operating costs, let alone service the loan for building the high-class infrastructure.

Another challenge facing the project is that many of the villagers displaced along the railroad's route are still waiting for compensation, according to Lao press accounts. More than two years after the project was launched in 2016 about 4,000 families impacted by the rail link were still waiting to receive compensation for losing their farmland, buildings, crops, and fruit trees. They also still do not know how much they will get and when the compensation will be paid.

Even before the project started, the villagers were prevented from airing their grievances at public meetings organized to explain the project. According to government estimates, nearly 10,000 acres of farm and forest land and more than 3,000 building were affected by the construction.[14] Frequent forced relocation for infrastructure or development projects and the long delays in getting compensation has become a source of irritation in Laos, according to observers in Vientiane.

Although only a few thousand villagers are being displaced by the high-speed rail, they add to the already significant numbers that are being resettled to make way for other foreign investment projects including hydropower dams, SEZs, plantations, and forestry projects. "People are angry," observes Holly High, an anthropologist at the University of Sydney who is doing research on resettlement in Laos. "It is certainly the number-one issue undermining the credibility of the ruling party in the eyes of ordinary people" in rural areas.

A United Nations special rapporteur had harsh criticism of the government's development model, much of which is based on huge Chinese infrastructure projects, following a March 2019 visit to Laos. The country's "rapid economic growth has not led to a commensurate reduction in poverty," wrote Philip Alston, the UN special rapporteur on extreme poverty and human rights.

---

14. Marwaan Macan-Markar, "China's Belt and Road Rail Project Stirs Discontent in Laos," *Nikkei Asian Review*, March 15, 2018, https://asia.nikkei.com/Politics-Economy/Policy-Politics/China-s-Belt-and-Road-rail-project-stirs-discontent-in-Laos.

"The government's single-minded focus on large infrastructure projects (such as dams and railways), land acquisition, resource extraction, and foreign investment has created too few jobs for Lao people, generated very large debt repayment obligations, and disproportionately benefited wealthy elites," Alston said. "Those living in poverty, ethnic minorities, and people in rural areas have seen very few benefits of the economic boom."[15]

Alston added that the displacement of people and the loss of access to land are serious social and environmental problems created by "mega" projects, including hydropower dams and infrastructure schemes. "There are serious environmental effects, which affect people's livelihoods, access to water, and food security, and there are also challenges that accompany construction such as dust, debris, coal, and an influx of workers from outside the community," the UN rapporteur said.[16]

Separately, the government also earns stunningly little revenue from some foreign investment and infrastructure projects. The country's 11 SEZs, most of which are Chinese projects, provided only $20 million to the Lao budget in 2017 and the hydropower dams generated only 1 percent of GDP as revenue for the government, Alston said. The SEZs established in the country have created less than 28,000 jobs and only one-third of those went to Lao workers.[17]

Toward the end of 2018, the World Bank began discussions with donor countries about launching a study to ensure that Laos gets optimal benefit from the high-speed train. The study would seek to highlight infrastructure gaps in connecting with Thailand. It will highlight "software" issues, including policy limitations that could make it difficult to take full advantage of the rail to boost cross-border trade and tourism and benefit from the Chinese SEZs. "The goal is to empower the government with information," says an official involved in the project.

---

15. "Statement by Professor Philip Alston, United Nations Special Rapporteur on Extreme Poverty and Human Rights on His Visit to Lao PDR, 18–28 March 2019," Vientiane, March 28, 2019, https://srpovertyorg.files.wordpress.com/2019/03/lao-pdr-end-of-mission-statement.pdf, 1.
16. Ibid., 6.
17. Ibid., 7.

TRANSFORMING VIENTIANE'S LANDSCAPE

Laos is one of the few countries in Southeast Asia that runs a trade surplus with China. In 2018, Lao exports to China reached $2 billion, while China's exports to Laos totaled $1.5 billion.[18] Despite its dominant role in the Laos economy, China is only the country's second largest source of imports behind Thailand. Laos's top export is hydropower to Thailand, which comprises nearly one-fifth of the country's exports. Copper ore and refined copper are the country's second and third largest exports and mainly go to China.

Most of the copper is extracted from two mines initiated and operated by Australian mining firms that were acquired by Chinese companies in recent years. One in the south was purchased by China Minmetals from Australian OZ Metals, which had long operated profitably in Laos.[19] Both mines are open-pit and slated to close in 2020 because they are running out of the minerals, which will have a significant impact on the government's revenue.[20] Economists in Vientiane wonder if this will prompt Laos to turn to its northern neighbor for more financial help.

Laos's largest imports, many of which come from or through Thailand, are refined petroleum products, cars and trucks.[21] Completion of the high-speed rail project will undoubtedly boost China's economic and political role in Laos as well as probably divert some trade from Thailand. China has already offered to export petroleum products, which are Laos's number-one import.

Laos's importance to Beijing is highlighted by the fact that the relatively small country ranks 17th among the nations receiving grants and low-interest loans from China. Beijing had financed some 764 projects in Laos through 2016, with over 552 being fully funded and the balance being joint ventures. China also provides Laos with some aid free of charge,

---

18. International Monetary Fund, "Exports, FOB to Partner Countries; Imports, CIF from Partner Countries," *IMF Data*, 2014–2018, http://data.imf.org/regular.aspx?key=61013712.
19. Shawn Crispin, "Laos Dances to Survive between China and Vietnam," *Asia Times*, January 9, 2018, https://cms.ati.ms/2018/01/laos-dances-survive-china-vietnam/.
20. Lao Economic Daily, "Sepon and Phu Bia Mines Set to Close Operations by 2020," *Laotian Times*, February 11, 2018, https://laotiantimes.com/2018/02/11/sepon-and-phubia-mines-set-to-close-operations-by-2020/.
21. "Laos Country Profile," The Observatory of Economic Complexity (OEC), https://atlas.media.mit.edu/en/profile/country/lao/ (accessed October 25, 2019).

including a bridge over the Mekong River at Houayxai in the north and a new three-story headquarters for the ruling party in Vientiane.[22]

But China's interest in Laos extends beyond the government and Communist Party. "Some of the investment comes down to Chinese developers," says Barney, the lecturer from the Australian National University who does research in Laos. "Chinese state-owned enterprises, as well as just everyday entrepreneurs, have a lot of interest in developing new markets. They're looking to turn a buck, including from wildlife trading and casinos."

Chinese president Xi Jinping included Laos among the several Southeast Asian countries he visited in late 2017, marking the first visit by a top Chinese leader in 11 years. The two countries signed agreements to establish a China–Lao Economic Corridor along their border and cooperate on electricity projects.[23] During and soon after Xi's visit, China pledged $800 million for foreign aid projects, including over $600 million to upgrade the country's health sector and $90 million to refurbish Vientiane's 100-year-old Mahasot Hospital.[24]

Not all of China's aid in the health space is winning Beijing kudos. In early 2019, Lao authorities closed four of seven Chinese clinics operating in Luang Namtha near China's border because unsanitary conditions and unqualified workers had resulted in the deaths of several patients.[25]

Chinese firms are transforming the Lao landscape. They are the largest investors in Laos in such areas as hydropower dams, SEZs, and real estate projects. Neither China nor Laos has published figures outlining how much Chinese companies have invested in Laos or how much China has provided under the BRI. But according to data assembled by the RWR Advisory Group in Washington, DC, China's investment reached $11.4 billion between 2013 and 2018. RWR assembled these figures from Chinese and Lao public announcements and media coverage. Andrew Davenport,

---

22. Zi Yang, "Securing China's Belt and Road Initiative," United States Institute of Peace Special Report, November 2018, https://www.usip.org/sites/default/files/2018-11/sr_436_securing_chinas_belt_and_road_initiative_web.pdf, 3.
23. "Xi Wraps Up State Visit to Laos with Strengthened Partnership," *Xinhua*, November 14, 2017, http://www.xinhuanet.com//english/2017-11/14/c_136752151.htm.
24. "China Pours Billions in Aid and Investment into Laos," *Radio Free Asia*, January 12, 2018, https://www.rfa.org/english/news/laos/billions-01122018160501.html.
25. "Authorities Shut Down Three Chinese-Owned Clinics in Laos," *Radio Free Asia*, March 19, 2019, https://www.rfa.org/english/news/laos/laos-chinese-clinics-closed-03192019171304.html.

RWR's chief operating officer, says that the company counts only "deals we believe have become real and official."

In addition to making Laos a key part of China's BRI, Chinese companies are also bringing Beijing's Digital Silk Road to its small landlocked neighbor. Beijing has helped Vientiane boost its Internet surveillance capabilities[26] and telecom giant Huawei has a contract to install up to 700 closed-circuit television (CCTV) cameras along main roads in the four southern provinces of Laos. Officials say the cameras are intended to help Lao police capture traffic violations and investigated crimes,[27] but this surveillance technology will also help Laos's security apparatus control any possible dissent.[28]

Chinese companies are the leading property developers in Vientiane and, particularly along the Mekong River, have significantly transformed the skyline of this city of roughly 800,000. At the east end of the city, overlooking the river, stands the Landmark Mekong Riverside Hotel, where Barack Obama stayed when he visited in 2016 and became the first U.S. president to visit the country. The imposing hotel looks like its architects brought their plans straight from Beijing without adapting them to more understated Vientiane. The hotel and the luxury apartment complex next door were developed by CAMCE Investment (Lao) Company, a joint venture between China CAMC Engineering Company Limited and a Lao construction firm, the Krittaphong Group.

Just up the Mekong stand 50 luxurious villas built to house the heads of state when Laos hosted the Asia-Europe Meeting Summit in 2012. The compound, also constructed by CAMCE Investment, includes the offices of several prominent Chinese companies operating in Laos such as

---

26. Zi Yang, "Securing China's Belt and Road Initiative," 3.

27. Phomphong Laoin, "Police Plan to Install CCTV Cameras in South," *Vientiane Times*, January 13, 2019. The online news article no longer exists, but its content can be found in a Vientiane Times Facebook post, https://www.facebook.com/vientianetimesonline/photos/a.430960606971398/2192463444154430/?type=3&theater.

28. This camera technology was not used to investigate the enforced disappearance in 2012 of Lao civil society leader Sombath Somphone. His family found CCTV footage in 2012 showing Sombath being removed from his vehicle and in 2015 of his vehicle being turned around and returned to the center of Vientiane. None of this footage appears to have been used to investigate Sombath's disappearance. Channel News Asia, "Family of Missing Laos Activist Sombath Somphone Reveal New Evidence Three Years after Disappearance," *Sombath Somphone* (blog), December 17, 2015, https://www.sombath.org/en/2015/12/family-of-missing-laos-activist-sombath-somphone-reveal-new-evidence-three-years-after-disappearance/.

PowerChina, a Chinese cultural center, and the Singapore ambassador's residence. Across the street on an outcrop on the Mekong is the Don Chan Palace Hotel, which was built by a Malaysian firm before it was sold to the CAMCE partnership.

North of the river near the morning market, Yunnan Construction Engineering Group Company Limited and Krittaphong Group opened the Vientiane Center Shopping Mall. It features retail shops, restaurants, a multiplex cinema developed by telecom titan Huawei, and an office block whose tenants include China Railway Materials and China's other telecom giant ZTE. The mall was largely empty during a visit in the middle of the week in late 2018.

Across the street, the joint venture CAMCE Investment (Lao), which earlier completed a number of large-scale construction projects along the Mekong, was scrambling to put the finishing touches on the even larger, $6 million World Trade Center for its soft opening in late 2018. The center sports retail shops, food outlets, a medical center, and an office tower and will be home to an InterContinental Hotel, scheduled to open in 2021.

Locating two shopping malls next to each other on a narrow and already busy street could create gridlock on big shopping days. Both malls have only limited parking underneath and next to their facilities, which could add another traffic nightmare.

In the northeastern part of Vientiane near the iconic That Luang stupa, the Shanghai Wanfeng Group, which develops shopping malls in China, has an agreement to develop 900 acres a stone's throw from the most sacred monument in Laos. The That Luang Marsh project is slated to cost $5 billion and to include residential towers, commercial buildings, and a tourist complex featuring a lake for fishing and boating.

Earlier reports suggested that a consortium of Chinese firms got access to a giant chunk of land around the That Luang in exchange for building Laos a sports stadium to host the 2009 Southeast Asian games. But this deal was apparently rescinded because of public protest against Chinese companies gaining control of such a prime piece of real estate.[29]

The current developer's plans included the construction of about 10 residential towers, six of which appeared to be in various stages of completion in late 2018. None of the apartments seemed to be occupied. Work had stopped some months earlier. There were no workers in sight and the

29. Storey, *Southeast Asia and the Rise of China*, 172.

temporary housing for workers from China had caved in and the yard around it was overgrown with tall weeds. A real estate agent in Vientiane said he had heard the developers faced "a problem with money."

Because Laos has plenty of land, Lao traditionally prefer individual houses near the ground, even if they are on stilts. The condos at That Luang Marsh are clearly targeting Chinese and possibly other foreign buyers. The project has SEZ status, so foreigners are allowed to buy condominiums, which they cannot do outside the zone.

That Luang Marsh is not the only Chinese project that has run into funding troubles. A three-tower, 32-story hotel and mall complex along the road north out of Vientiane was abandoned for the second time in mid-2018. The project is located across the road from the Chinese-built convention center where Laos held the summit of the Association of Southeast Asian Nations (ASEAN) in 2016 and the hotel was to be finished in time for Chinese president Xi to stay there during the meetings.[30] But construction of the hotel, which would have been the tallest building in the Lao capital, was halted months before he arrived and then restarted and abandoned again more recently. Some say the hotel project is a joint venture with the Lao military.

Chinese firms are also planning to build SEZs and casinos in southern Laos, which traditionally has been an area where neighboring Vietnam has more influence. One project, called the Mahanathy Siphandone SEZ, is slated for the Champassak Province. It is an over-the-top scheme being planned by the Laos Mahanathy Siphandone (Hong Kong) Investment Company. The firm says the first phase will cost $9 billion, develop nearly 500 acres, and include 35 five-star hotels and casinos, which are to be completed by 2021.

The project, the agreement for which was signed between representatives of the company and the Lao government in 2017, ran into its first major snag in 2019. At least 140 families from eight villages on the site of the SEZ were refusing to sell their land and relocate to make way for construction, although the developers had begun to build an access road for

30. Somewhat ironically, the Chinese-built convention center is located very near the former U.S.-style suburban residential compound known as KM6, where American embassy and aid officials lived until the U.S. Agency for International Development was shut down in May 1975. After the victory of the Lao People's Revolutionary Party later that year, party chief and prime minister Kaysone Phomvihane and his top lieutenants lived in the compound.

construction vehicles. "We are all for the economic growth, but if we give up the land, we will not have a place to live," the chief of one the affected villages told Radio Free Asia.[31]

The numbers of Chinese tourists visiting Laos has increased in recent years, but Thais and Vietnamese are still the largest groups of foreign visitors coming to the country. Chinese tourists are estimated to make up about 16 percent of the nearly 4 million foreign tourists who visited Laos in 2017.[32] Many of the Chinese arrive on direct flights from various locations in China, and in northern Laos many come by car or bus from Kunming.

Alipay, the large Chinese mobile and online payment service operated by Alibaba Group affiliate Ant Financial Services Group, has arrived with the growing number of Chinese visitors to Laos. The service is increasingly available in stores and food outlets in Vientiane and Luang Prabang.[33]

The old royal capital of Luang Prabang with its charming old Buddhist pagodas is a popular Chinese destination. A Chinese low-cost retail chain Miniso opened a shop in the city in mid-2018 and installed a flashing red and white sign to attract shoppers. The move set off Luang Prabang residents because neon signs are illegal in the city since UNESCO named it a world heritage site in 1995. The protests eventually convinced the owners of Miniso to replace the sign with a lower-tech wooden alternative.[34]

Some fear an invasion of Chinese tourists once the high-speed rail is completed, although others doubt that many tourists will take the train because it is expected to be relatively expensive and the cost of direct flights from China are quite cheap and faster. Laos is somewhat hampered in its efforts to attract tourists because it does not have the Angkor Wat temple complex of Cambodia or the beaches of Vietnam and Thailand.

---

31. Eugene Whong, "Lao Villagers Refuse to Yield Land for SEZ, Now Contend with Access Road," *Radio Free Asia*, May 9, 2019, https://www.rfa.org/english/news/laos/laos-sez-champassak-05092019173146.html.
32. "Laos Becomes Increasingly Popular Destination for Chinese Tourists," *Xinhua*, August 28, 2018, http://www.xinhuanet.com/english/2018-08/29/c_137427972.htm.
33. Company Announcement, "Alipay Rolls Out in Cambodia, Myanmar, Laos, and the Philippines," *Fintech News Singapore*, March 13, 2018, http://fintechnews.sg/17781/mobilepayments/alipay-rolls-out-in-cambodia-myanmar-laos-and-the-philippines/.
34. Peter Janssen, "Chinese Tourist 'Invasion' Feared as High-Speed Laos-China Railway Will Boost Visitor Numbers Dramatically," *South China Morning Post*, August 24, 2018, https://www.scmp.com/lifestyle/travel-leisure/article/2160947/chinese-tourist-invasion-feared-high-speed-laos-china.

THE PERIL OF CHINESE DAMS

The Mekong, the world's 12th longest river, is a critical economic lifeline for Laos. Four-fifths of the landlocked country's population lives along the river and on its watershed. For hundreds of years, people along the Mekong have depended on it for transport, fish for protein, and silt and water to nourish their rice fields and gardens. Laos's most important urban centers lie along the river. Thousands of tourists are attracted by cruises on the Mekong to see caves and the sunset near the former royal capital of Luang Prabang.

The Lao government is convinced that the only option it has to pull its economy out of underdeveloped status is to export electricity from a cascade of hydropower dams on the Mekong. Vientiane has already built over 60 dams on tributaries of the Mekong; it has completed two and plans as many as eight more on the river's mainstream. Countries downstream fret about the impact of dams have on the livelihoods of millions of living along the Mekong.

Cambodia (which plans its own dams) and Vietnam are anxious about the harmful consequences of Laos's dams on their economies down the river. The dams are expected to sharply reduce the movement of some 1,200 species of fish down the Mekong and restrict the flow of sediment that provides the nutrients for the rice and fruit crops in Vietnam's low-lying Mekong Delta and holds back encroaching saltwater from the South China Sea.

Western environmentalists in Laos say no good solution has been found for addressing the passage of fish. The builders of the Xayaburi Dam on the mainstream spent an estimated $300 million on a fish passage, but it does not seem to work. "Everyone is focused on getting the fish up" using fish ladders, says a Western environmentalist in Vientiane. "But their eggs get minced in the turbines, so the focus on getting fish up is pointless."

The trapping of sediment from upstream is a major threat to the fertile Mekong Delta in southern Vietnam and is critical to preventing the low-lying area from being submerged by the sea. "Sediment flushing is possible and works relatively well," says a foreign expert based in Vietnam. "Dams could be built to reduce the impact, but [China and Laos] are not doing it."

The political dynamics between Vientiane and Hanoi on Laos's dams are complicated. Laos has "snubbed Vietnam" on the construction of dams, says Baird, the University of Wisconsin-Madison geographer. "Vietnam doesn't want to push too hard and drive Laos closer to China."

The potentially damaging impact of hydropower power projects on the livelihoods of people who depend on the mainstream of the Mekong for transport, water, and fish has convinced the Asia Development Bank and other donors to suspend financing of dams.[35]

China has financed and/or built roughly half of the dams along the Mekong and its tributaries—and is heavily involved in those being planned—as Laos strives to become a key source of hydropower in mainland Southeast Asia. China's EXIM Bank and China Development Bank have provided several billion dollars in loans for dams on the Lao section of the Mekong and more are in the pipeline. Companies such as Power China Resources, Sinohydro Corporation, and China International Water and Electric Corporation have played roles in building Laos's hydropower facilities.

Laos's plans have created tension with its neighbors downstream. On the $3.5 billion Xayaburi Dam, Laos's first on the mainstream, Vientiane initially appeared to agree in 2011 to consult in advance with Cambodia and Vietnam under a process established by the Mekong River Commission, an intergovernmental agency that works with the governments of Laos, Thailand, Cambodia, and Vietnam for sustainable development and joint management of the river. But, in the end, Laos signed a contract with a Thai construction firm the following year to begin construction after Vientiane signed a power purchasing agreement with Thailand for the dam's electricity. Vietnam objected but construction continued.[36]

Similar controversy surrounded Laos's decision to construct the 240-megawatt Don Sahong Dam on one of the streams of Mekong just before it reaches the Khone Falls near the Cambodian border. Experts argued that the dam being developed by a Malaysian corporation would

35. Yukako Ono, "Mekong River Nations Face the Hidden Costs of China's Dams," *Nikkei Asian Review*, May 9, 2018, https://asia.nikkei.com/Spotlight/Cover-Story/Mekong-River-nations-face-the-hidden-costs-of-China-s-dams.

36. "MRC Vietnam Condemns Thai Company's Contract to Build Xayaburi Dam," *Thanh Nien News*, April 24, 2012, http://www.thanhniennews.com/politics/mrc-vietnam-condemns-thai-companys-contract-to-build-xayaburi-dam-7641.html; "Xayaburi Concerns Mount," *Radio Free Asia*, January 18, 2013, https://www.rfa.org/english/news/laos/xayaburi-01182013191811.html.

have a devastating impact on fish stocks in the river, seriously impacting villages depending on fish as their main source of protein.[37]

Under pressure from its neighbors, Laos agreed to a review of the dam before starting construction, but then two months into the study Vientiane announced that construction would begin. Thailand, Cambodia, and Vietnam requested an extension to allow more studies about the impact of the dam, but Laos moved ahead with construction. The minister of energy and mines declared that "if Laos wants to escape least developed status by 2020 this is our only choice."[38]

China was not involved in the construction of the Xayaburi Dam, but Sinohydro Corporation had the contract to build the Don Sahong Dam for the developers, including a Malaysian firm and the Lao government. China's Datang Corporation, in cooperation with companies from Thailand and Laos, is the lead developer in the 912-megawatt Pak Beng Dam planned for Laos's northernmost stretch of the Mekong. But in early 2018, Thailand, which was slated to buy most of the dam's power, decided to defer signing a power purchase agreement. Without a guaranteed buyer of the dam's electricity, its construction was put on hold.[39]

The next hydropower project in the queue is the $2.1 billion Pak Lay Dam. It is scheduled for construction by Power China Resources with a $1.7 billion loan from China's EXIM Bank.[40] The Mekong River Commission organized a series of stakeholder meetings beginning in 2018 to discuss concerns about the project ranging from dam safety to navigation and sediment flows to fisheries.[41]

But a grassroots group from Thailand calling itself the Network of Thai People in Eight Mekong Provinces boycotted the hearings, referring to them as an effort to "rubber stamp the dam to justify its construction." The group said it had participated in similar hearings for 10 years but

---

37. Ian Baird, "The Don Sahong Dam: Potential Impacts on Regional Fish Migrations, Livelihoods, and Human Health," *Critical Asian Studies* 43, no. 2 (2011): 211–235.
38. Creak, "Laos in 2013," 155–157.
39. International Rivers, "Press Release: Thailand Delays Decision on Power Purchase from Pak Beng Dam," March 13, 2018, https://www.internationalrivers.org/resources/press-release-thailand-delays-decision-on-power-purchase-from-pak-beng-dam-16784.
40. Marwaan Macan-Markar, "Chinese Dams Ramp Up Lao External Debt," *Nikkei Asian Review*, November 2, 2018, https://asia.nikkei.com/Economy/Chinese-dams-ramp-up-Lao-external-debt.
41. "Stakeholders Continue Debating Pak Lay Project," *KPL Lao News Agency*, January 24, 2019, http://kpl.gov.la/En/Detail.aspx?id=43082.

found "our concerns fell on deaf ears" and their opposition had no impact on the Lao government's decision to move ahead with the construction of other dams.[42]

PowerChina in 2010 began building a $2.4 billion cascade of seven dams on the Nam Ou River, north of Luang Prabang. The dams are slated to have a capacity of 1,156 megawatts of electricity. Some 70 percent of the project is being financed through loans, presumably from China's EXIM Bank and the China Development Bank, according to PowerChina subsidiary Sinohydro.[43] Lao officials, facing debt they need to repay and a lack of enthusiasm in Thailand about buying electricity from the Nam Ou, have started talking to Vietnam about buying it.

China, which refused to join the Mekong River Commission and weakened the organization by its abstention, in 2016 set up its own Lancang-Mekong Cooperation (LMC) forum in which all the commission countries, as well as Myanmar, participate. (Lancang is the Chinese name for the Mekong.) Countries from outside the region like the United States and Japan are excluded. Members of the LMC can, at least in theory, try to use the grouping to press China to increase the flow of water from the eight dams on the Chinese side of the border—completed before the body was established—during the dry season.[44]

China and the leaders of the LMC have mapped out a five-year development plan of projects for the participating countries. China has pledged billions of dollars, mostly in loans to support projects to establish water resource research stations and boost connectivity, trade, and agriculture as well as poverty alleviation along the river. Beijing has kicked in $400 million to support small and medium-sized enterprises operating along the Mekong.[45]

---

42. Anchalee Kongrut, "Group Snubs Hearing for Dam in Laos," *Bangkok Post*, December 14, 2018, https://www.bangkokpost.com/news/general/1593482/group-snubs-hearing-for-dam-in-laos.
43. "Lao PDR, Nam Ou Cascade Project," Sinohydro, http://eng.sinohydro.com/index.php?m=content&c=index&a=show&catid=42&id=398 (accessed April 22, 2019).
44. Shang-su Wu, "The Trouble with the Lancang Mekong Cooperation Forum," *The Diplomat*, December 19, 2018, https://thediplomat.com/2018/12/the-trouble-with-the-lancang-mekong-cooperation-forum/.
45. Laura Zhou, "Five Things to Know about the Lancang-Mekong Cooperation Summit," *South China Morning Post*, January 9, 2018, https://www.scmp.com/news/china/diplomacy-defence/article/2127387/five-things-know-about-lancang-mekong-cooperation.

To be sure, Laos enjoys an abundance of resources to generate power, including an estimated 18 gigawatts of exploitable hydropower potential, some 8.8 gigawatts of potential in solar power, and nearly 3 gigawatts of potential from wind, according to estimates by the Stimson Center in Washington.[46] By 2016, Laos had power purchase agreements with Thailand to supply about 7,000 megawatts by 2020. It had similar bilateral agreements to supply Vietnam with 5,000 megawatts by 2020 and Cambodia 200 megawatts.[47]

But Laos faces daunting challenges in meeting its energy production goals. Because it lacks its own investment capital, it must rely on the interest of investors in specific projects. Most power projects in Laos use the build-own-operate-transfer model under which Vientiane benefits from taxes and a share of export revenue from dams, but the projects are owned by investors to whom the profits are paid for the first 25 or so years. By the time a dam is transferred to Lao ownership, it may need to be refurbished or require costly maintenance.

Power purchase agreements with the importing country are the vehicle through which investors ensure that they will make a profit. The price and profit margin are key determinants of whether a project goes ahead. The uncertainties of the build-own-operate-transfer model make it difficult for Laos to plan projects both for export and for its domestic market.[48]

Thailand's decision to defer signing a power purchase agreement for output from the Pak Beng Dam was made in part because the Thai government had overestimated the country's energy needs until 2036. Another factor was the increasing integration of solar- and wind-generated electricity into Thailand's electricity supply. In the three years after 2015, Thailand doubled its solar capacity to 3,000 megawatts. Wind has also made significant gains, reducing the need for dam projects on the Mekong.[49]

---

46. Courtney Weatherby and Brian Eyler, *Letters from the Mekong—Mekong Power Shjft: Emerging Trends in the GMS Power Sector* (Washington, DC: The Stimson Center, June 2017), 10.
47. "Laos Country Profile," International Hydropower Association, last updated May 2016, https://www.hydropower.org/country-profiles/laos.
48. Weatherby and Eyler, *Letters from the Mekong*, 11.
49. Brian Eyler and Courtney Weatherby, "Pak Beng Dam Delay Paves Way for Cleaner solutions," *Bangkok Post*, March 17, 2018, https://www.bangkokpost.com/opinion/opinion/1429791/pak-beng-dam-delay-paves-way-for-cleaner-solutions.

Pak Beng had also faced strong opposition from Thai civil society organizations and villagers living along the Mekong who are concerned it would hinder the movement of fish and the flow of sediment downstream. Thai villagers brought a lawsuit against the dam in Thailand in 2017 charging that Thai agencies had failed to provide information about the dam and consult with communities that would be impacted; however, the Thai courts have not accepted the case for further hearings.[50]

Another challenge facing Lao dams is the country's whopping external public debt, which increased to $13.6 billion by the end of 2017. Debt to China had risen to 44 percent of Laos's public debt in 2015, reaching nearly 70 percent of GDP, and almost half was borrowed from China.[51] An estimated $2 billion of this debt is for hydropower dams, which is not sustainable if the country does not have guaranteed sales to major electricity customers.

Laos's hydropower ambitions could also soon face competition from the very companies that are now helping it build dams. China's Yunnan Province, just across the border from Laos, is producing a hefty electricity surplus itself and several Chinese power companies are exploring providing electricity to Myanmar's power grid and one, Rural Yunnan, is already selling surplus power to Laos and Vietnam.[52]

Electricity production in Yunnan totaled 262 terawatt hours in 2015 (1 terawatt hour is equal to 1,000 gigawatt hours), while consumption reached 167 terawatt hours, leaving a hefty surplus of 95-terawatt hours that could be exported to other parts of China and Southeast Asia.[53]

Ultra-high-voltage cable technology makes it possible for vast quantities of power to be transported commercially over long distances from Yunnan to Southeast Asia at lower costs than traditional transmission lines. This ultra-high-voltage technology, first deployed commercially by

50. International Rivers, "Briefing on Pak Beng Dam Lawsuit," June 8, 2017, https://www.internationalrivers.org/resources/briefing-on-pak-beng-dam-lawsuit-16498.

51. Macan-Markar, "Chinese Dams Ramp Up Lao External Debt."

52. Yimou Lee and Shoon Naing, "Exclusive: China in Talks to Sell Electricity to Myanmar amid Warming Ties," *Reuters*, August 3, 2017, https://www.reuters.com/article/us-myanmar-china-energy/exclusive-china-in-talks-to-sell-electricity-to-myanmar-amid-warming-ties-idUSKBN1AK011.

53. Darrin Magee and Thomas Hennig, "Hydropower Boom in China and along Asia's Rivers Outpaces Regional Electricity Demand," *The Third Pole*, April 28, 2017, https://www.thethirdpole.net/en/2017/04/28/hydropower-boom-in-china-and-along-asias-rivers-outpaces-regional-electricity-demand/.

Chinese firms, could also be used to move surplus power from Chinese-built mega-dams in Laos to neighboring countries beyond Thailand. This new technology opens a whole new area for Chinese investment: building and acquiring power transmission infrastructure.[54]

A critical question the Lao government and its Chinese and Thai creditors need to address is how much more debt Laos can take on considering the challenges and uncertainties facing its hydropower sector. If Yunnan has a hydropower surplus, does it make economic sense for Laos to continue hydropower development, particularly if China is looking to transmit electricity to mainland Southeast Asia? Might it make more sense for Laos to look at developing power from solar and wind renewables instead?

The public push in Thailand to sharply curtail investment in hydropower in Laos may result in Vietnam becoming the only significant new market to which Lao hydropower could be exported. Experts say this gives Vietnam leverage to negotiate an agreement with Laos to increase its imports in exchange for a commitment that Laos would stop building dams that block silt from reaching the fertile Mekong Delta and threaten the future of one of the most important rice baskets in Southeast Asia.

Vietnam, as part of its agreement, could step up its investment in renewable energy in Laos such as solar and wind by installing solar panels and wind turbines that Vietnam is increasingly manufacturing. Experts say this strategy would help Laos maintain its role as a major electricity producer while assisting Vietnam meet its growing energy demands and reduce its dependence on polluting Chinese-built coal plants.

The multiple opportunities for corruption in hydropower projects often create enthusiasm for dams among government officials, creditors, and construction companies. Corruption is a big problem in Laos—it ranks 135th out of 180 countries surveyed by Transparency International[55]—but there are no known figures estimating how pervasive it is hydropower projects and whether there is a difference between Chinese-built dams or those constructed by Thai or South Korean contractors.

A 2008 study on corruption in the water sector internationally by Transparency International concluded that in a best-case scenario

---

54. James Kynge and Lucy Hornby, "China Eyes Role as World's Power Supplier," *Financial Times*, June 6, 2018, https://www.ft.com/content/bdc31f94-68aa-11e8-b6eb-4acfcfb08c11.

55. "Laos Country Profile," Transparency International, 2018, https://www.transparency.org/country/LAO.

10 percent is siphoned off from the sector annually through corrupt practices but in a worst-case scenario that number reaches 30 percent.[56] "Huge budgets and opportunities to hide unseemly practices within complex administrative systems are the main drivers of corruption in hydropower projects," an expert wrote in the study.[57]

Resettlement of people displaced by the construction of a dam is another opportunity for officials to line their pockets. Many of those displaced by dams, including in Laos, are poor ethnic minorities who become further impoverished by the project. "Corruption is a major cause for impoverishment for resettlers who fail to receive promised compensation and development benefits," an anthropologist said.[58]

In some cases in Laos, the resettlement of ethnic minority villagers from highlands has a goal beyond building giant development schemes. Civil society representatives often criticize the resettlement of highland people along roads as destroying their traditional livelihoods and way of life. "Don't forget, some resettlement sites are an effort to concentrate state power over unruly upland people," says Barney of Australian National University, who has described this concept in a paper with David Blake, an independent scholar on Southeast Asia based in the United Kingdom.[59] Barney adds that resettlement helps Lao officials with their goals of nation building, providing security, and "buttressing the power and authority" of the government and ruling party.

The collapse of the billion-dollar Xe-Pian Xe-Namnoy hydropower dam in southern Laos following heavy rains in July 2018, which left some 40 dead, 31 missing, and thousands homeless, highlights the dangers that can haunt these projects.[60] The South Korean project in Attapeu Province makes clear the need for the Lao government to promote greater en-

---

56. Transparency International, *Global Corruption Report 2008: Corruption in the Water Sector* (Cambridge University Press, 2008), 10, https://www.gwp.org/globalassets/global/toolbox/references/global-corruption-report-2008-transparency-international-2008.pdf.
57. Ibid., 86.
58. Ibid., 96.
59. David J. H. Blake and Keith Barney, "Structural Injustice, Slow Violence? The Political Ecology of a 'Best Practice' Hydropower Dam in Lao PDR," *Journal of Contemporary Asia* 18, no. 5 (June 2018): 2–3.
60. "Laos Pays Compensation to Families of Dead and Missing in PNPC Dam Disaster," *Radio Free Asia*, January 29, 2019, https://www.rfa.org/english/news/laos/pnpc-dam-compensation-01292019132457.html.

vironmental protection for the rural population that lives in the shadow of giant development projects.[61]

The dam collapse prompted calls for Laos to consider alternative sources of energy. "The best risk mitigation strategy is to avoid barrages as much as possible—and focusing on other energy sources such as solar, wind, and biomass," Brian Eyler, an expert on the Mekong at the Stimson Center, wrote following the dam accident.[62]

In addition to the dams, people along the Mekong are also anxious about China's proposal to blast the rocks in the river to allow bigger ships to pass and increase trade. China's plan is to create a canal near Chiang Rai, Thailand, to allow 500-ton freighters to navigate down the Mekong from Yunnan to Luang Prabang in Laos. This plan would make it possible for commercial barges to operate year-around, including during the dry season.

Protestors in northern Thailand raised concerns that the rock blasting and dredging to create the channel for ships would threaten the ecosystem of the Mekong, which serves as a natural breeding ground for migrating birds.

China, Myanmar, Laos, and Thailand signed a "commercial navigation" agreement two decades ago, but not much happened until late 2016 when the Second Harbor Company, a subsidiary of the China Communications Construction Company (CCCC), requested a meeting with the local Thai environmental group. Within days the Thai cabinet had adopted a resolution supporting plans to "survey and design" the project, raising concerns that plans to implement the project remain active.[63] For now, the protestors appear to have convinced the Thai government to put the project back on hold, but analysts in Bangkok think it will not be long before the project moves ahead.

Since 2011, when 13 Chinese sailors were killed by a gang that had hijacked two cargo ships in Thai water along the Mekong, China has

61. Mike Ives, "Laos Dam Failure Exposes Cracks in a Secretive Government's Agenda," *New York Times*, July 29, 2018, https://www.nytimes.com/2018/07/29/world/asia/laos-dam-response-government.html.

62. Brian Eyler, "Rethink Plans to Dam Mekong after Laos Disaster," *Nikkei Asian Review*, August 10, 2018, https://asia.nikkei.com/Opinion/Rethink-plans-to-dam-Mekong-after-Laos-disaster.

63. Pianporn Deetes, "Troubled Waters: Mekong's Future Remains Uncertain as Thailand Lights Fuse on Rapids-blasting Project," *The Nation*, January 3, 2019, http://www.nationmultimedia.com/detail/opinion/30361510.

conducted monthly patrols on the river with token participation by police from Laos and Myanmar. By the end of 2018, some 76 so-called joint patrols had been carried out with the goal of increasing police visibility and targeting drug trafficking, smuggling, and other cross-border crimes. For years Beijing pressed Thailand to allow the boats to continue down the river into Thai territory, but Bangkok stood firmly opposed.

Some analysts in Thailand see the Chinese gunboats coming down the Mekong as serving another political purpose beyond interdicting drugs and stopping smuggling: intimidation. Elliot Brennan of the Institute for Security and Development told National Public Radio that gunboats from China "remind neighbors of the influence they can wield and that the hard power, the sharp power they hold is increasing, and I don't see it ebbing anytime soon."

"The control of both the South China Sea and the Mekong will strategically sandwich mainland Southeast Asia," Brennan said. "Beijing's control of Southeast Asian rivers is the other half of the so-called salami-slicing strategy in the region."[64] Salami-slicing refers to China in tiny increments constructing islands in the South China Sea and moving in military hardware to boost its control.

In the South China Sea Beijing has to compete with the United States, Japan, India, and other regional powers, but in the Mekong, China basically has the field to itself. China has completed 11 dams on its stretch of the Mekong and has others on the drawing board in China, Laos, and Cambodia. "This is a situation I feel can degenerate," said political scientist Thitinan Pongsudhirak of Thailand's Chulalongkorn University. "If more dams are built and water is more scarce, then . . . China can use its upstream position as a leverage and even as a coercive instrument."[65]

BALANCING HANOI AND BEIJING

Laos, which shares a 265-mile land border with China, is often perceived to be a near-client state of Beijing much like Cambodia, but Vientiane has a bit more political space thanks to its deep ties to Vietnam. Vietnamese communist forces helped their Lao counterparts snare power in 1975

64. Michael Sullivan, "China Reshapes The Vital Mekong River To Power Its Expansion," *National Public Radio*, October 6, 2018, https://www.npr.org/2018/10/06/639280566/china-reshapes-the-vital-mekong-river-to-power-its-expansion.
65. Ibid.

from the U.S.-backed regime in Vientiane and, over the years, Hanoi continued to have important influence on its smaller neighbor to the west. But in recent years, Beijing significantly stepped up its investment and aid, resulting in closer political links between China and Laos.

In the eyes of some of the country's political elite the country had drifted too sharply toward China. Some foreign analysts concluded that some of the leadership changes that took place during the once-every-five-years congress of the Communist Lao People's Revolutionary Party in January 2016 was an attempt to rebalance Laos's relations with Beijing and Hanoi, but the extent of the political transition can be overstated.

Party chief Choummaly Sayasone stepped down because he had served the maximum of two terms allowed under party rules. He was replaced by vice president Bounnyang Vorachith. Bounnyang hailed from southern Laos like all of his predecessors and had served in the military. He had profited generously from the timber industry earlier, had close ties to the business community, and had held various political posts, including that of prime minister.[66] The fact that he came from the south, where Vietnam has traditionally had significant influence, and had studied at the military and party training schools in Hanoi prompted some to conclude that Bounnyang would rebalance the country's foreign ties between Beijing and Hanoi.[67]

Deputy prime minister Somsavat Lengsavad, an ethnic Chinese and number eight in the party, was among four who left the politburo. Somsavat was widely associated with the Chinese high-speed rail project, the Chinese-built communications satellite launched in 2015,[68] the troubled That Luang Marsh project, and the Chinese casino projects first in Boten and then in Bokeo. He was widely speculated to have profited handsomely from all these projects. Some officials familiar with the thinking of party delegates said Somsavat was relieved of his position because he had made Laos too beholden to Beijing.

The appointment of Thongloun Sisoulith, the former deputy prime minister and foreign minister, as the new prime minister was seen as a

66. Soulatha Sayalath and Simon Creak, "Regime Renewal in Laos: The Tenth Congress of the Lao People's Revolutionary Party," *Southeast Asian Affairs* (2017): 189.
67. Luke Hunt, "Leadership Change in Laos: A Shift Away from China?," *The Diplomat*, January 25, 2016, https://thediplomat.com/2016/01/leadership-change-in-laos-a-shift-away-from-china/.
68. Soulatha and Creak, "Regime Renewal in Laos," 186.

step to have a polished leader serve as chair of ASEAN during a year when Vientiane would host the leaders of its neighboring countries as well as those of China, Japan, and the United States.[69] Thongloun, like most senior Lao officials today, had studied in both the former Soviet Union and Vietnam.

These political changes prompted some observers to speculate that the Lao leadership was tilting back to Vietnam and away from China, but this speculation is "a simplistic and often misguided exercise," argued Laos experts Soulatha Sayalath of Hiroshima University and Simon Creak from the University of Melbourne. "While China has continued to grow in importance since relations were normalized in the late 1980s, [Laos] has long understood the importance of maintaining close relations with all of its neighbors, particularly the two Communist nations with which it shares borders."[70]

Because of Laos's close ties to Vietnam, Vientiane's relations with Beijing were strained in the late 1970s by increasing rancor between Hanoi and Beijing. After China invaded Vietnam in 1979 in retaliation for Hanoi's ouster of the Khmer Rouge in Cambodia, Beijing-Vientiane ties cooled dramatically.

China apparently began actively supporting anti-government insurgency groups operating in Laos, including Hmong fighters, many of whom came from refugee camps in Thailand. China arranged with help of the Thai army to send large numbers of Hmong fighters to Thailand for training, weapons, and other supplies to resist the Lao government and their Vietnamese allies, according to Baird, the University of Wisconsin-Madison geographer. China reportedly also urged one Hmong group to adopt the name Ethnic Liberation Organization of Laos to resist the Lao government on behalf of highland ethnic minorities.[71] Baird says China's support appeared to wind down around 1985.

Vietnam-China relations started to normalize after Hanoi pulled its troops out of Cambodia in 1989, and once Laos's ruling party mounted economic reforms, the links between Beijing and Vientiane began warming up. However, Laos also started to look to the West and interna-

69. Ibid., 189.
70. Ibid., 192.
71. Ian G. Baird, "Chao Far Movies: The Transnational Production of Hmong American History and Identity," *Hmong Studies Journal* 15, no. 1 (2014): 8.

tional organizations for aid and support after the Soviet Union began unraveling in the late 1980s, and again when neighboring Thailand got hit by the 1997 Asian financial crisis.[72]

During the war involving the United States in the 1960s and 1970s, China provided assistance building roads critical for Lao and Vietnamese fighters in northern Laos. By the late 1990s and early 2000s, Laos started welcoming Chinese capital for infrastructure projects and investment in plantations, mines, and real estate, and the two countries began exchanging more officials, Communist Party cadre, and provincial delegations. In the years between 2000 and 2016, China and Laos exchanged some 158 official visits, the sixth largest number between Beijing and a Southeast Asian nation.[73]

Laos's hosting of the 10-nation ASEAN grouping in 2016 demonstrated Vientiane's efforts to carefully balance ties between its two larger communist neighbors. Four years earlier Cambodia as ASEAN chair, under pressure from Beijing, had failed for the first time in the group's nearly five-decade history to issue a communiqué after a summit because of differences between China and Vietnam and the Philippines over their claims in the South China Sea.

Lao officials said in advance of Vientiane hosting the summit that they did want to be repeat the diplomatic breakdown ASEAN experienced in Cambodia. The ASEAN statement agreed to in Vientiane in September 2016 did not mention the UN arbitral tribunal ruling rejecting Beijing's far-reaching claims in the South China Sea, but it did reference disquiet in some countries about ongoing island reclamation activities—a clear reference to China.

The statement said that ASEAN "took note of the concerns expressed by some leaders on the land reclamations and escalation of activities in the area, which have eroded trust and confidence, increased tensions and may undermine peace, security and stability in the region." Laos also managed to insert the phrase, which would not have pleased China, that

72. Storey, *Southeast Asia and the Rise of China*, 168–170.

73. Samantha Custer, Brooke Russell, Matthew DiLorenzo, Mengfan Cheng, Siddhartha Ghose, Harsh Desai, Jacob Sims, and Jennifer Turner, *Ties That Bind: Quantifying China's Public Diplomacy and Its "Good Neighbor" Effect* (Williamsburg, VA: AidData at William and Mary, June 2018), 16, https://docs.aiddata.org/ad4/pdfs/Ties_That_Bind--Full_Report.pdf.

"we further affirm the need to . . . pursue peaceful resolution of disputes in accordance with international law."[74]

Laos also demonstrated some symbolic diplomatic balance in the infrastructure used by foreign officials attending the summit. The *Nikkei Asian Review* noted that the meetings took place in a conference center built by China, but the visitors' planes landed at an airport terminal built by Japan and the visiting officials took walks along the Mekong on a boardwalk laid by South Korea.[75]

Laos and Cambodia have both had "long and complex histories" with Vietnam and China, but Vientiane today has more "diplomatic space and leverage" with China than Phnom Penh, according to Edgar Pang, who served as a visiting fellow at the ISEAS-Yusof Ishak Institute in Singapore. Pang attributed this to the fact that Laos today has less "contentious relations" with the two largest and most powerful nations on mainland Southeast Asia—Thailand and Vietnam.[76]

Despite China's economic clout in Laos, the government, in noteworthy Southeast Asian symbolism, gives the Vietnam Embassy higher-profile diplomatic treatment at its national day receptions by sending more senior-level officials to its festivities than it does to the Chinese Embassy, Pang noted.[77] After the party congress ended in 2016, a special envoy of the Vietnamese Communist Party leader called on the new Lao party chief immediately after the meeting ended. The Chinese special representative made his call on the new leader four days after the congress. When a new Lao president was appointed a few months later, he visited the capitals of both communist neighbors, but stopped in Hanoi before Beijing.[78]

"People in Laos welcome China's rise, they welcome [investment], Chinese tourists, and the opportunities for their kids to study," says a for-

74. Lao PDR ASEAN Chairman, "Turning Vision into Reality for a Dynamic ASEAN Community," Chairman's Statement of the 28th and 29th ASEAN Summits, Vientiane, September 6–7, 2016, https://asean.org/storage/2016/08/Final-Chairmans-Statement-of-the-28th-and-29th-ASEAN-Summits-rev-fin.pdf.

75. Yusho Cho, "Laos Showing Off Some Diplomatic Skills," *Nikkei Asian Review*, August 14, 2016, http://elb01-2039628332.us-west-2.elb.amazonaws.com/Features-archive/South-China-Sea-arbitration/Laos-showing-off-some-diplomatic-skills.

76. Edgar Pang, "'Same-Same but Different': Laos and Cambodia's Political Embrace of China," *ISEAS Perspective*, no. 66 (2017): 4, https://iseas.edu.sg/images/pdf/ISEAS_Perspective_2017_66.pdf.

77. Ibid., 5.

78. Soulatha and Creak, "Regime Renewal in Laos," 193.

eign ambassador in Vientiane. "Laos needs railways and roads. What options do they have?"

But Laos has not yet experienced the full force of Chinese-led development like in Sihanoukville and Phnom Penh in Cambodia. Nonetheless, a visitor privately hears considerable anxiety about China's outsized role in the economy, the lack of respect for the environment in Chinese projects, and the flood of ethnic Chinese into the north and into the capital. Lao also complain about corruption in Chinese ventures and point out that in recent years several province chiefs had been removed for flaunting their wealth, including the head of Bokeo Province on China's border.

From time to time Chinese nationals have been attacked in Laos, as has happened in other countries as China's firms increasingly move overseas. In 2017, a Chinese was killed by an unidentified gunman in Xaysomboun Province north of Vientiane in an area that has witnessed sporadic conflict between ethnic Hmong rebels and government forces since the war ended in 1975. Two Chinese nationals died in an apparent bomb blast against a vehicle in the same province in early 2016 and, a few months later, a Chinese worker was killed and several were wounded in an attack on a Chinese investment firm in Luang Prabang Province further north.

The Chinese Embassy responded to the 2017 incident by issuing a safety warning to Chinese nationals in Laos.[79] The attacks have prompted the Lao military to provide armed guards for Chinese companies and their project worksites, reported Zi Yang of Singapore's S. Rajaratnam School of International Studies.[80]

In recent years, the armed forces of China and Laos have sought to boost cooperation, particularly by increasing visits and exchanges on cross-border issues such as human and drug trafficking. Between 2003 and 2016, the two militaries had one joint exercise and 34 senior-level meetings, which ranks Laos behind six Southeast Asian countries but ahead of Cambodia, Philippines, and Brunei.[81]

---

79. "China Issues Security Alert in Laos after National Shot Dead," *Reuters*, June 18, 2017, https://www.reuters.com/article/us-china-laos-attacks/china-issues-security-alert-in-laos-after-national-shot-dead-idUSKBN19A09J.

80. Zi Yang, "Securing China's Belt and Road Initiative," 4.

81. Kenneth Allen, Phillip C. Saunders, and John Chen, *Chinese Military Diplomacy, 2003–2016: Trends and Implications* (Washington, DC: National Defense University Press, 2017), 62, https://ndupress.ndu.edu/Portals/68/Documents/stratperspective/china/ChinaPerspectives-11.pdf?ver=2017-07-17-153301-093.

Occasionally, the Lao media reports some aid deliveries by Chinese armed forces. In 2017, a Chinese military medical team visited Laos for 12 days and treated over 6,000 Lao military personnel and civilians in Vientiane and along the border with China. The Chinese team donated a clinical medicine training center to the army general hospital and brought them more than 20,000 boxes of medicines and medical equipment.[82] A Chinese army medical unit was sent to provide emergency services to people affected by the collapse of the Xe-Pian Xe-Namnoy hydropower dam in southern Laos in July 2018.[83]

Laos long depended on Russia for military equipment, but recently it acquired the Yitian anti-aircraft missile defense system produced by China North Industries Corporation (NORINCO).[84] China has also offered to sell its J-10 fighter jets to Laos to wean the country from Russian Yak-130 light fighters.[85] Most Lao combat aircraft are Russian MiG-21s.

China's attempts to bolster military ties with Laos are undoubtedly held back by the deep ties Lao armed forces have with their Vietnamese counterparts dating back to the critical help Hanoi provided Lao Communists in seizing power in 1975. Most Lao officers still go to Vietnam for training in its military academies.

Separately, Beijing has also stepped up its "soft power" efforts in recent years by giving scholarships to Lao to study in China and inviting Lao journalists and Buddhist monks on visits. The current foreign and education ministers of Laos studied in Australia. "Ten years from now they will all have studied in China," says a diplomat in Vientiane, but he adds that senior Lao officials continue to go to Hanoi for training for three months before they are promoted.

---

82. "China's PLA Peace Train Medical Team Completes Lao Task," *Xinhua*, August 6, 2017, http://www.xinhuanet.com//english/2017-08/06/c_136504032.htm.
83. "Chinese Army Medics Help to Ensure Health of Lao Victims following Dam Collapse," *Xinhua*, July 30, 2018, http://eng.chinamil.com.cn/view/2018-07/30/content_8103554.htm.
84. Global Defense Security Army News Industry, "Laos Displays Chinese-Made Yitian, or Tianlong 6, Air Defense Missile System," *Army Recognition*, January 2, 2019, https://www.armyrecognition.com/january_2019_global_defense_security_army_news_industry/laos_displays_chinese-made_yitian_or_tianlong_6_air_defense_missile_system.html.
85. "China Offering J-10 Fighters to Laos, Bangladesh as Rival to Russian Yak-130 Aircraft," *Defense World*, January 25, 2019, http://www.defenseworld.net/news/24152/China_Offering_J_10_Fighters_to_Laos__Bangladesh_as_Rival_to_Russian_Yak_130_Aircraft#.XJROt5hKjIV.

In 2016, Laos had 9,900 students studying in China, the fourth largest number from Southeast Asia, trailing only much larger Thailand, Indonesia, and Vietnam.[86] In 2010, China opened a massive Confucius Institute in Vientiane on the campus of National University of Laos to promote the Chinese language and culture.[87] The second Confucius Institute was opened in the northern city of Luang Prabang in 2018.[88]

Soochow University from Jiangsu Province in eastern China opened a branch in 2012 in a three-story French-style building in Vientiane teaching courses in finance and international economics and trade. Undergraduate students focus on introductory courses and Chinese in their first year and then transfer to the university's home campus in Suzhou for the final three years. By 2017, more than 200 Lao students had completed their undergraduate and postgraduate courses.[89]

Despite China's increased role in Laos, its people remain much more interested in Thai movies and music than those from China because of the similarities between the Thai and Lao languages and culture.

CHINESE "INVASION" OF LAOS

Over multiple square blocks of Vientiane, just north of the road to the airport, lies the Sang Jiang Chinese market where Chinese shopkeepers, many of whom do not speak Lao, sell products from China. They hawk everything from cooking ware to televisions and porcelain toilets to backhoes for construction. The market itself burned down in mid-2017, 10 years after it opened, so the selling now takes place in shop houses around the giant crater remaining after the fire.

The thousands of Chinese shopkeepers mostly appear to be relative newcomers who came in recent years since the ruling Lao party launched economic reforms in the late 1980s and China stepped up its aid and

86. Custer et al., *Ties That Bind*, 12.
87. Bien Chieng and Jean Chih-yin Cheng, "Changing Landscape and Changing Ethnoscape in Lao PDR: On PRC's Participation in the Greater Mekong Subregion Development Project," in *Impact of China's Rise on the Mekong Region*, ed. Yos Santasombat (Palgrave Macmillan, 2015), 97.
88. "First Confucius Institute in Northern Laos Inaugurated," *Xinhua*, July 15, 2018, http://www.xinhuanet.com/english/2018-07/15/c_137324317.htm.
89. Sun Ruifen, "Soochow University in Laos Pioneers Chinese Education Abroad," *China Report ASEAN*, September 4, 2017, https://chinareportasean.com/2017/09/04/soochow-university-in-laos-pioneers-chinese-education-abroad-china-asean/.

investment in the last decade or so. Some came to work on Chinese construction projects and stayed after they were completed. Others have come in search of economic opportunity. The number of Chinese children on the streets of the market suggest many of them have come with their families.

These shopkeepers are but the latest iteration of Chinese migration to Laos. The Chinese in Laos are divided into two broad groups: The "old" are those who arrived before the mid-twentieth century and maintain Chinese cultural identity but are Lao citizens. The "new" are those who came after 1990 when China and Laos normalized relations. Most of them remain Chinese citizens.[90]

Back in the fifteenth century, Muslim traders from China visited and provided landlocked Laos an outlet for valuable goods such as medicinal plants and rare timber to foreign markets. They were followed later by shopkeepers from Yunnan and, after 1949, by members of the defeated Kuomintang army in China. A second group from southern China settled in central and southern Laos during the French colonial period beginning in the late-nineteenth century. The numbers of ethnic Chinese in Laos in 1955 were estimated at about 32,500.[91]

The Chinese in Laos got a significant boost from the war that ended in 1975 during which the United States sought to prevent a communist victory in Vietnam, Laos, and Cambodia. Many ethnic Chinese profited from U.S. aid to the Vientiane government and from the robust opium trade during the war. In the north, some Chinese military units arrived in Laos in the 1960s to build a network of roads to help the Lao and Vietnamese communists control the northern areas of Laos.[92]

After the communist victory and with the deterioration of China-Laos relations, large numbers of ethnic Chinese fled, causing their numbers to plummet to about 10,000 by the early 1990s from an earlier estimated 100,000. But with the warming of Sino-Lao relations in the 1990s, the "old" Chinese who remained began opening shops again. As China launched aid ventures and Chinese state-owned enterprises

90. Chieng and Cheng, "Changing Landscape and Changing Ethnoscape in Lao PDR," 91.
91. Danielle Tan, *Trends in Southeast Asia: Chinese Engagement in Laos: Past, Present, and Uncertain Future* (Singapore: ISEAS-Yusof Ishak Institute, 2015), 4–5, https://www.iseas.edu.sg/images/pdf/trends_in_sea_2015_7.pdf.
92. Ibid., 6–8.

began investing in Laos, more Chinese arrived to work on these projects, while a new crop of migrants began settling in Laos's north and in Vientiane.

The migration of Chinese to Laos seems largely unregulated and creates irritation among some officials. "If I want to visit China, I have to go to the embassy in Vientiane and apply for a visa," says an official in Luang Nantha on the Chinese border with clear frustration in his voice. "If a Chinese comes to Laos, he gets a visa on arrival."

As in other countries in the region, some Chinese come to engage in illegal activities, including trafficking in protected wildlife and drugs and activities designed to defraud people. In early 2019, a group of 191 telecom and Internet fraud suspects were deported to China for allegedly defrauding people back home of $8.9 million. The suspects allegedly conned people into believing they could earn money by faking orders to help merchants increase sales online only to learn they could not make any money or recover their own money.[93] Some 104 telecom fraud suspects were returned to China a year earlier for pretending to be law enforcement officials to extort money from people in southern China.[94]

Virtually unchecked Chinese migration to Laos could have long-term implications for the country's demographics. Says a western diplomat in Vientiane: "You have to wonder what impact 25 years of colonization with Chinese characteristics will have on Laos."

SACRIFICING SOVEREIGNTY FOR PROSPERITY

Chinese and Lao authorities forced the Chinese casino in Boten to close because of abuses, but in the neighboring province of Bokeo, the Blue Shield Casino operated by Hong Kong–based Kings Romans Group continues to thrive. Its casino, plunked down in a clearing of jungle and rice fields and topped with a mammoth gold and turquoise crown, attracted international attention in 2018 when the U.S. Treasury imposed sanctions

93. "191 Telecom Fraud Suspects Escorted Back to China from Laos," *Xinhua*, January 11, 2019, http://www.xinhuanet.com/english/2019-01/11/c_137737074.htm.
94. "104 Telecom Fraud Suspects Returned to China from Laos," *Xinhua*, January 12, 2018, http://www.xinhuanet.com/english/2018-01/12/c_136891564.htm.

on the establishment for "engaging in drug trafficking, human trafficking, money laundering, bribery, and wildlife trafficking."[95]

Kings Romans controls four miles of prime real estate overlooking the Mekong River and 39 square miles of former farmland in the infamous Golden Triangle narcotics-smuggling region near where the borders of Laos, Thailand, and Myanmar converge.[96] The Treasury charged four company executives, including owner Zhao Wei, a Chinese national, with "an array of horrendous illicit activities."

The Treasury Department accused Zhao with distributing heroin, methamphetamines, and other narcotics for "illicit networks" that included the United Wa State Army[97] across the border in Myanmar. The statement said that since 2014, Thai, Lao, and Chinese officials had seized vast quantities of narcotics traced to Kings Romans.[98]

Zhao rejected the U.S. charges in a statement in Chinese and Lao calling them "a unilateral, extraterritorial, unreasonable and hegemonic act of ulterior motives and malicious rumor-mongering."[99]

Kings Romans has a 99-year lease on its land from the Lao government, which holds a 20 percent stake in the project. The casino permitted human trafficking and child prostitution, the Treasury statement charged, adding that the company used its resort to traffic "endangered and vulnerable animals, including Asiatic black bears, pangolins, tigers, rhinos and elephants."[100]

Treasury also sanctioned Zhao's Chinese wife, an Australian national, and a Thai national; it froze all assets belonging to Kings Romans' network within U.S. jurisdiction and banned American citizens from dealings with the group.

---

95. U.S. Department of Treasury, "Treasury Sanctions the Zhao Wei Transnational Criminal Organization," news release, January 30, 2018, https://home.treasury.gov/news/press-releases/sm0272.
96. "U.S. Slaps Sanctions on Laos Golden Triangle 'Casino' in Bid to Break Up Narco-Empire," *Reuters*, January 31, 2018, https://www.reuters.com/article/us-laos-sanction/u-s-slaps-sanctions-on-laos-golden-triangle-casino-in-bid-to-break-up-narco-empire-idUSKBN1FK1P1.
97. The United Wa State Army is the military wing of the United Wa State Party, the largest nonstate armed group in Myanmar. It runs a self-administered zone in Shan State bordering China and claims some 25,000 armed troops.
98. U.S. Department of Treasury, "Treasury Sanctions"; "U.S. Slaps Sanctions," *Reuters*.
99. "Lao Casino Operator Zhao Wei Rejects US Sanctions," *Laotian Times*, February 7, 2018, https://laotiantimes.com/2018/02/07/lao-casino-operator-zhao-wei-rejects-us-sanctions/.
100. U.S. Department of Treasury, "Treasury Sanctions."

The Chinese investors reportedly paid a concession fee to the Lao government of $850,000 for the first year of the lease. The first phase of the project was slated to cost $86.6 million, with the company saying it plans to invest $2.25 billion by 2020 to build an industrial park and ecotourism facilities. The developers have planted several vegetable fields to serve the casino, but they hope eventually to produce crops they can export.[101]

"The company claims that there is no drinking or prostitution in the casino, although a row of dubious-looking massage parlours and bars nearby, complete with giant signs displaying ladies in lascivious positions, suggests that these vices are not completely unrepresented," wrote Danielle Tan, a research associate at the International Institute for Asian Studies in France, in a study on Chinese engagement in Laos.[102]

The project marks an overlap between legal activities such as tourism development and illegal practices, including gambling, drug trafficking, and prostitution, on which "the Lao state has based its poverty alleviation policy," Tan noted.[103]

Barney of the Australian National University contrasts the SEZs next to the Chinese border, which attract only firms from China, with the Savan Park SEZ, which is a joint venture between the Lao government and a Malaysian firm. The SEZ is located near the town of Savannakhet in southern Laos along the East–West Economic Corridor that links Vietnam, Laos, Thailand, and Myanmar. The Savan Park SEZ has attracted investment from Japanese camera maker Nikon, Toyota for making seat covers, a French firm making optical products, and other foreign companies.[104] The SEZ "is trying to attract investment and is not linked to one country," Barney says. "That type of zone makes much more sense in the Laos context."

Laos's SEZ policy mainly involves renting border areas to Chinese firms for large-scale investment and allowing them access to natural resources, said Pinkaew Laungaramsri, an anthropologist at Chiang Mai University in Thailand who has visited the Bokeo project. Vientiane has turned over giant chunks of land to Chinese companies, allowed an influx of Chinese workers and entrepreneurs, permitted the use of Chinese

101. Tan, *Trends in Southeast Asia*, 22.
102. Ibid., 23.
103. Ibid., 24.
104. Manabu Ito, "Tax Breaks Lure Foreign Business to Laos," *Nikkei Asian Review*, April 17, 2015, https://asia.nikkei.com/Economy/Tax-breaks-lure-foreign-business-to-Laos.

currency, and tolerated an "unclear enforcement of legal jurisdiction" in the "name of modernization," she wrote.[105]

Laos's arrangement with China is a form of "extraterritoriality" in which the Lao government has "chosen to sacrifice its own sovereign rights in exchange for national prosperity," Pinkaew said. The special economic zones have "turned into a new frontier for the Chinese tycoon who has full rights and power to administer his territory; the influx of Chinese immigrants, massive deprivation of land and livelihoods, and expanded narcotics use and gambling have come to characterize the new economic border towns" of Laos.[106]

Zhao and some of the other Chinese operators on the border see themselves to be on a "civilizing mission," the Thai anthropologist observed. "When I first arrive here, it was a poor region. . . . There was nothing here," Zhao told journalists in interviews collected by Pinkaew. "I wanted to help them out of poverty. One day when I get old and look back here, it will have become the famous SEZ well known throughout the world."[107]

This notion of having something to teach the Lao goes beyond Chinese entrepreneurs. A Chinese expert on Laos wrote that the "mentality" of the Lao is an "obstacle" to economic development. Zhang Liang-min, a professor of the Lao language at the Beijing Foreign Studies University, said their "long-term isolation" from the outside world had left the Lao in a "locked up" condition, adding that they "are easy to feel content." Zhang wrote: "Laos is the country that receives the highest amount of per capita foreign aid, which nurtures a kind of dependent mentality and deprives people of the spirit of self-reliance and aggressiveness. [A] sense of urgency is wanting; the signature phrase of many [Lao] is 'no hurry, take it easy.'"[108]

Ironically, thousands of the people displaced by the Zhao's investment in Bokeo had better livelihoods before and now struggle to survive. "Being

105. Pinkaew Laungaramsri, "Commodifying Sovereignty: Special Economic Zones and the Neoliberalization of the Lao Frontier," in *Impact of China's Rise on the Mekong Region*, ed. Yos Santasombat (Palgrave Macmillan, 2015), 118.
106. Ibid., 118–119.
107. Ibid., 128.
108. Zhang Liang-min, "老挝经济社会发展现状" ["Lǎowō jīngjì shèhuì fāzhǎn xiànzhuàng, The Current Condition of Economic and Social Development in Lao PDR"], *国际论坛* [*Guójì Lùntán, International Forum*], no. 4 (1999): 71–75. Quoted in Chieng and Cheng, "Changing Landscape and Changing Ethnoscape in Lao PDR," 90 (translated from Chinese by authors).

deprived of their land and unable to get access to new resources for [their] livelihoods, the Lao people have been kept . . . in a state of suspension between two worlds, between traditional and modern realities, in neither of which they can fully take part," Pinkaew observed.[109]

When the Golden Triangle Special Economic Zone is completed, Kings Romans says it will have, in addition to the casino, a trade center, a five-star hotel, a bank, a golf course, a hospital, an airport, and a harbor. Owner Zhao promises it will serve as a hub connecting Laos, Thailand, and China and facilitate a surge of investment and tourists in the region.[110]

All of this will require the resettlement of nine Lao villages along the Mekong and the expropriation of their farmland, gardens, and pastures, Pinkaew found. Before Zhao's arrival in 2007, the Ton Phueng's farmers were well off and had been engaged in rice farming, cattle ranching, and river trade for generations.[111]

The farmers, from various ethnic groups, fought hard against being forced to abandon their land for a Chinese casino, but in the end they lost. By the time they were consulted, the Lao government had already decided that the first group would be moved to an area a little over six miles away.

In a highly unusual move in Laos, where protests are illegal, frustrated villagers raised money to send two representatives to Vientiane to ask the government to reconsider the SEZ and request fair compensation for grazing land and gardens already turned over to Kings Romans. But the representatives were told by officials that nothing could be done because the project had already been approved by the government.

From 2008 to 2012, the villagers struggled to get fair compensation for their houses and farmland. In the end, families got payment between $2,000 and $2,500 for their houses and between $26,000 and $34,000 if they owned a house, rice fields, gardens, cattle, grazing fields, and a granary. Some families rejected the compensation because they considered it to be too low.[112]

Villagers complained that government officials and village brokers sided with the Chinese investors in forcing people off the land and negotiating a compensation price. The relocated farmers also expressed frustration about the quality of the houses the Chinese company provided

109. Pinkaew, "Commodifying Sovereignty," 119.
110. Ibid., 123.
111. Ibid., 129.
112. Ibid., 131.

them. "The walls started to crack even before people moved in," Pinkaew said. "The house roofs also leak. Villagers have to spend the compensation they received from the company to repair the houses even before they move in."[113]

The company promised jobs but, in the end, the few people who got jobs were young people willing to work "odd hours" in the gambling complex. The firm promoted an organic farming venture and distributed seeds to farmers, but when the vegetables were ready to be harvested they could not find a market.

"I once thought that their occupation is one thing, ours is another," Nang Khai, the last person to leave the old village told Pinkaew. "But the fact that they took our land, the land where we used to grow corn, it means that they came to take away our jobs. That makes us upset." Nang Khai added that what made matters worse is that "now our properties are left idle. They didn't make use of them, just let the field [be] covered with grass."[114]

Later, in 2012, representatives of the company and province came to tell the original villagers and people in two nearby villages that all their rice fields would have to be turned over to the company to make way for an international airport and a 36-hole golf course. Villagers lined up in rows in their rice fields to block officials from measuring their land, prompting the government to bring in police and soldiers to move them.[115]

The Lao villagers who refuse to work in the casino are now "suspended" between "the vanishing world of traditional livelihoods" and economic development "designed by the Chinese," Pinkaew said. Surprisingly, she found that the "key engine" driving the casino and the SEZ are foreign workers from neighboring northern Myanmar, representing a failure of sorts for Zhao's "civilizing mission" in Laos.

The workers from Myanmar began arriving in 2008 to help clear land and work on construction of the casino. Later, some took jobs as dealers and cleaners in the casino. Pinkaew estimated there were around 10,000 workers living in four separate communities when she visited several years ago.[116]

---

113. Ibid., 133.
114. Ibid., 135.
115. Ibid., 136.
116. Ibid., 137–139.

Elsewhere along the Laos-China border, Chinese companies are investing in plantations. On both sides of the road south of Boten, giant swathes of farmland are covered with rubber trees, bananas, pumpkins, and other crops for export to China. The Lao export of bananas to China began in 2013 and within three years had grown to 250,000 tons valued at about $183 million, making Laos the second largest banana exporter to China.

Laos today has some 66,000 acres of banana farms, most of which are owned by Chinese investors who are attracted by Laos's abundant land and cheap labor.[117] Around Boten, Reuters found that Chinese companies paid farmers about $290 an acre ($720 per hectare) to rent their land.[118] This was more than they often earned from farming, allowing them to build new houses, buy pickup trucks, and send their children to school.

But the Chinese have used large quantities of pesticides and other chemicals on their crops. The Lao government in 2016 banned the opening of new banana plantations after a research institute found that the robust use of chemicals was making workers ill and polluting water sources. Many Lao stopped fishing in rivers near plantations because they feared the chemical runoff was harming the fish.[119]

Laos's banana export volume dropped somewhat in 2017 after plantations using pesticides were shut down. Several Chinese plantation operators told Reuters they were frustrated with the ban, insisting that the use of chemicals was necessary for their crops and was not causing workers to get sick.[120] In early 2018, Beijing separately introduced new regulations for banana imports that rejected bringing in fruit with dangerous levels of contaminants.[121]

Rubber was expected to be Laos's top agricultural export earner in 2018, reaching $115.6 million in the first 10 months of the year, while banana exports slipped to $99.7 million in the same period. Rubber exports

---

117. Poqmars, "China-Driven Banana Boom in Laos Faces an Uncertain Future," *Produce Report*, March 12, 2018, https://www.producereport.com/article/china-driven-banana-boom-laos-faces-uncertain-future.

118. Brenda Goh and Andrew R.C. Marshall, "Cash and Chemicals: For Laos, Chinese Banana Boom a Blessing and Curse," *Reuters*, May 12, 2017, https://www.reuters.com/article/us-china-silkroad-laos/cash-and-chemicals-for-laos-chinese-banana-boom-a-blessing-and-curse-idUSKBN187334.

119. Ibid.

120. Ibid.

121. Poqmars, "China-Driven Banana Boom."

have been rising because of the increasing number of rubber trees planted in areas such as northern Luang namtha Province.

Laos had over 740,000 acres of rubber trees at the end of 2018. But Lao producers have been worried in recent years as the price of rubber has fallen because of oversupply on the global market. This has prompted Lao farmers to cut down hundreds of acres of rubber trees to make way for other crops.[122]

Chinese rubber companies began entering northern Laos in 2003 to acquire cheap land for growing rubber. They were motivated in part by sizable subsidies, including grants and loans, that Beijing provided companies investing in the Golden Triangle area of Laos, Myanmar, and Thailand under China's opium replacement policy.[123] The China-Lao Ruifeng Rubber Company, which earlier focused on tourism, received a concession for 740,000 acres in Luang Namtha Province in a joint venture with the Lao military.[124]

Some Lao were anxious about the impact of rubber plantations because of environmental challenges they were seeing in southern China. The rubber plantations there required chemical fertilizers that, after the first few years, often contaminated nearby bodies of water and killed fish and other aquatic life. Rubber trees also used more water than native vegetation, especially during the dry season, impacting other crops and food security in the area.[125]

More than any other Southeast Asian country, Laos is witnessing the dramatic transformation of its landscape from Chinese investment. A high-speed train punching through mountains and riding on giant concrete pillars across valleys will run through the Lao countryside from China's border to the capital of Vientiane and alter the landlocked country's connections to the outside world. The leaders of underpopulated and heavily indebted Laos surprised many of their neighbors by negotiating for five

122. ASEAN Headline, "Rubber Farmers in Laos Quit Jobs due to Low Latex Prices," *Thai PBS*, February 9, 2016, http://englishnews.thaipbs.or.th/rubber-farmers-laos-quit-jobs-due-low-latex-prices/.

123. Tan, *Trends in Southeast Asia*, 17–18.

124. Ibid., 18.

125. Chris Horton, "That Stink Is the Smell of Money: China's New Rubber-Farming Dilemma," *The Atlantic*, May 6, 2013, https://www.theatlantic.com/china/archive/2013/05/that-stink-is-the-smell-of-money-chinas-new-rubber-farming-dilemma/275578/.

years and wrangling terms for the project out of the Chinese that they could live with.

China is also helping Laos build hydropower dams along the Mekong. Hydropower is providing desperately needed export income for the country. But the dams are threatening the flow of water, fish, and silt downstream—and the livelihoods of farmers and fishers around Cambodia's Tonle Sap Lake and Vietnam's fertile Mekong Delta. Environmental concerns are prompting Thailand, which imports most of Laos's hydropower, to explore more renewable sources of energy, which may force Vientiane to rethink its focus on dams.

One challenge Vientiane and Beijing will want to address is providing better livelihood opportunities for Lao displaced by the railroad, dams, and SEZs. Moving Lao farmers off their fields into housing settlements along roads without much land to farm is not a recipe for long-term happiness and prosperity. Another challenge is the seeming unfettered migration of ethnic Chinese into northern Laos, which over a few decades will transform the ethnic makeup and culture of the region.

5. VIETNAM: STANDING UP TO BEIJING IN THE SOUTH CHINA SEA

> China and Vietnam have the same political system,
> share the same [ideals] and belief[s], have common strategic interests, [so] we should be good comrades [with] mutual trust and mutual assistance.[1]
>
> —*Xi Jinping during 2015 visit to Vietnam*

Widespread anti-China protests erupted in Vietnam in June 2018, marking at least the third such incident in the past decade. The latest demonstrators took to the streets in opposition to the legislature's plans to consider a draft law on special economic zones (SEZs). An annex to the bill proposed granting land leases to Chinese investors for 99 years, fully 50 years more than any Vietnamese entity gets.

Vietnam's economy has benefited immensely from foreign investment since the late 1990s, but economic engagement with China easily raises hackles among the population. "No leasing land to China for even one day," read some of the banners at the anti-SEZ legislation protests. Even though the neighbors are Communist Party allies, every Vietnamese can recite the number of times Chinese rulers have invaded the country since colonizing it for over 900 years in the second century BC. "The draft law is now dead," insists a former official. "It was a betrayal of the fatherland's interests."

China's relations with Vietnam are more fraught than with any other Southeast Asian nation, given the more than two millennia of history between the countries. This history also colors the perceptions of Vietnamese people about China, even though Vietnam has more traits in

1. Quote and translation provided by a Chinese Vietnam scholar.

common with China than any of its neighbors. More than two-thirds of Vietnamese words are borrowed from Chinese, and both countries are heavily influenced by Confucianism.

But if Beijing wondered how focused the Vietnamese still are on China, it got a reminder in early 2019 when an embalmed turtle viewed as the symbol of the country's independence was displayed in a temple in Hoan Kiem Lake in the center of Hanoi. Former emperor Le Loi received a magic sword from the great grandfather turtle that he used to fight off Chinese forces in the fifteenth century and then returned it to the lake, according to Vietnamese legend.[2]

A late-2018 survey of Southeast Asian attitudes toward regional issues, conducted by the ISEAS-Yusof Ishak Institute in Singapore, found that nearly 61 percent of Vietnamese polled believe "China will become a revisionist power with an intent to turn Southeast Asia into its sphere of influence." Just under 59 percent believe China's Belt and Road Initiative (BRI) will draw Southeast Asian states closer into "China's orbit."

The survey, which canvassed the views of regional experts and business, civil society, and media communities, found that just over 73 percent of Vietnamese do not have confidence in China to "do the right thing" in contributing to global peace, security, prosperity, and governance. Some 52 percent of Vietnamese believe that China has the most political and strategic influence in Southeast Asia, turning upside down the conventional wisdom that China holds sway in the economic realm while the United States wields influence in the political-strategic domain.

Only 37 percent of Vietnamese thought U.S. engagement with Southeast Asia had declined under President Donald Trump compared to 68 percent across all of Southeast Asia. Nearly 55 percent of Vietnamese had confidence in the United States as a strategic partner and provider of regional security, which was the highest level across the 10 Southeast Asian nations.[3]

Much of the recent tension between China and Vietnam has been prompted by their overlapping claims in the South China Sea. A crisis erupted in 2014 after China moved its giant HYSY 981 oil rig off the coast

2. Mike Ives, "Vietnam Embalms a Sacred Turtle, Lenin-Style," *New York Times*, March 20, 2019, https://www.nytimes.com/2019/03/20/world/asia/vietnam-turtle-embalmed.html.
3. Tang Siew Mun, Moe Thuzar, Hoang Thi Ha, Termsak Chalermpalanupap, Pham Thi Phuong Thao, and Anuthida Saelaow Qian, *The State of Southeast Asia: 2019 Survey Report* (Singapore: ASEAN Studies Centre at ISEAS-Yusof Ishak Institute, 2019), https://www.iseas.edu.sg/images/pdf/TheStateofSEASurveyReport_2019.pdf.

of central Vietnam into waters controlled by both countries. In recent years, Beijing has reclaimed seven artificial islands in the Spratly grouping, boosting its ability to project military power throughout the South China Sea. Since mid-2017, under pressure from Beijing, Vietnam has suspended two oil and gas drilling projects by a Spanish company at a cost of several hundred million dollars each.

Despite these tensions, China is a pivotal player in Vietnam's economy. China is the country's largest import market, providing many of the inputs the once war-torn country needed to emerge as the world's twenty-first largest exporter since joining the World Trade Organization in 2007.[4] The United States, which maintained a postwar trade embargo against Vietnam until 1995, is the country's largest export market.

Like the rest of Southeast Asia, capital-starved Vietnam could benefit from China's heaps of investment capital. Despite bilateral tensions, China by 2017 had become Vietnam's eighth largest investor, behind nations like Japan, South Korea and Singapore. But some Chinese schemes such as a bauxite mine, a sky train in Hanoi, and a raft of coal-fired electricity plants have faced widespread complaints and street demonstrations for their environmental damage, cost overruns, shoddy workmanship, and delays.

Unlike some of China's other neighbors—notably Cambodia, Laos, and Malaysia—Vietnam has been slow to tap into China's massive Belt and Road Initiative (BRI), which aims to connect mainland Southeast Asia more closely with China. "Vietnam's reactions to the initiative remain largely ambivalent because of the complex political, economic and strategic relationship between the two countries," said Le Hong Hiep, a Vietnam expert at the ISEAS-Yusof Ishak Institute.[5]

Part of that is due to a general distrust of Beijing and rising anti-China sentiments in Vietnam, particularly because of China's pressure against Hanoi in the South China Sea. Vietnamese officials also say they find the commercial terms Beijing offers unattractive and are uneasy about being saddled with oceans of Chinese debt.[6]

---

4. "Vietnam Country Profile," The Observatory of Economic Complexity (OEC), https://atlas.media.mit.edu/en/profile/country/vnm/ (accessed October 20, 2019).
5. Le Hong Hiep, "The Belt and Road Initiative in Vietnam: Challenges and Prospects," *ISEAS Perspective*, no. 18 (2018): 2, https://www.iseas.edu.sg/images/pdf/ISEAS_Perspective_2018_18@50.pdf.
6. Ibid., 1.

Map 6. Vietnam

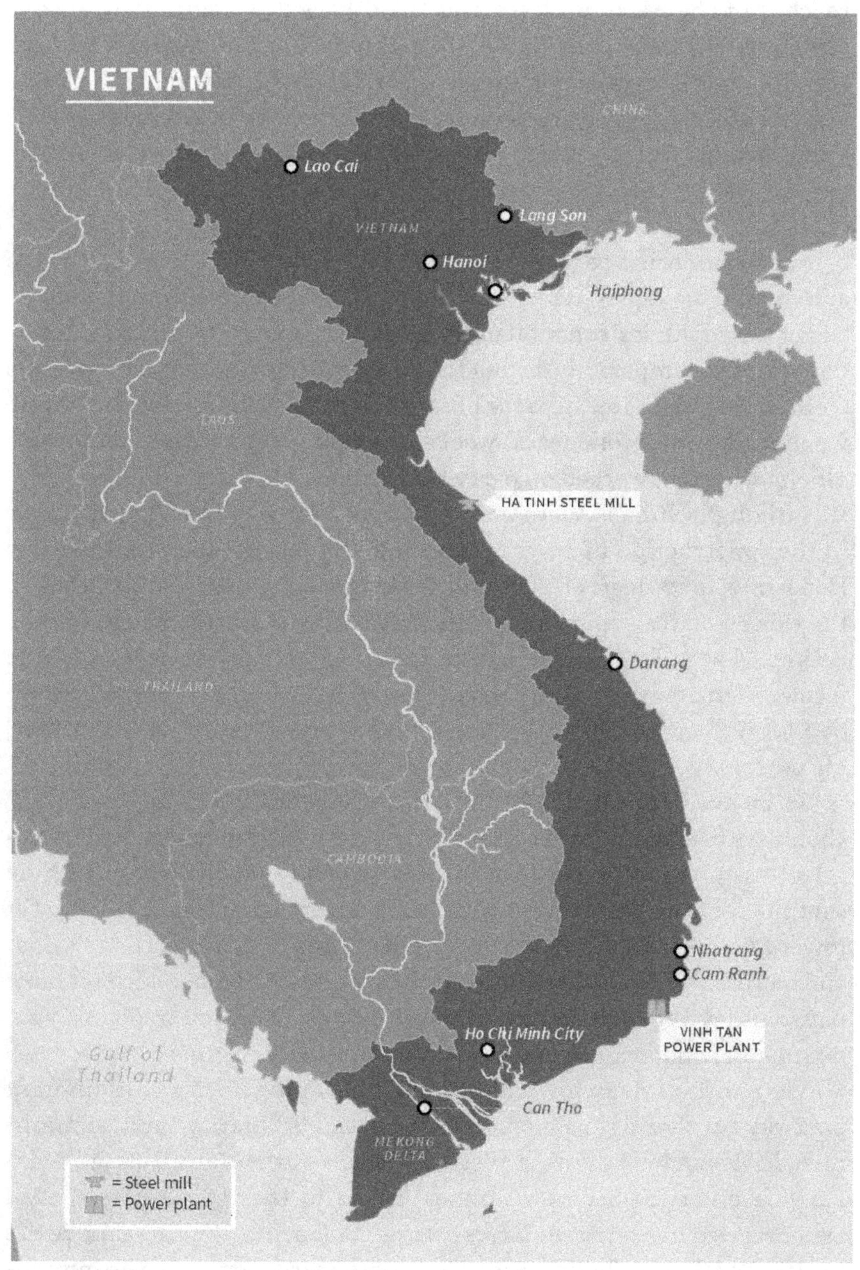

Vietnam is anxious about the 11 dams China has built in the upper reaches of the Mekong River and the others it is committed to constructing or financing in Laos and Cambodia. Environmentalists worry these dams will seriously reduce the arrival of fish supplying the lower reaches of the Mekong and sharply curtail the flow of silt into the low-lying Mekong Delta, reducing its fertility and threatening its low-lying "bread basket" with saltwater flooding as the ocean rises with climate change.

The Communist parties of the two countries have active exchanges and regular dialogues, which operate on a track separate from the activities of the countries' other bilateral links. Party-to-party relations broke down at least temporarily during the oil rig crisis in mid-2014. Phone calls from senior Vietnamese party officials to their counterparts in Beijing went unanswered for several weeks, according to a retired Vietnamese official who long worked on party ties with China.

Although China is Vietnam's top import partner and a major player in the construction of power plants, Beijing has not managed to draw Hanoi into its strategic orbit. Hanoi has long sought to balance its ties with the United States, Japan, and other Western nations as a hedge against Beijing. "The more friends we have, the more leverage we have," says the former Vietnamese party official with years of China experience. "To have better relations with China, we have to have good relations with [other] big powers."

To be sure, Vietnamese officials are constantly looking over their shoulders to ensure they are not irritating Beijing too much, but China's relentless pressure in the South China Sea and the virulent anti-China sentiment of the Vietnamese population ensures that Hanoi will not tilt toward Beijing any time soon. But facing China's growing military clout and increasing naval power projection capabilities, Hanoi realizes it must pay some levels of deference to China as long as it does not challenge Vietnam's independence or get too assertive in their maritime dispute.

Vietnam's strategy toward China is a changing mix of four different pathways, including "balancing," "deference," "solidarity," and "enmeshment," Alexander Vuving, a Vietnam expert at the Hawaii-based Asia-Pacific Center for Security Studies linked to the U.S. Department of Defense, wrote in an *Asian Survey* article. "Balancing," Vuving said, refers to Hanoi's effort at "building alliances with third parties on the international stage. Deference means that the weaker pursues its interests in a manner that corresponds to the stronger side's superior status."

Vietnam appeals to "solidarity" by stressing the shared communist ideology and similar political system between the two countries, Vuving said. Under "enmeshment," he said, paraphrasing Vietnamese officials, "Hanoi must interlock the diverse interests of different actors into situations that are favorable for Vietnam." Vietnam's goal of using these different "pathways" is to constrain Chinese aggressive actions, reassure Beijing of Hanoi's benign intentions, and build norms that govern relations between the two neighbors.[7]

The challenge of Vietnamese leaders in dealing with China is made more complicated by their uncertainty about relations with the United States under the Trump administration. "It's harder for Vietnam to stand up to China under Trump," says the retired party foreign policy expert in Hanoi. "If Trump doesn't pay enough attention to Southeast Asia, the region has no option but to bend to China."

"Vietnam has adapted to the unpredictability of U.S. policy under President Trump by boosting its hedge," says Vuving. "Hanoi has strengthened its ties with India, Russia, and Japan at the same time as it has strengthened ties with the United States."

Vuving says Vietnam is supportive of the Trump administration's emphasis on a "free and open Indo-Pacific (FOIP)," but Hanoi "does not put all its eggs into it." He adds that the Vietnamese see the FOIP as a necessary counterweight to China, but they are unsure about its real intent and actual implementation. "For the FOIP to be successful, it has to have a robust economic prong," Vuving says.

THE TALE OF TWO SUBWAYS

Vietnam has officially signed up for China's BRI and its president attended President Xi Jinping's infrastructure summit in Beijing in May 2017, but Hanoi has been super cautious about taking loans to build infrastructure under the scheme. "The BRI is too big, too ambitious, too expensive," says a Hanoi-based China expert, who asked not to be identified because of

7. Alexander L. Vuving, "Strategy and Evolution of Vietnam's China Policy: A Changing Mixture of Pathways," *Asian Survey* 46, no. 6 (November/December 2006): 806–810.

sensitive ties between the two countries. "When you are situated so close [to China], the best option is to wait and see."

To be sure, Vietnam is not shunning Chinese loans because it does not desperately need help financing infrastructure projects. The country faces an investment gap of $102 billion in meeting its staggering estimated infrastructure development needs of $605 billion between 2016 and 2040, according to the Global Infrastructure Hub, an initiative of the G20 grouping. Vietnam requires $265 billion to meet its electricity requirements, $134 billion for roads, $99 billion for telecommunications, and $72 billion for water.[8] Those are staggering sums for Hanoi, which has run critical government budget deficits in recent years.

Still, Hanoi holds China at arm's length because it is concerned about too much dependence on Beijing and giving China too much leverage should a conflict erupt down the road. Officials are troubled by the lack of transparency in many of China's projects in neighboring countries and the fact that Chinese companies have a poor record on the environment in many of their foreign ventures. They are concerned by the fact that the BRI's court for dispute settlement is based in Beijing and is staffed by eight judges, all of whom are Chinese.

Vietnamese officials complain that the interest rates for loans from Chinese banks are not cheap or concessionary. Often the interest rate offered for projects in Vietnam are 3.5 percent and they almost never fall below 3 percent, Vietnamese officials say. Most Chinese loans require the use of Chinese technology and expect that the work will be done by Chinese companies using workers from China.[9]

Residents of Hanoi have had a ringside seat to some shoddy work by Chinese companies—work that often falls behind schedule. Take the 7.5-mile elevated sky train project running through the heart of the Vietnamese capital. It is under construction by Chinese companies with credit from Beijing but is running way behind schedule and is already mightily over budget. Initially, when the project began in 2011, it was estimated to cost $552 million, for which Vietnam got a loan of just under $420 million from China's Export-Import (EXIM) Bank. When the subway

8. "InfraCompass Overview: Vietnam," Global Infrastructure Hub, https://www.gihub.org/countries/viet-nam/ (accessed October 20, 2019).
9. Hiep, "The Belt and Road Initiative in Vietnam," 4.

was still far from finished in 2017, its cost had risen to over $890 million and China provided another $250 million loan.[10]

Officials have no estimate when construction of the subway, which is headed by state-owned China Railways Sixth Group, will be completed. The current hold up: differences between the Vietnamese and Chinese contractors over safety certification of the project. Some officials say the project is now considered to be part of the BRI even though work on it began long before the initiative was launched.

Several accidents have dented the project's image in the eyes of the Vietnamese. In November 2014, some rolls of steel fell from the overhead construction, killing a motorcycle driver and injuring two other passersby. A month later a 30-foot section of scaffolding fell onto a taxi, trapping three people. In May 2017, an inspection team found rust developing on sections of the track which had not been covered with protective paint, further spoiling the project's reputation.[11]

Japan and China are competing head-to-head in a race to build infrastructure and boost connectivity in Vietnam and other Southeast Asian countries. Many Vietnamese contrast the Chinese subway venture in Hanoi with the 12-mile subway project being built by a Japanese consortium in Ho Chi Minh City, the commercial hub in Vietnam's south. This project, which is backed by funds and expertise from the Japan International Cooperation Agency and two Japanese conglomerates, has not reported any accidents. But the project has fallen way behind schedule and has faced funding shortages. The cost of the project has almost doubled to $2.5 billion, up from the initial projection of $1.4 billion.[12]

One sector in which Chinese companies have made significant inroads is in financing and building power plants. Economist Pham Sy Thanh of the Vietnam Economic and Policy Research Institute at the Vietnam National University in Hanoi, estimates that Chinese firms have financed

---

10. Vietnam Express, "Dự án đường sắt Cát Linh—Hà Đông trả nợ Trung Quốc 650 tỷ mỗi năm," *VNExpress*, January 24, 2018, https://vnexpress.net/thoi-su/du-an-duong-sat-cat-linh-ha-dong-tra-no-trung-quoc-650-ty-moi-nam-3703020.html, quoted in Le Hong Hiep, "The Belt and Road Initiative in Vietnam," 5.

11. Michael Tatarski, "Vietnam's Tale of Two Metros, One Built by the Japanese and the Other by the Chinese," *South China Morning Post*, July 30, 2017, https://www.scmp.com/week-asia/business/article/2104149/vietnams-tale-two-metros-one-built-japanese-and-other-chinese.

12. Ibid.

and constructed some 70 percent of the coal-fired power stations built in recent years for Vietnam Electricity, the country's largest power utility.

Thanh, who studied economics in China, says most of these plants are of "low quality and low technology," causing serious environmental damage. China is exporting this environmentally challenging coal-burning technology to Vietnam, even though it is installing more sustainable infrastructure back home.

Several rounds of protests have erupted in recent years against a series of coal-fired power plants in Binh Thuan Province, northeast of Ho Chi Minh City. The first phase called Vinh Tan 1 was built by China Southern Power Grid Company and China Power Investment Corporation. Vinh Tan 2 was constructed by Shanghai Electric Group, while Vinh Tan 3 is still under construction by China's CLP Group, Harbin Power Equipment Company of China, and Japan's Mitsubishi Corporation.[13]

The first protests against coal dust pollution caused by the power plants, including blocking Highway 1, the country's main north-south artery, erupted in 2015 against Vinh Tan 2. But some of the most violent protests against the draft special economic zone law in 2018 took place around the Binh Thuan power plants.

"Farmers complained that they could no longer grow vegetables due to pollution from the coal plant," says a former government official. "The protestors, who were led by retired colonels, destroyed police cars, fire trucks, and blocked traffic for several days." Some 21 protestors were sentenced from two to over four years in prison for attacking riot police with bricks and Molotov cocktails, destroying government vehicles and causing traffic jams.[14]

These environmental challenges can be expected to increase as Vietnam plans to build more coal-fired power plants in the coming years to meet the demands of its surging economy. By 2030 coal is projected to contribute 56 percent of the country's electricity mix, up from about 36 percent in 2015.[15] Chinese banks are not the only funders of coal-fired

---

13. "Vinh Tan Power Station," *Source Watch*, last edited on March 15, 2019, https://www.sourcewatch.org/index.php/Vinh_Tan_power_station.

14. "Vietnam Jails 15 Protesters for Violent Demonstration in Binh Thuan Province," *Radio Free Asia*, August 26, 2018, https://www.rfa.org/english/news/vietnam/vietnam-jails-15-protesters-for-violent-demonstration-09262018155849.html.

15. Mike Ives, "Vietnam Bets on Coal Power despite Rising Risks," *China Dialogue*, November 27, 2015, https://www.chinadialogue.net/article/show/single/en/8333-Vietnam-bets-on-coal-power-despite-rising-risks.

plants in Vietnam. Banks from Japan and South Korea are also major funders.[16]

China also plays a key role in hydropower dam construction in Vietnam. Hundreds of dams with capacities of less than 30 megawatts have been built over the past two decades, but most of them fly under the radar because they are small. Chinese companies have played a big role in designing and constructing these dams and are estimated to have supplied 90 percent of the equipment and much of the labor for these projects, according to environmental researchers.[17]

Tens of thousands of Chinese workers have entered Vietnam to work on these projects, with as many as one-third of them coming without work permits, according to Vietnamese government estimates. Sometimes Vietnamese villagers complain about not benefiting from construction projects, prompting Chinese firms to hire a few of them. But Chinese construction companies say that they prefer Chinese nationals because they are more willing to work long hours.[18]

Separately, China provides about 4 percent of the electricity used in Vietnam, for which the country's utility outfit often pays Chinese firms up to three times more than what it pays domestic producers. To avoid a backlash from the public, the government regularly publishes announcements about how much electricity it imports from China on any given day.[19]

Earlier, two rounds of anti-China protests erupted at an integrated steel mill in the north central province of Ha Tinh funded by Formosa Plastics Group, a top Taiwan chemicals producer, and built by Chinese state-owned China Metallurgical Group Corporation. In the early months of 2016, the discharge of chemicals, including cyanide, from the mill into the South China Sea killed fish and other marine life along a 120-mile stretch of the coastline, wiping out the livelihoods of fishers and sickening many people.

The disaster lead to wide-ranging public anger and prompted several weeks of demonstrations until the government explained the causes for

---

16. Green Innovation and Development Centre, *A Study on Financiers of Coal Power in Vietnam* (Hanoi: GreenID, October 2016).
17. Vanessa Lamb and Nga Dao, "Perceptions and Practices of Investment: China's Hydropower Investments in Mainland Southeast Asia," paper presented at conference on Land Grabbing, Conflict, and Agrarian-Environmental Transformations (Perspectives from East and Southeast Asia, Chiang Mai University, Thailand, June 5–6, 2015), 3.
18. Ibid., 9.
19. Ibid., 6.

the environmental disaster and announced that it was seeking compensation of $500 million from the mill operators.[20]

Anti-China protestors had attacked the steel mill three years earlier when China in May 2014 moved a giant oil rig belonging to state-run China National Offshore Oil Corporation about 120 miles off the coast of central Vietnam and in an area of the continental shelf claimed by both nations. The rig set off giant protests and riots against factories owned by Japanese, South Korean, Singaporean, and Taiwanese investors. The steel mill in Ha Tinh was attacked even though the owners were from Taiwan, not mainland China. As many as four Chinese workers constructing the mill are believed to have been killed.[21]

Some years earlier, a firestorm erupted in Vietnam when the government in 2009 granted Chinese mining company Chinalco the right to invest $15 billion to mine bauxite, a key mineral for producing aluminum, in central Vietnam. Environmentalists, war veterans, and religious leaders expressed fear that the mining activities would destroy the environment. In a surprising move, legendary General Vo Nguyen Giap, who led the Vietnamese military victories over France and the United States and was 97 at the time, joined the opposition, charging that the mining activities would wreck the local ecosystem, displace ethnic minority people, and result in the influx of Chinese workers.

Because senior Vietnamese party leaders reportedly had promised the project to their Chinese counterparts, officials refused to call off the scheme, although they did agree to study its environmental impact and slow its implementation.[22]

HOLDING THE BELT AND ROAD AT ARM'S LENGTH

Vietnam lags well behind some its Southeast Asian neighbors in signing up for the BRI. "Vietnam lacks trust," says Thanh, the economist. "We know China will not be very good to us and, yet at the same time, we face

20. Richard C. Paddock, "Taiwan-Owned Steel Factory Caused Toxic Spill, Vietnam Says," *New York Times*, June 30, 2016, https://www.nytimes.com/2016/07/01/world/asia/vietnam-formosa-ha-tinh-steel.html.
21. Austin Ramzy, "A View from the Sea, as China Flexes Muscle," *New York Times*, August 9, 2014, https://www.nytimes.com/2014/08/10/world/asia/a-view-from-the-sea-as-china-flexes-muscle.html.
22. Seth Mydans, "War Hero in Vietnam Forces Government to Listen," *New York Times*, June 28, 2009, https://www.nytimes.com/2009/06/29/world/asia/29iht-viet.html.

pressure from the Chinese [Communist] Party. We can't say no every time," the economist says. "Sometimes we say yes but do nothing."

At President Xi's BRI summit in May 2017, China signed some 270 projects with foreign delegations. Vietnam signed only two: one for completing the Hanoi sky train project and another for work developing e-commerce in Vietnam. "China was upset," says Thanh. "They say they pushed through initiatives with Myanmar, Thailand, Laos, and Cambodia, but in Vietnam we're stuck," says Thanh. "We say we need time to research the projects and think about them."

During Xi's visit to Hanoi in November 2017, the two sides signed a memorandum of understanding endorsing a "two corridors, one belt" framework to boost cross-border connections first proposed by China more than a dozen years earlier. One of the corridors was intended to link Kunming in southwestern China with Lao Cai, Hanoi, and Haiphong in northern Vietnam. The second would link Nanning in China's Guanxi Province with Lang Son, Hanoi, and Haiphong on the Vietnamese side of the border. The belt would boost economic cooperation between the areas of the two countries bordering on the Tonkin Gulf.[23]

Economic collaboration between the two countries is deepening, despite the widespread anti-China sentiment in Vietnam. Foreign direct investment by Chinese companies has picked up in recent years, reaching $2.4 billion in 2018, up from only $700 million six years earlier. China accounted for nearly 7 percent of the total foreign direct investment in 2018 and ranked fifth among investors behind Japan, South Korea, Singapore, and Hong Kong.[24]

Between 1993 and 2013, China's official development assistance (ODA) to Vietnam totaled $670 million and was focused primarily on the railway sector, fertilizer production, electricity, and some cultural projects, according to Thanh. Of these funds, Vietnam will not have to repay $50 million. It is uncertain whether China will require repayment of the rest. Beginning in 2007, China's ODA to Vietnam was combined with official credits and reached $417 million by 2013, Thanh estimates.

---

23. Hiep, "The Belt and Road Initiative in Vietnam," 3.

24. "Foreign Direct Investment Projects Licensed in 2018 by Main Counterparts," General Statistics Office of Vietnam, https://www.gso.gov.vn/default_en.aspx?tabid=776 (accessed October 20, 2019); Lam Thanh Ha, "Chinese FDI in Vietnam: Trends, Status and Challenges," *ISEAS Perspective*, no. 34 (2019), https://www.iseas.edu.sg/images/pdf/ISEAS_Perspective_2019_34.pdf.

Neither Beijing nor Hanoi have released figures on how much credit or assistance China has provided Vietnam under the BRI. RWR Advisory Group in Washington, DC, has estimated the amount at $4.5 billion in the six years through 2018. That is smallest amount among nine Southeast Asian countries, excluding Brunei. The next lowest is Thailand, which received $8.3 billion in credit. RWR calculates their figures from announcements or press articles in China or Vietnam and counts only those "deals that we believe have become real and official," says Andrew Davenport, the firm's chief operating officer.

China also provides Vietnam with commercial credit to fund imports and exports, mainly to state-owned enterprises working in telecommunications, electricity, and transport. Thanh says the Ministry of Planning and Investment estimates that these Chinese credits could be as high as $20 billion, and Vietnam could be expected to repay these funds in the future. The ministry found that Chinese loans to Vietnam had an interest rate of 3 percent compared to Japan's rate of 0.4 to 1.2 percent.

One of China's schemes for providing credit to Vietnam is through engineering, procurement, and construction (EPC) contracts. These schemes are subcontracted to state-owned Chinese corporate consortiums, which divvy up as much as 95 percent of the project value to companies from China that provide the contractors, technology, and services for the project. The Chinese subcontractors are financed by export credits and concessional loans from Chinese banks.[25]

The structure of these EPC contracts means there is little benefit to Vietnamese firms and workers. Because Chinese companies bidding on these contracts have no competition, they are under minimal pressure to ensure quality and to meet their deadlines, which results in troubled projects like the sky train in Hanoi. The requirement that a project must import technology and services from China contributes about 50 percent of the growing trade deficit Vietnam has with China, according to Thanh. Because Chinese contractors prefer using workers from China, these projects provide few jobs for Vietnamese.

Vietnam has also found that these EPC contracts are vulnerable to the vagaries of Beijing-Hanoi relations at any time. During the May 2014 pro-

25. Hiep, VNU, and UNSW@ADFA, "The Rise of Chinese Contractors in Vietnam," *East Asia Forum*, March 14, 2013, http://www.eastasiaforum.org/2013/03/14/chinese-contractors-rise-in-vietnam-causes-problems-and-implications/.

tests against the Chinese oil rig off the coast of Vietnam, Chinese lenders halted credit to EPC contracts in Vietnam, leaving a number of projects in limbo.[26]

The uncertainties of China's largesse add to Vietnam's concerns about accepting assistance from China. This was likely a factor in Hanoi's decision about how to fund a highway from Hanoi to Lao Cai on the Chinese border that was inaugurated in late 2014. Vietnamese officials say China offered to build the highway because it would help Chinese products intended for export from western China to reach a port more quickly. (Haiphong in northern Vietnam is the nearest port to the Chinese provinces of Yunnan and Guangxi.) Vietnamese officials say they suggested to China that it build the highway to the Vietnamese border, but that they would build the segment inside Vietnam with funds from the Asia Development Bank.

Vietnam is China's largest trading partner in Southeast Asia. China's exports to Vietnam in 2018 reached $84.2 billion and the closest competitor was Malaysia, which imported roughly half as much at $46.4 billion.[27] A government economist estimates that fully 70 percent of the inputs needed for Vietnam's exports by both domestic and foreign companies are imported from China.

China is also a major supplier for inputs in agriculture, which makes up nearly 20 percent of Vietnam's economy and a quarter of its exports. Chinese companies provide seeds, fertilizer, pesticides, fish seedlings, baby chickens, and much of the agricultural machinery used by Vietnamese farmers. "The price is quite good, but the quality sometimes isn't," says Hanoi-based agricultural expert Dang Kim Son. He says Vietnamese consumers are particularly concerned about the health effects of the extensive use of pesticides on Chinese farms.

Meanwhile, Vietnam's exports to China reached $64.4 billion in 2018, making China Vietnam's largest export market ahead of the European Union and the United States.[28] China's major imports from Vietnam were

---

26. Gavin Bowring, "Vietnam Yields Cautionary Tale over Chinese Investment," *Financial Times*, November 27, 2014, https://www.ft.com/content/6ea71dd6-ccea-3779-87be-d4654fc9379b.

27. International Monetary Fund, "Imports, CIF from Partner Countries," *IMF Data*, 2014–2018, http://data.imf.org/regular.aspx?key=61013712; International Monetary Fund, "Exports, FOB to Partner Countries; Imports, CIF from Partner Countries," *IMF Data*, 2014–2018, http://data.imf.org/regular.aspx?key=61013712.

28. Ibid.

electronic equipment, cotton, medical equipment, rubber, and footwear.[29] This gave China a $20 billion trade surplus with Vietnam, a figure that has risen rapidly in recent years.

Tensions between the two countries affect Vietnam's exports to China from time to time, says a government economist. During the oil rig crisis, China suspended the import of fruit and vegetables from Vietnam. In late 2016, China stopped importing live pigs from Vietnam, citing "quality" concerns, the economist says, adding, "This caused the domestic price to fall dramatically." He volunteers that Beijing may have suspended the trade in pigs to press Hanoi to suspend the oil exploration activities by Spanish oil company Repsol in the South China Sea.

When Vietnam joined the Trans-Pacific Partnership (TPP) trade talks with 11 other partners, including the United States and Japan, Beijing protested privately against Hanoi's move, according to Vietnamese officials. Interestingly, however, Chinese companies adopted a strategy different from their government: They moved some of their garment manufacturing operations to Vietnam to take advantage of the fact that Vietnam would be granted zero or near-zero tariffs for its clothing exports to the United States under the agreement. A government economist estimated that Chinese firms invested almost $1.3 billion in textile facilities in two provinces north of Ho Chi Minh City and one southwest of Hanoi to take advantage of the TPP.

It was Vietnam's heavy dependence on trade with China that prompted Hanoi to join the TPP in the first place. Trump's withdrawal from the trade deal within days of taking office in 2017 was a "shock" to Vietnam because it would have lowered tariffs for many Vietnamese exports, providing Vietnam's products a "huge benefit" in the U.S. market and helping balance the country's dependence on China, says Thanh. The TPP would also have provided more guarantees to investors from the United States and other member countries, giving non-Chinese foreign firms an incentive to invest in Vietnam, Hanoi hoped.

Washington's withdrawal prompted Hanoi to press ahead with the remaining 10 TPP members to launch the Comprehensive and Progressive Trans-Pacific Partnership that went into force at the end of 2018. Vietnam, a prolific negotiator of free-trade deals, also pursued other trade agree-

---

29. "Top China Exports," World's Richest Countries, 2019, http://www.worldsrichestcountries.com/top_china_exports.html.

ments with the European Union, Japan, and the Regional Comprehensive Economic Partnership with its Southeast Asian neighbors and Australia, China, Japan, Korea, and New Zealand.

Vietnam is expected to get at least an initial boost from the trade war that erupted in mid-2018 between China and the United States, two of the country's biggest commercial partners who combine to buy about a third of Vietnam's exports. In some sectors like garments, footwear, and furniture, China and Vietnam are competitors. Unless Chinese firms slash their costs, their Vietnamese competitors should benefit in the U.S. market.

"Vietnam will have a tiny benefit in the short run," says Thanh. "We will export more to both China and the United States, but in the long-term China will find replacement markets."

About $5 billion of Vietnam's exports to China, roughly 15 percent of the total, flow through the global supply chain that sells products on to the U.S. market. Domestic and foreign companies that export into the supply chain will likely be hurt by the trade war.[30]

The increased U.S. tariffs on Chinese goods has caused the U.S. dollar to appreciate against China's currency, which made Chinese goods cheaper in Vietnam, causing an initial surge of Chinese exports to Vietnam. Hanoi's central bank has devalued the Vietnamese currency against the U.S. dollar to increase the competitiveness of products from Vietnam, but economists warn this will also increase the cost of imports for domestic production. As the Trump administration has threatened more tariffs on Chinese goods, Vietnamese officials are anxious about a possible flood of Chinese clothing, furniture, and other products into their market.[31]

There have already been some signs of trade diversion of U.S. products from China to Vietnam, which benefits Vietnamese consumers. "Because U.S. goods can't find a market in China, chicken wings, chicken legs, beef, and soy beans are becoming cheaper in Vietnam," observes the China expert in Hanoi.

---

30. "Edmund Malesky on Vietnam Economy," *Asia Experts Forum*, October 23, 2018, http://asiaexpertsforum.org/edmund-malesky-vietnam-economy/.

31. Ibid.; Bloomberg, "Vietnam Goes on the Defence amid U.S.-China Trade War," *Straits Times*, July 18, 2018, https://www.straitstimes.com/asia/se-asia/vietnam-goes-on-the-defence-as-china-and-us-clash-on-trade?&utm_source=google_gmail&utm_medium=social-media&utm_campaign=addtoany.

Washington will be watching if there will be a diversion of Chinese products through Vietnam to avoid U.S. tariffs. Vietnam attracted the attention of U.S. trade officials a few years ago, ahead of the recent trade spat, as it became clear that dozens of factories around the southern coastal city of Vung Tau were importing steel from China, galvanizing it, and exporting it to the United States. This prompted Washington to slap tariffs on Vietnamese steel exports to the U.S. market.[32]

Vietnam is also expected to benefit as companies manufacturing in China shift their production bases to avoid U.S. tariffs. "We're getting more inquiries from manufacturing companies that want to relocate their facilities to Vietnam," says Dung Duong of CBRE Vietnam, whose U.S.-based parent company is one of the world's largest commercial real estate firms. Hang Sinh Business Service Center in Ho Chi Minh City guided some 80 manufacturers from China seeking tariff workarounds to set up shop in various industrial parks between September and late November 2018.[33]

China's GoerTech, an Apple equipment manufacturer, has informed suppliers that it plans to move its AirPod wireless earphone assembly to Vietnam.[34] Foxconn, another Apple contract manufacturer, is reportedly considering setting up a new facility in Vietnam to prevent the iPhone from being hit by U.S. tariffs.[35] Eclat Textile, which supplies apparel to Nike and Adidas, pulled out of China in late 2016 and has begun sourcing from Vietnam and Cambodia.[36]

---

32. Chuin-Wei Yap, Scott Patterson, and Bob Tita, "U.S. Accuses Chinese Firms of Rerouting Goods to Disguise Their Origin," *Wall Street Journal*, April 10, 2018, https://www.wsj.com/articles/for-chinese-steel-the-road-to-the-u-s-goes-through-vietnam-1523352601?shareToken=st58e59780836443aea6d50e3c4f44fd74&reflink=article_email_share; "Edmund Malesky on Vietnam Economy."

33. Megan Cassella, "Chinese Companies Find a Tariff Workaround," *Politico*, November 29, 2018, https://www.politico.com/newsletters/morning-trade/2018/11/29/chinese-companies-find-a-tariff-workaround-434691.

34. Cheng Ting-Fang and Lauly Li, "Apple Supplier Seeks to Escape Trade War Fallout with Shift out of China," *Nikkei Asian Review*, October 12, 2018, https://asia.nikkei.com/Economy/Trade-war/Apple-supplier-seeks-to-escape-trade-war-fallout-with-shift-out-of-China.

35. Malcolm Owen, "Foxconn Mulls Vietnam Move for iPhone Production to Avoid Effects of U.S. Tariffs," *AppleInsider*, December 4, 2018, https://appleinsider.com/articles/18/12/04/foxconn-mulls-vietnam-move-for-iphone-production-to-avoid-effects-of-us-tariffs.

36. Kenji Kawase, "How Asian Companies Are Navigating the Trade War," *Nikkei Asian Review*, September 19, 2018, https://asia.nikkei.com/Spotlight/Cover-Story/How-Asian-companies-are-navigating-the-trade-war.

While China's economic growth undoubtedly will be dented by the trade conflict with the United States, Chinese border provinces see a potential opportunity. Kunming and Guangxi are hoping to launch seven economic cooperation zones along their border with Vietnam. The Chinese think these zones could provide protection for industrial firms against Trump's tariffs.

The mayor of the Chinese border town of Pingxiang said he hopes these zones will allow for "a free flow of workers, capital and materials." He said the products produced in this zone could be labeled as "made in Vietnam" or "made in China." The mayor hopes U.S. tariffs and the establishment of these border zones will give the border region an economic shot in the arm. Local Chinese officials anticipate that working along the border will shield Chinese companies from the protests they face operating in more populated areas of Vietnam.[37]

So far, Vietnamese officials have been less enthusiastic about these zones than the Chinese. Hanoi wants to avoid Washington mounting an investigation into exports to the U.S. market from the border zones being labeled as originating in Vietnam to avoid American tariffs when the products were produced in China.

In real estate development in Vietnam, Chinese companies have played a more limited role than in Cambodia and Laos, where firms from China have invested heavily in hotels, apartment blocks, and office buildings. Vietnamese developers dominate the sector, at least in part because they have access to more developments sites. Anti-China sentiment among Vietnamese may also make Chinese investors wary of developing high-profile property projects.

But in the high-end condominium sector, the role of Chinese buyers jumped in 2018. In the first nine months of 2018, 31 percent of buyers of luxury condos sold by CBRE Vietnam were from mainland China, making them the single largest group of buyers. This figure is up from only 4 percent in 2017 and 2 percent in 2016, the year after Vietnam allowed

---

37. Bình Nguyên, "Tỷ lệ người Trung Quốc mua nhà ở TP.HCM tăng đột biến," *Zing.vn*, December 11, 2018, https://news.zing.vn/ty-le-nguoi-trung-quoc-mua-nha-o-tphcm-tang-dot-bien-post899322.html; He Huifeng and Keegan Elmer, "Has China Found a Trade War Loophole? Officials Tout 'Made in Vietnam' Zones on Border amid U.S. Tensions," *South China Morning Post*, July 9, 2018, https://www.scmp.com/news/china/economy/article/2154463/chinese-officials-tout-made-vietnam-zones-border-amid-trade-row.

foreigners to buy into this sector. In the two years before 2018, Vietnamese investors made up the single largest group of buyers.[38]

So why the sudden burst of interest in luxury condos in Ho Chi Minh City? Dung, CBRE Vietnam's senior director, says the first factor is that companies like hers started proactively marketing in China, particularly in Beijing and Shanghai. "We sell many units to people who never came to Vietnam before," she says.

A second reason, Dung says, is the fact that Chinese investors find that Ho Chi Minh City today reminds them of Shanghai three decades ago. A third is that prices for high-end apartments in Ho Chi Minh City cost only half of what they would have to pay in Bangkok and a third of the cost in Singapore.

So, are the Chinese not worried about the anti-China sentiment or renewed protests in Vietnam? "Most of the buyers are investors who don't live in Vietnam," says Dung. "After they buy a unit, they give it back to a professional firm to manage and lease it out." So far Chinese are mainly buying in Ho Chi Minh City and not in other cities like Hanoi and Danang and they are buying mainly luxury condos, not mid-level or lower-end apartments.

At least two Chinese developers, China Fortune Land Development and Country Garden, have opened offices in Vietnam and are exploring opportunities, but they do not seem to have launched any large-scale projects yet, says Matthew Powell of Savills Hanoi, a property management firm. Dung of CBRE says the assumption among real estate developers is that these companies are buying up land in the suburbs of major cities to develop mixed-use townships and industrial parks.

Vietnamese economists assume that Chinese firms are using Vietnamese or Chinese Vietnamese fronts to buy land in resort cities like Danang and Nhatrang because it is illegal for foreigners to buy land directly. Analysts also are convinced that Chinese money is supporting some Vietnamese companies, including ones owned by Chinese Vietnamese.

Vietnam's start-up environment still lags neighbors such as Indonesia and Singapore. But in Vietnam's e-commerce space, China's Alibaba

38. "Press Release about Foreigners Buying Property in Ho Chi Minh City," *CBRE (Vietnam) Co. Ltd.*, December 27, 2018.

Group Holding has been expanding rapidly and is running ahead of U.S. competitors like Amazon. Alibaba entered Vietnam in 2016 and claims to have gained tens of thousands of business partners, compared to some 200 working on the Amazon platform. Alibaba invested $1 billion in Singapore-based Lazada Group, an e-commerce firm that operates widely in Southeast Asia and is the largest e-tailer in Vietnam, controlling 30 percent of the country's online shopping.[39]

Chinese firms are also investing in Vietnamese start-ups. Tiki, an e-commerce platform and the fast-growing retailer in Vietnam, raised $54 million in 2017 from Chinese mega-retailer JD.com Inc. and a Korean investment fund to help consolidate Tiki's market foothold.[40]

Like elsewhere in Southeast Asia, a surge of Chinese tourists is visiting Vietnam. They reached nearly 5 million in 2018, up 24 percent over 2017.[41] But Vietnam, like its neighbors, complains that the local economy benefits little from Chinese "zero dollar" tours.

"A lot of tourists from China don't spend money in Vietnam," says a Vietnamese businessperson involved in the tourist business. "They enjoy our scenery in places like Quang Ninh but eat in Chinese restaurants and shop in Chinese shops," he says, referring to the coastal region of northern Vietnam famous for its thousands of towering limestone islands topped by rain forests. "They use Chinese tour guides who talk about Vietnam through Chinese eyes."

"Chinese tourists make a lot of noise," says an ethnic Chinese tour operator in Cholon, Ho Chi Minh City's Chinatown. "In restaurants they take a lot of food they can't finish. Some hotels want to set aside separate places for the Chinese to eat." In contrast to other tourists, he says "the Chinese like Chinese food more. They only want to try a little Vietnamese food."

The tour operator, who has an office in Beijing, caters mainly to higher-end tourists. He says most of the Chinese tourists prefer to visit the

39. Asia300 News, "Amazon to Enter Vietnam in Challenge to Alibaba," *Nikkei Asian Review*, March 12, 2018, https://asia.nikkei.com/Business/Companies/Amazon-to-enter-Vietnam-to-take-on-Alibaba.

40. "A Guide to Vietnam's Startup Scene," *Tech Collective*, October 8, 2018, https://techcollectivesea.com/2018/10/08/a-guide-to-vietnams-startup-scene/.

41. "Vietnam's Tourism Industry Continues Its Growth in 2018," *Vietnam Briefing*, January 18, 2019, https://www.vietnam-briefing.com/news/vietnams-tourism-industry-continues-growth-2018.html/.

beaches in Danang and Nhatrang, but they do not like visiting the country's mountains. "Today Vietnamese no longer like visiting Nhatrang," he says, about the beach town that was heavily frequented by Russian tourists a decade ago. "It's starting to look like a Chinese city." The tour operator says Danang along the central coast and Do Son in the north are popular destinations because they have casinos, which are important to Chinese tourists throughout Southeast Asia.

A group of Chinese tourists in May 2018 arrived in Cam Ranh, home to a deepwater port developed by the U.S. military during the war, wearing T-shirts depicting China's nine-dash-line claim to the South China Sea, which sparked widespread online anger in Vietnam. The tourists were stopped by immigration officials and told to take off the shirts before they left the airport.[42]

Some Vietnamese called for the tourists to be expelled. Others proposed that Hanoi should develop a code of conduct for Chinese arriving in Vietnam. Several Vietnamese also suggested the government should limit the number of Chinese allowed to visit.[43]

China earlier had begun featuring Beijing's nine-dash-line claims on a map of the disputed sea in Chinese passports. Some Vietnamese immigration officials reportedly have refused to stamp visas in passports depicting this map. In 2016, an immigration official in Ho Chi Minh City is reported to have written a welcome note on the map reading "F*** you."[44]

Chinese hackers responded by depicting messages on the display screens at the airports of Hanoi and Ho Chi Minh City criticizing Vietnam's claims in the South China Sea, Vietnam's Ministry of Transport said. For several hours, airport staff had to avoid using their computers and check passengers in manually.[45]

Despite the negative views of China, it is the top tourist destination for Vietnam's growing middle class. Just short of 2 million Vietnamese

---

42. Agence France-Presse, "Anger in Vietnam after Chinese Tourists Are Spotted in T-shirts with Controversial South China Sea Territory Map," *South China Morning Post*, May 15, 2018, https://www.scmp.com/news/asia/southeast-asia/article/2146258/anger-vietnam-after-chinese-tourists-arrive-airport-wearing.

43. "A Code of Conduct Proposed for Chinese Travelers," *VietNamNet Bridge*, June 15, 2018, https://english.vietnamnet.vn/fms/travel/202400/a-code-of-conduct-proposed-for-chinese-travelers.html.

44. Agence France-Presse, "Anger in Vietnam."

45. "South China Sea: Vietnam Airport Screens Hacked," *BBC News*, July 29, 2016, https://www.bbc.com/news/world-asia-36927674.

visited China in 2017, roughly half the number of Chinese who visited their southern neighbor.[46]

BRITTLE POLITICAL TIES

Despite their sometimes-brittle relations, Vietnam was the first country President Xi visited after he consolidated power at the Communist Party of China congress in October 2017. This was Xi's third visit to Vietnam in six years, and he received a 21-gun salute at the start of his visit to Hanoi the following month after the end of the Asia-Pacific Economic Cooperation (APEC) summit in Danang in central Vietnam.

Despite the pomp that greeted the Chinese leader, he was kept cooling his heels for half a day while Vietnam shoehorned U.S. President Trump into a lower-key visit ahead of Xi. He could not have missed the clear signal about Hanoi's dissatisfaction with how it has been treated in recent years.

The leaders of the two countries issued a joint communiqué, but roughly 90 percent of the content was identical to the communiqué after Vietnamese party chief Nguyen Phu Trong visited China in early 2017, an observation made by Hiep, the Singapore-based Vietnam expert.[47] They also signed a dozen cooperation agreements on building a border trade cooperation zone and setting up a working group on e-commerce collaboration. Shortly before Xi's visit, the two countries had signed over 80 deals worth nearly $2 billion that committed about 30 Chinese companies to invest in textiles, agriculture, and other projects.[48]

Hanoi made efforts to embrace a few joint economic initiatives with China during Xi's visit, says Vuving, the Vietnam watcher at the Asia-Pacific Center for Security Studies in Hawaii. "China was trying to use cooperative initiatives to bind Vietnam to China," he says. Beijing pledged to help Vietnam develop a new strain of rice resistant to saltwater in the

46. John Reed, "Rise of the Vietnamese Tourist Points to Growing Middle Class," *Financial Times*, February 13, 2018, https://www.ft.com/content/abaa894e-0fe2-11e8-8cb6-b9ccc4c4dbbb.
47. Hiep, "The Belt and Road Initiative in Vietnam," 4.
48. Kristin Huang, "China, Vietnam Sign Cooperation Pacts in Bid to Play Down South China Sea Tensions," *South China Morning Post*, November 14, 2017, https://www.scmp.com/news/china/diplomacy-defence/article/2119868/china-vietnam-sign-cooperation-pacts-bid-thaw-ties.

Mekong Delta in the south to help mitigate the impact of climate change in the fertile low-lying region.

"But China wanted much more," says a senior Vietnamese Communist Party official, who asked not to be identified. "They wanted us to declare Vietnam and China as a 'community of common destiny with strategic significance.'" (The phrase "with strategic significance" seems to have been added specifically for Vietnam, Cambodia, and Laos to the formulation about "a community of common destiny," which Xi used in a speech in 2013 at a conference discussing China's relations with its neighbors.)[49]

Vietnam stood its ground, but officials say they keep looking over their shoulders for more support from the United States in balancing China. "The presence of the U.S. Navy in the South China Sea is important, but it's not enough to change the picture on the ground," the senior party official said. "It does not prevent China's military buildup and [China] from expanding its control on the sea."

"In the absence of a clear U.S. strategy, Southeast Asian countries have no choice but to manage their relations with China and to try to avoid confrontation," the official continues. "The U.S. is the only power that can get China to adjust its strategy and policy. The U.S. needs a comprehensive approach, but Trump is focusing on the trade deficit."

Vuving says Vietnam has stepped up its contacts with both China and the United States since Trump's election, although the nature of Hanoi's relations with the world's two largest powers is very different. "Trips to the U.S. are focused on fact-finding because there's uncertainty about the Trump administration. They want to pull the administration into closer relations with Vietnam," he says. "Vietnam sees the U.S. as one way to get out of China's orbit and to help Vietnam modernize."

Furthermore, "on the China side, there's more of a Chinese demand to intensify contact at all levels in Vietnam," Vuving says. "The Chinese are using engagement as a way to nurture personal relations with Vietnam rather than as a way to strengthen friendship between the two countries. They use personal relations with individual officials and bribery as a way to buy people. People in Vietnam are very suspicious."

---

49. Jacob Mardell, "The 'Community of Common Destiny' in Xi Jinping's New Era," *The Diplomat*, October 25, 2017, https://thediplomat.com/2017/10/the-community-of-common-destiny-in-xi-jinpings-new-era/.

Considering the yawning gap between China and Vietnam, there is little likelihood that they can reestablish deep ties any time soon. The focus on economic reform and development by the Communist parties of both countries has weakened their shared communist ideology, Hiep said. Nationalism has become the key tenet of both parties' "domestic legitimacy" and has driven each of them to protect their national sovereignty and territorial integrity in the South China Sea. In the end, "national interests rather than shared communist ideals now dictate how the two communist parties view and manage bilateral relations," wrote Hiep.[50]

"As China keeps rising, its regional geostrategic rivals, most notably the United States, Japan and India, step up their strategic relations with Vietnam as part of their efforts to counteract China's increasing power and influence," Hiep continued. "Feeling mounting pressure from China in the South China Sea, Vietnam is open to such diplomatic and strategic powers, which tends to push Hanoi away from Beijing."[51]

As Vietnam deepens its ties with Washington, Tokyo, and other powers, China "feels the need to pull Vietnam back into its orbit," said the Singapore-based analyst. "While trying to expand in the South China Sea, China also tries to at least keep Vietnam within its reach and persuade Hanoi about the strategic benefits of maintaining close ties with Beijing, while staying away from its strategic rivals, especially Washington." On Vietnam's side, Hanoi feels the need to "embrace" China more closely to "assure Beijing of its balanced foreign policy while guarding against the latter's reactions," Hiep said.[52]

The oil rig crisis in 2014 marked the lowest point in China-Vietnam party relations in years. Senior leaders speaking at the Vietnamese Communist Party congress in January 2016 described the South China Sea as the biggest challenge facing Vietnam. At the Shangri-la Dialogue in Singapore that June, Deputy Defense Minister Nguyen Chi Vinh, a senior lieutenant general, said Vietnam must "struggle openly with a constructive spirit" in its relations with China while looking for "common points in strategic interests."[53]

50. Hiep, "The Belt and Road Initiative in Vietnam," 6.
51. Ibid.
52. Ibid.
53. Derek Grossman, "Can Vietnam's Military Stand Up to China in the South China Sea?," *Asia Policy* 13, no. 1 (January 2018): 117.

Before the January 2016 Vietnamese party congress, the Chinese party studied the situation in Vietnam, says the former party official who long worked on party-to-party ties. "They concluded that in economic reforms, China was ahead of Vietnam. But in political reforms Vietnam was ahead."

The Chinese comments about political reform in Vietnam referred, among other things, to the emergence of a raft of online petitions in the months leading up to the party congress. These petitions, posted by leading intellectuals and prominent personalities, covered topics ranging from bauxite mining by Chinese companies in the central highlands to land expropriation from farmers by Vietnamese officials and territorial disputes with China.

One petition by a group of 72 prominent intellectuals and former officials commented on the government's plans to revise the country's constitution. They prepared a draft constitution calling for a "society based on democracy, equality and rule of law," protecting human rights and limiting the state's ability to expropriate land. The draft, which was signed by some 15,000 people, omitted any reference to the party serving as the sole "force leading the state and society."[54]

Chinese officials confirm that these online petitions in Vietnam created heartburn in China. "Friends in China told me that democratic reform in Vietnam was too risky," the retired Vietnamese party official said. "I told them I didn't think political reforms in the two countries should be done in the same way. The two countries are very different," he said, adding, "They told me that what we were doing in Vietnam created pressure in China. Many were criticizing Xi's policies. They wanted democracy like we had in Vietnam."

The Chinese communists also warned their Vietnamese counterparts about getting too close to the Americans. "They told us to be careful with the United States," the former party and China expert said. "I responded that I fought against the Americans and you didn't. I understand them better than you do."

The former official says the two neighbors do not seriously discuss their relations with Cambodia and Laos, despite decades of competition between Hanoi and Beijing for influence in these two neighbors. "We just

54. Jason Morris-Jung, "Online Petitions: Promoting a Public Voice in Vietnamese Politics," *ISEAS Perspective*, no. 38 (2015): 4–6, https://www.iseas.edu.sg/images/pdf/ISEAS_Perspective_2015_38.pdf.

mention Laos and Cambodia as our 'mutual friends,'" says the former party official. Vietnamese analysts say Vietnam is gradually losing the battle thanks to China's growing economic clout. They see Phnom Penh under Cambodian prime minister Hun Sen as basically in "China's pocket," while they say Laos is still trying to balance ties between the two communist neighbors.

In recent years, the two parties have begun having annual dialogues between representatives of the two politburos focusing on issues such as communist theory and national development. The Chinese party offers the Vietnamese party scholarships to study in China and each year Hanoi sends a few students. On the government side, Hanoi and Beijing hold many ministerial exchanges each year. "These are beneficial to both sides and help us see what China is doing," the retired official says.

"The Chinese know Vietnam does not have a favorable attitude toward China and they know Vietnam doesn't like to be forced to do something," the former party official says. "The bigger China gets the more pressure we feel. One way we fight back is through party-to-party channels."

Since normalizing their relations in the early 1990s following their 1979 border war, the two countries have established a hotline linking their governments and parties and have launched annual consultations between party international affairs departments, foreign ministries, ministries of public security to discuss crime, and border provincial governments.[55]

In recent years, China has frequently hosted seminars on techniques for controlling online speech for foreign officials and journalists, including from Vietnam. Officials from Vietnam attended a seminar on media management in China in April 2017, and not long after Hanoi introduced a new cybersecurity law that was passed in mid-2018.[56] Still, Vietnam does not ban Facebook and Twitter, which are blocked in China, but Hanoi has put pressure on Internet companies to remove sensitive content. Unlike China, Vietnam also does not block Gmail accounts or access to the online editions of *The New York Times* and other foreign newspapers.

---

55. Le Hong Hiep, "Vietnam's Hedging Strategy against China since Normalization," *Contemporary Southeast Asia* 35, no. 3 (2013): 350.
56. Adrian Shahbaz, "Fake News, Data Collection, and the Challenge to Democracy," *Freedom House*, October 2018, https://freedomhouse.org/report/freedom-net/freedom-net-2018/rise-digital-authoritarianism.

Vietnam's cybersecurity law requires tech companies like Facebook and Google to store user data in Vietnam, bans users from organizing people for "anti-state purposes," and does not allow them to use the social media services to "negate the country's revolutionary achievements." Foreign tech companies are required to turn over user data to the Ministry of Public Security if it requests this information.[57]

In early 2019, Google agreed to remove a game from its app store in which players could combat characters named after the nation's political leaders.[58] Foreign companies are reluctant to cross swords with Vietnam because of its massive potential. A 2018 report by Google and Temasek Holdings of Singapore said that online commerce, ride hailing, media, and gaming in Vietnam in 2018 totaled $9 billion and was forecast to reach $33 billion by 2025.[59]

China and Vietnam may be communist comrades, but that does not mean that Beijing spares its neighbor from cyber hacking. In 2017, a Chinese hacker group spammed Vietnamese officials with phishing e-mails in an attempt to understand their strategy in upcoming trade talks, according to U.S. cybersecurity firm FireEye. The hackers e-mailed two Word documents in Vietnamese that contained malware in the hope officials would open them and effectively provide the attackers access to the user's computer or network.

What the hackers were after was Vietnam's negotiating tactics and talking points ahead of Hanoi's hosting of the APEC summit in November that would be attended by the U.S. and Chinese presidents, FireEye reported. They also wanted to understand Vietnam's stance ahead of upcoming talks in the Regional Comprehensive Economic Partnership, a

57. John Reed, "Vietnam Cyber Security Law to Restrict Facebook and Google," *Financial Times*, June 12, 2018, https://www.ft.com/content/28edfa20-6e26-11e8-92d3-6c13e5c92914.
58. Timothy McLaughlin, "Under Vietnam's New Cybersecurity Law, U.S. Tech Giants Face Stricter Censorship," *Washington Post*, March 16, 2019, https://www.washingtonpost.com/world/asia_pacific/under-vietnams-new-cybersecurity-law-us-tech-giants-face-stricter-censorship/2019/03/16/8259cfae-3c24-11e9-a06c-3ec8ed509d15_story.html?utm_term=.6401930b8081.
59. Rajan Anandan, Rohit Sipahimalani, Samuele Saini, Srikanth Aryasomayajula, and Well Smittinet, "e-Conomy SEA 2018: Southeast Asia's Internet Economy Hits an Inflection Point," Google-Temasek, November 2018, https://www.thinkwithgoogle.com/intl/en-apac/tools-resources/research-studies/e-conomy-sea-2018-southeast-asias-internet-economy-hits-inflection-point/, 7.

trade agreement that includes China, Vietnam, and 14 other Asia-Pacific nations.[60] Separate hacking attacks around the same time targeted a range of Vietnamese companies, including financial firms.[61]

Vietnamese officials, like their counterparts in some other Southeast Asian countries, say that a chunk of China's efforts to win investment or infrastructure projects or garner support for China's policies is conducted through bribes and offers of women. "China is the master of money and beautiful ladies," says a former Vietnamese official who was offered a suite in a hotel complete with a stunning female "roommate" when he visited on official business several years ago. When he rejected the woman assigned to his room, he said his visit became strained and was not very successful.

BEIJING STEPS UP PRESSURE IN THE SOUTH CHINA SEA

In June 2019, a massive Chinese coast guard ship, the *Haijing* 35111, arrived off the coast of southern Vietnam, in an area of the South China Sea called Vanguard Bank, where a Japanese rig was drilling an offshore well under a contract with Russian energy firm Rosneft. The coast guard vessel and other Chinese ships began harassing the rig and the ships servicing it and continued these activities on and off for several months. The Chinese vessels used provocative maneuvers to pressure Vietnam and Rosneft to end the drilling.

When the *Haijing* 35111 failed to convince Rosneft to stop its operations, another Chinese vessel, the *Haiyang Dizhi* 8, appeared off the Vietnamese coast and began conducting its own survey for oil and gas on the seabed. The area was within Vietnam's 200-nautical-mile exclusive economic zone (EEZ), but it also fell inside China's nine-dash-line claim. The survey ship was accompanied by vessels belonging to the Chinese coast guard and the People's Armed Forces Maritime Militia, a paramilitary force

---

60. Kevin Collier, "China Is Boosting Its Phishing Attacks—against Vietnam," *Buzzfeed News*, August 22, 2017, https://www.buzzfeednews.com/article/kevincollier/chinas-cut-its-cyber-attacks-on-us-now-vietnam-is-a-target#.wl6RlzZyl4.

61. Reuters, "Chinese Cyber Spies Broaden Attacks in Vietnam, Security Firm Says," *Straits Times*, August 31, 2017, https://www.straitstimes.com/asia/se-asia/chinese-cyber-spies-broaden-attacks-in-vietnam-security-firm-says?&utm_source=google_gmail&utm_medium=social-media&utm_campaign=addtoany.

using fishing boats. Vietnam sent its own coast guard vessels to protect its rig and trail the Chinese survey ship. The standoff created a tense situation in which a collision could have happened.

Similar harassment by Chinese vessels took place off the coast of Malaysia's Sarawak State where a Royal Dutch Shell subsidiary was conducting drilling operations. Later, another Chinese survey vessel began surveying an area of the continental shelf claimed by Malaysia and Vietnam. These maneuvers were tracked by the Asia Maritime Transparency Initiative of the Center for Strategic and International Studies (CSIS) using the identification signals transmitted by the vessels.[62]

Neither China nor Vietnam appeared ready to back down. Keeping Rosneft from buckling under Chinese pressure was critical to Vietnam's offshore energy industry, which supplies about one-tenth of the country's energy needs. Over the previous decade or so, several foreign oil companies had given up their offshore energy blocks off Vietnam's coast under pressure from China.

The goal of China's harassment activities off the coasts of Vietnam and Malaysia appeared aimed at convincing these two South China Sea claimant states to end their energy exploitation activities whether they were carried out by domestic firms or in partnership with international companies, says Collin Koh Swee Lean, a South China Sea expert at the S. Rajaratnam School of International Studies in Singapore. As China has developed its own offshore, deepwater energy exploration capabilities, Beijing hopes it "might be able to win over the cooperation of these South China Sea rivals in undertaking joint energy development, without the involvement of mostly Western multinationals," Koh says.

China's pressure against Vietnam appeared to have worked earlier. In March 2018, Vietnam abruptly suspended an oil and gas exploration project conducted by the Spanish oil firm Repsol off the country's southeastern coast in block 07-03. Just days before the project was halted about 40 Chinese naval vessels and submarines accompanied the Liaoning aircraft carrier from Hainan for a demonstration of China's naval power in South China Sea. It was one of the largest naval exercises ever conducted

---

62. Gregory B. Poling and Murray Hiebert, "Stop the Bully in the South China Sea," *Wall Street Journal*, August 28, 2019, https://www.wsj.com/articles/stop-the-bully-in-the-south-china-sea-11567033378.

Map 7. Vietnam's claims in the South China Sea

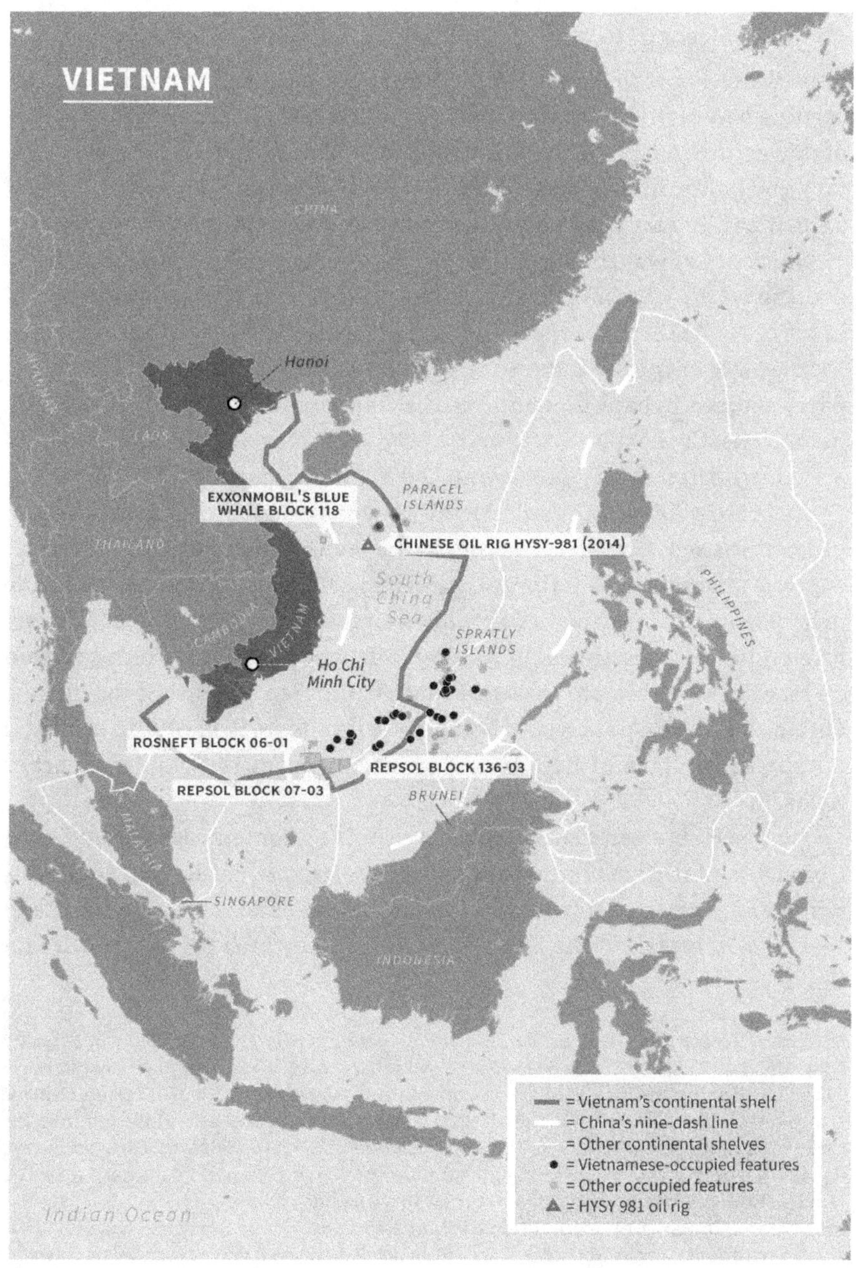

by China and it was operating only a few days' sail from the Repsol project site.[63]

But Vietnamese party leaders had decided to postpone drilling at the Repsol site a month before the Chinese flotilla set sail from Hainan, according Vuving. They made their decision based on "the overall balance of power," including the balance between Chinese and Vietnamese military and paramilitary forces at the Repsol drilling site. Vietnam's leaders agreed not "to take the risk at this time," Vuving says.

Block 07-03 was the second Repsol project where Vietnam suspended drilling within nine months. Work on the first block (136-03) was stopped in July 2017. At that time, Beijing had reportedly threatened to attack some Vietnamese outposts in the South China Sea. The politburo of Vietnam's party seemed to back down to avoid a confrontation with China shortly before the Chinese Communist Party congress met in October and Vietnam hosted the APEC summit the following month.

In a rare public comment, PetroVietnam said after the second Repsol project was scuttled that tensions in the South China Sea would hurt its exploration and exploitation work. "The East Sea is forecast to continue to have uncertainty this year . . . affecting the company's efforts to attract foreign investors to invest in its open offshore fields," the company said on its website. (Vietnam calls the South China Sea the East Sea.) PetroVietnam said the dispute would complicate its efforts to maintain crude oil output in the face of dropping production from the country's other fields.[64]

No issue between China and Vietnam is as contentious as the South China Sea. Maritime boundaries and sovereignty over the Paracel Islands (which Beijing snared from the former U.S.-backed regime in southern Vietnam in 1974) and the Spratlys (which are located further south and

63. James Pearson and Greg Torode, "Exclusive—Satellite Images Reveal Show of Force by Chinese Navy in South China Sea," *Reuters*, March 27, 2018, https://uk.reuters.com/article/uk-china-defence-exclusive/exclusive-satellite-images-reveal-show-of-force-by-chinese-navy-in-south-china-sea-idUKKBN1H3133; Bill Hayton and Chatham House, "China's Intimidation in the South China Sea Poses an Economic Threat to Vietnam," *East Asia Forum*, April 25, 2018, http://www.eastasiaforum.org/2018/04/25/chinas-intimidation-in-the-south-china-sea-poses-an-economic-threat-to-vietnam/.

64. Reuters, "In Rare Comment, PetroVietnam Says South China Sea Tension to Hurt Offshore Operations," *Straits Times*, April 3, 2018, https://www.straitstimes.com/asia/se-asia/in-rare-comment-petrovietnam-says-south-china-sea-tension-to-hurt-offshore-operations?&utm_source=google_gmail&utm_medium=social-media&utm_campaign=ad.

some of whose features are also claimed by Brunei, Malaysia, the Philippines, and Taiwan) remain intractable. Vietnam's efforts to exploit the hydrocarbon resources of the sea and China's determination to block Hanoi's moves have prompted frequent conflicts between these two neighbors.

The South China Sea is of critical strategic significance to Vietnam. The country has a 2,000-mile coastline with the South China Sea and the Gulf of Thailand. China invaded Vietnam from the sea several times between the tenth and thirteenth centuries, as did the French colonial forces in the mid-nineteenth century.

Hiep, the Singapore-based academic, said Vietnamese strategic planners are convinced that maintaining a hold on the South China Sea will help Hanoi restrain China despite its military superiority. The Vietnamese also fear that losing control of the Paracel and Spratly island groupings in South China Sea would hamper Vietnam's international trade routes to the Pacific and Indian Oceans and would make it possible for China to impose a blockade against the country, Hiep said.[65]

In a bid to bolster its dominance in the disputed 1.4 million-square-mile South China Sea, Beijing since 2013 has conducted extraordinary levels of dredging and artificial island building in the Spratlys, transforming seven reefs into island fortresses, including some complete with air and naval bases. The dredging generated some 3,200 acres of new land and three of the artificial islands in the Spratlys are fortified with anti-ship cruise missiles (YJ-12B ASCM) and surface-to-air missile systems (HQ-9B SAM) along with underground tunnels, missile shelters, and radar.[66]

China has also dredged hundreds of acres of new land in the Paracels,[67] deploying anti-ship and surface-to-air missiles and expanding harbors,

---

65. Hiep, "Vietnam's South China Sea Disputes with China: The Economic Determinants," *Korean Journal of Defense Analysis* 26, no. 2 (June 2014): 177.

66. Asia Maritime Transparency Initiative, "China Island Tracker," Center for Strategic and International Studies, https://amti.csis.org/island-tracker/china/#Spratly%20Islands;%20 https://missilethreat.csis.org/china-installs-first-missile-systems-in-spratly-islands/ (accessed October 20, 2019); Frances Mangosing, "Exclusive: New Photos Show China Is Nearly Done with Its Militarization of South China Sea," *Inquirer*, February 5, 2018, https://www.inquirer.net/specials/exclusive-china-militarization-south-china-sea.

67. Asia Maritime Transparency Initiative, "China Island Tracker: Paracel Islands," Center for Strategic and International Studies, https://amti.csis.org/island-tracker/china/#Paracel%20Islands (accessed October 20, 2019).

radar, and other infrastructure. In May 2018, Beijing aired footage of an H-6K long-range strategic bomber landing on Woody Island in the Parcels, a first for China's air force.[68] Beijing has also increasingly deployed advanced J11 fighters to Woody Island.

Hanoi is anxious that Beijing could use these enhanced military capabilities to seize other islands and features in the South China Sea currently controlled by Vietnam and the other Southeast Asian claimants. (In the Spratlys, Vietnam occupies twenty-one features, the Philippines nine, China seven, Malaysia five, and Taiwan one.)[69]

Beijing's naval, air, and missile modernization efforts allow China to project its power further and begin to challenge the United States in the South China Sea. Using radar, satellites, and missiles, Beijing has developed "anti-access" capabilities that have neutralized the edge that U.S. aircraft carrier groups long maintained. The commander of the U.S. Indo-Pacific Command, Admiral Philip Davidson, said in comments to the Senate in March 2018 that "China is now capable of controlling the South China Sea in all scenarios short of war with the United States."[70]

The United States, whose strategic interests in the South China Sea is to guarantee freedom of navigation and secure sea-lanes of communication, conducts freedom of navigation exercises and provides support to the Southeast Asian claimants in the disputed sea. Washington also supports the negotiations on a code of conduct between China and the 10 countries in the Association of Southeast Asian Nations (ASEAN).[71]

The U.S. Energy Information Agency has estimated that the South China Sea holds about 190 trillion cubic feet of natural gas and 11 billion barrels of oil in proved and probable reserves. It says that most of these

---

68. Ian Storey, "Vietnam under Increasing Pressure from China in the South China Sea," ISEAS-Yusof Ishak Institute, May 25, 2018, https://www.iseas.edu.sg/medias/commentaries/item/7647-vietnam-under-increasing-pressure-from-china-in-the-south-china-sea-by.
69. Alexander L. Vuving, "South China Sea: Who Occupies What in the Spratlys?," *The Diplomat*, May 6, 2016, https://thediplomat.com/2016/05/south-china-sea-who-claims-what-in-the-spratlys/.
70. U.S. Senate Committee on Armed Services, "Advance Policy Questions for Admiral Philip Davidson, USN Expected Nominee for Commander, U.S. Pacific Command," April 17, 2018, 11, https://www.armed-services.senate.gov/imo/media/doc/Davidson_APQs_04-17-18.pdf.
71. Council on Foreign Relations, "Territorial Disputes in the South China Sea," Global Conflict Tracker, https://www.cfr.org/interactive/global-conflict-tracker/conflict/territorial-disputes-south-china-sea (accessed October 20, 2019).

reserves are situated relatively near the countries that form the rim of the sea rather than under disputed islets and reefs.[72]

For Vietnam, access to the oil and gas resources in the sea is critical to help meet the growing energy needs of the country's surging economy. Repsol had estimated earlier that block 07-03 contained some 45 million barrels of oil and 172 cubic feet of gas.[73] Now, instead of boosting its hydrocarbon output, Vietnam is expected to owe the Spanish firm as much as $500 million for work already carried out on the two blocks.

But Vietnamese officials insist they have not given up interest in the two Repsol blocks. "We just stopped temporarily," says the China expert in Hanoi. "Maybe we'll push again at an appropriate time."

In recent years, Beijing has pressed countries with which it has overlapping claims in the South China Sea to jointly develop disputed areas even though the 1982 United Nations Convention on the Law of the Sea (UNCLOS) gives them the right to develop the areas on their continental shelf. A Chinese Vietnam expert describes China's policy regarding the dispute as based on the principle to "shelve differences and develop [resources] jointly." President Rodrigo Duterte of the Philippines has been exploring this possibility, but Vietnam has sought to go it alone.

In May 2018, China warned Russian oil company Rosneft against conducting oil exploration activities in block 06-01 issued by Vietnam in the South China Sea without Beijing's permission. Rosneft was drilling in a block from which Vietnam already gets 30 percent of the country's gas needs from operations begun 15 years earlier. Rosneft, which works on several ventures with Chinese firms in China, operates Vietnam's 06-01 which is jointly controlled with India's Oil and Natural Gas Corporation and state-owned PetroVietnam. So far, China does not seem to have tried to stop Rosneft's activities off the Vietnamese coast.[74]

---

72. South China Sea Expert Working Group, "A Blueprint for Cooperation on Oil and Gas Production in the South China Sea," Center for Strategic and International Studies—Asia Maritime Transparency Initiative, July 25, 2018, https://amti.csis.org/a-blueprint-for-cooperation-on-oil-and-gas-production-in-the-south-china-sea/.

73. Bill Hayton, "South China Sea: Vietnam 'Scraps New Oil Project,'" *BBC News*, March 3, 2018, https://www.bbc.com/news/world-asia-43507448.

74. Andrew Kemp, "Beijing Warns Rosneft over Drilling in South China Sea," *Newsbase*, March 23, 2018, https://newsbase.com/topstories/beijing-warns-rosneft-over-drilling-south-china-sea; James Pearson, "As Rosneft's Vietnam Unit Drills in Disputed Area of South China Sea, Beijing Issues Warning," *Reuters*, May 16, 2018, https://uk.reuters.com/article/us-rosneft-vietnam-southchinasea-exclusv/as-rosnefts-vietnam-unit-drills-in-disputed-area-of-south-china-sea-beijing-issues-warning-idUKKCN1II09H.

ExxonMobil in 2017 entered into an agreement with Hanoi for the Blue Whale (block 118) integrated-gas-for-power development project, some 55 miles off the coast of central Vietnam. According to the company's estimates, the field has enough gas to supply power to a city the size of Hanoi for more than 20 years. Production is slated to begin in 2023 and will be transported by pipeline to power four power plants planned for several locations around Danang in central Vietnam.[75]

ExxonMobil said in early 2019 that it had awarded Saipem, an Italian oilfield service provider, the contract for front-end engineering and design for the project, while the U.S. oil giant is filing permits and applications for the proposed work. Liam Mallon, president of ExxonMobil Development Company, said the project would bring "cleaner, reliable power to help drive economic growth" in Vietnam. Mallon said the project is expected to generate $20 billion revenue for the Vietnamese government along with thousands of local jobs and improved energy security.[76]

ExxonMobil's final investment decision is expected in 2020, depending on regulatory approvals, Vietnamese government guarantees and agreements on gas sales. Block 118 is about half inside and half outside China's nine-dash-line claim. But the area where ExxonMobil plans to drill is understood to be outside of China's nine-dash line and, so far, Beijing has not publicly protested the project.

"Vietnam very much wants to keep the Russian and American oil companies operating" off its coast, says a Western diplomat in Hanoi. "They believe that the U.S. government would offer strong support for a U.S. oil company" against any pressure from China.

It is only since the late 1980s when Vietnam began exploiting oil and gas in the South China Sea and developing fisheries and tourism that the disputed sea has taken on increased economic significance for Vietnam. In 2012, the National Assembly passed the country's sea law that affirms Vietnam's sovereignty over the Paracel and Spratly archipelagos and jurisdiction over the South China Sea in accordance with UNCLOS.[77]

75. "Ca Voi Xanh Project Overview," ExxonMobil, November 28, 2018, https://corporate.exxonmobil.com/en/Locations/Vietnam/Ca-Voi-Xanh-project-overview#projectOverview.

76. "Exxon Presses Ahead with Blue Whale Development with Saipem FEED Deal (Vietnam)," *Offshore Energy Today*, January 30, 2019, https://www.offshoreenergytoday.com/exxon-presses-ahead-with-blue-whale-development-with-saipem-feed-deal-vietnam/.

77. Hiep, "Vietnam's South China Sea Disputes with China," 178.

Vietnam's first commercial quantities of oil were pumped in 1986 from the Bach Ho well east of the Mekong Delta in the South China Sea. Vietnam's oil and gas production developed quickly, and by 2010 PetroVietnam had become the country's largest corporation, contributing some 20 percent of the country's economy and roughly a quarter of the government's revenue. As Vietnam's economy grew and oil and gas became more important to the country's development, PetroVietnam stepped up its exploration and exploitation of energy resources in the South China Sea, often through joint ventures with foreign oil firms.[78]

China started putting pressure on Vietnam's oil projects in the disputed sea as early 1992, when Beijing signed an agreement with Crestone Energy Corporation of the United States to launch exploration activities in the Tu Chin basin, which Vietnam claimed was on its continental shelf.[79]

Two years later, China sent two warships to block supplies being ferried to a Vietnamese oil rig operating in an area about 280 miles off the coast of southern Vietnam.[80] The site was being developed by a consortium of companies led by Mobil of the United States before it merged with Exxon. In 1997, China sent a floating oil platform to drill in block 113 off the coast of Hue in central Vietnam, but it withdrew the vessel after Hanoi mounted a diplomatic protest.

Hanoi moved in May 2009 to extend its claim to the South China Sea and the resources on its seabed by lodging two submissions (one was submitted jointly with Malaysia) with the United Nations Commission on the Limits of the Continental Shelf. Beijing rejected the submissions by Vietnam and Malaysia as a violation of China's sovereignty.

Beijing has long proposed to Hanoi the idea of shelving disputes for joint development in disputed areas. Hanoi rejected this proposal because China focused on Vietnam's EEZ and continental shelf, which the Vietnamese did not perceive as disputed areas. Hanoi views joint exploration with Beijing as "a trap," says Vuving.

---

78. Ibid., 179–180.

79. Nicholas D. Kristof, "China Signs U.S. Oil Deal for Disputed Waters," *New York Times*, June 18, 1992, https://www.nytimes.com/1992/06/18/world/china-signs-us-oil-deal-for-disputed-waters.html.

80. Philip Shenon, "China Sends Warships to Vietnam Oil Site," *New York Times*, July 21, 1994, https://www.nytimes.com/1994/07/21/world/china-sends-warships-to-vietnam-oil-site.html.

China opposes joint exploration in the Paracels, which China controls but Vietnam also claims, but Beijing is very interested in joint exploration on the continental shelves of Vietnam and the Philippines and in the Spratlys. "From the Vietnamese perspective, joint exploration would be tantamount to an implicit acknowledgment that the area of exploration is under dispute," Vuving says. "The Vietnam position is that its continental shelf is not a disputed area."

"If it was purely a commercial deal that would be fine," says Thanh, the economist. "But China won't admit to our sovereignty [even on our continental shelf]."

Not able to convince Vietnam to participate in joint development, China launched several actions to warn Hanoi to recognize the risks of operating unilaterally. In May 2011, Chinese maritime surveillance vessels cut the seismic cable of PetroVietnam's exploration vessel operating in block 148, 80 miles off southeast coast of Vietnam.[81] In December 2012, two Chinese fishing vessels cut the cables of the same vessel engaged in seismic exploration activities about 40 miles from Con Co Island off Vietnam's Quang Tri Province.[82]

In an attempt to restrain Chinese actions against Vietnam's oil exploration and exploitation activities, PetroVietnam actively pursued deals with foreign partners. In the dozen years after 1988, the Vietnamese oil firm signed nearly 100 contracts with companies from the United States, Russia, the United Kingdom, India, and several other countries.[83]

China responded by using its economic heft to press some of these foreign oil firms to abandon their work in Vietnam. Leaked cables from the U.S. Embassy in Hanoi reported that beginning in 2006, China lobbied oil companies, including ExxonMobil, BP, Chevron, and Petronas of Malaysia, to cancel oil exploration contracts with Vietnam.

ExxonMobil, for example, was told that if did not cancel its deal with Hanoi, it could risk losing business with China. The U.S. oil giant did not

81. Alex Watts, "Vietnam Accuses China of Sabotage," *Sydney Morning Herald*, June 2, 2011, https://www.smh.com.au/world/vietnam-accuses-china-of-sabotage-20110601-1fgec.html.
82. Jeremy Page, "Vietnam Accuses Chinese Ships," *Wall Street Journal*, December 3, 2012, https://www.wsj.com/articles/SB10001424127887323717004578157033857113510.
83. Hiep, "Vietnam's South China Sea Disputes with China," 180.

pull out, but the cables reported that five other contacts were suspended or canceled.[84]

Beyond hydrocarbons, the South China Sea is also rich in marine life. Bordered by a half dozen countries inhabited by roughly 2 billion people, the sea is one of the top-five most productive fishing areas in the world. It supports the livelihoods of people living near its shores, enhances food security, and boosts of the exports of nations along its rim.[85]

In 2012, the value of the catch in the South China Sea was estimated at about $21.8 billion, with China accounting for roughly 45 percent. Intensive fishing has reduced marine resources to about 5 to 30 percent of their levels in the 1950s. Illegal, unreported, and unregulated fishing accounted for about 8.1 million tons a year between 2000 and 2010 and seriously threatened the sea's ecosystem.[86]

Vietnam has an estimated one million fishers with some 120,000 fishing boats trying to make a living in Vietnam's EEZ and beyond.[87] As the fish stocks in the South China Sea have been depleted and neighboring countries have stepped up exploitation of the remaining marine life in the sea, more fishing spats have erupted, including between China and Vietnam. Since about 2005, both countries invested heavily in helping their fishing companies build high-capacity offshore fishing boats that they hoped would help defend their sovereignty around the Paracel and Spratly archipelagos.

Many incidents have taken place around the Paracels as Chinese law enforcement vessels chased or detained Vietnamese fishers operating around the Chinese-controlled islands. In the five years prior to 2010, China detained 63 fishing boats and 725 fishers from one province in central Vietnam alone.

The number of arrests of Vietnamese fishers has increased since 1999, when China began implementing a unilateral annual fishing ban in a

84. Greg Torode, "Beijing Pressure Intense in South China Sea Row," *South China Morning Post*, September 23, 2011, http://www.scmp.com/article/979876/beijing-pressure-intense-south-china-sea-row.

85. U. Rashid Sumaila and William W. L. Cheung, *Boom or Bust: The Future of Fish in the South China Sea* (Vancouver: University of British Columbia, 2015), 1, https://drive.google.com/file/d/0B_oUJE4kCTZrbVI4N2tTVjlpYTA/view.

86. Ibid., 1–2.

87. Grossman, "Can Vietnam's Military Stand Up," 115.

large swath of the South China Sea, a move Vietnam protests each year.[88] In May 2018, Beijing reported that 10 fishing boats from Vietnam had been expelled from a disputed area around the Paracels in the first joint operation involving the Chinese navy and coast guard.[89]

Vietnamese fishers often "serve on the frontlines" as they struggle to make a living in a competition with a bigger and better equipped Chinese fishing fleet, "one engaged in paramilitary work on behalf of the state rather than the commercial enterprise of fishing," Gregory Poling of CSIS said in a report released in early 2019. The study, a joint venture with Vulcan, Inc., used underutilized tracking technology such as Synthetic Aperture Radar and Visible Infrared Imaging Radiometer Suite to gather data on fishing in the South China Sea.

The report found "a significant amount of activity" around Vietnam-occupied reefs in the southwest area of the Spratlys, the central Spratlys where both China and Vietnam have outposts, and in the northeast around the island grouping where the Philippines and Vietnam occupy features. Poling and his colleagues concluded that the "imagery shows that Chinese fishing vessels account for the largest number of vessels operating in the Spratlys by far."

China makes no secret about the operations of its militia and that "some of the best-trained and equipped members engage in overt paramilitary activities such as the harassment of foreign vessels operating near Chinese-held islets," the study pointed out. "Their numbers in the Spratly Islands are much larger and much more persistent than is generally understood," Poling adds.

"As they race to pull the last fish from the South China Sea, fishers stand at least as much chance of triggering a violent clash as do the region's armed forces," Poling said. "And that has become even more likely as significant number of fishing vessels in the area forgo fishing full-time to serve as a direct arm of the state through official maritime militia."[90]

---

88. Hiep, "Vietnam's South China Sea Disputes with China," 183.
89. Storey, "Vietnam under Increasing Pressure."
90. Gregory B. Poling, "Illuminating the South China Sea's Dark Fishing Fleets," Center for Strategic and International Studies—Stephenson Ocean Security Project, January 9, 2019, https://ocean.csis.org/spotlights/illuminating-the-south-china-seas-dark-fishing-fleets/.

CHINA'S DAMS THREATEN THE MEKONG DELTA

The Mekong River, the longest river in Southeast Asia, could become another source of friction over water and resources between Beijing and Hanoi. China's efforts to harness the upper Mekong (known as the Lancang in China) for hydropower threatens the survival of the fertile Mekong Delta in southern Vietnam that produces half of Vietnam's rice and much of its fruit and seafood.

The 2,700-mile river begins in the Tibet plateau in northwestern China before flowing through Myanmar, Laos, Thailand, Cambodia, and Vietnam and out into the South China Sea. Fed by monsoon rains for six months a year, the Mekong provides livelihoods for some 60 million people along its banks and on its watershed, who rely on the river for water, silt and irrigation for their crops, fish, and transport.

In the Mekong Delta of southern Vietnam, the river supports one of the world's richest farming areas and some 18 million people. The low-lying plain of over 15,000 square miles intersected by rivers and canals has been created by mountains of silt, some of it carried down the river all the way from the Himalayas. The delta, roughly the size of Denmark, is covered by rice fields that produce three crops a year, feeding the country and supplying the rice that has turned Vietnam into one of the planet's largest rice exporters. Because the delta is barely above sea level, it is highly vulnerable to saltwater intrusion from the South China Sea, particularly during the dry season.

China in recent decades has expanded its influence over the Mekong by building 11 hydropower dams on the upper reaches of the river that produce about 15,000 megawatts of electricity. In addition, Chinese companies are building and financing about 6 of the 11 dams planned on the mainstream of the Mekong in Laos and Cambodia. Collectively, these dams have the potential to create an environmental and economic disaster for farmers forging their livelihoods in the Mekong Delta. The dams are prompting debate and creating controversy downstream because they are expected to curtail the arrival of fish and reduce the sediment that provides nutrients for crops and a buffer against saltwater intrusion from the sea.

Some security analysts see China's dam construction on the Mekong as the "second front" added to Beijing's militarization of the islands in the South China Sea to pressure Vietnam, the one country in Southeast Asia that has not been intimidated or bought up by Beijing. For China, "the dams have political objectives that go beyond financial justification," says a foreign analyst in Hanoi. By providing loans for the dams in Laos and Cambodia, "China has built interdependency" and in effect further isolated Vietnam.

China's "damming of the Mekong and gaining undue leverage over downstream countries is analogous and connected to its ongoing construction and weaponization of artificial islands in the South China Sea," said Thitinan Pongsudhirak, a political scientist at Thailand's Chulalongkorn University. Beijing's strategy in both the South China Sea and along the Mekong, he says, is to "build first, talk later."[91]

Water from the China section of the Mekong contributes about 18 percent of the water flow in the river in the Southeast Asian countries during the rainy season and up to 40 percent during the dry season, according to a study by Mekong River Commission (MRC), an intergovernmental body covering Laos, Thailand, Cambodia, and Vietnam, but not China.[92]

Nguyen Huu Thien, an independent Vietnamese ecologist and expert on the Mekong Delta, notes that in a normal year the Chinese-built dams that have storage reservoirs can reduce the "flood peaks" during the monsoon season and release more water during the dry season, thus helping reduce saltwater intrusion that threatens the delta's crops.

However, during a period of heavy floods, the dams will need to release water to protect their structures, causing "double flooding" downstream, says Thien, who studied conservation biology and sustainable development at the University of Wisconsin. During a drought, the dams will store water in their reservoirs, causing a worsening of the drought downstream.

In 2016 and 2017, the Mekong Delta faced its worst drought in 90 years, which devasted its crops. China offered to release some water from its reservoirs and Vietnam accepted the offer. But experts say no water made it. It takes roughly 28 days for water from China to reach the South China Sea, and as it travels down much of it is lost to tributaries along the way so that little water makes it to Cambodia, let alone the Mekong Delta.

91. Yukako Ono, "Mekong River Nations Face the Hidden Costs of China's Dams," *Nikkei Asian Review*, May 9, 2018, https://asia.nikkei.com/Spotlight/Cover-Story/Mekong-River-nations-face-the-hidden-costs-of-China-s-dams.

92. Mekong River Commission, *Mekong: Climate Change Adaptation Strategy and Action Plan* (Phnom Penh: Mekong River Commission, November 2017), 19, http://www.mrcmekong.org/assets/Publications/MASAP-book-28-Aug18.pdf.

But some of the biggest threats of the mainstream dams to the Mekong Delta are disruption to the sediment flows and fish migration. A study by the MRC found in 2014 that the sediment load was about 72 million tons a year, down from an earlier estimated 160 million tons a year. The authors attributed the sharp drop to "the capture of sediment in the Lancang cascade of hydropower dams" in China.[93]

Another MRC study shows that the cascade of dams expected to be completed by 2020, including in Laos and Cambodia, will cut sediment flows by another 10.2 million tons per year. The sediment load that will reach the Mekong Delta will be 33 percent of the 2007 level. The amount trapped by the mainstream hydropower dams in both Laos and Cambodia in 2040 is estimated at 47.1 million tons per year, or 97 percent of the total sediment load. In other words, only 3 percent of 2007 level of sediment will reach the Mekong Delta by 2040.[94]

The impact could be devastating. Thien says this "sediment hunger" will cause "severe erosion of river banks and along the coast in the Mekong Delta," allowing a surge of saltwater from the South China Sea to inundate fields and ravage crops. Thien warns that 50 percent of the delta could be "eroded away" by the end of this century. "The delta might disappear altogether in about 200 years."

Sediment flushing around the dams in China and Laos could help, but so far none of them have this capability. Experts are surprised that Vietnam apparently did not press for sediment flushing, particularly in Laos where it has considerable political clout.

But the dams in China, Laos, and Cambodia also create other challenges for people living along the river. Because the dams block the migration of fish, they will trigger a sharp decline in fisheries in the countries south of China of between $16.5 billion and $22.6 billion over 24 years, according a 2018 MRC study.[95] Thien, citing other MRC studies, estimates that the

93. Mekong River Commission Secretariat, "Summary Report of the Decision Support for Generating Sustainable Hydropower in the Mekong Basin," November 14, 2014, 3.

94. Mekong River Commission, "Short Technical Note: Mekong Sediment from the Mekong River Commission Study,"8, https://www.mrcmekong.org/assets/Publications/Mekong-sediment-from-the-MRC-Council-Study-Technical-notedocx.pdf (accessed August 12, 2019).

95. Mekong River Commission, *The Council Study: The Study on the Sustainable Management and Development of the Mekong River Basin, including Impacts of Mainstream Hydropower Projects: Macro-economic Assessment Report (Final Report)* (Phnom Penh: Mekong River Commission,

Mekong Delta's entire white fish catch of 220,000 to 440,000 tons a year, worth between $660 million and $1.3 billion, will be wiped out.

Beyond providing income, the fish are also an important source of protein for the delta population and their disappearance will create "an ecological disaster as many of the species of the biodiversity of the delta depend on the fish," Thien says. Other scholars estimate that the losses to fisheries from the dams on the Mekong are bigger than the gains from electricity.

"The Mekong is a national security issue as serious as the South China Sea," says Thien. "The Mekong is disappearing in a physical sense. I can't imagine how Vietnam is going to survive without the Mekong Delta. It's the food basket of the country."

With the upstream dams threatening the agricultural future of the Mekong Delta, environmentalists are perplexed why Hanoi, which is so strategic in building diplomatic support to oppose China's assertiveness in the South China Sea, has not harnessed its clout to slow the construction of mainstream dams in Laos and Cambodia. Vietnam has protested but work on the Xayaburi Dam in Laos, for example, continued at full throttle until it began operating in 2019.

Foreign environmental experts in Hanoi say recent developments in Laos and Thailand have created a new window of opportunity for Vietnam to promote lower-risk energy and water agreements with Laos and Cambodia that will not hobble economic growth. For starters, Thailand, which is the primary customer of electricity from the dams in neighboring Laos, is reviewing its power plans and is indicating it may stop investing in more hydropower in Laos.

Second, several dam collapses in Laos and Myanmar have highlighted the risks facing these barrages, which are likely to increase under climate change and more intense rainfall. Third, the cost of renewable energy sources such as solar and wind is now as cheap, if not cheaper, than hydropower. Fourth, with more sources for energy available, hydropower dams can be used to supplement intermittent supplies of electricity from solar and wind.

"The question . . . is not hydro versus no hydro," says one expert, "but which hydro projects, and how does hydro fit with an optimal energy mix."

2017), 7, http://www.mrcmekong.org/assets/Publications/Council-Study/Council-study-Reports-discipline/180207-Macroeconomic-Assessment-Report-final-5-MG-2.pdf.

If Thailand reduces its buying of hydropower from Laos, Vietnam could emerge as the only major export market for Laos. This hands Hanoi leverage to negotiate an agreement with Vientiane under which Vietnam would import more electricity in exchange for a commitment by Laos to stop considering construction of dams that threaten the future of the Mekong Delta.

As part of this agreement, Hanoi could offer to boost its investment in Laos in non-hydro renewables using Vietnam's increasing manufacturing capacity in solar panels and wind turbines. This could help Laos become a green "battery" of Southeast Asia in which both countries would benefit. Similar agreements could be negotiated with Cambodia, experts say.

This strategy would help Vietnam meet its soaring energy demand, which is expected to double to 90 gigawatts by 2030, and at the same time reduce the country's dependence on polluting coal plants installed by Chinese companies that are prompting protests in southern Vietnam.

"As the country with the most to lose from poorly planned hydropower development and the most [to] offer in terms of scientific and technological expertise, Vietnam is ideally placed to lead the negotiations," says Brian Eyler, a Mekong expert at the Stimson Center in Washington and author of a recent book on the Mekong. "But no agency has the mandate to coordinate an all-of-government response to take advantage of this window of opportunity."

Eyler adds that Vietnam could readily find support for this strategy from countries interested in "energy diplomacy," including Japan, the European Union, and the United States.

At a meeting in mid-2018, the ruling Communist Party of Vietnam is understood finally to have elevated the challenge facing the Mekong Delta to a national security risk facing the country. Some government offices are said to have been criticized for being "disorganized and complacent" in their handling of the issue.

To be sure, the dams are not the only threats the Mekong Delta faces. Another is climate change.[96] A 2016 report on climate change and

96. Mekong River Commission, *Mekong: Climate Change Adaption Strategy and Action Plan* (Phnom Penh: Mekong River Commission, 2018), 19, https://www.mrcmekong.org/assets/Publications/MASAP-book-28-Aug18.pdf.

sea-level rise scenarios in Vietnam by the Ministry of Natural Resources and Environment estimated the actual sea-level rise at only about three to four millimeters a year.[97]

But a more recent survey that calculated land elevation based on satellite readings produced by Climate Central, a New Jersey-based science organization, and published in the *Nature Communications* journal projected much more dire conclusions. It estimated that southern Vietnam, including much of Ho Chi Minh City, Vietnam's economic hub, would disappear and that the land on which over 20 million live on would be inundated.[98]

"Vietnam sees climate change as a security threat," says Eyler.

Another threat is overly intensive farming and large-scale irrigation practiced in the delta, which is depleting the soil and raising questions about the sustainability of the region as a farming powerhouse. These "development missteps" have prompted the government to shift from "focusing on maximizing production" to "focusing on quality and the [food] value chain," Thien says.

Still, the biggest challenge is the dams. "The impact from the dams will be permanent and irreversible once the dams are built," Thien warns. "The reduction of the sediment threatens the physical existence of the delta through erosion."

The dam developers have tried to calm public anxiety by talking about sediment gates to allow sediment to flow downstream uninhibited and fish ladders to allow fish to migrate. But, so far, "none of these are proven technologies for a large tropic river such as the Mekong," argues Thien. Unless effective alternatives are found, the inhabitants of the Mekong Delta could face a bleak future.

---

97. Tran Thuc, Nguyen Van Thang, Huynh Thi Lan Huong, Mai Van Khiem, Nguyen Xuan Hien, and Doan Ha Phong, *Climate Change and Sea Level Rise Scenarios for Viet Nam* (Hanoi: Ministry of Natural Resources and Environment, 2016), 35, https://www.researchgate.net/profile/Thuc_Tran/publication/318875854_Climate_Change_and_Sea_Level_Rise_Scenarios_for_Viet_Nam_-_Summary_for_Policymakers/links/5a3cadbaa6fdcc21d878b167/Climate-Change-and-Sea-Level-Rise-Scenarios-for-Viet-Nam-Summary-for-Policymakers.pdf.

98. Denise Lu and Christopher Flavelle, "Rising Seas Will Erase More Cities by 20150, New Research Shows," *New York Times*, October 29, 2019, https://www.nytimes.com/interactive/2019/10/29/climate/coastal-cities-underwater.html.

CHINA KEEPS VIETNAM'S MILITARY UP AT NIGHT

The militaries of China and Vietnam carry "a ton of historical baggage," observes a foreign military observer in Hanoi. Vietnamese officers remember well China's invasion of Vietnam's northern provinces in 1979 and the gunning down of more than 60 Vietnamese sailors at Johnson South Reef in 1988. More recently, they got heartburn from the arrival of a giant oil rig off the coast of Danang in 2014 and the threats in 2017 when Beijing was pressing Hanoi to abandon a Spanish oil company's exploration activity on Vietnam's continental shelf.

Military ties between the two countries are relatively superficial. "China claims they have brotherly ties," says the military analyst. "On the surface, Vietnam's military relations with China are good, but it keeps Vietnam awake at night."

As with other Southeast Asian countries, China has stepped up its military diplomacy with Vietnam in recent years, particularly through high-level meetings. The two countries' defense ministers launched an annual strategic defense dialogue in 2010 that serves as a venue for the two militaries to build trust and develop more levels of cooperation. A deliverable from one of these dialogues was the inauguration of a hotline in case of tensions in the South China Sea.[99]

Despite their strained ties, Vietnam had the sixth most frequent number of military encounters with China between 2003 and 2016, according to a 2017 study of China's military diplomacy published by the U.S. National Defense University's Center for the Study of Chinese Military Affairs.[100] In Southeast Asia, the frequency of Vietnam's encounters with the Chinese military were second only to Thailand.

By far, the largest number of encounters between China and Vietnam—54—were senior-level meetings. China had the same number of senior-level meetings during these years with Thailand, while holding 37 with Singapore, 33 with Indonesia, and 35 with Malaysia.[101] Despite their

99. Hiep, "Vietnam's Hedging Strategy," 349.
100. Kenneth Allen, Phillip C. Saunders, and John Chen, *Chinese Military Diplomacy 2003–2016* (Washington, DC: National Defense University Press, 2017), 45, https://ndupress.ndu.edu/Portals/68/Documents/stratperspective/china/ChinaPerspectives-11.pdf?ver=2017-07-17-153301-093.
101. Ibid., 62.

differences over the South China Sea, the Vietnamese and Chinese armed forces have adopted "guidelines on fundamental principles to settle maritime disputes." The two countries have also been talking about extending the boundary around the mouth of the Gulf of Tonkin, agreed to in 2000, and about implementing an oil and gas cooperation agreement in the gulf, but without making progress.[102]

"These meetings are more about meeting than substantial cooperation," says Vuving of the Asia-Pacific Center for Security Studies in Hawaii. "They can't really cooperate because they are enemies. They meet to make an impression that they are good neighbors." Vuving says the Chinese and Vietnamese deal with "three fronts" in their strategic planning: their land border, their disputes in the South China Sea, and their competition over Cambodia and Laos. "Vietnam and China are at loggerheads on all these fronts."

The two militaries also share a few activities that might qualify as low-level joint exercises. They have an annual joint border exercise that includes a border patrol with each side's soldiers operating on their own side of the border. The border patrol in 2017 was canceled at the last minute because Hanoi angered Beijing when it refused to agree to China's demands that Vietnam abandon the first Repsol exploration project. The joint patrols resumed in late 2018.

The communist neighbors had two military exercises between 2003 and 2016, compared to China's twenty-one with Thailand, of which five were combat exercises, and sixteen with Indonesia, which included three combat exercises.[103] The Chinese navy had four port calls to Vietnam in that fourteen-year period, in contrast to nine to both Singapore and Thailand and six each to Malaysia and Indonesia.

China hoped to have a naval ship port call to Vietnam in late 2018, some months after a U.S. aircraft carrier visited Danang, but the Vietnamese postponed the port call, saying the military was preoccupied with reorganizing the Ministry of National Defense.

Training of Vietnamese officers in China is limited. "It doesn't include any professional training," says the foreign military analyst in Hanoi. "The Vietnamese mainly learn Chinese."

102. Carlyle A. Thayer, "Background Briefing: Vietnam: Relations with the United States and China," Thayer Consultancy, May 3, 2018, https://www.scribd.com/document/380023942/Thayer-Vietnam-Relations-With-the-United-States-and-China, 2.
103. Allen, Saunders, and Chen, *Chinese Military Diplomacy 2003–2016*, 52.

China's moves since about 2000 to create a navy with more warships and submarines than those of the U.S. military, and largely focused on the South China Sea, worry Vietnam. Since late 2013, Beijing has built up four islands in the South China Sea equipped with radar, surface-to-air missiles, and runways long enough to land planes from China's air force.

Even though China's military today has an imposing high-tech cache of weapons, military analysts point out that its ability to use this hardware remains uncertain and untested. China's military has not been tested been since its army's border war with Vietnam in 1979 and its brief naval clash with Vietnamese sailors in 1988.

Timothy Heath, a defense analyst at the RAND Corporation, has written that China's "efforts to overcome the sizable gaps in the quality of its command, training rigor [and] integration . . . could prove important if a conflict drags on." Heath added that the outcome of a long war "will likely be decided by factors beyond the control of generals and admirals, such as economic strength, political cohesion and national resolve."[104]

Vietnam has responded by seeking to deepen its relations with major powers such as the United States, Japan, and India, as well as strengthen its involvement in regional multilateral groupings such as the ASEAN organization.

At the same time, Hanoi has taken steps since a Communist Party resolution in 2007 to boost spending to upgrade the country's maritime and air capabilities, including its coast guard, a significant move away from its earlier preoccupation with building ground forces.[105] Vietnam's goal is "not playing catch-up with China," but rather "minimal deterrence," says Vuving. "They want to build just enough capability to make potential aggressors think twice before attacking them."

Foreign analysts estimate Vietnam's defense budget at between $4.2 billion and $4.9 billion, or roughly 2.3 percent of its gross domestic product. These figures may well be bolstered by Vietnam's income from military-owned companies, which the Ministry of National Defense estimated at $13.7 billion in 2015.[106] One of biggest military companies is

104. Timothy R. Heath, "China's Untested Military Could Be a Force—or a Flop," *Foreign Policy*, November 27, 2018, https://foreignpolicy.com/2018/11/27/chinas-untested-military-could-be-a-force-or-a-flop/.

105. Grossman, "Can Vietnam's Military Stand Up," 117.

106. Ibid., 118.

the Viettel Group, which is the top mobile network operator in Vietnam, with operations in neighboring Laos, Cambodia, and Myanmar as well as in several African, Latin American, and Caribbean countries.

Hanoi realizes it can never hope to match China's technological superiority, so its military modernization is mainly focused on deterring China by convincing Beijing that it will face significant challenges in a battle against Vietnam in the South China Sea. The Vietnamese military has acquired six Kilo-class submarines and a fleet of Su-30MK2 strike fighters from the Russians. Vietnam has obtained K-300P Bastion-P shore-based anti-ship cruise missiles and S-300 surface-to-air missiles to strengthen its anti-access/area denial capabilities, including in parts of the Paracel and Spratly island groupings.[107]

In 2018, Vietnam engaged in modest expansion of Ladd Reef, the westernmost of the occupied rocks and reefs in the Spratlys, including the installation of a 100-foot platform and a channel to facilitate resupply and sheltering vessels. The construction on Ladd Reef brings modest upgrades in recent years to 21 of Vietnam's 49 outposts in the Spratlys.[108]

In addition, Hanoi reportedly reinforced several islands in the Spratlys with mobile EXTRA rocket artillery systems obtained from Israel that are capable of hitting China's runways and military installations in places such as Mischief Reef and Fiery Cross.[109] Vietnam has upgraded its coast guard, which today is larger than the combined coast guards of Indonesia, Malaysia, and the Philippines, and its maritime police forces in the disputed sea.[110]

"By fielding these capabilities, Vietnam has probably achieved its core objective, which is to demonstrate the ability to inflict great harm against [People's Liberation Army] forces in order to deter China from initiating

107. Hiep, "Vietnam's Hedging Strategy," 355. For a more complete list of Vietnam's military acquisitions, see Shang-su Wu, "The Development of Vietnam's Sea-Denial Strategy," *Naval War College Review* 70, no. 1 (Winter 2017): 151.
108. Asia Maritime Transparency Initiative, "Vietnam Expands Another Outpost," Center for Strategic and International Studies, June 13, 2018, https://amti.csis.org/vietnam-expands-another-outpost/.
109. Greg Torode, "Exclusive: Vietnam Moves New Rocket Launchers into Disputed South China Sea—Sources," *Reuters*, August 9, 2016, https://www.reuters.com/article/us-southchinasea-vietnam-idUSKCN10K2NE.
110. Grossman, "Can Vietnam's Military Stand Up," 119.

a confrontation in the first place," RAND Asia defense analyst Derek Grossman said.[111]

But not all military analysts agree that Vietnam has met its "core objective" of achieving "minimal deterrence." Vuving points out that Vietnam's six attack submarines are no match for China's South Sea fleet of 22 submarines, including 16 diesel-electric attack submarines, 2 nuclear-powered submarines, and 4 nuclear-powered ballistic submarines. Vietnam has nearly 50 fourth-generation air superiority aircraft; by comparison, China has nearly 200 similar aircraft in its southern theater air force and South Sea fleet naval air regiment.

If China deployed just 40 percent of its coast guard's estimated total tonnage (which in 2016 was 190,000 tons), it would be twice the size of Vietnam's coast guard, Vuving says. Despite all the military hardware Vietnam has acquired in recent years, "these efforts do not substantially alter the balance of forces between Vietnam and China in the South China Sea," Vuving argues.

Still, Vietnam faces several other critical challenges in the South China Sea, including figuring out what is happening in the sea, known as maritime domain awareness. Vietnam is exploring ways to leverage its significant fishers population to collect intelligence in the South China Sea and in 2013 acquired French-built long-range coastal surveillance radar that can detect ships over 100 miles away.

Vietnam has extended its runway and constructed two hangars on the Spratly Islands, presumably for landing transport and patrol aircraft to boosts its awareness of what is happening in the Spratlys.[112] Hanoi purchased a half dozen Canadian-built amphibious aircraft for medium-range surveillance and is exploring deploying unmanned aerial vehicles and space-based satellites. Despite these new technologies, Vietnam is still struggling to collect "basic intelligence" about what is happening in the disputed sea, Grossman said.[113]

Although Vietnam has achieved impressive results in acquiring and producing new weapons systems quickly, it continues to face challenges in integrating these systems and learning how to deploy them effectively

111. Ibid.

112. Asia Maritime Transparency Initiative, "Updated: Vietnam Responds with Spratly Air Upgrades," Center for Strategic and International Studies, last modified December 1, 2016, https://amti.csis.org/vietnam-responds/.

113. Grossman, "Can Vietnam's Military Stand Up," 128–129.

in air or sea battles. Because this will hobble Vietnam in any prolonged to high-intensity encounter in the South China Sea, Hanoi's top priority is to avoid military conflict at almost all cost. Instead, Vietnam has sought to deepen and expand its defense ties with the United States, Japan, Australia, and India as a hedge against China's assertiveness in the South China Sea.[114]

FRAUGHT HISTORY OF RELATIONS

Vietnam's relations with China are more complex and more regularly beset with disputes than those of any other nation in Southeast Asia, and much of this history continues to have a bearing on their relations today. Everyone in Vietnam remembers that their early history was marked by over 900 years as a Chinese colony.

Today, the Vietnamese admire China's stunning economic success and they often try to emulate Beijing's economic reforms, while at the same time deeply resenting their northern neighbor's frequent condescending attitude and attempts to browbeat them into hitching their destiny to that of China. The Chinese, for their part, often view the Vietnamese as ungrateful and deceptive.[115]

Part of what is northern Vietnam today was seized by the Han dynasty in 111 BC, and despite a few short periods of independence, it only broke free in the tenth century. The Han were attracted in part by the fertile plains and agricultural output of the Red River, but also by the international trade opportunities with Southeast Asia and the Indian subcontinent from the sea coast off northern Vietnam.[116]

The Han authorities could be brutal against locals who refused to submit to their imperial rule, but eventually they realized they would not be able to rule effectively without providing administrative roles to aristocratic families and warlords. Northern Vietnam achieved a new level of development as part of China, as new farming techniques, tools, and improved methods of irrigation were introduced.

Nearly a thousand years of Han influence brought new concepts of law, weapons, paper, architecture, character-based writing, and chopsticks.

114. Ibid., 130.
115. Ian Storey, *Southeast Asia and the Rise of China: The Search for Security* (New York: Routledge, 2011), 101.
116. Christopher Goscha, *Vietnam: A New History* (New York: Basic Books, 2016), 16–17.

Many Chinese words entered the Vietnamese language, and Mahayana Buddhism and Confucian concepts of governance and social harmony arrived during this period.[117]

But even during periods of independence, Vietnam was part of China's tributary system until the French arrived in the mid-nineteenth century. "All Vietnamese emperors sent diplomatic envoys every one or two years to show respect to the central kingdom's authority," says a Chinese Vietnam expert.

The Ming armies, after ousting the Mongols, marched into Hanoi in 1406 and reestablished a harsh Chinese rule that pressed cultural assimilation and burned local books "in an attempt to reset the Vietnamese clock to Chinese imperial time," wrote historian Christopher Goscha.[118] Predictably, resistance emerged against the Chinese occupation by leaders such as Le Loi, who built a strong military force that succeeded in driving out the Ming in 1427. After ousting the Chinese, Le Loi borrowed liberally from the old Chinese order using features from the Confucian model and establishing centralized control of the chaotic country.[119]

The centuries that followed were marked by territorial expansion south, civil wars, the rise of military houses, power grabs, and early waves of Chinese migrants to the region. Internally, instability and rivalry within the Vietnamese state in the nineteenth century allowed the French to move deeper into the region and in 1858 use the persecution of Catholics to justify an attack on the Nguyen dynasty. By 1887, the Vietnam had become a colony of France and part of the Indochinese Union, which also included Cambodia and Laos.[120]

The colonial period gave birth to communist movements in both Vietnam and China, which resulted in close ties developing between the Chinese and Vietnamese revolutionaries in the 1920s and 1930s. At the end of World War II, Vietnamese nationalist leader Ho Chi Minh looked to the Chinese for support to block the return of French rule in Vietnam.

Soon after the Communist Party of China's victory in 1949, Ho began seeking diplomatic support and military supplies from Beijing. China was

117. Ibid., 18–19.
118. Ibid., 30.
119. Ibid., 30–31.
120. Ibid., 45–55, 87.

open to Ho's request for ideological reasons as well as its strategic interest in having a friendly neighbor on its southern flank. The Chinese provided weapons, military advisers, and training that helped Vietnamese revolutionaries known as the Viet Minh defeat the French forces at Dien Bien Phu in 1954. Politically, Chinese advisers helped the Vietnamese communists train cadres to run the party and the state and introduced the concept of rectification campaigns and land reform.[121]

The Chinese led by Zhou Enlai played a critical role in Geneva in trying to help negotiate a political solution to the conflict. To get an armistice, Zhou pressed Ho and his colleagues to abandon plans to speak for their Indochinese neighbors, Cambodia and Laos, and to agree that the 17th parallel could serve a temporary dividing line in Vietnam in the hope this would prevent the Americans from intervening. Many Vietnamese considered this move as a betrayal by China and they became worried that Beijing opposed the creation of a unified Vietnam.[122]

Still, the Vietnamese communists looked to Beijing for military and financial support for the war in the south to which the United States sent more and more troops after 1965. China was also intent on keeping Vietnam from drifting into the Soviet camp after the split between Moscow and Beijing in 1960. As the United States got more involved in the south, the Soviet Union began providing more military hardware to the northern forces and their allies in the south, resulting in Hanoi becoming more dependent on Moscow.

Hanoi was offended when China moved to normalize relations with the United States in 1972 and feared the two governments were cooperating to press the northern Vietnamese forces to accept a peace settlement short of full reunification of the country. Following a peace agreement between the warring Vietnamese factions and Washington and the U.S. withdrawal from the south in 1973, China suspended further military assistance to Hanoi, leaving Vietnam dependent on the Soviets for the equipment it needed to launch its final offensive to topple the U.S.-backed regime in the south.

Then, in 1974, a year before the end of the Vietnam War, China seized the Paracel Islands in the northern reaches of the South China Sea from the regime in the south. By the time communist forces reunified Vietnam

121. Ibid., 252–254.
122. Storey, *Southeast Asia and the Rise of China*, 103–104.

in 1975, Beijing and Hanoi were firmly at loggerheads. Fearing that the Chinese Vietnamese would work with China to sabotage Vietnam's economy, Hanoi moved to nationalize private enterprise, prompting hundreds of thousands of ethnic Chinese, who had played a critical role in developing the south's economy for decades, to escape overland to China or flee by boat.

Khmer Rouge forces in Cambodia who were aligned with China began attacking across the border into southern Vietnam in 1977. To avoid feeling encircled by China, Vietnam signed a friendship treaty with Moscow in 1978 and then counterattacked Cambodia, toppling the Pol Pot regime in Phnom Penh in early 1979 and installing a regime friendly to Hanoi.

Some weeks later, China responded by sending its own troops to attack across Vietnam's northern border to teach their communist neighbor a lesson, heavily damaging five provincial capitals along the border. The Chinese troops faced surprisingly stiff opposition from the Vietnamese, resulting in heavy casualties on both sides. Sporadic fighting along the border continued for the next decade.

Meanwhile, on the Thai-Cambodian border, China worked with Thailand to arm Khmer Rouge and non-communist guerrillas in a fight to continue disrupting Vietnam's occupation of Cambodia. At the same time, the United States, Europe, Japan, and Vietnam's non-communist neighbors maintained economic sanctions against Hanoi to force its withdrawal from Cambodia.

Facing growing economic hardship at home, the Vietnamese Communist Party held a congress in 1986 and decided to withdraw its forces from Cambodia to improve relations with China and the United States, abandon hardline socialist economic policies, and court foreign investors. In 1988, Chinese naval forces attacked Johnson South Reef in the South China Sea and captured it from Vietnamese forces. Some 64 Vietnamese navy personnel died in the skirmish.

Hanoi completed the withdrawal of its troops from Cambodia in 1989, leading to a rapprochement between China and Vietnam two years later when their Communist Party chiefs met for a summit in southern China. Trade across the border blossomed. Beijing and Hanoi agreed in 1993 to begin working to resolve their border disputes, starting with their land border and the Gulf of Tonkin, which the two countries shared.

But the legacies of this border war have continued long after the guns fell silent. The last of hundreds of thousands of land mines laid in China's

Guangxi Province after 1979 were not cleared until October 2018.[123] Meanwhile, Vietnam continues to remember the sailors who died when China attacked on March 14, 1988, as they were delivering construction supplies to Johnson South Reef. Relatives of those killed and military veterans gather annually near Danang on the South China Sea to hold a prayer ceremony and lay wreaths in commemoration of those who died.[124]

The complicated history between China and Vietnam is depicted even in the stories that children are told in Vietnam, including about the outsized role of Chinese in their neighbor's economy. One story portrays China as putting great value on cats. This, the writer says, prompts many Vietnamese to round up cats in their neighborhoods to sell to China. The sharp drop in the number of cats causes the rodent population in Vietnam to soar, forcing the Vietnamese to look to China to buy mousetraps and poison to kill the mice, allowing the Chinese to make a profit.[125]

CHINESE MIGRANTS

Like its neighbors in Southeast Asia, Vietnam has had a significant surge of Chinese migrants in recent decades. The Chinese who live in Vietnam include two basic groupings: One consists of the early migrants who were pushed out of China by social conflict or poverty before and during the period of French colonial rule in Vietnam. A second group is comprised of newer migrants who came south after the two countries normalized relations in 1991, following their border war a dozen years earlier.

The newer migrants include contract workers who were recruited by Chinese companies as China's investment in and trade with Vietnam increased after about 2000. Others were migrants who went to Vietnam on their own seeking opportunity, according to Nguyen Van Chinh of Vietnam National University.[126]

---

123. "China Focus: China's Guangxi Completes De-mining Mission along Sino-Vietnam Border," *Xinhua*, October 26, 2018, https://www.xinhuanet.com/english/2018-10/26/c_137558535.htm.
124. "Vietnam Marks Anniversary of Naval Clash with China over Spratly Island Reefs," *Radio Free Asia*, March 13, 2018, https://www.rfa.org/english/news/vietnam/anniversary-03132018160914.html.
125. Lamb and Dao, "Perceptions and Practices of Investment," 3.
126. Nguyen Van Chinh, "Recent Chinese Migration to Vietnam," *Asian and Pacific Migration Journal* 22, no. 1 (2013): 8–9.

During the 1960s and first half of the 1970s, the Chinese living in the southern part of Vietnam controlled much of the country's rice-milling industry and import-export business. Most Chinese immigrants sought to move to the south, getting as far from China as possible. After Vietnam was divided as part of the peace process in 1954, some 50,000 Chinese from the north moved south.[127]

The Communist Party victory in southern Vietnam in 1975 led to the adoption of hardline economic policies that resulted in the nationalization of about 30,000 Chinese-owned enterprises. An estimated 1.5 million ethnic Chinese were living in Vietnam, of which about 300,000 lived in northern Vietnam in 1975. In the run-up to the 1979 border war, an estimated 300,000 Chinese left Vietnam for China or third countries.[128]

Meanwhile, thousands of ethnic Chinese who lost their businesses at the end of the war were relocated from cities to rural new economic zones. The shutting down of capitalist businesses in southern Vietnam after 1975 created tensions between Hanoi and Beijing as China announced policies to protect overseas Chinese. Beijing's support for ethnic Chinese business activities in Vietnam prompted more to flee as Hanoi moved to eliminate roles the ethnic Chinese had long performed in Vietnam.[129]

When Hanoi launched economic reforms in the late 1980s, many ethnic Chinese returned to doing business, albeit often on a smaller scale than before 1975. Some families began to import technology to modernize manufacturing facilities, leading to the reemergence of larger ethnic Chinese companies focused on hotels and restaurants, trading and services, and traditional medicine. Ethnic Chinese played an increasing role in Vietnam's economy and some reemerged as among the richest families in the country. Many ethnic Chinese businesses used the Chinese network abroad to mobilize capital, import technology, and develop distribution networks.[130]

According to Vietnamese census figures in 2009, just over 820,000 ethnic Chinese lived in Vietnam, down some 40,000 from 1999. About 85 percent of the Chinese lived in the south and around 500,000 lived in

127. Chinh, "The Rise and Revitalization of Ethnic Chinese Business in Vietnam," in *Chinese Capitalism in Southeast Asia: Cultures and Practices*, ed. Yos Santasombat (Singapore: Palgrave MacMillan/Springer Singapore, 2017), 259.
128. Chinh, "Recent Chinese Migration to Vietnam," 9.
129. Chinh, "The Rise and Revitalization," 266–267.
130. Ibid., 268–269.

Ho Chi Minh City.[131] Today the ethnic Chinese account for about 10 percent of the population of the southern commercial hub and run about 30 percent of the city's enterprises.[132]

Separately, as Chinese companies started securing construction projects in Vietnam in the 1990s, they brought contract workers from China, including engineers, managers, and workers. According to Ministry of Labor, Invalids, and Social Affairs statistics, some 75,000 Chinese workers were registered to work in Vietnam in 2010, more than three times the roughly 21,000 in 2005, Chinh said.[133]

Most of these workers were hired on short-term contracts for three months or more. Many Chinese workers said they had overstayed their contracts by one or more years and some had stayed longer than 10 years, moving from one project to the next.

Informally, many Chinese cross into Vietnam to farm or engage in informal trade. Some come to farm cash crops, renting land from Vietnamese farmers; others set up shops, restaurants, and massage parlors. Many Chinese come to offer traditional Chinese healing practices.

In 2005, there were some 168 Chinese clinics in Vietnam, including 52 in Hanoi, with 158 doctors who had studied at the Guangxi Institute of Chinese Traditional Medicine, just across the northern border of Vietnam. In Ho Chi Minh City, inspections of these clinics by the Department of Health found that many had practitioners working without a license and were selling drugs of unknown origin or that had expired, Chinh said.[134]

Many of the more recent migrants have come in search of economic opportunity rather than with the aim of settling in Vietnam. Most of them prefer to keep their Chinese passports rather than apply for citizenship in Vietnam.[135] There are no accurate figures on how many Chinese live in Vietnam today.

Many Vietnamese are anxious about the significant number of Chinese workers who come to Vietnam to work on Chinese projects or in search of economic opportunities. But some Vietnamese also cross the border to work in China, where they appear to be welcome. Chinese news-

131. Chinh, "Recent Chinese Migration to Vietnam," 9.
132. Ibid., 11.
133. Ibid., 14–15.
134. Ibid., 22.
135. Ibid., 24.

papers report that these workers help meet a labor shortage and work for lower salaries. Some 25,000 Vietnamese cross the border every day at the Dongxing crossing in Guangxi Province. While many of them come to trade, some 10,000 are day laborers working in China while living in Vietnam.[136]

Since China and Vietnam normalized their relations in the early 1990s, special economic zones have sprung up on the Chinese side of the border and attracted hundreds of thousands of entrepreneurs. Border towns like Hekou, in the southern tip of Yunnan Province, were transformed into trading hubs populated by local and migrant entrepreneurs engaging in activities ranging from petty trade to hospitality services and transport to construction. By late 2013, Hekou's yearly import-export revenue reached over $1 billion.

Hekou has two "Vietnamese markets" that sell imported goods and delicacies including tropical fruit, hardwood furniture, coffee, and sandals. The upper floors of these markets employ hundreds of young Vietnamese women offering services to satisfy the private needs and curiosity of male clients, according to researchers Caroline Grillot of the Netherlands and Juan Zhang of Australia.

Hekou's sex market is flourishing and has become a "unique attraction" in the border town. The researchers found that for Chinese traders the Vietnamese women "symbolize both the precarious nature of cross border engagement and the thrill of experimenting with illicit desires and pleasures."[137]

BEIJING'S SOFT POWER DIPLOMACY

Much of China's public diplomacy in Vietnam is focused on building support for its signature infrastructure investment projects. Beijing uses a range of "soft power" tools—from people-to-people exchanges to

136. Shan Jie, "Vietnamese Workers Ease Labor Shortage in Guangxi," *Global Times*, October 12, 2017, https://www.globaltimes.cn/content/1070016.shtml.

137. Caroline Grillot and Juan Zhang, "Ambivalent Encounters: Business and the Sex Markets at the China-Vietnam Borderland," in *Chinese Encounters in Southeast Asia: How People, Money, and Ideas from China Are Changing a Region*, ed. Pal Nyiri and Danielle Tan (Seattle: University of Washington Press, 2017), 99.

scholarships for students, official visits, and investment by companies—to bolster its often quite negative image in Vietnam.

When President Xi visited Hanoi in late 2017, he unveiled the $36 million Vietnam-China Friendship Palace—complete with a China Culture Center—in Hanoi. The groundbreaking ceremony was held in 2004 but construction did not begin for another 11 years. Le Hong Hiep, the Singapore-based Vietnam expert, said the palace should be seen "as part of China's 'charm offensive' to improve Vietnamese people's perceptions of China, which seriously deteriorated after the May 2014 oil rig crisis."[138]

The palace was also an attempt to expand China's cultural influence in Vietnam. "Ironically," wrote Hiep, "as the most Sinicized Southeast Asian country, Vietnam is now rather resistant to China's cultural influence, partly due to brewing anti-China sentiments generated by the South China Sea disputes." A proposal by the Ministry of Education and Training to teach Chinese in Vietnamese elementary schools has been rejected by the public, Hiep said.[139]

In tabulating overall levels of China's soft power, the College of William and Mary's AidData research lab's 2018 study on China's public diplomacy found that Vietnam, along with the Philippines, Myanmar, and Laos, receive "substantially lower" levels of engagement than their Southeast Asian counterparts, Indonesia, Cambodia, Malaysia, and Thailand. In this latter grouping, the first three countries receive significant levels of financial diplomacy while Thailand has a high number of Confucius Institutes.[140]

China has established one Confucius Institute based at the Foreign Languages Institute at Vietnam National University in Hanoi, compared with 15 in Thailand and six in Indonesia, to teach Chinese and Chinese culture.[141] "It's very strictly supervised," the Vietnamese China expert

138. Hiep, "Pull and Push: Sino-Vietnamese Relations and President Xi's Hanoi Visit," *ISEAS Perspective*, no. 92 (2017): 5, https://www.iseas.edu.sg/images/pdf/ISEAS_Perspective_2017_92.pdf.

139. Ibid., 5.

140. Samantha Custer, Brooke Russell, Matthew DiLorenzo, Mengfan Cheng, Siddhartha Ghose, Harsh Desai, Jacob Sims, and Jennifer Turner, *Ties That Bind: Quantifying China's Public Diplomacy and Its "Good Neighbor" Effect* (Williamsburg, VA: AidData at William and Mary, June 2018), 19, https://docs.aiddata.org/ad4/pdfs/Ties_That_Bind--Full_Report.pdf.

141. "About Confucius Institute/Classroom," Confucius Institute, 2014, https://english.hanban.org/node_10971.htm.

says of the Confucius Institute in Hanoi. "It is purely about teaching language and is not allowed to reach outside the university."

China promotes a variety of exchanges with Vietnam, from scholarships to study visits for elite Communist Party, government, and military officials as well as youth, journalists, business leaders, schoolteachers, and border guards. Between 2000 and 2015, 286 senior-level officials from China and Vietnam visited the other country, marking the largest number of exchanges among Southeast Asian countries. Thailand had 257, Cambodia 216, and Indonesia 194.[142]

Shortly before the National Assembly was scheduled to consider the ill-fated and wildly unpopular law on SEZs in mid-2018, the Chinese government invited about two dozen Vietnamese journalists to visit China and to explore that country's SEZs. A few of the journalists wrote articles on their return somewhat sympathetic to the Chinese SEZs and were sharply rebuked on Vietnam's social media platforms.

Vietnam had some 10,600 students studying in China in 2016 compared to 23,000 from Thailand and 14,700 from Indonesia.[143] A former Vietnamese party official estimates that about 90 percent of Vietnamese students find their own universities in China, with the balance recruited through government channels.

China's financial diplomacy creates considerable unease in Vietnam, but Beijing still is a significant provider of "official finance with diplomatic intent" for its southern neighbor, particularly in infrastructure. Vietnam ranks fifth among Southeast Asian countries receiving $3.7 billion between 2000 and 2016. Malaysia topped the list at $13.4 billion followed by Cambodia ($9.1 billion) and Indonesia ($9 billion).[144]

In the end, how effective is China's public diplomacy in Vietnam? On one of China's key goals—opening market opportunities for Chinese firms—Vietnam lags most other Southeast Asian countries, according to the AidData study. Vietnam is fifth among Southeast Asian countries in terms of Chinese financial diplomacy and is tied with much smaller Cambodia and Laos in having the lowest number of Confucius Institutes. But Vietnam ranks first in Southeast Asia in the number of diplomatic

142. Custer et al., *Ties That Bind*, 16.
143. Ibid., 13.
144. Ibid., 15.

exchanges with China and fourth in the number of students studying in China.

But in the end, China's public diplomacy efforts among the fiercely nationalistic Vietnamese appear to be severely hamstrung by Beijing's actions in the South China Sea. The 2017 Pew opinion survey found that fully four out of five Vietnamese perceive China's rise as a "major threat" and only one in four see China's expanding economy as a "good thing."[145]

Relations between Hanoi and Beijing have come a long way since they normalized ties in the 1990s. Trade has deepened rapidly, although China's investment, including under the BRI, is still much smaller than in many other Southeast Asian countries. As Storey has observed, "Vietnam has played its cards well: accommodating China's interests when necessary but unafraid to push back in the face of Chinese bullying."[146]

China's assertiveness in the disputed South China Sea leaves Vietnamese leaders with some formidable questions going forward. The repeated protests in Vietnam against China that sometimes turn violent make it clear that something must be done to address the tensions in the disputed sea. It is far from clear that Hanoi's military modernization and its efforts to balance its relations with China through deepened ties with the United States, Japan, and the European countries have weakened Beijing's determination to block Vietnam's attempts to develop its offshore resources.

Hanoi's conflict with a rising superpower on its northern flank that has modernized its military and militarized some of the islands it controls in the South China Sea is not one that Vietnam can expect to win in its wildest dreams. The question facing Hanoi's leaders is whether they can come up with a strategy for dealing with China that will secure its economic development, give it access to its offshore resources, and boost its security in a fraught and dangerous neighborhood.[147]

---

145. Laura Silver, "How People in the Asia-Pacific View China," *Pew Research Center*, October 16, 2017, https://www.pewresearch.org/fact-tank/2017/10/16/how-people-in-asia-pacific-view-china/.
146. Storey, *Southeast Asia and the Rise of China*, 123.
147. Huong Le Thu, "Vietnam Should Update Its South China Sea Strategy," Center for Strategic and International Studies—Asia Maritime Transparency Initiative, December 6, 2018, https://amti.csis.org/vietnam-should-update-south-china-sea-strategy/.

6. THAILAND: "SWIRLING IN THE WIND"

Not long after snaring power in Thailand in May 2014, military junta officials pledged to complete a 550-mile high-speed Chinese rail project within four years. The project, initially priced at nearly $6 billion for the first leg, was designed to connect the Thai northeast to the rail China is building from its southern city of Kunming across Laos to the industrial zone in Thailand's east and down to Malaysia and Singapore in the south.

Construction of the rail link along the length of Thailand, a critical cog in China's ambitious Belt and Road Initiative (BRI), seemed like a no-brainer as junta leaders stepped up their engagement with Beijing at a time when the United States and Europe harped on Thailand's quick return to democracy. But by late 2019, almost nothing had been built as officials from Thailand and China continued to haggle over the financial conditions, whose engineers would oversee the project, land-use rights, and other terms of the project.

China achieved significant advances in its military, economic, "soft power," and political ties with Thailand after the 2014 coup toppled a besieged democratically elected government, a move that prompted the United States and other Western democracies to turn a cold shoulder to Bangkok. No sector picked up steam as rapidly as military collaboration between Beijing and Bangkok as Washington cut funding for training military officers in the United States in response to the coup. The Thai and Chinese air forces for the first time organized a joint exercise in 2015, creating heartburn in Washington that Chinese officers might gain access to sophisticated American fighter jets procured by the Thais.

The joint exercise was soon followed by a $1 billion deal under which Thailand would purchase up to three Chinese-built submarines. U.S. officials were concerned that the subs, which would be accompanied by

Map 8. Thailand

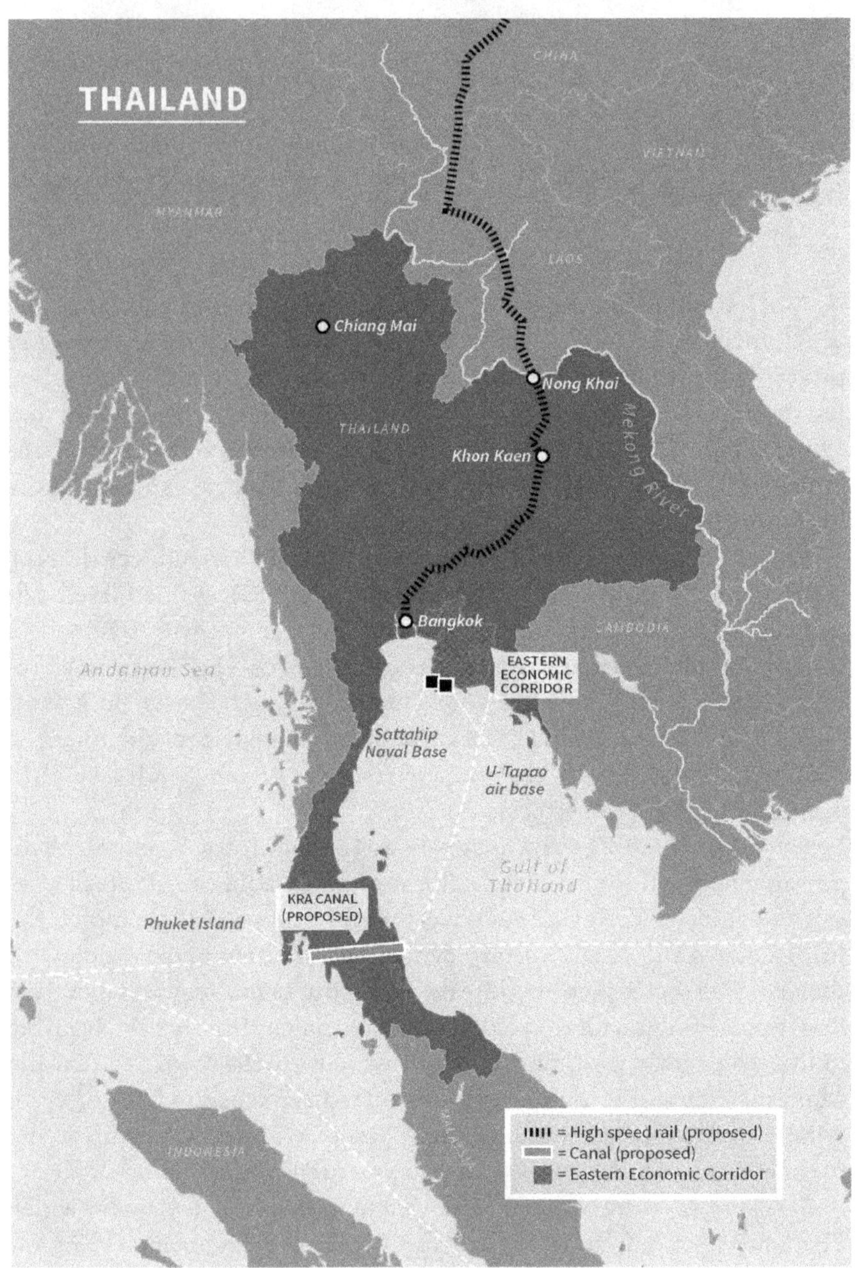

Chinese officers for several years of training, would operate out of Thailand's Sattahip Naval Base. Because many U.S. ships use the base on their way to the Gulf of Thailand, the Americans were concerned that the Chinese navy would be able to snare sensitive information about U.S. naval vessels.

Thailand, with its population of nearly 70 million and boasting Southeast Asia's second largest economy, was a whopping prize for China on the Southeast Asian mainland. Thailand is strategically located at the crossroads between the Pacific and Indian Oceans. It lies at the north end of the critical Strait of Malacca through which roughly one-fifth of global trade passes each year. Thailand is home to the U-Tapao air base, which since the end of the U.S. war in Vietnam, is often used as a stopover by transit flights to South Asia and the Middle East.

Still, Thais, like many of their Southeast Asian neighbors, have complicated views about China and the United States, as was highlighted in a late 2018 survey of regional experts, researchers, business and civil society representatives, and journalists by the ISEAS-Yusof Ishak Institute in Singapore. Just over 45 percent of Thais interviewed believe China will become "a revisionist power with an intent to turn Southeast Asia into its sphere of influence."[1]

Nearly 52 percent of Thais have "no confidence" or "little confidence" that China "will do the right thing" in contributing to global "security, prosperity and governance." (Almost 61 percent believe this about the United States.) Some 52 percent believe the BRI will bring the 10 Association of Southeast Asian Nations (ASEAN) countries closer into "China's orbit." Roughly 73 percent say their government should be cautious negotiating BRI projects to avoid getting into "unstainable debt with China" as happened to Sri Lanka and Malaysia.[2]

Forty-six percent of Thais believe China has "the most influence politically and strategically in the Southeast Asia" compared to nearly 34 percent who thought this about the United States. Two-thirds said that U.S. global power and influence had "deteriorated" or "deteriorated substantially" by the end of 2018. Nearly 71 percent thought that U.S. engagement with

1. Tang Siew Mun, Moe Thuzar, Hoang Thi Ha, Termsak Chalermpalanupap, Pham Thi Phuong Thao, and Anuthida Saelaow Qian, *The State of Southeast Asia: 2019 Survey Report* (Singapore: ASEAN Studies Centre at ISEAS-Yusof Ishak Institute, 2019), 18, https://www.iseas.edu.sg/images/pdf/TheStateofSEASurveyReport_2019.pdf.
2. Ibid., 19–20, 26.

Southeast Asia under President Donald Trump had "decreased" or "decreased substantially."[3]

Economic links between Thailand and China were surging even before the coup, and China has become Thailand's biggest trading partner. With the military in charge, high-profile Chinese business delegations flooded into Thailand as Western companies waited for the dust to settle after several years of political turmoil. But very few Chinese companies invested in Thailand and they continue to lag far behind investors from Japan and the United States.

A deepening of political engagement between Beijing and Bangkok began back in the early 2000s under ousted former prime minister Thaksin Shinawatra, and these ties were reinforced in the wake of the coup as Thailand was estranged from the United States and European Union. One noticeable trend is the growing number of Thai political party exchanges with the Chinese Communist Party.

But looking to Beijing for political cover as the United States shunned Bangkok in the wake of the coup created some anxiety in Thailand. "The Prayuth government felt isolated from the U.S. and many U.S. allies in 2014–2015," says Tom Parks of the Asia Foundation in Bangkok. "When the Thai government felt boxed in, China was able to provide an alternative, giving them some quick wins and bolstering their domestic standing."

But by 2017, the government seemed to be increasingly anxious about its dependency on China, which led the Thais to start "actively hedging," Parks observes. After Trump became president early that year, "the shift toward an emphasis on interests over values created an opening for renewed U.S. engagement, which was a big breakthrough for Thai-U.S. relations," says Parks.

Another area which has prompted unease in Thailand is China's growing footprint along the Mekong River, which starts in China and flows through Laos, Thailand, Cambodia, and Vietnam on its way to the sea. Thais are concerned that the 11 dams China has built at home on the mainstream of the Mekong and the two completed and seven others planned on the mainstream in Laos by Chinese and other builders could affect the flow of water and transform the shape and role of the river in Thailand.

3. Ibid., 15–16, 21.

Many in Thailand are nervous about the strategic and economic impact downstream if China follows through on its ambitions to blow up rocks in the river near the Thai city of Chiang Rai to allow large cargo vessels to come down the river from Kunming. Some Thais are anxious that the China-organized Lancang-Mekong Cooperation organization will give Beijing too much clout in determining how the Mekong region will be developed.

China appears to have invested more in Thailand in a "soft power" campaign than in any other nation in Southeast Asia. About half of the Confucius Institutes that Beijing has established in the region are in Thailand. More Thai students are studying in China than from any neighboring country. Beijing also sends more professors to teach in Thai universities than in any other nearby nation.

Chinese tourist numbers have exploded from roughly 1 million a year at the time of the 2014 coup to about 1 million a month five years later. These numbers could surge even higher with the completion of the rail, river, and road links to China, creating concerns in Bangkok about whether its transportation network and shopping malls could handle an even larger influx from China.

MILITARY TIES: HAVING THEIR CAKE AND EATING IT, TOO

Thailand today has the deepest and most long-standing military ties with China of any country in Southeast Asia, even though Thailand is one of five U.S. treaty allies in Asia. The Thais insist they are bolstering their defense engagement with Beijing with minimal impact on their connections with the U.S. armed forces.

Immediately after the 2014 military coup, the United States canceled about $3.5 million in financing for Thai purchases of U.S. military equipment, reduced the funding for training Thai military officers, and cut back the number of joint military exercises and visits by Thai military officers.[4] This prompted the Thai armed forces to move closer to China, which has been seeking to boost its relations with its Southeast Asian neighbors.

---

4. "Thailand: Background and U.S. Relations," Congressional Research Service RL32593, *EveryCRSReport.com*, July 31, 2015, https://www.everycrsreport.com/reports/RL32593.html.

In 2015, the Thai air force became the first in the region to engage in joint exercises with its Chinese counterparts. But Thai officers insisted the three-week "Falcon Strike 2015" exercise was not intended as a signal that Thailand was distancing itself from the United States. "We are not trying to use China to counter the U.S.," a major general told Reuters. "Our foreign policy is to have no enemies and to be friends with everyone."[5]

Thailand in 2016 ordered 28 VT-4 battle tanks from China North Industries Corporation (NORINCO) to replace aging U.S.-built tanks at a cost of $156 million, making it the first foreign customer for this Chinese tank. Bangkok, which sought initially to buy Ukrainian Oplot-T tanks until the contract unraveled because of delays and delivery challenges, ordered another 10 Chinese tanks the following year and was planning in 2019 to order 14 more, bringing the total to 52.[6]

This is not the first time Thailand bought Chinese tanks. In the 1980s, when Vietnam occupied Cambodia, Beijing offered Thailand 69 Chinese tanks at discounted "friendship prices." But quality issues and the lack of spare parts and after-sales support made it hard for the Thai armed forces to use the tanks. In 2010, the Thais jettisoned the tanks by sinking them in the Gulf of Thailand to serve as artificial reefs for fish.[7]

In 2017, the Thai military announced that it was establishing a jointly funded weapons maintenance center in Khon Kaen, in Thailand's northeast, with NORINCO, which in addition to tanks also manufactures other weapons systems.[8] The facility, 51 percent funded by the Thais, is slated to open in 2021 to maintain and repair Chinese military hardware. Plan-

---

5. Patpicha Tanakasempipat and Jutarat Skulpichetrat, "China, Thailand Joint Air Force Exercise Highlights Warming Ties," *Reuters*, November 24, 2015, https://www.reuters.com/article/uk-china-thailand-military/china-thailand-joint-air-force-exercise-highlights-warming-ties-idUKKBN0TD0CB20151124; Minnie Chan, "PLA Air Force Joins Thai Military for Joint drills," *South China Morning Post*, November 12, 2015, https://www.scmp.com/news/china/diplomacy-defence/article/1878048/pla-air-force-joins-thai-military-joint-drills.

6. Jon Grevatt, "Thailand Looks to Procure More VT-4 Tanks from China," *Jane's 360*, January 16, 2019, https://www.janes.com/article/85735/thailand-looks-to-procure-more-vt-4-tanks-from-china; Olli Suorsa and Koh Swee Lean Collin, "Thailand Takes Advantage of China's Arms Market," *The National Interest*, October 4, 2018, https://nationalinterest.org/feature/thailand-takes-advantage-chinas-arms-market-32647.

7. Suorsa and Koh, "Thailand Takes Advantage."

8. Panu Wongcha-um, "Thailand Plans Joint Arms Factory with China," *Reuters*, November 16, 2017, https://www.reuters.com/article/us-thailand-defence/thailand-plans-joint-arms-factory-with-china-idUSKBN1DG0U4.

ning is also under way to set up a warehouse for spare parts for Chinese-built defense equipment in nearby Nakhon Ratchasima Province.[9] No other Southeast Asian country shares these types of facilities with China.

In its most high-profile weapons deal in recent years, the Thai navy signed a contract with China Shipbuilding Industry Corporation (CSIC) in 2017 for a S26T diesel-electric submarine at a cost of $411 million. The sub is to be delivered in 2023 and Bangkok has the option to buy two more. The Chinese navy is expected to train Thai sailors on how to operate the sub.[10]

Many in Thailand have questioned whether the navy needs submarines, considering the country faces few maritime security threats. Thitinan Pongsudhirak, a political science professor at Chulalongkorn University, asked in an op-ed whether the submarine deal would result in a "lopsided embrace of Beijing" and mark a "shift in Thailand's geopolitical posture from its traditional hedging among the major powers."[11] Some Thai analysts say it is possible that the government set up after the 2019 elections could cancel the order for two of the three submarines.

As happens after many Thai coups, the military's defense budget has increased since 2014. It rose a little more than 4 percent in 2015 and roughly 5 percent the following year, compared to over 30 percent after the 2006 coup, according to Gregory Raymond, an expert on the Thai military at Australian National University (ANU).[12]

Interestingly, while boosting military engagement with China, the Thai military also continued to have some of the region's closest military cooperation with the United States. Since the coup, "the outcome has been the continuation of the recent trend of gradually increasing defense

---

9. Yukako Ono, "Russia Courts Southeast Asian Partners with Authoritarian Streaks," *Nikkei Asian Review*, January 16, 2018, https://asia.nikkei.com/Politics-Economy/International-Relations/Russia-courts-Southeast-Asian-partners-with-authoritarian-streaks?n_cid=NARAN012.

10. Liu Zhen, "Chinese Shipbuilder Starts Work on US$411 Million Submarine for Thai Navy," *South China Morning Post*, September 5, 2018, https://www.scmp.com/news/china/military/article/2162944/chinese-shipbuilder-starts-work-us411-million-submarine-thai.

11. Thitinan Pongsudhirak, "Subs Put Too Many Eggs in China Basket," *Bangkok Post*, July 13, 2015, https://www.bangkokpost.com/opinion/opinion/620800/subs-put-too-many-eggs-in-china-basket.

12. Gregory V. Raymond, "Competing Logics: Between Thai Sovereignty and the China Model in 2018," in *Southeast Asian Affairs 2019*, ed. Daljit Singh and Malcolm Cook (Singapore: ISEAS-Yusof Ishak Institute, 2019), 352.

engagement with China, but not at the expense of maintaining military ties with the United States," Raymond observed.[13]

Raymond said that Thailand's military planners have pursued "equidistance" in their relations with major powers since the days of King Chulalongkorn, who reigned for four decades beginning in the late 1860s. "Historically . . . , Thailand has tended to rely on its military power as a diplomatic tool, rather than seeking to develop a force capable of destroying or inflicting unacceptably high costs on an adversary," Raymond noted.[14]

Interestingly, in a 2017 survey of Thai military officers conducted by Raymond and his ANU colleague, John Blaxland, the researchers found ambivalent feelings about China among senior military officials. On one hand, when asked whether China's growing military posed a threat to Thailand, the officers scored their northern neighbor as a 7 on a scale of 10, with 10 indicating they were "very concerned."[15]

On the other hand, Thai officers viewed China as a potential protector against military threats, which they identified as more likely coming from nonstate actors such as the continuing conflict in Thailand's three southern provinces, globalization, illicit drugs, illegal migration, and climate change. Roughly 60 percent of the officers surveyed ranked Thailand's dependence on China for protection against threats between 7 and 10, with 10 indicating "a great deal" of reliance.[16]

In a sign of how much Thai officers' views of Beijing and Washington have evolved in recent decades, the United States as a military threat was ranked slightly higher than China at 8 out of 10 among the officers surveyed. The same number of officers scored Thailand's dependence on the United States against threats between 7 and 10, with 10 suggesting "a great deal" of reliance.[17]

In determining Thai military procurement choices, "price" was the most important factor in judging the attractiveness of Chinese military equipment and seemed to override geopolitical considerations.

13. Ibid.
14. Ibid., 351.
15. John Blaxland and Greg Raymond, "Tipping the Balance in Southeast Asia? Thailand, the United States, and China," The Centre of Gravity Series discussion paper, Australian National University, November 2017, 6.
16. Ibid., 8, 12.
17. Ibid., 6–7, 16.

"Availability" was a second factor, followed by "interoperability," in the Blaxland-Raymond survey. "Quality" was last.[18]

Although the Thais have been buying more defense hardware from the Chinese than the Americans in recent years, Thai military leaders still insist they prefer American equipment, calling it "the best, the most advanced," says Ian Storey, a senior fellow at the ISEAS-Yusof Ishak Institute in Singapore who recently conducted research on Sino-Thai military cooperation. But "they can't afford [U.S. hardware] due to their limited defense budget," Thai officers told Storey. "What the Chinese have to offer is good enough."

The United States began easing its sanctions against Thailand in 2016 and they were largely lifted after Prime Minister Prayuth Chan-ocha visited President Trump in the White House in October 2017. Nonetheless, Thai officers told Storey they were reluctant to request new military equipment from the United States because they did not know when Washington would again impose sanctions.

In the wake of Prayuth's Washington visit, the Thai army announced in 2018 that it would purchase four U.S.-built Black Hawk helicopters worth just over $23 million each, and the next year it agreed to buy 37 "refurbished" Stryker armored vehicles for $80 million.[19] Before the Thai elections in March 2019, U.S. officials said the return of an elected government would allow the United States to provide Thailand loans and grants for arms purchases and military training.

American officials told Bloomberg in early 2019 that the U.S. government had sold Thailand about $437 million of military hardware through foreign military sales since 2014. Despite recent procurements from China, the Thai air force also uses U.S. F-16 fighter jets.[20]

"On the defense side, there is a strong push to restore the relations of the past," says Parks of the Asia Foundation. "Security agencies [in Thailand]

---

18. Ibid., 13; Raymond, "Competing Logics," 352.
19. "U.S. Plans to Sell Black Hawk Helicopters to Thailand," *Reuters*, June 29, 2017, https://www.reuters.com/article/us-usa-thailand/u-s-plans-to-sell-black-hawk-helicopters-tothailand-idUSKBN19K193; "Army Seals Deal to Buy U.S. Armour," *Bangkok Post*, May 14, 2019, https://www.bangkokpost.com/news/general/1676940/army-seals-deal-to-buy-us-armour.
20. Natnicha Chuwiruch, "U.S. Is Ready to Boost Arms Sales to Thailand after Its Elections," *Bloomberg*, March 4, 2019, https://www.bloombergquint.com/global-economics/u-s-ready-to-boost-thai-arms-sales-after-vote-countering-china.

say that the strain in relations was minor and short-lived, in comparison to political relations [with the United States]."

The Thai purchase of submarines has raised a number of eyebrows both at home and among foreign military observers. The military has never adequately explained its security rationale. Some analysts say the Gulf of Thailand is too shallow for submarines to operate effectively. Many experts believe the Thai navy wanted them to "keep up with its neighbors," Malaysia, Singapore, Indonesia, and Vietnam, which all have subs, Storey points out.

The Thais have not yet decided finally where to base their subs, but one possibility is the Sattahip Naval Base, which creates heartburn in Washington. The United States has long used this base as a safe harbor for ships moving through the Gulf of Thailand.[21] The U.S. military is concerned that if Chinese engineers and naval officers are stationed nearby training the Thais on operating their sub, they will be able to pick up intelligence from U.S. naval vessels.

The Thai armed forces could soon face a tough choice about divvying up its military purchases between China and the United States. "The U.S. is starting to say to the Thais if you go down this road of buying Chinese weapons, there will be some U.S. systems you will no longer have access to," says Parks. "If there is a Chinese sub at the pier, probably being serviced by Chinese technicians, this would likely create an obstacle for a visit by the Seventh Fleet."

The Thai military is also doing more exercises and activities with China than the armed forces of other Southeast Asian countries. Beijing has recently upgraded its defense attaché in Bangkok to a two-star general from a one-star, Storey says. The only other countries that have two-star Chinese generals serving as military attachés in their capitals are the United States, the United Kingdom, France, and Russia.

"Compared to Thai-Chinese joint exercises, the Thai military has more substantial and more regular exercises with the U.S., more than double the number" than with China, says Parks.

21. Shawn W. Crispin, "China Can't Always Get What It Wants in Thailand," *Asia Times*, September 12, 2018, https://www.asiatimes.com/2018/09/article/china-cant-always-get-what-it-wants-in-thailand/.

Thailand is also the only Southeast Asian country that holds joint exercises with all three Chinese military services—the army, air force, and navy—Storey says. But the limited number of Chinese-speaking offices in the Thai armed forces is one issue that hobbles joint exercises. "They need interpreters at every level," Storey observes. "It slows things down."

Cobra Gold, the largest and longest-running annual military exercise in the Asia Pacific, is jointly sponsored by the Thai and U.S. armed services. Reflecting its closer ties with Thailand at a time when Washington and Beijing are increasingly at loggerheads, China recently asked the Thai military whether Chinese forces could participate in the amphibious landing component of Cobra Gold involving attack helicopters in early 2020, Storey reports.

The amphibious landing exercise is normally joined by only U.S.-friendly countries like Japan and Australia, while China and many other countries only participate in the humanitarian assistance and disaster relief component. The decision on whether China can participate in both parts of the exercise will be a joint one. In the current state of relations between Washington and Beijing, it seems unlikely that the Pentagon would agree to China's participation in the kinetic segment of the exercises.

Increasing numbers of Thai officers have been studying in Chinese military academies in recent years. Storey says the numbers average about 30 to 50 a year, roughly half the numbers the Thais send to U.S. military training institutions. Thai officers prefer to study in the United States followed by Australia and the United Kingdom. "Those going to China are not necessarily the best and the brightest," Storey says. Because language is a challenge for many Thai officers studying in China, its military academies are starting to offer some courses in English.

Will the trade war between Washington and Beijing affect Thai military cooperation with the two big powers? "It is too early to say how the rising geopolitical and geoeconomic competition between China and the United States will play out in Thailand," Raymond said. But within the Thai foreign policy establishment "the urge to 'balance' . . . remains strong."[22]

---

22. Raymond, "Competing Logics," 353.

Sino-Thai military relations were not always this cozy. In the days after the 1949 communist victory in China, Thai officials concluded that Beijing posed a "latent threat" to Thailand.[23] At the same time, Thai leaders were also making overtures to the new government in China, a frequently overlooked chapter in Beijing-Bangkok relations that suggests more continuity in these ties than is often understood. Soon after the communists seized power in China, Prime Minister Phibunsongkhram's closest adviser Sang Phathanothai launched secret efforts to establish links with China, a move he thought would protect Thailand's independence.[24]

At the Asian-African Conference organized in Bandung, Indonesia, in April 1955, which was attended by Chinese premier Zhou Enlai, Thai foreign minister Prince Wan made cautious overtures to China, which effectively launched Thailand into a new "two-track diplomacy." "The country would pursue informal relations with [China] while making public affirmations of continuing alliance with the United States," Mitchell Tan wrote in 2018 while studying history at Yale University.[25]

The Thai foreign minister made a speech at the conference expressing concern that Thai-speaking Chinese and Thais were being trained "for purposes of infiltration and subversion in Thailand." To dispel the minister's anxieties, Zhou invited him to send a delegation to southern China to investigate the existence of these activities. Prince Wan accepted Zhou's invitation for a private dinner, which resulted in a "paradigm shift" in Thai views of China.

"While fears of Chinese communist aggression were still not extinguished, the atmosphere of uncertainty and suspicion that had characterized the early 1950s gave way to a new era of opportunities for peaceful engagement," Tan said. "Thus began, 20 years before Bangkok's formal diplomatic recognition of Beijing, the opening chapter in Thailand's relations with [China]."[26]

23. Ang, *Southeast Asia's Cold War: An Interpretative History* (Honolulu: University of Hawai'i Press, 2018), 92.
24. Mitchell Tan, "Confronting Communism: Sang Phatthanothai and Thailand's Dynamic Relationship with the Cold War, 1948–1957," *Journal of Social issues in Southeast Asia* 33, no. 1 (March 2018): 62.
25. Ibid., 88.
26. Ibid., 89–90.

After the Bandung conference, Phibun put Sang in charge of orchestrating the Thai response to China. Sang turned to a long-term colleague Ari Phirom, who had translated Chinese newspapers until the early 1950s and had good contacts in China, to visit Beijing with a small Thai delegation in late 1955. They met Zhou and eventually Mao Zedong. In the meeting with Mao, he told the Thais about China's interest in establishing trade relations with Thailand. Mao said to the Thais that, as a small country, it should remain neutral and "not side with anyone" in relations between China and the United States.[27]

Soon after these meetings, Sang traveled to Burma to meet the Chinese ambassador, who expressed willingness to open economic and cultural exchanges with Thailand and to eliminate dual citizenship for ethnic Chinese in Thailand through a treaty. Sang and the Chinese ambassador signed a memorandum affirming "deep historical friendship between China and Thailand" and agreed to "establish contacts in the spheres of trade and culture."[28]

Based on these agreements, a host of Thai delegations including members of parliament, monks, journalists, artists, and business leaders visited China over the next two years. Sang decided in 1956 to send his two children, then ages 12 and 9, to live under Zhou's care in Beijing. They stayed for a decade and grew up among the children of high-ranking communist officials.[29]

While moving closer to China, Sang turned more critical of the United States. In his newspaper, Sang criticized Washington for organizing a military exercise in Thailand in early 1956. Sang wrote that U.S. aid to Thailand greatly benefited the U.S. military but hardly helped the Thai economy, and he criticized Washington for prohibiting Thailand from trading with China.[30]

A military coup in 1957 by Field Marshal Sarit Thanarat, who moved to suppress the Thai communists, abruptly reversed Thai overtures toward China and imprisoned Sang and Ari. "With the end of the Phibun era and Sang's imprisonment . . . , the opening episode in post-war Sino-Thai relations was closed," Tan wrote.[31]

27. Ibid., 90–91.
28. Ibid., 91–92.
29. Ibid., 92.
30. Ibid., 93–94.
31. Ibid., 97.

But that is not quite the end of Sang's story. In the mid-1960s as the war in Vietnam escalated, senior U.S. officials began pushing for more conciliatory measures toward China. In September 1966, U.S. diplomats were instructed to establish informal contacts with Chinese officials. A U.S. diplomat contacted Sang and asked him if he would travel to Beijing to convey a message on behalf of the U.S. government.

Sang, who had not seen his children in a decade, agreed and carried what his daughter referred to as an "extraordinary message" from President Lyndon Johnson communicating "his intention to open up direct talks with China on Sino-U.S. relations and the situation in Southeast Asia." But the U.S. message was never delivered, because the Cultural Revolution erupted and the "Red Guards" took over China's Foreign Ministry. Sang was dubbed a "running dog of the American imperialists" and expelled from China.[32]

Thailand became an unofficial base of operation for the U.S. war effort in Vietnam as early as 1961. After Sarit died in 1963, he was replaced by Field Marshal Thanom Kittikachorn, who sent the first Thai air force contingent to help train South Vietnamese pilots in 1964. By 1966, U.S. planes based in Thailand were being used to execute the war in Vietnam, and in early 1967 the first Thai troops were deployed to fight in South Vietnam.[33]

As Thailand increased its support for U.S. efforts to contain China and prevent communist victories in neighboring Southeast Asian countries in the 1960s, the Americans began providing massive economic and military assistance to Thailand. Beijing used a radio station based in southern China to step up its propaganda attacks against the Thai government. The United States began stationing troops in Thailand, prompting China to start sending rifles, small arms, and rocket launchers to the Thai communists through Laos.[34]

Once Washington began disengaging from the war in Vietnam in the early 1970s, Thailand moved to open trade and cultural ties with China. With the collapse of the U.S.-backed regime in South Vietnam in April 1975, the government in Bangkok moved quickly to recognize Bei-

32. Ibid., 98.
33. Ang, *Southeast Asia's Cold War*, 93, 107, 136.
34. Ian Storey, *Southeast Asia and the Rise of China: The Search for Security* (New York: Routledge, 2011), 125–128.

jing on July 1, 1975.[35] On the same day, the *Bangkok Post* honored Sang as the "first Thai to establish a people to people relationship with the People's Republic of China."[36]

"Vietnam's invasion of Cambodia in 1979 tipped the Thai military view of China from foe into friend," Blaxland and Raymond wrote about Vietnam's ouster of the Khmer Rouge regime.[37] On January 14, 1979, the Thai prime minister met Chinese politburo member General Geng Biao at the Thai U-Tapao air base where they hammered out a new strategic arrangement. Bangkok agreed to deliver Chinese weapons to Khmer Rouge fighters across the Thai border in Cambodia and in exchange Beijing pledged to sever its ties to the Thai communists.[38]

The weapons and supplies China sent to the Khmer Rouge through Thailand helped reconstitute the rebels into a force of some 40,000 guerrilla fighters by the mid-1980s. In 1985, China provided the Thai army with artillery pieces and ammunition and, two years later, Thailand became the first Southeast Asian country to buy Chinese weapons, including tanks, armored personnel carriers, and anti-aircraft guns for operating along the Thai-Cambodia border. In 1989, the Thai navy bought six Chinese-built frigates.[39] This cooperation "established strategic trust" between the two militaries, Blaxland and Raymond pointed out.[40]

With Vietnam's withdrawal from Cambodia and the 1991 Cambodia peace agreement, Sino-Thai defense ties pivoted quickly to focus on economic cooperation. By the mid-1990s, Thailand was uneasy about China's increasing supply of military equipment to the armed forces in neighboring Myanmar (formerly Burma), which frequently launched raids into Thailand in pursuit of ethnic armies along the border fighting the government. The Thai defense minister raised the arms buildup in Myanmar with Chinese leaders.[41]

In 2001, Thailand became the first Southeast Asian country to hold annual defense talks with China to discuss regional and international security challenges and cooperation between their militaries. Under these

---

35. Ibid., 128.
36. Tan, "Confronting Communism," 99.
37. Blaxland and Raymond, "Tipping the Balance in Southeast Asia?," 12.
38. Nayan Chanda, *Brother Enemy: The War after the War: A History of Indochina since the Fall of Saigon* (San Diego: Harcourt, 1986), 348–349.
39. Storey, *Southeast Asia and the Rise of China*, 130.
40. Blaxland and Raymond, "Tipping the Balance in Southeast Asia?," 12.
41. Storey, *Southeast Asia and the Rise of China*, 131–132.

talks the two militaries agreed to focus on observing each other's military exercises, Chinese arms sales to the Thais, educational exchanges, and joint training and exercises. Beginning in 2002, China sent military observers to watch the annual U.S.-Thai Cobra Gold military exercises and the Thais began sending observers to several large Chinese military exercises.[42]

The Thai military agreed in 2001 to buy Chinese grenade launchers and the following year it ordered two offshore patrol vessels built by a Chinese shipyard. The two armed forces also undertook various combined training exercises in the mid-2000s, with China offering land mine clearance training along the Cambodian border, and the navies simulated a rescue mission at sea.[43]

When the democratically elected prime minister Thaksin Shinawatra was ousted by the military in a coup in 2006, Beijing declared it to be an internal affair of Thailand. During a visit to Beijing by the coup leader, China offered $49 million in military credits, in contrast to the United States, which suspended $24 million in military aid. In May 2007, China and Thailand signed a 12-page joint action plan that outlined 15 areas in which they would boost strategic cooperation.[44]

LOOKING TO KICK-START A SLUGGISH ECONOMY

When Prime Minister Prayuth of Thailand attended Chinese president Xi Jinping's BRI summit in Beijing in April 2019, he told Chinese officials that Thailand would step up construction of the roughly $12 billion high-speed train project from Bangkok to the Lao border. The 375-mile stretch, which is slated to begin service in 2023, has been delayed through more than two dozen rounds of negotiations over four years. By mid-2019, hardly any work had been done, except for a 2.2-mile pilot stretch in Nakhon Ratchasima, about 160 miles northeast of Bangkok.[45]

Negotiations over the project have floundered over a phalanx of issues ranging from China's financial terms to whose companies would build the

42. Ibid., 138.
43. Ibid., 139.
44. Ibid., 140–141.
45. Online reporters, "Thailand to Speed Up Train Link with China," *Bangkok Post*, April 26, 2019, https://www.bangkokpost.com/business/tourism-and-transport/1667676/thailand-to-speed-up-train-link-with-china.

rail, which country's firms would design the project, and from where the equipment would come, according to Thai economists monitoring the discussions. These pesky differences were apparently key factors in China's decision not to invite Prayuth to the first BRI summit China organized in 2017. Thai bureaucratic inertia and domestic political differences, as well as Beijing's interest in bringing in Chinese workers, have also slowed the project.

More recently, the Thai government has begun to focus on building a high-speed rail link between the three major airports around Bangkok (Suvarnabhumi, Don Muang, and U-Tapao), which will have a much bigger impact on the Thai economy than connecting to the Lao border. A banker told the *Asia Times* that China has become so irritated at the slow progress that Beijing has pushed to have the transport minister, a career technocrat, removed from his job.[46]

Transport economists in Bangkok say that by late 2018, two contracts had been signed between the State Railway of Thailand (SRT), a state-owned rail company under the Ministry of Transport, and Chinese companies for project design and the hiring of a consulting firm to oversee the project. The Chinese company that snared the contract to design the project presented its proposal in Chinese and used Chinese specifications, says a Thai transport expert. This caused further delays as the design had to be translated into English and specifications had to be converted into standards commonly used internationally.

Once this was completed, the government expected to prepare tender documents on which companies would bid. SRT was supposed to give construction contracts to about a dozen firms to build sections of the rail from Bangkok to Nong Khai. Thai economists say a major cause for the delays is that SRT faces serious "capability limits" and has "too much work for too few people." One diplomat in Bangkok calls SRT "the worst performing state-owned enterprise in Thailand."

Because SRT already has land along existing Thai tracks, acquiring land for the rail will not be a big problem, except in urban areas where elevated stations will need to be built. In principle, the first leg from Bangkok to Nakhon Ratchasima, costing about $5.6 billion, could be built and operating in five to six years from late 2018, economists say.

46. Crispin, "China Can't Always Get What It Wants in Thailand."

Studies of the second 220-mile leg from Nakhon Ratchasima are now being prepared. But "if the section to Nong Khai is not financially feasible, it may not happen in the next 10 years," says a Thai economist who points out that SRT has already laid a double-track rail to this area for regular speed trains that adequately serve the northeast of Thailand. A delay of a decade, of course, would cause major heartburn for China and in Laos, where the high-speed train to the Thai border is slated to be completed in 2021.

China has offered funding from its Export-Import Bank at somewhere between 2 and 2.3 percent, but Thai economists believe the government in the end will rely on the robust Thai domestic debt market to fund the project. They say the government wants to avoid foreign debt (and foreign currency exchange costs) because the high-speed train is not expected to have a "good rate of return." For a railroad to pay for itself it needs a "high density of development" such as exists in roughly 60 miles around Bangkok, a Thai economist points out.

When the first railroad was built in Thailand beginning in the 1890s and early 1900s, much of it was constructed by workers from China, and Chinese firms in the country served as contractors supplying the rock and laying the ties, according to William Skinner, who wrote one of first histories of the Chinese in Thailand. Many ethnic Chinese settled in the larger towns that sprang up along the railroad.[47]

Observers expect this settlement pattern to happen again when the high-speed rail links southern China to Bangkok through Nong Khai, Khorat, and other cities in northeastern Thailand. "Thais are concerned that the railway will bring an increased influx of Chinese, some of whom can be expected to overstay," wrote Lin Renliang, a Chinese academic teaching at the National Institute of Development Administration in Bangkok.[48]

For China, the train project is about much more than being economically viable. It is all about "big linkages" from China to Southeast Asia, says a foreign economist based in Bangkok. "There's a perception that China is rolling over Southeast Asia. That might be true in some cases—Laos and Cambodia have been rolled over. But Thailand's not the same.

---

47. G. William Skinner, *Chinese Society in Thailand: An Analytical History* (Ithaca, NY: Cornell University Press, 1957), 89.

48. Li Renliang, "Dancing with the Dragon: The Trans-Asia Railway and Its Impact on Thailand," *ISEAS Perspective*, no. 9 (2016): 2, https://www.iseas.edu.sg/images/pdf/ISEAS_Perspective_2016_9.pdf.

China comes in thinking one size fits all. The Thais aren't impressed. The Chinese don't do their homework," the foreign economist said.

"China's BRI has not gone down all that well with partner countries," said Thai political scientist Thitinan. "China has a tendency to make and shape outcomes on the ground as a fait accompli, and then expect others to adjust to them. This is a mistake and will put China on problematic roads ahead."[49]

The Chinese are not the first to get frustrated trying to link to Thailand by rail. The British faced challenges from their colonies in Malaysia and Myanmar because the Thais adopted a different railroad gauge so their trains could not move easily into Thailand. The same happened with the French in Cambodia. "Thailand doesn't have a border with China, but a railroad makes the border much closer," notes a diplomat in Bangkok.

"Thais, especially small businessmen, worry that cheap Chinese goods will pour into Thailand," said Lin of the National Institute of Development Administration.[50] Many small and medium-sized businesses fear the flood of cheap Chinese products will put them out of business.

Chinese investors have run into a brick wall in Thailand on some earlier projects. Although many Thais are descendants from Chinese migrants, they are not always welcoming of Chinese capital. In 2011, Chinese investors from Yunnan Province proposed building a megamall in Bangkok that would serve as an outlet for Chinese products. But operators of small and medium-sized enterprises, many of whom were ethnic Chinese, viewed the new mall as a threat that would drive Thai companies out of business and called on the government to pull the plug on the project.[51]

"We have a country with our own mind," says a Thai China expert. "We can cooperate, but we will not take whatever they give us like Laos," he said. "We bend with our interests."

Although progress on the rail is slow, Thailand's sagging economy since the 2014 coup has Thai leaders looking to China to help jump-start growth in other areas.

49. Thitinan Pongsudhirak, "China's Belt and Road Needs to Listen More," *Bangkok Post*, November 30, 2018, https://www.bangkokpost.com/opinion/opinion/1584706/chinas-belt-road-needs-to-listen-more.

50. Li Renliang, "Dancing with the Dragon," 2.

51. "New Chinese Mall a Threat: Thai Traders—Bangkok Post," *Buriram Expats*, January 21, 2011, http://www.buriramexpats.com/forum/index.php?topic=3997.0.

China is Thailand's largest trading partner with two-way trade reaching $88.1 billion in 2018. China's exports to Thailand that year totaled $43.1 billion, up from $32.7 billion five years earlier. China's imports in 2018 stood at $45 billion, giving Thailand an almost $2 billion surplus, a rarity among Southeast Asian countries. China's imports five years earlier were $38.1 billion.[52]

Thailand's top exports to China include rubber, electrical and electronic equipment, plastics, optical and medical equipment, wood and wood products, chemicals, and machinery.[53] Thailand's top imports from China consist of electrical and electronic equipment, items made from iron or steel, machinery, iron and steel, plastics, chemical products, and vehicles.[54]

The China-U.S. trade spat will have several different impacts on Thailand's trade. Some economists believe Thai exports could drop by $1.2 billion to $4.4 billion in 2019, but others are convinced that China will step up its imports from Thailand of products such as cassava, soybeans, and plastic resins to avoid U.S. tariffs.[55]

Some in Thailand are concerned about possible dumping of Chinese imports denied access to the U.S. market. In early 2019 Thailand's domestic steel industry warned the government that thousands of workers could be laid off if the government did not stem the flood of Chinese steel exports into Thailand by imposing measures such as higher tariffs and implementing antidumping measures.[56]

China can be expected to turn to Thailand (and Malaysia) for auto parts manufacturing and imports for luxury cars like Mercedes-Benz and

---

52. International Monetary Fund, "Exports, FOB to Partner Countries; Imports, CIF from Partner Countries," *IMF Data*, 2014–2018, https://data.imf.org/regular.aspx?key=61013712.
53. "Thai Exports to China," *Trading Economics*, https://tradingeconomics.com/thailand/exports/china (accessed June 12, 2019).
54. Ibid.
55. "Trade War to Sap Thai Growth," *The Nation*, December 21, 2018, https://www.nationmultimedia.com/detail/Economy/30360853; Laura Villadiego and Laura Zhou, "Thailand Can Cash In on U.S.-China Trade War, but There's No Gain without Pain," *South China Morning Post*, December 19, 2018, https://www.scmp.com/news/china/diplomacy/article/2178373/thailand-can-cash-us-china-trade-war-theres-no-gain-without.
56. Apornrath Phoonphongphiphat, "Thai Steelmakers Warn of Job Cuts as Chinese Imports Flood Market," *Nikkei Asian Review*, February 13, 2019, https://asia.nikkei.com/Business/Business-trends/Thai-steelmakers-warn-of-job-cuts-as-Chinese-imports-flood-market.

BMW as trade woes with the United States drag on.[57] Star Microelectronics Thailand said its orders in 2018 were up 15 percent over the previous year because of U.S.-China trade tensions. Thailand expects its exports of canned tuna and canned fruit to benefit amid the chaos,[58] but Thailand's rubber industry, the world's largest, has become a casualty of the trade dispute.[59] Demand in China plummeted in 2018, compounding a long-term global oversupply causing prices to plunge.

If the trade row continues, some manufacturing facilities from China are expected to relocate to Thailand.[60] China's Shenzhen Besser Display Equipment, which manufactures liquid-crystal display products, announced in early 2019 that it would build a new plant in Thailand because of concern about U.S. trade tensions.[61] Sony Corporation of Japan said it would close its smartphone plant in China and move production to Thailand.[62]

Some Thai companies could do very well while the trade war plays havoc with other firms exposed to China. One outfit expected to benefit is Fabrient, which makes optical components for electronics firms. Its biggest customer is Lumentum Holdings Inc, which supplies 3-D sensing components for Apple's iPhone.[63]

---

57. Kenneth Rapoza, "Asian Countries Seen Benefiting Most from Trump Trade War," *Forbes*, November 2, 2018, https://www.forbes.com/sites/kenrapoza/2018/11/02/asian-countries-seen-benefiting-most-from-trump-trade-war/#467b01a846fc.

58. Michelle Jamrisko, Nguyen Dieu Tu Uyen, and Suttinee Yuvejwattana, "U.S.-China Trade Tussle Is Creating Winners in Southeast Asia," *Bloomberg*, September 18, 2018, https://www.bloomberg.com/news/articles/2018-09-18/u-s-china-trade-tussle-is-creating-winners-in-southeast-asia.

59. In the past, Thailand has largely exported raw rubber for use in the car tire industry, but more recently Thai officials urged companies to invest and innovate in the production of more finished rubber products such as condoms, gloves, and mattresses. Apornrath Phoonphongphiphat, "Thai Government Promotes Use of Rubber to Support Price," *Nikkei Asian Review*, April 3, 2018, https://asia.nikkei.com/Politics/Thai-government-promotes-use-of-rubber-to-support-price.

60. "Trade War to Sap Thai Growth," *The Nation*.

61. Lamonphet Apisitniran, "Trade War Causes Chinese LCD Maker to Relocate," *Bangkok Post*, April 9, 2019, https://www.bangkokpost.com/business/news/1658932/trade-war-causes-chinese-lcd-maker-to-relocate.

62. "Sony to Close Smartphone Plant in China, Shift Production to Thailand," *Reuters*, March 28, 2019, https://www.nasdaq.com/article/sony-to-close-smartphone-plant-in-china-shift-production-to-thailand-20190328-00060.

63. Jeran Wittenstein, "Trade War Is Boon for Thai Electronics Maker amid China Exodus," *Bloomberg*, January 10, 2019, https://www.bloomberg.com/news/articles/2019-01-10/trade-war-is-boon-for-thai-electronics-maker-amid-china-exodus.

Harley-Davidson said it plans to move manufacturing of its motorcycles bound for China out of the United States to Thailand by the end of 2019 to escape Chinese tariffs levied on U.S. vehicle imports.[64]

On foreign direct investment, China snags most of the headlines although it is only the fifth largest investor and is far behind Japan. Foreign investment in Thailand in 2018 totaled $235 billion, of which China contributed $4.9 billion or just over 2 percent. In comparison, Japan kicked in $86 billion, more than one-third of the total.[65] Over half of the capital invested in greenfield projects in Thailand from 2003 to 2017 came from Japan and the United States. Around 5 percent came from China.[66]

It is tough to find accurate figures on how much China has invested in BRI projects. By monitoring company announcements and press reports, RWR Advisory Group, a Washington consulting company, estimates the amount China plowed into infrastructure, power, transportation, shipping, and energy projects between 2013 and 2018 at $8.4 billion. Only Vietnam had a lower figure for BRI investments by China than Thailand. RWR Advisory says it only counts projects that "we believe have become real and official" and excludes deals that "have been announced but not finalized."

To kick-start an economy that has been sluggish since the coup, the junta has moved to turn the country's eastern seaboard into a high-tech hub with a 5G network, smart car plants, and a high-speed train. The Eastern Economic Corridor (EEC) is a flagship project aiming to attract over $50 billion, particularly from China and Japan, to boost economic growth. The zone will cover over 5,000 square miles in three eastern provinces and focus on several infrastructure projects, including the expansion of two deep seaports, a commercial airport at U-Tapao, and an

64. Shuji Nakayama, "Harley-Davidson Shifts Base for China Exports to Thailand," *Nikkei Asian Review*, April 24, 2019, https://asia.nikkei.com/Economy/Trade-war/Harley-Davidson-shifts-base-for-China-exports-to-Thailand.

65. Louise Moon, "Escalating Trade War a Boon for Thailand Industrial Property as Chinese Manufacturers Shift Production Overseas," *South China Morning Post*, May 14, 2019, https://www.scmp.com/business/article/3010010/escalating-trade-war-boon-thailand-industrial-property-chinese.

66. John Reed and Valentina Romei, "Who Dominates the Economies of South-East Asia?," *Financial Times*, April 30, 2018, https://www.ft.com/content/898fa38e-4882-11e8-8ee8-cae73aab7ccb.

airplane maintenance facility jointly developed by Airbus and Thai Airways.[67]

A key player at the center of the EEC is Thailand's Charoen Pokphand Group Company (CP), a sprawling conglomerate founded by a Chinese migrant that claims the title as the planet's largest producer of animal feed and shrimp and operates the leading telecom firm in Thailand. Chia Ek Chor, who arrived from China in 1921, established a small vegetable seed shop in Bangkok. His son Dhanin Chearavanont took the reins in 1969 and expanded the company into a giant animal feed firm and diversified into farm equipment and other agricultural products.

CP grew into the largest agribusiness company in Southeast Asia and became one of the first investors in China which stayed during the Cultural Revolution. The firm bolstered its credibility in China through actions such as providing Thai elephants for a Chinese tourist site. After China open its economy in the late 1970s, CP received foreign investment certificate 0001 in the Shenzhen Special Economic Zone and, by the 1990s, CP became the largest foreign investor in China.[68]

Under Dhanin, CP expanded its agriculture business into a globally diversified firm involved in retail, telecommunications, e-commerce, property development, automobiles, and finance. In 2017, Dhanin said the animal feed business in China accounted for nearly one-third of the group's global business and that in the years ahead China would receive the largest share of CP's investment overseas.[69] The Chearavanont family that controls CP is Thailand's richest with a fortune of $20.9 billion, according to the Bloomberg Billionaires Index.[70]

---

67. Apornrath Phoonphongphiphat, "Thai Parliament Passes Eastern Economic Corridor Law," *Nikkei Asian Review*, February 9, 2018, https://asia.nikkei.com/Economy/Thai-parliament-passes-Eastern-Economic-Corridor-law; Suttinee Yuvejwattana and Anchalee Worrachate, "Thai Junta Eyes Chinese Investment for $51 Billion Spending Plan," *Bloomberg*, July 11, 2018, https://www.bloomberg.com/news/articles/2018-07-11/thai-junta-eyes-chinese-investment-for-51-billion-spending-plan.

68. Joshua Kurlantzick, *Charm Offensive: How China's Soft Power Is Transforming the World* (New Haven, CT: Yale University, 2007), 74, 76.

69. Jitsiree Thongnoi, "Who Will Be Thailand's Next Prime Minister? Billionaire Dhanin Chearavanont of CP Group Might Have an Idea," *South China Morning Post*, May 9, 2019, https://www.scmp.com/week-asia/politics/article/3009493/who-will-be-thailands-next-prime-minister-billionaire-dhanin.

70. Blake Schmidt and Natnicha Chuwiruch, "Thailand's Richest Family Is Getting Richer Helping China," *Bloomberg*, April 24, 2019, https://www.bloomberg.com/news/articles/2019-04-23/richest-family-in-thailand-is-getting-richer-by-helping-china.

In August 2019, Dhanin bought three full-page newspaper advertisements in Hong Kong calling for an end to violence and a return to order in the city that had faced months of protests. The tycoon's ads, which he signed using his Chinese name Chia Kok Min, added his voice to those of Li Ka-shing, head of Hong Kong's richest family, and others. Dhanin's ads preceded the ouster of the Cathay Pacific chairman in September for the role some of the Hong Kong–based airline's staff had played in city-state's protest movement.

The ads prompted questions about how beholden some Asian leaders are to Beijing and about the impact it has on business even outside of China. An op-ed in the *Nikkei Asian Review* by a Singapore-based professor commented that "the fact that [Dhanin] felt forced to speak out in public shows how Asian business leaders far outside China are already adapting to the reality of China's rising influence in business affairs beyond its own borders." They are "doing so mostly by learning to self-police their activities and avoid perceived Chinese political red lines."[71]

CP has also become a diverse conglomerate in Thailand with a widespread economic footprint. It operates all 7-Eleven convenience stores in Thailand, True Corporation (the country's largest cable television and Internet provider), and one of the country's top mobile service companies.[72]

Sometimes in expanding its empire CP prompts criticism at home. In late 2018, when the company announced its 7-Eleven network would begin selling made-to-order food available 24 hours a day, a former commerce minister and senior Democratic Party official raised concerns that this move would harm smaller enterprises that make their living preparing food.[73]

Earlier, CP had come under criticism for trying to expand its empire into the pharmaceutical space by getting the government to adopt policies allowing 7-Eleven to sell more types of drugs in its convenience store

71. James Crabtree, "Southeast Asian Companies Fear China Reaching beyond Its Borders," *Nikkei Asian Review*, September 11, 2019, https://asia.nikkei.com/Opinion/Southeast-Asian-companies-fear-China-reaching-beyond-its-borders.

72. Masayuki Yuda, "Thailand's Richest Man Resigns as Chairman of CP's Core Business," *Nikkei Asian Review*, April 24, 2019, https://asia.nikkei.com/Business/Companies/Thailand-s-richest-man-resigns-as-chairman-of-CP-s-core-business.

73. *'อลงกรณ์' เตือน 'เจ้าสัวซีพี' อย่าหวังรวบตลาด ลั่นถ้าตนมีอำนาจระวังจะไม่มีโอกาสเสียใจ"* ["'Alongkorn' reminds 'CP Magnate,' Don't monopolize the market. If you're loud when you have power, then be aware you might not have the opportunity to be regretful"], *Sanook*, November 5, 2018, https://www.sanook.com/news/7565658/.

network rather than limiting their sales to pharmacies. This effort by CP was sharply criticized by pharmacists and doctors.[74]

The CP group has emerged as major conduit for Chinese investment in Thailand and these deals demonstrate just how deep into the Thai economy China's reach has extended. In April 2019, the SRT announced that a CP group-led consortium, which included China Railway Construction Corporation Limited, had been awarded the concession to build a $7.2 billion, 124-mile high-speed rail project to link the three airports around Bangkok. Analysts assume that the Chinese firm will provide the expertise for the railroad because CP has never ventured into transport before.[75]

The area around the EEC is one of Thailand's fastest-growing regions with manufacturing facilities, chemical plants, and a Toyota car factory. CP has announced plans for an automotive plant with SAIC Motor Corp. of China and a 1,200-acre industrial estate for Chinese investors with Guangxi Construction Engineering Group.[76]

Several Chinese automobile companies, telecom companies, and others signed over a dozen memorandums of understanding to establish ventures and next-generation industries in the EEC that will link to special economic zones in neighboring Cambodia, Laos, Myanmar, and Vietnam.[77] But actual work in the EEC has been slow to take off.

The origins of the EEC date back to the 1980s, when the Thai government developed the eastern seaboard and industrial zone and Japan kicked in financial support to develop the infrastructure to establish a platform for Thailand to export its products around the world. By 2017, the seaboard had some 23 industrial estates, one of which—the Thai-Chinese Rayong Industrial Zone—was established in 2006 as a joint venture by a Thai firm and the Holley Group, a privately held electrical parts enterprise from Hangzhou, China.[78]

---

74. "ระวัง!ซีพี-ปตท.ผูกขาดประเทศ ยึดรถไฟความเร็วสูง-ธุรกิจยา" ["Beware! CP-PTT are trying to monopolize the country, taking hold of high speed train and pharmaceutical industry"], คมชัดลึก [*Kom Chad Luek*], September 10, 2018, https://www.komchadluek.net/news/scoop/342924.
75. Jitsiree, "Who Will Be Thailand's Next Prime Minister?"
76. Schmidt and Natnicha, "Thailand's Richest Family Is Getting Richer Helping China."
77. Apornrath Phoonphongphiphat, "Thailand Rolls Out Red Carpet for 500 Chinese Companies," *Nikkei Asian Review*, August 24, 2018, https://asia.nikkei.com/Politics/International-relations/Thailand-rolls-out-red-carpet-for-500-Chinese-companies.
78. Romyen Kosaikanont, "Chinese Capital Going Global: Thai-Chinese Industrial Zone and Labor Conditions in Thailand," in *The Sociology of Chinese Capitalism in Southeast Asia*, ed. Yos Santasombat (Palgrave Macmillan, 2019), 170.

The goal of the zone was to help fire up the Thai economy, which was still weakened from the 1997 Asian financial crisis, and to provide a safe platform for Chinese companies looking to invest overseas. The zone provided corporate tax breaks, reduced import duties, and slashed utilities costs to attract Chinese investors.

By 2016, the zone had attracted 80 Chinese enterprises that had invested a total of $2 billion, generated $6.5 billion in annual sales, and created jobs for 20,000 Thais and 2,000 Chinese. One of the biggest investors is Zhongce Rubber Company, China's largest tire company that is state-owned and began operations in the zone in 2014. Chinese companies viewed Thailand as a "gateway" to other Southeast Asian countries and saw the zone as an opportunity to avoid antidumping measures and countervailing duties.[79]

The United States has strongly warned its allies to avoid using equipment from Huawei Technologies because of alleged security threats, but Thailand has turned to the Chinese telecom giant to build the next generation of the country's mobile network. Huawei launched a 5G test bed in Chonburi, inside the EEC, about 55 miles southeast of Bangkok in February 2019, marking its first such foray in Southeast Asia. Huawei is in talks with Thai telecom operators to establish partnerships before a national 5G rollout slated for late 2020. Huawei had earlier launched a $22.5 million cloud data center in the EEC.

Officials say cooperation with Huawei does not mean that Thailand is not concerned about potential security issues. "We keep a close watch on allegations worldwide," Thailand's minister of digital economy told Reuters. Because Huawei is establishing a test bed, "we can make observations which will be useful to either confirm or disconfirm the allegations."[80]

Some of Huawei's investment in Thailand runs through the CP group. The group's True Corporation is creating an Internet of things lab with Huawei, and CP used Huawei equipment to provide 4G service in

---

79. Romyen, "Chinese Capital Going Global," 174, 183, 177.

80. Patpicha Tanakasempipat, "Thailand Launches Huawei 5G Test Bed, Even as U.S. Urges Allies to Bar Chinese Gear," *Reuters*, February 8, 2019, https://www.reuters.com/article/us-huawei-thailand/thailand-launches-huawei-5g-test-bed-even-as-u-s-urges-allies-to-bar-chinese-gear-idUSKCN1PX0DY.

Thailand. Huawei says CP was invited to participate in the 5G test bed that the Chinese telecom giant is establishing in the EEC.[81]

One sector in which Chinese investors are outdueling their Japanese and American rivals is in investing in e-commerce, online banking, telecoms, and digital and high-tech start-ups. Alibaba Group Holding Limited announced in 2018 that it would invest $320 million in a digital free hub in the EEC to serve as a platform to connect global markets to Thai agricultural products.[82] The CP group is also a partner with Alibaba's Ant Financial, which has a 20 percent stake in Thailand's Ascend Corporation, an e-wallet and microloan service that uses CP's network of 7-Eleven stores.[83]

The Chinese Academy of Sciences has opened an international center in Bangkok as part of China's Digital Silk Road program. The center will focus on cooperation in such areas as climate change, disaster risk mitigation, and environmental research and is one of eight centers established by China in Pakistan, Italy, Morocco, Zambia, Finland, Russia, and the United States.[84]

Thais are big-time online bankers and shoppers, which lures Chinese investors to pour money into the country. Thailand ranked number one in the world in 2019 in mobile banking penetration, according to the annual Global Digital Overview 2019, prepared by Hootsuite, a social media management platform. Among Thai Internet users, 74 percent access banking services through their mobile devices.

The country placed fifth in e-commerce among global Internet users with 80 percent of Thais purchasing a product or service in January 2019. Some 47 percent of Thais used mobile wallets, the fifth highest global

81. Bloomberg, "The Chearavanonts, Thailand's Richest Family, Are Getting Richer Helping China," *South China Morning Post*, April 24, 2019, https://www.scmp.com/news/asia/southeast-asia/article/3007402/chearavanonts-thailands-richest-family-are-getting-richer.

82. "New Investment to Drive Growth in Thailand's E-Commerce Market," *Oxford Business Group*, November 29, 2018, https://oxfordbusinessgroup.com/news/new-investment-drive-growth-thailand%E2%80%99s-e-commerce-market.

83. Bloomberg, "The Chearavanonts, Thailand's Richest Family, Are Getting Richer Helping China."

84. Priyankar Bhunia, "New Centre Opened in Thailand as Part of China's Digital Belt and Road Program," *OpenGov*, March 13, 2018, https://www.opengovasia.com/new-centre-opened-in-thailand-as-part-of-chinas-digital-belt-and-road-program/.

percentage of Internet users who use their mobile phones to pay for goods and services each month.[85]

JD.com, China's second largest e-commerce firm, has formed a $500 million joint venture and online shopping platform with the Central Group, Thailand's top retailer. Tencent Holdings' popular mobile messaging app WeChat has formed a partnership with Kasikornbank Pcl to provide electronic payment services to Chinese visiting Thailand.[86]

Chinese firms are also active in supporting start-ups in Thailand. Alibaba participated with Thai conglomerate Siam Cement Group in a funding round for Getlinks, a Bangkok-based website that links technology professionals to companies like Tencent, Siam Commercial Bank, and Indonesia's Traveloka, a travel start-up.[87]

In 2018, Jack Ma, cofounder of Alibaba, launched a marketing campaign to sell Thai durian on the company's colossal online retailing website. The result: 80,000 of the large thorny and smelly fruit were snared within just one minute. The overwhelming success of Tmall.com, Alibaba's retailing website with access to over a billion consumers, awed but also worried Thai retailers who feared they could be overwhelmed by orders from China. Thanks to China's growing demand for durian, the price has surged in the Thai market in recent years.

In a move that would have been unimaginable a few years ago, Thailand has begun implementing a more tightly controlled vision of the Internet more akin to China's model than to the freewheeling U.S. paradigm. Thailand passed a new cybersecurity law in early 2019 that allows the government to seize data and electronic equipment in the name of national security without a court order.

The new law applies tight data controls, an appealing idea to authoritarian regimes that want to protect themselves against criticism. Like China's regulations, the Thai law insists that data be stored in the country and be accessible on demand by officials. Critics argue it will sacrifice pri-

---

85. Simon Kemp, "Digital in 2019," *We Are Social*, January 2019, https://wearesocial.com/global-digital-report-2019.

86. Patpicha Tanakasempipat, "Alibaba to Invest $320 Million in Thailand, as Rivals Boost Presence," *Reuters*, April 19, 2018, https://www.reuters.com/article/us-alibaba-thailand/alibaba-to-invest-320-million-in-thailand-as-rivals-boost-presence-idUSKBN1HQ1BI.

87. Chayut Setboonsarng, "You're Hired! Thai Startup Fills Gap in Tech Talent Recruiting," *Reuters*, January 27, 2019, https://www.reuters.com/article/us-world-work-thairecruit/youre-hired-thai-startup-fills-gap-in-tech-talent-recruiting-idUSKCN1PM05D.

vacy and the rule of law and stifle dissent, but the government insists it will protect networks from cyberattacks.[88]

Chinese investment in real estate, especially condominiums in Bangkok and Chiang Mai, is pouring into Thailand as families look to escape rising prices and polluted air in Beijing and Shanghai. Many come to take advantage of Bangkok's international schools for their children or to buy homes for vacations or retirement. Chinese buyers have topped the Japanese, who long were the number-one nationality snapping up condos in Bangkok. Chinese nationals now make up the second largest group of foreigners with work visas in Thailand, second only to Japan, which is also the largest investor in Thailand.[89]

Chinese are also attracted to Thailand because Beijing has imposed stricter conditions for property investment in China and because Thailand has lower taxes and fees than many competing markets. Some Chinese investors come to take advantage of Thailand's rental market in Bangkok, Chiang Mai, Pattaya, and Phuket.[90]

Much of the boom is driven by tech-savvy millennials, according to Uoolu.com, one of several online platforms used to help Chinese buy real estate overseas. Uoolu also assists buyers get mortgages from overseas banks, find tenants for buyers, and collect rent. Half of those who buy in Thailand do it without visiting the property, the company says.

Thailand does not allow foreigners to own land, but they can buy a condo or an apartment as long as more than 51 percent of a building is owned by Thais.[91] Nonetheless, the barriers to foreign property purchases

---

88. Lulu Yilun Chen and Yoolim Lee, "China Wins Allies for Web Vision in Ideological Battle with U.S.," *Bloomberg*, April 15, 2019, https://www.stripes.com/news/pacific/china-wins-allies-for-web-vision-in-ideological-battle-with-us-1.577028; Patpicha Tanakasempipat, "Thailand Defends Cybersecurity Law amid Concerns over Rights, Abuse," *Reuters*, March 1, 2019, https://www.reuters.com/article/us-thailand-cyber/thailand-defends-cybersecurity-law-amid-concerns-over-rights-abuse-idUSKCN1QI4KA.

89. "The Growth of Chinese Demand in the Thai Real Estate Market," *Retalk Asia*, March 22, 2019, https://www.retalkasia.com/news/2019/03/22/growth-chinese-demand-thai-real-estate-market/1553212854.

90. Suwatchai Songwanich, "Chinese Investors Fuelling Thailand's Property Market," *The Nation Thailand*, February 18, 2019, http://www.nationmultimedia.com/detail/opinion/30364287.

91. "Legal Restrictions: Can Foreigners Buy Property in Thailand?," *JustLanded.com*, https://www.justlanded.com/english/Thailand/Thailand-Guide/Property/Legal-restrictions (accessed June 12, 2019).

in Thailand are much lower than those in Australia or Singapore.[92] But some Thais are concerned that the surge of Chinese investment leaves the property market exposed to a potential property bubble.

In 2018, Thailand was the fourth most popular destination for Chinese property investors, who poured some $2.3 billion into the country, despite the fact that Thailand was preparing for elections and faced a still-uncertain political future. Even though property prices have roughly doubled over the past decade, Chinese buyers make up 70 percent of international sales by Sansiri, one of Thailand's biggest developers.[93]

Some Chinese investment projects have prompted protests against environmental damage. One of these was a potash mine in northeast Thailand. Thai authorities in 2015 granted state-owned China Ming Ta Potash Corporation an exploration license covering some 37,000 acres to study the feasibility of opening a potash mine in Sakon Nakhon Province in the northeast. Locals soon complained that they suffered contaminated water and sinking soil after salt mines were opened in the area.[94]

China's insatiable demand can have devastating consequences for the environment of its neighbors to the south. Take the "hed thob" mushroom, a small black fungus that grows in northern Thailand only during the dry season. It is wildly popular in China but develops only on the floor of the forest and is difficult to find under the thick layer of dried leaves on the ground.

Villagers can earn over $30,000 from these mushrooms in one short season. To uncover the mushrooms easily, farmers often light a fire to the underbrush and then search the cleared ground. Many of these fires burn out of control and add to the annual smog that distresses people living in northern Thailand.[95]

---

92. "Chinese Millennials Are Clicking Up a Storm Buying Asian Property Online," *Bloomberg*, March 6, 2019, https://www.bloombergquint.com/business/china-millennials-click-up-a-storm-buying-asian-property-online.
93. Huileng Tan, "Chinese Investors Pouring Money into Thailand Spending Billions on Property," *Chiang Rai Times*, February 12, 2019, https://www.chiangraitimes.com/chinese-investors-pouring-money-into-thailand-spending-billions-on-property.html.
94. Laura Villadiego, "Thai Villagers Continue to Fight Chinese Plans for Potash Mine," *South China Morning Post*, March 24, 2019, https://www.scmp.com/news/china/diplomacy/article/3002973/thai-villagers-continue-fight-chinese-plans-potash-mine.
95. Chaiyot Yongcharoenchai, "Amid Northern Haze, a Burning Desire for Wealth," *Bangkok Post*, March 29, 2015, https://www.bangkokpost.com/news/special-reports/511036/amid-northern-haze-a-burning-desire-for-wealth.

POLITICAL TIES "SWIRLING IN THE WIND"

During the cremation of Thai King Bhumibol Adulyadej in 2017, the top Chinese delegate irritated Thai officials by insisting on a meeting with the new king, Maha Vajiralongkorn, who was not accessible because of his leading role in the elaborate funeral ceremony. Vice Premier Zhang Gaoli of China then shifted his request for a meeting with Prime Minister Prayuth, who was also occupied with the cremation, which for Thais had deep religious and national symbolism.

In the end, in an account detailed by Shawn Crispin of *The Asia Times*, the Chinese vice premier was only mollified when Princess Sirindhorn, Bhumibol's second oldest daughter and the new king's sister, agreed to interpret some of the cremation ceremony chants, in a break with palace tradition. Thai officials say Zhang's goal was to use the ceremony as an opportunity to invite Vajiralongkorn to visit China first among foreign countries after his coronation in May 2019 as Beijing presses to boost its sway in Thailand.[96]

Bhumibol, who was born in the United States, never visited China during his over 60-year reign. Two years after he assumed the throne in 1946, the Chinese communists seized control of China and not long after that Beijing began providing ideological training and later sending arms through Laos to the Communist Party of Thailand.[97]

The key tenet of Thai foreign policy, according to popular wisdom, is an effort by the country's leaders to balance relations between the United States and China to avoid picking a side. That formula has been severely strained by the political turmoil that engulfed Thai politics since 2005, and particularly since the military's 2014 coup that toppled a democratically elected government. Washington's punitive response to the coup prompted the junta to tip the balance in Beijing's favor.

But Trump's invitation for Prayuth to visit the White House in October 2017 marked a significant step toward normalizing Thai-U.S. relations. Since then, Washington and Bangkok have engaged in a flurry of high-level meetings, led mainly by the U.S. military. Then-secretary of defense Jim Mattis visited Thailand shortly after Prayuth met Trump, and Mattis was followed to Bangkok in early 2018 by the then-chairman of the

96. Crispin, "China Can't Always Get What It Wants in Thailand."
97. Storey, *Southeast Asia and the Rise of China*, 126–127.

Joint Chiefs of Staff, Joe Dunford.[98] That April, Mattis welcomed then-Deputy Prime Minister and Defense Minister Prawit Wongsuwan to the Pentagon. Prawit was number two in the junta and is often described as tilting toward China.[99]

In early 2019, Dunford invited his counterpart—Thai Chief of Defense Forces (formerly known as the supreme commander), Army General Pornpipat Benyasri—for discussions on boosting Thai-U.S. military relations.[100] The annual Cobra Gold exercises, which were downgraded after the coup, were fully restored in early 2018. In another potential boost to U.S.-Thai relations, the army chief appointed in 2018 was General Apirat Kongsompong, who spent several stints studying in the United States and has deep ties Washington.[101]

These exchanges with senior U.S. officials gave Bangkok more breathing space. After the coup, "the Thais were looking for legitimacy that China was able to give them," says Parks of the Asia Foundation. "But the Thais got increasingly uncomfortable as China was getting more pushy and gaining more leverage," Parks observes. "When the thawing came with the U.S., they saw it as a big breakthrough."

Bangkok's efforts to balance its links between the two major powers are anything but static and fixed. "Thailand's relations with the U.S. and China are fluid in a moving mix and a function of Thai domestic politics and also U.S.-China dynamics," says Thitinan, the political scientist from Chulalongkorn University. "This is not uncommon for other states having to deal/hedge with the U.S. and China."

---

98. Jim Garamone, "Dunford Re-Energizing Military-to-Military Relations with Thailand," Joint Chiefs of Staff, February 6, 2018, https://www.jcs.mil/Media/News/News-Display/Article/1434639/dunford-re-energizing-military-to-military-relations-with-thailand/.
99. "Readout of Secretary James N. Mattis' Meeting with Thailand's Deputy Prime Minister and Minister of Defence General Prawit Wongsuwan," U.S. Department of Defense, news release, April 23, 2018, https://dod.defense.gov/News/News-Releases/News-Release-View/Article/1501350/readout-of-secretary-james-n-mattis-meeting-with-thailands-deputy-prime-ministe/.
100. Jim Garamone, "Dunford Welcomes Thai Counterpart for Talks on Military Relationship," U.S. Department of Defense, January 29, 2019, https://dod.defense.gov/News/Article/Article/1743177/dunford-welcomes-thai-counterpart-for-talks-on-military-relationship/.
101. Marwaan Macan-Markar, "Thailand Mends U.S. Military Ties after Post-Coup Tilt to China," *Nikkei Asia Review*, July 30, 2018, https://asia.nikkei.com/Politics/International-relations/Thailand-mends-US-military-ties-after-post-coup-tilt-to-China.

The academic adds, "For Thailand, the more China makes regional footprints and the more its BRI gains traction, Beijing's value in the Thai policymaking mix increases. But if the U.S. ups its heft, such as [through] the Asia Reassurance Initiative Act and the geostrategic frame[work] of the Indo-Pacific, China's weight and value would also be considered accordingly." The legislation he refers to is a strategy passed by the U.S. Congress that works to provide multifaceted security and economic engagement in the Asia Pacific.[102]

Thitinan makes clear that whether the Thai policy pendulum moves back roughly to the middle depends to a large extent on the actions of Washington and Beijing. His Chulalongkorn colleague Pongphisoot Busbarat argued in a 2016 article that Thai foreign policy has morphed in recent years into a strategy of "swirling in the wind" and away from its earlier long-standing and carefully honed policy of "bending in the wind" to balance China and the United States.[103]

But Pongphisoot said moves closer to China have not been without anxiety in Thailand. As Bangkok was stepping up economic cooperation with China, the Thai Foreign Ministry circulated a confidential document in the early 1990s warning about Beijing's intentions to expand its sphere of influence in mainland Southeast Asia, said Pongphisoot, who teaches political science. The document argued that in the "long run economic competition could lead to friction" and warned that "China was likely to become a security threat to Thailand" because "it could manipulate Thai policymakers and businessmen in favor of its national interests."[104]

The differences between Washington and Beijing in responding to the 1997 Asian financial crisis and to 2014 military coup in Thailand prompted the junta to play the "China card" against the United States, Pongphisoot said.[105] Despite that, Thailand was able to participate in the global war

102. Asia Reassurance Initiative Act of 2018, S.2736, 115th Cong. (2017–2018), https://www.congress.gov/bill/115th-congress/senate-bill/2736/text (accessed October 30, 2019); Ankit Panda, "Trump Signs Asia Reassurance Initiative Act into Law," *The Diplomat*, January 3, 2019, https://thediplomat.com/2019/01/trump-signs-asia-reassurance-initiative-act-into-law/.

103. Pongphisoot Busbarat, "'Bamboo Swirling in the Wind': Thailand's Foreign Policy Imbalance between China and the United States," *Contemporary Southeast Asia* 38, no. 2 (January 2016): 235.

104. Ibid., 239–240.

105. Ibid., 241.

against terror after 2001 by sending noncombat troops to Afghanistan and allowing the U.S. to refuel its aircraft at U-Tapao air base.[106]

But in 2012, when the U.S. National Aeronautics and Space Administration (NASA) asked to use U-Tapao for a purely scientific meteorological study, the government turned it down during a domestic debate about whether the project would negatively affect Thai relations with China, Pongphisoot noted.[107]

"China's rising power has created a dilemma for Thailand," Pongphisoot concluded. "Deepening ties with Beijing offer undeniable benefits to the Thai economy," but "Thailand's room for maneuver has become constrained," the academic said. On the other hand, "strengthening security ties with Washington is increasingly viewed in Thailand as participation in a containment policy against China."[108]

In his 2017 book *Thailand: Shifting Ground between the US and a Rising China*, Benjamin Zawacki argued that through years of benign neglect, the United States created a vacuum that China was able to exploit by stepping up economic, military, political, and soft power engagement with Thailand.[109]

Zawacki, an independent analyst who has long lived in Thailand, argued that the United States "has 'lost' Thailand more than China has gained it."[110] He cited a litany of U.S. "misdeeds" against Thailand to conclude that Washington no longer understands the Thai political ethos and is not able to connect with the current generation of Thai elites, citing the ho-hum U.S. response during the late 1990s financial crisis when China provided financial support.[111]

After the 2014 coup, the ruling junta complained bitterly that the United States had no empathy toward the complexities that had engulfed Thai politics.[112] Thai officials regularly complain that Washington accepted the 2013 coup in Egypt as "intervention to restore democracy,"

106. Ibid., 244.
107. Ibid., 247–248.
108. Ibid.
109. Benjamin Zawacki, *Thailand: Shifting Ground between the US and a Rising China* (London: Zed Books, 2017), 11–12.
110. Ibid., 301.
111. Ibid., 92–94.
112. Amy Sawitta Lefevre, "Thailand Warns U.S. to Mind Its Own Business over Politics," *Reuters*, January 28, 2015, https://www.reuters.com/article/us-thailand-politics/thailand-warns-u-s-to-mind-its-own-business-over-politics-idUSKBN0L10LZ20150128.

while Thailand was sanctioned for its coup that sought to end months of political turmoil, Zawacki said.[113]

The new military government turned increasingly to China for political and diplomatic support. In the months after the coup, while U.S.-Thai relations were sharply curtailed, Beijing and Bangkok stepped up high-level exchanges and conducted military exercises, and Thailand announced arms purchases from China. Thai leaders expressed gratitude that Beijing recognized that after years of political unrest only the armed forces could provide stability, Zawacki wrote.

"The Chinese have been more sophisticated in approaching Thailand," security expert Panitan Wattanayagorn, who served as an adviser to Deputy Prime Minister Prawit in the military government between 2014 and 2018, told Zawacki. "It is beyond a charm offensive, it has achieved another level in a very progressive approach to the relationship in terms of politics. The Chinese have been very quick in seeing the opportunities that have opened up since the coup . . . ," Panitan said. "They had been preparing for that opening up of opportunities."[114]

Zawacki argued that Thai military, political, and economic elites have increasingly embraced the "China model" of "an authoritarian government backed by a controlled market economy" because of the chaos that has engulfed Thai politics since the mid-2000s. A Thai general told Zawacki that "we now realize that simply mimicking the Western political system would inevitably lead us back to another dead-end."[115]

But Zawacki noted that Beijing does not seem actively to be promoting its model of governance to Thailand. He quoted former prime minister Thaksin Shinawatra as saying that "whoever becomes the government, [the Chinese] will do business with them. They are like entrepreneurs, they do business, they don't do politics."[116]

In contrast to Zawacki, Karl Jackson, a former Southeast Asia expert at Johns Hopkins School of Advanced International Studies, is not convinced that Thailand is bandwagoning with China. "Thailand always hedges rather than wholly committing itself to any emerging power or coalition, and that is exactly what Thailand has been doing with China and the U.S. during the twenty-first century," Jackson told a 2017 hearing

113. Zawacki, *Thailand: Shifting Ground*, 302.
114. Ibid., 300.
115. Ibid., 297.
116. Ibid., 297–299.

of the congressionally appointed U.S.-China Economic and Security Review Commission.

"China today will be told, and Americans may today mistakenly believe, that Bangkok is bandwagoning with Beijing," said Jackson, who previously served as senior director for Asia in the U.S. National Security Council. "As a small and militarily weak nation, Thailand must live by its wits as it confronts the emergence of China while continuing to cultivate the Americans to determine whether [they] will remain in the game."[117]

Thailand will seek to hedge its foreign relations among various powers. "In the end, unlike Cambodia and Laos, Thailand will likely diversify competing foreign powers—Japan, China, and the U.S," says Paul Chambers, a special adviser on international affairs at Naresuan University in northern Thailand. "But Japan and the U.S. need to maintain leverage against China's rising influence in Thailand."

Panitan, the former adviser during the military government who now teaches international relations at Chulalongkorn University adds: "As China rises, the U.S. is more important to Thailand. . . . Thailand can't afford to pick and choose a few friends. We're strategically located in the middle, so we have to engage in what I call a 'complex engagement' based largely on a buffer state mentality."

What about the United States policy toward Asia under Trump? "There's some concern but I don't think the U.S. will disappear. The U.S. position remains prominent in the region," the former adviser says. "What we're worried about is that it may take the U.S. too long to come up with a working formula to handle the rise of China. . . . We're in big trouble if it takes the U.S. too long. We can't cope with China or any other superpower alone."

One factor that sometimes makes it hard for Washington and Beijing to "read" Thailand is that the military, the Foreign Ministry, and other government agencies are divided into pro-United States and pro-China factions, as is the case in most governments in Southeast Asia, says Parks. "This plays out with different groups pushing against each other" and complicates decisionmaking.

117. Karl Jackson, "Changing Relations in a Brave New Asia: China, Thailand, and the U.S.," U.S.-China Commission Hearing on Mainland Southeast Asia, Washington, DC, June 8, 2017, 3, 5, https://www.uscc.gov/sites/default/files/Jackson_Written%20Testimony.pdf.

To be sure, all the apparent bonhomie between Beijing and Bangkok does not mean relations since the coup have had smooth sailing. Despite the various agreement signings between the two governments, the high-speed train project is still stuck, grounded by a host of differences and challenges.

Bangkok's ordering of submarines from China has faced anything but smooth sailing. Many in Thailand question whether the navy needs submarines considering that the country faces few maritime security threats. Political scientist Thitinan asked in an op-ed whether the submarine deal would result in a "lopsided embrace of Beijing" and mark a "shift in Thailand's geopolitical posture from its traditional hedging among the major powers."[118] It is also possible, some Thais point out, that the post-2019 election government could cancel the order for two of the three subs.

Bangkok's agreement in 2015 to deport to China over 100 Uighur refugees from restive Xinjiang Province after allowing over 170 to migrate to Turkey the previous year was sharply criticized by Thai civil society organizations, the United States, and the United Nations. A month later, an explosion at the popular Erawan Shrine in downtown Bangkok killed 20 and injured dozens, many of whom were ethnic Chinese tourists. Thai police arrested two ethnic Uighurs from China, but their trial in a military court has made little progress. More than a dozen other suspects are wanted following what was a widely criticized investigation.[119]

Despite the 2015 deportation of Uighurs, some remain in Thailand. The group deported was only about half of those detained in 2014. In November 2018, a group of 25 escaped from a detention facility in Songkhla in the south. Another group of seven escaped from detention in Mukdahan in the northeast.[120] It should be assumed that Beijing will continue to press Bangkok to repatriate those remaining to China.

More recently, Thais have become concerned about China's longer-term intentions on the Mekong River. More than a few analysts in Thailand and other Southeast Asia states see the Mekong as a possible next

---

118. Thitinan, "Subs Put Too Many Eggs in China Basket."
119. Jintamas Saksornchai, "Bangkok Bombing Trial Remains Stalled 3 Years On," *Khaosod*, August 17, 2018, http://www.khaosodenglish.com/featured/2018/08/17/bangkok-bombing-trial-remains-stalled-3-years-on/.
120. "China's Uighurs Still Caught in Jaws of Thai Immigration," *The Nation*, February 14, 2019, http://www.nationmultimedia.com/detail/opinion/30364100.

flashpoint between China and mainland Southeast Asia as Beijing steps up its activities down the river.

China has long pressed to send larger cargo vessels carrying up to 500 tons of goods down the river from Yunnan in southern China to Luang Prabang in Laos. But that would require blowing up some giant rocks and dredging the rapids near the Thai port of Chiang Saen, which environmentalists say would affect the river's ecosystem and wreck food security for people living along the river and for animals living in it.[121]

"Thailand's civil society organizations have been vocal about rock blasting and dredging of the Mekong to enable larger vessels from China to navigate downstream," says Thitinan of Chulalongkorn University. "But the Thai military government . . . is beholden to China on Mekong issues. In addition, Thailand is not as adversely affected as downstream communities in Cambodia and Vietnam, but they dare not to speak up publicly against China."

Not surprisingly, one of the main companies pursuing this project has been China Communications Construction Company, a major player in China's multibillion-dollar dredging operations to turn seven reefs in the Spratly archipelago into man-made islands.[122] In 2011, the World Bank had barred the company and its subsidiaries from involvement in any World Bank–funded projects for five years for fraudulent practices on a road improvement project in the Philippines.[123]

When three Chinese survey boats arrived in 2017, local villagers near the dredging site protested and after several months the Thai government put the project on hold. "While this decision may have been prompted by environmental concerns, it may also have been motivated by the trepi-

121. Andrew Stone, "Chinese Firm Fails to Convince Locals over Mekong Blasting," *The Third Pole*, January 29, 2019, https://www.thethirdpole.net/en/2019/01/29/chinese-firm-fails-to-convince-locals-over-mekong-blasting/.

122. Greg Torode and Brenda Goh, "China's State Firms Cementing Lucrative Role in South China Sea, New Research Shows," *Reuters*, August 9, 2018, https://www.reuters.com/article/us-southchinasea-china/chinas-state-firms-cementing-lucrative-role-in-south-china-sea-new-research-shows-idUSKBN1KU0MJ.

123. "World Bank Applies 2009 Debarment to China Communications Construction Company Limited for Fraud in Philippines Roads Project," World Bank, news release, July 29, 2011, http://www.worldbank.org/en/news/press-release/2011/07/29/world-bank-applies-2009-debarment-to-china-communications-construction-company-limited-for-fraud-in-philippines-roads-project.

dation at having large Chinese vessels moving freely down the Mekong into Thai territory," said ANU's Gregory Raymond.[124]

Since the death of 13 Chinese sailors during attacks on two cargo ships in Thailand's section of the Mekong, several armed Chinese police boats sail down the Mekong from China through Myanmar and Laos every month or so, announcing their arrival with a blast of their horns before turning around just before reaching the Thai part of the river. Thai patrol boats sit nearby, quietly observing. China has long pressed the Thais to allow their armed vessels to sail into the Thai section of the river, but Bangkok has pushed back concerned that this would extend China's economic and strategic reach, particularly since Beijing became more assertive in pressing its claims in the South China Sea.[125]

But many believe it is only a matter of time till China gets approval to move ahead with the project to blast rocks and dredge the Mekong. "For Thailand, this is something that China . . . has been demanding, and China has a heavy price to exact if you don't go along," Thitinan told National Public Radio. "The pressure is going to keep coming."[126]

Thais are also anxious about China's dam construction on its stretch of the Mekong in China and in neighboring Laos. Thais are concerned about the impact of the dams, which can reduce the water flow downstream, affect the ability of fish to spawn, and curtail the flow of nutrient-loaded silt needed for downstream farming.

"China also has carrots to play," Thitinan says. "Sometimes the Chinese release water in [the] dry season from upstream to quench the drought downstream." China's other "carrot," the political scientist notes, is the China-Indochina Peninsula Economic Corridor, Beijing's plan for roads and rail links connecting Cambodia, Laos, Malaysia, Myanmar, Thailand, and Vietnam to southern China.

At the same time, Thailand appears to be downgrading its enthusiasm for new dams in Laos in the wake of a dam collapse in southern Laos in 2018. Since then, Bangkok has deferred signing a power purchase

124. Raymond, "Competing Logics," 350.
125. Michael Sullivan, "China Reshapes the Vital Mekong River to Power Its Expansion," *National Public Radio*, October 6, 2018, https://www.npr.org/2018/10/06/639280566/china-reshapes-the-vital-mekong-river-to-power-its-expansion; Brian Spegele and Eric Bellman, "China Considers Armed Mekong Patrols," *Wall Street Journal*, November 10, 2011, https://www.wsj.com/articles/SB10001424052970203537304577027771282164912.
126. Sullivan, "China Reshapes the Vital Mekong River to Power Its Expansion."

agreement for the electricity output from the Pak Beng Dam planned in Laos. The Thai government took this step because it recognized it had overestimated the country's power needs and because the costs for solar and wind power had fallen dramatically. The government had also faced a lawsuit from villagers along the Mekong in 2017 charging that its agencies had failed to consult communities that would be impacted by the dam.

Some Thai analysts believe Bangkok appears to be hedging on China's Lancang-Mekong Cooperation (LMC) initiative, which Beijing established in 2015 and is promoting as the main vehicle for developing mainland Southeast Asia and linking it more closely to southern China. Beijing has used the initiative to host annual foreign ministers' meetings and has committed billions of dollars for water research centers and connectivity projects to boost border trade, industrial output, and agriculture as well as tackle poverty challenges.

While actively participating in Beijing's LMC forum, Thailand along with Laos, Cambodia, and Vietnam are continuing to work with the Mekong River Commission, which has existed in various incarnations for six decades with China as only an observer. In 2018, the countries along the lower Mekong lauded the commission's 1995 agreement not to launch any major projects without seeking input from all stakeholders under a "prior consultation process." China, of course, as observer can ignore this prior consultation provision.

Prime Minister Prayuth also used the 2018 meeting to express concern about environmental challenges facing the Mekong, including climate change and economic development. The Mekong River Commission has little legal clout or leverage to block any Chinese initiatives, but it can still set operating norms that China cannot risk violating without facing reputational risk.[127]

But Thitinan is not convinced that the other Mekong initiatives established over the years give the Mekong countries much leverage against the LMC. "The LMC now looks and feels like the only game in the Mekong town," the Chulalongkorn academic says. "China won't play by the other rules and frameworks set up in an earlier generation."

Thitinan adds that few other countries give the Mekong countries much of a hedge. "No other major powers are in the Mekong space, except

127. Raymond, "Competing Logics," 350.

Japan," he says. "Unlike the South China Sea, [the] Mekong mainland involves China and Japan as major power powers for available hedging among smaller riparian states." The Thai political scientist does not even mention Washington's Lower Mekong Initiative, a U.S. effort to promote economic development cooperation between the Mekong countries.[128]

The often-touted canal cutting the Kra Isthmus in southern Thailand could be another test of how far China will go in its relations with Thailand. Beijing would find the canal alluring because it would ease its "Malacca dilemma" of having to depend on the increasingly crowded strait between Malaysia and Singapore for roughly two-fifths of its global trade and shipments of much of its oil and gas from the Middle East.

In May 2015, Chinese media reported that the two governments had signed an agreement in Guangzhou to construct a 64-mile, $28 billion canal that would bypass the Malacca Strait and shorten the voyage for ships by 750 miles.[129] But within several hours, a Thai Transport Ministry official told Channel News Asia that the project was not in the pipeline and the Thai Foreign Ministry said no agreement had been signed between the two governments.[130] Many Thais wonder if China was floating a trial balloon.

But in 2018, the Thai government, in an apparent nod to Beijing, ordered another feasibility study, officially renaming the project the Klong Thai.[131] A *Bangkok Post* editorial, under the title *Kra Phoenix Rises Again*, noted that this study will add to what has become "literally hundreds of studies, papers, and recommendations and proposals of the past 341 years."[132]

Thai military officials for years have warned that the canal would divide Thailand, often citing the constitution, which "does not allow the dismemberment of the country."[133] The canal would be about 435 yards

128. "Lower Mekong Initiative," USAID, https://www.usaid.gov/asia-regional/lower-mekong-initiative-lmi (accessed June 13, 2019).
129. Chan Kai Yee, "China Announces Strategically Important Kra Isthmus Canal in Thailand," *China Daily*, May 17, 2015, https://chinadailymail.com/2015/05/17/china-announces-strategically-important-kra-isthmus-canal-in-thailand/.
130. Chris Husted, "China, Thailand Ink MOU for Kra Canal," *The Phuket News*, May 19, 2015, https://www.thephuketnews.com/china-thailand-ink-mou-for-kra-canal-52387.php#HvtBDQAJolu3fIKZ.97.
131. Editorial, "Kra Phoenix Rises Again," *Bangkok Post*, February 13, 2018, https://www.bangkokpost.com/opinion/opinion/1411502/kra-phoenix-rises-again.
132. Ibid.
133. Zawacki, *Thailand: Shifting Ground*, 313.

wide, so bridges could quite easily be built to cross the canal and move between the two parts as was done in the case of the Panama Canal.

A bigger question might be whether Thailand would benefit economically from the canal. Bangkok might want to continue to agree to do studies to buy time and avoid irritating China with an outright rejection, Raymond said.[134] Many Thais point out privately that the views of the new Thai king might be critical in any final decision.

CHINA'S SOFT POWER CAMPAIGN

China has spent more effort on public diplomacy in Thailand than in any other Southeast Asian nation. Of the 31 Confucius Institutes that China has set up in the region to teach the Chinese language and promote Chinese culture, fully 16 are in Thailand. The first institute in the region was established in Thailand in 2006.[135]

"China uses its own books [to teach at the Confucius Institutes]," says a Bangkok-based China expert. "I don't think these books are relevant to students in ASEAN countries. . . . Everything is about China."

The teachers in these institutes are volunteers from China, who get funded by Chinese Thais, says the Thai China specialist. "Many of them want to stay in Thailand. They speak Chinese, English, and Thai and want to stay in Southeast Asia."

The first Chinese Cultural Center in Southeast Asia was established in Bangkok in 2012. It is part of the Ministry of Culture and is located across the street from China's Embassy.[136]

Almost 45,000 Thai students studied in China in 2016, about 10.2 percent of the total of 440,000 foreign students in China. Thailand was the largest source of students from Southeast Asia, ahead of Indonesia (6.6 percent of the total) and Vietnam (4.7 percent). Thailand was the third largest source of all foreign students in China behind South Korea and the United States. In 2016, 40 percent of new students received scholarships from the Chinese government.[137]

134. Raymond, "Competing Logics," 351.
135. Kornphanat Tungkeunkunt, "China's Soft Power in Thailand," *ISEAS Perspective* (June 2013): 4.
136. Ibid., 6.
137. China Power Team, "Is China Both a Source and Hub for International Students?," *China Power*, September 26, 2017, https://chinapower.csis.org/china-international-students/.

"Most of the Thai [students] still want to go to the West or Japan," says journalist Kavi Chongkittavorn. "Only students who are serious in pursing higher education in languages and traditional Chinese medicines would go to China."

"Foreign students from Southeast Asian countries are the bridge and future of the relationship between ASEAN [countries] and China," Yang Xiping, the head of the ASEAN-China Center, said in explaining why Beijing puts so much effort into recruiting students from its neighboring countries to the south.[138]

Chinese students are also increasingly heading to Thailand to study, attracted by the country's cheaper tuition costs and easier visa regulations. Nearly 8,500 Chinese enrolled in Thai universities in 2017, double the number in 2012. Tuition in Thai universities is about $3,700 a year, less than half the cost in Singapore. Thai academics see Chinese students as part of China's soft power efforts to reach into Thailand.[139]

China also sends many scholars and experts from think tanks to Thailand and invites many Thai academics to China. "Thai academics told us that many universities have dozens of Chinese researchers and language teachers on campus, usually paid for by China," says Parks of the Asia Foundation. "By contrast, it's hard to find any Americans on faculty, and if they are there, they are usually being covered by the university and other sources. The comparison is overwhelming."

Beijing is also supporting a growing number of academic conferences in Thailand. "At these conferences there is no criticism of China," says Chambers of Naresuan University. "The purpose of these conferences is to increase Thai 'attachment' for China."

Separately, China has invested in several media outlets in Thailand in an effort "to build China's national image," according to Kornphanat Tungkeunkunt, a history lecturer at Thammasat University. In recent years, China started a newspaper funded by the Chinese Communist Party,

---

138. "China Seeks More Students from Southeast Asian Countries," *The Jakarta Post*, October 25, 2016, https://www.thejakartapost.com/youth/2016/10/25/china-seeks-more-students-from-southeast-asian-countries.html.

139. Reuters, "Chinese Students Are Flocking to Thai Universities, Drawn by Cheaper Fees and Friendlier Visa Rules," *South China Morning Post*, January 17, 2019, https://www.scmp.com/news/asia/southeast-asia/article/2182542/chinese-students-are-flocking-thai-universities-drawn.

launched a Facebook page of *Xinhua* news in Thai for "users interested in the China perspective" (even though Beijing blocks Facebook in China), and rebooted a former Thai-language radio station that earlier broadcast in support of the Thai communist insurgents.[140]

The ethnic Chinese population has published Chinese newspapers in Thailand since the start of the twentieth century, mainly to cover business developments. Eventually, many of the papers became vehicles to promote various political movements in China. In the 1950s, when China supported the communist movement in Thailand, the government closed pro-Beijing papers and news about China was banned. Since Thai-China relations were normalized in 1975, support by newspapers of the Chinese government has increased significantly, Kornphanat wrote.

Today there are six daily Chinese papers published in Bangkok, all of which claim they are funded by advertising. One paper supports the Kuomintang in Taiwan, while the others are "neutral" or pro-Beijing, Kornphanat said.[141]

In 2012, the *People's Daily*, the official newspaper of the Chinese Communist Party, launched its first overseas edition in Southeast Asia in Thailand to "promote [China's] image internationally in the Thai marketplace," in the words of Kornphanat. The paper is published monthly in Chinese and in Thai.[142]

China Radio International began broadcasting in Thai in 1950 in support of the Communist Party of Thailand. Today, "in a manner that is consistent with the Chinese government's new global policy," it broadcasts in cooperation with the three Thai universities, including Chulalongkorn University in Bangkok, according to Kornphanat.[143]

It is not known how effective Beijing's media experiment is in a country that has many other Thai, Asian, and Western sources of news. "News coverage from Chinese official media of the disputes between China and other neighboring countries including Southeast Asian nations makes China appear more aggressive than amicable," Kornphanat said. "Whether China's official media can challenge the existing media in Thailand and

140. Kornphanat Tungkeunkunt, "Culture and Commerce: China's Soft Power in Thailand," *International Journal of China Studies* 7, no. 2 (August 2016): 164.
141. Ibid., 165.
142. Ibid., 165–166.
143. Ibid., 166.

prove effective in creating a better impression of China among Thai people remains to be seen."[144]

Tourism is a critical pillar of both China's public diplomacy strategy and its economic footprint in Thailand. Chinese tourists totaled just over 10.5 million out of the slightly over 38 million in 2018, contributing about a quarter of Thailand's annual tourism revenue of $6 billion.[145] Growing numbers of Chinese no longer arrive on large, tightly organized group tours; they now travel alone or in small groups and are younger, better off, and more adventurous than those who came earlier.[146] So many Chinese are visiting that signs in some the largest department stores in Bangkok are no longer in Thai, but only in Chinese and English.

Thai tourist numbers from China got a giant boost in 2012 from the Chinese movie *Lost in Thailand*, which became the second biggest all-time box office money spinner in China. The movie is a comedy about two rival bumbling businessmen trying to track down their boss at a Buddhist temple in Thailand to acquire a patent on a revolutionary new fuel additive. The success of the movie fired up a surge of Chinese tourists that largely continues.[147]

Interestingly, the wave of Chinese tourists has changed a key dynamic in Thai tourism. For decades dating back to the Vietnam War, tourism in Thailand was dominated by men, at least some of them drawn to Bangkok's reputation as one of the world's "sex capitals." However, in 2016, the country attracted more women tourists than men for the first time, thanks to the tourist surge from China. Women totaled 52 percent of the tourist totals, up from only 42 percent four years earlier.[148]

---

144. Ibid., 166.
145. Jitsiree Thongnoi, "Tourists in Thailand Taking Phuket Airport Runway Selfies Could Face Death Penalty," *South China Morning Post*, April 9, 2019, https://www.scmp.com/news/asia/southeast-asia/article/3005343/tourists-taking-runway-selfies-thai-beach-risk-being-put; Xinhua, "38.27 Mln Foreign Tourists Visit Thailand in 2018," *China.org.cn*, January 28, 2019, http://www.china.org.cn/world/Off_the_Wire/2019-01/28/content_74418346.htm.
146. Thomas Sturrock, "In Pattaya, a New Breed of Chinese Tourist Emerges: Meet the FITs," *South China Morning Post*, February 8, 2019, https://www.scmp.com/week-asia/society/article/2185336/pattaya-new-breed-chinese-tourist-emerges-meet-fits.
147. Carl Berrisford, "Xu Zheng's 'Lost in Thailand' Film Spurs Chinese Tourist Boom," *South China Morning Post*, March 25, 2013, https://www.scmp.com/business/money/money-news/article/1199067/xu-zhengs-lost-thailand-film-spurs-chinese-tourist-boom.
148. Reuters, "Go-Go Going as Chinese Women Fuel Thai Tourism Boom," *Straits Times*, October 20, 2017, https://www.straitstimes.com/asia/se-asia/go-go-going-as-chinese-women

Thailand faced two incidents in the second half of 2018 that threatened to dislodge the country's standing as one of the top tourist destinations for Chinese. Just days before China's weeklong National Day holidays started on October 1, a Thai security guard slapped a Chinese national who could not produce a return ticket home and details about his accommodations in Thailand after he landed at Don Muang International Airport near Bangkok. The tourist, on the other hand, claimed the dispute broke out when he got into an argument about the cost of a fast-track visa.

Regardless, the Chinese national yelled about having been hit to attract attention and soon a video of the dispute went viral on Chinese social media. Anxious the incident would prompt Chinese tourists to cancel their visits to Thailand, the prime minister himself quickly "expressed regret" about the episode.[149]

Earlier, in July 2018, 47 Chinese tourists died when a boat capsized in the rough seas off the tourist island of Phuket in the south, in one of the worst maritime accidents in Thai history. A senior junta leader criticized the victims for not paying attention to the advance storm warnings, infuriating many Chinese. Thai and Chinese investigators mounted an investigation into the cause of the accident, which prompted Chinese tourist arrivals to fall nearly 9 percent in the third quarter of 2018.[150]

The decline in visitor numbers to the country's serene islands and charming beaches motivated Bangkok to waive normal visa-on-arrival fees for tourists from China and nearly two dozen other nations.[151] In early 2019, Thailand organized a number of welcome parties serving Thailand's famous dessert of mango and sticky rice to lure Chinese tour-

-fuel-thai-tourism-boom?&utm_source=google_gmail&utm_medium=social-media&utm_campaign=addtoany.

149. Masayuki Yuda, "Thai Tourism Hit Again after Airport Guard Slaps Chinese Visitor," *Nikkei Asian Review*, October 4, 2018, https://asia.nikkei.com/Business/Thai-tourism-hit-again-after-airport-guard-slaps-Chinese-visitor; "The Slap Heard Round the Region," *The Nation*, October 9, 2018, http://www.nationmultimedia.com/detail/opinion/30356091.

150. James Hookway, "Thailand Probes Boat Sinking, with Billions of Chinese Tourist Dollars at Stake," *Wall Street Journal*, November 21, 2018, https://www.wsj.com/articles/thailand-probes-boat-sinking-with-billions-of-chinese-tourist-dollars-at-stake-1542793831.

151. Mercedes Hutton, "Why Thailand Needs Chinese Tourists, Waives Visa Fee in Hope of Enticing Them Back," *South China Morning Post*, November 14, 2018, https://www.scmp.com/magazines/post-magazine/travel/article/2172952/why-thailand-understands-real-value-chinese-tourists.

ists back.[152] Thailand is also promoting the country as a venue for Chinese weddings and was expected to cater to about 5,000 of them in 2019.[153]

The benefits of the flood of Chinese tourists visiting Thailand is that they bring in buckets of cash. But they also create challenges: Places like Phuket and scenic destinations throughout the country are overwhelmed by gridlocked traffic and hordes of people, and hotels spring up willy-nilly to meet the soaring demand.[154]

Some 80 percent of the residents of the northern Thai city of Chiang Mai polled in 2014 were highly displeased with the behavior of Chinese tourists. They complained about littering, spitting, queue-jumping, and flouting traffic laws when driving or riding bicycles. Restaurant owners groused about Chinese clientele filling doggie bags at buffet meals.[155]

Sometimes the tourist tsunami also strains Thailand's sensitive ecosystems to the breaking point. Maya Bay in the south is a case in point. It was visited by only a handful of tourists a day until 2000, when a movie starring Leonardo DiCaprio featured the island; by 2018, some 5,000 arrived each day, causing serious damage to the reef from boats and snorkelers. The government closed the beach to visitors beginning in June 2018 and says it will remain shuttered until the damaged reefs have had time to recover and marine life returns to normal.[156]

The surge of Chinese tourists visiting Thailand has created a unique business phenomenon in Bangkok: a rush of new Chinese entrepreneurs arriving to cater to the millions of Chinese tourists. A 440-yard stretch along Pracha Rat Bamphen Road, not far from the Chinese Embassy in central Bangkok, is called Huai Khwang, but many inaccurately label it

---

152. Suchat Sritama, "Tourism Sector Dangles Mangoes for Chinese," *Bangkok Post*, December 4, 2018, https://www.bangkokpost.com/business/tourism-and-transport/1587166/tourism-sector-dangles-mangoes-for-chinese.

153. Akanksha Singh, "Thailand Expects up to 5,000 Weddings from China," *Thailand Business News*, April 17, 2019, https://www.thailand-business-news.com/tourism/71883-thailand-expects-up-to-5000-weddings-from-china.html.

154. Trefor Moss, "Thailand Loves Its Chinese Visitors, up to a Point," *Wall Street Journal*, February 15, 2018, https://www.wsj.com/articles/thailand-loves-its-chinese-visitors-up-to-a-point-1518690603?shareToken=st7120e69ea9f7427095ee34d030e80a5d&reflink=article_email_share.

155. "Survey Shows Chiang Mai Residents Unhappy with Chinese Tourists (Update)," *CityNews*, February 24, 2014, https://www.chiangmaicitylife.com/news/survey-shows-chiang-mai-residents-unhappy-with-chinese-tourists-update/.

156. Nithin Coca, "The Toll of Tourism: Can Southeast Asia Save Its Prized Natural Areas?," *Yale Environment 360*, April 18, 2019, https://e360.yale.edu/features/the-toll-of-tourism-can-southeast-asia-save-its-prized-natural-areas.

as a new Chinatown. Thai journalist Kavi pointed out that the new Chinese restaurants and coffee shops opened along the street give the area the appearance of a new Chinatown. But on closer inspection, the shops front for Chinese companies and traders who are selling rubber pillows, white-skin cream, butterfly amulets and other sacred objects, cosmetics, processed food and fruit, and other unusual Thai products to Chinese visitors.

Most of the Chinese doing business in Huai Khwang are from Yunnan, Guangxi, and Guangdong Provinces of southern China which border on mainland Southeast Asia, Kavi wrote in the *Bangkok Post*. "The Chinese newcomers have no intention of integrating into Thai society—they are here for new opportunities in business," Kavi said. "They like living in Thailand but remain loyal to China."

But the shops selling pillows, cosmetics, amulets, and processed food are really showrooms to prove to customers that they are Thai-registered companies selling genuine Thai products, Kavi wrote. Many of the new entrepreneurs use social media and the popular Chinese WeChat app to extol the merits of their products online. Often Chinese tourists order the pillows, skin cream, and amulets after they return home but, not surprisingly, many of them are fakes. They are made in China's Guangdong Province, sent to Thailand where they are repackaged, labeled as made in Thailand, and sold back to customers in China.[157]

ASSIMILATING THE ETHNIC CHINESE

Chinese migration to Thailand began nearly 800 years ago. Scholars identify five waves of migration between the mid-thirteenth century to the period after the communist victory in China in 1949 that prompted an exodus.[158] They came from Fujian, Guangdong, and other southern coastal provinces seeking economic opportunity or to escape political unrest, natural disasters, and poverty back home.

157. Kavi Chongkittavorn, "Is Huai Khwang Really a New Chinatown?," *Bangkok Post*, September 18, 2018, https://www.bangkokpost.com/opinion/opinion/1541986/is-huai-khwang-really-a-new-chinatown-.

158. Aranya Siriphon, "*Xinyimin*, New Chinese Migrants, and the Influence of the PRC and Taiwan on the Northern Thai Border," in *Impact of China's Rise on the Mekong River*, ed. Yos Santasombat (Palgrave Macmillan, 2015), 150.

Over the centuries, Thai governments encouraged assimilation of the Chinese into Thai society. In the 1930s, the government introduced compulsory Thai-language education, which officials believed would ensure that the second generation of Chinese would be "Siamese," said Skinner, who wrote an early history of the Chinese in Thailand.[159]

"The implication is clear that without a Chinese education grandchildren of Chinese immigrants . . . become Thai," Skinner wrote. "It is an interesting feature of Thai psychology that no matter how strong the prejudice against 'those Chinese,' the Thai are never inclined to reject anyone of Chinese ancestry who speaks and behaves like a Thai," Skinner said.[160]

Full assimilation was much harder in Indonesia because of Dutch "colonial attitudes and obvious physical differences" between Indonesians and Chinese, Skinner wrote. In Thailand, by contrast, the absence of sharp differences in physical appearance between Chinese and Thai made "full assimilation" possible.[161] Thai analysts say assimilation is also helped by the fact that many Chinese speak Thai at home and, like the Thais, practice Buddhism.

Precise numbers of ethnic Chinese in Thailand are difficult to determine because of their movement back and forth to China and their widespread intermarriage with Thais over the past few centuries. Official Thai figures gathered during the 2000s suggested that some 3.5 million lived in Bangkok—nearly a million in the central provinces, about 750,000 in the north, around 500,000 in the northeast, and a little over 300,000 in the south.[162]

All Chinese in Thailand identify themselves as *huaren*, of "Chinese nationality," but the earlier waves of migrants identified as ethnic Chinese whose citizenship is Thai. In contrast, *xinyimin* (recent arrivals) identify themselves as *zhonguo ren* (Chinese nationals or citizens).[163]

Like in Myanmar, Laos, Cambodia, and the Philippines, there has been a surge of new migrants from China arriving in Thailand in recent decades in search of economic and job opportunities. "There are often conflicts between the earlier and new generations," says the Thai China

159. Skinner, *Chinese Society in Thailand*, 249.
160. Ibid., 381.
161. Ibid., 300.
162. Aranya, "*Xinyimin*, New Chinese Migrants," 150.
163. Ibid.

expert. "The older generation mixed with locals well. The new generation doesn't mix well."

The recent arrivals often bring sizable amounts of capital to invest in start-ups, often live in their own enclaves, and have their own restaurants serving Yunnan or other southern food, Chinese beauty parlors, and retail stores.

Still, the most recent influx, including the numbers involved, is not yet very well understood. "It's important for Thailand to better understand the process, outcome and impact of the flow of migrants so we can adapt skillfully and peacefully to the influx," Yos Santasombat, a sociologist at the University of Chiang Mai, told the *Bangkok Post*.[164]

Life for ethnic Chinese who came to Thailand in earlier decades was not always harmonious. King Rama I provided swampland for Bangkok's current Chinatown, after expelling them from their settlement upriver, which was near the palace of his predecessor, King Taksin, who was of Chinese descent and was ousted in a military coup.[165]

A conflict broke out between the Thai government and ethnic Chinese at the end of World War II. At least seven Chinese died after riots flared up during a Chinese celebration in Chinatown when people hoisted the flags of China and some European countries, but not that of Thailand.[166]

Tensions erupted after the communist victory in China when Beijing began actively supporting communist rebels in Thailand in the 1960s in its efforts to topple the government in Bangkok. It was during this time that many Chinese adopted Thai names, said Supang Chantavanich of Chulalongkorn University's Institute of Asian Studies.[167] A second riot erupted in 1974 during the violent arrest by police of a Chinese taxi driver. Twenty-five Chinese were killed.[168]

---

164. Jon Fernquest, "New Wave of Chinese Coming to Live in Thailand," *Bangkok Post*, September 23, 2016, https://www.bangkokpost.com/learning/advanced/1093148/new-wave-of-chinese-coming-to-live-in-thailand.
165. Wasana Wongsurawat, "Rise of the Red Capitalists: PRC Influence and the New Challenge of the Royalist-Chinese Business Alliance in Thailand" (2017), 40.
166. Skinner, *Chinese Society in Thailand*, 279–280.
167. Nirmal Ghosh, "Little Distinction between Ethnic Thai and Chinese amid Close Ties," *Straits Times*, February 19, 2015, https://www.straitstimes.com/asia/se-asia/little-distinction-between-ethnic-thai-and-chinese-amid-close-ties.
168. Arnaud Leveau, ed., *Investigating the Grey Areas of the Chinese Communities in Southeast Asia* (Bangkok: Institut de recherche sur l'Asie du Sud-Est contemporaine, 2007).

Many of Thailand's business and political elites today are Thai Chinese. Several recent Thai prime ministers have been ethnic Chinese, including Banharn Silpa-archa, Chuan Leekpai, Abhisit Vejjajiva, Thaksin, and Yingluck Shinawatra.[169]

Nationalism in Thailand has a long-standing tradition of using overseas Chinese as "the other" against which "Thai-ness" is defined, said William Callahan, who teaches politics at the University of Manchester in the United Kingdom. Then prime minister Chaovalit Yongchaiyut tried to blame Sino-Thai capitalists for the 1997 financial crisis in Thailand, calling them "the nation's problem." His comments prompted a public outcry, forcing Chaovalit to apologize. His rapid about-face demonstrated the clout of Sino-Thai who are not only businesspeople, but also journalists, academics, and civil servants, Callahan observed.[170]

In Bangkok, "Chinese-ness" today is "a non-issue because the Chinese have mixed with the Thai to such an extent that you cannot easily tell one from the other," Callahan said. But in the provinces, many Chinese Thai "still figure Thai nationalism as an anti-Chinese activity and are suspicious about its morality and practicality."[171]

In northern Thailand, Thai academic Aranya Siriphon has identified three factors that encouraged Chinese to migrate to that region in significant numbers in recent decades. First, economic reforms in China in the 1980s opened China to the outside world and resulted in the shutting down of inefficient state-owned enterprises, prompting a massive migration to cities. A shortage of jobs caused many to seek new economic opportunities in the northern parts of Laos, Myanmar, and Thailand.[172]

A second factor encouraging Chinese migration was the increased economic integration and connectivity in the Greater Mekong subregion that includes southern China, Myanmar, Laos, Thailand, and Vietnam, which collectively has a population topping 300 million people. A third impetus was China's development aid, investment funds, grants, and loans to its southern neighbors, which brought Chinese to help implement these projects.

---

169. Ghosh, "Little Distinction between Ethnic Thai and Chinese."
170. William A. Callahan, "Beyond Cosmopolitanism and Nationalism: Diasporic Chinese and Neo-Nationalism in China and Thailand," *International Organization* 57, no. 3 (Summer 2003): 494–495.
171. Ibid., 503, 511.
172. Aranya, "*Xinyimin,* New Chinese Migrants," 151.

Aranya, a sociologist teaching at the University of Chiang Mai, said that part of China's strategy is associated with a "civilizing mission," adding, "The idea of Chinese and, specifically Han Chinese superiority in relation to less-civilized 'barbarians' in marginal areas has operated as an ideal throughout China's long history."[173]

Aranya, who did research on Chinese migrants in Mae Sai, a border-crossing town in the northernmost district in Chiang Rai Province, found that most of the new migrants are involved in various forms of business. The first group of medium-sized investors, who come from cities in southern China, invest in business and rent or buy land, including for agriculture to grow rubber and bananas to send back to China. Many move on to Bangkok and invest in transporting Chinese products to the capital and Thai products to China.[174]

The second group of entrepreneurs focus their business on wholesale and retail activities such as selling electronics from China in Mae Sai's markets. They frequently go back to China to buy more products. The third contingent are small traders who migrate to the Thai border to engage in petty trade with such products as dragon fruit, mangoes, and other fruit.

A fourth grouping includes professionals such as Chinese youth volunteers who teach in local Chinese schools. Many of them are supported by the Chinese government or the provincial government in Yunnan. Some Chinese young people also come to study in Thailand and some look for jobs in Thailand after graduating, often as Chinese tutors or translators.[175]

Aranya explored the role of *guanxi*, Chinese-style social connections and reciprocal relationships between people, which she argued greatly facilitated economic life for recent Chinese arrivals in Mae Sai. Newly arrived Chinese medium-sized investors find connections with relatives and friends with Thai citizenship particularly helpful for avoiding the prohibitions against buying land and houses under Thai property laws.

Chinese entrepreneurs and shop owners use these social connections to get relatives or friends they trust to staff their shops when they travel back to China to get new products or to run their shops back in China.

---

173. Ibid., 152.
174. Ibid., 153.
175. Ibid., 153–154.

These connections also help new arrivals to obtain official land registration certificates, Aranya said.[176]

New male arrivals adopt another popular *quanxi* strategy: marrying Thai women. These marriages help young Chinese men build a network of relationships that facilitate trade and banking, establish relations with Thai companies, and invest in land and property with official documents. Aranya found in her field research in Mae Sai that some of the marriages are real, while others are "fake" and are only arranged for business purposes. These marriages of convenience can carry risks because when fake documents are used the migrant can be cheated and lose his investment.[177]

Sometimes *guanxi* is established with Chinese associations in Mae Sai of which there are two main types. One is an association established by earlier waves of ethnic Chinese migrants that include the Teochiu, Hakka, and Hainaese sub-ethnic groups living in northern Thailand. This association is close to and receives assistance from the government in Beijing. The second is made up of Chinese from Yunnan, and this association was established by remnants of the Kuomintang army who escaped from China after the communist victory in 1949 and settled in over 50 villages in Chiang Rai Province. This association is affiliated with and gets help from the government in Taiwan.[178]

Without a doubt China's multifaceted ties with Thailand are deeper than those with any other state on mainland Southeast Asia, but that does not mean their relations face no tribulations. Beijing's military links have deepened rapidly since the 2014 coup, but long-standing ties with Washington also seem to be on the mend giving Bangkok more options. Although Chinese trade with Thailand is soaring and Chinese investment in the Thai digital economy is taking off, Chinese firms in other sectors still lag far behind their competitors from Japan and the United States.

Thailand is willing to give Huawei of China, which is shunned by the Americans, a role in establishing its 5G Internet infrastructure and to learn from Beijing's tough cyber standards to rein in freewheeling political criticism. But China has struggled mightily to get Thailand to

176. Ibid., 154–156.
177. Ibid., 156.
178. Ibid., 156, 157, 159, 160.

adopt its scheme for a high-speed train linking Kunming to Laos and down to Malaysia, and Beijing has not been able to figure out how to convince the Thais that the project is in the country's economic interests.

Along the Mekong River it is far from certain that Bangkok welcomes more Chinese dams on the river's mainstream or trusts Beijing's ambitions to dreg the river and send its big ships deep into mainland Southeast Asia. And, as Thailand lurches slowly back toward an elected government of sorts and the Trump administration steps up its engagement, Beijing no doubt recognizes that Bangkok will again work hard to balance its ties to the world's two major powers rather than remain more dependent on a China that is becoming more assertive in the region.

7. MALAYSIA: RESETTING THE DIAL WITH CHINA

China was on a roll in Malaysia. No other major economy in Southeast Asia had so enthusiastically embraced China's Belt and Road Initiative (BRI) as Prime Minister Najib Razak's Malaysia, which had signed loan and investment agreements worth more than $30 billion with Beijing. Then, in a stunning upset, Malaysian voters in May 2018 threw Najib out of office in a wave of discontent over his financial scandals and increasingly authoritarian rule.

Abruptly a cloud appeared over China's Southeast Asian BRI posterchild as the new prime minister, Mahathir Mohamad, pledged to review all of Najib's China projects, sending Beijing's mammoth infrastructure initiative, which has struggled mightily to get set for takeoff, into an uncertain funk. Mahathir, who had ruled Malaysia for 22 years until 2003, had himself begun Malaysia's deep economic engagement with China in the 1990s, but he now wanted to make sure that Najib's grandiose infrastructure plans were economically and financially viable.

"The change of government in Malaysia should serve as another wakeup call to China, that their previous approach of extensively cultivating relationship[s] only with powerholders and [the] elite is flawed," Ngeow Chow Bing of the University of Malaya's Institute of China Studies said shortly after the Malaysian electorate dumped Najib. "China should adjust this approach to be balanced more with a 'stakeholders approach,'" he says, suggesting that Beijing needs to engage a much broader swath of the Malaysian population.

A few months later Ngeow added that much of the analysis of how much Najib's ouster "will shift Malaysia away from China is not just premature, [but] . . . not very reflective of realities on the ground." Ngeow proved prescient. Eleven months after Mahathir had postponed the giant rail project down the east coast of peninsular Malaysia citing exorbitant costs, the prime minister had managed to renegotiate a hefty cost cut with China and declared the project back on track.

Another irritant has been China's repeated infringements on Malaysia's sovereignty in the South China Sea since 2013, especially near Malaysia's oil and gas wells off the coast of the eastern states of Sabah and Sarawak. Then, less than a month after Mahathir and the Chinese agreed to resume work on the rail project, Beijing upped the ante off the coast of Sarawak for several weeks by sending giant coast guard vessels to repeatedly harass an oil rig and service vessels contracted by a subsidiary of Royal Dutch Shell looking for hydrocarbons on Malaysia's continental shelf.

Malaysians have also taken umbrage at China's interference from time to time in the country's domestic political affairs. They have not been pleased at some implied threats by Chinese diplomats about how the sizable ethnic Chinese minority is treated. The Chinese ambassador's regular appearances with ruling party candidates ahead of the 2018 elections raised more than a few eyebrows. How Mahathir's government responds to these challenges will undoubtedly depend on how Beijing recalibrates its dealings with Malaysia.[1]

Najib's undoing was precipitated by his involvement after he took office in 2009 in setting up a state investment fund, 1 Malaysia Development Berhad (1MDB), from which billions of dollars disappeared. Investigators have said the fund was used by Najib as a political slush fund for his 2013 and 2018 reelection bids. It was also spent by people associated with him and the fund to buy high-end real estate, art, a yacht, and even finance movies in the United States and United Kingdom. The U.S. Department of Justice has alleged in civil lawsuits that some $4.5 billion was siphoned out of the fund between 2009 and 2015.[2]

Mahathir had a "very good relationship" with China when he was prime minister the first time, he said in an interview with the *South China Morning Post* a month after taking office. "There's nothing to be afraid of.

1. Prashanth Parameswaran, "What's Next for Malaysia-China Relations after the 2018 Elections?," *The Diplomat*, May 16, 2018, https://thediplomat.com/2018/05/whats-next-for-malaysia-china-relations-after-the-2018-elections/.

2. Justin Baer, Bradley Hope, and Nicole Hong, "Former Goldman Banker Is in Plea Talks over Malaysian 1MDB Scandal," *Wall Street Journal*, July 9, 2018, https://www.wsj.com/articles/former-goldman-banker-in-plea-talks-over-malaysian-1mdb-scandal-1531165030?shareToken=st097a2349756a43c19c4e9647d1e09498&ref=article_email_share.

Map 9. Malaysia

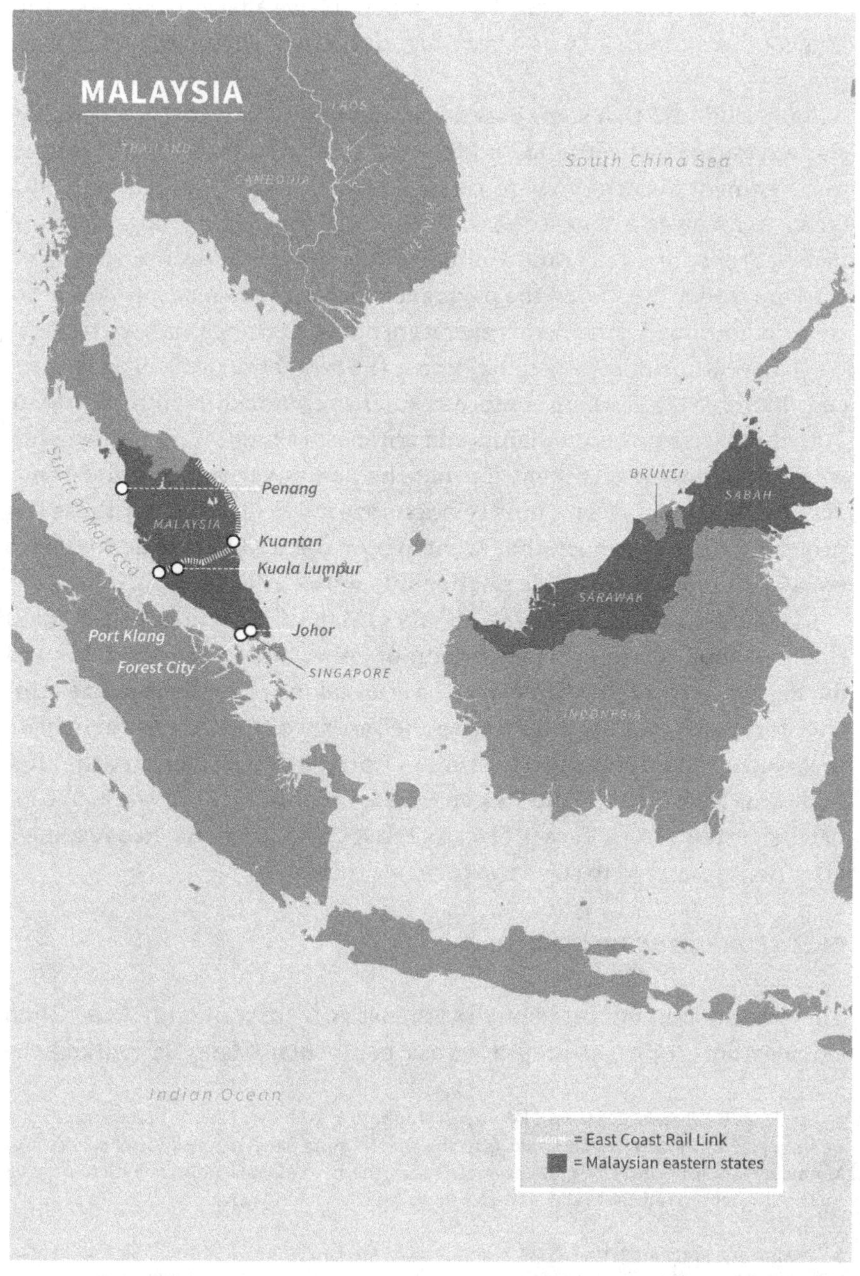

We have been neighbors for 2,000 years. You haven't conquered us yet," Mahathir told the Hong Kong–based paper. "I have always regarded China as a good neighbor, also as a very big market for whatever it is that we produce."[3]

Mahathir said that some past investment projects were "not to Malaysia's advantage or even good for Malaysia," but he added that he was open to investment "from anywhere, certainly from China." He continued: "But when it involves giving contracts to China, borrowing huge sums of money from China . . . , and China contractors prefer to use their own workers from China, even the payment is not here, it's made in China. So, we gain nothing. That kind of contract is not something that I welcome."[4]

Ngeow is optimistic that, in the end, the two countries will use the recent blunders to develop a more resilient relationship going forward. "Yes, there have been complaints and criticisms about China-related projects by the new government . . . , but the new government understands very well that Malaysia-China relations are not determined by these few projects only and, in fact, they want to move on and build a better, more equal, and more sustainable relationship with China."

Gradually, over his first year in office, Mahathir abandoned the shrill rhetoric about China's "new version of colonialism" that he had used during a visit to Beijing three months after taking office.[5] The prime minister tamped down his jargon when he returned to China to participate in President Xi Jinping's BRI summit in April 2019. Fourteen months after Mahathir took office, Najib was on trial for corruption, but work on China's biggest infrastructure project, the East Coast Rail Link, had resumed, after Beijing agreed to slash the cost by a third.

ELECTION UPSET JOLTS CHINA'S BRI

The groundbreaking ceremony in August 2017 for a roughly $20 billion Chinese-built railroad project across peninsular Malaysia marked the

3. Zuraidah Ibrahim and Bhavan Jaipragas, "Mahathir Mohamad Q&A: Malaysian PM on Beijing, Jack Ma, and Why Battleships in the South China Sea Are a Bad Idea," *South China Morning Post*, June 20, 2018, https://www.scmp.com/week-asia/politics/article/2151394/mahathir-mohamad-qa-malaysian-pm-beijing-jack-ma-and-why.
4. Ibid.
5. "Mahathir Warns against New 'Colonialism' during Visit to China," *Bloomberg*, August 20, 2018, https://www.bloomberg.com/news/articles/2018-08-20/mahathir-warns-against-new-colonialism-during-visit-to-china.

launch of one of the most expensive schemes initiated by China under the BRI. The project also cemented—at least for a time—Malaysia's standing as one of China's closest partners in Southeast Asia. The 418-mile East Coast Rail Link would start along the Thai border in Malaysia's northeast, move down the coast to the Kuantan Port, and then cut across the mountains of the country's central region to Malacca and Port Klang, just south of the capital.

Once completed in 2024, the rail was intended to provide the first land link between the contested South China Sea and the busy Strait of Malacca shipping corridor. The rail was to provide an alternate trade route for China around the congested strait and allow around 50 million tons of cargo to bypass the efficient port of Singapore, giving Malaysian ports a leg up to compete with its neighbor's port. Leaders hoped the rail line would give Malaysia's poorer east coast a boost by helping ease shipping with the more prosperous west coast.

The rail project, which had been directly negotiated by Najib with his Chinese counterparts during a visit in 2016, was to be built by China Communications Construction Company (CCCC) and financed by the Export-Import (EXIM) Bank of China at an interest rate of 3.5 percent.[6] Najib had hoped the railroad and a raft of other proposed connectivity projects with China would boost Malaysia's long-term economic development and help the country pull out of its apparent middle-income trap.

But according to Mahathir, the project's estimated cost was inflated to hide a scheme to divert funds to pay debt owed by the troubled 1MDB. Apparently, the project cost was increased by 50 percent to give the contractor some $5 billion to help meet some of the debt obligations of the state investment agency and additional funds to purchase two local construction firms. China's EXIM Bank was slated to fund over 90 percent of the total costs of the project.[7]

Malaysia has welcomed foreign investment for decades, but some officials and economists were starting to worry that the volume of Chinese investment was different from the earlier waves from Japan and the

6. Shannon Teoh, "East Coast Rail Link: Malaysia Touts Rail Trade Route as Rival to Singapore," *Straits Times*, August 10, 2017, https://www.straitstimes.com/asia/se-asia/east-coast-rail-link-malaysia-touts-rail-trade-route-as-rival-to-singapore.

7. The Edge Malaysia, "Mahathir Says the ECRL Project Contract Is Strange," *The Edge Markets*, June 4, 2018, http://www.theedgemarkets.com/article/mahathir-says-ecrl-project-contract-strange.

United States. "China comes with a lot of money and says you can borrow this money," Mahathir said in an interview with *The Wall Street Journal* shortly before the election that propelled him back into power. "But you must think, 'How do I repay?' Some countries see only the project and not the payment part of it. That's how they lose chunks of their country."[8]

Economist Jomo Kwane Sundar, a member of the council of eminent persons that Mahathir appointed to evaluate Malaysia's government programs and projects, said that "after discounting the original cargo and passenger projects to more realistic levels, the project would have implied permanent hemorrhag[ing] of operating costs, even after writing off the gargantuan development costs of [$20] billion plus interest." Jomo, a former senior United Nations official, added that the project had an "expedited" start and a few months later nearly $5 billion had "already been dispersed in dubious circumstances."[9]

To be sure, China drives a hard bargain, but how Beijing responded to the concerns of Mahathir's government on the suspended infrastructure projects would play a critical role in determining the future of Malaysia-China relations and would help other countries that had leaped to embrace the BRI figure out next steps. If China demonstrated that it was open to rejiggering the terms of projects, the contracts, the size of the loans, and interest rates, China could help ease the suspicions among BRI critics and the growing chorus of criticism within the international community.

Malaysian opposition politicians who now form the government had argued that the rail project, which was negotiated directly by Najib with his counterparts without an open tender, lacked transparency, facilitated corruption, and was not commercially viable. They also worried that mammoth projects like the rail link would become potential debt-traps and would add to the country's already heavy dependence on China. Some questioned whether the rail line would produce enough revenue to repay its loan and whether Malaysia could have snared a lower interest rate if it had gone directly to the international lending market.

8. James Hookway and Tom Wright, "Fall of Malaysia's Ruling Party, after Six Decades in Power, Shakes Vital U.S. Ally," *Wall Street Journal*, May 10, 2018, https://www.wsj.com/articles/fall-of-malaysias-ruling-party-after-six-decades-in-power-shakes-vital-u-s-ally-1525993571.

9. Jomo KS, "Jomo on Malaysia-China Ties," *Free Malaysia Today*, July 26, 2018, http://www.freemalaysiatoday.com/category/opinion/2018/07/26/jomo-on-malaysia-china-ties/.

Within two months of his election defeat, Najib was arrested and charged with three counts of criminal breach of trust. Mahathir suspended construction of the rail link and mounted a probe into whether at least some of the project's costs were going to pay the debts of scandal-ridden 1MDB or go into Najib's election coffers. The suspension of the rail project also focused a spotlight on China's often-opaque BRI projects for which little information is made public about financing arrangements, how the project's costs are determined, how the builders are selected, and from where the technology is coming.

After Najib's ruling coalition faced an earlier election setback in 2013 when it narrowly clung to power despite losing the popular vote, Najib pivoted to focus on issues of race and religion to consolidate support among his rural base. The former prime minister also turned increasingly to China to attract investment, capital, and technology to boost economic growth to open more opportunities for patronage-based politics, argued Kuik Cheng-Chee, an international relations expert at the National University of Malaysia.[10]

Then in mid-2015, the 1MDB scandal erupted into the open as some of the fund's debts came due. Beijing undoubtedly won a special place in Najib's heart when China General Nuclear Power Corporation bought 13 power plants in five countries from 1MDB for $2.3 billion. The purchase price was less than what the scandal-plagued fund paid for the assets, but the money helped 1MDB make some debt payments and reduce its $11 billion mountain of debt.[11]

Mahathir postponed or canceled other Chinese projects in addition to the East Coast Rail Link. In July 2018, Mahathir ordered the Finance Ministry to inform two Chinese state-owned enterprises, CCCC and China Petroleum Pipeline Bureau, that two oil and gas pipeline projects valued at about $2.3 billion would be suspended because of excessive costs.[12] The

---

10. Kuik Cheng-Chwee and Ithrana Lawrence, "A View from Malaysia," *The Asan Forum*, December 12, 2016, http://www.theasanforum.org/a-view-from-malaysia/.

11. "Malaysia's 1MDB sells power assets to China firm for $2.3 billion," *Reuters*, November 23, 2015, https://www.reuters.com/article/us-malaysia-1mdb/malaysias-1mdb-sells-power-assets-to-china-firm-for-2-3-billion-idUSKBN0TC0PT20151123; P. R. Venkat and Rick Carew, "Malaysia's 1MDB to Sell Energy Assets to China Nuclear Firm," *Wall Street Journal*, November 23, 2015, https://www.wsj.com/articles/malaysias-1mdb-to-sell-energy-assets-to-china-nuclear-firm-1448280084.

12. Stefania Palma, "Malaysia Suspends $22bn China-Backed Projects," *Financial Times*, July 4, 2018, https://www.ft.com/content/409942a4-7f80-11e8-bc55-50daf11b720d.

following day a third $813 million pipeline linking the port of Malacca with a state-owned refinery operated by Petronas, short for Petroliam Nasional Berhad, was suspended.[13]

Lim Guan Eng, Malaysia's first ethnic Chinese finance minister since the 1950s, said in June 2018 that the lion's share of the payments for these pipelines was based on dates on the calendar rather than on how much work had been completed. Lim said only about 13 percent of the work had been finished, but about 90 percent of the cost had been paid to the China Petroleum Pipeline Bureau, a subsidiary of China National Petroleum Corporation. The finance minister said Malaysia was trying to recoup money for work on the pipeline projects that had not been completed.[14]

Other projects facing uncertainty include the new proposed ports in Malacca and Selangor along the Strait of Malacca and a $7.4 billion energy port on the northwest coast of Malaysia that was slated to include a pipeline across peninsular Malaysia to Kelantan on the South China Sea.[15] Najib and his officials had hoped China would take major stakes in and provide financing for all three port projects, Ngeow says.

Jomo of the council of eminent persons added that "huge safety risks for the multi-product pipelines and the likely ecological damage in Sabah only exacerbate the familiar tale of economic infeasibility."[16]

Mahathir said that he would visit Beijing in August 2018 to discuss the "unfairness" of the terms of the contracts and of the loans in China-backed projects. "And the interest is also of concern to us because it is much higher than when governments borrow" from international banking institutions, Mahathir told journalists. The prime minster pledged to renegotiate the terms of these projects.[17]

But Mahathir's effort to reset relations with China faced some early turbulence. He sent Daim Zainuddin, his former finance minister who headed

13. Ibid.
14. Ibid.
15. Leslie Lopez, "Malaysia and China to Meet over Port Projects and Bandar Malaysia," *Straits Times*, May 31, 2017, https://www.straitstimes.com/asia/se-asia/beijing-kl-to-meet-over-port-projects-and-bandar-malaysia?&utm_source=google_gmail&utm_medium=social-media&utm_campaign=addtoany.
16. Jomo KS, "Jomo on Malaysia-China Ties."
17. Reuters, "Malaysia PM Mahathir to Raise 'Unfair' Contracts in August Visit to China," *Straits Times*, July 6, 2018, https://www.straitstimes.com/asia/se-asia/malaysia-pm-mahathir-says-will-raise-unfair-contracts-in-august-visit-to-china?&utm_source=google_gmail&utm_medium=social-media&utm_campaign=addtoany.

Mahathir's five-person council of eminent persons, to Beijing in July 2018 for bilateral talks with senior Chinese officials. But on the day of the meetings, Malaysia's anti-corruption agency launched raids on two Chinese state-owned companies involved in several large infrastructure projects. Neither governments' officials have commented on the raids, but Malaysian construction officials said their Chinese counterparts viewed the raids as a hardball strategy by the Mahathir government to extract concessions from China when renegotiating the infrastructure projects.[18]

Beijing has said little publicly about the dramatic developments in Malaysia, but Peter Chang of the Institute of China Studies at the University of Malaya said Beijing's "shock" at Mahathir's stunning victory "was tinged with unease as evidence is surfacing implicating China in collusion with the Najib administration's gross fiscal mismanagement." Chang said it is unlikely that this complication would "derail" China-Malaysia relations, but he speculated that "China's credibility may have been depreciated somewhat."

Chang wrote that the "Malaysia episode" underscores that China's "no-strings attached aid model no longer works . . . in countries that have achieved greater democratization." Along the way, as Malaysia achieved more civil liberties and a more vibrant civil society, "China lost the plot in this stunning Malaysia breakout story." Chang added, "Moving forward, Beijing has to recalibrate its economic-centric approach with greater care for issues pertaining to civil liberties and restore its lost credibility with 'cleaner' soft power."

The academic suggested that China needed to engage in a "domestic housecleaning exercise" to "clean up" its operations abroad. He urged Beijing to begin with "the explicit prohibition of any collusion between Chinese enterprises and corrupt regimes" overseas. Chang said China has "enormous potential to positively affect the world," but to do that it "must set in place stronger moral oversight of its fast expanding international footprints."[19]

Then, in April 2019, almost a year after the project was suspended, China, apparently recognizing that it had a great deal to lose in Malaysia,

---

18. Leslie Lopez, "Malaysia Stumbles in Rapprochement with China," *Straits Times*, July 22, 2018, https://www.straitstimes.com/asia/se-asia/malaysia-stumbles-in-rapprochement-with-china.

19. Peter T. C. Chang, "How China Lost Sight of Malaysia's Changes," *The Diplomat*, June 16, 2018, https://thediplomat.com/2018/06/how-china-lost-sight-of-malaysias-changes/.

struck an agreement to resume the East Coast Rail Link after shaving about one-third off the original cost and shortening the overall route. The new price was $10.5 billion, down from the original $15.8 billion, Mahathir said in a speech announcing the signing of a revised agreement.[20]

In the end, Mahathir made clear that China had given the government only two options under the terms agreed to by Najib earlier: either renegotiate the project or pay $5.2 billion in termination fees "with nothing to show for it." Mahathir said, "We chose to go back to the negotiation table and call for a more equitable deal." He added that it was the government's "belief" that the rail link would "serve as a stimulus for economic growth and development, especially in [the] east coast states."

CCCC, one of the biggest beneficiaries of the BRI globally, and Malaysian Rail Link Sdn, signed an agreement for the reduced costs after months of negotiations between the two governments and their companies. Under the new deal, the size and terms of Malaysia's loan from China's EXIM Bank will be reduced, although negotiations on the details were still under way when the agreement to resume the project was signed. This should save the government money in terms of repayment, interest costs, and fees. Malaysia had earlier agreed to take a loan for $13.5 billion or 85 percent of the original cost of the rail link.

CCCC agreed to refund nearly $1 billion of advance payments received from the Malaysian side. The Chinese also agreed to take a 50 percent stake with Malaysia Rail Link to operate and maintain the rail and bear half the risk if the project faces financial difficulties. CCCC agreed to increase local participation in the construction activities to 40 percent, up from 30 percent earlier, to address complaints that most of the work was being done by Chinese companies and workers.[21]

With the overall cost of the project reduced, Malaysia will pay $5.8 billion in interest, a saving of $3.1 billion from earlier projections. The rail link is now slated for completion in 2026, two years later than initially forecast.[22]

---

20. "ECRL Salient Points: RM1b Refund, More Locals and CCCC to Share Risk," *Malaysiakini*, April 15, 2019, https://www.malaysiakini.com/news/472336.
21. Ibid.
22. Hazlin Hassan, "Work Resumes on Malaysia's East Coast Rail Link," *Straits Times*, July 25, 2019, https://www.straitstimes.com/asia/se-asia/malaysia-restarts-rail-link-project-with-china-after-cost-cut.

The two Chinese firms resumed construction in July 2019 at a partially completed tunnel along the rail route. The revised plan will avoid some of the more rugged terrain to reduce tunneling costs and then connect to some existing rail networks near Kuala Lumpur.

The resumption of the rail deal could serve as a giant psychological boost for China's BRI, which has seen neighboring countries like Myanmar and Thailand delay decisions about Chinese infrastructure projects amid concerns about huge costs, expensive interest rates, and anxiety about the loss of sovereignty.

But the dispute over the two suspended pipelines continued. In July 2019, almost as if to send China a signal not to take Malaysia for granted despite the resumption of the rail project, officials seized more than $242.5 million from state-owned China Petroleum Engineering Limited (CPP), a unit of state energy giant China National Petroleum Corporation. The government ordered HSBC Bank to transfer the funds to Suria Strategic Resources, a company owned by the Ministry of Finance.

The Chinese firm responded, saying that "CPP firmly abides with the laws of Malaysia and is perplexed by the unilateral transfer of monies without notifying CPP." China Petroleum Engineering Limited had been awarded the pipeline project, including one 375-mile pipeline along the west coast of Malaysia costing $1.3 billion and a second 414-mile pipeline in Sabah in East Malaysia costing $984.6 million, in 2016.

The current Malaysian government has questioned why Suria Strategic Resources paid over 80 percent of the costs even though only 13 percent of the work was finished. Some Malaysian media reports have suggested that the firm sent the funds to a Cayman Island company linked to 1MDB, but the Chinese company has denied this assertion.[23]

It also appears that Mahathir will continue many of the massive Chinese real estate projects on the drawing board at the time of the elections. The 106-floor Tun Razak Exchange City (TRX City), Kuala Lumpur's new $1.7 billion financial district named after Najib's father, will be completed.

23. Leslie Lopez, "Malaysia Seizes $328 Million Held by Chinese State-Owned Unit in HSCB," *Straits Times*, July 13, 2019, https://www.straitstimes.com/asia/se-asia/malaysia-seizes-s328-million-held-by-chinese-state-owned-unit-in-hsbc?&utm_source=google_gmail&utm_medium=social-media&utm_campaign=addtoany; "Malaysia Seized $240 Million from Chinese Company over Pipeline Project: PM Mahathir," *Reuters*, July 15, 2019, https://www.reuters.com/article/us-malaysia-politics-china/malaysia-seized-240-million-from-chinese-company-over-pipeline-project-pm-mahathir-idUSKCN1UA1DU.

The new government decided to kick in the nearly $700 million needed to finish the project on which CCCC also has the lead contract. Finance Minister Lim Guan Eng said the alternative would have been to pay $921 million in compensation claims and leave "an eyesore of an abandoned mega project in the heart of Kuala Lumpur."[24]

The government also hopes to recoup about $790 million in misappropriated funds for the project that officials believe were used to pay off 1MDB debt.

The China-backed multibillion-dollar Bandar Malaysia project next to TRX City on over 300 acres of land that currently serves as an air force base in the southeast side of Kuala Lumpur is also back on track, two years after it was canceled. The project will resume with the original joint venture between Malaysia's Iskandar Waterfront Holdings and state-owned China Railway Engineering Corporation.

The original deal on the project was struck by Najib apparently to ease 1MDB's debt, but it collapsed in 2017 amid a dispute about payment. In the original plan, Bandar Malaysia was to serve as the end terminal for the 220-mile high-speed rail link between Singapore and Kuala Lumpur that was put on hold after Mahathir returned to power.

The new plan will include a "People's Park" and 10,000 affordable apartments. The project will focus on using Malaysian inputs and much of the work will be done by contractors from Malaysia's majority Malay community.[25]

Mahathir said in announcing the resumption of the project that he expected international financial institutions and multinational corporations to locate their offices in the complex. The prime minister said that a key reason he decided to resurrect the project was that 60 percent of the companies in the consortium building Bandar Malaysia belong to Malaysians.[26]

---

24. Arno Maierbrugger, "Kuala Lumpur's New Financial District 'Can Be Profitable': Ex-PM Najib," *Investvine*, June 22, 2018, http://investvine.com/kuala-lumpurs-new-financial-district-can-be-profitable-ex-pm-najib/.

25. "Malaysia to Revive Multi-Billion Dollar Project Linked to China," *Reuters*, April 19, 2019, https://www.reuters.com/article/us-malaysia-china-project/malaysia-to-revive-multi-billion-dollar-project-linked-to-china-idUSKCN1RV0K0.

26. Terence Tong, "Axed in 2017, Bandar Malaysia Back on Track as 'People-Centric' Project," *Malay Mail*, April 19, 2019, https://www.malaymail.com/news/malaysia/2019/04/19/axed-in-2017-bandar-malaysia-project-back-on-track/1744933.

Mahathir's agreement to resume two giant BRI projects that he had sharply criticized and canceled initially should give BRI a psychological boost in Malaysia and neighboring countries. It should also go some way to restore the goodwill between China and Malaysia that had been somewhat frayed in the early days after Mahathir returned to his former job.

Mahathir declared in a visit to Japan shortly after his election that Malaysia would remain friendly to Beijing, but he added that the country would not be "indebted" to China.[27] In his interview with the *South China Morning Post*, Mahathir said, "We welcome foreign investment from any country, so long as they bring in capital, they bring in the technology, they set up plants here, and they employ Malaysians, from workers to engineers, . . . and they produce goods for the domestic market, and for export."[28]

As a signal of his continuing interest in strong economic ties with China, Mahathir soon after taking office appointed Chinese Malaysian tycoon Robert Kuok, 94, founder of the Shangri-La Hotel chain and Malaysia's richest man, to his council of eminent persons. Because of Kuok's record of dealing with China dating back to the 1950s, when he ran a food trading business, he earned the nickname of "sugar king." At the end of the China's Cultural Revolution, Kuok was one of the first foreigners to bet on China's economic reforms by investing to refurbish the famous Hangzhou Hotel.[29]

Chinese billionaire Jack Ma of Alibaba, who had close ties with Najib, visited Mahathir a month after the elections in an apparent effort to help soothe relations between Beijing and Kuala Lumpur.[30] In 2017, Ma had opened a Digital Free Trade Zone, an electronic trading hub and logistics center, in Malaysia, the first outside of Alibaba's home base in China, to

---

27. Elaine Lies, "Malaysia Wants to Be Friendly, Not Indebted, to China: Mahathir," *Jakarta Globe*, June 12, 2018, http://jakartaglobe.id/international/malaysia-wants-to-be-friendly-not-indebted-to-china-mahathir/.
28. Zuraidah and Jaipragas, "Mahathir Mohamad Q&A."
29. Kenji Kawase, "Mahathir's 94-Year-Old Top Adviser Rekindles China Connections," *Nikkei Asian Review*, June 1, 2018, https://asia.nikkei.com/Spotlight/Asian-Family-Conglomerates/Mahathir-s-94-year-old-top-adviser-rekindles-China-connections?utm_campaign=RN%20Free%20newsletter&utm_medium=weekly%20newsletter%20free&utm_source=NAR%20Newsletter&.
30. Ben Bland, "Malaysian Backlash Tests China's Belt and Road Ambitions," *Financial Times*, June 24, 2018, https://www.ft.com/content/056ae1ec-7634-11e8-b326-75a27d27ea5f.

help companies to conduct cross-border trade with minimal bureaucratic hurdles.[31]

Beijing did not say much about Malaysia's demand to renegotiate Chinese projects after Mahathir returned to power, but the state-backed tabloid *Global Times* did weigh in. It warned that if Malaysia wanted to review projects, the affected Chinese companies would "have the right to claim compensation." The commentary added, "The Chinese government will . . . safeguard the interests and rights of Chinese enterprises. If Malaysia's new government fails to adhere to the spirit of the contract, it has to pay the price for its error."

The *Global Times* warned Malaysia that it is not the only global investment destination. The commentary said it would be "easy for Chinese companies to shift their focus to other countries," adding that it would be Malaysia's economy that would "suffer big losses."[32] In the end, the *Global Times* threat proved more difficult for China to carry out than the paper's editors thought.

Malaysia emerged as China's largest trading partner in Southeast Asia in 2009, although in more recent years it has fallen behind Vietnam. Two-way Malaysia-China trade reached $75.5 billion in 2018, up 8 percent over 2017, despite the disruption caused by the abrupt change of government. Malaysia's exports to China expanded to $33.4 billion, an increase of 10 percent over the previous year, while China's exports to the Southeast Asian nation totaled $42.1 billion, up more than 6 percent over 2017.[33]

China's major investments in Malaysia are relatively recent. Its first big investment project in Malaysia was the Kuantan Industrial Park launched in 2011 in Najib's home state of Pahang along the country's eastern coast. Much of the $1.6 billion investment was from Guangxi

31. Bhavan Jaipragas, "Alibaba's Electronic Trading Hub to Help Small and Medium-Sized Enterprises Goes Live in Malaysia," *South China Morning Post*, November 3, 2017, https://www.scmp.com/week-asia/business/article/2118304/alibabas-electronic-trading-hub-help-small-and-medium-sized.

32. "Scrapping HSR Bad for Beijing: Chinese Tabloid," *Straits Times*, June 2, 2018, https://www.straitstimes.com/asia/se-asia/scrapping-hsr-bad-for-beijing-chinese-tabloid?&utm_source=google_gmail&utm_medium=social-media&utm_campaign=addtoany.

33. "Trade Performance for 2018 and December 2018," Malaysia External Trade Development Corporation, http://www.matrade.gov.my/en/about-matrade/media/press-releases/4515-trade-performance-for-2018-and-december-2018 (accessed October 30, 2019).

Province in the south and the key project pieces included a steel plant, an aluminum processing plant, and a facility to process palm oil.[34]

China has been the largest foreign investor in the manufacturing sector since 2017. In 2018, China's foreign direct investment in manufacturing (not including investment in services) totaled $4.7 billion, almost one-quarter of total investment in the sector, despite the turmoil caused by the government change.[35] In 2017, Chinese investment in manufacturing reached $931.1 million, down from $1.1 billion in 2016.[36]

One of the key reasons Chinese investment began to pick up around 2016 was because Chinese companies were looking to Malaysia as a springboard into the larger Southeast Asian market. Firms from China invested in solar panels in Malaysia to get around U.S. antidumping duties on solar panels from China. Chinese companies stepped up investment in textiles during the negotiations for the Trans-Pacific Partnership trade agreement hoping to take advantage of provisions providing advantages to members of the agreement.

China does not release overall figures on the value of its BRI infrastructure projects in individual countries, but RWR Advisory Group, a Washington firm that tracks China's investment, estimates the total for Malaysia at $46.5 billion, the second largest in Southeast Asia behind Indonesia, between 2013 and 2018. RWR counts only those projects that "have become real and official" and does not include "deals that have been announced but not finalized," says Andrew Davenport, the group's chief operating officer.

Mahathir has announced that Malaysia will continue to use Huawei Technologies "as much as possible," despite the fact that the United States had decided to shun the Chinese tech giant. Mahathir said at a conference

34. Siva Sithraputhran and Stuart Grudgings, "China to Invest More than $1.6 Billion in Malaysia Steel, Port," *Reuters*, February 5, 2013, https://www.reuters.com/article/malaysia-china-investment/china-to-invest-more-than-1-6-billion-in-malaysia-steel-port-idUSL4N0B55RE20130205.

35. "Malaysia Investment Performance Report 2018," Malaysian Investment Development Authority, http://www.mida.gov.my/home/administrator/system_files/modules/photo/uploads/20190314161429_YBM%20Media%20Presentation%20Slides.pdf, 7 (accessed August 6, 2019).

36. "Approved Investments in 2017 Creates 129,520 Additional Job Opportunities in Malaysia," Malaysian Investment Development Authority, http://www.mida.gov.my/home/administrator/system_files/modules/photo/uploads/20170302155931_Slides%20Presentation%20Malaysia%20Investment%20Performance%202016.pdf, 3 (accessed August 6, 2019).

in Tokyo in May 2019 that Huawei has achieved a "tremendous advance over American technology." Washington has put Huawei on its Entity List, which includes foreign companies blacklisted for posing alleged national security threats. Axiata Group Berhad, Malaysia's largest wireless carrier, is working with Huawei on network technology, although it has not decided which companies it will partner with to roll out 5G services.[37]

Chinese tourists play an increasing important role in the economies of Southeast Asia. Over 2.9 million Chinese tourists visited Malaysia in 2018, an increase of nearly 30 percent over the previous year,[38] but still lagging Thailand, which is the most popular Southeast Asian tourist destination for Chinese with 10.5 million tourists in 2018.[39] Malaysia is the ninth largest global market for Chinese tourist spending according to online payment platform Alipay.[40]

To boost the number of visitors, Malaysia has introduced a visa waiver program and is partnering with China Southern Airlines to increase connections between the two nations. Currently some 470 weekly flights connect the two countries.[41]

Malaysia's famous pungent durian have become a major attraction for Chinese tourists. Chinese travel agents have started putting on special tours during the peak season, from early May in Penang in the north to early August in the south, for dedicated Chinese durian-lovers to savor such varieties as the Musang King and the Red Prawn.[42]

---

37. C. K. Tan and P. Prem Kumar, "Malaysia Will Use Huawei Tech 'as Much as Possible,' says Mahathir," *Nikkei Asian Review*, May 30, 2019, https://asia.nikkei.com/Spotlight/The-Future-of-Asia-2019/Malaysia-will-use-Huawei-tech-as-much-as-possible-says-Mahathir; Dave McCombs, "Malaysia's Mahathir Backs Huawei in Rare Public Rebuke of U.S.," *Bloomberg*, May 30, 2019, https://www.bloomberg.com/news/articles/2019-05-30/mahathir-backs-huawei-in-rare-public-rebuke-of-u-s-clampdown.

38. Syahirah Syed Jaafar, "Tourist Arrivals for 2018 Miss Target for Eighth Year," *The Edge Markets*, February 28, 2019, https://www.theedgemarkets.com/article/tourist-arrivals-2018-miss-target-eighth-year.

39. "Tourism Statistics Thailand 2000–2019," *Thaiwebsites.com*, http://www.thaiwebsites.com/tourism.asp (accessed August 4, 2019).

40. "Malaysia Ranked No. 9 for Chinese Tourists' Spending," *The Star*, May 22, 2018, https://www.thestar.com.my/news/nation/2018/05/22/malaysia-ranked-no-9-for-chinese-tourists-spending/.

41. "Interview: Malaysia Ramps Up Efforts to Attract Chinese Tourists," *Xinhua*, October 13, 2017, http://www.xinhuanet.com/english/2017-10/13/c_136676857.htm.

42. "Deduct Points for Football Violence, Says Khairy," *Free Malaysia Today*, August 7, 2016, http://www.freemalaysiatoday.com/category/nation/2018/07/16/durian-tours-gaining-popularity-with-chinese-tourists/dedu.

China sometimes uses tourism as an economic weapon to punish countries, as it did when the Philippines brought an arbitral tribunal case against China after it seized Scarborough Shoal in 2012. Occasionally, Chinese tourists shun a destination on their own for some time, as happened after Malaysia Airlines Flight 370 disappeared flying from Kuala Lumpur to Beijing in March 2014. In the following weeks, Chinese arrivals in Malaysia declined by 50 percent.[43]

Complaints erupted in Malaysia in recent years when the surge of Chinese tourists appeared to attract the arrival of tour guides from China, particularly on the island resorts of Penang and Langkawi. Local tour guides grumbled that Chinese competitors were affecting their ability to find work, prompting a pledge from China's ambassador to Malaysia that the embassy would investigate these charges.[44]

As in other markets, Chinese tourists sometimes get in trouble in Malaysia. In 2018, two Chinese nationals clad in shorts were fined just under $10 each and escorted to the airport for a return flight to China after they danced disrespectfully in front of the city mosque in Kota Kinabalu in Sabah.[45]

CHINA PRESSES MARITIME CLAIMS

China and Malaysia have overlapping claims in the South China Sea, but Beijing in recent years has put less pressure on Malaysia than on Vietnam and the Philippines in the maritime dispute. But on May 10, 2019, only a month after the two governments had agreed to resume work on their postponed rail project, the hulking Chinese coast guard vessel *Haijing* 35111 arrived over the horizon near Luconia Shoals off the coast of the eastern state of Sarawak.

---

43. Zhang Hong and Laura Zhou, "Chinese Tourists Boycott Malaysia in Wake of MH370 Disappearance," *South China Morning Post*, March 26, 2014, https://www.scmp.com/article/1457902/malaysia-tourism-hit-sharp-drop-chinese-visitors-wake-mh370-incident.
44. "China Embassy to Probe Claims of Chinese Tour Guides Operating in Malaysia," *Straits Times*, February 3, 2018, https://www.straitstimes.com/asia/se-asia/china-embassy-to-probe-claims-of-chinese-tour-guides-operating-in-malaysia?&utm_source=google_gmail&utm_medium=social-media&utm_campaign=addtoany.
45. The Star/Asia News Network, "Chinese Tourists Fined $8.50 Each for Disrespectful Dance in Front of Malaysia Mosque Wall," *Straits Times*, June 28, 2018, https://www.straitstimes.com/asia/se-asia/chinese-tourists-fined-850-each-for-disrespectful-dance-in-front-of-malaysia-mosque.

In the following days, the vessel circled and provocatively approached within 90 yards of the two supply ships contracted by a subsidiary of Royal Dutch Shell to service an oil rig leased from Supura Drilling. For the next two weeks the *Haijing* 35111 harassed and impeded Shell's drilling operations at natural gas field 14, one of three fields the Shell subsidiary was developing in block 2016, according to the vessels' signals tracked by the Asia Maritime Transparency Initiative (AMTI) at the Center for Strategic and International Studies (CSIS).

"Given the close-quarters and provocative behavior on display, there is a clear risk that an accidental collision could lead to escalation," AMTI warned.[46]

The location where the Chinese coast guard vessel approached the ships contracted by Shell was on Malaysia's continental shelf in an area where the Malaysian oil company Petronas and its partners have pumped oil and gas for decades. Chinese blog posts that were later removed claimed that a second coast guard vessel, *Haijing* 46302, was also involved in the operations around the oil rig. After two weeks, *Haijing* 35111 returned briefly to its base on China's Hainan Island for several days before heading to the coast of Vietnam to harass another oil rig.

But this was not the end of China's pressure on energy exploration activities off the coast of Malaysia. By early August 2019, the Chinese Academy of Science's survey ship *Shiyan* 2 was operating near Luconia Breakers in Malaysia's exclusive economic zone.[47] The *Shiyan* 2 does exploration that is primarily oil and gas related.[48] It was operating in an area near where the Shell subsidiary had leased the Deepwater Nautilus to drill six wells between May 2019 and January 2020.[49]

46. Asia Maritime Transparency Initiative, "China Risks Flare-Up over Malaysian, Vietnamese Gas Resources," Center for Strategic and International Studies, July 16, 2019, https://amti.csis.org/china-risks-flare-up-over-malaysian-vietnamese-gas-resources/.

47. Ryan Martinson (@rdmartinson88), Twitter, "The Chinese Academy of Science survey ship 'Shiyan 2' is currently operating in Malaysia's exclusive economic zone, near the Luconia Breakers," August 4, 2019, 7:41 a.m., https://twitter.com/rdmartinson88/status/1157979954312896512.

48. "Scientific Research Ship," Key Laboratory of Ocean and Marginal Sea Geology, Chinese Academy of Science, http://www.omg.scsio.ac.cn/document.action?docid=31521 (accessed November 26, 2019).

49. "Transocean Secures More Work for Its Rigs, Adds $373 Million in Contract Backlog," *OffshoreEnergyToday.com*, https://www.offshoreenergytoday.com/transocean-secures-more-work-for-its-rigs-adds-373-million-in-contract-backlog/ (accessed August 5, 2019).

Map 10. Malaysia's claims in the South China Sea

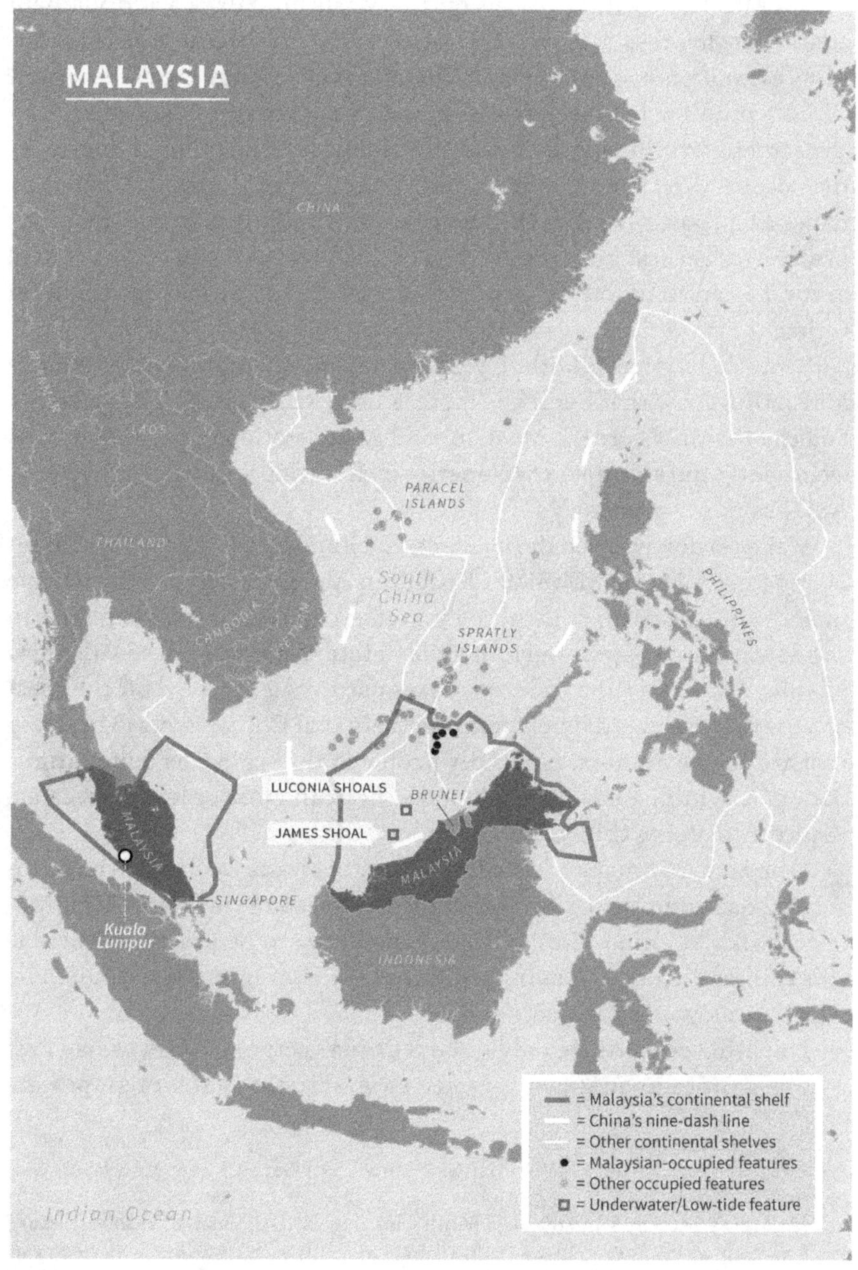

Analysts see the swarming of China's coast guard and People's Armed Forces Maritime Militia vessels off the coasts of Malaysia and Vietnam as an effort to press these countries to abandon unilateral projects to develop oil and gas even on their continental shelves if the area falls within China's nine-dash-line claim. In 2017 and 2018, Beijing had convinced Vietnam to terminate exploration efforts by Spanish oil firm Repsol off the coast of Vietnam after reportedly threatening force against Vietnamese outposts nearby. Off the coast of the Philippines, China has pressed for several years for Manila not to develop the natural gas field around Reed Bank on its own but instead do the project jointly with China.

"China's actions off both the Malaysian and Vietnamese coasts since May [2019] show that Beijing is increasingly willing to employ coercion and the threat of force to block oil and gas operations by its neighbors, even while pursuing its own energy exploration in disputed waters," AMTI said in statement.[50]

Malaysia downplayed the incident, and its domestic media avoided reporting on it. Foreign Minister Saifuddin Abdullah had provided some insights into Malaysia's thinking in remarks about China's behavior in the South China Sea in April in a video interview with the *South China Morning Post* before the Chinese coast guard vessel arrived off the coast of Sarawak. "Things happen here and there that China seems to be doing that are seen by others, especially people in the region, as quite intimidating," the minister said. "And I hope they can more or less de-escalate their way of doing things."

"The South China Sea issue is one very big issue that we have not resolved," Saifuddin said, adding that the issue is on the table each time Malaysia talks to China. "But, of course, you have to be practical. There is this thing called low-hanging fruits and whichever one you can handle first, I think you try and settle it."[51]

Mahathir said little in public about China's actions. When he had first assumed office in 2018 he suggested several times that foreign powers

50. Asia Maritime Transparency Initiative, "China Risks Flare-Up over Malaysian, Vietnamese Gas Resources."

51. "Malaysia's Foreign Minister Says South China Sea Still a Major Unresolved Issue," *South China Morning Post*, video, 2:17, April 22, 2019, https://www.scmp.com/video/asia/3007174/malaysias-foreign-minister-says-south-china-sea-still-major-unresolved-issue.

should keep warships out of the sea and deploy only small patrol vessels instead. "I think there should not be too many warships. Warships create tension," Mahathir told the *South China Morning Post*. "Someday, somebody might make some mistakes and there will be a fight, some ships will be lost, and there might be a war."[52]

Mahathir did not make clear whether his warships reference alluded to China or the United States. Likely it was to both. China has constructed half a dozen artificial islands in the Spratlys and equipped four of them with runways for handling military planes and missile stations, and China's giant coast guard vessels regularly sail through Malaysian waters. Washington, meanwhile, frequently sails navy ships near disputed islands in "freedom of navigation" exercises.

Interestingly, Mahathir did refer to the South China Sea in his speech at the BRI summit in Beijing in April shortly after Malaysia agreed to resume the east coast rail project with China. "Everyone will benefit from the ease of travel and communication that the development of the belt and road project will bring," Mahathir said. "An essential element is the freedom of passage along these routes. . . . Both the sea and land routes will pass through many countries. . . . It is essential therefore for these passages to be free and open to all."[53]

In late June 2019, a month after China's coast guard and maritime militia vessels pivoted from the coast of Malaysia to that of Vietnam, the Chinese military conducted missile tests in a disputed region of the South China Sea. The missiles reportedly were anti-ship ballistic missiles and the tests marked the first time the missiles had been fired over open water. The significance of these weapons is that China would now be able to put at risk the naval assets of the United States and other countries operating in the disputed waters.[54]

---

52. Bhavan Jaipragas, "Forget the Warships: Malaysian PM Mahathir's Peace Formula for the South China Sea," *South China Morning Post*, June 19, 2018, https://www.scmp.com/week-asia/geopolitics/article/2151403/forget-warships-malaysian-pm-mahathirs-peace-formula-south.

53. Kinling Lo, "Malaysia's Mahathir Backs China's Belt and Road but Insists on Open Trade Routes," *South China Morning Post*, April 26, 2019, https://www.scmp.com/news/china/diplomacy/article/3007874/malaysias-mahathir-backs-chinas-belt-and-road-insists-open.

54. Ankit Panda, "How Chinese Missile Tests Could Up the Stakes for the U.S. in the South China Sea," *South China Morning Post*, July 14, 2018, https://www.scmp.com/news/china/diplomacy/article/3018520/how-chinese-missile-tests-could-stakes-us-south-china-sea.

In advance of the exercise, China warned ships not to enter a designated area between the disputed Spratly and Paracel Islands for five days. Pentagon officials said the missile launch took place from one of the half dozen islands China has built up and to which it has added military capabilities in the South China Sea.[55]

Surprisingly, Malaysia did its own missile launches shortly after China's. In mid-July 2019, Malaysia's air force conducted live-fire missile exercises in Sabah State and the waters in the South China Sea. The air force exercise followed a similar test by the Malaysian navy some days earlier that had fired guided missiles from a ship to a helicopter. The missile firings by the air force and navy were part of larger military exercises. The last time Malaysia had tested its anti-ship missiles was in 2014.[56]

In December 2019, some months after the missile launches, Malaysia submitted information to the UN Commission on the Limits of the Continental Shelf expressing its rights to an extended continental shelf beyond 200 nautical miles. This new submission nearly doubled the range of the continental shelf from Malaysia's earlier 1979 government map.

Beijing rejected Malaysia's submission, declaring that it "seriously infringed China's sovereignty, sovereign rights and jurisdiction in the South China Sea." Malaysia's Foreign Minister Saifuddin responded: "For China to claim the whole South China Sea belongs to China, I think that is ridiculous."[57]

Much of China's charm offensive toward Southeast Asia of the late 1990s and early 2000s began to unravel in April 2010, when Beijing asserted its "undisputable claim" on the South China Sea by claiming it was a "core interest" similar to China's claims on Taiwan and Tibet.[58] In May 2011, Chinese patrol boasts confronted a Vietnamese vessel exploring

---

55. "U.S. Criticizes Chinese 'Missile Launches' in the South China Sea," *BBC News*, July 3, 2019, https://www.bbc.com/news/world-asia-china-48850085.

56. Ridzwan Rahmat, "Malaysia Flexes Missile Capabilities in the South China Sea amid Fresh Tensions," *Jane's 360*, July 16, 2019, https://www.janes.com/article/89904/malaysia-flexes-missile-capabilities-in-south-china-sea-amid-fresh-tensions.

57. Sean Quirk, "Water Wars: Stare Decisis in the South China Sea," *Lawfare*, January 6, 2020, https://www.lawfareblog.com/water-wars-stare-decisis-south-china-sea; Ted Regencia, "Malaysia FM: China's 'Nine-Dash Line' Claim 'Ridiculous,'" *Aljazeera*, December 21, 2019, https://www.aljazeera.com/news/2019/12/malaysian-top-envoy-china-dash-line-claim-ridiculous-191221034730108.html.

58. Mark Landler, "Offering to Aid Talks, U.S. Challenges China on Disputed Islands," *New York Times*, July 24, 2010, https://www.nytimes.com/2010/07/24/world/asia/24diplo.html.

for oil and gas in the South China Sea, snapping its seismic cables.[59] Over several weeks beginning in April 2012, Chinese cutters effectively dislodged Philippine vessels from Scarborough Shoal and seized full control of the fertile fishing ground.[60]

Earlier, China had seized from Vietnam the Paracel Islands in 1974 and Johnson South in the Spratly group further south in 1988 and captured Mischief Reef from the Philippines in 1995. But Beijing has not moved against any disputed Malaysian-occupied features that fall within China's nine-dash line, even though it appears to cut as near as 34 nautical miles off the coast of Sarawak in eastern Malaysia.

Malaysia claims 11 maritime features in the Spratlys and occupies eight of them, including Swallow Reef, which it seized in 1983 and then moved to build an artificial island, complete with an airstrip and 90-room resort for scuba diving.[61]

Compared to its frequent confrontations with the Philippines and Vietnam, China had not until May 2019 objected to Malaysia's oil and gas exploitation off the coast of Sabah and Sarawak, even though some of the area lies within Beijing's nine-dash line. Analysts speculate this is because the Malaysian area is much further from China than the areas disputed with the Philippines and Vietnam, so it has taken longer for Beijing to project its growing maritime heft that far south.

Malaysia, at least initially under Najib's leadership, seemed to have adopted a "play it safe" approach of saying little publicly about China's policies and actions in the South China Sea. Instead, Kuala Lumpur pursued "a combination of diplomatic, legal, economic, and security initiatives that secure its interests as a claimant state while being careful not to disrupt its vital bilateral relationship with China," observed Prashanth Parameswaran of *The Diplomat*.[62]

---

59. "Update 1-Vietnam Says Chinese Boats Harassed Oil Exploration Ship," *Reuters*, May 27, 2011, https://af.reuters.com/article/energyOilNews/idAFL3E7GR1HL20110527.

60. Michael Green, Kathleen Hicks, Zack Cooper, John Schaus, and Jake Douglas, "Counter-Coercion Series: Scarborough Shoal Standoff," Center for Strategic and International Studies—Asia Maritime Transparency Initiative, May 22, 2017, https://amti.csis.org/counter-co-scarborough-standoff/.

61. Pek Koon Heng, "Testimony: Hearing on China's Relations with Southeast Asia," The U.S.-China Economic and Security Review Commission, May 13, 2015, https://www.uscc.gov/sites/default/files/Heng_Written%20Testimony_5.13.2015%20Heaing.pdf, 7–8.

62. Prashanth Parameswaran, "Playing It Safe: Malaysia's Approach to the South China Sea and Implications for the United States," Center for a New American Security, February 2015,

Malaysia, which is Southeast Asia's second largest oil and natural gas producer, gets a significant chunk of its energy resources from the South China Sea. Oil and gas revenue contributes about a third of the government's budget, so hydrocarbons are critical to the state's operations.[63]

Some of the disputed sea's most productive oil and gas deposits are off the northern coast of Sarawak and Sabah in East Malaysia. About nine oil and gas blocks are pumping energy with investors such as Royal Dutch Shell, Murphy Oil Corporation, and ConocoPhillips operating joint ventures with Malaysia's state-owned oil company.[64]

Malaysia and China have well-developed energy relations. The Southeast Asian country is China's third largest supplier of liquified natural gas. In 2014, China Petroleum and Chemical Corporation, or Sinopec, partnered with Petronas in an oil sands project in Canada.

But Kuala Lumpur had some earlier hints that its hydrocarbon projects off the coast of eastern Malaysia had appeared on Beijing's radar. For over a year between 2013 and early 2014, Chinese naval patrols hung around James Shoal (Beting Serupai in Malay), some 43 nautical miles off the coast of Sarawak State.

"The government responded with a baffling array of silence, denial, and nonchalance," noted Elina Noor, who was then director for foreign policy and security studies at the Institute of Strategic and International Studies in Kuala Lumpur. "Malaysian authorities had been caught off balance by China's audacity, which they had not expected given Kuala Lumpur's perceived special relationship with Beijing."[65]

Separately, a Chinese coast guard vessel arrived at South Luconia Shoals in September 2013 and stayed there until just before Malaysia was slated to host the Association of Southeast Asian Nations (ASEAN) summit in November two years later. While there, the coast guard vessel chased away Malaysian fishers, prompting complaints by the Sarawak government and a local fishers' association.

---

https://s3.amazonaws.com/files.cnas.org/documents/CNAS-Maritime-6_Parameswaran_Final.pdf?mtime=20160906081622, 4.

63. Ibid., 4.

64. Eric Yep and Simon Hall, "Malaysia, China Keep Low Profile on Conflicting Sea Claims," *Wall Street Journal*, June 24, 2014, https://www.wsj.com/articles/malaysia-china-keep-low-profile-on-1403622597.

65. Elina Noor, "Malaysia: Recalibrating Its South China Sea Policy," Center for Strategic and International Studies—Asia Maritime Transparency Initiative, January 8, 2016, https://amti.csis.org/malaysia-recalibrating-its-south-china-sea-policy/.

The Chinese coast guard vessel prompted hearings in Malaysia's Parliament and complaints from several government officials, including from a minister in the Prime Minister's Department who posted aerial photos of the vessel on Facebook in June 2015. Malaysian naval and maritime enforcement vessels responded by stepping up their patrols in the area to 345 days in 2015, up from 269 the previous year.[66]

But a month after the ASEAN summit, China's coast guard vessels had returned to Luconia Shoals and until late February 2017, at least three different coast guard vessels had appeared over the 60-day period.[67]

"It's a wake-up call that it could happen to us and it is happening to us," Malaysian foreign policy expert Tang Siew Mun, of the ISEAS-Yusof Ishak Institute in Singapore, told Reuters about the incidents around James Shoal in 2014. "For some time we believed in this special relationship. . . . James Shoal has shown to us over and over again that when it comes to China protecting its sovereignty and national interest it's a different ball game."[68]

The Chinese ship intrusions upset Malaysian defense officials and political leaders, but they said little publicly to protest China's actions. At least in part, China's moves were possible because the Malaysian navy had little or no physical presence in the area.[69]

But Malaysia responded by "beefing up its security presence in the area (albeit limited by budgetary resources), enhancing security partnership[s] with the United States and Japan, voicing . . . its unhappiness in several international fora, [and] upholding ASEAN unity and ensuring ASEAN's collective engagement in the dispute," Ngeow said. He added that "somewhat ironically," Malaysia tried to strengthen its "defense relations with China so as to increase mutual trust and confidence." Ngeow pointed out that Malaysia now has to live with "a changed

66. Ibid.

67. Asia Maritime Transparency Initiative, "Tracking China's Coast Guard off Borneo," Center for Strategic and International Studies, April 5, 2017, https://amti.csis.org/tracking-chinas-coast-guard-off-borneo/.

68. Stuart Grudgings, "Insight: China's Assertiveness Hardens Malaysian Stance in Sea Dispute," *Reuters*, February 26, 2014, https://www.reuters.com/article/us-malaysia-china-maritime-insight/insight-chinas-assertiveness-hardens-malaysian-stance-in-sea-dispute-idUSBREA1P1YX20140226.

69. Asia Maritime Transparency Initiative, "Tracking China's Coast Guard off Borneo"; Ngeow, "A 'Model' for ASEAN Countries," in *China and Southeast Asia in the Xi Jinping Era*, ed. Alvin Cheng-Hin Lim and Frank Cibulka (Lanham, MD: Lexington Books, 2019), 116.

reality on the ground" of "a constant Coast Guard presence in Luconia Shoals."[70]

In March 2015, as China was mounting its island reclamation and militarization activities in the South China Sea, a Malaysian deputy foreign minister described China in surprisingly strong terms as "as an aggressive nation" in the sea and called on ASEAN to stand together against this source of aggression.[71] The following month when Malaysia hosted the ASEAN leaders summit, Najib in a chairman's statement said that China's island reclamation activities were eroding "trust and confidence and may undermine peace, security, and stability in the South China Sea."[72]

Malaysians found other ways to let Beijing know privately that they were frustrated. During the last few years of the Najib regime, the foreign minister, a parliamentarian from Sabah, had sent what one defense analyst called annual "love letters" to his Chinese counterpart listing China's "sins" during the previous year. The references included the dates when Chinese ships had blocked Malaysia's coast guard vessels in Malaysian waters, conducted boat-ramming incidents, and interfered with fishing operations by Malaysian fishers. The foreign minister also cited examples of when Chinese vessels had pilfered oil from Malaysian boats or fishers and used Chinese vessels to pressure oil platforms off the coast of Sabah and Sarawak.

The analyst also said that in 2017, the Malaysian coast guard had planted coconut trees on the only feature above water during high tide in Luconia Shoals. He said Chinese forces responded by pulling out the trees and smearing oil on the beach to ensure that nothing would grow there in the future.

At the end of that year, a Chinese vessel passed near an oil rig off Luconia Shoal, "spooking our people," the defense analyst said. "That is the only place within [China's] nine-dash line that there's an unoccupied feature above high tide. I don't know why it's not occupied, but if we did it now, it would be escalatory."

70. Ngeow, "A 'Model' for ASEAN Countries," 117.

71. Rahimy Rahim, "Malaysia to Push Drafting of Code of Conduct with China to Settle Dispute," *The Star*, March 12, 2015, https://www.thestar.com.my/news/nation/2015/03/12/parliament-coc-malaysia-china/.

72. Manuel Mogato and Praveen Menon, "China Maritime Tensions Dominate Southeast Asia Summit," *Reuters*, April 27, 2015, https://www.reuters.com/article/us-asean-summit-southchinasea/china-maritime-tensions-dominate-southeast-asia-summit-idUSKBN0NI0BH20150427.

In early 2018, Malaysian media reported public calls for Malaysia to follow the example of other South China Sea claimants in renaming parts of the disputed sea near Malaysia.[73] The Philippine government had renamed the sea around its country the West Philippine Sea. Indonesia, which does not have overlapping claims with China but has disputes over Chinese fishers operating in its waters, called its area the North Natuna Sea. The Najib government, which had followed a nonconfrontational approach to China in the disputed sea, did not act on this recommendation before it left office.

Ngeow summarizes China's policy toward Malaysia "as one of offering inducements through economic and, to a lesser extent, cultural charm offensives" with a policy that "is balanced by maintaining and asserting China's position in the South China Sea dispute." The academic argues that any Malaysian leader, whether Najib before or Mahathir today, has to face "contradictory policy dynamics from China." Ngeow says that, while many critics described Najib as "too much aligned with China," in reality he did not pursue a Beijing-friendly policy at the expense of relations with China's rivals such as the United States, Japan, and India. The China expert argues that Mahathir will likely continue similar engagement with all major powers.[74]

To hedge against China's increasing assertiveness, Najib moved to deepen political, security, and economic relations with the United States when the administration of President Barack Obama launched its rebalance to Asia around 2011. Najib bolstered Malaysia's military ties with Washington by welcoming more U.S. naval ship visits to Malaysia and having its military forces join the annual U.S.-led Cobra Gold military exercises in Thailand as full members instead of only observers. Najib also looked to the United States to help build a marine corps in Malaysia and hosted the first exercise with U.S. marines in Sabah in 2014.[75]

As a hedge against China's increasingly dominant economic role in Malaysia, Kuala Lumpur joined the 12-nation Trans-Pacific Partnership (TPP) trade agreement, which included the United States and Japan but not China

73. Prashanth Parameswaran, "Should Malaysia Rename Its Part of the South China Sea?," *The Diplomat*, March 9, 2018, https://thediplomat.com/2018/03/should-malaysia-rename-its-part-of-the-south-china-sea/.
74. Ngeow, "A 'Model' for ASEAN Countries," 119.
75. Heng, "Testimony: Hearing on China's Relations with Southeast Asia," 12; Grudgings, "Insight."

(until U.S. President Donald Trump pulled out in 2017). The United States is Malaysia's fourth largest trading partner and the largest foreign investor on a cumulative basis.[76] Najib also looked to the TPP to help pull Malaysia out of the middle-income trap and become an advanced economy by 2020.

Asked about China's role in the South China Sea after he returned to office, Mahathir responded: "So we want to retain, of course, about four or five islands that we have occupied. . . . It is something if China claims the South China Sea is theirs, but those islands have been regarded as ours for a long time. So we want to retain them."[77] Ngeow believes Mahathir's comments suggest that, off the coast of Sabah and Sarawak, Mahathir will "continue to tolerate the presence of Chinese ships, as long as this does not disturb Malaysia's economic interests" such as fishing and oil and gas exploitation.

In his first public comments on the South China Sea, Mahathir's foreign minister, Saifuddin, said in July 2018 that Malaysia would adopt a firmer stand on the South China Sea, in apparent reference to the previous government that rarely criticized Beijing. The foreign minister said that the prime minister "was sending a signal that we want to be more firm, more serious" in handling the dispute. Saifuddin told Parliament that the 2002 Declaration of a Code of Conduct in the South China Sea between China and the Southeast Asian countries has "no fangs," adding that Beijing's militarization of the sea could escalate regional tensions.[78]

CHINA AND THE ETHNIC CHINESE

Malaysia's ties with China date back to the fifteenth century when the Malacca Sultanate became a protectorate and tributary state of the Ming dynasty to defend itself against Thailand and other neighboring powers. The port of Malacca emerged as an important trading center, warehousing facility, and harbor to protect ships against monsoon rains along Chinese trading routes through the Strait of Malacca.[79]

---

76. U.S. Department of State, "U.S. Relations with Malaysia: Bilateral Relations Fact Sheet," Bureau of East Asian and Pacific Affairs, July 17, 2018, https://www.state.gov/r/pa/ei/bgn/2777.htm.
77. Zuraidah and Jaipragas, "Mahathir Mohamad Q&A."
78. Eileen Ng, "Malaysia to Be Firmer in Row over South China Sea," *Associated Press*, July 24, 2018, https://www.seattletimes.com/nation-world/malaysia-to-be-firmer-in-row-over-south-china-sea/.
79. Barbara Watson Andaya and Leonard Y. Andaya, *A History of Malaysia* (Macmillan, 1982), 41–42.

The descendants of the Chinese migrants who came to the Malay Archipelago between the fifteenth and seventeenth centuries are known as Peranakan, or Straits-born Chinese, who adopted many elements of Malay culture from the largest ethnic group, including aspects of their language. The ancestors of many of the ethnic Chinese living in Malaysia today came to work on rubber plantations and in tin mines during the British colonial period that began in the early 1800s.

When Malaysia gained independence in 1957, the country still faced an insurrection by the Malayan Communist Party supported by China. As a result, the new government viewed China as one of Malaysia's top security threats. The ethnic Chinese in Malaysia at the time comprised 38 percent of the population and many of them were working-class people whose loyalty was considered to be pro-China, increasing the government's anxiety about the threat from the communist rebels. This challenge prompted Kuala Lumpur to adopt a strong pro-West foreign policy and seek to maintain close ties with Britain and the United States to boost the country's security and economic development.

The fighting largely ended by the late 1950s and, in 1974 Malaysia, under Najib's father, Prime Minister Abdul Razak, became the first ASEAN country to normalize diplomatic relations with China. This move was prompted by Washington's steps toward rapprochement with Beijing and the U.S. withdrawal from the war in Vietnam. Two key changes by China made this policy shift possible: Beijing's decision to severe links with the Malaysian communists (although it did not formally happen until 1978) and its adoption of new citizenship laws that stopped recognizing overseas Chinese as citizens of China.[80]

Despite their disputes over islands in the South China Sea, Malaysian leaders, beginning with Mahathir during his first stint as prime minister, dubbed China an opportunity rather than a threat. "Why should we fear China?" Mahathir famously said in 1997. "If you identify a country as your future enemy, it becomes your present enemy—because then they will identify you as an enemy and there will be tension."[81]

---

80. Heng, "Testimony: Hearing on China's Relations with Southeast Asia," 1–3.

81. Asiaweek, "I Am Still Here: Asiaweek's Complete Interview with Mahathir Mohamad," *CNN*, May 9, 1997, http://edition.cnn.com/ASIANOW/asiaweek/97/0509/cs3.html, quoted in Cheng-Chwee Kuik, "Malaysia between the United States and China: What Do Weaker States Hedge Against?," *Asian Politics and Policy* 8, no. 1 (2016): 160, https://www.researchgate.net/publication/291748126_Kuik_2016_APP_What_Do_Weaker_States_Hedge_Against.

Malaysian Chinese businesspersons, led by entrepreneurs such as William Cheng of the Lion Group and Robert Kuok, were among the first wave of foreign companies to invest in China after the government launched reforms in the late 1970s. The second wave of investment from Malaysia began after the Asian financial crisis in 1997 when Malaysian government-linked companies such as Khazanah Nasional, the country's sovereign wealth fund, and Sime Darby, the world's biggest palm oil plantation owner, began to invest in China.

The stock of Malaysian foreign investment in China reached $7.5 billion by 2017, which is the second highest amount from Southeast Asia behind Singapore, according to Chinese government figures.[82]

The ethnic Chinese in Malaysia today number about 7 million or nearly a quarter of the population, making the country's ethnic Chinese diaspora one of the largest in Southeast Asia. The ethnic Chinese exercise considerable economic clout, although exactly how much is not known. The last time the government released corporate equity ownership figures by ethnic group was in 2008. That year, the equity owned by the Chinese was 34.9 percent. "I don't think that figure has changed much over the past decade," says economist Edmund Terence Gomez of the University of Malaya.

The Chinese heritage in Malaysia has survived to a considerable extent thanks to Malaysia's multiculturalism. The national educational system allows ethnic minorities to study and maintain their mother languages. This has made it possible for the Chinese community in Malaysia to keep alive its culture, beliefs, and language in ways largely unmatched in other Southeast Asian countries.[83]

At the same time, the country's ethnic diversity has also slowed assimilation and has kept Malaysia's politics divided along racial lines. Violent race riots erupted in Kuala Lumpur in May 1969 after opposition parties backed by the ethnic Chinese community made major gains in general elections. About 200 people are believed to have been killed in the clashes, although some estimates are higher.

---

82. "China-Malaysia Economic and Trade Cooperation," Ministry of Commerce of the People's Republic of China, September 27, 2017, http://yzs.mofcom.gov.cn/article/t/201709/20170902651400.shtml.

83. Peter T. C. Chang, "Ethnic Chinese in Malaysia Are Celebrating China's Rise—but as Multicultural Malaysians, not Chinese," *South China Moring Post*, May 11, 2018, https://www.scmp.com/comment/insight-opinion/article/2145521/ethnic-chinese-malaysia-are-celebrating-chinas-rise.

To address these racial cleavages, the government in 1971 implemented the new economic policy (NEP), an affirmative action program for ethnic Malays (or bumiputra), who comprise about two-thirds of the population. The NEP granted the majority special political privileges, set aside a 30 percent share for Malays in initial public offerings, and created quotas for Malays in university admission.

The fact that many of the NEP provisions remain in force over four decades later frustrates many ethnic Chinese and prompts significant numbers to leave for Singapore and Australia, creating a brain drain of some of Malaysia's best talent. Of the nearly 57,000 Malaysians who gave up their citizenship in the decade to 2016, just under 50,000 were ethnic Chinese, according to figures from Malaysia's Home Affairs Ministry.[84]

In Southeast Asian nations like Myanmar and Cambodia, the local ethnic Chinese community has often played a bridging role in facilitating investment from China. But at least so far, ethnic Chinese entrepreneurs are frustrated that they have been left out of the bonanza from China. "The Kuantan Chamber of Commerce complains that their companies don't get much" from China's investment, says Kuik of the National University of Malaysia. "They say Malaysia's bureaucracy follows a double standard by pursuing Chinese from the mainland. Some ethnic Chinese are not very happy."

Interestingly, the ethnic Chinese in Malaysia have benefited little from China's investment surge. A 2015 study by geographer Guanie Lim of the University of Singapore found that 50 percent of mainland Chinese firms collaborated with Malay government-linked companies (GLCs) while only 28 percent worked with Malaysian Chinese firms.[85] Breaking down these numbers by economic sector, 76 percent of the companies from China involved in construction cooperated with GLCs and only 12 percent with ethnic Chinese firms.

Lim said the heavy dependence on GLCs in construction stems from the need for projects to acquire land and get government approvals, which mainland Chinese firms are convinced will be easier for GLCs because

84. Tashny Sukumaran, "What's Causing Malaysia's Ethnic Chinese Brain Drain?," *South China Morning Post*, May 20, 2017, https://www.scmp.com/week-asia/politics/article/2095012/whats-causing-malaysias-ethnic-chinese-brain-drain.

85. Guanie Lim, "China's Investments in Malaysia: Choosing the 'Right' Partners," *International Journal of China Studies* 6, no. 1 (April 2015): 18.

their ties to the government are by definition closer than those of ethnic Chinese companies.[86]

The outsized reliance of Chinese firms on GLCs can be attributed to the dominant role GLCs play in Malaysia's economy, thanks at least in part to the affirmative action policies. These policies prompted the government to support the creation of giant government-linked conglomerates to promote greater equality between the Malay and ethnic Chinese.[87]

Meanwhile, in manufacturing, companies from China worked with Malaysian Chinese firms in 43 percent of ventures and only 29 percent with GLCs. Lim says this difference is due to ethnic Chinese firms "exploiting their expertise in the manufacturing industry despite their lack of state support."[88]

Since at least 2014, China's policy has been to engage more actively with ethnic Chinese abroad. At a conference of Overseas Chinese Associations in June that year, Chinese leader Xi Jinping gave a speech in which he declared that "the rejuvenation of the Chinese nation is the common dream" of the "sons and daughters of China within and outside China."[89] The following January, politburo member Yang Jiechi in a speech to the National Overseas Chinese Conference called on the Chinese government to strengthen "overseas Chinese patriotic friendly forces" in the "great rejuvenation" of China.[90]

Then in March 2018, the United Front Work Department of the central committee of the Chinese Communist Party took the Overseas Chinese Affairs Office under its wing.[91] These moves are widely interpreted by analysts as a call by Beijing to persuade ethnic Chinese overseas "into accepting allegiance to China as at least part of their identity," former senior Singaporean diplomat Bilahari Kausikan argued in a speech at a June 2018 conference in Singapore.[92]

---

86. Ibid., 19.
87. Ibid., 19–20.
88. Ibid., 20.
89. Leo Suryadinata, *The Rise of China and the Overseas Chinese* (Singapore: ISEAS-Yusof Ishak Institute, 2017), 19.
90. "Amid Rise of Identity Politics, S'poreans Need to Beware Foreign Manipulation: Bilahari Kausikan," *Today*, July 12, 2018, https://www.todayonline.com/singapore/amid-rise-identity-politics-sporeans-need-beware-foreign-manipulation-bilahari-kausikan.
91. Ibid.
92. Ibid.

Since China stepped up its efforts to engage overseas Chinese, Chinese diplomats have sometimes found themselves in political situations that created controversy in Malaysia. In September 2015, the Chinese ambassador ran into a buzz saw of protest when he said on Petaling Street, Kuala Lumpur's Chinatown, that China opposes discrimination against ethnic groups. Two weeks earlier, this area had been the focal point of a pro-Malay demonstration and another one had been planned a day after the ambassador's visit. The diplomat warned that China would not "sit idly by" if others "infringe upon the legal rights of Chinese citizens and companies."[93]

Many Malaysians read the ambassador's comments as interference in Malaysia's internal affairs and a reminder of the early days after independence, when China supported Chinese communist insurgents in their effort to topple the government. Malaysia's deputy foreign minister summoned the ambassador to a meeting, but his aides responded that he was busy and said the ministry should send officials to the embassy. The ambassador instead went to meet other Malaysian officials who effectively let him off the hook, at a time when the foreign minister was at the United Nations in New York.[94]

A few days later, the Malaysian Chinese newspaper *Sin Chew Daily* responded to China's frequent references to ethnic Chinese as *huaqiao* (overseas Chinese) by saying that "this does not suit the Chinese in Malaysia" because it prompts Malays to question their loyalty. The paper, which is normally friendly to China, added: "The new generation of Malaysian Chinese regard themselves as Malaysians. They don't like to be called *Huaqiao*. . . . We do not want the Malays to keep doubting our loyalty to Malaysia and suspecting that we do not identify ourselves with Malaysia."[95]

Some academics think China got the message. "Yes, the ambassador's behavior was controversial, but he learned his lesson now and is making up by busily making friends with the [new ruling coalition] parties," says Ngeow, the China expert at the University of Malaya. The academic im-

93. "China's Envoy to Malaysia Visits Petaling Street Day before Rally," *Malay Mail*, September 15, 2015, https://www.malaymail.com/s/976463/chinas-envoy-to-malaysia-visits-petaling-street-day-before-rally; Suryadinata, *The Rise of China and the Overseas Chinese*, 112–114.

94. Parameswaran Ponnudurai, "China Flaunts Political Clout in Malaysia with Envoy's Defiance," *Radio Free Asia*, August 29, 2015, https://www.rfa.org/english/news/china/diplomacy-09292015182941.html.

95. Suryadinata, *The Rise of China and the Overseas Chinese*, 117–119.

plies that the ambassador ran into problems because he followed China's "traditional approach of cultivating ties with whoever is the powerholder of the day" instead of relating to a broad cross section of Malaysians.

Separately, at the time of the lunar year festivities in early 2018, China's new ambassador, Bai Tian, was very active in attending and giving speeches at celebrations organized by the Malaysian Chinese community around the country. Some Malaysian observers criticized him for attending only festivities linked to the Malaysian Chinese Association (MCA) and the then-ruling party and not those tied to the then-opposition and largely ethnic Chinese Democratic Action Party (DAP) headed by Lim Guan Eng, the current finance minister.

Soon after the ambassador arrived in Malaysia in late 2017, he visited Bentong in Pahang, the constituency of then MCA chief Liow Tiong Lai, ostensibly to savor the area's famous durian and promote the town as an area for ecotourism among Chinese tourists.[96] Because of the timing of the visit, some observers interpreted it as a campaign stop for Liow. Analysts quoted by *The Star* newspaper, which has long been affiliated with the MCA, said "it is so obvious that the present and past ambassadors" were supporting the then-ruling coalition. But the Chinese Embassy spokesman insisted that China's policy is one of "no interference in the domestic politics of host countries."[97]

The ambassador also visited constituencies of Malay candidates of the ruling coalition, giving many people the impression that he supported their candidacies in the 2018 elections. One that grabbed attention was the ambassador's participation at an event in the constituency of then deputy prime minister Ahmad Zahid Hamidi in Perak State, north of the capital, during which he offered scholarships to residents and made donations to local schools.[98]

---

96. Malay Mail, "After Durian Feast, Chinese Envoy Promises to Promote Bentong to Countrymen," *Malay Mail*, January 6, 2018, https://www.malaymail.com/s/1547329/after-durian-feast-chinese-envoy-promises-to-promote-bentong-to-countrymen.
97. Ho Wah Foon, "China Factor Looms Ahead of Election," *The Star*, March 25, 2018, https://www.thestar.com.my/news/nation/2018/03/25/china-factor-looms-ahead-of-election-the-china-card-was-flashed-in-almost-every-general-election-in/.
98. Samantha Custer, Brooke Russell, Matthew DiLorenzo, Mengfan Cheng, Siddhartha Ghose, Harsh Desai, Jacob Sims, and Jennifer Turner, *Ties That Bind: Quantifying China's Public Diplomacy and Its "Good Neighbor" Effect* (Williamsburg, VA: AidData at William and Mary, June 2018), 31, https://docs.aiddata.org/ad4/pdfs/Ties_That_Bind--Full_Report.pdf.

A 2018 study of China's public diplomacy by the College of William and Mary in the United States noted that the "lack of sensitivity to Malaysia's domestic context on the part of Chinese companies and the Chinese embassy can undercut the efficacy of Beijing's public diplomacy overtures."[99]

In other cases during the 2018 election campaign, ethnic Chinese political parties tried to play the "China card." For instance, the MCA put up billboards depicting party chief Liow, not with then prime minister Najib but with Chinese president Xi. The MCA head and transportation minister seemed to be promoting his party's ties with the Chinese leader and implied that voters would stand to benefit from ties with China if they elected the ethnic Chinese party's candidates. In the end, Liow lost his seat and only one MCA candidate survived.[100]

Separately, in the run up to the elections, some Malay politicians of the then-ruling party threw insults at Robert Kuok, the ethnic Chinese tycoon now serving on Mahathir's council of eminent persons, opening a racial and religious rift in the country. They charged Kuok with funding a majority-Chinese opposition party, the DAP, to topple the Najib government. Kuok denied the allegations and threatened legal action, prompting Najib to intervene.

The firestorm erupted after Kuok released his memoirs in late 2017 in which he criticized the ruling coalition's affirmative action policies that favored the majority Malays over minority ethnic Chinese and Indians. Many ethnic Chinese saw the criticism against Kuok as race-baiting in a hotly contested election.[101]

Beijing in recent years has worked to boost its standing in the international media landscape around the globe and snare influence over the international narrative about China, including by using the Chinese-language media to appeal to overseas Chinese to support the mainland. In Malaysia, China got considerable support from a Chinese Malaysian tycoon who invested in Chinese-language newspapers, but he seems not to have fully succeeded in bringing the papers under Beijing's sway.

---

99. Ibid.

100. Foong Pek Yee and Tho Xin Yi, "Liow Will Not Seek Re-Election in MCA Polls," *The Star*, May 11, 2018, https://www.thestar.com.my/news/nation/2018/05/11/liow-will-not-seek-re-election-in-mca-polls/.

101. Bhavan Jaipragas, "Malaysian Election: Hong Kong Billionaire Robert Kuok Targeted by Anti-Chinese Whispers," *South China Morning Post*, February 27, 2018, https://www.scmp.com/week-asia/politics/article/2134932/malaysian-election-hk-billionaire-robert-kuok-targeted-anti.

Chinese Malaysian billionaire Tiong Hiew King, a timber tycoon from Sarawak in East Malaysia, acquired the money-losing *Sin Chew Daily*, the second largest Chinese newspaper in Malaysia, in 1988 during a domestic political crisis in the country. His motives were "purely from the business point of view more than anything," according to Kou Yok Liong, who served as an editor of the paper.

Within two years, the paper had recovered financially and Tiong emerged as "the leading Chinese community leader in Malaysia" and presented himself as "representing the view of Chinese Malaysians toward mainland China," Kuo recalls. As the paper grew in prestige, Tiong was "entertained by many Chinese Communist leaders."

In his youth, Tiong apparently had pro-communist sympathies. He was detained by the British colonial government in Sarawak for two years after being identified as supporting "communist activities" in what today are the Malaysian states of Sabah and Sarawak, according to Kou. Even before he bought into newspapers, Tiong had invested in a timber sawmill factory in Dalian along with various mining and oil projects, property development, and operating a toll road in China.[102]

In 1996, Tiong purchased the financially troubled Ming Pao Group in Hong Kong. "He definitely wished to turn *Ming Pao* into [a] pro-mainland paper," says Kou, who transferred to Hong Kong to work as an editor at the paper. But Tiong was "barred" from doing that by a close friend from Singapore "who escaped from China after he realized that the Communist regime was not what he wanted." This friend's stand made it possible for the paper's editors to adopt a "very neutral editorial policy on mainland China matters," Kou recalls.

In the early 1990s, Ming Pao expanded to Vancouver and Toronto with support from ethnic Chinese who "migrated to Canada with [a] negative view on [the British] handover of Hong Kong" in 1997, Kou says. Tiong tried to expand the paper to New York and San Francisco, the latter of which failed and shut down. Tiong also expanded to Chinese newspapers in Cambodia and Indonesia.

In 2007, Tiong merged two of the largest Chinese-language outlets in Malaysia, Xin Chew Media Corporation and Nanyang Press, with the remaining assets of Hong Kong's Ming Pao Group at a cost of nearly

102. "Tan Sri Tiong Hiew King—Rimbunan Hijau," *Fortune.my*, December 31, 2014, https://www.fortune.my/tan-sri-tiong-hiew-king-rimbunan-hijau.htm.

$500 million.[103] "From what I know, Tiong did not get instruction from mainland China to expand his newspaper empire worldwide," Kou notes. "It was purely Tiong's own ambition as he wanted to be seen by [the] mainland regime as a man who could influence the overseas Chinese."

Chang Teck Peng, a lecturer in the Faculty of Communication in the Tunku Abdul Rahman University College in Kuala Lumpur, believes that some Ming Pao publications softened their tone toward Beijing under Tiong's tenure. Ming Pao "used to be critical [of] China and power[s]-that-be," but the media outlet "became softer after Tiong took it over," argues Chang. *Yazhou Zhoukan* (Asia Weekly), also published by Ming Pao Group, became "significantly pro-China, especially when it comes to issues [that] involved Taiwan and U.S.-China conflicts."

Chang says that "occasionally" the weekly was critical of Beijing on "topics that would not affect politics in China." For example, the publication raised questions about the Chinese government "doing nothing in safeguarding Chinese Indonesians" during the riots in Jakarta in 1998.

Chinese-language newspapers in Malaysia, including those owned by Tiong, are generally "China-friendly," Chang says, which is "understandable" because "older generations of Malaysians are more inclined to China than to Taiwan" and because "the main sources of news on China are from Xinhua News Agency, Phoenix TV, [and] pro-China Hong Kong media."

Tiong suffered a stroke and stepped down from executive roles in his company in 2018 at the age of 83.[104]

POLITICAL TIES

Najib visited China in early November 2016 as the pressures on his 1MDB fund were building. One of his top goals was to snare more investment to bolster Malaysia's flagging economy. He signed a whopping $33 billion worth of deals, including for some infrastructure projects and for four littoral navy ships, with his Chinese counterparts.[105]

---

103. Adela Ma, "Bid for All of Ming Pao," *South China Morning Post*, October 13, 1995, https://www.scmp.com/article/135098/bid-all-ming-pao.
104. Oo Tee China, "MCIL: Hiew King Quits Executive Chairman Post," *New Straits Times*, March 28, 2018, https://www.nst.com.my/business/2018/03/350469/mcil-hiew-king-quits-executive-chairman-post.
105. Kuik and Lawrence, "A View from Malaysia."

Interestingly, he also wrote an editorial in a state-run Chinese daily calling on "former colonial powers" to cease interfering in the internal affairs of smaller nations. "It is not for them to lecture countries they once exploited on how to conduct their internal affairs today," Najib wrote.[106] It was not certain what precisely his motive was, but it may have been an effort to play China against the United States, whose Justice Department had mounted a criminal investigation into 1MDB.

China-Malaysia ties had faced several major tests in the previous two years. In 2013 and 2014, Chinese military vessels showed up at James Shoal, off the coast of the Sabah, where the Malaysian oil and gas company and its foreign partners were pumping hydrocarbons.

In March 2014 an ill-fated Malaysia Airlines plane flying from Kuala Lumpur to Beijing disappeared in the Indian Ocean, resulting in the loss of 154 Chinese nationals. Although the Chinese government was relatively restrained in its criticism of Malaysia's handling of the crisis, it put considerable pressure on Malaysia by allowing family members of the victims to protest in front of Malaysia's Embassy in Beijing and complain about the airlines handling of the missing airplane. Some called for boycotting Malaysian products.[107]

The airline disappearance was followed by two kidnappings of Chinese tourists from resorts in Sabah over the following two months by insurgents from the southern Philippines, which prompted the numbers of Chinese tourists visiting Malaysia to drop for about 18 months.[108] But neither the plane disappearance nor the kidnappings appear to have created longer-term problems in relations between Beijing and Kuala Lumpur.

Soon after Najib got back to Kuala Lumpur from his trip to Beijing, opposition politicians began criticizing China's growing economic clout in Malaysia. "I'm sure Chinese Malaysians won't feel comfortable seeing mainland Chinese come here with tons of cash to buy up Bandar Malaysia [real estate project] and make us work for them," former deputy prime minister Muhyiddin Yassin, who was fired by Najib for criticizing 1MDB,

---

106. Ibid.

107. Celia Hatton, "Malaysia Airlines MH370: Relatives in Beijing scuffles," *BBC*, March 25, 2014, https://www.bbc.com/news/world-asia-26728045; Asiaweek, "I Am Still Here," quoted in Kuik, "Malaysia between the United States and China," 161.

108. AP, "Chinese Tourist Kidnapped in Malaysia Is Rescued by Security Forces," *South China Morning Post*, May 31, 2014, https://www.scmp.com/news/asia/article/1522303/rescue-chinese-tourist-and-filipino-worker-held-hostage-2-months-after.

told a Malaysian Chinese newspaper. (Muhyiddin now serves as home affairs minister in Mahathir's the new government.)

China's ambassador quickly shot back: "These are people, when they were in power, pushed for friendly ties with China and welcomed Chinese investments to Malaysia. But when they are no longer in power, they strenuously fan anti-China sentiments and deliberately dismiss Chinese investments as China 'robbing rice bowls of locals.'"[109]

It was becoming clear that Malaysia's relations with China could no longer be fenced off from domestic Malaysian politics. In earlier election cycles, Malaysia's foreign policy was not a key campaign issue. When the "China card" had been played previously, it was used by the ruling coalition to try to win support from ethnic Chinese voters. In the 2018 elections, the opposition took advantage of the China issue to provoke anti-government sentiment among Malay voters, especially in rural areas, said Ngeow of the University of Malaya.[110]

The criticism of China's projects also created a quandary for Beijing. China read Najib's interest in Chinese investment as a great opportunity to build economic ties with a key Southeast Asian nation. But as Beijing was criticized for investing too much in one person, China risked potentially jeopardizing its relations with Kuala Lumpur. To avoid this, Ngeow said, Beijing needed to "be more transparent in its economic dealings with Malaysia."[111]

In July 2017, eight months before the election that swept Najib and his ruling coalition from power, China sent a delegation of academics to Malaysia to assess the political, financial, and legal situation and determine if there were any risks to China's projects. "We are here to study the response to Belt and Road projects," delegation head Zhang Yuyan, director of the Institute of World Economics, told journalists. "We have heard there are opposition noises and we hope to clear our doubts."

Another member of the delegation told journalists that Malaysia's political situation appeared to be "more stable now" than it was two years

109. Trinna Leong, "Beijing Rebuts Critics Who Say It Is Stealing Locals' Rice Bowls," *Straits Times*, January 25, 2017, https://www.straitstimes.com/asia/beijing-rebuts-critics-who-say-it-is-stealing-locals-rice-bowls.

110. Ngeow Chow Bing, "The Domestic Frays in Sino–Malaysian Ties," *East Asia Forum*, January 26, 2017, http://www.eastasiaforum.org/2017/01/26/the-domestic-frays-in-sino-malaysian-ties/.

111. Ibid.

earlier. What the group concluded or reported back to Beijing is not publicly known, but it would appear the scholars completely missed the level of public anger about the 1MDB scandal and the role that massive Chinese investments played in helping to bail out Najib.[112]

Between taking office in 2009 and his toppling in 2018, Najib visited China eight times, including five times after Xi took power in 2013, making China Najib's most visited country. His deputy and the ministers of defense and foreign affairs also visited frequently. President Xi and his predecessor, and Premier Li Keqiang and his predecessor, also visited Malaysia once each, while other senior Chinese political, military, and provincial officials traveled to Malaysia frequently.[113]

On a visit in 2013, Xi urged Malaysia to step up party-to-party cooperation; the following year the Chinese Communist Party signed agreements with the United Malay Nasional Organization (UMNO) and the MCA, two of the main component parties of the ruling coalition that Najib headed. This paved the way for the Chinese and Malaysian parties to mount regular visits, exchanges, and training for Malaysian party officials about China's economic development experience and political governance in Chinese cadre-training institutions.[114]

Party-to-party ties between the two countries had begun two decades earlier. In 1992, a Chinese Communist Party delegation visited Malaysia and was received by Mahathir and five of his top deputies. A reciprocal visit took place in 1994 and included representatives of 12 of the 14 parties in the ruling coalition. The visit signaled that despite the ideological differences between the Malaysian and Chinese parties, political ideology would no longer hamper relations, Ngeow observed.

Mahathir, in his earlier two decades in office, distrusted Western values and institutions and his "Asian values" philosophy was admired by Chinese leaders. In their meetings, political leaders of the two countries found much common ground in areas such as the importance of order, stability, economic growth, nationalism, and anti-Western sentiments, Ngeow noted. On top of that, neither country's ruling party was

112. Ho Wah Foon, "Asean Belt and Road Risks under Scrutiny," *The Star*, July 30, 2017, https://www.thestar.com.my/news/nation/2017/07/30/asean-belt-and-road-risks-under-scrutiny-china-is-signalling-that-it-will-not-be-splashing-money-ind/.
113. Ngeow, "A 'Model' for ASEAN Countries," 106.
114. Ibid., 107–108.

interested in a free media, government transparency, civil liberties, and opposition politics.[115]

Since 2000, the MCA, which has now been decimated, sent many delegations to China to learn about party building, crisis management, and public relations. Mutual visits and exchanges took place almost annually from the mid-2000s and played an important role in changing the views within Malaysian political circles about China no longer posing a communist threat to Malaysia.[116]

In a sign of new times, Mahathir took his first overseas trip to Japan after returning to power in a signal that Malaysia would shift from its dependence on Chinese investment and return to his earlier "Look East" policy by strengthening relations with Japan. Undoubtedly, Mahathir hoped to tap into Japan's vast pots of low-cost capital. Despite China snaring most of the headlines for memorandums of understanding, Japan kicked in $13 billion in 2017 to remain the largest investor in Malaysia.[117]

In another possible test for Malaysia-China relations, the Muslim-majority nation in October 2018 freed 11 ethnic Uighur Muslims who had escaped from detention in Thailand the previous year to travel to Turkey, despite Beijing's request that they be repatriated to China. "They have done nothing wrong in this country, so they were released," Mahathir said. "These people are all Chinese nationals," the Chinese Foreign Ministry insisted. "We resolutely oppose them being deported to a third country."[118]

The next group of Uighurs that arrive in Malaysia may not be as confident that they will not be sent back to China. In a July 2019 interview with a Turkish news outlet after resumption of the Chinese rail project, Mahathir apparently had a change of heart and said that criticizing Beijing over its treatment of the Uighur Muslim minority "would not achieve

115. Ngeow Chow Bing, "Barisan Nasional and the Chinese Communist Party: A Case Study in China's Party-Based Diplomacy," *The China Review* 17, no. 1 (February 2017): 60–62, https://www.jstor.org/stable/44160409?seq=1#page_scan_tab_contents.
116. Ibid., 63, 68.
117. Praveen Menon and Anshuman Daga, "In Mahathir's Malaysia, Japan Is Back amid Doubts over Chinese Funding," *Reuters*, June 10, 2018, https://www.reuters.com/article/us-malaysia-japan/in-mahathirs-malaysia-japan-is-back-amid-doubts-over-chinese-funding-idUSKBN1J60AZ.
118. Nile Bowie, "Mahathir Puts Uighur Rights above China Ties," *Asia Times*, October 16, 2018, https://www.asiatimes.com/2018/10/article/mahathir-puts-uighur-rights-above-china-ties/.

anything." The prime minister added that "we need to verify certain things of what [the Chinese] are accused of. Of course, they deny," said Mahathir, who when he first took office was also strongly outspoken in his criticism of Myanmar's treatment of Rohingya Muslims.

"We believe that the approach should not be confrontation," he said. "It should be through negotiation and exposure of what is actually happening in China." A few weeks earlier, Mahathir's Islamic affairs minister was criticized for describing a Uighur camp as a "training and vocation center" and posting pictures on Facebook that showed Uighurs sitting at school desks in a room surrounded by artificial flowers.[119]

The Najib government had arrested 29 Uighurs in Malaysia after 2011 using biometric information provided by China. Six of them were repatriated to China, despite having refugee-status applications pending.[120]

TENTATIVE MILITARY LINKS

Military relations between Malaysia and China evolved much more tentatively than economic and political ties, but defense cooperation did begin to pick up in recent years with stepped-up exchanges, dialogues, joint military exercises, and staff training. Military contacts increased despite growing concern in Malaysia about China's more assertive behavior in the South China Sea, especially around James and Luconia Shoals after 2013.

Perhaps it was because of Beijing's more pushy behavior that Malaysia pressed for more defense engagement. Still, Malaysia's military exchanges with China lagged behind those of some of its neighbors. China's weapons sales to Indonesia, Thailand, and Myanmar are greater than arms transfers to Malaysia. China conducted joint military exercises with Indonesia, Thailand, Singapore, and Vietnam before beginning them with Malaysia.[121]

---

119. "Malaysia: Mahathir Careful Not to Condemn China's Treatment of Uyghurs," *Radio Free Asia*, July 31, 2019, https://www.rfa.org/english/news/uyghur/malaysia-uyghurs-07312019175631.html.

120. Bowie, "Mahathir Puts Uighur Rights above China Ties."

121. Ngeow, "Comprehensive Strategic Partners but Prosaic Military Ties: The Development of Malaysia-China Defence Relations 1991–2015," *Contemporary Southeast Asia: A Journal of International and Strategic Affairs* 37, no. 2 (August 2015): 291–292, https://umexpert.um.edu.my/file/publication/00011812_126395.pdf.

On top of that, Malaysia's defense cooperation with China still lags that with the United States and Australia. In response to China's aggressive naval actions off the eastern states of Sabah and Sarawak, Malaysia increased its military cooperation with the United States, including joint exercises and port visits by U.S. Navy ships.

One joint military exercise in 2014 involved the F-22 Raptor, the United States' most advanced fighter. U.S. officials said the same year that Malaysia had offered to allow U.S. P-8 Poseidon aircraft, designed for long-range surveillance missions, to operate out of a base in East Malaysia, likely the air force facility on the island of Labuan, on a case-by-case basis. Malaysian officials never confirmed this, apparently out of desire not to anger China.[122] U.S. arms sales to Malaysia from 1990 to 2014 totaled $724 million while those from China were just over $6 million.[123]

In June 2019, shortly after a Chinese coast guard vessel spent two weeks off Malaysia's Luconia Shoals, where it interfered with an oil rig and service vessels contracted by Royal Dutch Shell, the United States announced that it was selling as many as 12 surveillance drones to Malaysia. The Boeing-manufactured ScanEagle drones would cost about $19 million and help Malaysia gather intelligence on China's activities in the South China Sea.[124]

Kuik of the National University of Malaysia said that the government's decision to increase military engagement with China at the time when it is becoming militarily more assertive may reflect an effort by Kuala Lumpur to "develop closer military cooperation and a more comprehensive partnership with the proximate giant, than to counter-balance it militarily." Kuik said Malaysia simultaneously sought to "ensure that its revitalized defense partnership with Washington will not harm its robust economic ties with Beijing."[125]

In 2012, the defense ministries of China and Malaysia held their first defense and security consultation in Kuala Lumpur. One of the

122. Trefor Moss, "Malaysia Offers to Host U.S. Navy Aircraft," *Wall Street Journal*, September 12, 2014, https://www.wsj.com/articles/malaysia-offers-to-host-u-s-navy-aircraft-military-official-says-1410524618.

123. Ngeow, "Comprehensive Strategic Partners but Prosaic Military Ties," 295–296.

124. Mike Stone, "U.S. to Sell 34 Surveillance Drones to Allies in South China Region," *Reuters*, June 3, 2019, https://www.reuters.com/article/us-usa-defense-drones/u-s-to-sell-34-surveillance-drones-to-allies-in-south-china-sea-region-idUSKCN1T42ST.

125. Kuik, "Malaysia between the United States and China," 157.

suggestions by the Chinese side included deepening ties in the defense industry, a priority for Malaysia. The second defense consultation was held in 2015. These forums, headed at the vice-ministerial level, are mainly platforms for discussing regional security issues such as political violence in the southern Philippines. The two sides also explain their respective defense policies, discuss plans for future joint exercises, and explore cooperation on ways to tackle nontraditional security threats.[126]

During a visit by the Malaysian defense minister to China in 2013, the two sides agreed to hold joint exercises, exchange military personnel, and cooperate in the defense industry. In late 2014, the first joint tabletop simulation exercise was held in Kuala Lumpur involving about 40 military personnel from both sides. The following year the first-ever joint search-and-rescue exercise with live troops took place in the Strait of Malacca and included from China over 1,000 troops, two destroyers, a hospital ship, four transport vessels, and three amphibious helicopters.

This exercise marked the largest-ever military collaboration between China and a Southeast Asian country. In 2016, China sent 195 soldiers to form a joint expeditionary team with Malaysian troops to conduct a land-based exercise in Selangor, south of the capital, including jungle tracking and survival tactics.[127]

"The Malaysians complain that they don't learn much from joint exercises with China," says a Malaysian defense analyst who requested not to be named. "They are a very set piece. Language is a huge issue" because few Malaysian military personnel speak Chinese, he said. "You can't do adventurous stuff. They say they learn much more from working with the Aussies and the Americans."

The frequency and level of strategic significance of Chinese ship visits to Malaysian ports has also increased in recent years. In late 2016, a Chinese naval escort task force including two frigates paid a call at Port Klang. In early 2017, a Chinese submarine and a support ship docked at the Sepanggar naval base in the eastern state of Sabah, which is the headquarters of Malaysia's Navy Command Region 2 and is responsible for the country's interests in the South China Sea. Sepanggar is also the base at

126. Ngeow, "Comprehensive Strategic Partners but Prosaic Military Ties," 292.
127. Ngeow, "A 'Model' for ASEAN Countries," 115; Kuik, "Malaysia between the United States and China," 171–172.

which U.S. ships conducting freedom-of-navigation operations in the disputed sea often dock.

"Opening up this base for Chinese naval vessels [signifies] Malaysia's commitment to neutrality despite the [fact that the] ongoing South China Sea dispute would have made China a likely potential security threat," wrote Ngeow of the University of Malaya. He said the submarine visit also signifies a "level of trust that is perhaps higher than expected."[128]

A few months later a small Chinese naval fleet, including a destroyer and frigate, visited Penang in the north, and then in September two more Chinese submarines again docked at Sepanggar,[129] at the very time when Najib was in Washington for meetings with Trump. This visit marked the fourth Chinese naval ship visit to a Malaysian port in the year after October 2016.

Among Southeast Asian countries, Thailand, Indonesia, and Myanmar have had more arms transfers from China than Malaysia. The two countries concluded their first arms deal in 2004 when China agreed to provide FN-6 very short-range air defense systems that would be assembled in Malaysia, but the deal was not completed until five years later, at which time Malaysia paid $6.6 million for 16 sets of FN-6s.[130]

Beijing and Kuala Lumpur discussed possible arms transfers, including defense industry cooperation, over the years, but it was not until 2016 that Malaysia agreed to purchase four littoral mission ships from China at an estimated cost of $277 million. The first two are to be built in China and the next two in a Malaysian shipyard, involving technology transfer from and training by China.[131]

The two militaries started exchanging military students in the late 2000s when Malaysian officers began attending courses offered in regular Chinese military institutions. As was the case with other Southeast Asian military students attending training in China, Malaysians were not very impressed by the quality of their education and many of them preferred to attend military colleges in Western countries.

Beginning in 2008, three senior Malaysian military officers, one from each branch, started studying at China's National Defense University each

128. Ngeow, "A 'Model' for ASEAN Countries," 115–116.
129. "Chinese Sub Docks at Malaysian Port for Second Time This Year," *Reuters*, September 13, 2017, https://www.reuters.com/article/us-china-malaysia-southchinasea/chinese-sub-docks-at-malaysian-port-for-second-time-this-year-idUSKCN1BO17P.
130. Ngeow, "Comprehensive Strategic Partners but Prosaic Military Ties," 290.
131. Ngeow, "A 'Model' for ASEAN Countries," 115.

year. And since the late 2000s, one or two Malaysian military officers a year began studying at the People's Liberation Army Command College in Nanjing. China has also offered nonmilitary courses such as engineering and medicine to some Malaysia military students.[132]

Many fewer Chinese officers have attended Malaysian military institutions. Since 2007, one or two officers have studied each year at the Malaysian Armed Forces Staff College. Some Chinese officers also take short courses of a few months at Malaysian institutions.

To protect its claims in the South China Sea, Malaysia maintains several military outposts on its islands in the Spratlys and uses warships and submarines to patrol within its 200-nautical-mile exclusive economic zone and track foreign ships showing up in the areas that Malaysia claims. As China has increased its incursions into Malaysia's waters, Kuala Lumpur has quietly stepped up its intelligence cooperation with partners such as the United States to boost its maritime domain awareness. Malaysia also set up a new naval base in Bintulu in Sarawak.[133]

But Malaysia's navy is severely limited with only 39 aging ships and two submarines to cover the country's vast surrounding water.[134] As China increased its forays off the coast of Malaysia in 2013, Japan gave the Malaysia coast guard a boost by donating two former Japanese cutters that arrived in 2017. The Malaysia Maritime Enforcement Agency in 2017 received the first two of six new-generation patrol craft ordered in 2015. After Chinese vessels stunned Kuala Lumpur by showing up at James and South Luconia Shoals, Malaysia's coast guard ordered three new *Damen*-class offshore patrol vessels that are expected to be delivered in 2021.[135]

As Malaysia and other claimants in the South China Sea take steps to modernize their navies, air forces, and coast guards, some analysts argue that there is an arms race brewing between the countries bordering on the disputed sea. But Alexander Vuving, a military expert at the Asia-Pacific Center for Security Studies in Hawaii, insisted that countries like Malaysia, which reduced its military spending in 2016 to 1.4 percent of

132. Ngeow, "Comprehensive Strategic Partners but Prosaic Military Ties," 286–287.
133. Parameswaran, "Playing It Safe," 8.
134. Ibid.
135. Alexander L. Vuving, "Tracking Malaysia's Force Build-Up in the South China Sea," *cogitASIA*, October 17, 2017, https://www.cogitasia.com/tracking-malaysias-force-build-up-in-the-south-china-sea/.

gross domestic product, down from 2.6 percent in 2003, have no intention of developing military parity with China, let alone superiority.

"Instead, their long-term ambition is what can be called 'minimal deterrence,'" Vuving said. "They want to build just enough capability to make potential aggressors think twice before attacking them."[136]

Malaysia's stepped-up military engagement was taking place at the same time as its alarm about China's growing assertive behavior around the disputed Spratlys was increasing, including the presence of Chinese naval ships at James Shoal beginning in 2013. Kuik said this "paradox" reflects Malaysia's realization that "protecting its maritime interests requires it to pragmatically adapt, adjust, and move closer to—rather than reject, ignore, and keep away from—China's growing power projection and strategic outreach."[137]

Malaysia under Najib, argued Kuik, tried to "hedge by concurrently enhancing Malaysia's relations with America and China, building stronger bilateral relationships with both powers without departing from its nonalignment stance." In the South China Sea, Malaysia has chosen to continue to "downplay the 'China threat' and not overplay the U.S. card." Kuik dubbed that "light-hedging."[138]

MALAYSIAN PERCEPTIONS OF CHINA

The opposition victory in May 2018 can be attributed in part to the fact that many Malaysians are starting to feel overwhelmed by the tsunami of Chinese investment. "At the grassroots level, people are getting more uncomfortable," Kuik of the National University of Malaysia said shortly before the elections. "Nurul Izzah [Anwar] keeps saying it's 'too much, too fast, too soon,'" he says about the former opposition parliamentarian whose party became a member of the ruling coalition with the recent elections. "She captures Malaysian sentiment very well," Kuik says. (Nurul Izzah Anwar is the daughter of longtime opposition leader Anwar Ibrahim, who is often touted as the likely successor to Mahathir.)

136. Alexander L. Vuving, "Force Buildup in the South China Sea: The Myth of an Arms Race," *cogitASIA*, October 12, 2017, https://www.cogitasia.com/force-buildup-in-the-south-china-sea-the-myth-of-an-arms-race/.
137. Kuik, "Malaysia between the United States and China," 168.
138. Ibid., 169.

Some Malaysian critics of China's projects cite concern about the country falling into a neocolonial-style debt trap as happened when a Chinese company took control of a port in Sri Lanka in 2017 after the government was not able to service its loans from China.[139] At the local level, Malaysians express alarm about the increasing presence of Chinese workers in the country, particularly in the construction and services sector. Local contractors complain that little of the work in China's projects goes to Malaysian companies and workers, because Chinese investors tend to control the entire supply chain and price out small and medium-sized local enterprises in the process.[140]

"The Chinese tend to bring their own skilled and unskilled workers, importing supplies such as steel and machinery from China, and carrying out projects with a speed and scale unmatched by most Malaysian companies," Malaysian business representatives told *The Straits Times* of Singapore. Because Chinese firms mostly import their own inputs for their projects, Malaysian companies were not able to compete until the Malaysian government imposed some local-content rules to limit this process.[141]

Malay and Muslim nongovernmental organizations host events and frequently raise concerns about Malaysia becoming more Chinese with the influx of Chinese migrants. The Islamic group Ikatan Muslimin Malaysia (ISMA) claims that the first ethnic Chinese were brought into Malaysia to help the British colonize Malaysia and to "weaken the Malay identity." The group's leaders add that if Chinese wish to stay in Malaysia and become citizens they must be loyal to the Malay king, agree that Islam is the religion of the country, and accept the sovereign rights of the Malays.[142]

In a late-2018 poll of opinion makers conducted by ISEAS-Yusof Ishak Institute in Singapore a little more than six months after the Malaysian

---

139. Kiran Stacey, "China Signs 99-year Lease on Sri Lanka's Hambantota Port," *Financial Times*, December 11, 2017, https://www.ft.com/content/e150ef0c-de37-11e7-a8a4-0a1e63a52f9c.
140. Tham Siew Yean, "Chinese Investment in Malaysia: Five Years into the BRI," *ISEAS Perspective*, no. 11 (2018): 6, https://www.iseas.edu.sg/images/pdf/ISEAS_Perspective_2018_11@50.pdf.
141. Shannon Teoh and Trinna Leong, "Chinese Deals in Malaysia under Scrutiny," *Straits Times*, May 7, 2017, https://www.straitstimes.com/asia/se-asia/chinese-deals-in-malaysia-under-scrutiny.
142. Malay Mail, "Isma: Chinese Migration into Tanah Melayu 'a Mistake' Which Must Be Rectified," *Malay Mail*, May 6, 2014, https://www.malaymail.com/s/664033/isma-chinese-migration-into-tanah-melayu-a-mistake-which-must-be-rectified.

elections that toppled the ruling party, nearly 43 percent of those surveyed thought China "will become a revisionist power with an intent to turn Southeast Asia into its sphere of influence." Those polled included policy experts, researchers, business representatives, civil society leaders, and people from the media.

Over 44 percent thought Beijing with provide "alternative regional leadership in the wake of perceived U.S. disengagement," but just under 10 percent believed China would be a "benign and benevolent power."

A hefty 78 percent said China has the "most influence economically" in the region (while less than 6 percent thought that about the United States). Almost 44 percent thought China has the "most influence politically and strategically in Southeast Asia" (compared to just under 30 percent who thought this about the United States).

A little more than 39 percent of Malaysians believed China's BRI projects would benefit "regional economic development" and nearly 52 percent thought these projects would bring Southeast Asian countries "closer into China's orbit." But a whopping 84 percent said their government "should be cautious in negotiating BRI projects to avoid getting into unsustainable financial debts with China."[143]

China favorability standing was down from earlier surveys. A poll conducted in April 2016 by the Institute of China Studies at the University of Malaya found that fully 70 percent of Malaysians had a favorable impression of China and 67 percent felt that Malaysia-China relations were headed in the right direction.

On economic relations, 45 percent viewed China as "an advantage" to Malaysia, while 15 percent saw it as a "potential threat." On the question of China's emergence as a military power, 28 percent viewed China as a potential ally, 22 percent as neutral, and 20 percent as a potential threat. Some 45 percent viewed China's territorial claims in the South China Sea as a threat.[144]

---

143. Tang Siew Mun, Moe Thuzar, Hoang Thi Ha, Termsak Chalermpalanupap, Pham Thi Phuong Thao, and Anuthida Saelaow Qian, *The State of Southeast Asia: 2019 Survey Report* (Singapore: ASEAN Studies Centre at ISEAS-Yusof Ishak Institute, 2019), 18, 21, 22, 19, https://www.iseas.edu.sg/images/pdf/TheStateofSEASurveyReport_2019.pdf.

144. Ho Wah Foon, "Malaysians Give China the Thumbs Up," *The Star*, August 18, 2016, https://www.thestar.com.my/news/nation/2016/08/18/msians-give-china-the-thumbs-up-bilateral-relationship-heading-in-the-right-direction-according-to/.

A survey of residents in the Malaysia's southernmost state of Johor, where China has several luxury real estate development projects, was conducted by the Merdeka Center for Opinion Research in early 2018 shortly before the elections. It found that residents generally welcomed foreign investment. Some 69 percent said they approved of investment from neighboring Singapore, but that number fell to 56 percent for investment from China. About 29 percent of the respondents were dissatisfied with the Chinese investments.[145]

Respondents said they did not see themselves benefiting from China's increasing economic presence in the state because much of the investment was focused on giant property development projects. Some of the complaints were likely targeted at the futuristic $100 billion Forest City project, which is being erected by China's Country Garden Holdings Company. It features ritzy apartments, glitzy shopping malls, luxury hotels, and state-of-the-art golf courses on four reclaimed islands in the Straits of Johor between the Malaysian city of Johor Baru and Singapore. The developers are targeting Chinese from China to buy these apartments.[146]

"We don't feel the positive effects," a 32-year-old executive told the pollsters about Chinese real estate projects. "The only thing they have done is drive up the local property prices and make it harder for people like me to buy a home." Others complained that China's projects do not provide local job opportunities.[147]

Mahathir, as an opposition candidate running for election, was uneasy about the fact that Forest City, a joint venture with the sultan of Johor and located near the strategic Strait of Malacca shipping lane, would soon serve as home for thousands of ethnic Chinese. "We should realize that once we sell land to others, we no longer have ownership over it," Mahathir said.[148]

---

145. "Johoreans Prefer Singapore Investment over China's: Survey," *Straits Times*, February 23, 2018, https://www.straitstimes.com/asia/se-asia/johoreans-prefer-singapore-investment-over-chinas-survey?login=true.

146. Sylvain Orbis, "Chinese Flood Johor in Malaysia to Invest in US$100b 'Eco City' Billed as the 'Next Shenzhen,'" *South China Morning Post*, September 1, 2017, https://www.scmp.com/magazines/post-magazine/long-reads/article/2109110/chinese-flood-johor-malaysia-invest-us100b-eco.

147. "Johoreans Prefer Singapore Investment over China's," *Straits Times*.

148. Brook Larmer, "A Malaysian Insta-City Becomes a Flash Point for Chinese Colonialism—and Capital Flight," *New York Times*, March 13, 2018, https://www.nytimes.com/2018

Local fishers complain about Forest City because they say the project has devastated fishing in the Johor Strait between Malaysia and Singapore. Because the apartments are built on reclaimed islands, fishers say their fish supplies have lost their natural habitat.

SOFT POWER OFFENSIVE

Beijing has dramatically stepped up its public diplomacy activities since Xi became president to tackle its trust deficit in Malaysia. Its activities include Confucius Institutes that teach Chinese, exchange diplomacy comprised of sister cities, financial diplomacy, and official visits with the goal of increasing bilateral ties and boosting China's international image, according to a June 2018 report on China's public diplomacy activities released by AidData of the College of William and Mary in Virginia.[149]

Malaysia has been the biggest beneficiary of China's financial diplomacy, receiving $13.4 billion in "official finance with diplomatic intent" between 2000 and 2014, according to the authors of *Ties That Bind: Quantifying China's Public Diplomacy and Its "Good Neighbor" Effect.*[150] In comparison, Indonesia, Southeast Asia's largest country, and Cambodia, China's closest ally, got around $9 billion each in the same time period. Under financial diplomacy, the report included infrastructure investments, humanitarian aid, budget support, and debt relief.

What are China's public diplomacy objectives? The AidData report said a key driver was "to open market opportunities for Chinese firms and sway natural resource 'gatekeepers.'" Countries that represent greater economic opportunities for China and "openness to Chinese goods, services, and investments" tend to receive more of its public diplomacy attention.[151]

Interestingly, *Ties that Bind* found that China has considerably fewer official visitors to Malaysia than many other countries, including some where Beijing faces significant diplomatic challenges. Malaysia received

/03/13/magazine/a-malaysian-insta-city-becomes-a-flash-point-for-chinese-colonialism-and-capital-flight.html.

149. Custer et al., *Ties That Bind*, 1.

150. Max Walden, "Malaysia Is the Largest Beneficiary of Chinese Cash Diplomacy," *Asian Correspondent*, June 28, 2018, https://asiancorrespondent.com/2018/06/malaysia-is-the-largest-beneficiary-of-chinese-cash-diplomacy/#D8u8wMFP7f68bqF5.97.

151. Custer et al., *Ties That Bind*, 40.

only 145 official visits between 2000 and 2015, many fewer than Vietnam with 286, Thailand with 257, and Cambodia with 216.[152] On the other hand, Malaysia has more sister city exchanges—40—than any other country in Southeast Asia. Vietnam has 35, Thailand 34, and the Philippines 29.[153]

China uses Confucius Institutes among its public diplomacy tools to promote language and culture. Malaysia has two compared to six in Indonesia and four in the Philippines.[154] The first one opened at the University of Malaya in 2009 and a second one at the private SEGi University, just south of Kuala Lumpur, in 2015.

Because the name "Confucius" could carry sensitive religious overtones in Malaysia, the institutes are called Kong Zi Institutes in Kuala Lumpur. With almost one-quarter of Malaysia's population being ethnic Chinese, many of whom are Chinese-educated, the Confucius Institutes mainly targeted the Malay Muslim majority and ethnic Indian minority, said Kuik. China also opened a new China Cultural Center in Malaysia in early 2020.[155]

Malaysia and China actively promote educational and cultural exchanges. Despite the large number of ethnic Chinese in Malaysia, the numbers of Malaysians studying in China is smaller than the numbers from at least four Southeast Asian neighbors. Some 6,900 Malaysians studied in China in 2016 compared to 23,000 from Thailand and 14,700 from Indonesia.[156] (Malaysia also has a much smaller population—less than half the size of Thailand and about a tenth the size of Indonesia.)

Some Chinese universities such as Jinan University in Guangdong Province have begun putting recruitment notices on their websites targeting Malaysians.[157] The majority of students studying in China are ethnic Chinese who use their own funds or are sponsored by private

152. Ibid., 16.
153. Ibid., 9.
154. Ibid., 10.
155. Leisure Pursuit Reporting Desk, "China Cultural Center opens in Kuala Lumpur," *Belt & Road News*, January 22, 2020, https://www.beltandroad.news/2020/01/22/the-china-cultural-center-officially-opens-in-kuala-lumpur/.
156. Custer et al., *Ties That Bind*, 13.
157. Sin Chew Daily/Asia News Network, "Institutions of Higher Learning in China Compete to Recruit Malaysian Students," *Straits Times*, August 24, 2017, https://www.straitstimes.com/asia/se-asia/institutions-of-higher-learning-in-china-compete-to-recruit-malaysian-students?login=true&utm_source=google_gmail&utm_medium=social-media&utm_campaign=addtoany.

sources. Most of the ethnic Malays studying in China receive scholarships or are sponsored by either the Chinese or Malaysian governments, Ngeow says.

In 2016, Xiamen University became the first Chinese university to open an overseas campus in Malaysia, just south of the capital. It is fully funded by China, teaches courses in English, and was expected to graduate its first students in 2019.[158] When it opened in 2017, the $300 million university had 1,900 students, mostly ethnic Chinese, and it is aiming to have 5,000 by 2020.[159]

"Exporting education is a way to promote China's soft power," Zhang Baohu, an international affairs expert at Lingnan University in Hong Kong, told the *South China Morning Post.* "It reflects China's quest for broader influence in the world."[160]

So far, students at Xiamen reportedly are allowed to discuss sensitive subjects such as the South China Sea dispute. Only about one-third of the teachers are from China. But the university faced some criticism because it brought many of its staff, including cafeteria workers, from China. The menus are in Chinese and the waiters take orders in Mandarin, limiting the multiplier effect of the investment in Malaysia's economy.[161]

In 2017, the first Southeast Asia-China film festival was organized in Malaysia. A total of 11 movies from China and 10 from Southeast Asia were entered in the competition.[162] In 2018, a concert celebrating the BRI was performed in Kuala Lumpur featuring Malaysian pianist Claudia Yang and China's National Symphony Orchestra.[163]

The Chinese Embassy has made donations of academic books and yearbooks to the University of Malaya's Institute of China Studies and

158. Ngeow, "A 'Model' for ASEAN Countries," 113.
159. Coco Liu and Tashny Sukumaran, "Belt and Read: How China Is Exporting Education and Influence to Malaysia and Other Asean Countries," *South China Morning Post*, July 30, 2017, https://www.scmp.com/week-asia/politics/article/2097965/belt-road-and-books-how-chinas-trying-soft-power-outreach?utm_content=buffer26e90&utm_medium=social&utm_source=twitter.com&utm_campaign=.
160. Ibid.
161. Teoh and Leong, "Chinese Deals in Malaysia under Scrutiny."
162. Seto Kit Yan, "First Asean-China Film Festival to Take Place in Malaysia in December," *Star2*, November 6, 2017, https://www.star2.com/entertainment/2017/11/06/first-asean-china-film-festival-happening-malaysia-next-month/.
163. Xinhua, "'Belt and Road' Malaysia-China Friendship Piano Symphony Concert Held in Kuala Lumpur," *Global Times*, March 18, 2018, http://www.globaltimes.cn/content/1093867.shtml.

provided some support for organizing conferences. Still, perhaps not surprisingly, China studies among Malaysian scholars "remains wanting," in the words of Ngeow. Initially, the Chinese Communist Party's support for Communist parties in Southeast Asia created concern in Malaysia that the various ethnic Chinese communities in the country would become an "extension of the Communist giant." It was believed that by studying China, academics would be "advocating the interests of that country," Ngeow said.[164]

Even after China stopped supporting the Malaysian communists and the travel ban was lifted, China remained a sensitive topic in Malaysia and its students were reluctant to study domestic political, economic, and social developments in the country. Identity politics in Malaysia, which focused on different ethnic communities, further hindered the development of China studies.

Much of the early push for China studies came from top Malaysian political leaders who promoted inter-civilizational dialogue and a Malaysia-China friendship agenda rather than seriously pursuing understanding about what was happening in contemporary China, Ngeow said. In recent years, research has focused more on China's economic rise and its foreign policy toward Southeast Asia rather than what is happening politically and socially in China itself.[165]

Although China Central Television (CCTV), the predominant state broadcaster in China, and the official Chinese Xinhua News Agency have a presence in Malaysia, China seems to make greater use of local Chinese media, especially *Sin Chew Daily*, which runs regular articles by China's ambassador and statements put out by the embassy. The embassy also reaches out to the English media but does not do much with Malay-language news outlets.[166] The English-language *The Star*, which is partly owned by the MCA, carries China Daily's *Asia Weekly*. Phoenix Television of Hong Kong is carried on Malaysia's Astro Satellite service.

Separately, on some occasions, pro-Beijing views seem to gain access to some surprising media outlets in Malaysia. For example, on March 6, 2019, Wu Xiangi, who is not identified but appears to be a Chinese journalist or academic, had a long article in *Malaysiakini*, a normally

164. Chow, Tek Soon Ling, and Pik Shy Fan, "Pursuing Chinese Studies amidst Identity Politics in Malaysia," *East Asia* 31, no. 2 (June 2014): 116–117.
165. Ibid., 118–120.
166. Custer et al., *Ties That Bind*, 31.

independent-minded online news portal that was founded following the 1997–1998 financial and political crisis. The article raised questions about the government's decision to send 11 Uighur Muslims to Turkey instead of China, which had requested them.

The writer said Kuala Lumpur had "unexpectedly violated the will of the Chinese government" and cited a statement from the Chinese Embassy that claimed that "the Chinese government respects religious freedom" and emphasized that "Islam enjoys good development in China." Representatives of the World Uighur Congress, an organization of exiled Uighur groups that supports the interests of this ethnic group and that had received some support from the U.S. National Endowment for Democracy, the writer said, had visited Malaysia in January 2019 and met with political party and civil society leaders. After this visit, the Chinese Embassy had taken out a full-page color advertisement in the Chinese-language *Sin Chew Daily* under the heading, "Real Xinjiang," which provided a short history of the province and summarized the Chinese government's long-standing respect for Islam.

For 10 days beginning on February 18, 2019, the writer of the *Malaysiakini* article said, a delegation of five Malaysian and six Indonesian journalists were invited to tour Xinjiang. This group was followed by a visit by a delegation of political party leaders that included representatives from Malaysia. Curiously, the Malaysian politicians invited were representatives of the former Malay ruling party and the ethnic Chinese party that were ousted in May 2018, rather than representatives from the new ruling coalition.

The writer concluded the article by saying, "The soft diplomacy response used by China . . . will take some time to be effective, but it remains to be seen whether it can calm the issue of Xinjiang."[167]

China-Malaysia ties in 2020 are a relationship in transition. Economic cooperation will remain a key driver in the bilateral relationship. It will be fascinating to watch progress on the East Coast Rail Link and whether the two governments and their companies can stick to the agreement hammered out. Because the rail project is the most ambitious BRI scheme in

167. Wu Xiangi, "Looking at China's Soft Diplomacy about the Uyghur Subject," *Malaysiakini* (Chinese language), March 6, 2019, https://www.malaysiakini.com/news/466898?fbclid=IwARoZs2HzqRjM384jzpdac-g7seYYyMJujvwL2ub8SMiUHalaWCtd9c8Iq-8 (accessed June 4, 2019).

Southeast Asia, China will want to keep the costs within the limits the two sides agreed to and ensure that Malaysian contractors and workers get the jobs and share of the project that the two sides negotiated.

How relations between Beijing and Kuala Lumpur unfold in the South China Sea will be critical. Will China allow Petronas to continue developing oil and gas resources off the coast of Sarawak in partnership with international oil majors, or will Beijing try to press Malaysia into joint development with China as it has in Vietnam and the Philippines? If China strongly challenges Malaysia's rights to develop oil and gas within the nine-dash line of the South China Sea, Kuala Lumpur may conclude that it has no option except to step up its hedging with other powers and increase military cooperation with the United States.

8. SINGAPORE: "YOU ARE ETHNIC CHINESE, SO YOU SHOULDN'T OPPOSE US"

Singapore has many firsts in Southeast Asia—the freest and most vibrant economy, the busiest and most efficient port, the least corruption—but the first that Beijing seems to care about most is that it is the only country in Southeast Asia with a majority ethnic Chinese population. The fact that three-quarters of the city-state's population traces its heritage back to China often prompts it to assume that Singapore will define its interests in ways comparable to Beijing. When the Lion City does not respond according to Chinese expectations, tensions sometimes erupt.[1]

The most recent incident flared up after the arbitral tribunal ruling in The Hague in July 2016 in a case which determined that Beijing had no historic rights in the waters of the South China Sea and had violated the Philippines' sovereign rights with its activities. Singapore issued a statement saying that all sides should respect the tribunal ruling, avoid conducting any activities that may raise tensions in the region, and support the maintenance of a rules-based order.[2]

China was livid and for a year shunned engagement with senior Singapore leaders. *The Global Times*, a state-owned nationalist newspaper, got into a tiff with Singapore's ambassador to China in September 2016 over

---

1. Amy Qin, "Worries Grow in Singapore over China's Calls to Help 'Motherland,'" *New York Times*, August 5, 2018, https://www.nytimes.com/2018/08/05/world/asia/singapore-china.html.
2. "Singapore Urges Respect for Court Ruling on South China Sea," *Today*, July 12, 2016, https://www.todayonline.com/singapore/singapore-south-china-sea-ruling-reaction.

whether Singapore had tried to include a reference to the tribunal ruling in a Non-Aligned Movement summit document.[3]

In November, Hong Kong customs officials seized nine Singapore armored vehicles that transited the port as they were being shipped from Taiwan to Singapore after military exercises, which had been conducted regularly since the 1970s.[4] The following May, Singapore prime minister Lee Hsien Loong did not get an invitation to a summit on China's Belt and Road Initiative (BRI) in Beijing in which two dozen other heads of state participated.[5]

Singapore finally escaped its period of "reprimand" when President Xi Jinping and Lee met at a Group of 20 (G20) summit in July 2017 as Singapore prepared to chair the Association of Southeast Asian Nations (ASEAN) grouping in 2018. But the following month the tiff continued when Singapore expelled a Chinese American professor for allegedly trying to influence the city-state's foreign policy on behalf of an unnamed government, widely assumed to be China's.[6] Beijing again took umbrage in mid-2018 when an outspoken former Singapore diplomat described China's public diplomacy campaign in Singapore and the region in rather blunt terms.[7]

Despite occasional political rows, the countries remain top economic partners. Like with most countries in the Southeast Asia, China is Singapore's largest trading partner and the two countries are major investors in each other's economies. Singapore also has invested in at

3. Peh Shing Huei, "How China Is Using Its Global Times Attack Dog to Intimidate Singapore," *South China Morning Post*, October 1, 2016, https://www.scmp.com/week-asia/opinion/article/2024088/how-china-using-its-global-times-attack-dog-intimidate-singapore.

4. Bhavan Jaipragas, "Hong Kong to Return Seized Armoured Vehicles to Singapore," *South China Morning Post*, January 24, 2017, https://www.scmp.com/week-asia/geopolitics/article/2065027/hong-kong-return-singapores-seized-armoured-vehicles.

5. Bhavan Jaipragas, "What New Silk Road Snub Means for Singapore's Ties with China," *South China Morning Post*, May 18, 2017, https://www.scmp.com/week-asia/geopolitics/article/2094781/what-belt-and-road-snub-means-singapores-ties-china.

6. Zuraidah Ibrahim, "What Singapore Is Saying by Expelling China Hand Huang Jing," *South China Morning Post*, August 12, 2017, https://www.scmp.com/week-asia/opinion/article/2106497/what-singapore-saying-expelling-china-hand-huang-jing.

7. "China Does Not Manipulate Other Countries: Chinese Ambassador Responds to Remarks from Former Singapore Diplomat Bilahari Kausikan," *Channel News Asia*, July 12, 2018, https://www.channelnewsasia.com/news/singapore/china-does-not-manipulate-countries-ambassador-bilahari-kausikan-10522578.

least three major government-to-government business initiatives in China. On top of that, chunks of China's funding to BRI projects goes through Singapore where many of the deals are structured and project financing is worked out.[8]

CHINA CHASTISES SINGAPORE

The strong response of China's Singapore ambassador in July 2018 to comments about Beijing's "influence operations" in the city-state highlights the conflicts facing Singaporean Chinese as they connect with their cultural heritage but seek to avoid serving Beijing's political interests. Speaking at a conference on China's public diplomacy, Bilahari Kausikan, former permanent secretary of the Ministry of Foreign Affairs, warned Singaporeans that China was not only trying to influence their actions but also to condition their behavior.

"China does not just want you to comply with its wishes; more fundamentally, China wants to shape your thinking so that you will do [what] it wants without having to be told what to do," the straight-speaking retired diplomat said at a conference on China's public diplomacy co-organized by the S. Rajaratnam School of International Studies (RSIS), Washington-based Center for Strategic and International Studies, and two other U.S. organizations.[9]

"When the Chinese try to impose a Chinese identity on Singapore, we must resist, because modern Singapore is based on the idea of being a multiracial country," Kausikan said.[10] This policy has been in place since independence and reflects the fact that Singapore is made up of people with Chinese descent (74 percent), Malays (13 percent), and Indians (9 percent).[11]

8. Shiwen Yap, "Risk and Opportunities: Singapore's Role in China's Belt and Road," *Medium.com*, June 27, 2018, https://medium.com/venture-views/risk-opportunities-singapores-role-in-china-s-bri-ff6377d035b7.
9. Bilahari Kausikan, "Chinese Public Diplomacy in East Asia and the Pacific," lunch keynote, Singapore, 2017. Speech notes received from the speaker.
10. "China Does Not Manipulate Other Countries," *Channel News Asia*.
11. Department of Statistics Singapore, *Population Trends 2015* (Singapore: Ministry of Trade and Industry), 5, https://web.archive.org/web/20151010202531/http://www.singstat.gov.sg/docs/default-source/default-document-library/publications/publications_and_papers/population_and_population_structure/population2015.pdf.

China's ambassador to Singapore Hong Xiaoyong responded by declaring that Kausikan's speech was a "far cry from reality and leaves an unfavorable impression of China on others." The ambassador protested that "every country hopes to gain recognition and support" and in that sense "China is no different." He said in recent years China has made "great efforts in carrying out its international responsibilities" and had put forward cooperative initiatives such as the BRI.

These initiatives have "gained a positive response from many countries, not because of manipulation but because they meet the interests of other parties and provide opportunities for common development," Hong said. China opposes "big bullying" of small countries and "interference in other's internal affairs."[12]

The ambassador avoided Kausikan's most poignant message about the challenge facing Singaporeans of Chinese descent because Beijing assumes they will align their interests with those of China. Although three-quarters of Singaporeans are ethnic Chinese, they have become very different from mainland Chinese over the five decades plus since Singapore achieved independence. With one-quarter of the population being non-Chinese, Singapore has developed a "multiracial social compact," which Kausikan said in other interviews he does not think Beijing understands. He notes that as a "small country" Singapore will always be "subject to multiple influences," but added that "we have to have the gumption and courage to be ourselves."[13]

One of the examples of narratives that China uses against Singaporeans is that "Singapore has no claims in the South China Sea, so why is the Singapore government taking sides against China?" Kausikan said in his speech.[14] It was precisely Singapore's comments in support of the arbitral ruling about the maritime dispute and call for all sides to support it that prompted Beijing to send its relations with Singapore into a deep freeze in 2016.

Prime Minister Lee said in an August 2016 speech, a few weeks after the tribunal ruling, that Singapore had three issues at stake in the dispute:

12. "China Does Not Manipulate Other Countries," *Channel News Asia*.

13. Wong Kim Hoh, "Bilahari Kausikan, the Diplomat Who 'Writes and Speaks without Hedging,'" *Straits Times*, July 9, 2017, https://www.straitstimes.com/singapore/diplomat-who-writes-and-speaks-without-hedging?&utm_source=google_gmail&utm_medium=social-media&utm_campaign=addtoany.

14. Kausikan, "Chinese Public Diplomacy in East Asia and the Pacific."

freedom of navigation, the "rules based international order," and the unity of ASEAN. "If rules do not matter, then small countries like Singapore have no chance for survival," Lee said in his national day address. He reminded China that their relations had begun decades earlier and are "much broader than the South China Sea."[15]

Beijing's opening salvo landed in a September 2016 article in *The Global Times*, which often reflects the more hawkish views of some Chinese officials, that charged that Singapore had sought to include an endorsement of The Hague's South China Sea ruling in the final communiqué of the just-concluded Non-Aligned Movement (NAM) summit in Venezuela.

Singapore's ambassador to China, Stanley Loh, accused the newspaper of making up the report in two open letters to the editor. "We are disappointed that an established newspaper published this irresponsible report replete with fabrications and unfounded allegations with no regard for fact," Loh wrote.[16]

A Chinese Foreign Ministry spokesperson defended *The Global Times* report by saying that an unspecified "nation" had insisted that a reference to the maritime dispute be included in the summit document.[17] Singapore officials say a consensus statement prepared by ASEAN was read out by a Singapore diplomat at the request of Laos, which chaired the grouping at the time. The verbal jousting seemed to reflect China's frustration with Singapore for claiming neutrality in the dispute, but in the eyes of Beijing, largely supporting Washington's efforts to pressure China into accepting the ruling.

Separately, a Chinese academic close to the government told this writer during the dispute that frustration was mounting in Beijing about Singapore's apparent tilt toward Washington in the city-state's long-standing balancing act between the United States and China. In addition to Singapore's view on the arbitral tribunal ruling, the academic, speaking off the record, cited the fact that U.S. P-8 surveillance planes fly out of Singapore's

15. "NDR 2016: Singapore Must Choose Its Own Place to Stand on South China Sea Issue, Says PM Lee," *Channel News Asia*, June 12, 2017, https://www.channelnewsasia.com/news/singapore/ndr-2016-singapore-must-choose-its-own-place-to-stand-on-south-c-7884434.

16. "Singapore Accuses Chinese Paper of Fabricating South China Sea Story," *Reuters*, September 27, 2016, https://www.reuters.com/article/us-southchinasea-china-singapore-idUSKCN11X10N.

17. Peh, "How China Is Using Its Global Times Attack Dog to Intimidate Singapore."

Paya Lebar Air Base to "spy on China's coastline" and U.S. littoral combat ships rotate through Singapore's naval base.

Even though Singapore has no territorial claims in the South China Sea like China and four of the city-state's Southeast Asian neighbors, its concerns about the maritime dispute date back to the early 1990s. China's increasing assertiveness in the South China Sea in the mid-1990s and again since 2009 created anxiety in Singapore because of its dependence on the free flow of maritime trade for its survival. Singapore officials fretted that fishing disputes or efforts to exploit hydrocarbons on the seabed have increased the risks of incidents at sea that could create instability and threaten trade flows.

Beijing's second salvo came in November 2016, when nine Singapore Terrex armored vehicles being shipped on a commercial vessel from Taiwan to Singapore following military exercises made a stop in Hong Kong and were seized by customs officials and held for two months. Hong Kong authorities said they found "suspected controlled items" on the vessel during a routine search and warned that the private carrier might faces criminal charges.[18] The incident drove relations between Beijing and Singapore to a new low.

China has long complained about Singapore's close relations with Taiwan and the city-state's use of training facilities in Taiwan, which Beijing considers a breakaway province of China. Singapore established close political ties with Taiwan after it separated from Malaysia in 1965. Because Singapore lacked space to carry out military maneuvers, it signed an agreement to use Taiwan for some of its training exercises. Economic ties between the two islands soared following Singapore's independence, as Taiwan became one of city-state's most important trading partners and foreign investors.[19]

China finally released the nine Terrex troop carriers to return to Singapore in late January 2017, auspiciously just before the lunar new year.[20]

---

18. Jermyn Chow, "SAF Armoured Vehicles Seized in Hong Kong Port, Mindef Expects Shipment to Return to Singapore 'Expeditiously,'" *Straits Times*, November 24, 2016, https://www.straitstimes.com/asia/se-asia/9-saf-armoured-vehicles-seized-at-hong-kong-port.
19. Ian Storey, *Southeast Asia and the Rise of China: The Search for Security* (New York: Routledge, 2011), 246.
20. Jaipragas, "Hong Kong to Return Seized Armoured Vehicles to Singapore," *South China Morning Post*.

Singapore officials say they did not negotiate with Beijing or make any concessions for the return of the military equipment.

But the extent of Beijing's involvement in this case is disputed by some academics in Singapore. One China expert who asked not to be identified points out that the commercial shipping company committed a "technical glitch" and "failed to send the complete paperwork to Hong Kong" before the armored vehicles arrived.

The analyst says he is "skeptical" about whether Beijing played a role in the seizure of the military vehicles because "in the past Chinese arms dealers have encountered similar problems in Hong Kong." So have South Korean weapons companies. But the academic adds that "if it was only a legal issue, it should have been resolved in a few weeks," not after more than two months.

Ian Storey, an Asian security expert at ISEAS-Yusof Ishak Institute in Singapore, is convinced that "Beijing wanted to send a message to Singapore to end its military training in Taiwan."

The next incident on the dispute timeline was the fact that Lee was not invited to Beijing in May 2017 for President Xi's BRI forum, which involved 29 national leaders, including the heads of state of seven of Singapore's Southeast Asian neighbors. Even though Singapore is expected to play a critical role in the BRI as a financial hub, its delegation was led by National Development Minister Lawrence Wong.

Xue Li, a senior fellow at the Chinese Academy of Social Sciences, told the *South China Morning Post* that China's decision not to invite Lee probably reflected the conclusion in Beijing that Singapore only sought economic advantages from China while "relying on the U.S. for security."[21]

Some Singapore and Chinese scholars believe that at least some of China's animus is targeted at Lee personally. The prime minister, the son of founding Singapore prime minister Lee Kuan Yew, who died in 2015 and is credited by Chinese officials as having adroitly dealt with their leaders, had faced Beijing's wrath at least once before. In 2004, shortly before the younger Lee became prime minister he was rebuked by Beijing after he made a private visit to Taiwan.

When news of Lee's visit to Taiwan leaked, China reacted with anger and accused him of encouraging Taiwan's independence movement. Beijing canceled several senior-level exchanges, including preliminary talks

21. Jaipragas, "What New Silk Road Snub Means for Singapore's Ties with China."

on a bilateral trade agreement. Singapore insisted it remained committed to the One China policy and, after the younger Lee became prime minister he gave a major foreign policy speech in which he declared that his government would not recognize Taiwan if it declared independence. Relations normalized in 2005.[22]

Lee apparently also irritated Beijing with some jokes made during comments he delivered at an after-dinner speech to business representatives in Washington in 2013. "Beijing residents joke that to get a free smoke all they have to do is open their windows," Lee quipped. He followed that with a reference to pig carcasses appearing in Chinese rivers. "In Shanghai, if you want some pork soup, you just turn on the tap," he said. When the audience appeared to wonder if they would be in good taste if they laughed, he added, "That's their joke, not mine."[23]

Chinese academic Xue told a Hong Kong newspaper that the current government in Singapore is "different from the generation of Lee Kuan Yew." Xue said today's leaders are "used to dealing with China from their Western perspective that is being a teacher of China rather than a follower of China."[24]

But some Singapore officials and academics insist that the fact that Lee was not invited was not an issue. "We had one minister there," says a Singapore official. "China never sends a letter until the other side says yes. They don't want to lose face."

The China expert says China's invitation was sent to the Singapore government without designating an invitee, just like the invitations sent to other participating countries. He said there was some uncertainty among Singapore officials about "whether China was trying to discourage Prime Minister Lee from attending" so they sent another minister instead. The China expert is convinced that Lee would have been welcomed to attend if the Singapore government had proposed that.

In the end, Xi and Lee had an opportunity to meet on neutral turf at the G20 leaders' summit in Germany in July. The two leaders "affirmed the substantive bilateral relationship" and cited "good progress" in cooperation between the two countries, according to a statement released by the Singapore government. They also discussed how Singapore could

22. Storey, *Southeast Asia and the Rise of China*, 248–249.
23. Matthew Pennington, "Singapore PM Draws Laughs in U.S. Speech," *Associated Press*, April 3, 2013, https://www.apnews.com/0763d799da3d4cad9a60f838c3427d2b.
24. Jaipragas, "What New Silk Road Snub Means for Singapore's Ties with China."

work with Beijing to implement the BRI and agreed to step up economic cooperation.[25]

But bilateral relations faced one more jolt before getting back on track: the expulsion in August 2017 of a prominent American academic who had been born in China. Huang Jing was charged in a statement released by the Ministry of Home Affairs with being "an agent of influence for a foreign country," which was not identified. But observers in Singapore assume the reference was to China.

The ministry said that Huang used his position at the Lee Kuan Yew School of Public Policy, where he taught courses on China-U.S. relations, to "deliberately and covertly advance the agenda of a foreign country at Singapore's expense." The ministry charged that Huang gave "privileged information" about a foreign country to a senior member of the Lee Kuan Yew School who passed it on the Singapore government. "The clear intention was to use the information to cause the Singapore government to change its foreign policy," the ministry statement said. "This amounts to subversion and foreign interference in Singapore's domestic politics."[26]

Huang told the *South China Morning Post* that "it's nonsense to identify me as an 'agent of influence' for a foreign country." He asked why Singapore did not "identify which foreign country they're referring to? Is it the U.S. or China?" Huang added that "if they have evidence, they should take me to court."[27]

Huang previously had taught at Harvard University, where he received his doctorate, and Utah State University. He also served as a fellow at the Brookings Institution and Stanford University. He published on topics ranging from China's elite politics to Beijing's foreign and military policy and U.S.-China relations.[28] Academics familiar with his writings say they often reflected a Beijing-friendly point of view.

---

25. Royston Sim, "PM Lee Hsien Loong Meets Chinese President Xi Jinping in Hamburg ahead of G-20 Summit," *Straits Times*, July 7, 2017, https://www.straitstimes.com/singapore/pm-lee-meets-chinese-president-xi-jinping-in-hamburg-ahead-of-g-20-summit.
26. Royston Sim, "LKY School Professor Huang Jing Banned, Has PR Cancelled, for Being Agent of Influence for Foreign Country," *Straits Times*, August 4, 2017, https://www.straitstimes.com/singapore/lky-school-professor-huang-jing-banned-has-pr-cancelled-for-being-agent-of-influence-for.
27. Jun Mai, "Chinese-American Professor and His Wife to Be Expelled from Singapore," *South China Morning Post*, August 4, 2017, https://www.scmp.com/news/china/policies-politics/article/2105475/chinese-professor-and-his-wife-be-expelled-singapore.
28. Sim, "LKY School Professor Huang Jing Banned."

At a panel on the South China Sea hosted by the Lee Kuan Yew School in August 2016, a month after the tribunal negated most of Beijing's claims, Huang highlighted his view that the ruling had undermined the "political situation" in the Asia Pacific. A summary of his views published by the school paraphrased him as saying that "the ruling makes the situation look like an end between two extremes for China, making it into a take it or leave it situation."[29]

Academics in Singapore say that Huang in debates regarding policy toward China in recent years had been publicly "very critical" of Singapore. One Asia expert said the memo that Huang passed to the government through a senior Lee Kuan Yew School official had warned that Singapore needed to change its policy toward the South China Sea, otherwise Singapore could face negative consequences. These academics said that Huang told the school official to whom he passed the memo that he had received the information from important officials in China. One scholar said this convinced Singapore officials that Huang was acting as an agent of a foreign country.

Huang has since been named academic dean of the National and Regional Research Institute of Beijing Language and Culture University.[30]

The events in 2016–2017 were not the first time Beijing put Singapore in the deep freeze. In June 2011, a Chinese maritime surveillance vessel Haixun 31 visited Singapore during a time when China was quite assertive in pressuring Singapore's neighbors in the South China Sea. The ship visit raised "an unusual number of enquires," which prompted Singapore's Foreign Ministry to issue a statement on the purpose of the port call.

"It is obvious that what ought to have been a routine visit has occasioned a high level of attention because of recent incidents between China and Vietnam and China and the Philippines in the South China Sea," the statement said. It continued that Singapore is not a claimant in the disputed sea and takes no position on the various claims by China and the other disputing nations.

---

29. Global-is-Asian Staff, "In Search of Solutions for the South China Sea," Lee Kuan Yew School of Public Policy—Global IS Asia, October 11, 2016, https://lkyspp.nus.edu.sg/gia/article/in-search-of-solutions-for-the-south-china-sea.

30. "Huang Jing," Beijing Language and Culture University, November 8, 2018, http://www.blcu.edu.cn/art/2018/11/8/art_5733_1134571.html.

"But as a major trading nation, Singapore has a critical interest in anything affecting freedom of navigation in all international sea lanes," the statement added. It said that Singapore believes it is in "China's own interests to clarify its claims in the [sea] with more precision," adding that "the current ambiguity . . . has caused serious concerns in the international community," which is why the Haixun 31's visit has "provoked so much interest."

The Foreign Ministry told China that completing negotiations on the Declaration of a Code of Conduct with its ASEAN neighbors, which had been ongoing "for almost a decade," would be "a good start." Singapore urged Beijing to look at "some new proposals" that ASEAN had recently made and said it hoped they would be "received in the spirit of goodwill and cooperation." The statement ended: "Then perhaps a routine port call will not arouse so much excitement."[31]

China was livid at Singapore's pointed comments. At the Chinese National Day celebration in Singapore several months later, China's ambassador gave a speech in which he pointedly talked about "China's indisputable sovereignty" in the South China Sea, according to a Singapore-based academic who attended the event. The embassy played the Singapore and Chinese national anthems as is customary at these events, but it cut the Singapore anthem to only one verse and dropped the second one. The ambassador also deliberately turned his back to the Singapore minister attending the celebration, the academic recalls.

"We know we will have bush fires regularly," Kausikan says. "So you have to prepare yourself." The former diplomat says, "China is at once very confident and very insecure. It's a mistake to only focus on one."

Malaysian academic Kuik Cheng-Chwee, who writes extensively about hedging by Southeast Asian nations in the face of China's rise, has argued that it was Singapore's "heavy hedging" between Washington and Beijing beginning in 2016 that prompted China's ham-fisted response. As indicators of Singapore's heavy hedging, Kuik cited the city-state's repeated and strong support for the arbitral tribunal ruling against Beijing in the South China Sea and its deepening of defense ties with Washington. China

31. "MFA Spokesman's Comments in Responses to Media Queries on the Visit of Chinese Maritime Surveillance Vessel Haixun 31 to Singapore," Ministry of Foreign Affairs, Singapore, June 20, 2011, https://www.mfa.gov.sg/Newsroom/Press-Statements-Transcripts-and-Photos/2011/06/MFA-Spokesmans-Comments-in-responses-to-media-queries-on-the-visit-of-Chinese-maritime-surveillance.

countered Singapore's "defiance by imposing higher costs," said Kuik, who teaches international relations at the National University of Malaysia.[32]

"A NEW HISTORIC CHAPTER"

Once the Huang incident died down, China-Singapore relations returned to a more normal state. In September 2017, Lee finally got his visit to Beijing, one month before the critical 19th Chinese Communist Party congress and three months before Singapore assumed the ASEAN chair. The leaders, in a meeting which Xi described as marking a "new historical chapter," agreed to build cooperation in the financial, judicial, legal, and defense sectors, according to a Singapore government statement. Xi expressed appreciation that Singapore was an early supporter of the BRI.[33]

During Lee's trip, Singapore Defense Minister Ng Eng Hen had talks with his Chinese counterpart to step up military relations, including through combined training exercises between the two countries' navies and armies. The two armed forces also agreed to increase military dialogues and promote confidence-building measures. The two militaries in 2015 had begun a new bilateral naval exercise called Exercise Maritime Cooperation.[34]

Still, defense ties between Singapore and China are less developed than Beijing's military links with some of Singapore's neighbors. In 2005, the two countries agreed to establish a defense dialogue and cooperate in less sensitive areas such as humanitarian aid and disaster relief. In 2007, war ships from China, Singapore, and eight other nations conducted a combined maritime exercise. After their first annual Defense Policy Dialogue in 2008, the first Singapore frigate visited China and the following year the two militaries organized a nine-day counterterrorism exercise. Despite these exchanges, Singapore-China military exercises still lag far

---

32. Kuik Cheng-Chwee, "A Southeast Asian Perspective," *The Asan Forum*, September 5, 2017, http://www.theasanforum.org/a-southeast-asian-perspective/#a4.
33. Lim Yan Liang, "Chinese President Xi Jinping and Singapore PM Lee Hsien Loong Discuss New Areas of Cooperation," *Straits Times*, September 20, 2017, https://www.straitstimes.com/asia/east-asia/pm-lee-meets-chinese-president-xi-jinping-other-top-leaders-on-china-trip.
34. Lim Yan Liang, "Singapore and China to Deepen Defence Ties with More Bilateral Exercises," *Straits Times*, September 22, 2017, https://www.straitstimes.com/asia/se-asia/singapore-and-china-reaffirm-commitment-to-deepen-defence-ties.

behind those Singapore has with the United States, Australia, and the United Kingdom.[35]

Singapore ranked eighth on the list of China's most frequent military diplomatic partners around the world between 2003 and 2016, according to a 2017 study by Center for the Study of Chinese Military Affairs of the National Defense University in Washington. Among Southeast Asian countries, only Thailand and Vietnam had more engagements than Singapore, whose activities included 10 joint military exercises, nine Chinese naval port calls, and 37 senior-level meetings.[36]

Elite diplomacy, including high-level official visits, is another prominent feature of China's diplomatic outreach in the region. Between 2000 and 2015, some 176 high-level exchanges took place between the two countries. That is fewer exchanges than Vietnam, Thailand, and Indonesia had, but more than Beijing had with the Philippines and Malaysia.[37]

Singapore also occasionally takes umbrage at the China's actions in Singapore. During a visit by a Chinese destroyer to Changi Naval Base in 2013,[38] the Chinese Embassy apparently organized Chinese nationals working in Singapore to wave Chinese flags at a reception ceremony, irritating some in Singapore. Soon afterward a Chinese oceanographic vessel stopped over in Singapore before cruising into the South China Sea to "underline" Beijing's sovereignty. Political scientist Ian Chong of the National University of Singapore says the negative perceptions around these two visits caused China subsequently to make "less high key" port visits to the city-state.

Singapore was the second to last country in Southeast Asia to recognize China in October 1990, followed by Brunei a year later. After Singapore separated from Malaysia in 1965 during a political dispute over the

---

35. Storey, *Southeast Asia and the Rise of China*, 241.

36. Kenneth Allen, Phillip C. Saunders, and John Chen, *Chinese Military Diplomacy 2003–2016* (Washington, DC: National Defense University Press, 2017), 45, https://ndupress.ndu.edu/Portals/68/Documents/stratperspective/china/ChinaPerspectives-11.pdf?ver=2017-07-17-153301-093.

37. Samantha Custer, Brooke Russell, Matthew DiLorenzo, Mengfan Cheng, Siddhartha Ghose, Harsh Desai, Jacob Sims, and Jennifer Turner, *Ties That Bind: Quantifying China's Public Diplomacy and Its "Good Neighbor" Effect* (Williamsburg, VA: AidData at William and Mary, June 2018), 16, https://docs.aiddata.org/ad4/pdfs/Ties_That_Bind--Full_Report.pdf.

38. "Chinese Naval Escort Task Force Calls at Singapore Port," *Xinhua*, September 5, 2013, http://www.china.org.cn/world/2013-09/05/content_29944651.htm.

rights of ethnic Chinese, the new state was much more focused on stabilizing troubled relations with its two much larger Muslim-majority neighbors, Indonesia and Malaysia, than on China.

Indonesia at the time was in a period of military confrontation with Malaysia that finally ended in 1966. Malaysia was in a battle with domestic communists supported by China, while Indonesia charged Beijing with allegedly supporting a domestic communist attempt to seize power in a coup in 1965.[39]

Indonesia and Malaysia feared that China would use Singapore as a Chinese client state in the region. Singapore responded by pledging not to normalize diplomatic ties with Beijing until Jakarta took that step. The city-state also highlighted the multicultural make up of its society while downplaying its ethnic Chinese majority population. Singapore's government adopted a stridently anti-communist ideology and strongly backed the U.S. military campaign to contain the spread of communism in Vietnam.[40]

Singapore cautiously supported Malaysia's move to normalize relations with China in 1974, although the city-state remained anxious about Beijing's goals in Southeast Asia. It was also concerned that a security vacuum might develop if the United States withdrew from the region after its defeat in Vietnam the following year. After Chinese paramount leader Deng Xiaoping launched economic reforms in 1978 (he visited Singapore a month before kicking off the reforms) and Vietnam invaded Cambodia to oust the Khmer Rouge in 1978, opportunities emerged for Singapore to develop more cooperative ties with Beijing in the 1980s.[41]

Thanks to Deng's economic opening, Singapore became Southeast Asia's largest trading partner with China; by the mid-1980s it was also the region's largest investor in the country. But Singapore waited until 1990, the year Jakarta recognized Beijing, to establish diplomatic ties with China. Singapore's leaders early on projected that China would in the next few decades achieve economic preeminence in the Asia Pacific.[42]

---

39. Storey, *Southeast Asia and the Rise of China*, 231.
40. Ibid., 232.
41. Ibid., 233. See also Teo Chee Hean, "Singapore-China Ties: Breaking New Ground," *Straits Times*, September 20, 2018, https://www.straitstimes.com/opinion/singapore-china-ties-breaking-new-ground.
42. Storey, *Southeast Asia and the Rise of China*, 235.

"As China rose, Singapore viewed a U.S. security umbrella as critical for stable balance of power in the Asia-Pacific," wrote Storey, of ISEAS-Yusof Ishak Institute in Singapore.[43] Just weeks after establishing formal relations with Beijing, Singapore signed an agreement with the United States allowing more frequent ship and aircraft visits.

After the Philippines moved to close two U.S. bases in the early 1990s, Singapore started to construct a pier at Changi Naval Base to accommodate port calls by the U.S. Navy. In 2005, Singapore and Washington signed a Strategic Framework Agreement that provided for an annual strategic dialogue, increased military training and exercises, and gave the city-state access to sensitive defense technology.[44]

Despite their sharp differences over the South China Sea and the city-state's military engagement with the United States, Singapore has long actively supported engaging China in the Asia Pacific. It believes that cooperation between ASEAN and Beijing will boost regional security.

The question going forward is whether Singapore, which works hard to balance its relations with Washington and Beijing, will be able to avoid being impacted by the China-U.S. trade war. "Singapore will try its best to stay out of the way, but it could start affecting the way we invest in China and the ways our production networks operate," says Chong.

"The U.S.is our largest investor, and much U.S. investment goes toward the creation of components, products, and services subsequently sold to China, our largest market." Chong adds, "As our political space shrinks, how will Singapore try to thread the needle? It may be difficult as it becomes easier to upset one side or the other, or potentially even both leading powers."

Despite the deep engagement between China and Singapore, Singaporeans have considerable anxiety about China's role in the region, according to poll findings released by Singapore's ISEAS-Yusof Ishak Institute in early 2019 after surveying academics, think tankers, and representatives of business, civil society organizations, and the media in the 10 ASEAN countries. Some 57 percent of Singaporeans surveyed said they thought "China will become a revisionist power with an intent to

43. Ibid., 236.
44. Ibid., 237.

turn Southeast Asia into its sphere of influence." More than nine in ten thought that China would "most likely vie for regional leadership in response to perceived growing indifference of the U.S. towards Southeast Asia."

A little less than 47 percent of Singaporeans polled had "no confidence" or "little confidence" that China "will do the right thing" in contributing to global security and prosperity. (The number for the United States was almost identical at 48 percent.) About 60 percent of Singaporean respondents thought China's BRI would bring Southeast Asian nations "closer into China's orbit" and roughly 42 percent thought the scheme "provides needed infrastructure funding for countries in the region."

Shifting to Washington, almost 73 percent of Singaporean elite thought in late 2018 that U.S. global power and influence had "deteriorated" or "deteriorated sharply" over the previous year. More than three-quarters of Singaporeans polled said "U.S. engagement with Southeast Asia under the Donald Trump administration" had "decreased substantially" or "decreased." Just over 38 percent had "no confidence" or "little confidence" in the United States as "a strategic partner and provider of regional security."

Nearly three out of four Singaporeans said the U.S. Free and Open Indo-Pacific concept "is unclear and requires further elaboration."[45]

PIVOTAL ROLE IN BELT AND ROAD

The closest ties between China and Singapore are economic, as is the case with most Southeast Asian countries. Singapore was long China's top trade and investment partner in Southeast Asia, but in recent years Vietnam has overtaken the city-state as China's largest trading partner in the region. Singapore's two-way trade with China reached $82.7 billion in 2018, up from $2.9 billion in 1990, the year the countries normalized diplomatic relations.[46]

---

45. Tang Siew Mun, Moe Thuzar, Hoang Thi Ha, Termsak Chalermpalanupap, Pham Thi Phuong Thao, and Anuthida Saelaow Qian, *The State of Southeast Asia: 2019 Survey Report* (Singapore: ISEAS-Yusof Ishak Institute, 2019), https://www.iseas.edu.sg/images/pdf/TheStateofSEASurveyReport_2019.pdf.

46. International Monetary Fund, "Exports, FOB to Partner Countries; Imports, CIF from Partner Countries," *IMF Data*, 2014–2018, http://data.imf.org/regular.aspx?key=61013712.

A China and Singapore free-trade agreement, Beijing's first with another Asian country, went into effect in 2009.[47] The two countries signed an upgraded agreement at the end of 2018 that, among other things, was expected to provide Singapore companies increased market access in services and greater investment protection in China. Chinese companies were granted increased access to invest in education services in Singapore.[48]

Interestingly, political irritations between Singapore and China do not appear to have much impact on the trade and investment climate between the two countries as has happened to other countries. For example, a wave of anti–South Korean sentiment erupted across China after Seoul agreed to install a U.S. missile defense system in 2017. Boycotts of stores like Lotte Mart started and Chinese tour groups canceled their trips to South Korea.[49] Similar incidents have engulfed Japanese and Taiwanese companies.

"At the moment, I don't think Singapore has the same high stakes for Beijing that the other countries have," political scientist Chong says. "China doesn't appear to get as upset with Singapore as it does with Japan or Korea, for instance."

Singapore overtook the United States in 2017 to become the top investment destination for China.[50] But China's cumulative stock of investment in Singapore by the end of 2016 reached only $18.1 billion, making China the 13th largest investor with less than a 10th of the U.S. total of $206.7 billion.[51] Singapore has more cumulative investment from U.S. companies than from its Japanese and Chinese counterparts combined.

Excluding Hong Kong and Taiwan, Singapore has emerged as China's largest foreign investor. Much of Singapore's investment in China is in

---

47. Teo, "Singapore-China Ties: Breaking New Ground."
48. Piet Flintrop, "Singapore Signs Upgraded Free Trade Agreement with China," *ASEAN Briefing*, December 6, 2018, https://www.aseanbriefing.com/news/2018/12/06/singapore-signs-upgraded-free-trade-agreement-china.html.
49. Javier C. Hernández, Owen Guo and Ryan Mcmorrow, "South Korean Stores Feel China's Wrath as U.S. Missile System Is Deployed," *New York Times*, March 9, 2017, https://www.nytimes.com/2017/03/09/world/asia/china-lotte-thaad-south-korea.html.
50. Stephanie Luo, "Singapore Top Destination for China Investments," *Straits Times*, December 8, 2017, https://www.straitstimes.com/business/economy/spore-top-destination-for-china-investments.
51. Department of Statistics Singapore, *Foreign Direct Investment in Singapore 2016* (Singapore: Ministry of Trade and Industry, January 2018), https://www.singstat.gov.sg/-/media/files/publications/trade_and_investment/fdi2016.pdf.

contract manufacturing and implemented by small and medium-sized enterprises looking for lower production costs than they face back home. Many of these factories produce components for the electronics supply chain that runs through China and could get squeezed by the "tariff war" as China retaliates against U.S. tariffs imposed by the Trump administration.

Singapore will end up being a huge beneficiary of the BRI, even though it is not looking for help from China to bolster the city-state's already first-class infrastructure. Rather, Singapore will provide its neighbors with banking, legal, and insurance services for building roads, ports, airports, and power stations. It is often in Singapore where the consortium of companies doing the project will be cobbled together, where the bonds will be raised, and where lending from Singapore and Japanese banks will originate.[52]

In 2018, China and Singapore signed an agreement to expand Singapore's involvement in BRI projects to include financial connectivity and collaboration in training officials in nations where BRI projects will be implemented.[53] Singapore is already the largest clearing center for Chinese renminbi payments outside of China and Hong Kong.[54]

Chinese banks in Singapore by 2018 had committed about $73 billion to finance Singaporean and Chinese companies involved in BRI projects.[55] "There's a promise [in the BRI] of higher end design and service," says Chong, adding that it's not clear "how much of this will be realized. . . . Cambodia and Thailand, for example, may not need or want stuff that fancy," he says.

Another critical Singapore role is providing legal services to resolve commercial disputes in the often-complicated contracts. "China prefers

52. Takashi Nakano, "Singapore Aims to Be Hub for Belt and Road Deal Signings," *Nikkei Asian Review*, October 25, 2018, https://asia.nikkei.com/Spotlight/Belt-and-Road/Singapore-aims-to-be-hub-for-Belt-and-Road-deal-signings.

53. Danson Cheong, "Singapore and China Sign Deal to Boost Cooperation on Belt and Road Initiative," *Straits Times*, April 12, 2018, https://www.straitstimes.com/asia/east-asia/singapore-and-china-sign-deal-to-boost-cooperation-on-belt-and-road-initiative.

54. Claire Huang, "How Singapore Can Gain from Silk Road Project," *Straits Times*, March 5, 2018, https://www.straitstimes.com/asia/east-asia/how-spore-can-gain-from-silk-road-project?&utm_source=google_gmail&utm_medium=social-media&utm_campaign=addtoany; Akane Okutsu, "Singapore Signs Deal with China on Belt and Road," *Nikkei Asian Review*, April 9, 2018, https://asia.nikkei.com/Politics/International-Relations/Singapore-signs-deal-with-China-on-Belt-and-Road.

55. Teo, "Singapore-China Ties: Breaking New Ground."

Singapore after a company requests third-party help" in resolving a dispute, a Singapore official says.

Singapore since 2013 has emerged as a large investor in China's real estate development. CapitaLand, which owns a chain of shopping malls and office buildings across China, in early 2019 completed a $3.6 billion mega-commercial complex, boasting eight skyscrapers with a nearly 1,000-foot "horizontal skyscraper" lying across the top of four of them. The complex in Chongqing in southern China, called Raffles City Chongqing, has 450 shops and views of the Yangtze and Jialing Rivers, along with offices, apartments, a hotel, and a transport hub with ferry, subway, and bus stations.[56]

One of Singapore's biggest early investments in China was the $20 billion, 27-square-mile Suzhou Investment Park launched by both governments in 1994. Located outside the ancient city of Suzhou west of Shanghai, the park was intended to bring together Singapore's managerial expertise and capital with China's low labor costs. Singapore initially held a 65 percent stake in the project with China holding the balance.

But five years later, the project faced serious challenges as Singaporean officials said Chinese authorities began developing a rival economic zone in Suzhou, prompting competition for investment by multinationals. Singapore elder statesman Lee Kuan Yew complained about "municipal shenanigans" and government flip-flops on tax exemptions for imported equipment, prompting Singapore to scale back its investment.

The Economist found, however, that the second industrial park actually predated the one set up by Singapore by three years. Nonetheless, Chinese officials responded by lauding the Singapore project as a critically important example of economic cooperation between the two countries and began to investigate Lee's criticisms.[57] Eventually the project recovered, inspiring Lee to dub it a "success" on its 10th anniversary, and by 2006 it had started turning a profit.[58]

56. Tracy You, "Chinese Workers Have Nearly Completed a £2.7 Billion Mega Commercial Complex with an Incredible 'Horizontal Skyscraper' Almost 1,000 Ft across the Top," *Daily Mail*, February 27, 2019, https://www.dailymail.co.uk/news/article-6751491/Chinese-city-nearly-completed-enormous-2-7bn-complex-horizontal-skyscraper-top.html?ito=social-facebook.

57. "The Trouble with Singapore's Clone," *The Economist*, January 1, 1998, https://www.economist.com/asia/1998/01/01/the-trouble-with-singapores-clone.

58. Storey, *Southeast Asia and the Rise of China*, 243.

The Suzhou park has ranked as the second-best industrial zone in China in recent years. In the early days, the park focused primarily on labor-intensive manufacturing, but more recently high-tech (e.g., nanotechnology) and service industries have become more prominent. Over the years, Singapore's share of the park has been reduced to 28 percent.[59]

By the early 2000s, China posed another challenge to the economic clout of Singapore and its neighbors as China gained increased access to more sophisticated technology. Coupled with relatively low labor costs in China, Southeast Asian companies found it hard to compete with Chinese-made goods as they snared ever-larger market share. In addition, growing levels of foreign investment in China prompted concerns in the region that China was diverting investment from the economies of other countries.[60]

Ever-nimble Singapore responded by working to restructure its economy and cooperate with its Southeast Asian neighbors to promote greater economic integration. The government decided the country would need to focus on niche areas where China would find it harder to compete. These included pharmaceuticals, biomedicine, environmental technology, financial services, and top-end manufacturing. Beyond that, Singapore encouraged its companies to invest in new developing markets, including in China and Vietnam, promote innovation at home, and bolster training and human capital.[61]

Singapore advocated for the establishment of the ASEAN Economic Community (AEC). The intended goal was to turn the region into a single market through the free flow of goods, services, and capital, notionally by 2015. The AEC would achieve greater economies of scale, lower trade costs, a more business-friendly environment, and better connectivity and become a single production base to attract foreign investment.[62] Progress, however, has been incremental and slow. Tariffs between member countries have largely been slashed, but services, for

59. "Suzhou Industrial Park: 10 Things to Know about the China-Singapore Project," *Straits Times*, October 25, 2014, https://www.straitstimes.com/asia/east-asia/suzhou-industrial-park-10-things-to-know-about-the-china-singapore-project.
60. Storey, *Southeast Asia and the Rise of China*, 244.
61. Ibid.
62. "What Is the ASEAN Economic Community?," *Business Times*, August 29, 2018, https://www.businesstimes.com.sg/hub-projects/deepening-asean-economic-integration/what-is-the-asean-economic-community.

example, remain largely closed and, in some cases, new nontariff barriers have been introduced.

Beyond Suzhou, Singapore invested in two other major projects intended to promote rapid economic increases using sustainable development techniques. One is the Tianjin Eco-City, near Beijing, which is a three-square-mile area that includes industrial parks, residential areas, community centers, schools, and a hospital. The next phase will include smart bus stops, driverless cars, and bicycles to promote green transport.[63]

A second Sino-Singapore project is the Chongqing Connectivity Initiative in the upper reaches of China's Yangtze River. The project will facilitate the movement of container cargo shipped via the river to the Southern Transport Corridor railway network. The aim of the initiative is to spur economic growth in less developed western China.[64]

In late 2018, Singapore companies signed 22 deals with Chinese firms to provide business with greater access to western China in such sectors as technology and innovation, education, logistics, and tourism. One plan is for a Singapore fintech incubator to launch start-ups in Sichuan Province. By the end of 2017, Singapore's investment in Sichuan totaled $6.7 billion. Trade that year stood at just over $1 billion.[65]

Singapore has become an important target for investment by Chinese tech companies. In early 2019, Shanghai-based artificial intelligence firm Yitu Technology announced that it was launching a research and development center in Singapore. The company, which claims its facial recognition platform can recognize 1.8 billion faces in three seconds, said it was exploring bidding with partners to invest in Singapore's surveillance camera program.

---

63. Olivia Siong, "Tianjin Eco-City to Develop New Central District, City Centre," *Channel News Asia*, July 1, 2018, https://www.channelnewsasia.com/news/singapore/tianjin-eco-city-to-develop-new-central-district-city-centre-10487778.

64. Chong Koh Ping, "Singapore-Chongqing Logistics Hub under Chongqing Connectivity Initiative Takes Shape," *Straits Times*, July 4, 2018, https://www.straitstimes.com/asia/east-asia/singapore-chongqing-logistics-hub-under-chongqing-connectivity-initiative-takes-shape.

65. "Singapore Firms Sign 22 Deals with Sichuan Companies for Greater Access to Western China," *Business Times*, September 14, 2018, https://www.businesstimes.com.sg/asean-business/singapore-firms-sign-22-deals-with-sichuan-companies-for-greater-access-to-western.

Under its "Lamppost-as-a-Platform" pilot project, Singapore is planning to install more than 100,000 cameras to help officials pick out and recognize people in crowds as part of its broader "Smart Nation" plan.[66] Singapore had earlier rolled out facial recognition technology in Terminal 4 at Changi Airport to provide self-service options such a check-in, customs and immigration, and boarding for passengers.[67]

China's two leaders in the digital space, Alibaba and Tencent, have been investing aggressively in Singapore. Alibaba by 2018 invested a hefty $4 billion in Lazada, the Singapore-based e-commerce company, and tapped a senior Alibaba executive to run the business as it takes on rival Amazon from the United States, which in 2017 launched two-hour delivery in the city-state. Alibaba's Ant Financial earlier had acquired Lazada's payment affiliate helloPay and rebranded it under the Alipay platform.[68] Alibaba in 2018 also set up in Singapore its first research center outside of China to focus on artificial intelligence.

Tencent, the gaming-and-social-media giant, has taken a 34 percent stake in Singapore-based SEA Ltd., which operates the Shopee e-commerce site and Garena gaming platform. Chinese tech unicorns Didi Chuxing and Meituan Dianping have invested in Singapore's Grab, a tech company that offers ride hailing, ride sharing, and food delivery and logistics services.[69]

Singapore also capitalized on the growing numbers of tourists from China. In 2017, 3.2 million tourists visited from China, beating out Indo-

66. Ardhana Aravindan and John Geddie, "Singapore to Test Facial Recognition on Lampposts, Stoking Privacy Fears," *Reuters*, April 13, 2018, https://www.reuters.com/article/us-singapore-surveillance/singapore-to-test-facial-recognition-on-lampposts-stoking-privacy-fears-idUSKBN1HK0RV; Rami Blachman, "China's Tech Companies Are Taking a More American Approach to International Expansion," *VentureBeat*, February 16, 2019, https://venturebeat.com/2019/02/16/chinas-tech-companies-are-taking-a-more-american-approach-to-international-expansion/.

67. Jason Thomas, "Facial Recognition and the Big Picture," *The ASEAN Post*, January 9, 2019, https://theaseanpost.com/article/facial-recognition-and-big-picture.

68. Cate Cadell and Aradhana Aravindan, "Alibaba Doubles Lazada Investment to $4 Billion in Aggressive Southeast Asian Expansion," *Reuters*, March 18, 2018, https://www.reuters.com/article/us-alibaba-lazada-funding/alibaba-doubles-lazada-investment-to-4-billion-in-aggressive-southeast-asian-expansion-idUSKBN1GV09W.

69. Chua Kong Ho and Zen Soo, "Southeast Asia Becomes a Target for China Technology Companies but Is a Tough Nut to Crack," *South China Morning Post*, July 6, 2018, https://www.scmp.com/tech/enterprises/article/2153876/southeast-asia-becomes-target-china-technology-companies-tough-nut.

nesia, as Singapore promoted tourism beyond the major city markets of Beijing and Shanghai. Chinese tourists comprised over 18 percent of the total numbers of tourists that arrived in Singapore and spent $2.3 billion, making them the biggest spenders for the third year in a row.[70] In late 2018, Alipay and the Singapore Tourism Board offered tourists from China "cashless" trips to Singapore using Alibaba's mobile payment service.[71]

But the Singapore Tourism Board wants to make sure that Singapore does not become too dependent on Chinese tourists, so it seeks to diversity by promoting other markets as well. The occasional rude behavior of Chinese tourists has not created the popular backlash incidents it has in some other places, at least for now. Often incidents that cause problems in other markets are not reported in the city-state because "Singapore has a more controlled media," Chong says.

"OVERSEAS CHINESE SHOULD IDENTIFY THEIR INTERESTS WITH CHINA'S"

Roughly three-quarters of Singaporeans are ethnic Chinese, most of whose ancestors were Hokkien immigrants from Fujian in southern China and landed in the first half of the nineteenth century when Singapore was a British settlement. Many Indians and Malays arrived around the same time and make up nearly 25 percent of Singapore's population, but it is the size of the ethnic Chinese population that played a critical role in the development of Singapore.

Singapore has long attracted newcomers with its liberal visa program. In 2013, the government introduced plans to increase the population to 6.5 million by 2030 from about 5.3 million. The goal was to reshape Singapore into a global knowledge hub and to make up for the local ethnic

70. Tiffany Fumiko Tay, "Tourist Arrivals, Spending in Singapore Hit Record High for 2nd Straight Year; China Top Source of Visitors," *Straits Times*, February 12, 2018, https://www.straitstimes.com/singapore/tourist-spending-in-singapore-hit-record-268b-in-2017-china-top-source-of-visitors; Jose Hong, "China Beats Indonesia as Singapore's Top Tourist Source," *Straits Times*, February 12, 2018, https://www.straitstimes.com/singapore/china-beats-indonesia-as-singapores-top-tourist-source.

71. Luke Barras-Hill, "Chinese Visitors Make First 'Cashless' Trip to Singapore," *TR Business*, September 17, 2018, https://www.trbusiness.com/regional-news/asia-pacific/chinese-visitors-make-first-cashless-trip-to-singapore/149968.

Chinese population's plummeting birth rate.[72] It was assumed that much of the increase in numbers would come from China. Large numbers of ethnic Chinese were also expected from Indonesia and Malaysia.

The numbers of new Chinese migrants are estimated to have grown to 700,000 to 800,000 from 300,000 in 2011. These new migrants consist of two main groups: affluent Chinese coming as investors to start companies and Chinese who worked or studied in Singapore first and returned to set up their own firms. Many of the new immigrants consider both China and Singapore as their "homes" and are tied to both.[73]

The Hua Yuan General Association of New Immigrants from China was established in 2001 by China-born professionals with the purpose of helping members to integrate better into Singapore's multiethnic society and promote commercial relations between China and Singapore. In the 1990s, China emphasized that its citizens study overseas and were "returning to China to make a contribution." Over the past two decades, Beijing's focus has shifted to Chinese nationals "contributing to China from overseas," and it encourages them to integrate into the society where they live.[74]

Close geographical and political ties facilitate the ability of Chinese entrepreneurs to operate in both China and Singapore. By the end of 2017, Changi airport had direct links to 34 Chinese cities served by 13 airlines.[75] Deep economic links also helped as bilateral trade soared and more companies from Singapore invested in China and vice versa.

A car accident in downtown Singapore in May 2012 highlighted the tensions brought on by the surge of new Chinese immigrants from China. A speeding Ferrari driven by a 31-year-old wealthy Chinese investor blew through a red light and crashed into a taxi, killing three people. Many Sin-

---

72. Brenda S. A. Yeoh and Weiqiang Lin, "Multiplying Diversities: How 'New' Chinese Mobilities Are Changing Singapore," in *Chinese Encounters in Southeast Asia: How People, Money, and Ideas from China Are Changing a Region*, ed. Pal Nyiri and Danielle Tan (Seattle: University of Washington Press, 2017), 45.

73. Liu Hong and Ren Na, "Transnational Social Underpinnings of New Chinese Capitalism: Immigrant Entrepreneurship in Singapore," in *Chinese Capitalism in Southeast Asia: Cultures and Practices*, ed. Yos Santasombat (Palgrave Macmillan), 61.

74. Ibid., 64.

75. Karamjit Kaur, "Changi Airport Set for Record Year in Passenger Traffic, with Some 130 New Flights a Week till December," *Straits Times*, October 29, 2017, https://www.straitstimes.com/singapore/changi-airport-set-for-record-year-in-passenger-traffic-with-some-130-new-flights-a-week.

gaporeans saw the wreck as a symbol of an immigration policy gone too far, allowing Chinese migrants to compete for jobs with locals and changing the ethos and culture of Singapore.[76]

As more newcomers from China arrived, online forums emerged in which Singaporeans complained that Chinese from the mainland were rude and uncivilized. People from the mainland grumbled that Singaporeans, who study English as their first language, are aloof and lack fluency in Mandarin.[77] In an informal poll in 2011 carried out by a blog visited by Chinese nationals in Singapore, 48 percent said that Singaporeans are the most "disgusting" and "irritating" among eight choices.[78]

"The result of this tension is an uneasy two-way xenophobia, with each side accusing the other of racism even though both are Han Chinese," writer Tash Aw said in a 2015 commentary in *The New York Times*.[79]

Aw said that in the past the Chinese focused on their Chinese-ness to distance themselves from Malaysia, but today they are using it to separate themselves from mainland China. "Yet in harnessing its ancient heritage to a newer national identity, the Chinese diaspora in Singapore has created a hybrid culture that questions the idea of a single Chinese identity," Aw wrote.

Singaporeans complain that new arrivals drive up real estate prices and clog up the subway system and roads. Sometimes newer arrivals get caught in a public spat, as happened in 2011 when a family newly arrived from China complained about the smell of curry from an ethnic Indian family's apartment. Nearly 60,000 supporters of the Indian family vowed to cook curry on a subsequent Sunday in a campaign organized on Facebook to highlight rising anger about increasing immigration.[80]

In 2012, 171 bus drivers from China launched a strike by refusing to leave their dormitories to report to work, marking Singapore's first strike in over two decades. Their complaint: They were paid less than their

---

76. Yeoh and Lin, "Multiplying Diversities: How 'New' Chinese Mobilities are Changing Singapore," 42.
77. Tash Aw, "Being Chinese in Singapore," *New York Times*, February 12, 2015, https://www.nytimes.com/2015/02/13/opinion/tash-aw-being-chinese-in-singapore.html.
78. Yeoh and Lin, "Multiplying Diversities: How 'New' Chinese Mobilities Are Changing Singapore," 54.
79. Aw, "Being Chinese in Singapore."
80. Harry Suhartono, "Singaporeans' Culinary Anti-Immigration Protest: Curry," *Reuters*, August 21, 2011, https://www.reuters.com/article/us-singapore-curry/singaporeans-culinary-anti-immigration-protest-curry-idUSTRE77K0TB20110821?feedTy.

counterpart drivers from Malaysia and Singapore. At the time just over a fifth of the slightly more than 2,000 bus drivers were from China. Twenty-nine of the drivers were deported back to China and five others were sentence for up to seven weeks in prison for the two-day strike.

Strikes in Singapore are illegal in "essential services" like transport unless the workers give 14 days' notice. The worker walkout highlighted the challenges the government faces as it seeks to defuse public irritation over a surge of immigrants, many of whom come from China, and complaints by lower-skilled foreign workers, who are critical to the transport and construction sectors, about getting lower pay than locals.[81]

For decades, Singapore leaders promoted a Singaporean national identity while supporting efforts by citizens to link to their Chinese cultural and linguistic heritage. More recently, some academics have become concerned that Beijing may be using its soft power efforts to promote greater allegiance to the homeland of their ancestors.

In addition to China's efforts to influence the Singapore government, Kausikan in his mid-2018 talk on China's public diplomacy highlighted Beijing's endeavors to influence ordinary overseas Chinese, including those in Singapore. Kausikan focused on the activities of the Overseas Chinese Affairs Office and pointed out that its goals were encapsulated in the title of the 2014 speech by President Xi to a conference of overseas Chinese associations: "The rejuvenation of the Chinese nation is a dream shared by all Chinese."

Four years later, another Communist Party politburo member, in a speech to the national Overseas Chinese Conference, urged the government to increase and bolster "overseas Chinese patriotic friendly forces" in the service of the "great rejuvenation" of China. The goal as outlined by Xi and the second official is that "overseas Chinese should identify their interests with China's interests and the [Communist Party's] interests," Kausikan said.

To emphasize the importance of its work, the Overseas Chinese Affairs Office in early 2018 was brought under the umbrella of the United Front Work Department, the section of the party that seeks to influence various

81. "Singapore Jails Bus Drivers for Inciting Strikes," *BBC News*, February 25, 2013, https://www.bbc.com/news/world-asia-21571053; John O'Callaghan and Kevin Lim, "Strike by China Bus Drivers Tests Singapore's Patience," *Reuters*, November 28, 2012, https://www.reuters.com/article/uk-singapore-strike/strike-by-china-bus-drivers-tests-singapores-patience-idUSLNE8AR01J20121128.

groups in China and overseas Chinese.[82] Kausikan said China uses a diverse toolkit of tactics ranging from "legitimate diplomacy" to more "covert operations," employing "agents of influence" to convince key "decisionmakers and public opinion shapers."

Political scientist Chong says China is energized in promoting public diplomacy activities among the raft of different Chinese organizations in Singapore, including the scores of clan associations set up to support new arrivals from Fujian, Guangdong, and so on dating back to the early nineteenth century. More recently these clan associations have morphed gradually into groups focusing on "preservation of our rich Chinese heritage" and promoting the Chinese language.[83]

The leadership and membership of these clan associations often overlap with business groupings such as the Singapore Business Federation and the Singapore Chinese Chamber of Commerce and Industry. During tense periods Chinese officials will impress on the business groups its views, such as "Singapore's position on the South China Sea is not helpful and could lead to business costs," Chong says. Association leaders reportedly shared these views with government officials.

China uses public diplomacy to say "you are ethnic Chinese, so you should understand our position and shouldn't oppose us" on issues such as the dispute in the South China Sea. "If not, bad things could happen," Chong notes. China's approach is "more threatening than the North American or European approaches, which tend to focus on persuasion, bridging differences, and finding common ground, at least in Singapore," Chong says. "They don't expect you to necessarily agree. They say, 'Here is a way to help us understand each other and perhaps help each other out.'"

China opened a Confucius Institute at Nanyang Technological University in Singapore in 2005 to teach Mandarin and Chinese culture. In 2015, Xi opened a Chinese cultural center on a visit to Singapore.[84] Two years later, Prime Minister Lee opened a separate Singapore Chinese

---

82. Chris Buckley, "China Gives Communist Party More Control over Policy and Media," *New York Times*, March 21, 2018, https://www.nytimes.com/2018/03/21/world/asia/china-communist-party-xi-jinping.html.

83. "The History of Clan Associations in Singapore," Singapore Federation of Chinese Clan Associations, http://www.sfcca.sg/en/node/446 (accessed October 29, 2019).

84. "President Xi Jinping Gets an Early Start Opening the China Cultural Centre at Queen Street," *Straits Times*, November 7, 2015, https://www.straitstimes.com/singapore/president-xi-jinping-gets-an-early-start-opening-the-china-cultural-centre-at-queen-street.

Cultural Center nearby to highlight the cultural differences between a Chinese person in Singapore and one in China, Malaysia, or Taiwan. "Indeed, we can now speak of a Singaporean Chinese culture," Lee said at the official opening. "In the same way, I think we can speak of a Singapore Malay culture or Singaporean Indian culture."[85]

Like in other Southeast Asian countries, China has ramped up people exchanges with Singapore in recent years, organizing conferences, academic exchanges, study tours, and visits back to the home of their ancestors for Chinese Singaporeans. In 2016, about 5,000 Singaporean students were studying in China.[86] China "does not seem to be the destination of choice" for many Singaporean students, in contrast to, say, Myanmar or Laos, says Chong. "Singapore students are mostly richer and can afford a fancier degree" in Europe, Australia, or North America.

The number of Chinese studying in Singapore is also limited because the city-state has sought to "manage growth," says Chong, due to "a lot of unhappiness" around 2011 that "too many scholarships and school places were going to non-Singaporeans."

China in recent years has invested hundreds of millions of dollars on media platforms around the world, including in Southeast Asia, to "influence international opinion" and "bolster China's image" with a strong focus on overseas Chinese, according to a 2019 report published by the Hoover Institution. Beijing's efforts have included expanding Xinhua News Agency, China Global Television Network, China Radio International, and other state-run media to penetrate foreign markets.[87]

One of the ways Chinese views enter Singapore is through television stations closely allied to Beijing. Singapore's two cable providers, Starhub and Singtel TV, each offer about a half dozen Mandarin news, documentary, and variety channels from Taiwan and Hong Kong through their basic service packages. Some of these channels, several of which accept

---

85. Mayo Martin, "New Arts Centre Will Promote Chinese Culture That Is Singaporean-Centric: PM Lee," *Channel News Asia*, May 19, 2017, https://www.channelnewsasia.com/news/singapore/new-arts-centre-will-promote-chinese-culture-that-is-singaporean-8864144.

86. Custer et al., *Ties That Bind*, 13.

87. Larry Diamond and Orville Schell, eds., *China's Influence and American Interests: Promoting Constructive Vigilance* (Stanford, CA: Hoover Institution Press Publishing, 2019), 99, 100, 103. https://www.hoover.org/sites/default/files/research/docs/00_diamond-schell-chinas-influence-and-american-interests.pdf.

funding from Beijing, actively push China's official views in their target markets.

One of them, CTi TV in Taiwan, is owned by Want Want China Holdings, which reportedly received $586.7 million in subsidies from China since 2004 for its television and print operations in Taiwan, according to *Nikkei Asian Review*. A senior Taiwan government minister said taking subsidies from Beijing "does not violate Taiwan's laws," but he added that it would be a concern "if the money comes with political agenda against Taiwan."[88]

Brian Hioe, founding editor of *New Bloom* magazine, which describes itself as providing "radical perspectives on Taiwan and the Asia Pacific," portrayed CTi's reporting as largely aimed at "damaging the reputation" of Taiwan President Tsai Ing-wen's administration. Hioe said CTi is helping "politically benefit" Tsai's opponents in the opposition Kuomintang party and broadcasting views that "depict Taiwan as directly part of China." Hioe said 60 percent of the network's coverage was dedicated to covering populist Kaohsiung mayor Han Kuo-yu, from the opposition Kuomintang party, who was running for president of Taiwan in the 2020 elections. Han promoted closer links between his city and China.[89]

What is not known is "whether the unwavering pro-Beijing stance adopted by Want Want's media outlets" and its "tendency to attack Beijing critics and generate/amplify disinformation" is a direct result of the [China's] subsidies," wrote J. Michael Cole of the Taiwan Studies Program of the University of Nottingham in the United Kingdom. "At this point, this cannot be demonstrated, nor is there concrete evidence that the Chinese Communist Party has directly meddled in the editorial decisions of Want Want's media outlets or coordinated those with Beijing-controlled media." Cole noted that CTi has received numerous fines from Taiwan's National Communications Commission for spreading "fake news" and

88. Kenji Kawa Se, "Chinese Subsidies for Foxconn and Want Spark Outcry in Taiwan," *Nikkei Asian Review*, April 30, 2019, https://asia.nikkei.com/Business/Companies/Chinese-subsidies-for-Foxconn-and-Want-Want-spark-outcry-in-Taiwan; Sophia Yang, "Taiwan's Want Received NT$2.8 Billion State Grant from China in 2017," *Taiwan News*, April 23, 2019, https://www.taiwannews.com.tw/en/news/3686238.

89. Brian Hioe, "Recent Incidents Point to Increasing Chinese Influence on Taiwanese Media," *New Bloom*, May 13, 2019, https://newbloommag.net/2019/05/13/tw-cn-media-influence/; Chris Horton, "The Taiwanese Populist Advancing China's Interests," *The Atlantic*, April 16, 2019, https://www.theatlantic.com/international/archive/2019/04/taiwanese-populist-han-kuo-yu-china/587146/.

various other violations of the country's broadcast laws that would easily have been covered by the huge subsidies that Want Want has received from China.

Cole also documented meetings between senior Want Want officials and United Front officials in China but said that these interactions in themselves do not prove that the company is engaging in United Front activities in Taiwan. But, he added, this interaction "certainly raises questions and encourages the view that the subsidies may serve as an incentive to reflect Beijing's wishes."[90]

Separately, in May 2019, the Want Want group and Beijing Newspaper Group organized a trip to China for 70 representatives of Taiwan media organizations. Much of the trip was focused on cross-strait relations between China and Taiwan. In a meeting with Wang Yang, chair of the Chinese People's Political Consultative Conference National Committee, the official reportedly tried to convince the participants from Taiwan that they had no guarantees that the United States would intervene on behalf of Taiwan if China invaded.[91]

Other Mandarin-language channels available in Singapore that have close ties to the Chinese government are TVBS Media (Taiwan), Eastern Broadcast Corporation (Taiwan), Television Broadcasts Limited (Hong Kong), and Phoenix Hong Kong Channel. Eastern Broadcast Corporation is reported to have links with the Chinese People's Liberation Army. In 2015, the Carlyle Group reportedly sold its 61 percent stake in the company to U.S. filmmaker Dan Mintz, coproducer of the action movie *Iron Man 3* and cofounder of Shenzhen-listed DMG Entertainment and Media Company for $600 million. Mintz's partner in the company is Peter Xiao, who reportedly has links through his father to the Chinese military.[92]

Singapore political scientist Chong says the programs in the "Mandarin-language [television] news/documentary diet that gets piped straight into Singaporean homes are from those colored with [China] in-

---

90. J. Michael Cole, "An Analysis of Possible Chinese Influence Operations against Taiwan: The Want-Want Case," *The Prospect Foundation Newsletter*, no. 9 (May 3, 2019), https://www.pf.org.tw/article-pfch-2049-6473.

91. Hioe, "Recent Incidents Point to Increasing Chinese Influence on Taiwanese Media."

92. Faith Hung, "Hollywood Producer Dan Mintz Agrees to Buy Carlyle Stake in Taiwan Broadcaster," *Reuters*, November 22, 2015, https://www.reuters.com/article/taiwan-television-ma/update-1-hollywood-producer-dan-mintz-agrees-to-buy-carlyle-stake-in-taiwan-broadcaster-idUSL3N13I04J20151123.

fluence activities in Hong Kong and Taiwan." The political scientist notes that when cable providers first began including these channels in the 1990s and 2000s, "they initially did not have such strong Beijing-leaning tendencies, but [they] became increasingly so as Chinese capital bought into them."

Why does the airing of China-influenced channels in Singapore concern observers? "Because they push the idea of a Greater China, that ethnic Chinese ought to have an affinity to the People's Republic of China," the political scientist says. There is the implication that "on contentious issues like the South China Sea, a party like Singapore should not resist China's position." Other messaging from China suggests "the U.S. is in trouble, so Singapore should focus on its relations with China," Chong says.

China-backed media "decreases sympathy for Taiwan and Hong Kong's distinction from China. This makes [readers and viewers] less open to the positions and complexities facing these societies and governments," says Chong. "In effect, this pushes China's unification agenda onto ethnic Chinese communities in third countries for which the issue should not be of concern and unnecessarily draws these communities into Beijing's cross-strait politics," he observers. "Playing on ethnic loyalties in a region with a history of communal tensions is risky."

In addition, the main key free-to-air channels and Mandarin-language print media in Singapore have begun recruiting more journalists, editors, and television anchors from China, because fewer Singapore young people want to get into Mandarin-language news and documentary production. "One thing I noticed about this crop of media professionals is that their language and sometimes editorializing seems to have an increasingly [pro-Beijing] slant. This could simply be unconscious and due to upbringing, but it is probably useful to try to rule out other possibilities," Chong says.

Mandarin media outlets operating in Singapore appear to increasingly pick up news feeds or wires from China's Xinhua News Agency and China News Service. These outlets provide news reports, editorials, and layout for overseas news organizations around the world on a pro bono basis and reduce costs for Chinese media abroad. At the same time more democratic-leaning liberal media from Taiwan and Hong Kong such as Apple Daily, Formosa Television, SET News, and Liberty Times are for the most part kept out of Singapore. So too are even-handed public broadcasters like Public Television Service and Radio Television Hong Kong.

The Chinese government is also inviting Southeast Asia journalists to visit China to get Beijing's spin into stories for the Chinese-language media. On April 23, 2019, Singapore's *Lianhe Zaobao* ran a story about a visit to Xinjiang Province by a reporter identified as the "Beijing special rapporteur" because the newspaper rejected the reports about the mass incarceration of Uighur Muslims by Western media and human rights organizations.

At the vocational skills training center in Kashgar, "the students seem to . . . play games happily" and "welcomed the reporters with songs and dances and musical instruments," the journalist reported. "All the interviewees took the initiative to tell reporters that they [had] volunteered" to come to the center. Two "students" said they had been "infected [with] extreme thoughts" by their grandparents. The 800 students at the center were being taught skills ranging from cooking to home appliance repair and animal husbandry.[93]

Singapore will undoubtedly continue to face some "bumpy" times with China as the city-state feels compelled to remind Beijing that no country should do anything that will affect freedom of navigation along the South China Sea's trade routes and hobble the free flow of commerce. Singapore will irritate Beijing by not being "Chinese" enough and remembering how that means it should act. China will not be impressed by the city-state's almost religiously zealous efforts to balance its ties between the United States and China and refuse to take sides in their competition for regional influence.

So far Singapore has escaped being punished economically for standing up to Beijing, in contrast to some of its neighbors. Singapore will benefit economically from supporting China on the BRI by structuring loans and providing legal and accounting support for these projects. Sin-

93. "The Mystery of the Xinjiang Education and Training Center Was Gradually Unveiled by the West," *Lianghe Zaobao*, April 23, 2019, http://m.unzbw.com/shiju/20190423/56455.html?fbclid=IwAR31myA9L-aNE3lJoPx-nMoovkNBPOeoZDxXndIiWImDvo6CDJnoy3xPi5A.

gapore's role will help burnish China's checkered reputation on some of the first infrastructure projects Beijing has supported in the region.

Singapore will want to ensure it escapes tarnishing its own relatively pristine image by working with China on the BRI. Singapore will want to avoid getting involved in projects that create unsustainable levels of debt or involve massive corruption and payoffs to government officials, as has been the case in some early BRI projects in countries neighboring Singapore.

9. INDONESIA: CHINA TIES ENTANGLED BY DOMESTIC POLITICS

Indonesia has managed in recent years to do what its neighbors bordering the South China Sea have had trouble doing: stand up to an increasingly assertive China without incurring the full wrath of Beijing and while still keeping the Chinese investment pipeline open. In the first half of 2016, Indonesia's maritime policing vessels were involved in several skirmishes with Chinese fishing boats near the resource-rich Natuna Islands, off the northwestern coast of the country. Days after the third skirmish President Joko Widodo, or Jokowi, conducted a cabinet meeting on a warship near the Natunas.

At the same time, Jokowi has developed close personal ties with President Xi Jinping of China with the hope of courting investors from China to fund infrastructure projects in the planet's fourth most populous nation, a far-flung archipelago of some 17,000 islands and vast natural resources. Jokowi hoped these projects would connect Indonesia with the global economy and convince voters to reelect him president in 2019. China has become Indonesia's most important trading partner, is a major buyer of such commodities as palm oil, and has propelled itself into the role as the Southeast Asian country's second largest investor.

But all this has been anything but an easy slog for either China or Jokowi. Beijing is frustrated by how slow it has been to get projects off the ground. Jokowi has been surprised at how much blowback he got at home for becoming so friendly with China. His critics charge that massive numbers of Chinese workers are flooding into the country to work on investment projects, complain that China is sending poor-quality technology, and warn that not all the Chinese partners coming to Indonesia are financially sound.

Map 11. Indonesia

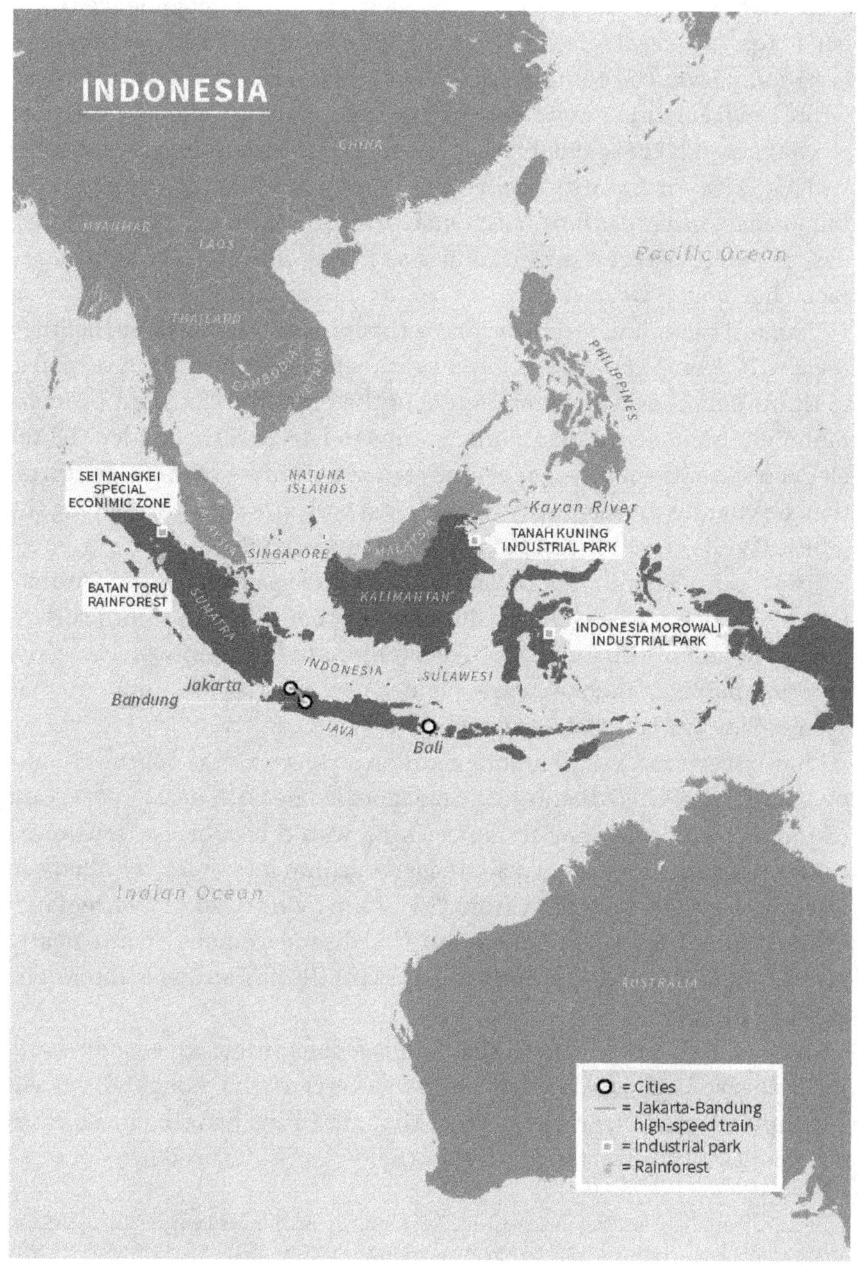

China's influence remains a sensitive issue in Indonesia where ethnic violence has erupted twice since Indonesia gained independence in the late 1940s. "Bilateral relations between Indonesia and China have always been complicated by being entangled with Indonesian domestic politics," wrote Dewi Fortuna Anwar, research professor at the Indonesia Institute of Sciences in Jakarta and former aide to Jokowi's first vice president.

"The rise in identity politics in Indonesia has again conflated Indonesia-China relations with tensions over the role of Chinese Indonesians, thereby threatening Indonesia's hard-won and still fragile interracial harmony," Dewi said.[1]

Some of the country's ethnic Chinese population are anxious that they seem to be facing growing negative sentiment at least in part in response to China's increasing economic role in the country. The giant protests mounted by conservative Islamic groups in late 2016 that ended the reelection bid of the former Jakarta governor, a Chinese Indonesian Christian, on charges of blasphemy were at least partially aimed at keeping the political and economic clout of non-Muslims in check.

Dewi said, "Relations with China to a lesser or greater degree continue to impinge on domestic affairs, due among other things to significant influence of Chinese-Indonesians." She pointed out that opinions among the elite and public in Indonesia are "divided over the rise of China, which is seen as both a threat and an opportunity."[2]

In a survey conducted among opinion shapers across Southeast Asia by ISEAS-Yusof Ishak Institute in Singapore in late 2018, nearly 38 percent of Indonesians said they thought China would become "a revisionist power with an intent to turn Southeast Asia into its sphere of influence." Some 36 percent thought China "would provide alternative regional leadership in the wake of perceived U.S. disengagement," while nearly 29 percent said it was "too early to ascertain China's strategic intentions at the moment."

Almost 82 percent said China "had the most influence economically in Southeast Asia" compared to less than 4 percent who thought this about the United States. Nearly 41 percent thought China had the "most influence politically and strategically" in the region, compared to 33 percent

---

1. Dewi Fortuna Anwar, "Indonesia-China Relations: To Be Handled with Care, *ISEAS Perspective*, no. 19 (2019): 1, https://www.iseas.edu.sg/images/pdf/ISEAS_Perspective_2019_19.pdf.
2. Ibid., 2.

who thought this about the United States. Just under 69 percent thought China "would most likely vie for regional leadership in response to the perceived growing indifference of the U.S. towards Southeast Asia."

About 64 percent of Indonesians thought China's Belt and Road Initiative (BRI) would "benefit regional economic development" or would provide "needed infrastructure funding for countries in the region." But nearly 73 percent said their government should be "cautious in negotiating BRI projects to avoid getting into unsustainable financial debts with China" in light of the debt problems facing Sri Lanka that forced it to turn over a port to China for 99 years.[3]

CHINESE INVESTORS FIND INDONESIA A TOUGH SLOG

A Chinese consortium beat out a Japanese grouping in 2015 for the contract to build a 90-mile high-speed rail from Jakarta to Bandung, Indonesia's third largest city. The $5.5 billion project was to be completed before Jokowi faced the electorate again in 2019. But four years later, just under one-third of the rail had been completed.

The Chinese high-speed rail project is struggling. Acquiring land is the number-one problem, says a senior Indonesian official. Indonesians have a deep attachment to their land and often the country's land ownership records are outdated or unreliable. On top of that, speculation has driven up the cost of land prices along the railroad's route. By late 2018, the expected costs of the project had risen to $6.1 billion because of the rising cost of supplies and labor in Indonesia.

Nearly all the land had been acquired by the end of 2019 by the construction consortium led by state-owned China Railway Corporation and Indonesian state-owned firm PT Wijaya Karya, Indonesia's largest construction firm. The Indonesian group controls a 60 percent stake and the Chinese hold the balance.[4]

---

3. Tang Siew Mun, Moe Thuzar, Hoang Thi Ha, Termsak Chalermpalanupap, Pham Thi Phuong Thao, and Anuthida Saelaow Qian, *The State of Southeast Asia: 2019 Survey Report* (Singapore: ASEAN Studies Centre at ISEAS-Yusof Ishak Institute, 2019), 18, 21, 22, 23, 20, https://www.iseas.edu.sg/images/pdf/TheStateofSEASurveyReport_2019.pdf.

4. Takehiro Masutomo and Teng Jing Xuan, "Indonesia's China-Financed High-Speed Rail Project Off Track," *Caixin*, October 11, 2018, https://www.caixinglobal.com/2018-10-11/indonesias-china-financed-high-speed-rail-project-off-track-101333896.html.

In contrast to his Southeast Asian counterparts, Jokowi has looked to state-owned domestic companies to obtain funding from China for big infrastructure projects to avoid having the government take on sovereign debt. But this model is stretching state-owned construction firms. In 2017, the debt of the four biggest companies jumped almost 60 percent to $11.3 billion, raising concerns among credit agencies about excessive borrowing.[5]

Under this funding model, the high-speed train project "may not be financially feasible," says the senior government official. "We may have to change the business model from a business-to-business to a government-to-government [arrangement]," he says. With one-way tickets expected to cost about $13 and riders having other train and bus options, the official wonders if the government will not have to consider subsidizing the rail's operating costs, which is difficult if it is owned by companies.

Another problem identified by the official is the "challenging landscape" along the rail route, which will add to the costs of the project. "It is mountainous. The rail needs a straight road," the official says.

China is discovering what American, European, and other businesses have learned in recent decades: investing in Southeast Asia's biggest economy can be daunting and is not for the faint of heart. "Indonesian bureaucrats are often equally skeptical of foreign investors regardless of which country they come from," says Douglas Ramage, who heads up the BowerGroupAsia business consulting firm in Indonesia.

In the run-up to the April 2019 elections, Jokowi's presidential challenger, former army general Prabowo Subianto, who was named defense minister in Jokowi's second term, charged that forcing state-owned enterprises (SOEs) to seek financing for infrastructure projects had caused them to take on increasing debt. He said Indonesia "has put our main SOEs in financial risks."[6]

Prabowo's vice presidential candidate Sandiago Uno said if the opposition team won it would "review and check" the train project's progress.

---

5. Wataru Suzuki, "Debt at Indonesian State Contractors Soars in Infrastructure Push," *Nikkei Asian Review*, March 16, 2018, https://asia.nikkei.com/Business/Business-trends/Debt-at-Indonesian-state-contractors-soars-in-infrastructure-push.

6. Shotaro Tani, "Widodo Slammed for Infrastructure Policy in Second TV Debate," *Nikkei Asian Review*, February 18, 2018, https://asia.nikkei.com/Politics/Widodo-slammed-for-infrastructure-policy-in-second-TV-debate.

Sandiago, a billionaire businessman, said the construction process benefited only Chinese interests, not ordinary Indonesians.[7]

A former Indonesian cabinet official who served in an earlier administration raises concerns about Jakarta's growing dependence on China and Indonesian SOEs to build infrastructure. "To sign a [memorandum of understanding] with China is easy, you can do it in one day, but it is hard to implement," says the former senior official, a trained economist. "The use of Chinese workers is one issue. On equipment, if you don't do due diligence, they will send you second- or third-grade quality. It's better to pay for more expensive equipment [from other sources] and get good quality."

"Finding financing is not an issue," the former official says. "There's plenty of liquidity" on the international capital market. The multilateral banks and Japanese agencies are "looking for projects. A lot of projects are not commercially viable," he says, suggesting that the fact that only Beijing is interested in financing a project might say something about its bankability. "You can only fund very few good projects. The rest are not viable."

Japan was livid at losing the rail contract to China, but Jokowi promised Japanese companies alternative projects, including the extension of the Jakarta mass rapid transit system and the development of the new Jakarta port. The president also offered Japan visa-free travel for its tourists. "Indonesia has honed balancing major powers to a fine art," says Ramage.

China-Indonesia economic relations got a huge boost since Jokowi took office. China has become Indonesia's largest trading partner in recent years, and like most of its Southeast Asian neighbors, Indonesia has a perennial trade deficit with China. Indonesia's exports to China in 2018 reached $34.1 billion while its imports from China topped $43.4 billion, leaving it with a sizable deficit. Both figures were up significantly from the previous year when Indonesia's exports to China were $28.5 billion and its imports reached $34.9 billion.[8]

Many in Indonesia have been worried about the disruption of the domestic economy caused by the flood of cheap, sometimes illegal Chinese

7. Ibid.

8. International Monetary Fund, "Exports, FOB to Partner Countries; Imports, CIF from Partner Countries," *IMF Data*, 2014–2018, http://data.imf.org/regular.aspx?key=61013712.

products. The business community and civil society organizations called on Indonesia to withdraw from the Association of Southeast Asian Nations (ASEAN) free-trade agreement with China before it took effect in 2010, fearing that it would cause a hollowing out of domestic manufacturing and create large numbers of job losses.[9]

Indonesia's export figures to both China and the United States were expected to take a hit from the U.S.-China trade war. But Indonesia can expect at least some new investment as a result of the tensions. Pegatron, a key iPhone assembler, picked Indonesia for its first move to diversify from China. The company announced in late 2018 that it would move non-iPhone products affected by U.S. tariffs on exports from China to a factory on Batam Island in western Indonesia.[10]

In 2017, China became Indonesia's second largest investor with $5.5 billion in foreign direct investment, trailing Singapore's $8.4 billion but overtaking Japan, which invested $5 billion, according to figures released by Indonesia's Investment Coordinating Board. China's investment slowed during the first half of 2018, reaching only $120 million, less than one-quarter of the $507 million in the first half of the previous year.

Some analysts attributed this drop to Beijing imposing new rules on foreign investment to prevent capital flight from China. Others thought Chinese companies could be channeling more of their investment through subsidiaries in Singapore and Hong Kong. In addition, considerable Chinese investment arrives in the form of loans, so it does not show up in investment figures.[11]

How much of China's investment under its BRI shows up in Indonesia's investment figures is not clear. According to estimates by RWR Advisory Group, a Washington-based consultancy, China announced infrastructure deals in Indonesia totaling $84.4 billion in the six years through 2018. This is nearly 40 percent of all the deals China has announced for Southeast Asian countries and would make Indonesia the largest BRI recipient in the region.

9. Dewi Fortuna Anwar, "Indonesia-China Relations," 4.

10. Lauly Ly, "Pegatron Shifts from China to Indonesia as Trade War Bites," *Nikkei Asian Review*, December 5, 2018, https://asia.nikkei.com/Economy/Trade-war/Pegatron-shifts-from-China-to-Indonesia-as-trade-war-bites.

11. Pierre van der Eng, "Chinese Investors in Indonesia Seem to Be Tightening Their Belts," *East Asia Forum*, September 28, 2018, http://www.eastasiaforum.org/2018/09/28/chinese-investors-in-indonesia-seem-to-be-tightening-their-belts/?utm_source=newsletter&utm_medium=email&utm_campaign=newsletter2018-09-30.

Andrew Davenport, RWR's chief operating officer, recognizes that tabulating investment from China is "an imperfect science." He says his company counts "as real" any deal "announced as signed, barring any information we find that refutes this assumption." The firm does not include signings of memorandums of understanding.

"Chinese investment is real and flowing heavily," says Ramage of BowerGroupAsia. "It has been important in recent years in keeping economic growth above 5 percent." Jokowi "doesn't want to make too much of Chinese investment" to avoid ramping up domestic concern, Ramage says. "As an investor, China is like a secret friend you don't want to tell anyone about."

Jokowi has made infrastructure development one of country's top priorities since he took office. Indonesia's woefully underdeveloped infrastructure hobbles its efforts at integrating into the global supply chain and adds significant costs to its economy. The World Bank has estimated that Indonesia has an infrastructure gap of $1.5 trillion that it needs to reduce transport costs and generate economies of scale. The quantity of its roads and ports is among the lowest in Southeast Asia and the quality lags Indonesia's emerging market peers, the World Bank said.[12]

The government's aim was to spend $327 billion during Jokowi's first term (2014–2019), of which $15 billion was slated to come from the state budget and nearly $46 billion from SOEs.[13] The large remaining gap needed to come from the private sector and foreign investors, including China's BRI.

The Jakarta-Bandung high-speed rail is one of the first projects in Indonesia under the BRI. Jakarta has also proposed a 62-mile east-west line of mass rapid transit that would link Jakarta to two neighboring provinces as well as a 945-mile railway that would connect the north and south of the island of Sulawesi, northeast of Java.

Much of China's investment comes to Indonesia through joint ventures with Indonesian companies, particularly state-owned projects,

---

12. The World Bank, *Indonesia Economic Quarterly: Closing the Gap* (Washington, DC: The World Bank, 2017), 35–37, http://pubdocs.worldbank.org/en/677741506935868706/IEQ-Oct-2017-ENG.pdf.

13. Karlis Sana, "Indonesia Needs $157 Billion for Infrastructure Plan," *Bloomberg*, January 25, 2018, https://www.bloomberg.com/news/articles/2018-01-25/indonesia-seeks-to-plug-157-billion-gap-in-nation-building-plan.

but some funding comes in the form of loans, especially for infrastructure projects.

The massive role of firms from China in these projects has prompted wild rumors whirling around Indonesia about a "flood" of Chinese workers coming to work on investment projects, says economist Yose Rizal Damuri of the Center for Strategic and International Studies (CSIS) in Jakarta. In 2015 and 2016, "fake news" stories reported that millions of Chinese workers were inundating the country and "increased negative sentiment against Chinese projects," Yose Rizal says.

Not long before the 2017 Jakarta governor elections, *The Jakarta Post* ran several stories about a Chinese-Indonesian joint venture investing in an industrial park in Central Sulawesi using large numbers of workers from China. The articles ran under headlines such as "Morowali: a tale of China's grip on the rich region" and "Anti-Chinese spectre raises head in C. Sulawesi regency."[14]

Indonesia in 2018 offered China a menu of $60 billion worth of potential BRI projects, but the government has targeted Chinese investment mainly away from the sprawling capital of Jakarta and densely populated Java, the economic and geographic center of Indonesia and home to half the country's people. The government has selected three provinces to be the focal points for Chinese investors. All three have significant economic potential that has not yet been exploited and all are located "far from the South China Sea," says a senior government official.

One area is North Kalimantan located on the large island of Borneo north of Java. It is blessed with vast amounts of natural resources and hydropower potential.

In 2018, Power Construction Corporation of China (China Power) signed a memorandum of understanding with Indonesia's PT Kayan Hydro Energy to build a cascade of five hydropower dams on the Kayan River in the north of the province over a 20-year period. The cascade, estimated to cost $17.8 billion and to be funded under the BRI, is expected to produce 9,000 megawatts of electricity.[15]

The first dam will supply electricity to the Tanah Kuning Industrial Park, which will be built by China's Gezhouba Group International En-

---

14. Dewi Fortuna Anwar, "Indonesia-China Relations," 5.

15. "Agreement Signed to Construct Kayan River Cascade, Indonesia," *Hydropower & Dams*, May 22, 2018, https://www.hydropower-dams.com/news/agreement-signed-to-construct-kayan-river-cascade-indonesia/.

gineering Company in partnership with Indonesia's PT Adhidaya Suprakencana at a cost of $10 billion. Chinese and Indonesian companies have signed agreements under the BRI for a smaller hydropower plant, an industrial park, an international airport, and a dimethyl ether processing plant to turn coal into gas in North Kalimantan.[16]

A second region targeted for Chinese investment is North Sumatra located across the Strait of Malacca from Malaysia. It also is rich in natural resources, including palm oil and rubber. The government recently established the Sei Mangkei Special Economic Zone to target palm oil and rubber-based industries and is looking for Chinese investment in industrial estates, a port, and light industries.

A $1.6 billion dam project situated in the Batan Toru rainforest has sparked concern about the impact on the Tapanuli orangutan. The dam, a joint venture between PT North Sumatra Hydro Energy and Sinohydro, the state-owned enterprise that built the Three Gorges Dam in China, will cut through the heart of the orangutan habitat, which is also home to gibbons and Sumatran tigers. Indonesia environmental groups have launched a legal bid to stop construction of the dam charging that the environment assessment of the project's impact was fraudulent.[17]

A third area is North Sulawesi on Sulawesi Island. The government is convinced that this area has tremendous potential as a tourist hub because Manado, the provincial capital, is only five hours by air from Beijing, Tokyo, and Seoul. But the region is desperately short of infrastructure. Much of its economy is centered around agriculture, livestock, and forestry. The government is courting Chinese investors for such projects as an international airport, tourist resorts, and an industrial estate.

One sector in which Chinese investment has picked up is in mining and mineral processing in Sulawesi, particularly after Jakarta banned the export of unprocessed minerals in 2014 to gain more value from its

---

16. "Five Chinese Companies to Invest in North Kalimantan Province," *AntaraNews.com*, April 18, 2018, https://en.antaranews.com/news/115410/five-chinese-companies-to-invest-in-north-kalimantan-province.

17. Augustinus Beo Da Costa, "Indonesia NGO Appeals Ruling on China-Funded Dam in Endangered Orangutan Habitat," *Reuters*, March 13, 2019, https://www.reuters.com/article/us-indonesia-orangutan/indonesia-ngo-appeals-ruling-on-china-funded-dam-in-endangered-orangutan-habitat-idUSKBN1QU16S.

mineral assets. In 2015, Chinese steelmaker Tsingshan began constructing the $4 billion, almost 5,000-acre Indonesia Morowali Industrial Park in the town of Morowali in Central Sulawesi to process raw nickel.

By 2019, the park was turning out 3 million stainless steel slabs a year, about 6 percent of global output of stainless steel. The park employs nearly 26,000 workers, and almost 19,000 of them are Indonesians. The rest are Chinese nationals. The park has increased the province's exports to $5 billion a year from less than $300 million five years earlier.[18]

Although the mining and smelting activity will boost Indonesia's economy, environmentalists are worried about the impact on water and air. Earlier strip-mining had already caused silt runoff that turned the sea around southeastern Sulawesi red. The Chinese cranes and monster trucks used in the construction of roads are kicking up choking quantities of red dust and the new smelters are expected to add sulfur dioxide and ash to the air.[19]

Chinese investment has more than a few detractors. "I'm critical of Chinese investment, it's not purely clean business," says Fahri Hamzah, who was deputy speaker of the Indonesian House of People's Representatives when we talked before the 2019 elections. "Chinese investment in infrastructure is . . . not of high quality, abuses human rights, and makes pollution."

Disputes break out from time to time between Chinese and Indonesian workers. In early 2018, two videos went viral showing fights between local and Chinese workers at the Morowali Industrial Park. One video depicted Chinese nationals blocking Muslim workers from conducting Friday Muslim prayers. Indonesian workers also complained that their

18. Wahyudi Soeriaatmadja, "Central Sulawesi Sees Gains from Tie-Up with China Firm," *Straits Times*, February 25, 2019, https://www.straitstimes.com/asia/se-asia/central-sulawesi-sees-gains-from-tie-up-with-china-firm; "Growing Manganese Capacity in Indonesia to Shrink China's Exports There," *SMM Insight*, February 20, 2019, https://news.metal.com/newscontent/100876983/growing-manganese-capacity-in-indonesia-to-shrink-china%E2%80%99s-exports-there/; Tom Daly, "China Battery Firms Set Up $700 Million Nickel Joint Venture in Indonesia," *Reuters*, September 28, 2018, https://www.reuters.com/article/us-china-mining-indonesia/china-battery-firms-set-up-700-million-nickel-joint-venture-in-indonesia-idUSKCN1M80ON.

19. Melati Kaye, "Indonesia's Ore-Smelting Ambitions Augur Rain of Poison in Sulawesi," *Mongabay*, January 19, 2016, https://news.mongabay.com/2016/01/indonesias-ore-smelting-ambitions-augur-rain-of-poison-in-sulawesi/.

counterparts from China earned two to four times more for working 12 hours shifts compared the salaries of locals for working eight hours.[20]

China has invested heavily in coal power plants, totaling $5.8 billion in 2015 and 2016.[21] Earlier, Indonesia had some bad experiences with Chinese investors in coal power plants. In 2006, Chinese companies agreed with Indonesia's state electricity company to provide the financing, construction, and equipment for plants to produce 6,000 megawatts of electricity over the next four years. "Many of them failed to deliver and the program was never completed," says economist Yose Rizal of CSIS Jakarta.

Indonesians also complained that these coal-fired plants use old, dirty coal-burning technology creating large-scale environmental problems. "We're very dissatisfied" with these projects, says a senior official. Adds Ramage, "These power projects badly damaged China's brand."

Indonesia has been a top target for Chinese investment in the digital marketplace. Officials hope Chinese investment in the Digital Silk Road will help the country leapfrog to the next level of development. Investment in the digital economy now accounts for roughly one-fifth of all foreign investment, according to Tom Lembang, chair of the government's investment coordinating board until late 2019.[22]

After long fighting for market share and consumers in China, Chinese tech firms are now engaged in all-out battle in Southeast Asia. Companies like Alibaba, Tencent, and JD are investing billions of dollars—and their brands—in funding and acquiring Indonesian start-ups in the tech sector.

These firms are attracted by Indonesia's population of over 260 million—including 150 million Internet users—and the increasing purchasing power of the country's growing tech-savvy middle class.[23]

20. Ardi Wirdana, "Anti-Chinese Sentiment among Factory Workers Escalates in Central Sulawesi," *Indonesia Expat*, January 31, 2018, https://indonesiaexpat.biz/news/anti-chinese-sentiment-among-factory-workers-escalates-central-sulawesi/.

21. Edward Ng, "The Rise of Chinese FDI into ASEAN," *Nikko Asset Management*, October 5, 2017, https://www.nikkoam.com.sg/articles/2017/10/the-rise-of-chinese-fdi-into-asean?nk-route.

22. Kenjji Kawase, "Indonesia Wants 20 More Unicorns Like Go-Jek and Tokopedia by 2025," *Nikkei Asian Review*, January 24, 2019, https://asia.nikkei.com/Editor-s-Picks/Interview/Indonesia-wants-20-more-unicorns-like-Go-Jek-and-Tokopedia-by-2025.

23. Nadine Freischlad, "China's Growing Appetite for Indonesia Shouldn't Discourage Local Founders, Says VCs," *Tech in Asia*, November 1, 2017, https://www.techinasia.com/china-hearts-indonesia.

Indonesia's Internet economy, the biggest and fastest-growing in Southeast Asia, hit $27 billion in 2018 and is set to top $100 billion by 2025, according to a 2018 report on Southeast Asia's e-Conomy by Google and Temasek of Singapore.

E-commerce sales in Indonesia in 2018 totaled $12 billion, accounting for fully half of money spent in online purchases in Southeast Asia. The country's online media market, including online advertising, gaming, and subscription music and video on demand, reached $11 billion, while its online travel market hit $8.6 billion. Online transport and food delivery were worth $3.7 billion.

In the three years beginning in 2015, Indonesian Internet companies raised $3 billion (albeit not all from Chinese firms), compared to Singapore's $16 billion and only $2 billion in the rest of Southeast Asia.[24]

Investors from China and other countries have helped nurture four dynamic Indonesian unicorns valued at over $1 billion: Go-Jek, Tokopedia, Traveloka, and Bukalapak. Alibaba is focused on e-commerce, while Tencent seems more fixed on online games, ride-sharing, and online shopping. Mobile payments could be their next frontier.

Alibaba bet on Tokopedia, leading a $1.1 billion funding round for Indonesia's largest e-commerce firm. Tencent invested in Go-Jek, Indonesia's motorbike-on-demand service that has expanded into a car-hailing service and led a funding round that raised $1.2 billion in 2017. Go-Jek not only carries people but has expanded to include parcel delivery and ferrying masseurs to waiting clients. It has also aggressively promoting its mobile wallet, Go-Pay, which allows users to store money and make transactions digitally. Go-Pay entered this e-money space early and aggressively and, in an increasingly competitive environment, appears to be far ahead of its competitors.[25]

Traveloka, an Indonesia-based travel marketplace, was valued at $2 billion in 2017 after it raised $500 million from a group that included

---

24. Google Temasek, "e-Conomy SEA 2018: Southeast Asia's Internet Economy Hits an Inflection Point," Google Temasek, 2018, https://www.thinkwithgoogle.com/_qs/documents/6870/Report_e-Conomy_SEA_2018_by_Google_Temasek_121418_cpsLjlQ.pdf, 5, 8, 11, 13, 16, 21.

25. Clay Chandler and Eamon Barrett, "Alibaba v. Tencent: Taking the Fight to Southeast Asia," *Fortune*, June 21, 2018, https://fortune.com/2018/06/21/alibaba-tencent-southeast-asia/; "Indonesia's E-Wallet Race Is Heating Up. Here Are the Main Players," *Finch Capital*, April 25, 2019, https://news.finchcapital.com/post/102fhye/indonesias-e-wallet-race-is-heating-up-here-are-the-main-players.

China's JD.com, China's largest retailer.[26] JD.com is partly owned by Tencent and is China's second largest e-commerce company. In 2019, JD .com launched the first government-approved flight of a drone aircraft in Indonesia that delivered backpacks of books to schoolchildren in a remote village.[27]

Bukalapak, or "open stall," is another Indonesian online retailer that claims an impressive 2 million orders a day. Alibaba's Ant Financial along with Indonesian telco Emtek and Singapore sovereign fund GIC were Bukalapak's early backers. The firm today also offers streaming and fintech services.[28]

Chinese fintech firms, which help provide credit to those who do not have access to bank lending, are looking for opportunities in Indonesia. China's Hexindai Inc., which listed on Nasdaq in 2017, acquired a 20 percent stake in Indonesian online lender Musketeer in 2018 with the goal of capitalizing on the market opportunities in Indonesia.

But not all Chinese fintech firms arriving in Indonesia in recent years bother to register with authorities and many employ aggressive debt-collecting tactics, alarming regulators. Some Chinese fintech lenders have begun aggressively calling and threatening the relatives, colleagues, and friends of clients who fall behind in their payments.

Reuters talked to a 24-year-old secretary near Jakarta who said that Chinese debt collectors were repeatedly calling and threatening her boss and her boyfriend. By September 2018, Indonesian regulators had published a list of 407 blacklisted fintech lenders and more than half of them were from China.[29]

Huawei of China, the world's top manufacturer of telecom equipment, signed partnerships with state-controlled PT Telekomunikasi Indonesia and PT XL Axiata in early 2019 to provide network maintenance and

---

26. Elaine Huang, "Traveloka in Funding Talks to Snag $400M Led by GIC at $4B Valuation," *KrASIA*, October 5, 2018, https://kr-asia.com/traveloka-in-funding-talks-to-snag-400m-led-by-gic-valuation-at-4-1b.
27. R. J. Frometa, "JD.com Uses Drones in Indonesia," *Vents Magazine*, February 13, 2019, https://ventsmagazine.com/2019/02/13/jd-com-uses-drones-in-indonesia/.
28. Jon Russell, "Indonesian E-Commerce Unicorn Bukalapak Raises $50M," *TechCrunch*, January 2019, https://techcrunch.com/2019/01/18/bukalapak-raises-50m/.
29. Fanny Potkin, Shu Zhang, and Tabita Diela, "A Call to the Boss: Indonesia Contends with Aggressive Chinese Online Traders," *Reuters*, September 21, 2018, https://www.reuters.com/article/us-china-p2p-indonesia/a-call-to-the-boss-indonesia-contends-with-aggressive-chinese-online-lenders-idUSKCN1M10T7.

equipment. Rudiantara (he uses only one name), who was communications minister until late 2019, told Reuters that Indonesia "can't be paranoid" about many Indonesian telecom companies using Huawei's technology, despite intense scrutiny and warnings by the U.S. government that the telecom giant has close ties to Beijing and could be used for espionage.[30]

Chinese tourists are also playing a growing role in Indonesia's economy as more visit Indonesia attracted by the country's unspoiled beaches and scattered islands. More direct flights from Chinese cities to Bali and Sulawesi are boosting tourism numbers. In 2018, 2.1 million Chinese visited the country, up from 1.97 million the previous year, despite the fact that Indonesia was hit by several earthquakes and tsunamis. Bali is by far their favorite destination, and the surge of Chinese tourists now tops visitors from Australia who were long number one.[31]

Some Indonesian tourist officials complain that 70 percent of the Chinese visitors come on "zero dollar" tours in which most of the profits are returned to tour operators from China.[32] Recent visitors who have gone diving off the coast of Sulawesi say local authorities have banned the use of gloves by divers. The goal: make it harder for Chinese tourists to break off and steal pieces of coral.

Like other Southeast Asian nations, Indonesia in recent years has frequently arrested and deported groups of Chinese nationals allegedly involved in multimillion-dollar fraud rings that target wealthy businesspersons and government officials in China. One group of 153 deported in 2017 had made about $425 million since the end of 2016. Members of the group contacted their victims pretending to be Chinese police

30. "Indonesia Cannot 'Be Paranoid' about Curbing Huawei as Telcos Sign Deals: Minister," *Reuters*, February 27, 2019, https://www.reuters.com/article/us-indonesia-huawei/indonesia-cannot-be-paranoid-about-curbing-huawei-as-telcos-sign-deals-minister-idUSKCN1QG1C7.

31. Tassia Sipahutar, "More Tourists Visited Indonesia Last Year than Ever Before," *Bloomberg*, February 1, 2019, https://www.bloomberg.com/news/articles/2019-02-01/malaysians-chinese-lead-record-influx-of-tourists-to-indonesia; "Indonesia among Chinese tourists' favorite destinations for Chinese New Year," *The Jakarta Post*, January 24, 2019, https://www.thejakartapost.com/travel/2019/01/24/indonesia-among-chinese-tourists-favorite-destinations-for-chinese-new-year.html.

32. Mercedes Hutton, "Chinese Tourists Are Changing Bali, but They Are Not the First Ones to Do So. Who Made Kuta 'the Worst Place' on the Island?," *South China Morning Post*, August 29, 2018, https://www.scmp.com/magazines/post-magazine/travel/article/2161683/chinese-tourists-are-changing-bali-they-are-not-first.

or legal authorities and offered to help resolve their legal woes in return for immediate cash transfers.[33]

CHINA TIES OFTEN ENTANGLED WITH DOMESTIC POLITICS

Rumors spread quickly in Indonesia in early 2019 claiming that seven containers of ballots from China had been found at Indonesia's Tanjung Priok port. All were allegedly cast for incumbent president Jokowi and his running mate. The supposed goal of the Chinese-marked ballots was to help tilt the election to Jokowi. The only problem was that the story was false, but before it could be disproved by officials visiting the port, the rumor had been retweeted 17,000 times.[34]

Even if China did not send fake marked ballots to Indonesia, its hackers (along with some from Russia) allegedly were active in attacking Indonesia's voter database to disrupt the elections, according to the head of Indonesia's election commission. Arief Budiman said attacks originating in China and Russia tried to "manipulate or modify" content and create ghost voters or fake voter identities.

"They try to hack our system," Budiman told Bloomberg. "Not only every day. Almost every hour." He added, "Voter behavior can be changed by de-legitimizing the organizer of the election."[35]

China was a shadow hanging over the campaign in the run-up to the elections. Jokowi's challenger Prabowo called for a review of Indonesia's trade policies with China, arguing that its unfair policies hurt the economy. His vice presidential running mate criticized delays on a Chinese high-speed train project. And social media continued to spread rumors about Chinese workers pouring into the country.

During the previous election campaign in 2014, Jokowi had been charged with false claims that he was of ethnic Chinese descent and a

33. "Indonesia to Deport 153 Chinese for S$610M Scam," *Straits Times*, August 1, 2017, https://www.straitstimes.com/asia/se-asia/indonesia-to-deport-153-chinese-for-s610-million-scam.

34. Nithin Coca, "The New Bogeyman in Indonesia's Coming Elections: China," *Ozy*, March 15, 2019, https://www.ozy.com/fast-forward/the-new-bogeyman-in-indonesias-coming-elections-china/92836.

35. Viriya Singgih, Arys Aditya, and Karlis Salna, "Indonesia Says Election under Attack from Chinese, Russian Hackers," *Bloomberg*, March 13, 2019, https://www.bloomberg.com/news/articles/2019-03-12/indonesia-says-poll-under-attack-from-chinese-russian-hackers.

Christian. In the run-up to the 2019 elections, Jokowi came under criticism for the fact that dependence on China for building infrastructure projects had become a hallmark of his first term in office and that these projects often involved huge numbers of workers from China. "People ask 'why is he dealing so much with China,'" says Shafiah Muhibat, head of the international relations department at CSIS Jakarta.

Although the charges did not seem to dent his popularity much, "there were real concerns that in the increasingly charged political climate, the rise in anti-Chinese sentiments may again be manipulated for political purposes," Dewi Fortuna Anwar, of the Institute for Social Sciences, said shortly before the April 2019 voting. "Great care must . . . be taken to address all the issues that have arisen in Indonesia-China relations, for if left unattended they may jeopardize all the gains that have been made," including the country's sometimes still tenuous interracial accord.[36]

Indonesia has had more politically fraught relations with China than most of its Southeast Asian neighbors have had. Indonesia formally got independence from the Dutch in December 1949 a few months after the Communist Party seized control of China. The two countries established diplomatic ties in April 1950, but Indonesian society remained deeply suspicious of Beijing. Indonesian Islamic groups were wary of China because the new ruling party was opposed to organized religion.[37]

Anti-communism was a key factor driving popular perceptions about China. Another was attitudes toward ethnic Chinese, who made up about 3 percent of the population at the time of independence. Many Indonesians viewed the Chinese Indonesians as having supported the Dutch during colonial rule and the Japanese occupiers during World War II. At the time of independence there was widespread perception that the loyalty of Chinese Indonesians was focused on China.[38]

In 1959, President Sukarno issued a ruling banning Chinese Indonesians from certain rural trades, which prompted a sharp rebuke from Beijing and caused it to send ships to pick up Chinese Indonesians and bring them back to China. Leo Suryadinata, an expert on ethnic Chinese in Southeast Asia at the ISEAS-Yusof Ishak Institute in Singapore, says more

36. Dewi Fortuna Anwar, "Indonesia-China Relations," 6.
37. Ian Storey, *Southeast Asia and the Rise of China: The Search for Security* (New York: Routledge, 2011), 192.
38. Ibid., 192–193.

than 100,000 left Indonesia, but other studies suggest that only about 10,000 chose to return to China.[39]

Relations, however, thawed when Sukarno swung Indonesian politics sharply to the left in the early 1960s. He positioned Indonesia as a defender of the developing world, pulled out of the United Nations, and set up the Jakarta-Phnom Penh-Hanoi-Pyongyang-Beijing axis. As Sukarno moved to the left, he launched a period of military confrontation with the newly established Federation of Malaya and increasingly turned to the Communist Party of Indonesia, which had emerged as one of the largest Communist parties in Asia, for support.[40]

But Sukarno's moves distressed the armed forces, who were not enamored by the conflict with Malaysia. A power tussle emerged between the military and the Communist Party, and on September 30, 1965, a half dozen generals were killed by left-leaning officers. Beijing denied any involvement, but the military, led by Suharto and supported by Islamic organizations, moved to oust the communists from political power and remove Sukarno from the presidency.

Over the next six months, at least a half million alleged communist sympathizers—including some 2,000 ethnic Chinese, relatively few of whom were members of the Indonesia Communist Party—were killed, and Suharto moved to seized power.[41] A batch of U.S. diplomatic cables declassified in 2017 made clear the deep American involvement in the brutal anti-communist purge launched by Suharto in an effort to halt the spread of communism as the war in Vietnam was heating up.[42]

The new government of President Suharto pivoted abruptly toward the West and blamed China for orchestrating the coup attempt and ethnic Chinese of being collaborators and linked to the Indonesian Communist

---

39. Leo Suryadinata, *The Rise of China and the Chinese Overseas: A Study of Beijing's Changing Policy in Southeast Asia and Beyond* (Singapore: ISEAS-Yusof Ishak Institute, 2017), 55; James Jian Hua, *Qiaowu: Extra-Territorial Policies for the Overseas Chinese* (Netherlands: Brill Academic Publishers, 2014), 228; Richard Borsuk and Nancy Chng, *Liem Sioe Liong's Salim Group: The Business Pillar of Suharto's Indonesia* (Singapore: Institute for Southeast Asian Studies, 2014), 50–52.

40. Storey, *Southeast Asia and the Rise of China*, 193.

41. Ibid., 193–194; Suryadinata, *The Rise of China and the Chinese Overseas*, 55.

42. Vincent Bevins, "What the United States Did in Indonesia," *The Atlantic*, October 20, 2017, https://www.theatlantic.com/international/archive/2017/10/the-indonesia-documents-and-the-us-agenda/543534/; Hannah Beech, "U.S. Stood by as Indonesia Killed a Half-Million People, Papers Show," *New York Times*, October 18, 2017, https://www.nytimes.com/2017/10/18/world/asia/indonesia-cables-communist-massacres.html.

Party. As the Cultural Revolution engulfed China, Red Guards attacked the Indonesian Embassy in Beijing, prompting retaliation against the Chinese Embassy in Jakarta and Suharto's government to suspend diplomatic ties with China.[43]

Suharto's government closed Chinese newspapers and banned the teaching of Chinese, the use of Chinese characters, and the celebration of Chinese festivals. Ethnic Chinese were barred from serving in the military or civil service and becoming teachers and journalists, leaving them few options other than engaging in business.[44]

Despite these harsh policies, Suharto relied on some key ethnic Chinese business leaders to help him build his regime. One of these was Liem Sioe Liong, who migrated from China in the late 1930s and built the Salim Group, thanks to his ties to Suharto. In its heyday, the group controlled Indonesia's largest nonstate bank, ran the country's biggest cement company, and became the world's largest producer of instant noodles.[45]

While Indonesia's Southeast Asian neighbors began normalizing ties with Beijing, the Suharto government continued to insist that China apologize for its alleged involvement in the events of 1965. Jakarta sharply criticized China for its attack on northern Vietnam in 1979 after Hanoi ousted the brutal Khmer Rouge regime in Cambodia.[46]

Hoping to take advantage of China's economic growth, Indonesia established direct trade relations with China in 1985. Diplomatic relations were finally restored in 1990, but it took time for the decades of distrust and suspicion to dissipate. China's assertiveness in the South China Sea in the early 1990s prompted Jakarta to ask for clarification about Beijing's claims on the Natuna Islands, which fell partially within China's nine-dash line even though they were mainly within Indonesia's 200-nautical-mile exclusive economic zone.[47]

---

43. Storey, *Southeast Asia and the Rise of China*, 194–195.

44. Johannes Herlijanto, "'Search for Knowledge as Far as China!' Indonesian Response to the Rise of China," in *Chinese Encounters in Southeast Asia: How People, Money, and Ideas from China Are Changing the Region*, ed. Pal Nyiri and Danielle Tan (Seattle: University of Washington Press, 2017), 198–199.

45. Richard Borsuk and Nancy Chng, *Liem Sioe Liong's Salim Group: The Business Pillar of Suharto's Indonesia* (Singapore: Institute for Southeast Asian Studies, 2014).

46. Storey, *Southeast Asia and the Rise of China*, 195–196.

47. Ibid., 196, 198.

The 1997–1998 Asian financial crisis, which ravaged the Indonesian economy leading to protests that prompted the toppling of Suharto,[48] also led to a sharp improvement in Jakarta's relations with Beijing. China provided Indonesia a $200 million line of credit and contributed another $500 million to an International Monetary Fund package to bail out the economy.

Beijing was relatively restrained in its complaints after riots broke out against Chinese Indonesian businesses and dozens of Chinese Indonesian women suffered sexual assaults and some were killed.[49]

"It was sadly fitting [that] the New Order should later collapse amid the rubble of anti-Chinese riots," Jusuf Wanandi, who is ethnic Chinese, served as a foreign affairs adviser to Suharto, and was one of the founders of CSIS Jakarta, wrote in a memoir about the Suharto period. "We were treated as minor wives, enjoyed but not recognized."[50]

Relations between China and Indonesia warmed dramatically in the post-Suharto era as a multiparty democracy emerged and the military's role in politics was reduced. Many of the former discriminatory policies against Chinese Indonesians were gradually abolished. The ban against Chinese newspapers and schools was lifted, celebration of Chinese festivals such as the lunar new year were allowed, and Confucianism was designated as Indonesia's sixth official religion. Chinese Indonesians were allowed to play a role in politics.[51]

Indonesia's foreign policy elite were offended that the United States had pressed Jakarta to accept an austere International Monetary Fund economic restructuring plan in 1998. They were also irritated that Washington had imposed an arms sales ban against the Indonesian military in response to its troops' brutal actions in East Timor as it struggled for independence from Jakarta.[52]

---

48. Seth Mydans, "The Fall of Suharto: The Overview; Suharto, Besieged, Steps Down after 32-Year Rule in Indonesia," *New York Times*, May 21, 1998, https://www.nytimes.com/1998/05/21/world/fall-suharto-overview-suharto-besieged-steps-down-after-32-year-rule-indonesia.html.
49. Ibid.; Storey, *Southeast Asia and the Rise of China*, 200; Borsuk and Chng, *Liem Sioe Liong's Salim Group*, 381–385.
50. Jusuf Wanandi, *Shades of Grey: A Political Memoir of Modern Indonesia, 1965–1998* (Jakarta: Equinox, 2012), 126–127, quoted in Borsuk and Chng, *Liem Sioe Liong's Salim Group*, 513.
51. Storey, *Southeast Asia and the Rise of China*, 200–201.
52. Ibid., 202.

Frustrations with Washington played a role in drawing Indonesia closer to China and, under the country's fifth president, Megawati Soekarnoputri, Sukarno's daughter, Beijing provided a $400 million concessional loan for the construction of a critical bridge. Bilateral trade also took off under Megawati and Indonesia began exporting liquified natural gas to China and PetroChina began operating an oil field in Indonesia.[53]

After Susilo Bambang Yudhoyono, a retired general, was elected in 2004, he sought to build a more comprehensive relationship that included a focus on political and security ties in addition to trade and investment. In 2005, President Hu Jintao became the first Chinese leader to visit Indonesia in a trip that produced a joint declaration on building a "strategic partnership" that provided a roadmap for deepening political, economic, security, and cultural ties. Hu also committed funds for the reconstruction of the western province of Aceh, which had been devastated by a tsunami the previous year.[54]

Although diplomatic relations improved between the two countries, Beijing's mounting assertiveness in the South China Sea beginning in 2009 raised concerns about whether China's rise would be peaceful and whether Beijing would undermine the unity of ASEAN by splitting off countries to block consensus within the grouping.[55] In 2010 Indonesia submitted a letter to the United Nations questioning the legal justification for the nine-dash-line map that Beijing submitted to the United Nations Commission on the Limits of the Continental Shelf.[56]

Even though Jakarta's suspicions of China eased, Indonesia remained "uncertain and anxious regarding China's long-term role and intentions in the region," according Rizal Sukma, who then headed CSIS Jakarta. Rizal was alluding to the perception in Indonesia that China had longer-term aspirations to play a leading role in the Asia Pacific, which explains why Jakarta was willing to see the United States play an active political, economic, and military role to balance China's influence in the region.[57]

---

53. Ibid., 203–204; Herlijanto, "'Search for Knowledge as Far as China!,'" 203.
54. "China to Mark Emergence as Leader of Third World," *New York Times*, April 9, 2005, https://www.nytimes.com/2005/04/09/world/asia/china-to-mark-emergence-as-leader-of-third-world.html.
55. Dewi Fortuna Anwar, "Indonesia-China Relations," 4.
56. Storey, *Southeast Asia and the Rise of China*, 206.
57. Rizal Sukma quoted in Storey, *Southeast Asia and the Rise of China*, 207.

Jokowi visited China four times during his first five-year term. That's one less visit than he had to Singapore and tied with the number to Malaysia, both of which he visited repeatedly when they chaired the ASEAN grouping. He only visited Washington once, but is estimated to have met Chinese president Xi at least six or seven times.

A "marked change" has taken place in public attitudes toward China since Jokowi took office in 2014 and turned increasingly to China to fund his ambitious infrastructure projects, wrote Dewi. Jokowi "has been criticized for not sufficiently protecting Indonesia's wider national interests in his drive to attract foreign investment from China."

Dewi added that "the rise in identity politics . . . has again conflated Indonesia-China relations with domestic political competitions for power." She wrote that Jokowi has "become the target of massive social media campaigns accusing him of being a handmaid of both China's and the local Chinese community's interests."[58]

Even though the allegations against Jokowi have not had significant traction, Dewi said there is a danger that "the rise in anti-Chinese sentiments may again be manipulated for political purposes."[59]

SUSPICIONS ABOUT ETHNIC CHINESE LINGER

About 3 million people, less than 2 percent of Indonesia's population, are of ethnic Chinese descent,[60] but they play an outsized role in the country's economy through their control of many large conglomerates. Despite their relatively small numbers, political candidates pay considerable attention to ethnic Chinese. Candidates look for financial support, while wealthy ethnic Chinese hope to reap economic opportunities down the road.

---

58. Dewi Fortuna Anwar, "Indonesia Election: Widodo Has Courted Chinese Cash. He's About to Find Out the Cost," *South China Morning Post*, March 29, 2019, https://www.scmp.com/week-asia/opinion/article/3003794/indonesia-election-widodo-has-courted-chinese-cash-hes-about-find.

59. Ibid.

60. According to estimates in Taiwan, the actual number of ethnic Chinese in Indonesia is over 8.4 million—which, if accurate, would make them one of the largest populations of ethnic Chinese in the world. These estimates suggest that 1.6 million live in Jakarta and half a million live in both northern Sumatra and western Kalimantan. Cited in Bien Chiang and Jean Chih-yin Cheng, "Ethnic Chinese Enterprises in Indonesia: A Case Study of West Kalimantan," in *Chinese Capitalism in Southeast Asia: Culture and Practices*, ed. Yos Santasombat (Palgrave Macmillan, 2017), 132.

Ahead of the 2019 elections, some ethnic Chinese businesspeople supported incumbent Jokowi's opponent Prabowo because they felt that the incumbent's anti-corruption campaign and heavy taxes had dented the business environment. A group of Chinese business representatives in late 2018 organized a gala dinner in Prabowo's honor at a hotel in Jakarta's Chinese business district. Prabowo told the group that, if elected, he would "defend" "any ethnic group or religion" that was "being ill-treated and receives no justice." He said he appreciated China and Chinese culture.[61]

At the end of the dinner, 15 donors contributed a modest $30,000 to Prabowo's election campaign. One Chinese billionaire, Hary Tanoesoebibjo, publicly supported Prabowo in both the 2014 and 2019 elections. Most other Chinese tycoons avoided expressing support for either candidate because they believed "this would not serve their interest," said Suryadinata of ISEAS in Singapore who was born in Indonesia.[62]

Overall, relatively few Chinese Indonesians supported Prabowo. Many older ethnic Chinese opposed Prabowo because of his purported role in the anti-Chinese violence that erupted after Suharto was toppled in 1998. Prabowo, who was head of the special forces (Kopassus) at the time, has denied the charges.[63] By some estimates, up to 1,000 ethnic Chinese died.[64]

"In general, while Chinese Indonesian businessmen contribute to both sides, they also tend to be reluctant to take any side openly, for fear that a wrong decision would adversely affect their business in the future," Suryadinata said.[65]

In 2017, Prabowo actively backed a Muslim candidate in the Jakarta governor election in opposition to the Chinese Christian incumbent Basuki Tjahaja Purnama, or Ahok, although the former general had supported Ahok's bid as deputy governor five years earlier when he ran with

61. Leo Suryadinata, "Which Presidential Candidate Will Chinese Indonesians Vote for in 2019?—Analysis," *Eurasia Review*, February 13, 2019, https://www.eurasiareview.com/13022019-which-presid ential-candidate-will-chinese-indonesians-vote-for-in-2019-analysis/.
62. Ibid.
63. Ibid.
64. Jeffrey Hutton, "Indonesian Chinese Still Face Discrimination 20 Years after Reformasi," *South China Morning Post*, May 19, 2019, https://www.scmp.com/week-asia/politics/article/2146841/indonesian-chinese-still-face-discrimination-20-years-after.
65. Suryadinata, "Which Presidential Candidate."

Jokowi. Prabowo openly supported Islamic conservatives who mounted two massive protests in late 2016 in which they highlighted divisive issues of race, ethnicity, and religion by charging Ahok with alleged blasphemy for comments he made in response to Muslims who argued that the Qur`an barred Muslims from voting for a non-Muslim.

Many ethnic Chinese were anxious about the faith-based politics that surfaced during the prosecution of Ahok and expressed concern that this might lead to a new wave of discrimination against Chinese Indonesians. But others blamed Ahok for some of what happened, saying he was "arrogant" and "divisive" in some of his public comments. "Ethnic Chinese families are split over Ahok," says a Chinese Indonesian businessman who asked not to be identified.

Two decades after Suharto was toppled, most of the official discrimination he instituted such as the bans on Chinese culture or celebrating the lunar new year have long been lifted. But distrust about the apparent affluence and clout of the ethnic Chinese seems to continue to percolate within the society. The imprisonment of Ahok on blasphemy charges worried some ethnic Chinese, reopening old scars and resurrecting fears that communal frictions could resurface.

Shortly after Ahok was convicted in 2017, an Islamic campaign was mounted calling for the tearing down of the 100-foot statute of third-century Chinese general Guan Yu, who is worshipped as a Chinese deity in East Java Province. A solution was found by covering the statue with a huge white tarp. On social media, Muslim opponents of the statue, which had been installed only a month earlier, called it an "uncivilized" insult to Islam.[66]

Suspicions against ethnic Chinese continue within Indonesian society. Part of the issue is linked to their wealth. On the Forbes list of Indonesia's richest businesspersons in 2018, eight of the top 10 are ethnic Chinese.[67] "I have heard people openly express their resentment towards the fact that many ethnic Chinese appear to be richer than them," says Shafiah of CSIS Jakarta.

---

66. Russell Goldman, "In Indonesia, Chinese Deity Is Covered in Sheet after Muslims Protest," *New York Times*, August 10, 2017, https://www.nytimes.com/2017/08/10/world/asia/indonesia-chinese-statue-islam-muslims-protest-guan-yu.html?emc=eta1.

67. "Indonesia's 50 Richest: Forbes 2018 Ranking," *Forbes*, https://www.forbes.com/indonesia-billionaires/list/#tab:overall (accessed October 30, 2019).

Yet ethnic Chinese also play critical political and social roles. During Jokowi's first term, Tom Lembong, a dapper Harvard-educated ethnic Chinese man, served first as trade minister and then as chair of the Investment Coordinating Board responsible for courting foreign investors. Jokowi turned to Chinese Indonesian tycoon Mochtar Riady when he needed help convincing wealthy Indonesians to bring their money home and pay their taxes after his government launched its $300 billion tax amnesty program.[68]

When Jakarta was having difficulty completing the sports facilities needed to host the Asian Games in 2018, the president recruited Erick Thohir, the brother of ethnic Chinese billionaire business leader Garibaldi Thohir. Erick Thohir served as campaign team chair during Jokowi's reelection campaign and was named minister of state-owned enterprises in the president's second term in the beginning of 2019.

His father, Teddy Thohir, co-owner of the Astra International automobile group with another ethnic Chinese tycoon, converted to Islam and raised his sons as Muslims. Eric Thohir is "ethnically Chinese, but what matters more is religious identity," says Ramage. "He is rarely referred to as 'Chinese Indonesian.'"

Chinese traders began making the journey to a port on Java's northern coast as early as the fourteenth century and by 1351 had established a Chinese trading settlement. These early traders brought clothing and textiles that they exchanged for rice to bring back to China. Many of these earlier traders settled in Java permanently, trading, acquiring land to farm, and introducing bright colors and Chinese motifs like dragons into Indonesian batik cloth. In 1413, one of the captains under Chinese Admiral Zheng He traveled to Indonesia to spread Islam among the Confucian-practicing Chinese population.[69]

Ethnic Chinese have been the targets of violence quite frequently since they first started arriving in Indonesia. The most recent case erupted during the protests that toppled Suharto. The violence claimed 1,200 lives, dozens of Chinese women were raped, and large numbers of malls and

---

68. Hutton, "Indonesian Chinese Still Face Discrimination."

69. Randy Mulyanto, "Chinese Indonesians Work to Preserve 700 Years of History in Lasem, a 'Little China' in Central Java," *South China Morning Post*, May 28, 2018, https://www.scmp.com/lifestyle/travel-leisure/article/2147773/chinese-indonesians-work-preserve-700-years-history-lasem.

shop houses were destroyed.[70] Suryadinata said the riots were "unique" because they were aimed at ethnic Chinese, not against China, which had been the case in previous violent outbreaks. Many ethnic Chinese fled the country taking their capital with them.[71]

China's response to the violence was "noticeably restrained," Suryadinata said, adding that its response must be understood within the framework of Beijing's broader foreign policy goals. China had "no desire to jeopardize" its relations with Jakarta, which had only been restored eight years earlier. Beijing was also seeking to gain "acceptance" within Southeast Asia more broadly, according to Suryadinata.[72]

During the protests against Ahok in 2016, one of the leaders of the movement declared that the wealth of the country's ethnic Chinese posed a problem and recommended that an affirmative action program be introduced for native Indonesians, like that practiced in Malaysia. Bachtiar Nasir, who chaired the National Movement to Safeguard the Fatwas of the Indonesian Ulemas Council that led the protests, said Ahok was convicted to "ensure that [the state] does not sell Indonesia to foreigners, especially China."[73]

When the new governor of Jakarta, Anies Baswedan, was sworn in to succeed Ahok the following year, he called on the "pribumi" Indonesian majority to become "masters of their own house."[74] Anies is touted as a possible presidential candidate in 2024 when Jokowi's term ends.

Despite their relatively small numbers, ethnic Chinese in Indonesia are not a homogenous group and have different cultures, politics, and economic backgrounds. The first Chinese arrived in the far western island of Sumatra in 942 and brought agricultural tools, introduced tea cultivation, and perfected the techniques for growing pepper.[75] Later, the Chinese arrived in two new waves: The first came in the early 1800s, picked up the Dutch language, and often stopped speaking Chinese. The second wave came in the early 1900s before Indonesia gained its independence.

70. Hua, *Qiaowu*, 232.
71. Suryadinata, *The Rise of China and the Chinese Overseas*, 56.
72. Ibid., 60–61.
73. Tom Allard and Augustinus Beo Da Costa, "Exclusive—Indonesian Islamist Leader Says Ethnic Chinese Wealth Is Next Target," *Reuters*, May 12, 2017, https://www.reuters.com/article/uk-indonesia-politics-cleric-exclusive/exclusive-indonesian-islamist-leader-says-ethnic-chinese-wealth-is-next-target-idUSKBN18817N.
74. Hutton, "Indonesian Chinese Still Face Discrimination."
75. Borsuk and Chng, *Liem Sioe Liong's Salim Group*, 49.

Indonesian writer Pramoedya Ananta Toer, writing in 1960, blamed much of the anti-Chinese sentiment that developed among indigenous Indonesians on the Dutch colonial authorities. In a book of letters to a Chinese friend, Pramoedya said the Dutch introduced a raft of regulations to limit the immigration of Chinese. "Since then, the Chinese have been treated like a rubbish bin into which every kind of filth has been thrown: insults, humiliations, degradation, agitation, torture, murder," he said. "They were just peaceful people not after anything else but a bowl of rice."[76]

"Many [recent] Chinese investors are very aggressive in coming to Indonesia," says a Chinese Indonesian business executive in Jakarta who asked not to be identified. "They tried to work with Chinese Indonesians, maybe because they have money and [business] know-how, even though many of them can't speak Chinese," he said. But in the end, because Jokowi is pushing Chinese investors to partner with Indonesian state-owned firms, the Chinese have only consummated a few deals with Chinese Indonesian companies, the businessman says.

Some Chinese Indonesian conglomerates are also investing in China. In 2018, the Lippo Group invested $44.4 million in Chinese Internet giant Tencent Holdings Ltd.[77] Lippo's health care arm has a joint venture agreement with China Changjiang National Shipping Group Co. to establish a hospital in Shanghai in addition to the 10 clinics that Lippo is already operating in China.[78]

FISHING SPAT IN THE NATUNAS

Alarmed at China's increasingly assertive actions in the southern fringes of the South China Sea, Indonesia's maritime police in March 2016 boarded a Chinese trawler fishing illegally in Indonesian waters, ordered eight crew onto the police boat, and began towing the fishing vessel to port. Twelve hours later, a Chinese coast guard vessel arrived, rammed

76. Pramoedya Ananta Toer, *The Chinese in Indonesia* (Singapore: Select Books, 2008), 89, quoted in Borsuk and Chng, *Liem Sioe Liong's Salim Group*, 49.
77. "Indonesia's Lippo Group Says Invests $44 Million in China's Tencent," *Reuters*, June 25, 2018, https://www.reuters.com/article/us-lippo-group-tencent-holdings/indonesias-lippo-group-says-invests-44-million-in-chinas-tencent-idUSKBN1JM08Z.
78. Desk Editor Insider, "Indonesia Lippo, China Merchants to Operates First Hospital in Shanghai," *The Insider Stories*, July 3, 2018, https://theinsiderstories.com/indonesia-lippo-china-merchants-to-operates-first-hospital-in-shanghai/.

the fishing boat, and pried it free from the Indonesian police north of the Natuna Islands, nearly 1,100 miles from China's Hainan Island.[79]

Indonesia's blunt-speaking maritime and fisheries minister at the time said the Chinese coast guard action was "arrogant." Foreign Minister Retno Marsudi called in a senior Chinese Embassy representative in Jakarta and handed him an official letter of protest. Ryamizard Ryacudu, who was defense minister at the time, pledged a few weeks later that he would deploy U.S.-made F-16 fighter jets to the islands to fend off "thieves" from the resource-rich islands, which are well inside Indonesia's exclusive economic zone but partly overlap with China's claimed nine-dash line.[80]

A Chinese Foreign Ministry spokesperson called the area where the vessel was detained "traditional Chinese fishing grounds" and rejected claims that its coast guard ship had crossed into Indonesian territorial waters.

A similar incident erupted in December 2019. Again, Chinese coast guard vessels accompanied several dozen Chinese fishing boats into the waters around Natuna. Jakarta sent half a dozen warships and F-16 jet fighters to drive the Chinese out of the area. When the Indonesian vessels tried to detain the Chinese fishing boats, Chinese coast guard ships blocked them. About two weeks into the standoff, Jokowi visited the islands to meet with local fishers. A day or two later, the Chinese vessels started heading north.[81]

"(T)he recurrence of maritime incidents is eroding the strategic capital that China has accumulated in Indonesia," Evan Laksmana, a senior researcher at CSIS Jakarta, said. "No amount of economic benefits or prosperity could beat 'sovereignty and autonomy' in domestic political contests."[82]

---

79. Joe Cochrane, "China's Coast Guard Rams Fishing Boat to Free It from Indonesian Authorities," *New York Times*, March 21, 2016, https://www.nytimes.com/2016/03/22/world/asia/indonesia-south-china-sea-fishing-boat.html.

80. Chris Brummitt and Rieka Rahadiana, "Indonesia Will Defend South China Sea Territory with F-16 Fighter Jets," *Bloomberg*, March 31, 2016, https://www.bloomberg.com/news/articles/2016-03-31/indonesia-to-deploy-f-16s-to-guard-its-south-china-sea-territory.

81. Niharika Mandhana, "In South China Sea Confrontation, Indonesia Resists China, Cautiously," *Wall Street Journal*, January 17, 2020, https://www.wsj.com/articles/in-south-china-sea-confrontation-indonesia-resists-chinacautiously-11579257004.

82. Evan A. Laksmana, "Beijing's Dubious Claims Undermine Indonesia's Role as South China Sea's Honest Broker," *South China Morning Post*, January 20, 2020, https://www.scmp.com/week-asia/politics/article/3046611/beijings-dubious-claims-undermine-indonesias-role-south-china.

Similar confrontations between Jakarta and Beijing over Chinese fishing boats had happened repeatedly over the years, but before the 2016 incident Indonesia had largely sought to tackle the issue quietly through diplomatic channels without alerting the media. An analogous incident took place in 2013 when an Indonesian Maritime Ministry vessel caught a Chinese fishing boat in roughly the same place. But when the Indonesian vessel was confronted by an armed Chinese ship, the captain freed the boat. Little was said about the incident publicly.[83]

The Natuna Islands are rich in fish and hydrocarbons. East Natuna is believed to hold some 46 trillion cubic feet of natural gas, making it one of the world's largest reserves of untapped natural gas. ExxonMobil of the United States was in discussions with Jakarta about developing the block for several years, but eventually abandoned the talks in mid-2017.[84] The company did not explain whether it dropped out because of rising natural resource nationalism in Indonesia, depressed global gas prices, or because the East Natuna block is near the southern edge of Beijing's claims in the South China Sea.

Unlike, say, in Vietnam, the Indonesian public does not seem "very interested" in the Natunas, except if it is "blown up" by the media or by those promoting "nationalist sentiments," says Shafiah of CSIS. "If the media stops reporting, attention dies down."

What prompted the new hardened Indonesian position? Was it that Beijing was using its coast guard more to protect fishers operating increasingly in waters claimed by China's neighbors? Was the tougher response a sign of anxiety about Beijing reclaiming more islands in the South China Sea on which it could land fighter planes and warships? Or was it that the Indonesian navy and air force were looking for a foreign threat to convince parliament that they needed to modernize their equipment?

The harder line could have been driven by Indonesia's more aggressive efforts against illegal fishing in its waters in recent years. Susi Pudjiastuti, who was minister of maritime affairs and fisheries and the most popular cabinet member in Jokowi's first term, mounted a campaign under which she blew up hundreds of fishing boats from neighboring

83. Cochrane, "China's Coast Guard Rams Fishing Boat."

84. Wilda Asmarini, "ExxonMobil Says Will Drop Discussions over Indonesia's East Natuna Gas Field," *Reuters*, July 18, 2017, https://www.reuters.com/article/us-indonesia-gas-exxon-mobil/exxonmobil-says-will-drop-discussions-over-indonesias-east-natuna-gas-field-idUSKBN1A30JB.

countries caught poaching in Indonesian waters, even if she has targeted the vessels from neighboring Southeast Asian countries more than those from China.[85] (By mid-2019, it appeared the minister had toned down her campaign and was working more closely with other ministers to tackle the illegal fishing problem.)

The minister's tough measures against illegal, unreported, and unregulated fishing appeared to pay off. A report in 2018 by experts at the University of California, Santa Barbara, found an 80 percent drop in the number of foreign vessels fishing in Indonesian waters—and evidence that the catches by Indonesian fishers are increasing.[86]

In addition, one of Jokowi's top foreign policy goals is to boost connectivity between the islands of the archipelagic nation and turn Indonesia, which lies at the crossroads between the Pacific and Indian Oceans, into a maritime hub. The surging number of Chinese navy, coast guard, and maritime militia vessels sailing to the southern reaches of the South China Sea could challenge some of Jokowi's plans for Indonesia to become what he calls a maritime "fulcrum."

Planning to upgrade Indonesia's military capabilities in Natuna began before Chinese fishers became more active around the Indonesian island chain. Jakarta has extended the runway making it easier for larger military aircraft to land and it has increased the capacity of the main port to accommodate bigger ships. After the third skirmish in 2016, Jokowi convened a cabinet meeting on a warship in an apparent effort to demonstrate his resolve to Beijing.

"Jokowi has to make his challenges to China public," says Ramage. "He has to reassure the armed forces that he is fully aligned with their position. . . . The military still sees China as a threat," Ramage says, alluding to events in 1965 when China was accused of supporting a communist uprising.

In July 2017, Indonesia's armed forces signed an agreement with the Ministry of Energy and Mineral Resources to provide warships to protect

85. Hannah Beech and Muktita Suhartono, "A 'Little Bit of a Nut Case' Who's Taking on China," *New York Times*, June 8, 2018, https://www.nytimes.com/2018/06/08/world/asia/indonesia-fishing-boats-china-poaching.html.

86. Nithin Coca, "Tough Policing Is Restoring Indonesia's Fisheries," *Chinadialogue Ocean*, February 12, 2019, https://chinadialogueocean.net/6412-tough-policing-is-restoring-indonesia-fisheries/; Reniel B. Cabral, Juan Mayorga, Michaela Clemence, et al., "Rapid and Lasting Gains from Solving Illegal Fishing," *Nature Ecology & Evolution* 2 (2018): 650–658, https://www.nature.com/articles/s41559-018-0499-1.

offshore oil and gas production and the country's fishing grounds. On the same day, the Ministry of Maritime Affairs and Fisheries released a new national territory map that depicted the newly named North Natuna Sea for the first time.[87] China protested the name change, saying it would result in "complication and expansion of the dispute" and not be "conducive" for peaceful ties between the two countries.[88]

Laksmana sees the renaming of the area as largely an "empty gesture." He points out that "Jokowi is in good relations with Xi and calls Xi more often than any other foreign leader." Jokowi's predecessor would have had a "much more stern response in public," Laksmana says.

The Indonesian military in late 2018 inaugurated a new base at Natuna Besar, the largest of several hundred islands on the southern fringes of the South China Sea that will significantly bolster the Indonesia armed forces' presence in the South China Sea. Air Chief Marshal Hadi Tjahjanto, commander of the Indonesian National Armed Forces, said the base was meant to provide a "deterrence effect" against border threats, prompting speculation that the base was aimed at China, given the recent incidents at Natuna. But deterring China is "not the primary goal of the new base," Laksmana said.

Instead, the base, called the Natuna Integrated TNI Unit, is "a pioneering project to develop greater tri-service integration and joint operational capabilities," Laksmana wrote. The base had been planned since Indonesia's strategic defense review in 2009. When it is completed, Laksmana said the sprawling facility would host battalions from the army and marines along with advanced platforms including submarines, unmanned aerial vehicles, warships, fighter jets, and missile systems. Four other tri-service integrated units will be established in other parts of Indonesia and form the backbone of the military's Joint Regional Defense Commands.[89]

87. Joe Cochrane, "Indonesia, Long on Sidelines, Starts to Confront China's Territorial Claims," *New York Times*, September 10, 2017, https://www.nytimes.com/2017/09/10/world/asia/indonesia-south-china-sea-military-buildup.html.

88. Associated Press, "U.S. May Upset Beijing after It Backs Indonesian Claim on South China Sea near Natuna Islands," *South China Morning Post*, January 24, 2018, https://www.scmp.com/news/asia/southeast-asia/article/2130258/us-may-upset-beijing-after-it-backs-indonesian-claim-south.

89. Evan Laksmana, "Why Indonesia's New Natuna Base Is Not about Deterring China," Center for Strategic and International Studies—Asia Maritime Transparency Initiative, January 25, 2019, https://amti.csis.org/indonesias-natuna-base-not-about-deterring-china/.

More recently, Indonesia has announced plans to develop a fishing hub in the Natunas in an effort to assert its sovereignty over waters in which it has clashed with China. The government planned by the end of 2019 to build cold-storage facilities and use satellites and drones to help Indonesian fishers operating in the water surrounding the Natunas, according to Maritime Affairs Coordinating Minister Luhut Pandjaitan. He said the government would also provide refueling tankers to supply fishing boats, "so no one can claim that [the area is their] traditional fishing zone."[90]

Jakarta has long insisted that Beijing's territorial claims in the South China Sea have no legal standing under international law. Unlike its neighbors Brunei, Malaysia, the Philippines, and Vietnam, Indonesia is not a claimant in the disputed sea. Still, Indonesian analysts say, China's nine-dash line that claims roughly four-fifths of the sea seems to overlap with the northern edge of the 200-mile exclusive economic zone around the Natunas. Jakarta has asked Beijing for clarification since the 1990s about whether the line includes part of the exclusive economic zone around the Natunas but has never received an explanation from China.

LINGERING DISTRUST HOLDS BACK MILITARY TIES

Even though Indonesia is not a claimant in the South China Sea, China's rising assertiveness in nearby disputed waters has driven Indonesia to realize that the strategic environment around its islands is changing. This has prompted Jakarta to work at modernizing the military and make efforts to step up its military engagement with Beijing.

Already under Yudhoyono, Jokowi's predecessor, the Indonesian military bought billions of dollars of weapons and its budget was nearly tripled, Laksmana has pointed out.[91] Stockholm International Peace Research Institute estimates Indonesia's defense spending in 2017 at $8.2 billion, up from $5.8 billion in 2012.[92] Some of this funding has been used

90. Karlis Sana, "Indonesia Seeks to Assert Authority in Waters in South China Sea," *Bloomberg*, February22, 2019, https://www.bloomberg.com/news/articles/2019-02-23/indonesia-seeks-to-assert-authority-in-waters-in-south-china-sea.

91. Evan Laksmana, "Indonesia's Modernizing Military: Suharto's New Order Is Old News," *Foreign Affairs*, September 3, 2015, https://www.foreignaffairs.com/articles/indonesia/2015-09-03/indonesias-modernizing-military.

92. Stockholm International Peace Research Institute, "Military Expenditure by Country, in Constant (2016) US$ M., 1988–1997," SIPRI 2018, https://www.sipri.org/sites/default

to boost its air and naval forces, shifting away from relying on the army as the country's main defense force.

Jakarta and Beijing agreed in 2005 to establish a strategic partnership to boost their security ties and promote cooperation between their militaries, including helping develop each other's defense industries, establishing defense dialogues, and increasing cooperation between law enforcement and intelligence agencies in the battle against transnational security threats.[93] But progress has been slow.

In the mid-2000s, Indonesia was interested in developing defense ties with China to step up collaboration in the arms industry. At least in part, this was a response to an arms embargo imposed by the United States against Indonesia after its military was accused of taking part in violence in East Timor as it voted for independence from Indonesia in a UN-sponsored referendum in 1999.[94] The United States began partially lifting the ban in 2005.

Indonesia also wanted to develop a domestic weapons manufacturing capability to modernize the armed services with limited impact on the government's defense budget. During the visit of Yudhoyono to Beijing in 2005, the two nations signed an understanding on defense technology cooperation. Indonesia agreed to buy C-802 anti-ship missiles costing $11 million, marking the first purchase of Chinese weapons since the 1960s.[95]

Defense security consultation talks began in 2006 to discuss regional and international developments and joint military exercises. Two Chinese warships visited Jakarta in 2007, the first such visit in more than a dozen years. At the second round of security talks that year an agreement was signed on defense cooperation that included military student exchanges and possible additional arms sales.

China's then defense minister Cao Gangchuan visited Jakarta twice in 2007 and 2008. China offered training for about two dozen Indonesian

---

/files/1_Data%20for%20all%20countries%20from%201988%E2%80%932017%20in%20constant%20%282016%29%20USD.pdf.

93. Associated Press, "U.S. Lifts Arms Embargo against Indonesia," *NBC News*, November 23, 2015, https://www.nbcnews.com/id/10168487/ns/world_news-south_and_central_asia/t/us-lifts-arms-embargo-against-indonesia/.

94. Ibid.

95. Ian Storey, "China and Indonesia: Military-Security Ties Fail to Gain Momentum," *China Brief* 9, no. 4 (February 2009), https://jamestown.org/program/china-and-indonesia-military-security-ties-fail-to-gain-momentum/.

officers, but little other defense cooperation has taken place, despite the signing of various agreements.[96]

Strategic dialogue between China and Indonesia is "very formalized" with both sides making "preset statements," says Laksmana. When these talks started under former president Yudhoyono, the two sides tried to "figure out what to discuss," but it was difficult because of "ideological resistance" from the Indonesian navy and air force to technical military cooperation. Still, Laksmana says, military relations are improving, and they have explored the possibility of joint exercises in the maritime domain that will include law enforcement agencies.

For Jokowi security cooperation with China is far less of a priority than infrastructure projects. "Jokowi is more focused on the economy and infrastructure," says Laksmana. "On the defense side, they're just going through the motions." He adds: "Defense and security ties with China are good compared to 10 years ago, but they're not close to what exercises Indonesia does with Australia and the United States."

Ramage thinks China-Indonesia military engagement is also held back by the fact that the Indonesian military still carries considerable negative baggage about China. "They still exercise against China," Ramage points out. "They still see China as a threat. This holds them back" from bolstering military ties.

According to a 2017 study of China's military diplomacy published by the U.S. National Defense University, Indonesia ranks ninth among countries with the most military diplomatic exchanges between 2003 and 2016. These exchanges included 16 military exercises (of which three involved combat exercises), six naval port calls, and forty-three senior-level meetings. In Southeast Asia, only Thailand, Vietnam, and Singapore had more engagement with the Chinese military.[97]

Modernization of the military began under Yudhoyono and has continued under Jokowi as he has sought to turn Indonesia into maritime power. Jokowi's 2017 "sea policy" rests on five key pillars including managing marine resources, developing maritime infrastructure and

96. Ibid.

97. Kenneth Allen, Phillip C. Saunders, and John Chen, *Chinese Military Diplomacy 2003–2016* (Washington, DC: National Defense University Press, 2017), 45, https://ndupress.ndu.edu/Portals/68/Documents/stratperspective/china/ChinaPerspectives-11.pdf?ver=2017-07-17-153301-093.

connectivity, boosting maritime diplomacy, and bolstering maritime defense forces, Laksmana wrote.[98]

To improve the country's maritime defense forces, the navy has stepped up the acquisition of submarines. In 2019, the navy launched its third submarine, the KRI Alugoro-405 attack sub, built by Indonesian shipbuilder PT PAL Indonesia. The first two subs, the KRI Nagapasa-403 and KRI Ardadedali-404, were built in South Korea in 2017 and 2018 in a joint venture between the Indonesian shipbuilder and Daewoo Shipbuilding and Marine Engineering.

The navy estimates that it needs 12 submarines to protect Indonesian territorial waters and signed a $1 billion contract with Daewoo Shipbuilding for three more Nagapasa-class subs in early 2019.[99]

Beginning in 2017, Indonesia received the first of eight Boeing AH-64E Apache Guardian attack helicopters under the U.S. Foreign Military Sales program. The helicopters are equipped with radar from Northrop Grumman and 140 anti-tank missiles from Lockheed Martin at a cost of $1.4 billion. Indonesia officials said at least some of the Apaches will be stationed on the Natuna Islands bordering the South China Sea.[100]

Separately, Indonesian defense officials have said they intend to buy five C-130J Super Hercules transport aircraft produced by Lockheed Martin and some CH-47 Chinook heavy-lift helicopters from Boeing to boost the military's airlift capacity.[101]

Between 2014 and 2018, the United States delivered 24 Lockheed Martin F-16 Fighting Falcon aircraft to Indonesia under the U.S. Excess

---

98. Evan Laksmana, "Indonesian Sea Policy: Accelerating Jokowi's Global Maritime Fulcrum?," Center for Strategic and International Studies—Asia Maritime Transparency Initiative, March 23, 2017, https://amti.csis.org/indonesian-sea-policy-accelerating/.

99. Amir Baihaqi, "Kapal Selam Pertama Buatan Indonesia Alugoro-405 Diluncurkan," *Detik News*, April 11, 2019, https://news.detik.com/berita-jawa-timur/d-4506139/kapal-selam-pertama-buatan-indonesia-alugoro-405-diluncurkan; Franz-Stefan Gady, "Indonesia Launches Third Nagapasa-Class Diesel Elective Attack Submarine," *The Diplomat*, April 11, 2019, https://thediplomat.com/2019/04/indonesia-launches-third-nagapasa-class-diesel-electric-attack-submarine/; Franz-Stefan Gady, "Indonesia, South Korea Ink $1 Billion Contract for 3 Diesel-Electric Submarines," *The Diplomat*, April 15, 2019, https://thediplomat.com/2019/04/indonesia-south-korea-ink-1-billion-contract-for-3-diesel-electric-submarines/.

100. Mike Yeo, "First AH-64E Apache Guardian for Indonesia Arrives from U.S.," *Defense News*, December 18, 2017, https://www.defensenews.com/air/2017/12/18/first-ah-64e-apache-guardian-for-indonesia-arrives-from-us/.

101. Mike Yeo, "Indonesia Plans to Buy C-130-J Super Hercules, CH-47 Chinooks," *Defense News*, September 14, 2018, https://www.defensenews.com/air/2018/09/14/indonesia-plans-to-buy-c-130j-super-hercules-ch-47-chinooks/.

Defense Articles program after they were refurbished to meet modern standards.[102]

Indonesia signed a contract in 2018 to buy 11 Sukhoi Su-35 fighter jets from Russia for $1.1 billion. Officials in Jakarta have said delivery of these planes may be delayed or terminated to avoid possible U.S. sanctions prompted by legislation that threatens to penalize countries that procure Russian military equipment in response to Moscow's annexation of Crimea.[103]

Lingering distrust about Beijing's long-term goals, including around the Natunas, undoubtedly holds the military back from buying much military equipment from the Chinese. But, occasionally, the Indonesian military goes shopping for hardware in China. In 2018, Jakarta equipped two of its domestically built KCR-60M fast attack craft with Chinese sensors, consoles, combat information systems, and Type 630 30-millimeter close-in weapon system turrets. The Type 630 weapons system is intended to engage low-flying aircraft and sea-skimming missiles and can fire more than 4,500 rounds per minute.[104]

Jakarta seems to make a virtue of buying military hardware from many different sources at least in part to ensure the country is not dependent on any one major source for weapons. "Indonesia is not a big arms spender," says Ramage. "But when they spend, they spread it around," he says, pointing out that Indonesia recently bought training jets from the Czech Republic. "Indonesia buys very little from China, despite signing a defense agreement with China. Balancing is more important than interoperability" to the Indonesian military, says Ramage.

Beginning in 2006, Washington provided funds to help Indonesia install maritime surveillance systems in the Strait of Malacca, the Sulawesi Sea, and the Moluccas Strait around Indonesian islands.[105] Washington

---

102. Mike Yeo, "F-16 Fighter Jets to Begin Journey to Indonesia following U.S. Regeneration Work," *Defense News*, December 8, 2017, https://www.defensenews.com/air/2017/12/08/f-16-fighter-jets-to-begin-journey-to-indonesia-following-us-regeneration-work/.
103. Jon Grevatt, "Indo Defence 2018: Indonesia's Su-35 Procurement Faces CAATSA Hurdle," *Jane's 360*, November 9, 2018, https://www.janes.com/article/84427/indo-defence-2018-indonesia-s-su-35-procurement-faces-caatsa-hurdle.
104. Ridzwan Rahmat, "Indonesia Reveals Details of Chinese Sensors Installed Onboard KCR-60M Vessels," *Jane's 360*, July 27, 2018, https://www.janes.com/article/82032/indonesia-reveals-details-of-chinese-sensors-installed-onboard-kcr-60m-vessels.
105. "Fact Sheet: DoD-funded Integrated Maritime Surveillance System," U.S. Embassy and Consulates in Indonesia, https://id.usembassy.gov/our-relationship/policy-history

has also provided some patrol boats for the Indonesian marine police and, under the Maritime Security Initiative, Washington has helped increase Indonesia's patrol capacity and build the coast guard's organizational capacity.[106] The United States conducts annual exercises with Indonesia through the Cooperation Afloat Readiness and Training (CARAT) and Southeast Asia Counterterrorism Training.[107]

During a visit to Indonesia in 2018, then U.S. secretary of defense Jim Mattis told journalists that the U.S. military engages the Indonesian military more than any other country in military-to-military engagements.[108] Mattis offered to help Indonesia "maintain maritime domain awareness in the South China Sea, the North Natuna Sea," implying that he accepted Jakarta's renaming the area around the Natuna Islands, despite the protests from Beijing.[109]

COURTING HEARTS AND MINDS

China's crackdown against the minority Muslim Uighurs in Xinjiang Province in the west is a sensitive topic among Indonesian Muslims. In late 2018, several hundred demonstrators gathered outside the Chinese Embassy in Jakarta, demanding an end to the detentions of Uighur Muslims and chanting "God is great" and "Get out, Communist." The protest was organized by the Islamic Defenders Front, a group that was the driving force in organizing the protests against Jakarta governor Ahok.[110]

/embassy-fact-sheets/fact-sheet-dod-funded-integrated-maritime-surveillance-system/ (accessed October 30, 2019).

106. "Fact Sheet: U.S. Building Maritime Capacity in Southeast Asia," White House, Office of the Press Secretary, November 17, 2015, https://obamawhitehouse.archives.gov/the-press-office/2015/11/17/fact-sheet-us-building-maritime-capacity-southeast-asia.

107. Storey, "China and Indonesia."

108. Secretary of Defense James N. Mattis, "Press Gaggle by Secretary Mattis En Route to Indonesia," U.S. Department of Defense, transcript, January 22, 2018, https://dod.defense.gov/News/Transcripts/Transcript-View/Article/1420752/press-gaggle-by-secretary-mattis-en-route-to-indonesia/.

109. Associated Press, "U.S. May Upset Beijing after It Backs Indonesian Claim on South China Sea near Natuna Islands," *South China Morning Post*, January 24, 2018, https://www.scmp.com/news/asia/southeast-asia/article/2130258/us-may-upset-beijing-after-it-backs-indonesian-claim-south.

110. "Indonesian Muslims Protest China's Detention of Uighurs," *Associated Press*, December 21, 2018, https://www.apnews.com/b37f2e7a4bb145e58e2c8e9316aaf8eb.

But the Indonesian government has been reluctant to criticize China for its handling of the Uighurs, presumably because it is concerned that it could dent Chinese investment or perhaps prompt Beijing to support pro-independence separatists in the far eastern province of Papua.[111] In late 2018, shortly after the protest at the embassy, Indonesia's foreign minister Retno Marsudi called in the Chinese ambassador and asked him to explain what was happening in Xinjiang.

In other instances involving the mistreatment of Muslims, Indonesia has not been so reserved. Jakarta was sharply critical of the Myanmar government's handling of the Muslim Rohingya population, which prompted over 700,000 to flee the country since late 2017. Indonesia has long offered support for the Palestinians and sharply criticized the U.S. government's decision to move its embassy in Israel to Jerusalem.

In the 2019 election campaign, Jokowi's opponent criticized Jokowi for his failure to challenge China on its treatment of the Uighurs. "As a country with the largest Muslim population, Indonesia should have significant bargaining power to address such humanitarian tragedy," Prabowo's foreign policy spokesman said, adding that the president's silence is "proof that China holds Jokowi hostage."[112]

Beijing has sought to be proactive with diplomats of countries that could face pressure to speak out against the crackdown. At the end of 2018, Beijing invited diplomats from 12 countries, including from Indonesia and Malaysia, which have large Muslim populations, to visit Xinjiang. While Western governments have urged Beijing to stop its alleged detention of the Uighurs, most Muslim majority countries, except for Turkey, have avoided making criticisms.[113]

Jokowi, on a trip to China for the BRI summit in 2017, visited the Niuje Mosque in Beijing where he honored Chinese Muslim traders who had

111. Ibid.

112. Max Walden, "Indonesia's Opposition Takes Up the Uighur Cause," *Foreign Policy*, February 5, 2019, https://foreignpolicy.com/2019/02/05/indonesias-opposition-takes-up-the-uighur-cause/.

113. Karen Leigh (Bloomberg), "China Takes Diplomats to Tour 'Re-Education Camps' as Pressure Builds over Mass Detention of Uighurs," *Time*, January 8, 2019, https://time.com/5496435/china-12-diplomats-tour-xinjiang/; Reuters, "China Invites Waves of Diplomats to Visit, Seeking to Head Off Xinjiang Backlash," *The Epoch Times*, February 21, 2019, https://www.theepochtimes.com/wary-of-xinjiang-backlash-china-invites-waves-of-diplomats-to-visit_2810097.html.

engaged with Indonesia beginning in the fourteenth century and established a trading settlement on northern Java.[114]

China had launched a campaign several years earlier to convince Indonesian Muslims that all is well in Xinjiang. In April 2016, Beijing invited five leaders of Indonesia's largest Muslim social organization, Nahdlatul Ulama, to visit Xinjiang on an all-expenses-paid trip in an attempt to show that Uighur Muslims have religious freedom. Following the tour, which included meetings with Uighur religious leaders and visits to mosques, the visitors said publicly that China's government "guarantees freedom of religion to all religions."[115]

The following year, the Chinese government helped Nahdlatul Ulama build sanitation facilities in Banten in western Java.[116] Nahdlatul Ulama has established a special branch in China, much like it has in some 20 foreign countries, to serve Indonesian Muslims studying and working in China. The Chinese consul general in 2015 opened a Center for Cultural Development of Islam and China at the Grand Mosque in Semarang City in Central Java belonging to Nahdlatul Ulama, according to Christine Tjhin, who was a China researcher at CSIS Jakarta when we talked.

Shortly after the visit by Muslim leaders, China invited an editor of the news site *Liputan 6* to visit Xinjiang. She wandered the streets of the provincial capital of Urumqi on her own and visited schools and mosques. She talked to people with government-provided interpreters and concluded that the issues surrounding the ethnic clashes in 2009 had been resolved.

China's treatment of Muslims Uighurs is particularly sensitive in Indonesia, where ethnic Chinese are viewed with some uncertainty by conservative Muslims. Former Jakarta governor Ahok, who is ethnic Chinese, raised hackles when he banned public schools from forcing female students to wear head coverings. The conservative Islamic De-

---

114. "Jokowi Recalls Past Trade Relations with Chinese Muslims," *The Jakarta Post*, May 15, 2017, https://www.thejakartapost.com/news/2017/05/15/jokowi-recalls-past-trade-relations-with-chinese-muslims.html.

115. Jon Emont, "China Goes All Out to Win Favor with Indonesian Muslims," *Washington Post*, July 1, 2016, https://www.washingtonpost.com/world/asia_pacific/china-goes-all-out-to-curry-favor-with-indonesian-muslims/2016/06/30/caee52d4-3e08-11e6-9e16-4cf01a41decb_story.html.

116. Nurmulia Rekso Purnomo, "Pemerintah Tiongkok Gandeng NU Bangun Sanitasi di Banten," *TribunNews.com*, June 2, 2017, https://www.tribunnews.com/nasional/2017/06/02/pemerintah-tiongkok-gandeng-nu-bangun-sanitasi-di-banten.

fenders Front linked the head scarves to Xinjiang by tweeting, "China's government restrictions Muslim worship in Xinjiang. In Jakarta Ahok forbids mandatory head scarf. . . . Draw your own conclusion."[117]

In June 2016, Xie Feng, China's ambassador to Indonesia, visited an Islamic boarding school in Jakarta during the Muslim fasting month with a leader of Nahdlatul Ulama, who had been on the trip to Xinjiang. The ambassador donated money to a scholarship fund for orphans and handed out books, while the Nahdlatul Ulama leader said in his speech that "China is our friend. Nothing is to be feared from China." The ambassador said about the Uighurs: "Their religious freedom has all along been valued, respected, and protected by the Chinese government."[118]

Beyond reaching out to Muslim religious leaders, China has stepped up its broader public diplomacy activities in Indonesia in recent years. The embassy holds elaborate Chinese New Year celebrations. More academics working with think tanks were invited to China especially in 2016. "The invitations from all kinds of Chinese institutions were overwhelming," says Shafiah of CSIS, although she adds these activities have slowed since 2017.

Tjhin, who is Chinese Indonesian and has participated in many Chinese-sponsored trips organized by different Chinese agencies, says "some [are] good, some bad, others meh" or not very interesting. She adds that those organized for foreign academics in China by agencies of the Ministry of Commerce often involved "long speeches, and not enough time was allowed for discussion. Many of the speakers didn't have a deep enough understanding of the issues" such as the BRI they were discussing with their visitors.

China has repeatedly offered scholarships to Indonesian reporters to study journalism in China, but Endy Bayuni, a longtime editor with *The Jakarta Post*, says none of his journalists were interested. China has been inviting so many of his reporters to visit China on all-expenses-paid tours, he says, that his paper has had to start turning them down.

China has also provided political training in its Communist Party training schools for 10 officials each year from the Indonesian Democratic Party of Struggle (PDIP), Jokowi's party, and the Democrat Party affiliated

117. Emont, "China Goes All Out to Win Favor with Indonesian Muslims."
118. Emont, "China Goes All Out to Win Favor with Indonesian Muslims."

with former president Yudhoyono. Some PDIP officials have come home thinking that the more ideological training methods of the Chinese Communist Party might have some useful applications in Indonesia, says Laksmana, a researcher at CSIS Jakarta.

As China has developed its economy, it has also transformed the country into a magnet for students from Southeast Asia. Many Indonesians are attracted to China to study language and others are drawn to study medicine and other technical fields. In 2016, China had over 14,700 students from Indonesia, the third largest group globally behind South Korea (70,500) and Thailand (23,000). The total from all of Southeast Asia reached 68,000.[119]

"China is the fastest-growing place for Indonesian overseas education," says Laksmana. "China can also be political on this issue, informally saving some scholarship spots for [students affiliated with] Nahdlatul Ulama and Muhammadiyah, for example," he adds, referring to two of the largest Muslim organizations in the country.

But it is not always smooth sailing for Indonesian students in China. "For some Muslim students in China it's often a challenge to eat and pray," says Laksmana, alluding to Islamic restrictions against eating pork, which is popular in China, and the difficulty of finding quiet places for Muslims to pray five times a day. "This is very sensitive," he says.

Anxiety about China and the ghost of communism in Indonesia sometimes follow students studying in China. In 2018, the Indonesian online newspaper *Republika* published an article quoting the rector of a university run by Muhammadiyah, which is often actively trying to shape politics in Indonesia, charging that Indonesian students in China study communist ideology.

The article was quickly denied by Indonesian student groups in China and the alleged source denied making the comment and said he had never been interviewed by the paper. Nonetheless, the story could have poi-

119. China Power Project, "Is China Both a Source and Hub for International Students?," Center for Strategic and International Studies, https://chinapower.csis.org/china-international-students/; Muhammad Zulfikar Rakhmat, "China's Educational Expansion in Indonesia," *The Diplomat*, February 15, 2019, https://thediplomat.com/2019/02/chinas-educational-expansion-in-indonesia/; Samantha Custer, Brooke Russell, Matthew DiLorenzo, Mengfan Cheng, Siddhartha Ghose, Harsh Desai, Jacob Sims, and Jennifer Turner, *Ties That Bind: Quantifying China's Public Diplomacy and Its "Good Neighbor" Effect* (Williamsburg, VA: AidData at William and Mary, June 2018), 13, https://docs.aiddata.org/ad4/pdfs/Ties_That_Bind--Full_Report.pdf.

soned the environment among students studying in China. "It reinforces existing communist phobia in Indonesia and gives credence to the prevalent spate of related fake news, particularly related to a 'communist threat' and China's influence in Indonesia," Tjhin, was quoted as saying.[120]

China and Indonesia agreed in 2010 to establish Confucius Institutes at six Indonesian universities. Setting up these institutes was complicated and required protracted negotiations. One sensitivity was over the name. Even though Confucianism is considered one of the religions of Indonesia, it carries considerable political and historical baggage. In the end, the two sides agreed that the name of the institutes would be the Mandarin Language Center in Indonesian while Confucius Institute would be used in English.[121]

Indonesia is also a target of China's elite diplomacy. Indonesia had some 194 high-level exchanges between 2000 and 2015, trailing Vietnam (286), Thailand (257), and Cambodia (216) in Southeast Asia.[122]

Despite Beijing's stepped up "soft power" efforts, the views of China among Indonesians remain complicated and often seem contradictory. Thanks to a raft of opinion polling in recent years, more is known about the attitudes of Indonesians toward China than about the views of their neighbors regarding the rising giant to the north. Part of that can no doubt be attributed to the fact that Indonesia is, for the most part, more democratic than its neighbors and has a fairly lively press, which means opinion polls are not as "foreign" in Indonesia as in more authoritarian Southeast Asian countries.

A survey conducted in May 2017 by Lembaga Survey Indonesia on behalf of the ISEAS-Yusof Ishak Institute in Singapore found that nearly 77 percent of Indonesians admired China and about the same number viewed China as an important country for Indonesia.[123] Despite China's popular showing, it trailed Japan (83 percent) and the United States (81 percent) as the country most important to Indonesia. Johannes Herlijanto, a political scientist at the Pelita Harapan University in Jakarta,

120. Aisyah Llewellyn, "Student Politics: Indonesians Confront China Prejudice," *Lowey Institute*, May 31, 2018, https://www.lowyinstitute.org/the-interpreter/student-politics-indonesians-confront-china-prejudice.

121. Rikko Theo and Maggi W. H. Leung, "China's Confucius Institute in Indonesia: Mobility, Frictions, and Local Surprises," *Sustainability* 10, no. 530 (2018): 6.

122. Custer et al., *Ties That Bind*, 2.

123. Johannes Herlijanto, "Public Perceptions of China in Indonesia," *ISEAS Perspective*, no. 89 (2017): 4, https://www.iseas.edu.sg/images/pdf/ISEAS_Perspective_2017_89.pdf.

who analyzed this data for ISEAS, was surprised how well China fared despite the various negative narratives at work in Indonesian society.

Asked about the impact of China's rise on Indonesia, 41 percent of those surveyed thought it would be positive and almost the same number thought it would be negative.[124] One-quarter of Indonesians are totally opposed to Chinese investment in the country, while one-fifth believe investment should be allowed, Herlijanto reported.[125]

Some 28 percent have a positive view of Indonesia-China economic relations, while just over 62 percent believe that Indonesia will only receive a "little benefit" from close ties with China.[126]

Despite the stories about Chinese workers inundating Indonesia, Herlijanto reported that only 27 percent of Indonesians told the pollsters that Chinese workers should not be allowed to work in Indonesia.[127]

Survey respondents were also asked about the 2016 fishing disputes between Jakarta and Beijing around the Natuna Islands. Nearly 60 percent avoided answering this question, but of those who did answer it, almost 51 percent said they regarded the incidents as alarming. About 32 percent said the incidents were not serious because they were caused by illegal fishing rather than by a territorial dispute.[128]

In questions about Chinese Indonesians, who make up about 2 percent of the country's population, the poll found that 42 percent thought they had too much political influence and 62 percent said they had too much economic clout. Some 48 percent of those polled said they believed that Chinese Indonesians might still harbor loyalty toward China even though almost all of them were born in Indonesia and are Indonesian citizens. Just over 64 percent said they were uncomfortable with electing a Chinese Indonesian for a position of political leadership.[129]

With the reelection of Jokowi for a second five-year term in April 2019, Indonesia's ties with China will likely continue to focus most actively on

---

124. Ibid.
125. Ibid., 7.
126. Ibid., 5.
127. Ibid., 6.
128. Ibid., 8.
129. Diego Fossati, Hui Yew-Foong, and Siwage Dharma Negara, *The Indonesia National Survey Project: Economy, Society and Politics* (Singapore: ISEAS-Yusof Ishak Institute), 25–27.

economic collaboration as Jakarta looks to Beijing for investment in power plants, industrial parks, and information technology start-ups.

China will no doubt continue to get heartburn from the tough slog foreigners face when investing in Indonesia, but Beijing will not want to give up its toehold in the market that makes up nearly half of the total economy of Southeast Asia. Chinese companies will need to limit the numbers of Chinese workers they bring in to work on their projects and provide quality technology and workmanship at competitive prices if they hope to overcome China's sizable trust deficit in Indonesia.

The two countries will find it challenging to fashion deeper political and military relations as long as Indonesians who lived through the turmoil and bloodshed of 1965 are still around (even though China's involvement in the apparent communist coup attempt at that time has never been proven). Although the earlier state-sanctioned discrimination against ethnic Chinese has ended, resentment continues among indigenous Indonesians about the wealth and hefty role of ethnic Chinese in the economy. Often these sentiments are conflated with China's role in the country as the economic footprint of the powerhouse to the north increases in Indonesia.

Indonesia has long viewed itself as the natural leader of Southeast Asia, even if Jokowi has been mainly domestically focused. The regional leadership ambitions of Beijing and Jakarta could collide down the road if China picks off more countries like Cambodia to side with Beijing rather than with its Southeast Asian neighbors. As Ian Storey of the ISEAS-Yusof Ishak Institute in Singapore has said, "Indonesia would find a China-centric regional order with itself subordinate to Beijing a deeply unpalatable prospect."[130]

130. Storey, *Southeast Asia and the Rise of China*, 211.

10. PHILIPPINES: DUTERTE'S STRATEGIC DALLIANCE WITH BEIJING

China could hardly have wished for a better outcome in its endeavor to snare control of the South China Sea than the election of Rodrigo Duterte as president of the Philippines in May 2016. The longtime mayor of the southern city of Davao took office two weeks before the July 12, 2016, ruling by the Hague-based arbitral tribunal which determined that China's outsized claims in the South China Sea had no legal basis.

But Duterte soon declared that he would "set aside" the ruling in a case brought by his predecessor, Benigno Aquino, in the hope of courting Chinese investment and aid. The case initiated in 2013 prompted the wrath of Beijing and turned the Philippines into something akin to a frontline state in the maritime dispute. The new president said his goal was to mend relations with China that had become severely strained after Manila took the dispute to the international tribunal following China's 2012 seizure of the Scarborough Shoal from the Philippines.

Beijing, after long shunning Aquino, invited Duterte to visit China in October 2016, a few months after he assumed office. He returned home with $24 billion in investment and loan pledges, including for infrastructure projects such as rail links, ports, and hydropower plants. China also agreed to lift an advisory against travel by its citizens to the Philippines, drop restrictions on Philippine agricultural exports,[1] and allow Philippine fishers to return to fish around Scarborough Shoal.

Following his meeting with Chinese president Xi Jinping, Duterte told a business forum in the Great Hall of the People that "I announce my sep-

1. Willard Cheng, "Duterte Heads Home from China with $24 Billion Deals," *ABS-CBN*, October 21, 2016, http://news.abs-cbn.com/business/10/21/16/duterte-heads-home-from-china-with-24-billion-deals.

Map 12. Philippines

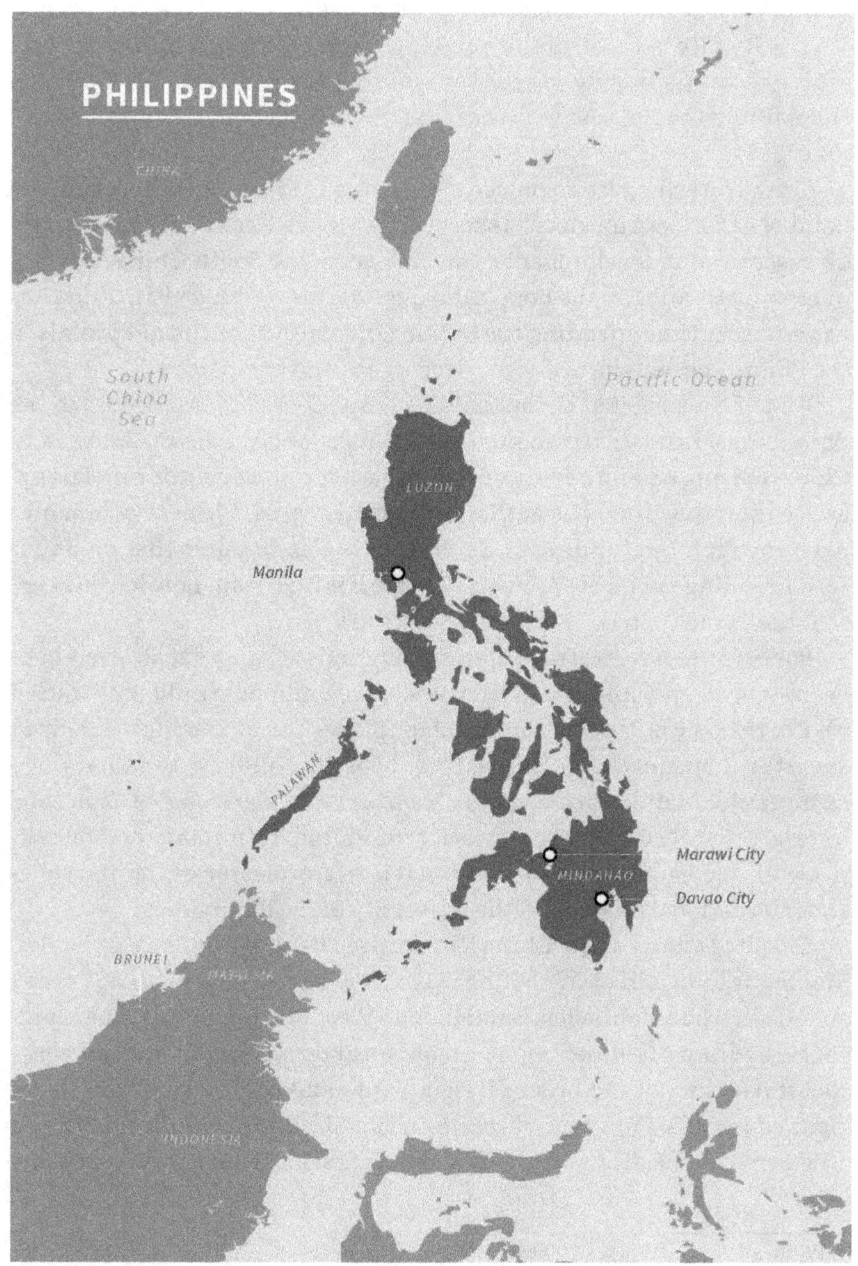

aration from the United States both in military—not in social—both in military but economic" relations. Duterte was livid with the Philippines' U.S. treaty ally because of the outgoing Barack Obama administration's criticism of his bloody crackdown on illegal drug dealers and users. Duterte told the Chinese audience that "I will be dependent on you for all time."[2]

Since Duterte's rise to power, Philippine trade with China is up, the number of Chinese tourists has surged, and the two countries have begun discussing joint development of oil and gas in the South China Sea. But, interestingly, after all the hoopla during Duterte's Beijing visit, China has had a harder time spending the billions in investment and aid promised the Philippines by the Chinese government and companies.

Part of the problem is one that has long affected many donors to the Philippines: Infrastructure projects often get bogged down. Sometimes Chinese firms run into Philippine regulations, or economic officials exercise their due diligence authority. In other cases, Chinese companies have encountered funding difficulties. It is also possible that Beijing is slow in rolling out its big projects because it is uncertain how long its current honeymoon in the Philippines will last.

Political ties have warmed dramatically and exchanges at all levels have been stepped up. China has given rifles to the Philippine military (which it gave to the police), landed some military planes and an intelligence ship in Duterte's hometown of Davao, and boosted military-to-military exchanges. But Manila's armed forces "remain very suspicious" of China and have largely held off Duterte's calls for the Philippine military to reduce its ties with the Pentagon, says Aileen Baviera, a professor of China studies and international relations at the University of the Philippines.

Despite Duterte's pro-China tilt, the president in August 2018 let Beijing know loud and clear that he is far from supportive of all of China's actions in what Manila has renamed the West Philippine Sea. The blunt-speaking leader told Beijing in unequivocal terms that he did not agree that it has the right to order foreign planes and boats away from its reclaimed islands. "You cannot create an island . . . and you say that the air above this artificial island is yours," Duterte said. "That is wrong because

2. Willard Cheng, "While in China, Duterte Announces 'Separation' from U.S.," *ABS-CBN*, October 20, 2016, https://news.abs-cbn.com/news/10/20/16/while-in-china-duterte-announces-separation-from-us.

those waters are what we would consider international sea. And the right of innocent passage is guaranteed."[3]

Duterte seemed to be responding to a leaked internal report of the Philippines' armed forces, which detailed that its military planes had received radio warnings at least 46 times in the last half of 2017 while patrolling near artificial islands constructed by China in the Spratly Islands of the South China Sea. These outposts have been equipped with powerful surveillance and communications equipment.[4]

China rejected Duterte's call for Beijing to rethink its behavior in the disputed sea, insisting in a Foreign Ministry statement that "China has a right to take necessary steps to respond to foreign aircraft and ships that deliberately get close to or make incursions into our air and waters near China's relevant islands." It urged Manila "to meet China halfway, and jointly protect the present good situation that has not come easily in the South China Sea."[5]

It is far from certain that Duterte's sharp pivot toward China marks a long-term Philippine policy trend. The next presidential elections are scheduled for 2022, when Duterte's six-year term ends. "Whoever wins won't go back to a confrontational approach," says Malcolm Cook, a Philippine expert at ISEAS-Yusof Ishak Institute in Singapore. "I expect the pendulum to swing back [toward the middle]. It won't go back to the 2012 to 2016 period."

"Strong anti-China sentiment" remains among Philippine voters and could have a bearing on the next national elections, Baviera says. Factors that she thinks will influence Philippine views include the harassment of Philippine fishers by the Chinese maritime law enforcement agencies, China's blocking of oil and gas development off the Philippine coast in the South China Sea, and its use of artificially created islands for military purposes.

---

3. Associated Press, "'Someone Will Press a Trigger': Duterte Says China's Claim to Disputed Islands' Airspace 'Is Wrong' and Could Be 'Flashpoint' for Conflict," *South China Morning Post*, August 14, 2018, https://www.scmp.com/news/asia/southeast-asia/article/2159719/duterte-chinas-claim-airspace-above-disputed-islands-wrong.

4. Renato Cruz De Castro, "Duterte's China Policy Isn't Paying Off," *East Asia Forum*, September 18, 2018, http://www.eastasiaforum.org/2018/09/18/dutertes-china-policy-isnt-paying-off/?utm_source=newsletter&utm_medium=email&utm_campaign=n.

5. "China Rebuffs Philippines President's South China Sea Rebuke," *Reuters*, August 16, 2018, https://www.reuters.com/article/us-china-southchinasea-philippines/china-rebuffs-philippines-presidents-south-china-sea-rebuke-idUSKBN1L10M4.

Baviera believes that "what China does" in the next few years and whether there are "further provocations" will play "an important role in shaping [Philippine] views. . . . Any change in leadership will have to respond to the pressure of public sentiment" in setting China policy, she argues.

Despite Duterte's push to develop closer ties with China, Filipinos remained quite skeptical about Beijing. A survey of elite opinion conducted by ISEAS in Singapore in late 2018 (after Duterte's first 30 months in office) found that over 66 percent of Filipinos believed "China will become a revisionist power with an intent to turn Southeast Asia into its sphere of influence." This was the highest percentage among Southeast Asia respondents and ahead of Vietnam at 61 percent.

In the survey of the views of policy experts, researchers, businesspeople, civil society officials, and media representatives in the Philippines, just over 61 percent thought China had the most economic influence in Southeast Asia (compared to nearly 12 percent who thought this about the United States). Almost 41 percent said China had the most political and strategic influence in Southeast Asia (slightly ahead of the United States at a little over 36 percent).

Asked which country would "do the right thing in contributing to global peace, security, prosperity and governance," fully two-thirds of Filipinos interviewed had "no confidence" or "little confidence" that China would meet these standards. (Almost 45 percent doubted that the United States would fill this role.)

On China's Belt and Road Initiative (BRI) megaprojects, 27 percent of Filipinos thought the projects would benefit regional economic development, and nearly 39 percent said the projects would bring Southeast Asian country "closer into China's orbit."

In light of the Sri Lanka's experience of having to give China a 99-year lease to the Hambantota Port because it was unable to make its loan payments, almost 79 percent of Filipinos said their government should be "very cautious" in negotiating BRI projects with China "to avoid getting into unsubstantiated financial debts." Only Malaysia had a higher percentage at over 84 percent.

About the United States with which the Philippines has a treaty alliance, just over three-quarters thought U.S. global power and influence had "deteriorated" or "deteriorated substantially" in the year prior to late

2018. Almost 71 percent believed U.S. engagement with Southeast Asia under the Donald Trump administration had "decreased" or "decreased substantially." Around 37 percent had "full confidence" or "some confidence" in the United States as "strategic partner and provider of regional security."[6]

DUTERTE'S BEIJING PIVOT

Duterte's ruling PDP-Laban Party celebrated its 36th anniversary in a ballroom in the luxury Manila Hotel in Manila Bay in February 2018. What set the event off from other political party celebrations is that it did not mark the exploits of the party in the country's recent elections or discuss its upcoming legislative priorities. The guests of honor seated at the head table with Duterte were a handful of Philippine party leaders and trio of senior Chinese officials.

One was a Chinese vice minister, another was the Chinese ambassador to the Philippines, and the third was a prominent Chinese professor who gave a keynote speech honoring the life and thought of Chinese leader Xi. An English translation of Xi's book, *The Governance of China*, was handed out to the dinner guests.[7] The unusual optics took on added significance among Filipinos given that Duterte sometimes jokes about turning the Philippines into a Chinese province.

By the time of this party celebration, the international tribunal ruling in July 2016, two weeks after Duterte had replaced Aquino as president, seemed but a distant memory. The judges had issued a decision overwhelmingly in favor of most of the Philippine claims in the South China Sea. One of the key issues facing the panel was the legality of Beijing's claim to the water within China's nine-dash line that includes roughly 90 percent of the disputed sea. The tribunal said that any claims to historic rights in the entire sea were overruled by the United Nations

---

6. Tang Siew Mun, Moe Thuzar, Hoang Thi Ha, Termsak Chalermpalanupap, Pham Thi Phuong Thao, and Anuthida Saelaow Qian, *The State of Southeast Asia: 2019 Survey Report* (Singapore: ASEAN Studies Centre at ISEAS-Yusof Ishak Institute, 2019), 18, 21, 22, 26, 19, 20, 13, 16, 17, https://www.iseas.edu.sg/images/pdf/TheStateofSEASurveyReport_2019.pdf.

7. "In Photos: Ruling PDP-Laban celebrates 36th anniversary," *Rappler*, February 27, 2018, https://www.rappler.com/nation/197049-pdp-laban-anniversary-china.

Convention on the Law of the Sea (UNCLOS), which both countries had ratified.[8]

On the issue of Scarborough Shoal, which China snared from the Philippines in 2012, the court ruled that it was a rock entitled to only 12 nautical miles of territorial sea. The judges said China had violated the traditional fishing rights of Filipinos by barring them from fishing at the shoal. The tribunal declared that none of the Spratly Islands, including the largest features such as Itu Aba, generate exclusive economic zones or continental shelves because they cannot sustain human habitation or independent economic life.

The ruling rebuked Beijing for its environmental destruction in the process of constructing artificial islands and said that China had violated Philippine sovereign rights by interfering with oil and gas exploration at Reed Bank (called Recto Bank in the Philippines). The bank lies on the Philippines' continental shelf northwest of Palawan Island.

Although the ruling is legally binding, the tribunal has no vehicle to enforce its findings. China condemned the ruling and said that it would not accept its conclusions. Considering the years of legal research and the treasure the Philippines had invested in the tribunal, Duterte's comments must have sounded like music to Beijing's ears. "In the play of politics, now, I will set aside the [tribunal] ruling," Duterte said a few months after taking office. "I will not impose anything on China."[9]

Right after the ruling, hackers from China targeted several Philippine organizations using malware designed to steal sensitive information from government agencies, according to Finnish security firm F-Secure. Two prime targets were employees at the Department of Justice and lawyers at an international law firm that was supporting the Philippines in the arbitral case.[10]

---

8. Much of this summary of the ruling is based on Gregory Poling, Michael Green, Murray Hiebert, Chris Johnson, Amy Searight, and Bonnie Glaser, "Judgment Day: The South China Sea Tribunal Issues Its Ruling," Center for Strategic and International Studies—Asia Maritime Transparency Initiative, July 11, 2016, https://amti.csis.org/arbitration-ruling-analysis/.

9. Jim Gomez, "Duterte Says He'll Set Aside Sea Feud Ruling against China," *Philippine Star*, December 17, 2016, https://www.philstar.com/headlines/2016/12/17/1654340/duterte-says-hell-set-aside-sea-feud-ruling-against-china.

10. David Gilbert, "Chinese Hackers Thought to Target Philippines over South China Sea Dispute," *Motherboard Vice*, August 4, 2016, https://motherboard.vice.com/en_us/article/vv7zy3/chinese-hackers-thought-to-target-philippines-over-south-china-sea-dispute.

Duterte's strategy was to de-emphasize the country's territorial disputes with China in the hope of wooing Chinese investment and aid to boost the Philippines economic development. He also hoped China would relax some of its pressure tactics against the Philippines in the South China Sea. Shortly before visiting Beijing in October 2016, Duterte, to convince a skeptical China that he was serious about deepening ties, announced that he was suspending joint patrols with the U.S. Navy in the Philippines' exclusive economic zone to avoid offending China.[11]

Philippine foreign policy is very much determined by the perceptions and views of whoever is president. Some describe Manila's policy toward China since the late 1990s as "bipolar," as it has swung from a "golden age" under Gloria Macapagal Arroyo during most of the 2000s, to frosty during Aquino in the six years to 2016, and highly friendly under Duterte. Each president seems to seek a new equilibrium in recalibrating relations between Asia's two most prominent competitors, China and the United States.[12]

Duterte's arrival in the presidency signaled a major Philippine foreign policy shift, particularly toward the country's "chief security partner (America) and chief security concern (China)," commentator/writer Richard Javad Heydarian said in his 2017 book, *The Rise of Duterte: A Populist Revolt against Elite Democracy*. "Under Duterte, relations with America became no longer special and ties with China became no longer as hostile."[13]

To appreciate Duterte's abrupt pivot requires understanding that his election and political success were based on "a full-fledged 'antiestablishment' brand of populism" that rejected "the Philippine political elite and their entire policy paradigm," Heydarian said. Like other strongmen such as Turkey's Recep Tayyip Erdogan, Duterte promised an "alternative form

11. Trefor Moss, "Philippine President's Shift on U.S. Alliance Worries Military," *Wall Street Journal*, September 16, 2016, https://www.wsj.com/articles/philippine-presidents-shift-on-u-s-alliance-worries-military-1474058666; Renato Cruz De Castro, "The Duterte Administration's Appeasement Policy on China and the Crisis in the Philippine-U.S. Alliance," *Philippine Political Science Journal* (2017): 11.

12. Samantha Custer, Brooke Russell, Matthew DiLorenzo, Mengfan Cheng, Siddhartha Ghose, Harsh Desai, Jacob Sims, and Jennifer Turner, *Ties That Bind: Quantifying China's Public Diplomacy and Its "Good Neighbor" Effect* (Williamsburg, VA: AidData at William and Mary, 2018), 25, https://docs.aiddata.org/ad4/pdfs/Ties_That_Bind--Full_Report.pdf.

13. Richard Javad Heydarian, "Duterte's Art of the Deal," *The National Interest*, October 22, 2017, 1, https://nationalinterest.org/feature/dutertes-art-the-deal-22840.

of governance and political worldview under a firm and decisive leadership style."[14]

The U.S. government's refusal to "clarify whether it would come to the Philippines rescue in an event of conflict with China in the South China Sea" under the terms of the two countries' 1951 Mutual Defense Treaty was another factor leading to Duterte's victory, Heydarian argued. A poll a few months before the 2016 elections taken by Pulse Asia found that half of the respondents were either undecided or disagreed when asked if defense ties with the United States had been beneficial to the Philippines. Asked if Manila should explore defense cooperation with other countries such as China, fully 47 percent expressed support.[15]

Beijing had clearly spelled out to the Aquino administration the sticks and carrots of continuing confrontation with China on the South China Sea. Chinese officials made clear that Manila risked continuing military confrontation and diplomatic isolation and would forgo important investment opportunities from China if it continued to challenge Beijing, Heydarian said. While Washington criticized Duterte's signature antidrug campaign, China expressed support for the effort and offered help in terms of equipment, criminal investigations, and the establishment of drug rehabilitation centers.[16]

Still, on the Philippines' policy toward China and the United States, "there is a significant gap between Duterte's often-hyperbolic rhetoric, on one hand, and the more subdued policy of his administration, on the other," Heydarian said. He pointed out that key players in the Philippine security establishment like Secretary of Defense Delfin Lorenzana, the former longtime veteran's affairs attaché in the Philippine Embassy in Washington, have sought to ensure that Duterte's extreme rhetoric does not necessarily become government policy. "The military brass, which is largely American trained and equipped, consistently lobbies for maintenance of the foundation of existing security ties with Washington," Heydarian wrote.[17]

Still China's standing in Manila has changed dramatically. "The Chinese ambassador is regularly present at events with the president," says Cook, alluding to the envoy frequently cutting ribbons at ceremonies and

14. Ibid., 2.
15. Ibid.
16. Ibid.
17. Ibid.

meeting with Philippine officials all over the country. "That's unprecedented. Ambassador Zhao [Jianhua] must be the happiest man in the Philippines." Many are convinced that he has a direct line to Duterte.

Diplomats in Manila say China has staffed its embassy with some of its savviest diplomats who speak flawless English to take advantage of the new opening. "China is moving from the West Philippine Sea to the halls of congress," a veteran Philippine journalist jokes about the transition from Aquino to Duterte.

Politically, Duterte's ruling party has signed an agreement with China's Communist Party to step up exchanges and training for Philippine party and government officials in Fujian. The two countries have agreed to hold a bilateral strategic dialogue every six months to plan next cooperative steps and to air grievances. More Chinese official delegations are visiting the Philippines and more Philippine groups are visiting China these days. Many Chinese delegations bypass the capital and engage with provincial government officials directly. China opened a consulate in Duterte's hometown of Davao in late 2018.[18]

At the beginning of his first trip to China as president in 2016, Duterte played up his Chinese heritage saying that his grandfather came from Xiamen in Fujian Province. He added that many Filipinos are part Chinese and that 2 million ethnic Chinese are living and working in the Philippines. "So we might be asking for your help, asking the Chinese people to help Chinese people here," Duterte said. "They are Filipinos, but they are also Chinese."

The grandfather of Aquino's mother also migrated from Fujian Province, but Duterte's predecessor quickly learned that a Chinese heritage does not necessarily guarantee good relations with China.[19]

While in Beijing, where Duterte was accompanied by hundreds of Filipino business leaders, many of whom were ethnic Chinese, the president signed 13 cooperation agreements with his Chinese counterparts, including between economic agencies and ministries, drug enforcement agencies, and their coast guards. China's State Council Information

18. "China Opens Consulate in Davao City," *ABS-CBN News*, October 28, 2018, https://news.abs-cbn.com/news/10/28/18/china-opens-consulate-in-davao-city.

19. Liu Zhen, "Will Playing the Chinese Ancestry Card Help Rodrigo Duterte Win over Beijing?," *South China Morning Post*, October 20, 2016, https://www.scmp.com/news/china/diplomacy-defence/article/2038385/will-playing-chinese-ancestry-card-help-rodrigo-duterte.

Office promised to provide training to the Philippine president's communications office.[20]

The Philippines held the rotating chair of the Association of Southeast Asian Nations (ASEAN) in 2017, half a year after Duterte took office, and often seemed to use its lead role to protect China from criticism by other Southeast Asian countries for its assertive actions in the South China Sea. Duterte and his second foreign secretary, Alan Peter Cayetano, kept the arbitral ruling off the table during ASEAN deliberations throughout the year. Both men regularly downplayed Chinese actions in the maritime dispute in contrast to the Philippine military and media, which often criticized Beijing's moves.

After Cayetano was elected speaker of the House of Representatives of the Philippines in mid-2019, China's foreign minister Wang Yi and the ambassador to the Philippines congratulated the former foreign secretary for his "significant contributions" in promoting relations between Manila and Beijing "as an old and good friend of the Chinese people."[21]

Duterte's position frustrates some of the country's Southeast Asian neighbors, particularly the Vietnamese, who "sees the Philippines as a threat to their own interests in the maritime dispute with China," says Jose Custodio, a military analyst and historian. Hanoi feels that "the Philippines is helping China consolidate the South China Sea and is not cooperating with ASEAN" in challenging China's moves in the disputed sea.

Duterte rarely criticizes China in public about its actions in the South China Sea, but he has "raised the [arbitral] ruling in private with both Xi and [Premier] Li Keqiang," says an official in the president's office.

Cayetano, the former foreign secretary, said Manila had informed Beijing about Philippine "redlines" in the South China Sea dispute. One is if China starts building on Scarborough Shoal. A second is trying to remove the Philippine *Sierra Madre* navy ship anchored at Second Thomas Shoal or interfering with Philippine efforts to resupply the troops on the ship. A third is seeking to exploit resources in areas of the South China Sea claimed by the Philippines. If any of these redlines are violated, Cayetano

20. Frances Roberto, "Timeline: Philippines-China Relationship under Duterte," *Rappler*, August 7, 2018, https://www.rappler.com/newsbreak/iq/209026-timeline-philippines-china-relationship-duterte-administration.

21. Sofia Tomacruz, "In a Rare Move, China Congratulates House Speaker Cayetano," *Rappler*, July 30, 2019, https://www.rappler.com/nation/236686-china-congratulates-house-speaker-cayetano.

said Duterte had made clear "he will go to war."[22] What Cayetano did not explain is how Duterte would militarily confront China with his much weaker and poorly equipped navy.

Many Filipinos are convinced that Duterte received financial support from China, perhaps through ethnic Chinese businesspersons, for his 2016 election campaign, but no evidence has surfaced publicly proving this assertion. Some speculate that China supported online trolls to post disinformation in support of the president and harass his opponents with "fake news."[23]

As it supported Myanmar against criticisms for the abuse of its Rohingya minority, so China has defended Duterte from criticisms by the United Nations human rights chief for Manila's brutal crackdown against drug addicts and sellers. When a UN official said Duterte needed a "psychiatric evaluation," China's Foreign Ministry spokesman responded that "anyone without bias can see" that the Philippine president has made "achievements" in dealing with illegal drugs and improving people's lives.[24]

It is more than a little ironic that China plays a leading role in the Philippine drug crisis that Duterte is seeking to tackle with brute force. Although Chinese businesses have built several giant drug rehabilitation centers in the Philippines, China is a key source of the methamphetamines, *shabu* locally, to which many Filipinos are addicted, and the precursors used to make the drugs in laboratories in the Philippines are often produced by Chinese nationals.[25]

---

22. Patricia Lourdes Viray, "Philippines, China Draw 'Red Lines' in South China Sea Dispute," *Philippine Star*, May 29, 2018, https://www.philstar.com/headlines/2018/05/29/1819745/philippines-china-draw-red-lines-south-china-sea-dispute; John Reed, "Philippines Claims It Would 'Go to War' over China Incursions," *Financial Times*, May 29, 2018, https://www.ft.com/content/1e36de52-62ec-11e8-90c2-9563a0613e56.

23. For a description of political trolling in the Philippines, see Jonathan Corpus Ong and Jason Cabanes, "In the Philippines, Political Trolling Is an Industry—This Is How It Works," *openDemocracy*, February 20, 2018, https://www.opendemocracy.net/digitaliberties/jonathan-corpus-ong-jason-cabanes/in-philippines-political-trolling-is-industry-this.

24. Paterno Esmaquel II, "China Defends Duterte from U.N. Rights Chief's Tirades," *Rappler*, March 13, 2018, https://www.rappler.com/nation/198016-china-defends-duterte-un-human-rights-chief-psychiatric-test.

25. John Chalmers, "Meth Gangs of China Play Star Role in Philippines Drug Crisis," *Reuters*, December 16, 2016, https://www.reuters.com/investigates/special-report/philippines-drugs-china/; "China-funded: Duterte Opens Biggest Drug Center in Mindanao," *Politiko*, August 4, 2018, http://politics.com.ph/china-funded-duterte-opens-biggest-drug-center-in-mindanao/.

Duterte's son was called to testify before a senate inquiry in September 2017 after an opposition senator charged that the son had links to a seized shipment of $125 million worth of narcotics from China interdicted by Philippine customs agents. The son, Paolo Duterte, who was the vice mayor of Davao City, where his father long served as mayor, insisted the charges were "baseless."[26] But in late 2017 the younger Duterte resigned his post citing the fact that opponents had linked him to the drug smuggling case.[27] In the 2019 mid-term elections he was elected as a member of the Philippines House of Representatives.

China's "biggest nightmare is that Duterte dies in office," Custodio says, alluding to Vice President Leni Robredo, a lawyer and former social activist who comes from the opposition Liberal Party. She has condemned Duterte's war on drugs[28] and has said "China's encroachment on Philippine territories is the most serious threat to our country since World War II."[29]

LAWYERING FOR BEIJING IN THE SOUTH CHINA SEA

Despite Duterte's pivot toward China, Beijing has given him anything but an easy ride in the South China Sea. The list of China's continuing encroachment against the Philippines is long and almost nonstop.

During the night of June 9, 2019, a large Chinese fishing trawler collided with a small wooden boat, Gem-Ver 1, carrying 22 Filipino fishers anchored near Reed Bank, some 168 nautical miles off Palawan Island, northeast of Luzon Island. As the fishers struggled to stay afloat for hours in the dark sea, the Chinese ship, potentially a maritime militia vessel,

26. "Philippine President's Son Denies Links to $125-Million Drug Shipment," *Reuters*, September 7, 2017, https://www.reuters.com/article/us-philippines-drugs/philippine-presidents-son-denies-links-to-125-million-drug-shipment-idUSKCN1BIoKA.
27. "Philippines' Duterte's Son Quits as Vice Mayor of Hometown Davao," *Reuters*, December 25, 2017, https://www.reuters.com/news/picture/philippines-dutertes-son-quits-as-vice-m-idUSKBN1EJoI1.
28. "Philippine VP Decries Duterte's Drug War Tactics in Video to U.N.," *Reuters*, March 15, 2017, https://www.reuters.com/article/us-philippines-drugs-robredo/philippine-vp-decries-dutertes-drug-war-tactics-in-video-to-u-n-idUSKBN16MoWM.
29. Cliff Venzon, "Duterte under Pressure to Press South China Sea Claims," *Nikkei Asian Review*, July 12, 2018, https://asia.nikkei.com/Politics/International-Relations/Duterte-under-pressure-to-press-South-China-Sea-claims; Mara Cepeda, "Robredo: China Presence in West PH Sea 'Most Serious External Threat since WWII,'" *Rappler*, June 11, 2018, https://www.rappler.com/nation/204681-leni-robredo-speech-west-philippine-sea-china-militarizationred.

sped off abandoning the struggling fishers. Eventually, a Vietnamese fishing boat operating nearby came and rescued the stranded men.

The incident appeared to mark the first time that a Chinese vessel is known to have rammed a Filipino fishing boat. Similar ramming incidents by Chinese militia vessels had taken place for years against Vietnamese fishers further north around the disputed Paracel Islands.

Defense Secretary Lorenzana on June 12 charged the Chinese vessel with intentionally ramming the Philippine boat near Reed Bank, where China had some years earlier blocked Philippine efforts to explore for oil and gas. "We condemn in the strongest terms the cowardly action of the Chinese fishing vessel and its crew for abandoning the Filipino crew," he said in a statement first reporting the incident.[30]

But Duterte said nothing about the incident for more than a week, even though the Chinese vessel was illegally fishing in Philippine waters and violated international maritime law by abandoning the fishers in distress. Finally, on June 17, Duterte referred to the incident as "a little maritime accident" and said he would need to investigate what happened and give Beijing a chance to explain its position. He added that going to war with China would be the "most stupid thing,"[31] repeating his common theme that Beijing might attack the Philippines if Manila tried to stand up to China.

Duterte's remarks downplaying the incident echoed the comments delivered five days earlier by the Chinese Foreign Ministry spokesman, who called the incident "an ordinary maritime traffic accident."[32]

Then, on July 4, Duterte's third foreign secretary, Teodoro Locsin Jr., said the fishers shared the blame for what happened. They had been asleep and did not know what happened, he said, adding they should have had more lights on their boat to make it easily visible and had a lookout while they slept. However, Locsin added that there was "no question" that

30. Jason Gutierrez, "Philippines Accuses Chinese Vessel of Sinking Fishing Boat in Disputed Waters," *New York Times*, June 12, 2019, https://www.nytimes.com/2019/06/12/world/asia/philippines-china-fishing-boat.html.

31. Alexis Romero, "Duterte on the Sinking: It Was a Little Maritime Incident," *Philippine Star*, June 18, 2019, https://www.philstar.com/headlines/2019/06/18/1927498/duterte-sinking-it-was-little-maritime-accident.

32. Jamie Laude, "Philippine Fishing Boat Was Rammed—Navy Chief," *Philippine Star*, June 15, 2019, https://www.philstar.com/headlines/2019/06/15/1926641/philippine-fishing-boat-was-rammed-navy-chief.

Map 13. The Philippines's claims in the South China Sea

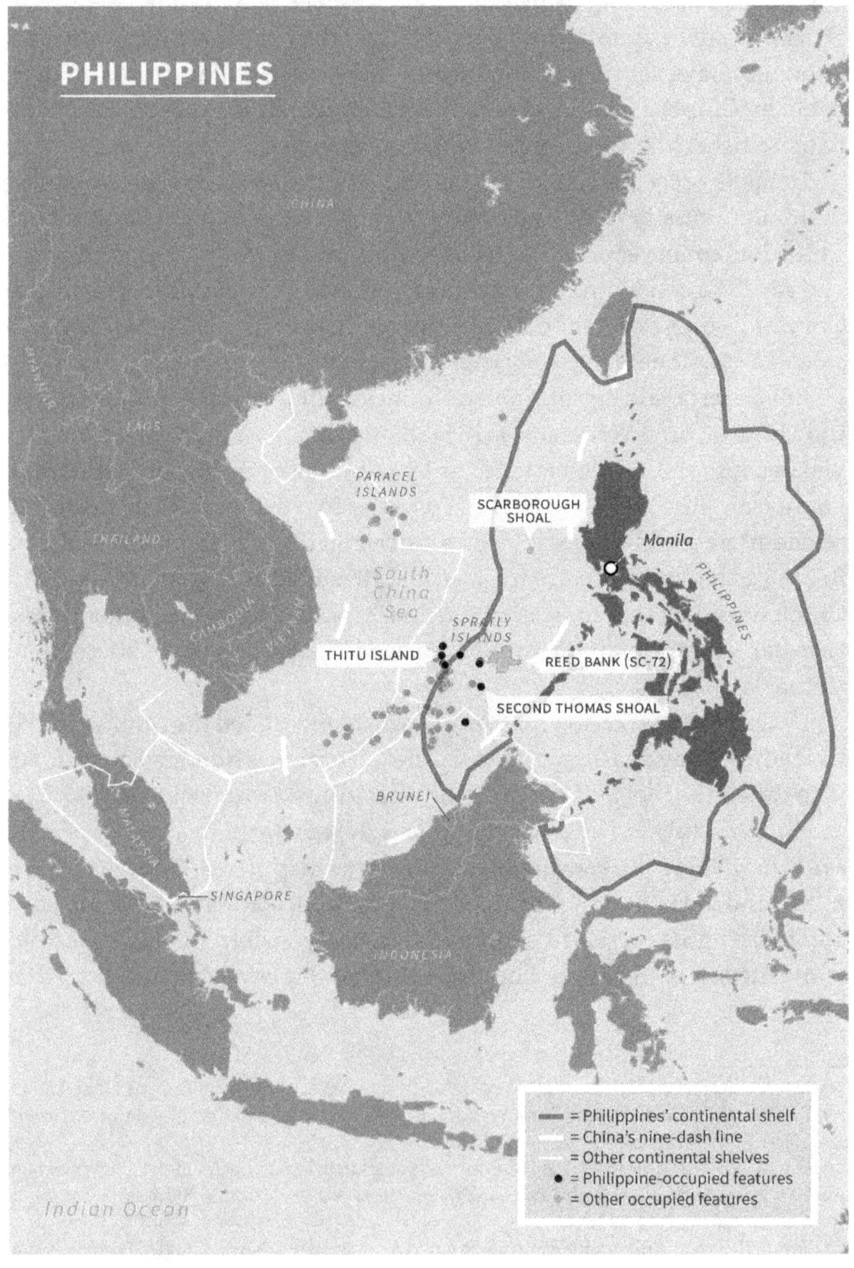

the Chinese vessel had abandoned the fishers in the open sea in the dark, behavior he had earlier denounced as a "felony."[33]

Duterte's top aides, who raised doubts about the fishers' version of events, offered several explanations about why the president was reluctant to challenge China's behavior. His press secretary said on June 27 that Duterte was trying to ensure that China's aid and investment in infrastructure projects continued. "He is protecting the interest of the Filipino people," the press secretary said. "The 'Build, Build, Build' Program is precisely designed to uplift our economy, and necessary to uplift the lives of Filipinos,"[34] referring to Duterte's flagship economic project.

In his State of the Nation Address on July 22, 2019, Duterte said that China was "in possession" of the South China Sea. But the following day his national security adviser revised that to say China was only "in position" in the disputed sea, an apparent reference to the outposts and reclaimed islands complete with military runways and missiles that Beijing controls in the resource-rich waterway.[35]

The Philippine president's response to the fishing vessel incident underscored the extent to which he has accommodated to Beijing's concerns and interests. "The Duterte administration risks replacing a foreign policy perceived as too deferential to U.S. interests with one that is too deferential to Chinese ones," Cook of ISEAS said in an analysis of the fishing boat ramming incident. "This at a time when the unlawful activities of vessels from China (and others) in the West Philippine Sea undermine Philippine territorial integrity."[36]

Duterte generous attitude toward China despite its assertive actions toward the Philippines is jarringly out of step with much of the Philippine population. A poll of Philippine attitudes by Social Weather Survey

---

33. Dona Z. Paxxibugan, "Locsin: Probe Shows PH Crew Share Blame in Recto Bank Hit," *Inquirer.net*, July 4, 2019, https://globalnation.inquirer.net/177468/locsin-probe-shows-ph-crew-share-blame-in-recto-bank-hit.

34. "Duterte Cites Need to Preserve China Relations after Collision," *BusinessWorld*, June 27, 2019, https://www.bworldonline.com/duterte-cites-need-to-preserve-china-relations-after-collision/.

35. Nestor Corrales, "Palace: China Has 'Legal and Constructive Possession' of South China Sea," *Inquirer.net*, July 24, 2019, https://globalnation.inquirer.net/178260/palace-china-has-legal-and-constructive-possession-of-south-china-sea.

36. Malcolm Cook, "The Duterte Administration's China Tensions," *ISEAS Perspective*, no. 62 (2019): 2, https://www.iseas.edu.sg/images/pdf/ISEAS_Perspective_2019_62.pdf.

a few weeks after the boat incident found that China had the lowest trust level among seven foreign nations, including the United States.[37] Fully 59 percent "strongly agree" and another 28 percent "somewhat agree" that the Philippine government should "assert its right to the islands in the West Philippine Sea as stipulated in the 2016 decision of the Permanent Court of Arbitration."[38]

But the boat ramming incident did not take place in isolation. A month earlier, a giant Chinese coast guard vessel, backed by maritime militia boats, showed up off the coast of Malaysia's eastern state of Sarawak and for two weeks harassed the operations of a subsidiary of Royal Dutch Shell, which had an oil rig exploring for oil and gas under contract with Malaysia's state-owned oil and gas company.

On June 16, the same Chinese coast guard vessel, supported by militia boats, moved near Vanguard Bank off the coast of southern Vietnam and tried to interfere with exploration activities of Russian oil firm Rosneft under contract with Vietnam. Looking at the incidents off the Philippines, Malaysia, and Vietnam together, Beijing seemed to send other claimants in the South China Sea a strong signal that it would increasingly use the threat of force to block oil and gas operations and press fishers in neighboring countries to suspend their activities in the South China Sea.

The boat ramming in the Philippines in June 2019 was preceded by scores of Chinese vessels patrolling near Philippine-occupied Thitu Island (known as Pag-asa Island in the Philippines) in the Spratly grouping for at least several months. The island, the second largest natural landmass in the Spratlys, lies about 280 nautical miles off the Philippine coast and was occupied by Philippine forces in 1974.

Between January and March, the Philippine military spotted 275 Chinese vessels near Pag-asa. Then, over two days in July, Philippine "military intelligence" counted 113 Chinese vessels "swarming" around the island. This prompted Manila to fire off a diplomatic protest note to China,

37. "Second Quarter 2019 Social Weather Survey: Trust in China Falls to Net −24 (Poor)," Social Weather Stations, July 19, 2019, https://www.sws.org.ph/swsmain/artcldisppage/?artcsyscode=ART-20190719100415.

38. "Second Quarter 2019 Social Weather Survey: 87% of Adult Filipinos Believe Government Should Assert Its Right to Disputed Islands in the West Philippine Sea," Social Weather Station, July 12, 2019, https://www.sws.org.ph/swsmain/artcldisppage/?artcsyscode=ART-20190712122047.

a much stronger response than the Philippine government had to the boat ramming incident near Reed Bank a month earlier.[39]

Pag-asa is the one island in the South China Sea occupied by the Philippines about which Duterte drops his normal placating tone toward Beijing and threatens to send Filipino troops to protect it against Chinese intervention. "This is not a warning, this is a word of advice to my friend [China]," Duterte said during a visit to Palawan Island in April 2019. "I will not plead or beg but I'm just telling you [to] lay off the Pag-asa," the president said. "If you mess with that, it's a different story. I will tell my soldiers 'Prepare for suicide missions.'"

Two years earlier, Duterte threatened to visit Pag-asa, but he canceled his trip after China protested. In the end, he sent his defense secretary instead. *Rappler* has reported that Pag-asa is "special" to Duterte in ways that some other features China has captured from the Philippines like Scarborough Shoal are not, because it has about 100 civilian Filipinos living on it.[40]

Duterte's dramatic overtures toward China after he took office did little to slow Beijing's assertive behavior in the South China Sea. After his first trip to China as president in late 2016, his national security adviser announced that the two sides had reached a "friendly" understanding that Philippine fishers, who had been blocked from fishing in Scarborough Shoal since China seized the feature, would again have the right to fish in the shoal.[41] But satellite photos released a week after the trip showed that at least 17 Philippine fishing boats were still barred by a Chinese coast guard vessel[42] anchored just inside the mouth of the lagoon.[43]

39. "Philippines Protests 'Swarming' of More than 100 Chinese Vessels," *Aljazeera*, July 31, 2019, https://www.aljazeera.com/news/2019/07/philippines-protests-swarming-100-chinese-vessels-190731041056198.html.

40. Pia Ranada, "Dissecting Duterte's Amped-Up West Philippine Sea Rhetoric," *Rappler*, April 20, 2019, https://www.rappler.com/newsbreak/in-depth/229034-dissecting-duterte-amped-up-west-philippine-sea-rhetoric.

41. Agence France-Presse, "China, Philippines in 'Friendly' Understanding on Shoal—Official," *Rappler*, October 31, 2016, https://www.rappler.com/nation/150893-china-philippines-friendly-understanding-scarborough-shoal.

42. Bloomberg, "Philippine President Duterte Says China's Xi Jinping Won't Allow His Removal from Office," *Straits Times*, May 16, 2018, https://www.straitstimes.com/asia/se-asia/philippine-president-duterte-says-chinas-xi-jinping-wont-allow-his-removal-from-office?&utm_source=google_gmail&utm_medium=social-media&utm_campaign=addtoanymedium=social-media&utm_campaign=addtoany.

43. Asia Maritime Transparency Initiative, "Updated: Imagery Suggests Philippine Fishermen Still Not Entering Scarborough Shoal," Center for Strategic and International Studies, October 26, 2017, https://amti.csis.org/china-scarborough-fishing/.

In March 2017, the mayor of China's Sansha City, the administrative base for the features Beijing controls in the South China Sea, unilaterally announced that the Chinese would begin preparatory work to build an environmental monitoring station on Scarborough Shoal, 140 nautical miles west of the Philippines' Luzon Island. The previous month a Philippine minister had said that Xi had promised Duterte that China would not build any structures on the outcrop still claimed by the Philippines.[44]

The blunt-speaking Duterte made clear his options in blocking the monitoring station were limited. "What do you want me to do? Declare war against China? I can't. We will lose all our military and our policemen tomorrow and we [will be] a destroyed nation."[45]

A week earlier, Lorenzana, the defense secretary, said that a Chinese survey ship had plied the area around Benham Rise (renamed Philippine Rise by Duterte), an underwater plateau that belongs to the Philippines, for three months the previous year. The 32-million-acre area, located east of Luzon and not part of the South China Sea, is believed to be rich in minerals and possibly natural gas.[46]

Not long after Manila learned that China had gained approval from the International Hydrographic Organization to rename five undersea features at Benham Rise. This led to a Philippine Senate hearing in February 2018 and prompted Duterte's office to announce that it would not recognize China's names of the features, all five of which are within 200 nautical miles of the coast of Luzon.[47]

On May 11, 2018, a Chinese helicopter harassed a civilian vessel contracted by the Philippine navy at Second Thomas Shoal (Ayungin Shoal in the Philippines) in the Spratly Islands as it sought to resupply a handful

---

44. "China to Build on Disputed Shoal in South China Sea," *Reuters*, March 17, 2017, http://news.trust.org/item/20170317095411-h903t.

45. Agence France-Presse, "PH 'Can't Stop' China from Building on Scarborough," *Rappler*, March 19, 2017, https://www.rappler.com/nation/164634-duterte-philippines-cannot-stop-china-building-scarborough-shoal.

46. Carmela Fonbuena, "Lorenzana: China Showed Interest in PH's Benham Rise," *Rappler*, March 9, 2017, https://www.rappler.com/nation/163729-lorenzana-china-survey-ship-philippines-benham-rise.

47. Pia Ranada, "Philippines Rejects Chinese Names for Benham Rise Features," *Rappler*, February 14, 2018, https://www.rappler.com/nation/196018-philippines-rejects-chinese-names-benham-rise-features.

of Philippine marines living aboard the *Sierra Madre*, a rusting World War II ship beached on the shoal. Duterte's then foreign secretary Cayetano labeled China's activity an "incident" rather than harassment but said Manila had issued a complaint to Beijing. The shoal is an underwater reef about 120 nautical miles northwest of the Philippine island of Palawan.[48]

On May 19, 2018, China's official *People's Daily* uploaded a video to Twitter showing several Chinese bombers, including the sophisticated H-6K, landing on and taking off from Woody Island, China's largest base in the Paracel grouping in the South China Sea.[49] The Paracels are not claimed by the Philippines but most of the country, its capital, and all five Philippine bases earmarked for development under a 2014 U.S.-Philippines defense agreement would be within range of the bombers on Woody Island.[50]

In addition, China's coast guard has reportedly been seizing fish from Filipino fishers near Scarborough Shoal since early 2018. In June *GMA News* obtained video of officials in a Chinese coast guard speedboat boarding a Philippine vessel to take the fishers' catch.[51] In some instances, coast guard officials compensate the fishers with bottled water, cigarettes, or packages of stale noodles. Duterte referred to this unbalanced exchange as "barter."[52]

Chinese fishers also were harvesting protected giant clams and destroyed reefs inside Scarborough Shoal, according to a report by *ABS-CBN News*.[53] This prompted former foreign secretary Albert del Rosario and former ombudsman Conchita Carpio Morales to raise concerns about

48. Paterno Esmaquel II, "China Chopper Harasses PH Rubber Boat in Ayungin Shoal—Lawmaker," *Rappler*, May 30, 2018, https://www.rappler.com/nation/203720-chinese-helicopter-harass-rubber-boat-ayungin-shoal-spratly-islands.

49. Roberto, "Timeline: Philippines-China Relationship under Duterte."

50. Asia Maritime Transparency Initiative, "China Lands First Bomber on South China Sea Island," Center for Strategic and International Studies, May 18, 2018, https://amti.csis.org/china-lands-first-bomber-south-china-sea-island/.

51. Carmela Fonbuena, "Video Captures China Coast Guard Taking PH Fishermen's Catch," *Rappler*, June 8, 2018, https://www.rappler.com/nation/204383-china-coast-guard-taking-filipino-fishermen-catch-scarborough-shoal-video.

52. Pia Ranada, "Duterte: China Taking of PH Fisherman's Catch 'Not Outright Seizure,'" *Rappler*, June 18, 2018, https://www.rappler.com/nation/205225-duterte-china-filipino-fishermen-catch-panatag-shoal-not-outright-seizure.

53. Chiara Zambrano, "Chinese Harvesting Giant Clams in Scarborough Shoal," *ABS-CBN News*, April 15, 2019, https://news.abs-cbn.com/news/04/15/19/exclusive-chinese-harvesting-giant-clams-in-scarborough-shoal.

these Chinese activities in disputed waters before the International Criminal Court.[54]

"Everything China has been doing is making [the 2016 arbitral tribunal] ruling irrelevant," says Jay Batongbacal, law professor at the University of the Philippines and director of the university's Institute of Maritime Affairs and Law of the Sea. To many analysts it appeared that Duterte's foreign policy had effectively ended efforts in Southeast Asia to stand up to China and handed the South China Sea to Beijing, although others argue that doomsday verdict is still premature.

CHINA SNARES SCARBOROUGH SHOAL

Duterte's predecessor Aquino had also come into office seeking to bolster ties with Beijing and court Chinese investors. Manila boycotted the Nobel Peace Prize ceremony in Norway for Chinese dissident Liu Xiaobu in late 2011 to avoid irritating Beijing. A few months later, Aquino agreed to extradite to China 14 Taiwanese accused by Beijing of operating electronic fraud operations against Chinese nationals.[55]

But Philippine-China relations were severely strained two months after Aquino assumed the presidency in mid-2010, when a former Manila policeman hijacked a bus carrying 21 tourists from Hong Kong. The bungled rescue effort, which was covered live on television, resulted in the deaths of eight tourists. The Hong Kong government responded by urging travelers to avoid the Philippines.[56]

In early 2011, Manila accused Chinese vessels of "bullying" Philippines ships and firing on unarmed fishers in the South China Sea. The Philippines responded by changing the name of the Philippine part of the disputed sea to the West Philippine Sea. Soon after, China executed three Filipinos on drug charges despite the government's appeal for clemency.[57]

54. Arianne Merez, "China's Harvest of Giant Clams an 'Affront' to Philippines," *ABS-CBN News*, April 16, 2019, https://news.abs-cbn.com/news/04/16/19/chinas-harvest-of-giant-clams-an-affront-to-philippines-palace.

55. De Castro, "The Duterte Administration's Appeasement Policy on China," 5.

56. Greg Hughes and Kevin Voigt, "Hong Kong Angry, Sad at Handling of Manila Siege," *CNN*, August 24, 2010, http://www.cnn.com/2010/WORLD/asiapcf/08/23/hongkong.hostages.reaction/index.html.

57. Xiaoni Chen, "Aquino Seeks Chinese Business, Improved Relations," *CNN*, August 31, 2011, http://www.cnn.com/2011/WORLD/asiapcf/08/31/philippines.china/index.html.

In March 2011, two Chinese patrol ships harassed a Philippine Department of Energy oil exploration vessel at Reed Bank, prompting Manila to file an official protest.[58] By the time, a Philippine surveillance plane and patrol ships arrived a few hours later, the Chinese vessels had left. So had the survey ship, the *Veritas Voyager*.

Foreign and domestic oil companies had conducted exploration activities at Reed Bank since the mid-1970s. Earlier survey results had suggested that the area had about 96 billion cubic meters of natural gas and 440 million barrels of oil, roughly equivalent to the Philippines' proven gas reserves.

The incident marked a turning point for the Aquino administration. The president hardened his position on sovereignty rights, pursued closer relations with the United States, and stepped up efforts to upgrade the country's poorly equipped military.[59]

Beijing had begun stepping up its assertiveness in the South China Sea in 2009, the year it submitted its nine-dash-line claim to a United Nations body for the first time and claimed that most of the sea its islands had belonged to China for centuries. The Reed Bank incident was followed by China's 2012 seizure of Scarborough Shoal, about 120 nautical miles west of the former U.S. naval base at Subic Bay, which marked a dramatic deterioration in China-Philippines relations.

The incident began on April 8, 2012, when a Philippine aircraft spotted a cluster of Chinese fishers anchored in the shoal, over which Manila exercised control.[60] The Philippine navy dispatched its largest vessel, the BRP *Gregorio del Pilar*, which had recently been acquired from the United States, to disrupt what Manila considered to be illegal fishing.

Two days later, armed Philippine sailors boarded the Chinese fishing vessels, prompting them to issue a distress call to Chinese authorities.

---

58. Jaime Laude, "China Gunboats Harass RP Vessel," *Philippine Star*, March 4, 2011, https://www.philstar.com/headlines/2011/03/04/662502/china-gunboats-harass-rp-vessel.

59. Randy Fabi and Manuel Mogato, "Insight—Conflict Looms in South China Sea Oil Rush," *Reuters*, February 27, 2012, https://www.reuters.com/article/oukwd-uk-china-spratlys-philippines-idAFTRE81R03820120228; De Castro, "The Duterte Administration's Appeasement Policy on China," 6.

60. This scenario of events borrows heavily from Michael Green, Kathleen Hicks, Zack Cooper, John Schaus, and Jake Douglas, "Counter-Coercion Series: Scarborough Shoal Standoff," Center for Strategic and International Studies—Asia Maritime Transparency Initiative, https://amti.csis.org/counter-co-scarborough-standoff/.

Two unarmed Chinese marine surveillance vessels were patrolling nearby and quickly took up positions near the mouth of the shoal's lagoon. The Philippines attempted to demilitarize the situation on April 12 by moving in a vessel from the Bureau of Fisheries and Aquatic Resources to replace the navy frigate.

The following day, as the two sides promised diplomatic talks, two Chinese cutters escorted Chinese fishing boats out of the shoal, leaving each nation with one vessel inside the shoal. Negotiations quickly broke down as Manila rejected a Chinese request that their fishers be able to leave with their fish catches.

On April 17, Manila changed its strategy and announced that it would pursue arbitration of the dispute. The Philippines appealed to the ASEAN grouping to "take a stand." China rejected the effort and charged that Manila was violating the agreement to resolve the standoff bilaterally.

Chinese media on April 23 announced that Beijing had withdrawn two vessels to demonstrate that it was ready to resolve the dispute through dialogue. Manila rejected the overture and instead sent a second fisheries boat into the lagoon. Three days later, the Philippines said it would seek to involve the United States.

On April 30, Philippine and U.S. officials met in Washington to discuss the incident and American officials pledged to help the Philippines boost their maritime capacity. U.S. officials did not, however, make clear if the U.S.-Philippines Defense Treaty covered the South China Sea or pledge to intervene in the dispute.

China began employing economic tools on May 3, when it blocked Philippine fruit from entering the country, citing the need for quality control tests. Beijing also increased its forces around the shoal. Five cutters and more than a dozen fishing boats faced two Philippine vessels by May 21. Aquino appointed a Philippine senator to serve as a back-channel negotiator with Chinese vice foreign minister Fu Ying. The senator met her and other Chinese officials roughly 16 times.

Two months later, on June 15, Manila pulled its two vessels out of Scarborough Shoal, citing a coming typhoon. But two days later, the Philippines protested that China had not left as was expected under a joint "agreement."

According to one version of what happened, a senior U.S. State Department official had negotiated with Fu Ying an immediate withdrawal by both sides in early June. In the end, the Philippines followed through on the commitment, but China kept its ships at the shoal. A second version has it that the Chinese official only agreed to pass the suggestion along to her bosses in Beijing and that the two sides never reached an agreement.

Regardless, Philippine officials never succeeded in restoring Manila's control of the shoal. Once it was clear that the Chinese ships were not leaving, the Philippines decided not to resume the standoff, resulting in the de facto transfer of control of the shoal to China. By July, China was expelling Filipino fishers from Scarborough.

China's seizure of the shoal marked a significant disruption to stability in the South China Sea. Beijing could be forgiven for concluding that its hardball tactics to intimidate the Philippines had worked. At the same time, China's muscle flexing rallied the often-fractious Philippine population to unite against Beijing's bullying and the next year take the diplomatic step to challenge the legality of its neighbor's move, which caught China off guard.[61] By 2014, the standoff had pushed Manila closer to Washington and the Philippines agreed to the Enhanced Defense Cooperation Agreement, which was intended to allow the United States to rotate troops through several agreed-on Philippine bases.

In early 2013, the Philippines filed its case before the international tribunal. China rejected Manila's case, charging that the claim "carried unacceptable allegations against Beijing."[62]

Not long after the Philippines filed the case, China began large-scale dredging operations around seven reefs it controls in the Spratly Islands, including three of which—Fiery Cross, Subi, and Mischief Reefs—are claimed by the Philippines. Over the next few years, China added some 3,000 acres to these features. Beijing justified its move by charging that the other disputing nations, the Philippines, Malaysia, Vietnam, and Taiwan, had also expanded features they occupied. But China created in a 20-month period 17 times as much land as the others had built up over four decades, the Pentagon reported in 2015.[63]

---

61. Aileen S. Baviera, "The Domestic Meditations of China's Influence in the Philippines," in *Rising China's Influence in Developing Asia*, ed. Evelyn Goh (Oxford University Press, 2016), 125–126.
62. "Timeline: The Philippines-China Maritime Dispute," *Rappler*, July 12, 2016, https://www.rappler.com/world/regions/asia-pacific/139392-timeline-west-philippine-sea-dispute.
63. "China's Land Reclamation in South China Sea Grows: Pentagon Report," *Reuters*, August 21, 2015, https://www.reuters.com/article/us-southchinasea-china-pentagon-idUSKCN0QQ0S920150821.

SHOW ME THE MONEY

One of the most visible transformations in Manila since Duterte mounted his Beijing charm offensive in 2016 is the surge of new arrivals from China. In Makati, the city's financial hub, new dumpling restaurants, shops, money changers, and payment centers targeted at Chinese customers are opening. Property prices are soaring and reshaping the real estate market.

Some estimates suggest that roughly 200,000 migrants, mostly from China, have descended on Manila since 2016, but Philippine officials do not know or will not disclose the official numbers. In a Philippine Senate hearing in late 2018, Senator Joel Villanueva scolded officials from the Bureau of Immigration and Department of Labor and Employment. "It's glaring," he said. "Your records show you are issuing few alien employment permits but there's a flood [of Chinese workers] and from their numbers, it's clear there are illegal workers."

Recent Chinese migrants are a sensitive topic among many Filipinos because they create competition for jobs and housing. "The Chinese have invaded our islands in the West Philippine Sea and now they're in my condo," one Manila resident told the *South China Morning Post*. "It's a home invasion." Senator Villanueva said at his hearing that he "thought I was born in China" because of the large numbers of Chinese in the gigantic Mall of Asia near Manila Bay.[64]

Many of the new arrivals have come to staff the more than 50 online gaming operators, or POGOs, that have received licenses since Duterte came to power. These POGOs are aimed at clients in China where online gaming is illegal. Many of the gaming tables are staffed by Filipino women, who are viewed online, but the bets are placed offshore—mostly in China—requiring the gaming firms to employ Chinese speakers to market the gambling products and process payments to punters overseas.[65]

China bans gambling and Philippine law forbids targeting a country were gambling is illegal, but both governments look the other way as the industry thrives. Revenue for online gaming catering to players in China

64. Raissa Robles, "Chinese Workers 'Flood' the Philippines, yet Duterte's Officials 'Don't Know' How Many There Are," *South China Morning Post*, December 22, 2018, https://www.scmp.com/week-asia/economics/article/2178749/chinese-workers-flood-philippines-yet-dutertes-officials-dont.

65. "Chinese Money Triggers a Dizzying Rally in Manila Property," *Bloomberg*.

was expected to drive gambling revenue in the Philippines up to $4.1 billion in 2019, compared to just over $1 billion three years earlier, according to Philippine government estimates. The annual licensing fees reached $140 million the previous year, up more than 10 times the figure three years earlier, and represent the third largest source of government revenue after taxes and customs.[66]

Between 2016 and 2018, some 335,800 working visas and special work permits were issued to Chinese, which is over half of the total number of permits issued to foreigners.[67] International companies and schools complain that they have a hard time bringing foreign bankers and teachers into the Philippines, while online gaming firms seem to find it relatively easy to bring in Chinese nationals on a short-term basis.

The online gaming operations are creating jobs and generating income for the economy, but they are also bolstering prostitution and conflicts between Filipinos and Chinese. In July 2019, the government established a task force to clamp down on tax avoidance by the gaming companies. A senior official of the Bureau of Internal Revenue told *The Financial Times* that the online gaming operations provide jobs for over 100,000 Chinese citizens who owe about $39 million in taxes on their wages each month. But collecting this money could be difficult. Most of the gaming firms are headquartered offshore and many of the workers are undocumented.

Some of the Chinese migrant workers tell journalists that they are subjected to "slave-like conditions" in the Philippines. They report that they are forced to work 12-hour shifts seven days a week and only get off one day a month. In the case of gaming operator Oriental Group, the workers said the company had taken their passports and housed up to 12 people in a single dormitory room.[68]

The surge of new arrivals is firing up the Philippine property market in parts of Manila and attracting Chinese real estate developers. Qiang Huang, a realtor from the Chinese city of Hefei, came to Manila to gamble

---

66. David Pierson and Alice Su, "China Has a New casino: The Philippines," *Los Angeles Times*, July 1, 2019, https://www.latimes.com/world/asia/la-fg-philippines-china-gambling-20190701-story.html.

67. Cliff Venzon, "Duterte under the Gun over Chinese Influx into Philippines," *Nikkei Asian Review*, March 5, 2019, https://asia.nikkei.com/Spotlight/Asia-Insight/Duterte-under-the-gun-over-Chinese-influx-into-Philippines.

68. Ella McDonald, "Philippines Gambling Industry Treating Migrants 'Like Slaves,'" *Legal Gambling and the Law*, August 16, 2018, https://www.legalgamblingandthelaw.com/news/philippines-gambling-industry-treating-chinese-migrants-like-slaves/.

at the Solaire Resort and Casino in 2017 and recognized the opportunities. He decided to open a showroom in Manila to attract Chinese real estate projects to begin marketing apartments in two sites. "I chose an area with a booming gambling business, as properties there have the largest potential to appreciate," he told Bloomberg.[69]

Chinese investment in real estate rose to over $190 million in the first 10 months of 2018 compared to only $13 million in 2017, according to real estate firm Santos Knight Frank. Prices in the Manila Bay area rose 65 percent in 2018 compared to about 15 percent in some business districts, the company said.[70]

Gaming operators are also pushing up commercial demand at a time when the footprint of outsourcing companies is shrinking. Leechiu Property Consultants estimates that offshore gaming outfits tripled their demand for office space to 20 percent of the total in 2017 while outsourcing firms reduced their share to 46 percent.[71]

Ayala Land, the Philippines' largest real estate firm, said that its international sales, many to Chinese, accounted for 34 percent of the companies $2.2 billion in real estate sales in 2018. SM Prime Holdings said that Chinese buyers comprised 60 percent of the international sales at one of its properties and 50 percent of another in 2018, which is up from only 10 percent the previous year.[72]

The Philippines has witnessed some economic benefit from China in other areas like trade, tourism, and foreign investment since Duterte announced that he was setting aside the South China Sea ruling. But beyond effusive Chinese rhetoric, almost none of the $24 billion that Beijing pledged during Duterte's visit in late 2016 has translated into the big-ticket infrastructure projects the then new president was looking for. The slow takeoff is provoking anxiety in some quarters that Duterte undercut the nation's sovereignty with not much to show for his efforts.

---

69. "Chinese Money Triggers a Dizzying Rally in Manila Property," *Bloomberg*, May 3, 2018, https://www.bloomberg.com/news/articles/2018-05-03/in-china-s-new-gambling-hot-spot-property-prices-are-on-a-tear.
70. Jessica Fenol, "Influx of Chinese Investments 'Encouraging' for PH Property Market: Consultant," *ABS-CBN News*, January 30, 2019, https://news.abs-cbn.com/business/01/30/19/influx-of-chinese-investments-encouraging-for-ph-property-market-consultant.
71. "Chinese Money Triggers a Dizzying Rally in Manila Property," *Bloomberg*.
72. Alvin Camba, "The Winners and Losers in Duterte's China Play," *South China Morning Post*, September 30, 2018, https://www.scmp.com/week-asia/economics/article/2166070/winners-and-losers-dutertes-china-play.

China's exports to the Philippines jumped significantly between 2015 and 2017, but Philippine exports to China had only a surprisingly minor uptick. Foreign investment from Chinese firms in 2018 totaled $198.7 million, slightly behind Japan but up significantly from 2017 when it reached only $28.8 million,[73] leaving China's cumulative investment behind many of its competitors like Japan, Taiwan, Singapore, and the United States.[74] Chinese bilateral aid resumed but reached less than $100 million in 2017.

During his visit to Beijing in 2016, Duterte inked 27 deals, procuring pledges that China would give investments worth $15 billion in infrastructure schemes for railroad, port, energy, and mining projects. Beijing committed another $9 billion in soft loans, including a $3 billion credit line from the Bank of China.[75] The projects ranged from a railway project between the former U.S. bases at Clark and Subic to a biomass energy project in North and South Negros, a banana plantation project, and a cable manufacturing facility.[76]

One controversial Chinese firm whose subsidiaries bagged several memorandums of understanding (MOUs) for infrastructure projects with Philippine partners during Duterte's 2016 Beijing visit was state-owned China Communications Construction Company (CCCC), one of biggest investors in China's BRI. One of its subsidiaries, Tianjin Dredging Company, operated the giant barges digging sand from the seabed of the South China Sea and piling it on coral atolls including Mischief, Subi, and Fiery Cross Reefs claimed by the Philippines and Vietnam.[77] Earlier CCCC had been blacklisted by the World Bank in 2009 for fraudulent bidding

73. "Net Foreign Direct Investment Flows," Bangko Sentral Ng Pilipinas, http://www.bsp.gov.ph/statistics/spei_pub/Table%2010.pdf (accessed August 19, 2019).

74. "Philippines (The): Foreign Investment," Santander Bank Trade Portal, last updated March 2019, https://en.portal.santandertrade.com/establish-overseas/philippines/foreign-investment.

75. Jason Koutsoukis and Cecilia Yap, "China Hasn't Delivered on Its $24 Billion Philippines Promise," *Bloomberg*, July 25, 2018, https://www.bloomberg.com/news/articles/2018-07-25/china-s-24-billion-promise-to-duterte-still-hasn-t-materialized.

76. Amy R. Remo, "Itemized List of PH Projects Covered by China's $15-B Investment Pledges to Duterte," *Philippine Inquirer*, October 23, 2016, https://business.inquirer.net/217269/itemized-list-ph-projects-covered-chinas-15-b-investment-pledges-duterte#ixzz4XabVCPwQ.

77. Laura Zhou, "Chinese Island-Building Firm Wins Contract with South China Sea Rival Claimant, the Philippines," *South China Morning Post*, October 26, 2016, https://www.scmp.com/news/china/diplomacy-defence/article/2040256/chinese-firm-helped-build-islands-disputed-area-south.

practices on a highway project in the Philippines.[78] The ban was lifted in January 2017.[79]

But most of the preliminary deals signed by CCCC's subsidiaries unraveled over the ensuing months. CCCC's dredging operation signed an MOU to implement an almost 500-acre land reclamation project in the Davao harbor to build new government offices, port terminals, factories, and houses.[80] Davao mayor Sara Duterte-Carpio terminated the project signed by her father some months later after reviewing its social and environmental impact.[81]

Another CCCC-linked firm, China Road and Bridge Corporation, signed an MOU with a Philippine firm to develop a segment of the Metro Manila Bus Rapid Transit project.[82] The Chinese corporation withdrew from the rapid transit project after the Philippine government guidelines were released.[83]

Since Duterte's trip, Beijing has completed only one $62 million loan contract to build an irrigation scheme north of the capital. This loan attracted public criticism because it carried interest of 2 percent and will mature in 20 years. In contrast, Japanese loans charge between 0.25 percent to 0.75 percent interest.[84]

China has also provided $73 million in no-interest loans for four bridges. Considerable controversy has surrounded a proposed $91 million friendship bridge intended to ease traffic in the Chinatown area of Binondo; this project has repeatedly been delayed. A prominent leader of

---

78. Sheridan Prasso, "A Chinese Company Reshaping the World Leaves a Troubled Trail," *Bloomberg*, September 18, 2018, https://www.bloomberg.com/news/features/2018-09-19/a-chinese-company-reshaping-the-world-leaves-a-troubled-trail.
79. "Are 'Blacklisted' Chinese Firms on Board Duterte's Infra Projects?," *ABS-CBN*, April 24, 2017, https://news.abs-cbn.com/business/04/24/17/are-blacklisted-chinese-firms-on-board-dutertes-infra-projects.
80. "China's CCCC to Build Artificial Islands for Duterte-Backed Scheme in Philippines," *Global Construction Review*, October 27, 2016, http://www.globalconstructionreview.com/news/chinas-cccc-build-artifi7cial-isla7nds-dut7erte/.
81. Ace June Rell S. Perez, "Davao City Backs Out of Mega Harbour Project," *SunStar*, July 25, 2017, https://www.sunstar.com.ph/article/155127.
82. Nikko Dizon, "Chinese Company Banned by World Bank Bags PH Infrastructure Project," *Philippine Inquirer*, October 26, 2016, https://business.inquirer.net/217467/chinese-company-banned-by-world-bank-bags-ph-infrastructure-project.
83. "Are 'Blacklisted' Chinese Firms on Board Duterte's Infra Projects?," *ABS-CBN*.
84. Ralf Rivas, "Philippines 'Extra Careful' with China Loans—NEDA," *Rappler*, June 27, 2018, https://www.rappler.com/business/205903-philippine-government-extra-careful-china-loans-neda.

Kaisa, a Filipino Chinese civil society group, told the *South China Morning Post* that "we need that bridge like we need a hole in the head." She and others raised questions about whether it would ease traffic flow because there are already two other bridges within 165 yards of the new bridge. She also warned that it could damage buildings along the narrow streets of the walled city of Intramuros, a Philippine heritage site.[85]

Other projects have struggled mightily to get liftoff. Power China Guizhou signed an agreement to build a $1 billion, 300-megawatt hydropower plan with Greenergy Development Corporation on the southern island of Mindanao. But Greenergy had trouble getting funds from shareholders because of uncertainty related to the Bangsamoro Organic Law that would provide considerable autonomy to the Muslim areas of Mindanao, according to Alvin Camba, a nonresident fellow at the Alberto Del Rosario Institute in Manila who focuses on Chinese investment.[86]

Baiyin Nonferrous Group signed an agreement in October 2016 with Global Ferronickel, one of the Philippines biggest nickel-mining firms, to build a $700 million stainless steel plant. But the project has been kept in the deep freeze because the government imposed a ban on new mining projects soon after Duterte took office.[87]

Expectation of massive largesse on infrastructure projects is one reason Duterte cited in putting the arbitral ruling on the back burner. Still, Philippine citizens could be forgiven for wondering why both Beijing and Duterte are not moving heaven and earth to get a few of these signature ventures up to demonstrate the benefits of rebalancing to China's camp.

A raft of factors seems to be slowing these schemes down. Senior Philippine officials says that the experiences of other countries in accepting Chinese loans for infrastructure has made Manila prudent. "Given the various experiences already felt by other countries that dealt with China, we are even more cautious, we are extra careful in having projects funded

85. Raissa Robles, "'We Need It Like We Need a Hole in Our Head': Chinese Friendship Bridge in Manila Not So Popular with the Locals," *South China Morning Post*, January 18, 2018, https://www.scmp.com/news/asia/southeast-asia/article/2129448/we-need-it-we-need-hole-our-head-chinese-friendship-bridge.

86. Alvin Camba, "What Happened to the Billions China Pledged the Philippines? Not What You Think," *South China Morning Post*, August 5, 2018, https://www.scmp.com/week-asia/business/article/2158237/what-happened-billions-china-pledged-philippines-not-what-you.

87. Koutsoukis and Yap, "China Hasn't Delivered on Its $24 Billion Philippines Promise."

by China," Ernesto Pernia, the economic planning secretary, said at a briefing for journalists in mid-2018.[88]

Beijing has felt compelled to reassure the Philippines that it will not allow the country to descend into the debt trap that has plagued some recipients of Chinese loans. "China's loans to finance infrastructure projects will not make the Philippines fall into a debt trap," Ambassador Zhao told participants at the groundbreaking for two bridges in Manila in 2018. "We will do our utmost to prove that President Duterte's independent foreign policy, particularly friendly and cooperative policy toward China, will produce more tangible benefits to the people of the Philippines."[89]

"Big infrastructure projects [in the Philippines] always get bogged down," says Baviera, the Chinese studies professor at the University of the Philippines, with "the Finance Department and the economic planning agency exercising due diligence on projects."

"Duterte doesn't give orders to fast-track Chinese projects," says an official working in the president's office. "His instructions are to be nice to the Chinese, but don't give in," he says, suggesting that Duterte does not want officials to bend the country's regulations to accommodate Chinese investors. The official said it is worth noting that the government approved a $7 billion Manila subway project to be built with Japanese financing, rather than with Chinese loans, to help relieve some of the gridlock in this megacity of 13 million.[90]

Some Chinese projects have run into funding problems; others were found not to be viable or bumped into changing Philippine regulations and the country's limited capacity, said Camba of the Alberto Del Rosario Institute. He pointed out that in August 2018, Philippine government data showed that Chinese aid projects were making some progress, with two contracts signed, four approved, and another 14 in the pipeline. Camba wrote that MOUs for foreign investment and aid are often "cancelled,

88. "Philippines Says Cautious on Infrastructure Loans from China," *Reuters*, June 27, 2018, https://www.reuters.com/article/philippines-china-loans/philippines-says-cautious-on-infrastructure-loans-from-china-idUSL4N1TT3J9.

89. "China Won't Allow Philippines to Fall into a 'Debt Trap': Envoy," *Reuters*, July 17, 2018, https://www.reuters.com/article/uk-philippines-china-loans/china-wont-allow-philippines-to-fall-into-a-debt-trap-envoy-idUSKBN1K717W.

90. Mikhail Flores, "Japan-Backed Manila Subway Project Gets Green Light," *Nikkei Asian Review*, September 13, 2017, https://asia.nikkei.com/Politics/Japan-backed-Manila-subway-project-gets-green-light2.

modified, or delayed after the initial signing process—and this is not unique to China."[91]

Others speculate that China could be intentionally slow in rolling out its projects. Duterte swung the country's policy toward Beijing without making any demands up front, so the "deal is already done" in Beijing's eyes, argues Cook, the Philippines expert at ISEAS Singapore. A Philippine national security official adds: "China is holding back [in its investment and aid in the Philippines]. It knows Duterte will only be here for six years."

One thing that concerns Filipinos is the terms of the projects, including the interest rates for loans and the repayment terms, which have not been made public, much like Chinese projects in neighboring countries. "How much will the loans from China cost? 2 percent? 3 percent?" asks a former national security adviser. "From Japan, loans cost from 0.25 to 0.75 percent. China loans are much more expensive."

"Other factors are the price [of equipment], quality, and the risk of renminbi versus yen [loans]," he says. "And what about the issue of Chinese workers?" he asks, referring to China's demand that Chinese contractors and workers play key roles on the projects that Beijing funds.

Despite all the hype about China's largesse, Japan is providing about $8.8 billion to fund nine infrastructure projects, including a high-speed rail link from Manila to the former U.S. base at Clark in central Luzon, a flood management project in southern Luzon, and an irrigation project in Mindanao.[92]

Still, Chinese businesses were the most successful in snaring appointments with Duterte during his first two years in office, despite their relatively low investment numbers. Of the 32 meetings with business leaders or groups, 14 were with Chinese, 13 with Filipinos, 3 with Americans, and 2 with Japanese, according to tabulations by *Rappler* news network.[93]

---

91. Camba, "What Happened to the Billions China Pledged the Philippines? Not What You Think."

92. Flores, "Japan-Backed Manila Subway Project Gets Green Light."

93. Pia Ranada, "Chinese Businessmen Flock to Duterte's Malacañang," *Rappler*, June 2, 2018, https://www.rappler.com/newsbreak/in-depth/203898-duterte-chinese-businessmen-meetings-malacanang.

CHINA TELECOM HOOKS UP WITH CHINESE-FILIPINO TYCOON

One new foreign investor gunning to break into the Philippines is state-owned China Telecom. In late 2018, just before a visit by President Xi, the deep-pocketed Chinese company and its partner firms held by a Chinese Filipino tycoon aligned with Duterte were confirmed as winners of a third telecom license, beating out the bids by several rivals.[94] China Telecom had hooked up with businessman Dennis Uy, whose firms are involved in a raft of businesses, from real estate to shipping and logistics to energy, to form Mislatel Consortium.

Duterte had announced the government was offering a third telecom license in 2017 to improve spotty service and break the grip that PLDT, which has a partnership with Japan's NTT Group, and Globe Telecom, which is partially owned by Singapore Telecommunications, have on the market. The president was very interested in having a Chinese firm enter the domestic telecommunications market.[95]

The partners of the consortium (since renamed the Dito Telecommunity), signed a $5.4 billion investment deal to set up and operate the Philippines' third telecom provider.[96] The Chinese stake in the company will be 40 percent and 60 percent will be held by two firms linked to Uy, holding company Udenna Corporation and Chelsea Logistics Holdings.

Uy, 46, has close links to the President Duterte and contributed $1.5 million to his 2016 election campaign, according to Duterte's statement of contributions and expenditures submitted to the Commission on Elections.[97] Uy had 11 companies in 2016, but has added three dozen more since Duterte took office, according to analysis by *Rappler*, the online news

94. John Reed, "Philippines Taps China Telecom-Led Group as Third Telecoms Provider," *Financial Times*, November 19, 2018, https://www.ft.com/content/47628b82-ebf9-11e8-8180-9cf212677a57.
95. Cliff Venzon, "China Telecom and Duterte Ally Set for Philippine Telecom License," *Nikkei Asian Review*, November 7, 2018, https://asia.nikkei.com/Business/Companies/China-Telecom-and-Duterte-ally-set-for-Philippine-telecom-license.
96. Ralf Rivas, "Mislatel Now Called Dito Telecommunity," *Rappler*, July 8, 2019, https://www.rappler.com/business/234889-mislatel-now-officially-called-dito-telecommunity; Ralf Rivas, "Dennis Uy, China Telecom Ink $5.4 Billion Deal for 3rd Telco," *Rappler*, April 26, 2019, https://www.rappler.com/business/229094-udenna-corp-china-telecom-ink-deal-3rd-telco.
97. Michael Bueza, "Who's Who in Duterte's Poll Contribution List," *Rappler*, December 9, 2016, https://www.rappler.com/newsbreak/iq/155060-duterte-contributors-list-2016-presidential-elections.

website. Uy in recent years bought the license to operate the Japanese-owned convenience-store chain FamilyMart in the Philippines, the digital start-up Pos!ble.net, the Conti's restaurant chain, and water utility firm H2o ventures.[98]

The Philippine military in September 2019 signed a preliminary agreement with Dito Telecommunity allowing this joint venture with China Telecom to install communications equipment and towers on its army bases. The Armed Forces of the Philippines (AFP) said in a statement that it received "guarantees that the devices, equipment, and/or structures installed at the site provided by the AFP shall not be used to obtain classified information." This statement was made to address concerns about electronic espionage.[99]

Senator Francis Pangilinan of the opposition party sharply criticized the deal, charging that the government has "laid the red carpet" for the telco, including China Telecom, "inside our military camps." The senator said the arrangement "raises fears of electronic espionage and interference given the record of some Chinese firms for engaging in this illegal activity."[100]

A national security official said shortly before the deal was signed that the military is worried about "ceding sovereign rights" to a firm that takes instructions from a foreign government and does not feel compelled to strongly protect the network from outside interference. Military analyst Custodio warned that the Chinese presence on Philippine military bases would make the United States, which has an agreement to use several Philippine military bases on a rotational basis, reluctant about dealing with the armed forces.[101]

The Philippines has become a haven for Chinese tech companies at a time when they are being shunned by the United States and some of its

---

98. Ralf Rivas, "Dennis Uy's Growing Empire (and Debt)," *Rappler*, January 3, 2019, https://www.rappler.com/newsbreak/in-depth/219039-dennis-uy-growing-business-empire-debt-year-opener-2019.

99. "Philippines to Allow China-Backed Telco to Build Towers on Military Bases," *Reuters*, September 11, 2019, https://www.reuters.com/article/us-philippines-telecoms-security/philippines-to-allow-china-backed-telco-to-build-towers-on-military-bases-idUSKCN1VW1H5.

100. J. C. Gotinga, "'Absurd': Why Build China-Backed Telco Towers in Military Camps?," *Rappler*, September 13, 2019, https://www.rappler.com/nation/239994-china-backed-telco-access-afp-camps-questioned.

101. Ibid.

allies. In addition to China Telecom, another giant Chinese telecom firm, Huawei Technologies, is setting up 5G network equipment for the other two mobile carriers in the Philippines, PLDT and Globe Telecom.[102]

Some Philippine senators raised an alarm in late 2018 about a China-funded surveillance project with the Department of Interior. The Safe Philippines Project will install a 12,000-camera surveillance system. Huawei will supply the equipment while an affiliate of China Telecom is slated to install the system.[103]

Philippine exports to China reached $8.8 billion in 2018, up from $6.2 billion in 2015.[104] Before Duterte visited China in 2016, China lifted some of the earlier restrictions against Philippine exports of bananas and pineapple imposed after the Scarborough Shoal standoff. It also opened the market for mangoes, coconut, and dragon fruit, particularly from Mindanao. But these fruit agreements resulted in only a minor boost to fruit exports, which totaled $221 million in 2017. Electronic equipment and machinery exports made up the lion's share of Philippine exports to China.

Meanwhile, China's exports to the Philippines ballooned to $22 billion in 2018, double the figure of $11.5 billion three years earlier.[105] As the Philippines trade deficit with China expanded, economists expressed concern that it was contributing to the weakness of the Philippine peso and driving up inflation.[106]

Separately, Chinese aid to the Philippines resumed in 2017, but by June 2018 China's share of official development assistance accounted for

---

102. Kenji Kawase, "China Telecom Downplays Philippine Entry as U.S. Pressure Mounts," *Nikkei Asian Review*, March 20, 2019, https://asia.nikkei.com/Business/Companies/China-Telecom-downplays-Philippine-entry-as-US-pressure-mounts.

103. Camille Elemia, "Senators Sound Alarm over China-Funded DILG Surveillance Project," *Rappler*, December 13, 2018, https://www.rappler.com/nation/218831-dilg-china-telecom-affiliate-partnership-video-surveillance-system-philippines.

104. "Goods Trade Up 10.5% amid Large Deficit with Top Partner China; Electronics Still Top Export," *BusinessWorld*, May 6, 2019, https://www.bworldonline.com/goods-trade-up-10-5-amid-large-deficit-with-top-partner-china-electronics-still-top-export/.

105. Andreo Calonzo, "'I Need China': Duterte's Pivot to Beijing Shows Signs of Payoff," *Bloomberg*, April 11, 2018, https://www.bloomberg.com/news/articles/2018-04-11/duterte-s-pivot-to-china-shows-some-signs-of-economic-payoff; "China Allows PH Banana, Pineapple Exports Ahead of Duterte Visit," *ABS-CBN*, October 10, 2016, https://news.abs-cbn.com/business/10/08/16/china-allows-ph-banana-pineapple-exports-ahead-of-duterte-visit; "Top Philippines Exports to the World," World's Richest Countries, 2019, http://www.worldsrichestcountries.com/top_philippines_exports.html.

106. Jose Galang, "Analysis: The Perils of a Surging Trade Imbalance with China," *ABS-CBN*, February 13, 2018, https://news.abs-cbn.com/business/02/13/18/analysis-the-perils-of-a-surging-trade-imbalance-with-china.

0.8 percent of the $13 billion the Philippines had received, the National Economic and Development Authority reported. Japan, meanwhile, accounted for over 40 percent.[107]

"China moves quickly and publicizes it," says a foreign diplomat in Manila. "It tailors its aid to fit Duterte's interests. When the U.S. trims back aid to the police, China offers to build two [drug] rehab centers with over a thousand beds," he says.

China donated some $21.8 million in cash and about $3 million worth of excavators, bulldozers, and dump trucks in late 2017 for the reconstruction of Marawi, a largely Muslim city of about 200,000 residents on the southern island of Mindanao. The city was devastated during months of siege by Islamic State–affiliated fighters, the Philippine military's battle to reclaim the city, and U.S.-helped airstrikes.[108] Officials estimated the reconstruction costs at about $1.5 billion.

A consortium of five Chinese and four Filipino companies, including China State Construction Engineering Corporation, was selected in early 2018 to spearhead the reconstruction.[109] The tapping of a Chinese-led group angered many former Marawi residents who insisted they wanted to be consulted in advance about reconstruction plans.[110] In the end, the consortium failed to hammer out details of the reconstruction and consideration was passed to a second China-led group. But two years after the fighting ended, the government appears somewhat overwhelmed by the task of reconstruction.[111]

---

107. Bienvenido S. Oplas, Jr., "The Meager Truth of China's Aid to the Philippines," *Asia Times*, December 5, 2018, https://www.asiatimes.com/2018/12/article/the-meager-truth-of-chinas-aid-to-the-philippines/.

108. Dharel Placido, "China Announces P1.1-Billion Marawi Aid," *ABS-CBN*, November 15, 2017, https://news.abs-cbn.com/news/11/15/17/china-announces-p11-billion-marawi-aid; Patricia Lourdes Viray, "China Turns Over Construction Equipment for Marawi Rehabilitation," *Philippine Star*, October 24, 2017, https://www.philstar.com/headlines/2017/10/24/1751983/china-turns-over-construction-equipment-marawi-rehabilitation.

109. Leila B. Salaverria, "Chinese Firms Join Rebuilding of Marawi," *Philippine Inquirer*, April 4, 2018, http://newsinfo.inquirer.net/979898/chinese-firms-join-rebuilding-of-marawi.

110. Shawn Crispin, "Anti-Chinese Sentiment Rises from the Ashes of Marawi," *Asia Times*, April 18, 2018, http://www.atimes.com/article/anti-china-sentiment-rises-ashes-marawi/.

111. Joseph Franco, "Philippines: Addressing Islamist Militancy after the Battle for Marawi," *International Crisis Group*, July 17, 2018, https://www.crisisgroup.org/asia/south-east-asia/philippines/philippines-addressing-islamist-militancy-after-battle-marawi.

Chinese tourist numbers jumped to 1.3 million in 2018, more than double the 570,000 in 2015, according to the Department of Trade and Industry. Chinese numbers still trail South Korea as the Philippines' biggest source of tourists.[112]

One of the changes Chinese tourists are bringing to the Philippines is the rapid growth of Chinese cashless payment systems, Tencent's WeChatPay and Alipay from Alibaba. Philippine banks are introducing platforms for these two mobile phone platforms and more hotels, restaurants, and shops are accepting these cashless payments.[113] Even the U.S. fast-food chain McDonald's accepts Alipay, including for its delivery of food orders.

Many of the Chinese tourists are gamblers who come to enjoy the country's casinos. Some analysts believe the uptick in Chinese arrivals could turn the Philippines into one of the next Asian gaming destinations alongside Macau and Singapore. Three large gaming resorts are operating in Entertainment City near Manila Bay, including Solaire Resort and Casino operated by Bloomberry Resorts, which belongs to Philippine port tycoon Enrique Razon and opened in 2013.

The numbers of Chinese gamblers patronizing Solaire doubled between 2016 and 2018 and now make up half of the resort's patrons, according to company officials. Some Chinese come on their own, but most are brought from China in small groups by independent agents.

Duterte created some confusion among Chinese casino investors in August 2018 when he declared he would not allow the opening of any new casinos in the Philippines. His comments landed as Macau casino operator Galaxy Entertainment Group was planning to develop a gambling resort on the popular tourist island of Boracay. A day before his comments condemning casinos, Duterte had fired the management and board of directors of the Philippine foundation that owned a site on Manila Bay where Hong Kong–listed Landing International Development was planning to build a $1.5 billion casino.

---

112. Charina Clarisse Echaluce, "DOT Targets 1.5-M Chinese Tourists for 2018," *Manila Bulletin*, February 23, 2018, https://news.mb.com.ph/2018/02/23/dot-targets-1-5-m-chinese-tourists-for-2018/; Koutsoukis and Yap, "China Hasn't Delivered on Its $24 Billion Philippines Promise."

113. Michelle Ong, "Chinese Tourists Driving WeChat Pay, Alipay Growth in Philippines," *ABS-CBN*, February 19, 2018, https://news.abs-cbn.com/business/02/19/18/chinese-tourists-driving-wechat-pay-alipay-growth-in-philippines.

"You don't give gambling license franchises for 75 years," Duterte said in sharp rebuke of the Philippine casino-regulating body, although Landing International insisted it only had a 25-year lease. "I will not allow it. I hate gambling. There will be no casinos outside of what is existing."[114]

IS AN ENERGY JOINT VENTURE IN THE WORKS?

One of the biggest prizes China is hoping for in the Philippines is that the government will agree to a joint oil and gas venture in a swath of the South China Sea long disputed between the two countries. In early 2018, Manila said it was considering this possibility and had agreed to establish a panel to work out details on how to explore in disputed waters without resolving the issue of sovereignty, a move many Philippine maritime experts said would be very tricky. Duterte said that joint exploration in the South China Sea would be "like co-ownership" and would be preferable to war.

During Xi's visit to Manila in November 2018, the two sides signed a memorandum of understanding on joint oil and gas development in the West Philippine Sea. A purported Chinese version of the agreement stated that the joint project "should not affect the respective positions on sovereignty and maritime rights and interests of the two parties," according to press reports.[115]

In mid-2019, Foreign Secretary Locsin announced that Manila had accepted the terms of reference on joint exploration of oil and gas proposed by China in the disputed sea. "I accepted China's version of the terms of reference as superior to our own," the secretary said. "Everything is going well." Locsin said the negotiations were ongoing but denied reports that the two sides were looking for a late 2019 deadline.[116]

The two governments are considering the 2-million-acre block SC-72 at Reed Bank, where the Department of Energy had earlier explored for gas. In 2011 Chinese vessels had driven away a Philippine survey ship

---

114. Cliff Venzon, "Duterte Vows No New Casinos, as Chinese Investors Push On," *Nikkei Asian Review*, August 8, 2018, https://asia.nikkei.com/Business/Companies/Duterte-vows-no-new-casinos-as-Chinese-investors-push-on.

115. Christina Mendez and Paolo Romero, "Philippines, China Sign MOU on Joint Gas, Oil Development," *Philippine Star*, November 21, 2018, https://www.philstar.com/headlines/2018/11/21/1870458/philippines-china-sign-mou-joint-gas-oil-developement.

116. Dona Z. Pazzibugan, "DFA Chief Accepts Beijing's Terms as 'Superior,'" *Inquirer.net*, July 8, 2019, https://globalnation.inquirer.net/177636/dfa-chief-accepts-beijings-terms-as-superior.

from this area hired by Forum Energy PLC, which is 70 percent owned by the Philippine company PXP Energy Corporation. But in 2016 the tribunal ruling made clear that the area, 85 nautical miles off the coast of the Philippines, was in the country's exclusive economic zone (EEZ) and on its continental shelf.[117]

Philippine legal experts argued that any deal between the two countries to jointly explore for gas in Reed Bank would be illegal unless China recognized Manila's sovereign rights over the area. Antonio Carpio, the Supreme Court justice who played a leading role in Manila's submission to the tribunal, said it was legal for the Philippines Energy Ministry to talk to state-owned China National Offshore Oil Corporation (CNOOC) as a subcontractor as long as it recognizes that Reed Bank is in the Philippine EEZ. "But that is the problem, because CNOOC will not recognize [Philippine jurisdiction]," Carpio said.[118]

Philippine constitutional provisions related to natural resources make joint development of the block problematic. Maritime legal expert Jay Batongbacal wrote that "joint development in practice usually means the two share the contested resource, the rights and jurisdictions over it, including its exploration and exploitation, pending final settlement of their dispute."

To make a deal with China work, Batongbacal said Manila would need to overcome two legal hurdles. Internationally, it needs to justify how it accepts that "China contingently shares the petroleum resources within its continental shelf after an international arbitration award clearly declared that no plausible claim exists." Domestically, the government needs to explain how it will accommodate oil and gas development in Philippine waters "on a shared, co-equal basis with another state."

Under Philippine law, including under a service contract with a foreign company, the project must remain under Philippine control, super-

---

117. "Philippines Earmarks Two Sites for Possible Joint Oil Exploration with China," *Reuters*, March 2, 2018, https://www.reuters.com/article/philippines-china-southchinasea-energy/philippines-earmarks-two-sites-for-possible-joint-oil-exploration-with-china-idUSL4N1QK4CW.

118. Reuters, "Philippine Judge Rules Out South China Sea Gas Deal unless Beijing Recognises Manila's Sovereignty," *South China Morning Post*, March 5, 2018, https://www.scmp.com/news/china/diplomacy-defence/article/2135731/philippine-judge-rules-out-south-china-sea-gas-deal.

vision, and jurisdiction, Batongbacal said, adding "these conditions would never be acceptable to China."[119]

But Beijing has Manila over the barrel. The Philippines badly needs another source of gas soon. Its Malampaya gas field, which fires almost a third of the electricity supplied to Luzon Island, will begin to be depleted by 2024. Without progress in developing Reed Bank, the Philippines faces a severe energy crisis in a few years, much higher costs of importing liquefied natural gas, or turning to coal or nuclear power.

Carpio told *The Wall Street Journal* that a deal with China was possible in which the Philippines offered China about half the gas or proceeds from selling the resource but did not offer sovereign rights. The judge said Manila could contract a Chinese state-owned company and share the output or the profit with the firm. But in the end, Carpio was not optimistic. "China is using the nine-dash line to bully us into giving up half of our resources," he said. "They'll get what they want."[120]

Batongbacal adds, "All China needs is for the Philippines not to explore for oil. The longer the talks take the better for China." He is convinced that Beijing is not really interested in joint development on the eastern side of the South China Sea because it would "financially be a money-losing proposition for China." Reed Bank is far from land-based facilities, so a joint exploitation project would need to service its operations. "It's location and the costs of lifting the gas would probably make it unprofitable for China," he says. Economically, the project only makes sense if the gas is piped to the Philippines.

In a joint venture, Manila would want to nominate its service contractors, but because the Philippine National Oil Company does not have the "competencies or resources," the Philippines would likely nominate "foreign oil companies to operate on its behalf," Batongbacal says. "That would be problematic for China precisely because they want to elbow extra-regional interests out of the South China Sea."

---

119. Jay Batongbacal, "Philippine-China Joint Development Talks Still at an Impasse, despite Green Light," Center for Strategic and International Studies—Asia Maritime Transparency Initiative, April 13, 2018, https://amti.csis.org/philippine-china-joint-development-impasse/.

120. Niharika Mandhana, "China Poised to Win Major Victory in Sea Dispute With Help of Philippine Resources Deal," *Wall Street Journal*, September 10, 2018, https://www.wsj.com/articles/oil-and-gas-pact-poised-to-hand-china-a-victory-in-sea-dispute-1536571801?shareToken=st41978036cce24056937b31f06b52c4bc&ref=article_email_share.

Duterte's moves to negotiate a joint energy development framework with China in the South China Sea prompted a public spat with members of the previous Philippine administration. Former president Aquino, who brought the arbitral tribunal case against China, told Duterte that thanks to the ruling "we have no obligation to share with [China]." Aquino asked if the Philippines was getting into an unfair arrangement with Beijing in which it says, "What is ours is ours, and what is yours, we share." Albert del Rosario, Aquino's foreign secretary, accused the current government of wasting an overwhelming legal victory in exchange for uncertain benefits.

Duterte's former foreign secretary Cayetano fired back: "We lost many opportunities for cooperation in fields like science and technology, protection of the environment . . . , all because of the approach you [Aquino], together with former secretary del Rosario . . . chose to adopt and implement."[121]

After Duterte visited Beijing in late August 2019, he said Chinese President Xi had told him that Manila could have a controlling stake in a joint venture and that China would agree to be a junior partner in an agreement to exploit the gas reserves at Reed Bank if Manila agreed to set aside the arbitral tribunal award that ruled against China.

"Set aside your claim," the Philippine president said his Chinese counterpart told him. "Then allow everybody connected with Chinese companies. They want to explore. If there is something, they said, we will be gracious enough to give you 60 percent, only 40 percent will be theirs. That is the promise of Xi Jinping." Duterte did not say if he had accepted Xi's proposal, but he said that references to the EEZ in the arbitral award "we will ignore to come up with economic activity."[122]

A Philippine agreement to ignore the arbitral ruling and work with China to develop a hydrocarbon project would be a giant blow to the other claimants in the South China Sea, particularly Malaysia and Vietnam,

---

121. Richard Javad Heydarian, "Pro- and Anti-China Lines Harden in the Philippines," *Asia Times*, August 7, 2018, http://www.atimes.com/article/pro-and-anti-china-lines-harden-in-the-philippines/.

122. Martin Petty, "Philippines' Duterte Says Xi Offering Gas Deal If Arbitration Case Ignored," *Reuters*, September 10, 2019, https://www.reuters.com/article/us-philippines-china-southchinasea/philippines-duterte-says-xi-offering-gas-deal-if-arbitration-case-ignored-idUSKCN1VW07O.

which have also come under Chinese pressure on their continental shelves.

MILITARY STICKS WITH THE PENTAGON

If Duterte had his druthers, Philippine military ties with China would really be sizzling by now. In a meeting with President Xi at the Boao Forum in April 2018, the Philippine leader called for intensified defense cooperation with Beijing to tackle the threats of terrorism and transnational crime.[123] Two months earlier, in a speech to the Chinese Filipino Business Club in Manila, Duterte said that Philippine soldiers should start training in China to gain skills in counterterrorism and balance the training the troops receive in the United States.[124]

Somewhat surprisingly, Duterte's calls for stepped-up military cooperation followed a comment by Xi in May 2017 in which the Chinese president allegedly warned his Philippine counterpart that Beijing would go to war with the Philippines if it "forces the issue" of the 2016 tribunal ruling in the South China Sea. When Duterte told Xi that the Philippines would eventually want to drill for oil in the West Philippine Sea, the Chinese leader replied, "Well, if you force the issue . . . we will go to war. We will fight you," the Philippine president quoted his Chinese counterpart as saying.[125]

The irony of getting his soldiers trained by a military whose leader threatens to attack the Philippines if it explores for oil in an area the arbitral tribunal had ruled was part of his country's territory seems lost on Duterte. Progress toward closer military cooperation is slower than the Philippine leader might wish, at least in part because of opposition from his generals who have decades of experience with China.

---

123. Genalyn Kabiling, "PH Pushes for Intensified Military, Defense Cooperation with China," *Manila Bulletin*, April 11, 2018, https://news.mb.com.ph/2018/04/10/ph-pushes-for-intensified-military-defense-cooperation-with-china/.
124. Catherine Wong, "Rodrigo Duterte Wants to Create 'Balance' by Sending Troops to China for Training," *South China Morning Post*, February 21, 2018, https://www.scmp.com/news/china/diplomacy-defence/article/2134157/rodrigo-duterte-wants-create-balance-sending-troops.
125. Pia Ranada, "Duterte Claims Xi Warned of War If PH 'Forces Issue' in Disputed Sea," *Rappler*, May 19, 2017, https://www.rappler.com/nation/170388-duterte-xi-war-south-china-sea.

The Philippine military has long distrusted China because of its support for the Philippine communist rebels against which many soldiers fought until the end of the 1970s. The military's suspicions were further reinforced in 1995 when China seized Mischief Reef from the Philippines and in 2012 when Beijing took control of Scarborough Shoal.

The views of the military toward China were in sharp contrast to Duterte's perceptions in the country's 2017 national security policy. It called the dispute in the South China Sea the country's "foremost security challenge to the Philippines' sovereignty and territorial integrity" and referred to the U.S. role in the region as a "stabilizing force."[126]

Despite Duterte's enthusiasm, Philippine security analysts doubt that Manila will send many Philippine officers to study in China any time soon. "We're talking about a different doctrine, different weapons systems, and a difficult language barrier," says a former national security official referring to the decades of close cooperation with the United States. "What can we learn from China about the war on terrorism. We've had continuous war against the New People's Army and various secessionists for decades. We know more about handling terrorist threats [than China]," he said.

Between 2003 and 2016, the Philippines had the second lowest number of military diplomatic interactions with the Chinese armed forces of any of its counterparts in Southeast Asia, except for tiny Brunei. During 14 years, the two countries had only three joint naval exercises, five port calls, and 20 senior-level meetings, according to a 2017 study by the Center for the Study of Chinese Military Affairs at the National Defense University in Washington.[127] China has raised the possibility of holding joint military exercises with the Philippines, particularly focused on counterterrorism, but so far none have taken place.[128]

Duterte came to power pledging to scale down military exercises with the United States and suspend joint naval patrols in the South China Sea

---

126. Custer et al., *Ties That Bind*, 25.

127. Kenneth Allen, Phillip C. Saunders, and John Chen, *Chinese Military Diplomacy 2003–2016* (Washington, DC: National Defense University Press, 2017), 63, https://ndupress.ndu.edu/Portals/68/Documents/stratperspective/china/ChinaPerspectives-11.pdf?ver=2017-07-17-153301-093.

128. Dharel Placido, "China Open to Joint Military Exercises with PH," *ABS-CBN*, June 28, 2017, https://news.abs-cbn.com/news/06/28/17/china-open-to-joint-military-exercises-with-ph.

to avoid irritating China.[129] Despite that, the Philippine and U.S. navies conducted a joint naval patrol in July 2017, but in the somewhat lawless Sulu Sea between the Philippines, Indonesia, and Malaysia, rather than in the South China Sea disputed with Beijing.[130] Another round of Philippine-U.S. Sama Sama (together jointly) naval exercises were held in July 2018 in an area of the South China Sea west of Luzon Island.[131]

The United States and the Philippines simulated in April 2019 the repelling of a foreign power that had seized control of a Philippine-controlled island in the South China Sea as part of the annual Balikatan (shoulder to shoulder) exercises. But Duterte's press spokesman insisted that the exercise was not meant to send a message to Beijing, even though in the months prior, China and the Philippines had been at odds over Beijing's sending a large contingent of vessels to Philippine-held Thitu Island. Security analysts believe Beijing's goal has been convince Manila to abandon plans to build any military features on the island.[132]

The Balikatan exercises on land in 2017 were scaled back with only about 5,000 U.S. and Filipino military participants, down from 9,000 the previous year.[133] But these drills in May 2018 featured 8,000 American and Filipino personnel along with some forces from Australia and Japan. The exercises were aimed at tackling urban terrorism and natural disasters and included live-fire maneuvers and combat drills in mock urban settings.[134]

---

129. Cris Larano, "Philippines Leader to End Joint Military Exercises, Naval Patrols with U.S.," *Wall Street Journal*, September 29, 2016, https://www.wsj.com/articles/philippines-leader-to-end-joint-military-exercises-joint-naval-patrols-with-u-s-1475086567.

130. Ben Otto, "U.S., Philippines Conduct Naval Patrol in Southeast Asian Waters," *Wall Street Journal*, July 1, 2017, https://www.wsj.com/articles/u-s-philippines-conduct-naval-patrol-in-southeast-asian-waters-1498917226.

131. U.S. Department of Defense, "U.S., Philippines Strengthen Alliance with Maritime Training Activity Sama Sama," July 9, 2018, https://dod.defense.gov/News/Article/Article/1569455/us-philippines-strengthen-alliance-with-maritime-training-activity-sama-sama/.

132. Raissa Robles, "U.S.-Philippine Balikatan Military Exercises in the South China Sea 'Not a Message to Beijing,' Insists Manila," *South China Morning Post*, April 15, 2019, https://www.scmp.com/news/asia/southeast-asia/article/3006271/us-philippine-balikatan-military-exercises-south-china-sea.

133. "U.S., Philippines Scale Back Next Month's Military Drills, No More 'War Games,'" *Reuters*, April 24, 2017, https://www.reuters.com/article/us-philippines-usa-defence-idUSKBN17Q120.

134. Jim Gomez, "U.S., Philippines Launch Largest Military Drills under Duterte," *Military Times*, May 7, 2018, https://www.militarytimes.com/news/your-military/2018/05/07/us-philippines-launch-largest-military-drills-under-duterte/.

Some progress also continues under Duterte to implement the 2014 Enhanced Defense Cooperation Agreement between the Philippines and the United States under which Washington was granted access to five military bases to store relief supplies and to rotate military ships and aircraft. In April 2018, officials engaged in a groundbreaking ceremony for the first major project under the arrangement, a warehouse for disaster relief supplies, at an air base in Pampanga, some 40 miles northwest of Manila.[135] Under the agreement, the United States will upgrade infrastructure at some Philippine bases, pre-position some relief supplies to respond to disasters, and provide training to Philippine military units.[136]

Washington removed one major irritation in its relations with Manila in 2019 when the United States made a verbal pledge that U.S. forces would defend Philippines vessels in the South China Sea under a Mutual Defense Treaty dating back to 1951. U.S. Secretary of State Mike Pompeo said in Manila that "any attack on Philippine forces, aircraft, or public vessels in the South China Sea would trigger mutual defense obligations."

The Philippines was disappointed that Pompeo did not pledge to defend the Philippines' islands in the South China Sea, where Beijing claims all the islands within its nine-dash line and has built up its military capacity to challenge the claims of its neighbors. The Philippines had in the months before the U.S. pledge threatened a review of its military alliance with the United States. Manila had long believed that the lack of U.S. clarity had left the Philippines without protection and support should a conflict with China erupt.[137]

China has begun providing some military equipment to the Philippines. In 2017, Beijing sent two shipments of 3,000 assault rifles to the Philippines worth about $6.6 million. The weapons were initially intended for the military, which was battling Islamic militants who had captured the city of Marawi on the island of Mindanao in May that year.

135. "First EDCA Facility Breaks Ground in Pampanga," *Philippine Star*, April 18, 2018, https://www.philstar.com/headlines/2018/04/18/1807117/first-edca-facility-breaks-ground-pampanga.

136. Renato Cruz De Castro, "EDCA and the Projection of U.S. Air Power in the South China Sea," Center for Strategic and International Studies—Asia Maritime Transparency Initiative, May 20, 2016, https://amti.csis.org/edca-projection-u-s-air-power-south-china-sea/.

137. Jake Maxwell Watts and Michael R. Gordon, "Pompeo Pledges to Defend Philippine Forces in the South China Sea," *Wall Street Journal*, March 1, 2019, https://www.wsj.com/articles/pompeo-pledges-to-defend-philippine-forces-in-south-china-sea-11551425469.

In 2018, China donated four 40-foot boats and some 30 rocket-propelled grenade launchers to the military.[138]

In the end, the Chinese assault rifles were turned over to the Philippine police, who were engaged in a fierce war on drugs in which thousands were killed. The guns reportedly helped overcome a police weapons shortage after the U.S. Congress blocked 26,000 M4 rifles from being sold to the Philippine police because of concern about human rights violations.[139]

When China delivered the first allotment of rifles in mid-2017, Duterte personally went to receive them.[140] However, in a clear signal of the president's attitudes toward Washington, he drove past the handover ceremony a few weeks later at the Davao airport when the United States delivered two surveillance planes to boost the country's ability to patrol its sprawling maritime borders and detect ships in the South China Sea, but he did not stop.

The two planes and their surveillance, intelligence, and reconnaissance equipment cost $30 million and were transferred to Manila as part of the United States' $425 million Maritime Security Initiative to help Southeast Asian countries boost their awareness about what is happening in the South China Sea.[141]

Duterte credits China with playing a significant role in putting down the uprising in Marawi in which several hundred Filipino and foreign militants loyal to the Islamic State seized Marawi in May 2017, forcing hundreds of thousands of residents to flee. After five months, the Philippine military was finally able to put down the revolt with airstrikes, artillery fire, and ground attacks with assistance from American and Australian surveillance planes.

---

138. Reuters, "China Donates Small Boats and RPG Launchers to Philippines," *South China Morning Post*, July 30, 2018, https://www.scmp.com/news/asia/diplomacy/article/2157406/china-donates-small-boats-and-rpg-launchers-philippines.

139. "China Gives Guns to Philippines to Show It's a friend, Not a Foe," *Reuters*, October 5, 2017, https://uk.reuters.com/article/uk-philippines-china-defence/china-gives-guns-to-philippines-to-show-its-a-friend-not-a-foe-idUKKBN1CA0OK.

140. Reuters, "Duterte Receives Sniper, Assault Rifles from China," *ABS-CBN*, June 29, 2017, https://news.abs-cbn.com/news/06/29/17/duterte-receives-sniper-assault-rifles-from-china.

141. "U.S. Transfers Surveillance Planes to the Philippines," *Reuters*, July 27, 2017, https://www.reuters.com/article/us-philippines-usa-planes-idUSKBN1AC1S0.

Duterte claims that it was Chinese sniper rifles that were used to kill two militant leaders in Marawi that led to the end of the occupation in October 2017. Speaking at a business conference at which the Chinese ambassador was a guest, Duterte said: "I would like to officially inform you, Ambassador Zhao, that the rifle that killed [Isnilon] Hapilon was a sniper rifle made in China."

However, Reuters reported earlier that the Scout Rangers' Facebook page claimed that troops had used an armored vehicle's thermal imaging to shoot the top militant leader at night from a 50-caliber machine gun mounted on the vehicle. The deputy commander of the task force deployed to retake the city told the news agency that he did not know the origin of the gun used to kill the two militant leaders because his troops were using weapons from China, the United States, and other countries at the time of the attack.[142]

Despite Duterte's gravitation toward Beijing, he agreed to support funding for the second phase of a 15-year military modernization program that will prioritize acquisitions to provide territorial defense, largely against moves by China, at a cost of roughly $5.6 billion, according to analysis by Renato Cruz De Castro, an international affairs professor at De La Salle University in Manila.[143] This modernization phase, which will run from 2018 to 2022, will provide equipment primarily for the navy and the air force for defending the world's fifth longest coastline around some 7,600 islands.

The navy will procure two new missile-capable frigates, amphibious assault vehicles, anti-submarine helicopters, multi-role vessels, and submarines. The big-ticket items for the air force will be two squadrons of multi-role fighters, possibly the Gripen from Saab in Sweden and a dozen FA-50 lead-in fighter planes from South Korea.[144]

It is interesting that Duterte is continuing the shift toward territorial defense despite his rebalance toward China. De Castro argued that one

142. Meme Buster, "Duterte Says China-Made Rifle Killed Maute, Hapilon but Marawi Task Force Commander Says He couldn't Say for Sure," *Meme Buster*, October 22, 2017, https://memebuster.net/duterte-says-china-made-rifle-killed-maute/.

143. Renato Cruz De Castro, "The Next Phase of Philippine Military Modernization: Looking to External Defense," Center for Strategic and International Studies—Asia Maritime Transparency Initiative, July 12, 2018, https://amti.csis.org/the-next-phase-of-philippine-military-modernization-looking-to-external-defense/.

144. De Castro, "The Next Phase of Philippine Military Modernization."

reason he is doing this is to "maintain support from the military, especially as he seeks to shift the country away from its historic reliance on the United States and toward a closer relationship with China driven by economic concessions."[145]

Chinese Premier Li Keqiang and Duterte signed a defense industrial agreement in November 2017 that is intended to boost Chinese exports and technology transfers to the Philippines.[146] But China's arms supplies are still small compared to those of the United States, which has been a Philippine treaty ally since 1951.

Between 2009 and 2015, Washington provided Manila some $211 million in foreign military financing, over half of the total grants and aid given to all of the Asia Pacific to purchase weapons and defense equipment from the United States.[147] During the same years, the Philippines received $12 million in International Military Education and Training funds out of a total of $65.4 million, almost one-fifth of the total for East Asia, to fund the training of military officers in the United States.[148]

The United States in 2018 offered $300 million in new funding for the Indo-Pacific region to strengthen maritime security, develop peacekeeping capabilities, and counter transnational threats. A chunk of this money will be available to the Philippines. Washington offered to sell F-16 fighter jets to the Philippines, but Duterte rejected them as "utterly useless." He said the country needs lighter combat aircraft to fight insurgents.[149]

Earlier, military ties with China had warmed somewhat during the Arroyo administration in the early 2000s, and in 2004 the two militaries signed a memorandum of understanding to boost military cooperation, including exchanges of military delegations, discussion of issues such as

---

145. Ibid.

146. Pia Ranada, "LIST: 14 Deals Signed during Chinese Premier Li's Manila Visit," *Rappler*, November 15, 2017, https://www.rappler.com/nation/188578-list-14-deals-china-premier-li-keqiang-visit-philippines.

147. U.S. Department of State, "Foreign Military Financing Account Summary: FY 2009–FY 2015," https://2009-2017.state.gov/t/pm/ppa/sat/c14560.htm.

148. "International Military Education and Training Account Summary," FY 2009–FY 2015, U.S. Department of State, https://2009-2017.state.gov/t/pm/ppa/sat/c14562.htm.

149. Jim Gomez, "Duterte Says Buying U.S. F-16 Jets 'Utterly Useless,'" *Bloomberg*, August 24, 2018, https://www.bloomberg.com/news/articles/2018-08-24/duterte-says-buying-us-f-16-jets-utterly-useless.

counterterrorism, disaster relief, and the launching of annual defense talks.[150]

In late 2017, the Philippines and China restarted their annual defense and security talks to discuss deepening ties, which had been in the deep freeze after the previous administration brought a case against Beijing to the arbitral tribunal in The Hague.[151]

During 2018, several Chinese ships and aircraft landed in Davao, Duterte's hometown in Mindanao. In August, a maritime tracking ship docked to refuel and restock the crew's food supplies, marking the fifth Chinese vessel to visit the Philippines since Duterte became president.[152] A Chinese navy research and surveillance ship, reportedly used for tracking and support of satellites and intercontinental ballistic missiles, visited the city in July. In April, a guided missile frigate stopped on a goodwill visit. A Chinese military transport plane, designed to conduct tactical and strategic airlift missions, stopped in Davao twice in June for refueling on its way to and from New Zealand.[153]

The Chinese ship and aircraft visits to Davao, rather than to ports or bases closer to Manila, are widely interpreted in the Philippines as a Chinese gesture to the president. When a Chinese missile destroyer visited Davao on a goodwill visit in May 2017, the first Chinese port call in the Philippines since 2010, Duterte personally boarded the ship, which raised some eyebrows. Gary Alejano, then an opposition member of the Philippines congress and a former military officer, said "the visit shows the president is trying everything to appease China."[154] When the U.S. aircraft carrier *Carl Vinson* visited Manila Bay in early 2018, Duterte's defense secretary Lorenzana boarded the vessel, but Duterte stayed away.[155]

---

150. Prasanth Parameswaran, "What's With the 'Revival' of the China-Philippines Military Dialogue?," *The Diplomat*, December 19, 2017, https://thediplomat.com/2017/12/whats-with-the-revival-of-the-china-philippines-military-dialogue/.
151. Parameswaran, "What's With the 'Revival' of the China-Philippines Military Dialogue?"
152. "Chinese ship docks in Davao City for refueling, tour," *ABS-CBN*, August 31, 2018, https://news.abs-cbn.com/news/08/31/18/chinese-ship-docks-in-davao-city-for-refueling-tour.
153. "Chinese research ship docks in Davao City," *ABS-CBN*.
154. Agence France-Presse, "Duterte visits Chinese warships in hometown Davao in first Philippines port call since 2010," *South China Morning Post*, May 1, 2017, https://www.scmp.com/news/asia/diplomacy/article/2092036/duterte-visits-chinese-warships-hometown-davao-first-philippines.
155. Jim Gomez, "Philippine Leaders Visit U.S. Carrier on Disputed Sea," *SFGATE*, March 4, 2017, https://www.sfgate.com/world/article/Philippine-leaders-visit-U-S-carrier-on-disputed-10977387.php.

Despite the warming of ties between the Philippines and China, Chinese navy ships, coast guard vessels, and maritime militia boats continue patrolling inside the Philippines' EEZ area of the South China Sea. "They maintain a permanent presence and challenge any Philippine aircraft and vessels that go near features" claimed by China, says a national security official. "On the sandbars near Pag-asa Island, there's a significant presence of Chinese fishing vessels backed by [People's Liberation Army Navy] and coast guard vessels," he says.

CHINA'S FIRST OVERTURES UNRAVEL

The first encounters between China and the Philippines date back to 1417, when the Muslim sultan of Sulu, today part of the Philippines, sailed to China to pay tribute to the third emperor of the Ming dynasty. The sultan became ill and died on his way home, prompting the emperor to build an elegant tomb for the Sulu leader in Shandong Province. The sultan's wife and two children stayed to take care of his tomb, and some of his ancestors continue to live in the city of Dezhou, south of Beijing.[156] The tomb was refurbished by a prominent Chinese Filipino business leader in 2017 to mark the 600 years since the voyage.[157]

The Philippines, which gained independence from the United States after World War II, was the second ASEAN member country to recognize the communist government in China in 1975. Like many of its Southeast Asian neighbors, the Philippines viewed China as a domestic threat in the early decades after the Mao Zedong victory because of Beijing's support for the Communist Party of the Philippines in its fight against the government. It was not until the U.S. rapprochement with China began in the early 1970s that Manila started to explore closer ties with Beijing, although China continued

156. "Next 'Balangay' Adventure: Voyage of Sulu Sultan to China," *Philippine Daily Inquirer*, April 7, 2017, https://globalnation.inquirer.net/154466/next-balangay-adventure-voyage-sulu-sultan-china; Carmen Pedrosa, "A Sultan of Sulu Is Buried in China," *Philippine Star*, September 11, 2015, https://www.philstar.com/opinion/2015/09/11/1498840/sultan-sulu-buried-china.

157. Teresita Ang See, "Commemorating 600 years of a Royal Voyage," *Philippine Star*, September 23, 2017, https://www.philstar.com/other-sections/starweek-magazine/2017/09/23/1741989/commemorating-600-years-royal-voyage.

financial support for the communist movement until late in the decade.[158]

Beijing offered Manila cheap oil supplies at the height of the 1973 oil crisis, but it was not long before overlapping claims in the South China Sea became an irritant in bilateral relations. When UNCLOS came into force in 1994, competition in the sea intensified as the disputing countries sought control over land features and their nearby maritime resources.[159]

Beijing's seizure in 1995 of Mischief Reef in the Spratly Islands, 130 nautical miles west of the Philippine island of Palawan, provoked a crisis in bilateral ties and had a major impact on attitudes among Filipinos toward China. Beijing's takeover of the reef took place three years after the Philippines had forced the United States to close two major bases in the country. Manila sought to garner international and regional support in condemning China's move but with discouraging results, as Beijing consolidated its occupation by building structures on Mischief Reef.[160]

When Gloria Macapagal Arroyo became president in 2001 she mounted a major effort to expand ties beyond the focus on maritime disputes. Arroyo sought to build on a bilateral agreement the previous year to increase official exchanges, bolster trade and investment, and expand defense cooperation. Trained as an economist at Georgetown University in the United States, she focused on boosting the Philippines economy by exploring links to China's flourishing economic growth engine and courting investment in her country's dilapidated infrastructure.

Two signature projects proposed by Chinese investors were the North Rail project and ZTE Corporation's offer of a $330 million upgrade of the national broadband network. Jinchuan Non-Ferrous Metal Corporation planned to invest billions in the Nonoc Mines in Surigao del Norte in the north of Mindanao. The Industrial Bank of China nearly reached an agreement with the government to invest billions of dollars and open over 30 branches across the country.

---

158. Ian Storey, *Southeast Asia and the Rise of China: The Search for Security* (New York: Routledge, 2011), 251, 253.
159. Baviera, "The Domestic Meditations of China's Influence in the Philippines," 101.
160. Storey, *Southeast Asia and the Rise of China*, 251, 253, 257, 258.

In the end, the only major project to take off was State Grid Corporation of China's purchase of a 40 percent stake in the National Grid Corporation of the Philippines. Most of the other big projects crumbled amid wide-ranging corruption charges and because of squabbles between officials, some of whom were vying for rent-seeking opportunities within the Arroyo administration, said Alvin Camba, the economist.[161]

Arroyo also signed a resource-sharing agreement with China and Vietnam in the South China Sea named the Joint Maritime Seismic Undertaking in 2005. The deal put China National Oil Corporation in charge of conducting seismic exploration of oil and gas resources in an area where the three countries' claims overlapped. The Philippine National Oil Company and its Vietnamese counterpart were left with the role of interpreting the Chinese data. There was opposition in the Philippines because the deal was seen as undermining the country's sovereignty. Protests and deteriorating relations between Hanoi and Beijing caused the deal to unravel when it expired in 2008.[162]

Beijing was interested in mending its ties with Manila as part of China's charm offensive in the wake of the irritation in Southeast Asia about the giant neighbor's seizure of Mischief Reef. China worked with ASEAN to sign in 2002 a Declaration on the Conduct of Parties in the South China Sea, an agreement that had no real impact on developments in the maritime dispute. A leaked report that year by the Philippine military, which has long had close links to the Pentagon, concluded that China was intent on continuing its strategy of "talk and take," a reference to its efforts to negotiate while at the same time continuing to build new installations in the Spratlys.[163]

---

161. Alvin Camba, "The Philippines' Chinese FDI Boom: More Politics than Geopolitics," *New Mandela*, January 30, 2018, http://www.newmandala.org/duterte-philippines-chinese-investment-boom-politics-geopolitics/; Alvin Camba, "Why Did Chinese Investment in the Philippines Stagnate?," *East Asia Forum*, December 12, 2017, http://www.eastasiaforum.org/2017/12/12/why-did-chinese-investment-in-the-philippines-stagnate/.

162. "PNoy: JMSU with China, Vietnam 'Shouldn't Have Happened,'" *ABS-CBN News*, January 5, 2011, https://news.abs-cbn.com/nation/01/04/11/pnoy-jmsu-china-vietnam-shouldnt-have-happened; Richard Javad Heydarian, "The Perils of a Philippine-China Joint Development Agreement in the South China Sea," Center for Strategic and International Studies—Asia Maritime Transparency Initiative, April 27, 2018, https://amti.csis.org/perils-philippine-china-joint-development-scs/.

163. Storey, *Southeast Asia and the Rise of China*, 259.

ROLE OF CHINESE FILIPINOS

Duterte's abrupt swing toward China poses both opportunities and potential challenges for Philippine ethnic Chinese. By some estimates, the mix of old and new migrants among Chinese Filipinos make up roughly 2 percent of the Philippines population,[164] but they control about 60 percent of the economy. If people of mixed heritage such as Duterte and Aquino are included, their numbers could make up over 20 percent of the population.[165] The new migrants, who comprise about a tenth of the total, include those who came in the 1980s to join their Hokkien relatives and a newer group that came in the early 2000s as part of China's "going out" policy.[166]

Some Chinese migrants were already living in the Philippines when the Spanish arrived in the sixteenth century. Because they were not allowed to own land, most Chinese became active in small business activities. Many intermarried with Filipinos. After Manila recognized the communist regime in China, the government changed its nationality laws to allow Chinese Filipinos to become citizens and assimilate into the larger society.

Chinese Filipinos have economic clout disproportionate to the size of their population. They have long played leading roles in sectors from financial services to semiconductors and airlines to shopping malls and hotels. The Jollibee fast-food chain was founded by a Chinese Filipino. Nine of the country's 15 billionaires, including Henry Sy of SM Malls and Lucio Tan of the LT Group, are Chinese Filipino and, in fact, are pure Chinese. By 2014, Chinese Filipinos owned 41 percent of the top 100 firms in the Philippines and six of the top 10 Philippine banks, including China Banking Corporation and Metrobank.[167]

Investment in China by Philippine companies founded by Chinese migrants has long been larger than Chinese investment in the Philippines. Most Chinese Filipinos have maintained ties to their home communities

164. Ellen Huang Palanca, "Politics, Policy, Culture and China: The Growth of the Top Ethnic Chinese Businesses in the Philippines since the 1990s," in *Chinese Capitalism in Southeast Asia*, ed. Yos Santasombat (Palgrave Macmillan, 2017), 105.
165. Solita Collas-Monsod, "Ethnic Chinese Dominate PH Economy," *Philippine Inquirer*, June 22, 2012, https://opinion.inquirer.net/31223/ethnic-chinese-dominate-ph-economy.
166. Palanca, "Politics, Policy, Culture and China," 105.
167. Ibid., 110, 112.

in China and sent money home even during the hard times after the communist revolution. Today many of them invest in business ventures in their hometowns, particularly in Jinjiang, home area for 90 percent of the Chinese Filipinos, and Xiamen.[168]

Henry Sy of SM Investments Corporation built supermalls in both cities as well as in Chengdu, Suzhou, and Chongqing. Lucio Tan built a 30-story banking center in Xiamen. Carlos Chan has established 15 food-processing factories all over China.[169]

Some researchers who have interviewed Filipinos have found "growing discontent" about the outsized role of the Chinese Filipino community in key sectors of the economy, in contrast to the poverty and economic insecurity found elsewhere in the country. Those interviewed made a distinction between Chinese Filipinos who have lived in the Philippines for generations and recent "new arrivals."[170]

On Philippine relations with China, the Chinese Filipino community today is roughly divided between the second and third generation of migrants, who closely identify themselves with the Philippines and are mostly neutral on Manila's relations with Beijing, and newer arrivals who still have closer ties with China and are more active in establishing business partnerships with their country of birth.[171]

"Some Chinese Filipinos are more Filipino than Chinese, while others work to facilitate relations between China and the Philippines," says a national security official in Manila. Adds a former security official: "Some Chinese Filipinos believe it is better to do business with China than to fight for rocks in the middle of nowhere," referring to the South China Sea dispute.

The Federation of Filipino-Chinese Chambers of Commerce and Industry has long called for China and the Philippines to establish mutually beneficial relations. In 2015, it urged the Aquino government to "set aside its differences" with Beijing and counseled the president against "further antagonizing" China. After Benigno Aquino likened China to Nazi Germany for its actions in the South China Sea in 2015, the federation canceled celebrations commemorating the 40th anniversary of diplomatic relations between the two countries. It has been much more

168. Ibid., 107.
169. Ibid., 120–121.
170. Custer et al., *Ties That Bind*, 25.
171. Palanca, "Politics, Policy, Culture and China," 105.

enthusiastic about Duterte and his turn toward China. Over 100 of the 400-plus business leaders who accompanied Duterte on his first trip to Beijing in late 2016 were federation members.

It is not clear that the Chinese Filipino community played a significant role in opening doors for Duterte to China. "My bet is that Duterte is not beholden to Chinese oligarchs," says Baviera of the University of the Philippines, alluding to the fact that the president's base is in Davao while many of the Chinese tycoons are based in Manila.

Baviera says that "new migrants" have been more "active in facilitating economic exchange with China" and are "facing some pushback from old migrants." She adds that the competition of doing business with China is causing some earlier migrants to "resent the entry of new Chinese" to the Philippines.

Newspaper commentaries on Chinese Filipinos run the gamut from calls that they need to protect Philippine independence against Chinese actions to supporting China and Duterte against the broadsides of critics. One op-ed writer credits Chinese Filipinos with being "midwives to China's economic expansion in the region" and the "pivot to Beijing by president Rodrigo Duterte." But the writer argues that for the "Philippines to maintain its economic independence from China, the Chinese-Filipinos must remain clear-eyed in defending the interests of the country where they have made their home."[172]

Other commentaries call on Chinese Filipinos to play a bigger role in combating criticisms of China and of Duterte's turn toward Beijing. One writer criticized the hanging of red banners with the words "Welcome to the Philippines, Province of China" on footbridges around Manila at the time of the second anniversary of the arbitral tribunal ruling against China in 2018. "The anti-Duterte groups are promoting their racist anti-China platform in order to destroy the government's efforts to have friendlier ties with China," the writer said. The author argued that it is time for Filipino Chinese to "start speaking up, which will help counterbalance the bias and racism being promoted by the opposition against China."[173]

---

172. Clinton Palanca, "Manila's Pivot to Beijing Spells Peril—Not Just Opportunity—for Chinese-Filipinos," *Quartz*, November 10, 2017, https://qz.com/1116029/manilas-pivot-to-beijing-spells-peril-not-just-opportunity-for-chinese-filipinos/.

173. Getsy Tiglao, "Filipino-Chinese Must Step Up to Help the Country," *Manila Bulletin*, July 18, 2018, https://news.mb.com.ph/2018/07/18/filipino-chinese-must-step-up-to-help-the-country/.

Cook of ISEAS Singapore says these differing views about Chinese Filipinos and the role they should play regarding China have at least some of them concerned about a possible "backlash" if "Duterte plays [relations with Beijing] wrong" in the eyes of the larger Philippine population. Chinese Filipinos are concerned they could face criticism and anger from Filipino nationalists if Duterte is seen as too accommodating to China and his moves are seen as supported by the Chinese Filipino community.

CHINA BATTLES FOR HEARTS AND MINDS

Duterte's election opened a yawning opportunity for China to reboot its relations with the Philippines, defuse a sharp critic of Beijing's actions in the South China Sea, and unlock a new market for Chinese companies. Despite Duterte's enthusiasm about the prospects of ties with China, Beijing still faces two key hurdles: widespread misgivings about China among Filipinos and the possibility that the Philippines will elect a less-Beijing friendly leader in 2022.[174]

Despite Duterte's moves toward rapprochement with Beijing, Filipinos still have deep-rooted philosophical differences dating back to the Cold War and distrust China's communist ideology, according to a June 2018 report by AidData, a research lab at William and Mary College in Virginia. The language barrier also makes it hard for people in the Philippines to consume Chinese culture and media.[175]

Like in Malaysia and other Southeast Asian neighbors, much of China's public outreach is focused on financial diplomacy, although three years after Duterte signed a raft of aid and loan agreements very little has happened on the ground, despite considerable Chinese hype by officials and the media. Between 2000 and 2016, Beijing provided the Philippines financing of only $1.1 billion compared with $13.4 billion to Malaysia and around $9 billion each to Cambodia and Indonesia.[176]

Beijing has also stepped up elite diplomacy including visits by Chinese officials and invitations for Philippine officials and congresspersons to visit China. Elite visits by Chinese officials between 2000 and 2016 reached 148, lower than Vietnam (286), Thailand (257), and Cambodia

174. Custer et al., *Ties That Bind*, 24.
175. Ibid., 25.
176. Ibid., 15.

(216).[177] Duterte has visited China four times as president and President Xi and Premier Li have both visited Manila.

Beijing has increased its exchange programs in recent years for businesspersons, academics, civil society representatives, and journalists to visit China for conferences, study tours, and training to "socialize" them to Chinese values and positions and accrue greater empathy and understanding of China's global role. China is doing many of the things the United States used to do in public diplomacy two decades ago, before its foreign aid budget was cut.

Beijing has also bolstered the number of scholarships for Filipino students to study in China, although so far it appears that supply is topping demand.[178] De Castro of De La Salle University says that one group targeted by China are the children of military officers, many of whom are quite skeptical about Beijing's intentions.

In 2016, 3,100 Filipino students were studying in China, lagging far behind such neighbors as Thailand (23,000), Indonesia (14,700), and Vietnam (10,600).[179] Graduates from China face some challenges in the workplace after they return to the Philippines. "Many students coming back from China lack critical thinking [skills]," says a business executive in Manila who said one of his recent hires who graduated from a Chinese university had to be retrained before she could perform her duties.

China has established four Confucius Institutes in the Philippines to teach Mandarin and Chinese history and philosophy.[180] One of the institutes is on the campus of the University of the Philippines, "where it does not have much demand," says Batongbacal, who teaches law at the university. "The student population is a hotbed of nationalism and isn't welcoming to either the Chinese or the Americans." Chinese Filipinos do not use these institutes because they have their own Chinese-language schools that have been operating on weekends for decades.

Beijing's use of the media in the Philippines is relatively muted. China Central Television broadcasts content in Mandarin, but it is only available as a paid channel, which limits viewership. *China Daily* provides news and content from China for paid inserts in newspapers, including the *Philippine Daily Inquirer*, which "promotes the goodness of China in the

177. Ibid., 16.
178. Ibid., 27.
179. Ibid., 13.
180. Ibid., 27.

region," in the words of a diplomat in Manila. China's Ministry of Foreign Affairs provides weekly updates and official statements that are included in the newspapers such as the *Philippine Star* and *Manila Bulletin*.[181]

More recent efforts on television display a softer side of China. In mid-2018, Philippine state network PTV-4, a channel that is a not widely watched, announced that it would begin showing Chinese documentaries, cartoons, and movies dubbed in Tagalog, the Philippine national language. The Filipino Chinese community has also launched a news program that will seek to depict China as more than a communist giant looking to take over Asia.[182]

Chinese ambassador Zhao told *The Straits Times* that the Chinese programming is intended to open "a new window to millions of people in the Philippines to better understand China, its people, their long history, their rich culture, their daily lives, their endeavor[s], and their dreams." Some members of the country's congress are less confident about China's ambitions and tried to block the airing of "invasive foreign agenda" on Philippine television. Six senators filed a resolution in 2018 in which they said the "airing of the Chinese shows may subtly inculcate among Filipinos the authoritarian, one-party state, anti-democratic and atheist ideology and principles of the Chinese Communist Party."[183]

No Southeast Asian nation in recent decades has changed its policies toward Beijing as often and as dramatically as the Philippines. "The flip-flops in Philippine policy toward China over the last quarter century have become larger" with each presidential election, Cook of ISEAS points out. Arroyo, who was president from 2001 to 2010, was more accommodating toward Beijing than Fidel Ramos, who served from 1992 to 1998. Aquino, in office from 2010 to 2016, took a firmer line against China but pursued closer ties with the United States than Ramos. Today, Duterte is taking a more accommodating stance toward China than Arroyo.

What prompts these abrupt shifts? Cook believes "this is predominantly due to China's growing power and aggressiveness."

---

181. Ibid.
182. Raul Dancel, "China Turns to TV for Charm Offensive to Woo Filipinos," *Straits Times*, July 13, 2018, https://www.straitstimes.com/asia/se-asia/china-turns-to-tv-for-charm-offensive-to-woo-filipinos.
183. Ibid.

Where does this leave the Philippines in 2022, when the next presidential elections are scheduled? Unless China manages to change the narrative, recent polling of Filipinos suggests that the country in the next elections may look for a candidate who will seek to again rebalance the country's relations between Beijing and Washington. "Under Aquino, relations with China turned into a contest between the Philippines and China. Under Duterte, relations with China is a contest within the Philippine state," Cook notes.

11. BRUNEI: CHINA'S INVESTMENT DRIVES RELATIONS

Brunei's economic ties with China have flourished more rapidly than political, defense, and cultural cooperation over the past decade. The tiny sultanate, with a population of roughly 430,000 wedged between the two East Malaysian States of Sabah and Sarawak, was the last of the 10 members of the Association of Southeast Asian Nations (ASEAN) to normalize ties with China in 1991.

Brunei received independence from the United Kingdom in 1984 but delayed establishing relations with Beijing because of lingering distrust dating back to China's earlier support for communist movements in the region. Officials were also concerned that Beijing might use the country's proportionately large ethnic Chinese population to destabilize Brunei.[1]

Still, Brunei's earliest encounters with China may date back the furthest among Southeast Asian countries. Allegedly, the second sultan of Brunei, Abdul Majid Hassan, visited China in 1408, where he died at the age of 29, according to Chinese records researched by the Brunei History Center, says Jatswan Singh, a Brunei expert at the University of Malaya in Kuala Lumpur. The sultan was believed to have been buried near the city of Nanjing, where his tomb was discovered in 1958. The only problem is that there is no mention of this sultan in the Brunei Annals to authenticate the claim, Singh says.

Even though Brunei and China exchanged regular visits, economic cooperation was slow to take off after they normalized relations. But by 2018, China was Brunei's largest trading partner, its largest foreign

1. Ian Storey, "President Xi Jinping's Visit to Brunei Highlights Progress and Problems in Bilateral Relations," *ISEAS Perspective*, no. 83 (2018): 2, https://www.iseas.edu.sg/images/pdf/ISEAS_Perspective_2018_83@50.pdf; Ian Storey, *Southeast Asia and the Rise of China: The Search for Security* (New York: Routledge, 2011), 269.

investor, and the most important source of tourists. Two-way trade reached $1.4 billion in 2018, roughly double the level of 2011. Yet Brunei's exports hit only $247 million, as the sultanate's trade deficit with China has ballooned in recent years.[2]

The reason for the deficit: Brunei imports much greater volumes of manufactured products from China than its giant northern neighbor imports oil and liquified natural gas from Brunei. With oil and gas contributing a little over half of Brunei's $16.7 billion gross domestic product (GDP) and nearly 90 percent of its exports in 2017, Brunei clearly has little else to offer China.[3] (Brunei is the world's fourth largest producer of liquified natural gas and third largest producer of oil in Southeast Asia after Indonesia and Malaysia).

Just over 65,000 Chinese tourists visited Brunei in 2018, up more than 20 percent over the previous year.[4] Tourist arrivals from China have received a boost thanks to the increasing numbers of direct flights to Brunei from Chinese cities in recent years. Royal Brunei Airlines, which already had flights from Shanghai, Nanning, Haikou, Hangzhou, and Changsha, was slated to resume direct flights from Beijing in October 2019. China's budget airline Lucky Air has direct flights to Brunei from Kunming and Nanning.[5]

Since about 2010, Chinese firms have emerged as the largest foreign investors in the country. "Brunei is hard pressed for investments and in dire need to diversify its economy from overt dependence on the hydrocarbon industry," says Singh, the Brunei expert. Officials are increasingly concerned that the country will run out of fossil fuels, which drive much of the country's revenue, within the next two decades.

---

2. International Monetary Fund, "Exports, FOB to Partner Countries; Imports, CIF from Partner Countries," *IMF Data*, 2014–2018, http://data.imf.org/regular.aspx?key=61013712.
3. "Brunei Darussalam Key Indicators 2017," Department of Statistics, Department of Economic Planning and Development and the Prime Minister's Office (2018), 9, 19, 25, http://www.depd.gov.bn/DEPD%20Documents%20Library/DOS/BDKI/BDKI_2017.pdf.
4. "Tourism Industry 2019: Towards Brunei Wawasan 2035," Tourism Development Department, Ministry of Primary Resources and Tourism, http://www.tourism.gov.bn/Brochures%20Library/Tourism/Tourism%20Industry%202019.pdf (accessed August 31, 2019).
5. "Brunei Air to Launch Direct Flight to Beijing in October," *XinhuaNet*, July 11, 2019, http://www.xinhuanet.com/english/2019-07/11/c_138218373.htm; "Direct Flight Connects China, Brunei," *XinhuaNet*, July 18, 2017, http://www.xinhuanet.com/english/2017-07/18/c_136452728.htm.

Map 14. Brunei

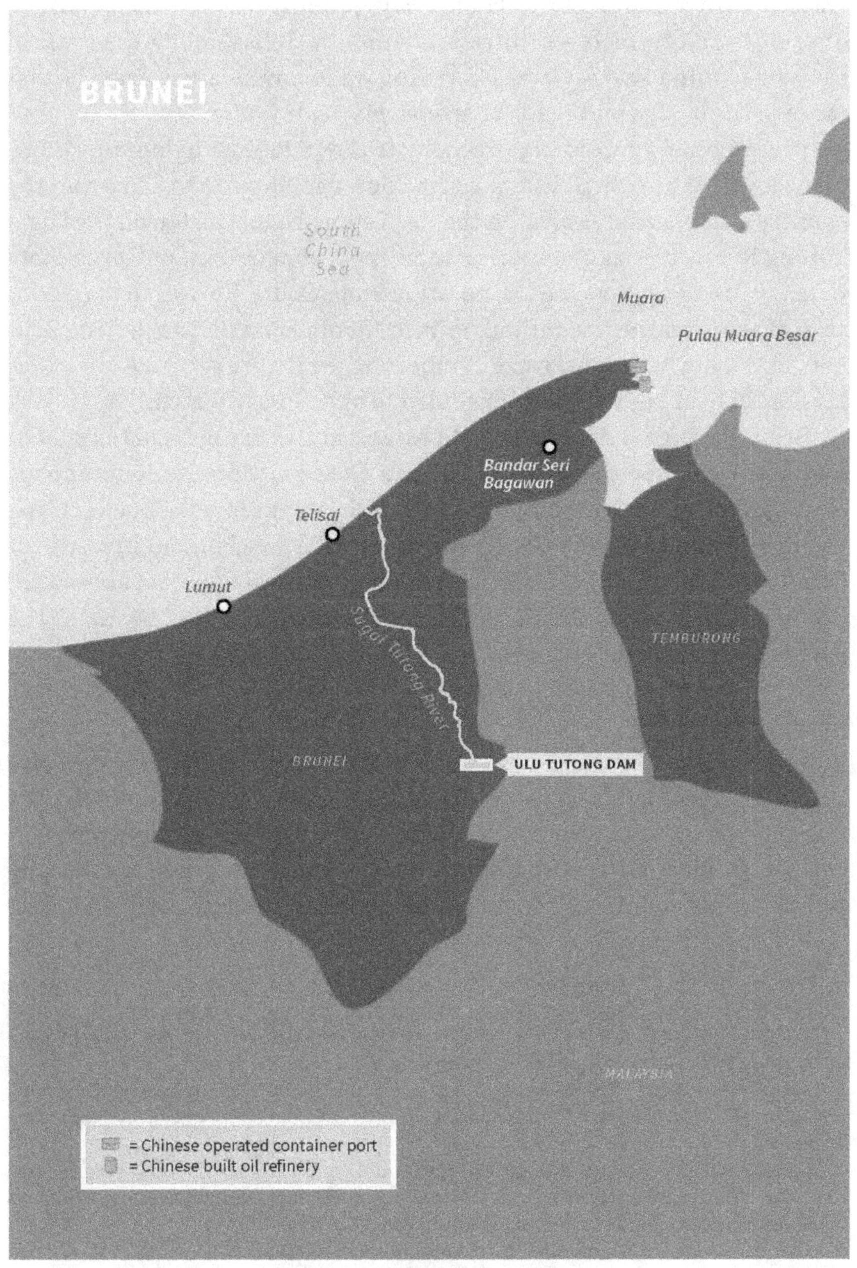

State-owned China Construction Company snared a $123 million contract in 2010 to build a 19-mile highway—almost half of which consists of bridges and tunnels—connecting Lumut to Telisai along the coast of the South China Sea. A viaduct carrying water covers about half the distance of the bridge and road.[6] It opened six years later.

PowerChina, a subsidiary of Sinohydro Foundation Engineering Company, and a Brunei firm won a $85 million deal in 2010 to construct the country's largest water project, the Ulu Tutong Dam, located on the Sugai Tutong River. It began operating in 2017.[7] A consortium of China State Construction Engineering Corporation and a South Korean firm in 2014 started work on the $1.6 billion, 19-mile Temburong Bridge linking Brunei's mainland to the enclave of Temburong, which are separated by a Malaysian strip of land.[8] It was scheduled to open in early 2020.

Brunei signed a deal in 2014 to establish the Brunei–Guangxi Economic Corridor with southern China's Guangxi Zhuang Autonomous Region. One of the corridor's initiatives is an agreement between the Guangxi Beibu Gulf Port Group and the Brunei government investment firm to manage the Muara Container Terminal and boost its annual capacity to 1 million containers, up from the current 220,000, by 2021.[9] The partners are expected to invest over $500 million to upgrade the port and build an industrial park, an agricultural park, and a medicine park nearby.[10]

The biggest Chinese investment is an oil refinery at Pulau Muara Besar, a project led by privately held textiles and petrochemical giant Hengyi Industries International. The refinery in its first phase, which will cost $3.4 billion, will process some 175,000 barrels of crude per day and produce large quantities of paraxylene, benzene, gasoline, and jet fuel for

6. "Bridges in Brunei," *SkyscrapperCity.com*, June 3, 2013, https://www.skyscrapercity.com/showthread.php?p=134220740; Storey, "President Xi Jinping's Visit," 4.

7. "Ulu Tutong Golden Jubilee Dam to Supply Water for 250K People," *The Scoop*, July 20, 2018, https://thescoop.co/2018/07/20/ulu-tutong-golden-jubilee-dam/.

8. Quratul-Ain Bandial, "China Keen to Aid Brunei Economy," *The Jakarta Post*, April 22, 2016, https://www.thejakartapost.com/seasia/2016/04/22/china-keen-to-aid-brunei-economy.html.

9. "China-Brunei JV Starts Running Brunei's Container Terminal—Xinhua," *Reuters*, February 21, 2017, https://www.reuters.com/article/china-shipping/china-brunei-jv-starts-running-bruneis-container-terminal-xinhua-idUSL4N1G660Q.

10. "Brunei–Guangxi Economic Corridor Supports Vision 2035," *ASEANAffairs.com*, April 22, 2016, http://www.aseanaffairs.com/brunei_news/economy/brunei_guangxi_economic_corridor_supports_vision_2035.

export to China and other Asian markets.[11] Some of the output will be reserved for use in Brunei. The first phase was scheduled to come onstream in late 2019 and contribute some $1.3 billion to Brunei's economy in its first year of operation.

Hengyi, which owns 70 percent of the refinery in a venture with Damai Holdings, a subsidiary of the Brunei government's trust fund Strategic Development Capital Fund, is projecting to invest another $12 billion in the second phase. This phase will produce downstream products such as aromatics and industrial chemicals used to make garments and plastics and could generate an estimated additional income of $10 billion, nearly 60 percent of Brunei's GDP.[12]

Interestingly, all of the refinery's crude will be imported rather than using Brunei's oil. Its first shipment of nearly 600,000 barrels of Seria Light arrived in May 2019.[13]

Sultan Hassanal Bolkiah, who has ruled the country since 1967, abruptly reshuffled his cabinet in 2018, replacing six top ministers, including the ministers of energy, finance, and foreign affairs.[14] He offered no explanation, but Brunei-based diplomats attributed the move to allegations of corruption, including senior officials granting family members contracts linked to some Chinese-backed projects.

Neither Brunei nor Beijing has released information about the terms of any of these investment projects, including whether China is providing loans and, if so, at what rates. China has sent thousands of workers to Brunei during the construction of the refinery and infrastructure project but promises to turn over many of the slots to Bruneians once the project is completed. Brunei tightly controls dissent, so until now no public complaints or protests have emerged like they have in Myanmar, Malaysia, Thailand, and even Cambodia about the

11. Danial Nojidi, "A Look at Hengyi's Pulau Muara Besar Project," *Borneo Bulletin*, April 3, 2017, https://borneobulletin.com.bn/look-hengyis-pulau-muara-besar-project/.

12. Ali Bandial and Rasidah Hj Abu Bakar, "Hengyi Refinery to Be Operational by End of 2019," *The Scoop*, March 1, 2019, https://thescoop.co/2019/03/01/hengyi-refinery-to-be-operational-by-end-of-2019/.

13. "Hengyi Prepares to Start Trial Run at Brunei Crude Oil Refinery," *Reuters*, May 9, 2019, https://www.reuters.com/article/brunei-refinery-hengyi/hengyi-starts-trial-runs-at-brunei-crude-oil-refinery-idUSL3N22L0YP.

14. "Brunei Ruler Replaces Top Ministers in Surprise Cabinet Reshuffle," *Reuters*, January 30, 2019, https://www.reuters.com/article/us-brunei-politics/brunei-ruler-replaces-top-ministers-in-surprise-cabinet-reshuffle-idUSKBN1FJ19K.

inflated costs of infrastructure schemes, the environmental damage caused by the projects, or the dislocation of villagers from their land with minimal compensation.

Most, if not all, of China's projects have been brought under the umbrella of the Belt and Road Initiative (BRI), launched in 2013. Brunei's sultan, who has visited China frequently, laid a wreath in 2017 at the monument at Tiananmen Square that commemorates those who died in the revolutionary struggle in the nineteenth and twentieth centuries.[15] Chinese president Xi Jinping made his first visit to Brunei the following year. The two leaders signed a memorandum of understanding (MOU) pledging to boost bilateral cooperation.

The two countries regularly hold foreign ministry consultations and have established modest defense cooperation. Since the early 2000s, they have had military educational exchanges and since 2006 have sent officers to attend development programs or courses at each other's military schools. In 2013, China and Brunei exchanged military attaches.[16] Between 2003 and 2016, they had three military exercises, one port call, and 14 senior-level meetings.[17]

"Brunei is close to China," says a senior Brunei official, who requested not to be identified. "We're called China lovers . . . , but we're not aligned to China's policy. We want to be friends with everybody." He adds: "Regional architecture depends on balancing major powers in the region. We can't take sides."

The ethnic Chinese in Malay-dominated Brunei, who are mainly of Hokkien decent, make up roughly one-tenth of the population. They play a dominant role in the business sector, controlling the hotel, garment, fishing gear, plumbing, and gravel pit industries. "Every Chinese [family] had their business monopoly in the small economy," says a diplomat who formerly served in Brunei. The ethnic Chinese were early investors in China and for years had more investment in China than Chinese companies had in Brunei.

---

15. "Brunei's Sultan Lays Wreath to Monument to People's Heroes in Beijing," *Xinhua*, September 13, 2017, http://en.people.cn/n3/2017/0913/c90000-9268591.html.

16. Storey, *Southeast Asia and the Rise of China*, 273.

17. Kenneth Allen, Phillip C. Saunders, and John Chen, *Chinese Military Diplomacy, 2003–2016: Trends and Implications* (Washington, DC: National Defense University Press, 2017), 63, https://ndupress.ndu.edu/Portals/68/Documents/stratperspective/china/ChinaPerspectives-11.pdf?ver=2017-07-17-153301-093.

Ethnic Chinese first began arriving in the seventeenth century and their numbers surged after Brunei became a British protectorate in the late 1880s and then again after oil was discovered in the late 1920s. Another surge of newer Chinese migrants has unfolded since China and Brunei stepped up their economic ties. "The old [time] Chinese are very unhappy about how China is given all kinds of business concessions," says the former diplomat, implying that the local Chinese feel left out of much of the economic action.

For Brunei, the issue of overlapping claims in the South China Sea is much less contentious than is the case of the other claimants: Vietnam, the Philippines, and Malaysia. China's nine-dash line, which Beijing uses to make its claims to four-fifths of the disputed sea, reaches down to about 35 nautical miles off Brunei's coast where much of the country's oil and gas activities take place. Brunei has not been as vocal as its neighbors in rejecting China's nine-dash-line claim as being incompatible with the United Nations Convention on the Law of the Sea. But the country's domestic laws and its 2009 submission to the UN Commission on the Limits of the Continental Shelf make clear that Brunei has rights to its exclusive economic zone (EEZ) and the seabed under it.[18]

In 1988 Brunei claimed a long and narrow 200-nautical-mile EEZ and an extended continental shelf.[19] Louisa Reef is in Brunei's EEZ, while Owen Shoal and Rifleman Bank are on its extended continental shelf beyond 200 nautical miles. Brunei does not claim sovereignty over these submerged features, but it claims rights to them as part of the seabed belonging to its continental shelf, says Gregory Poling, a South China Sea expert at the Center for Strategic and International Studies.

These features are also claimed by China, Taiwan, and Vietnam, which currently occupies Rifleman Bank. Brunei is the only claimant that does not occupy any of features in the disputed sea and does not have a military presence in the area that it claims, Singh of the University of Malaya pointed out.[20]

---

18. "Brunei Darussalam's Preliminary Submission concerning the Outer Limits of Its Continental Shelf," https://www.un.org/Depts/los/clcs_new/submissions_files/preliminary/brn2009preliminaryinformation.pdf (accessed October 20, 2019).
19. R. Haller-Trost, "The Brunei-Malaysia Dispute over Territorial and Maritime Claims in International Law," *Maritime Briefings* 1, no. 3 (1994), https://www.dur.ac.uk/ibru/publications/view/?id=226.
20. The Editors, "Brunei Maintains a Low Profile in Pressing Its South China Sea Claims," *World Politics Review*, January 28, 2016, https://www.worldpoliticsreview.com/trend-lines/17799/brunei-maintains-a-low-profile-in-pressing-its-south-china-sea-claims.

Malaysia and Brunei formerly had overlapping claims that have now mostly been resolved, and the two countries cooperate to jointly develop fossil fuel resources in areas of Brunei earlier claimed by Malaysia.[21]

Chinese coast guard and maritime militia vessels are not reported to carefully monitor or harass Brunei's oil and gas development sites in the South China Sea as they regularly do neighboring Malaysia's projects operated by state-owned Petronas and Royal Dutch Shell subsidiaries off the coasts of Sabah and Sarawak near Brunei. Illegal Chinese fishing boats are not reported to fish in Brunei's EEZ like they do off Indonesia or the Philippines, and maritime law enforcement vessels are not reported to harass Brunei fishers.

Beijing began pressing Brunei to consider joint development of fossil fuels around 2005, when former president Hu Jintao visited the sultanate. In 2011, the two countries signed an MOU on energy cooperation between China National Offshore Oil Corporation (CNOOC) and Brunei National Petroleum. Shell reportedly was told by officials to try to work out a joint venture with CNOOC but, in the end, "the sultan said no, saying it infringed on Brunei's sovereignty," says a diplomat who worked in Brunei until recently.

During Xi's visit in 2018 the Chinese leader again urged Brunei to consider joint development, but no apparent progress has been made in negotiating an agreement. "The sultan recognizes it would be a red line to the U.S. and to Vietnam," says the former diplomat.

On the recent reclamation and militarization of islands in the Spratly grouping by China, Brunei is softer than the other claimants. "Everyone has done their part in reclamation" of islands, the Brunei official says, referring to China, Vietnam, the Philippines, and Malaysia. "We've said everyone should stop militarization of the South China Sea."

Brunei seems to suggest a high level of equivalence to the reclamation activities of all parties in the dispute, even though the 3,200 acres of artificial islands China has built up through dredging and landfill are many multiples larger than that done by any of its neighbors. In addition, only China has moved missile systems and prepared to deploy combat aircraft to the artificial islands it has built in the disputed sea.

Brunei has also been quiet when China's recent assertive behavior in the South China has been discussed within ASEAN. When Malaysia,

21. Storey, "President Xi Jinping's Visit," 5.

the Philippines, and Vietnam organized the first ASEAN Claimants Working Group Meeting in Manila in 2014, Brunei promised to attend. But, in the end, it did not send a representative from the local embassy to fill the chair behind the name tent the organizer had placed on the table.[22]

22. The Editors, "Brunei Maintains a Low Profile in Pressing Its South China Sea Claims."

EPILOGUE: FOR SOUTHEAST ASIA, HOW CLOSE TO CHINA IS TOO CLOSE?

What will Southeast Asia look like in, say, 2030 in the wake of China's sweeping ambitions and stepped-up economic, diplomatic, military, and cultural engagement? Will Chinese navy vessels have regular access to the Cambodian navy base at Ream on the Gulf of Thailand or Myanmar's Kyaukphyu port on the Indian Ocean? Will China have built up Scarborough Shoal off the Philippines and transformed it into a base for deploying radar and missile batteries?

Will a Chinese-built and financed high-speed rail link Kunming in southern China through Laos, Thailand, and Malaysia to Singapore, further tying these economies to the supply-chain economy running through China? Will the United States' move to ban Huawei and Chinese supercomputer companies have resulted in a bifurcation of the global digital system, with most Southeast Asian countries relying on Huawei to lay the undersea cable grid and develop their successor to the 5G network?

Will Chinese oil rigs be pumping oil and gas from wells near Vanguard Bank off Vietnam's southern coast, Luconia Breakers off the Malaysian state of Sarawak, and Reed Bank off the Philippines after having dislodged by the early 2020s the international companies operating in those areas under contracts with these Southeast Asian countries? Will Myanmar, Laos, Thailand, Cambodia, and Vietnam be linked increasingly into China's highly developed electricity grid to meet their domestic power shortages?

Will the dams in China and the ones it has built and financed in Laos on the Mekong River have cut off enough water, silt, and fish to shrink the Tonle Sap in Cambodia to a fraction of its former self and cause the fertile Mekong Delta in southern Vietnam to slip under saltwater from the South China Sea? Will these developments have prompted millions of environmental refugees to flee their homes? Will China's dredging and blasting of rocks in the Mekong near the Thai town of Chiang Rai make it possible for 500-ton ships and military vessels to sail directly from Kunming to Luang Prabang in Laos or even down to Vientiane, the capital?

Will China's increasing economic and military heft have convinced most Southeast Asian nations to abandon the global rules-based trading system and bandwagon with Beijing to promote a Sino-centric trading system using Chinese norms and rules? Will the migration of Chinese into northern Myanmar and Laos over decades have turned these regions effectively into new provinces of China?

To be sure, some of these scenarios might be a bit far-fetched and perhaps more than Beijing's leaders would wish for even in their wildest dreams. Still, like the ghost of Christmas yet to come in Charles Dickens's compelling *A Christmas Carol* novel, they do provide warnings of what could happen if Southeast Asian nations, the United States, and regional players like Japan, India, and Australia do not get their acts together.

Southeast Asia may sometimes feel that it bears the full brunt of Beijing's assertiveness and ambition, but it does have considerable agency and could do more if the countries were less competitive and more cooperative with each other.

The Association of Southeast Asian Nations (ASEAN) works overtime to keep China engaged with the grouping diplomatically, and ASEAN did negotiate a free-trade agreement with Beijing and has wrapped up the Regional Comprehensive Economic Partnership (RCEP) with China and five other nations including Japan, South Korea, and Australia after India pulled out in late 2019.

But beyond their trade agreements with China and the 2018 joint maritime military exercise between ASEAN and China, the 10 nations largely seem to be competing among each other and pretty much going it alone bilaterally with China. Each of their relations with Beijing are unique and different from that of their neighbors. These differences are determined by their geographic proximity to China, their size and economic clout, the history of their relations, their domestic politics, and the strength of their militaries.

Comparing notes among each other, for example, could be immensely helpful in addressing China's infrastructure projects under the Belt and Road Initiative (BRI). Then Malaysia would have learned that it was paying

China at least 1 percent more for its loans for the East Coast Rail Link than Beijing, after years of haggling, agreed to charge Laos and Thailand for loans for rail projects in their countries.

Laos might not have agreed to take out a sizable loan from China and pay hundreds of millions of dollars from its own budget to build a high-speed train from southern China if Vientiane had realized Thailand had no plans any time soon to connect a high-speed rail from its border with Laos to the border with Malaysia. Thailand has other rail priorities, so Laos could have agreed to a less costly regular speed train to transport rice and mangoes to Kunming.

Myanmar had to struggle mightily to figure out how to scale back China's outsized ambitions for a giant port in Kyaukphyu on the Indian Ocean. Naypyidaw could have learned some lessons if it had talked to the Lao and the Thais, but instead it turned to economists from Western countries for ideas on how to scale back the project and make it more manageable. To be sure, Myanmar struck much more appropriate deals than it likely would have had it gone off on its own.

When China's coast guard and maritime militia vessels began harassing oil exploration rigs off the coasts of Vietnam and Malaysia in mid-2019, ASEAN could not agree on a statement even mildly calling out China's actions so the association said nothing. That is not surprising because Beijing has been able to divide ASEAN and buy off Cambodia to block consensus within the grouping with pledges of new assistance.

But it also appears that Hanoi and Kuala Lumpur did not talk with each other when oil exploration vessels they had contracted to work off their coasts in the South China Sea came under pressure from Chinese ships in mid-2019. Malaysian officials did not even mention publicly or suggest that their journalists cover the fact that vessels exploring for oil and gas off their coast were tailed, monitored, and harassed by Chinese ships for weeks at a time, presumably because government officials were trying to court more infrastructure projects from Beijing.

In 2014, before Rodrigo Duterte was elected president of the Philippines and decided to pivot to China, the foreign ministers of Malaysia, the Philippines, and Vietnam met in Manila to discuss their disputes with China in the South China Sea, but Brunei, the fourth Southeast Asian claimant, did not even send a representative from its embassy to fill the sultanate's seat.

Southeast Asian nations have a host of overlapping territorial and maritime claims with each other in the South China Sea. Parts of the maritime border north of Borneo are claimed by Malaysia, the Philippines, and Brunei. Vietnam claims all the Spratlys, some of which are claimed by Malaysia and the Philippines, and parts of the sea off Sabah have overlapping claims between Malaysia and the Philippines. The Philippines and Malaysia have a dispute over northern Sabah itself. If the Southeast Asians could resolve some of these territorial and maritime disputes among themselves, it would set an example to China of what is possible.

The ASEAN countries and China are in the process of negotiating a code of conduct, a framework for resolving disputes in the South China Sea through dialogue. A Chinese leader said in 2019 that his government would like to see the code hammered out within the next three years. Beijing is undoubtedly confident little real progress will be made because the ASEAN countries will be hard-pressed to hammer out a consensus on a code with enforcement provisions among themselves before they can present a unified stance to China.

China is intensely aware of the rifts and distrust between Southeast Asian nations, so it gets away with working with each of them bilaterally rather than as a group to "divide and conquer" and play them off against each other.

For the most part that is how ASEAN prefers to work with Beijing. The "reality is that as a multilateral organization, ASEAN has always prized sovereignty of independent member states above all else. And this organizational structure lends itself to bilateralism," says Joseph Chinyong Liow, professor of comparative and international politics at the S. Rajaratnam School of International Studies (RSIS) in Singapore.

The ASEANs are often somewhat defeatist in dealing with China, asking how they can possibly compete against China's power and resist its agenda. But Paul Heer, who previously served as the U.S. National Intelligence Officer for East Asia, suggests that they can address that "by undermining Beijing's assumptions and premises. Don't let the Chinese exploit your differences or assume that you can't agree on how to approach Beijing," he says.

"Shelve your differences and devise a unified position with which to confront Beijing. Don't use the excuse that Beijing will obstruct it. Beijing doesn't like to be viewed as the obstructionist party—because this invites broader international attention and pressure on China," Heer says. "This is where ASEAN has leverage."

SOUTHEAST ASIAN HEDGES

As China steps up its influence in Southeast Asia and the region has become less confident about the depth of future engagement by the United States, the grouping has worked overtime to establish ties to other powers to hedge its links with the major powers. It has sought to build out its relations with the European Union, but particularly with countries closer to home—Japan, India, and Australia.

Japan

Japan has long been a major investor, official aid donor, and trader with Southeast Asia, but in recent years it has also built out its political and security engagement with the region as Tokyo has sought to balance its own complicated relations with Beijing and uncertainties about Washington. Japan's political, economic, and security engagement with Southeast Asia got a boost in 2017 after the administration of President Donald Trump announced the "Free and Open Indo-Pacific" (FOIP), which U.S. officials borrowed from Tokyo (with a few changes), according to Kei Koga, who teaches public policy and global affairs at RSIS.[1]

Southeast Asians have a more positive attitude about Japan than about the United States and China. A survey of foreign affairs experts and leaders of civil society, media, and business communities in Southeast Asian countries in late 2018 conducted by the ISEAS-Yusof Ishak Institute in Singapore gave Japan a high "trust" ranking compared to the United States and China. When asked which countries will "do the right thing" in contributing to global peace, security, prosperity, and governance, 66 percent of survey respondents said they were "confident" or "very confident" in Japan. Some 27 percent said that about the United States and just under 20 percent about China.[2]

1. Kei Koga, "The Emerging Indo-Pacific Era," *Pacific Forum: Comparative Connections* 21, no. 1 (May 2019), http://cc.pacforum.org/2019/05/the-emerging-indo-pacific-era/.
2. Tang Siew Mun, Moe Thuzar, Hoang Thi Ha, Termsak Chalermpalanupap, Pham Thi Phuong Thao, and Anuthida Saelaow Qian, *The State of Southeast Asia: 2019 Survey Report*

When Singapore and other ASEAN countries informed Japan that they would not join groupings related to the FOIP strategy unless it incorporated the concept of "ASEAN unity and centrality," Japan moved to integrate this principle into its larger strategy. Some ASEAN members also warned that referring to the FOIP as a strategy suggested that it was aimed at China, prompting Tokyo to drop the word strategy and just call it the Indo-Pacific, Koga said.[3]

Japan has bolstered its defense commitments to Southeast Asia in recent years, says Ken Jimbo, a Southeast Asia expert at Keio University. In 2012, shortly before China captured Scarborough Shoal from the Philippines, Japan announced that it would provide Manila with 10 patrol vessels for its coast guard in one of Tokyo's "most visible commitments" to promote "maritime capacity building in Southeast Asia," Jimbo says. In 2016, Japan promised to supply Manila with two large patrol vessels and to loan it as many as five used TC-90 surveillance planes to counter China's expansion in the South China Sea.[4] The following year, Japan said it would provide six patrol vessels to Vietnam as part of a $1.1 billion loan package.[5]

Japan also stepped up its own naval operations in the region. For two months in 2018, three Japanese destroyers sailed through the South China Sea and Indian Ocean making port calls in Indonesia, Singapore, and the Philippines to "promote cooperation and interoperability with partner navies."[6] In 2019, two Japanese destroyers launched joint exercises in the Indo-Pacific region "to improve tactical capabilities and strengthen coordination with foreign forces" during stops in Brunei, Malaysia, the Philippines, Singapore, and Vietnam.[7]

(Singapore: ISEAS-Yusof Ishak Institute, 2019), 31, 29, 26, 30, https://www.iseas.edu.sg/images/pdf/TheStateofSEASurveyReport_2019.pdf.

3. Koga, "The Emerging Indo-Pacific Era."

4. Robin Harding and Michael Peel, "Japan Provides Ships for Philippines to Help Counter China at Sea," *Financial Times*, September 6, 2016, https://www.ft.com/content/6bdb1cdc-7422-11e6-b60a-de4532d5ea35.

5. Kyodo, Reuters, Bloomberg, "Abe Pledges Fresh Security-Related Aid to Vietnam," *Japan Times*, January 16, 2017, https://www.japantimes.co.jp/news/2017/01/16/national/politics-diplomacy/abe-jokowi-unite-south-china-sea-disputes-plan-two-plus-two-meeting/#.XXZulShKhhE.

6. "Indo Southeast Asia Deployment 2018," Japan Maritime Self-Defense Force, https://www.mod.go.jp/msdf/en/operation/operation2018.html (accessed September 9, 2019).

7. Ibid.

Tokyo also stepped up its political ties with Southeast Asian nations, particularly with Vietnam, which will be the ASEAN chair in 2020 and serves as Japan's country coordinator in ASEAN in the three years until 2021.

Japan was long the largest investor and largest official aid donor in Southeast Asia, but in recent years China has started to give Japan a run for its money. Indonesia completed the first $1.1 billion leg of the Jakarta subway in 2019 with a loan from the Japan International Cooperation Agency (JICA). The second leg of the subway is under construction and will be completed in 2024.[8] Japan is also providing loans for the construction of the Patimban Deep Sea Port in West Java, near an industrial park where many Japanese firms have factories.

Japan pledged in 2017 to provide the Philippines with $8.8 billion to rebuild the battle-scarred city of Marawai on the island of Mindanao and upgrade the country's infrastructure. Tokyo agreed to modernize the country's rail network, including the first subway system to help relieve Manila's notorious traffic jams. Japan pledged to help the country boosts its power generating capabilities.[9]

Japan has also promised to support a Thai-led initiative awkwardly dubbed the Ayeyawady-Chao Phraya-Mekong Economic Cooperation Strategy (ACMECS) to boost cooperation among the countries linked to these three rivers—Cambodia, Laos, Myanmar, Thailand, and Vietnam. ACMECS is clearly an example of Thailand wanting to work with its neighbors to provide a homegrown balance to China's overwhelming dominance in developing infrastructure along the Mekong.

China dislodged Japan as the region's largest trading partner in 2009 and in recent years China's exports have been up to four times higher than Japan's. Four Southeast Asian countries—Brunei, Malaysia, Singapore, and Vietnam—are members of the Comprehensive and Progressive Agreement for the Trans-Pacific Partnership, which includes Japan, but not China. The agreement went into effect at the end of 2018, but it is not

8. Agence France-Presse, "Gridlocked Jakarta Inaugurates Its First MRT System," *South China Morning Post*, March 24, 2019, https://www.scmp.com/news/asia/southeast-asia/article/3003032/gridlocked-jakarta-inaugurates-its-first-mrt-system.

9. Masayaki Yuda, "With Its Eye on China, Japan Pledges $9 Billion in Philippine Aid," *Nikkei Asian Review*, November 2, 2019, https://asia.nikkei.com/Politics/With-its-eye-on-China-Japan-pledges-9-billion-in-Philippine-aid.

yet known what impact that will have on trade of the Southeast Asian members with China and Japan.

"Southeast Asia is not completely vulnerable to China economically," says Koga, "because it can rely on ASEAN investment," which has risen exponentially in recent years and reached $26.6 billion in 2017. But Japan remains the largest investor from outside Southeast Asia. In 2017, Japan invested $13.2 billion in the ASEAN countries while China invested $11.3 billion.[10] However, in Cambodia, Laos, and Myanmar, China is now the largest investor.

Even though Washington and Tokyo often cooperate under the FOIP, they also have significant differences. For example, Japan takes a "softer approach" toward the nondemocratic Southeast Asian countries, Myanmar and Cambodia, and human rights Koga noted.

The differences in priorities and threat perceptions between Washington and Tokyo sometimes make it difficult for them to capitalize fully on the opportunities for collaboration in Southeast Asia

India

As Southeast Asia faces concerns about both Beijing and Washington, the grouping has also looked to deepen strategic ties with India, a process that has been considerably slower than that with Japan.

Prime Minister Narendra Modi has sought to boost India's political and economic ties with Southeast Asian nations under a policy one of his predecessors dubbed "Act East," which was intended to pick up the pace of the previous government's "Look East" policy. Commenting on New Delhi's somewhat erratic engagement with Southeast Asia, Pramit Pal Chaudhuri, foreign editor of the *Hindustan Times*, joked that "India suffers from attention deficit disorder."

In 2018, Modi invited the 10 ASEAN leaders as guests to India's annual national day celebrations in New Delhi to jump-start closer ties between India and the ASEAN grouping. One outcome was an agreement between the leaders to hold a maritime security dialogue.

---

10. The ASEAN Secretariat and United Nations Conference on Trade and Development, *ASEAN Investment Report 2018* (Jakarta: ASEAN Secretariat, November 2018), 6, https://asean.org/storage/2018/11/ASEAN-Investment-Report-2018-for-Website.pdf.

Singapore is one of India's closest defense partners and the two countries have a growing strategic partnership. They signed their first defense cooperation agreement in 2003 and a memorandum of understanding on joint army exercises in 2005. The two countries have annual joint army and navy exercises and, given Singapore's limited space for military training, India has opened its air force and artillery firing ranges to Singapore's armed forces. Since 2015, Singapore and New Delhi have had three defense minister dialogues a year.[11]

Singapore is India's largest foreign investor and the two countries have agreed to review their 2005 Comprehensive Economic Cooperation Agreement, New Delhi's first with another country. The agreement cut tariffs and doubled two-way trade to $25 billion. Singapore has announced that it will open a Singapore-India incubation program to help start-ups break into the Indian market.[12]

Further west, New Delhi several decades ago promised to build a road from India through Bangladesh to Myanmar, but progress has been glacially slow at least in part because it would go through remote underdeveloped northeastern India. India's record on infrastructure construction has not been good, says Chaudhuri, who also serves on the prime minister's national security advisory board. But he adds that this could begin to change as India deepens its ties with Japan, which has a long history of building infrastructure in Southeast Asia.

In early 2019, Myanmar's military for the first time drove ethnic Naga rebels out of a sanctuary in northern Myanmar from where they long launched raids into northeastern India and then retreated into Myanmar when Indian security forces counterattacked. Some analysts say the Myanmar military is hoping the move will convince India to take a bigger role in balancing Beijing. China again has a stronger position in Myanmar after Western countries soured on the country in the

---

11. Rajeswari Pillai Rajagoplan, "Army Exercise Showcases Growing India-Singapore Defense Collaboration," Observer Research Foundation, April 18, 2019, https://www.orfonline.org/research/army-exercise-showcases-growing-india-singapore-defence-collaboration-50004/.

12. Chuang Peck Ming, "India and Singapore to Forge Deeper Economic Ties," *Straits Times*, June 1, 2018, https://www.straitstimes.com/business/companies-markets/india-and-singapore-to-forge-deeper-economic-ties.

wake of the military's expulsion of hundreds of thousands of Rohingya Muslims in 2017.[13]

Vietnam has some of the oldest and deepest ties to India. Hanoi has discussed procuring defense equipment such as surface-to-air missiles from India as Vietnam seeks to bolster its naval defenses at a time when China is stepping up pressure in the South China Sea. India offered Vietnam's defense industry a $500 million line of credit several years ago, but the two sides have been slow to agree on a framework for the loan.[14] Their two militaries do some joint military exercises and Indian sailors have trained Vietnamese to operate the six Kilo-class submarines Hanoi bought from Russia.

Southeast Asian countries would like to develop deeper defense ties with India, including doing more military exercises, but progress has been limited. "Sixty percent of our military equipment is obsolete," says Aparna Pande, an India expert at the Hudson Institute in Washington. "Most of the military budget goes for salaries and pensions," she says. "We don't have military hardware to send abroad."

India's Oil and Natural Gas Corporation (ONGC) in a venture with PetroVietnam explored for oil and gas in two blocks in the disputed South China Sea for several years but did not find anything, notes Chaudhuri. "They tried to pull out, but the Foreign Ministry told them they couldn't leave," the editor says, implying that India did not want to concede that the oil company had failed literally in China's backyard. "Vietnam took pity and gave them another, better block," he says about the 2019 talks between both sides about swapping blocks.

Modi visited Indonesia for the first time in 2018 and while there elevated India's bilateral ties with Indonesia to a comprehensive strategic partnership. Modi and President Joko Widodo signed 15 agreements, including one to boost defense cooperation. The two leaders also pledged to boost bilateral trade that in 2017 reached $18 billion, less than a third of China's trade with Indonesia that year. India is also building its first-ever

13. Bertil Lintner, "Myanmar and India Becoming Brothers in Arms," *Asia Times*, June 12, 2019, https://www.asiatimes.com/2019/06/article/myanmar-and-india-becoming-brothers-in-arms/.

14. Saurav Jha, "Can India Break into Vietnam's Defense Market?," *The Diplomat*, December 5, 2019, https://thediplomat.com/2018/12/can-india-break-into-vietnams-defense-market/.

overseas deep-sea port in Sabang in Aceh Province near the Andaman Sea in a joint venture with Indonesia.

ASEAN aspirations to boost trade with Indian floundered when it pulled out of the RCEP trade agreement after six years of talks. India apparently worried the deal, which would have reduced tariffs, would prompt a flood of Chinese products. The Southeast Asian countries often blamed India for slowing down the agreement before it withdrew from the talks. "We're not good on trade," says Chaudhuri. "India is very protectionist."

Most of India's foreign policy and security goals are targeted on meeting India's domestic needs, argues Pande. "Our focus is domestic," she says. "Relations with the world are important but only to achieve our goals."

Australia

Australia in 2018 hosted its first-ever summit with the leaders of Southeast Asia. For many observers, the summit signified that smaller Asia-Pacific countries want to deepen their partnership at a time when China is becoming more assertive and the United States' commitment to the region remains uncertain under President Trump.

Indonesian president Joko Widodo startled the conference when he proposed that Australia should consider full membership in ASEAN. His proposal suggested to many that the grouping wanted to boost its clout at a time of considerable uncertainty. In their concluding Sydney Declaration, the 11 leaders reaffirmed their support for trade and investment and promised to resist "all forms of protectionism," a clear chiding of U.S. trade policies.

The leaders also emphasized "the importance of non-militarization" and "self-restraint" in the South China Sea, a reference to Beijing's activities in the disputed sea. A year earlier in his speech to the Shangri-la Dialogue security forum, then prime minister Malcolm Turnbull had declared that "in this brave new world we cannot rely on great powers to safeguard our interests."

Australia sees its "stability, security, and prosperity" directly tied to Southeast Asia, a senior official in the Indo-Pacific Strategy Division of the Department of Foreign Affairs and Trade said in a speech in mid-2019. "Southeast Asia frames Australia's northern approaches and our key trade routes flow through it," he said. "ASEAN lies at the nexus of the Indo-Pacific, geographically, diplomatically, and strategically." The official said an "ASEAN centered architecture" takes on greater significance as the collective "we" seeks to "shape a region that adheres to law, rule, and norm."[15]

Prime Minister Scott Morrison summed up the importance of Southeast Asia to Australia in a speech in June 2019: "Our special relationship with ASEAN since its inception has plugged us into a critical network of independent and dynamic developing economies working together to create their own norms and rules for intra-regional growth, critical to the interests of all Indo-Pacific members."

But Morrison also expressed concern about rising tension between the United States and China. "The world's most important bilateral relationship—the U.S.-China relationship—is strained. Trade tensions have escalated. The collateral damage is spreading. The global trading system is under real pressure," Morrison warned. "Global growth projections are being wound back."[16]

Analysts note that Australia is somewhat ambivalent about both the FOIP concept and the Quadrilateral Security Dialogue—the "Quad," for short—made up of Australia, India, Japan, and the United States, because it has only limited confidence in Tokyo and New Delhi in an Asia-Pacific–wide strategy.

"Australian [foreign policy] institutions have a huge focus on Southeast Asia," says Aaron Connelly, who until recently headed up Southeast Asia research at the Lowy Institute in Sydney. As an American who has worked in Washington, Connelly was implying a considerable contrast between Australia's foreign policy agencies and their counterparts in the United States, who see Southeast Asia as only one among many priorities.

Like Japan and India, Australia takes a less strident stance on human rights problems in the region. "Australia is not as outspoken at the U.S.,"

15. Philip Green, "Australia–Japan-ASEAN: Strengthening the Core of the Indo-Pacific," Australian Government, Department of Foreign Affairs and Trade (speech, Perth USAsia Centre, March 22, 2019), https://dfat.gov.au/news/speeches/Pages/australia-japan-asean-strengthening-the-core-of-the-indo-pacific.aspx.

16. Scott Morrison, "Where We Live," Asialink Bloomberg Address (speech, Sydney, NSW, Australia, June 26, 2019), https://www.pm.gov.au/media/where-we-live-asialink-bloomberg-address.

says Connelly, who is now with the International Institute for Strategic Studies in Singapore. "It holds back more on human rights." He points out that Australia continues training programs for the military in Myanmar in such areas as teaching English, peacekeeping, and the rule of law at a time when Washington is shunning Myanmar's armed forces for their abuses of the Rohingya.

The ASEAN-Australia-New Zealand Free Trade Agreement, which was signed in 2009, is one of deepest economic agreements ASEAN has signed with its dialogue partners, but its economic impact has been less than overwhelming. Australia has separate bilateral trade agreements with Singapore, Thailand, and Malaysia, which turned these countries into Australia's third largest trading partners.

Australians often say that no country is more important to them than Indonesia. In 2019, the two countries signed an Indonesia-Australia Comprehensive Economic Partnership that will deepen ties between these two neighbors. This agreement followed several months of diplomatic tensions after Australia announced plans to move its embassy in Israel to Jerusalem. The trade deal is expected to provide new impetus for Australian trade with Indonesia. The two countries also have an annual leaders' meeting and a 2 + 2 meeting of foreign and defense ministers.

In addition to their deep trade and investment ties, Australia and Singapore hold regular joint exercises and Australia provides training facilities where the land-short Singaporeans can conduct training exercises. Canberra upgraded its ties with Malaysia to a comprehensive strategic partnership in 2016.

In 2018, Australia launched three new cooperative assistance initiatives in ASEAN. The first is an economic governance and infrastructure project under which Australia will support infrastructure project selection and preparation and help mobilize financing.

The second is a water resources project that will support more equitable, transparent, and effective water resource management, which is particularly important as Laos and Cambodia plan more dams along the Mekong and the region faces challenges posed by climate change. A third initiative will deepen Australia's investment in helping the region tackle illegal, unreported, and unregulated fishing and boost maritime domain awareness.

Prime Minister Morrison in August 2019 paid an official visit to Vietnam, a strategic partner, and announced commitments to increase economic ties and strengthen defense and security cooperation. But the visit took place while a Chinese survey ship and supporting coast guard vessels were hassling a Vietnam-sponsored oil rig exploring for oil and gas near Vanguard Bank off the coast of southern Vietnam. China's actions were discussed in Hanoi, but Morrison avoided calling out Beijing's behavior, presumably to avoid offending China, which is Australia's most important economic partner.

The reluctance of the Australian prime minister to call Beijing out suggests that nations in China's crosshairs cannot expect much support from countries like Australia that are highly dependent on China economically, said Huong Le Thu of the Australian Strategic Policy Institute.[17]

U.S.-CHINA STRATEGIC COMPETITION

Southeast Asians desperately want the mounting strategic rivalry between China and the United States resolved soon. Countries like Vietnam have picked up some increased trade as other nations look for other markets to avoid tariffs from the trade war. Some factories from China have moved to Thailand and Vietnam as alternative manufacturing hubs. But overall in Southeast Asia most leaders fret that the strategic competition will cause a global economic slowdown and result in a more troubled and fractured world.

Voicing the concerns of many in the region, Singapore prime minister Lee Hsien Loong in mid-2019 appealed to the United States and China to "reconcile" their differences. He told those attending the annual Shangri-la defense summit in Singapore that the U.S.-China relationship is "the most important in the world today." He adds, "How the two work out their tensions and frictions will define the international environment for decades to come."

Lee said the rest of the world will have to accept that "China will grow and strengthen and that it is neither possible nor wise for them to prevent this from happening." He recognized that the United States has "the most difficult adjustment," but added that "it is well worth the U.S. forging

17. Huong Le Thu, "Morrison Bolsters Bilateral Ties While Avoiding China Rhetoric in Vietnam," *The Strategist*, August 28, 2019, https://www.aspistrategist.org.au/morrison-bolsters-bilateral-ties-while-avoiding-china-rhetoric-in-vietnam/.

a new understanding that will integrate China's aspirations with the current system of rules and norms."

But Lee worried that the global community is "headed for a more divided and troubled world." He said attitudes in both Washington and Beijing have been hardening and noted that there is a "growing bipartisan consensus" among Americans that "China has taken advantage of the U.S. for far too long," adding that "Americans now talk openly about containing China."

Lee appealed to both countries to "understand the other's point of view and reconcile each other's interests" to avoid upending the global system. "Even short of outright conflict, a prolonged period of tension and uncertainty will be extremely damaging," the Singapore leader warned. "In economic terms the loss will be not just a percentage point or two of world GDP, but the huge benefits of globalized markets and production chains, and the sharing of knowledge and breakthroughs that enable all countries to progress together."[18]

Many in Southeast Asia agree with Singapore's prime minister, but others take a more strident view. "Some policymakers used to think that the more you engage China, the more you can make China a responsible stakeholder," says a senior Southeast Asian official who asked not to be identified. "We need to change this perception. The truth is that China is trying to break the international order where it is weak."

"Some think China can respect the role of the U.S. [in the Asia Pacific]," the official said. "That's not true. It wants to replace the U.S. and be number one."

A giant complicating factor for Washington in Southeast Asia is that these countries all want different things from Washington and they also have very different threat perceptions about China.

While many in the United States support Washington taking an "adversarial stance" toward China, others still advocate for continuing engagement with Beijing. About 100 former U.S. officials, China experts, and business leaders sent an open letter to Trump in July 2019 expressing concern about the "growing deterioration" in U.S. relations with China. The signatories said that "although we are very troubled by Beijing's recent

18. "PM Lee Hsien Loong's Speech at the 2019 Shangri-La Dialogue," *Channel News Asia*, May 31, 2019, https://www.channelnewsasia.com/news/singapore/lee-hsien-loong-speech-2019-shangri-la-dialogue-11585954.

behavior, which requires a strong response, we also believe that many U.S. actions are contributing directly to the downward spiral of relations."

The letter signers—who included Stapleton Roy, the former U.S. ambassador to China, Indonesia, and Singapore; Susan Thornton, former acting assistant secretary of state for East Asian and Pacific affairs; and the preeminent Asia scholar Ezra Vogel—said "a successful U.S. approach to China must focus on creating enduring coalitions with other countries in support of economic and security objectives."

"Ultimately, the United States' interests are best served by restoring its ability to compete effectively in a changing world and by working alongside other nations . . . rather than by promoting a counterproductive effort to undermine and contain China's engagement in the world," the group argued.[19]

More than a few officials in the U.S. administration, even many that worked on Asia and China in previous administrations, characterize Prime Minister Lee's speech and the letter to Trump from former officials and China experts as advocating only engagement. But people who signed the letter insist that seriously mischaracterizes the letter's message. "We recognize that much more is required in the U.S. response to China," one signer says. "The fact that disengagement and decoupling [from China] would be counterproductive is only a starting point."

THE UNITED STATES AND SOUTHEAST ASIA

Washington is half a world away from Southeast Asia, which limits its ability to influence China's relations with its southern neighbors, and for a long time it has not been sure exactly how to respond to a more forceful China. This stems in part from the United States' uncertainty about what China's Southeast Asian neighbors would like beyond not wanting to take sides between Washington and Beijing. U.S. uncertainties about what Southeast Asians want feeds the region's uncertainty about and lack of confidence in the United States.

19. M. Taylor Fravel, J. Stapleton Roy, Michael D. Swaine, Susan A. Thornton, and Ezra Vogel, "China Is Not an Enemy," *Washington Post*, July 3, 2019, https://www.washingtonpost.com/opinions/making-china-a-us-enemy-is-counterproductive/2019/07/02/647d49d0-9bfa-11e9-b27f-ed2942f73d70_story.html.

Most Southeast Asia countries look to the United States to provide some sort of counterbalance to China, but they have increasing doubts about Washington's dependability, know-how, resources, and staying power. These uncertainties affect their strategic thinking and planning in their relations with Beijing. "The U.S. needs to have a long-term consistent, comprehensive, bipartisan approach to the Asia Pacific," says an ASEAN diplomat. "Countries in the region believe the U.S. will change its policy depending on who the next president is."

Broadly speaking, most Southeast Asians want the United States to remain active in the region, engaging a diversity of economic, political, security, and public diplomacy tools. They would like to strengthen their strategic relationships with Washington, but they experience varying levels of ambivalence and frustration in achieving that.

Economic growth and development are of paramount importance to all Southeast Asian countries. With the U.S. withdrawal from the Trans-Pacific Partnership (TPP), Southeast Asian officials say Washington must find new vehicles through which to deepen economic engagement, take down trade barriers, and press for rules in new sectors such as digital commerce that would ensure the free flow of information and protect consumers.

But what are the options now that Washington has effectively taken regional or multilateral trade agreements off the table saying it wants to negotiate bilateral agreements? Bilateral agreements are incredibly difficult to negotiate between a giant economy like that of the United States and a relatively small one like, say, Vietnam, which has limited options for making concessions that would excite the United States. That is precisely the reason the previous U.S. administration tried to negotiate the TPP so that concessions could be horse-traded among different partners.

With Trump very focused on U.S. deficits in goods trade with countries in Southeast Asia, one Southeast Asian official suggests that Washington "needs to tell us how we can open our markets to more U.S. products."

The Trump administration began dinging Vietnam in 2019 for its surging trade in goods surplus with the United States that reached almost $40 billion the previous year. This prompted Trump to call Vietnam "the single worst abuser" that "takes advantage of us even worse than China." U.S. trade officials told Vietnam to reduce its trade deficit by importing more goods from the United States and resolving market access challenges facing American products, implying they could be next on Trump's tariff list.[20] Vietnamese officials do not miss the irony that some of the "unfair trade barriers" U.S. officials have warned Hanoi about were resolved in the TPP, which Trump jettisoned.

At the same time, Vietnam is one country in Southeast Asia that is very interested in deepening its strategic partnership with Washington, and yet this relationship is now threatened by the administration's very narrow focus on Vietnam's trade surplus. Instead of taking advantage of Vietnam's tensions with China to boost ties with Hanoi, Washington is threatening new tariffs that could unravel the close relations built up painstakingly over the last quarter century. Beijing is undoubtedly watching this development and cheering on the China-leaning leaders in Vietnam's Communist Party and the military.

Vietnam is not alone. Most other Southeast Asian countries would also like to deepen their strategic links with the United States, but they have bumped into differing levels of ambivalence and frustration in doing so.

Several Southeast Asian officials suggested that Washington ought to focus more on Southeast Asia's smaller countries, Laos and Cambodia. Some in Cambodia might welcome a bit of balance from Washington amid Phnom Penh's near-total dependence on Beijing, particularly as the country prepares for a transition from long-serving prime minister Hun Sen.

"No matter how big or small the country, they each have one voice in ASEAN. When one country opposes [a measure or statement], you don't have consensus," a Southeast Asian diplomat says, alluding to Cambodia's frequent blocking of ASEAN's consensus on its South China Sea statements. Even when a country is small, you must pay attention to it because of the competition between the United States and China, he says.

Infrastructure

Washington cannot compete with Beijing on financing or building infrastructure projects. But U.S. government plans under way to combine several government agencies and boost spending on infrastructure projects to $60 billion to counter China's increasing influence is a helpful

20. Doug Palmer, "Lighthizer Warns Vietnam over Trade Deficit with U.S.," *Politico*, July 29, 2019, https://www.politico.com/story/2019/07/29/lighthizer-vietnam-trade-deficit-1439780.

first step.[21] The Build Act, signed into law in late 2018, will establish a new agency, the U.S. International Development Finance Corporation (DFC), by expanding roles previously played primarily by the Overseas Private Investment Corporation. The DFC was slated to open for business in October 2019, but it did not get off to an auspicious start. It was postponed due to delays in Congress approving annual funding measures.

Washington's goal in establishing the DFC is to respond to China's BRI and China's increasing economic influence in developing countries. The DFC will work to promote private investment as an alternative to China's state-directed model of investment. The DFC will have more tools to provide investment support and more funding capacity with its cap doubled to $60 billion.[22]

Many in the United States view China's BRI as predatory and corrupt, but most in Southeast Asia do not view it that way. Despite its problems, they see the BRI as providing much-needed infrastructure and financing. "I detect in ASEAN circles a view that China's seeming honesty about recalibrating the BRI, as articulated by Xi Jinping in the second BRI forum, should be taken seriously," says Joseph Liow of RSIS.

Washington will have to accept that the BRI is very competitive and quite attractive to many countries in the region. Some Southeast Asian officials argue that the United States should consider joining China's BRI to have a voice inside to press for transparency, rein in corruption, and ensure that projects are environmentally friendly and economically sustainable. Joining might provide opportunities for U.S. construction, engineering, and consulting firms to win some contracts, particularly in environmental and energy projects.

Others would like to see the Washington join the Asia Infrastructure Investment Bank, the Chinese-established development bank. They argue that working with the United Kingdom, Australia, and others, the United States could help dilute China's voting power and press the bank to boost its governance standards and lobby for higher environmental and labor standards.

---

21. Josh Zumbrun and Siobhan Hughes, "To Counter China, U.S. Looks to Invest Billions More Overseas," *Wall Street Journal*, August 31, 2018, https://www.wsj.com/articles/to-counter-china-u-s-looks-to-invest-billions-more-overseas-1535728206.

22. "BUILD Act: Frequently Asked Questions about the New U.S. International Development Finance Corporation," *Congressional Research Service*, January 15, 2019, https://fas.org/sgp/crs/misc/R45461.pdf.

Some of the initiatives that Secretary of State Mike Pompeo outlined in a July 2018 speech on the America's Indo-Pacific economic vision focused on infrastructure. One was a digital connectivity and cybersecurity partnership that would be kicked off with a $25 million initial investment to improve digital connectivity and boost opportunities for U.S. technology exports.

A second initiative is called Asia EDGE, short for Enhancing Development and Growth through Energy, which was slated to spend $50 million in its first year to help Indo-Pacific partners import, produce, store, and deploy energy resources. The third initiative Pompeo listed was infrastructure under which the United States would promote connectivity that is "physically secure, financially viable, and socially responsible."[23]

The Center for Strategic and International Studies released a study in 2019 reporting on the findings of a bipartisan infrastructure task force of experts that outlined a strategy suggesting ways in which the United States could play a critical role in supporting the buildout of the global infrastructure. The group was cochaired by former U.S. trade representative Charlene Barshefsky and former national security adviser Stephen Hadley.

One of the task force's recommendations was that the United States should work with allies and partners to be a force multiplier by cooperating with the multilateral development banks, the G20 grouping, and the Asia-Pacific Economic Cooperation forum to develop infrastructure projects. Another recommendation was that the United States should lead in the digital space by promoting American strengths in information and communications technology (ICT) infrastructure to prevent other countries, presumably China, from monopolizing this space and dictating the standards and rules governing it.

The report suggested that the United States support the development of infrastructure using cleaner-burning natural gas, wind, solar, and other clean energy technology. Another key recommendation was that the United States leverage private-sector financing to move more money off the sidelines into the global infrastructure effort.

---

23. Michael R. Pompeo, "Sec. Pompeo Remarks on 'America's Indo-Pacific Economic Vision,'" U.S. Mission to ASEAN (speech, Indo-Pacific Business Forum, Washington, DC, July 30, 2018), https://asean.usmission.gov/sec-pompeo-remarks-on-americas-indo-pacific-economic-vision/.

The study said the United States should help boost the capacity of officials in developing countries and urge them away from automatically picking the lowest bid and instead promote the benefits of employing life-cycle cost analysis and objective criteria for making procurement decisions.[24]

Mekong River

As tensions rise over the environmental challenges of dam building on the Mekong, security analysts fret that the river will emerge as the next potential flashpoint between China and Southeast Asia and Beijing and Washington, much like what is happening in the South China Sea.

The United States seemed to step up its interest in the Mekong River in 2019 and sought to reinvigorate the U.S.-backed Lower Mekong Initiative, which had languished in recent years. Secretary of State Pompeo hosted a meeting of the organization in Bangkok in August that included representatives of the five ASEAN Mekong countries. His welcoming remarks reflected some of the strongest U.S. criticism to date of China's actions in the Mekong.

"We see a spree of upstream dam building which concentrates control over downstream flows," Pompeo said. "The river has been at its lowest level in a decade—a problem linked to China's decision to shut off water upstream," he said. The secretary was referring to the severe El Niño–induced drought facing the Mekong countries in mid-2019 and China's decision to store water by shutting off the flow from some of the 10 dams it has built on its section of the Mekong.

"China has plans to blast and dredge riverbeds," Pompeo continued, alluding to a proposal by a Chinese company to blast rocks in the Mekong near the Thai city of Chiang Rai, which would allow 500-ton vessels to travel from southern China to Luang Prabang in central Laos. Environmentalists are worried this would seriously impact the river's ecosystem.

Pompeo also charged that "China operated extra-territorial river patrols." This was a reference to China sending police patrol boats down the Mekong about once a month into Myanmar and Lao territories. Thailand

24. Matthew P. Goodman and Daniel F. Runde, "The Higher Road: Forging a U.S. Strategy for the Global Infrastructure Challenge," *CSIS Briefs*, April 2019, https://csis-prod.s3.amazonaws.com/s3fs-public/publication/190423_Hadley%20et%20al_HigherRoads_Brief_WEB_0.pdf.

so far has refused to allow the patrol boats to continue into the Thai section of the Mekong. Beijing refers to them as joint patrols because one or two police from each country participate in the roughly 300-mile mission. The patrols were established as a show of force after 13 Chinese sailors were killed by a drug-smuggling operation in 2011. The penetration of Chinese vessels deep into mainland Southeast Asia prompt longer-term security concerns among officials of countries along the Mekong.

"And we see a push to craft new Beijing-directed rules to govern the river, thereby weakening the Mekong River Commission," Pompeo said, alluding to the Lancang-Mekong Cooperation organization China established in 2016. It includes all five Mekong countries and China but pointedly excludes participation from countries like the United States and Japan and is seen by many as a direct rival of the Mekong River Commission, which excludes China but cooperates with Washington and Tokyo.[25]

"In addition, criminal groups—some active in casinos and special economic zones—are using the Mekong as their major artery to traffic drugs, wildlife, and even human beings," Pompeo said. The U.S. Treasury Department in 2018 slapped sanctions on the Chinese owner and several top executives of the company operating the Kings Romans Casino and special economic zone along the Mekong in northern Laos for drug, wildlife, and human smuggling.[26]

Pompeo announced several new U.S.-backed initiatives for the Mekong. One initiative is the Japan-U.S. Mekong Power Partnership, which will help develop regional electricity grids. Washington made an initial commitment of nearly $30 million, but much more will be needed.

A second program would support law enforcement efforts to counter transnational crime and trafficking, support victims of trafficking in persons, stop financial flows for wildlife traffickers, and counter methamphetamine and other drug activity in the tri-border area between Laos, Thailand, and Myanmar. This project, to which Washington would

---

25. Michael R. Pompeo, "Opening Remarks at the Lower Mekong Initiative Ministerial," U.S. Department of State, speech, Centara Grand, Bangkok, Thailand, August 1, 2019, https://www.state.gov/opening-remarks-at-the-lower-mekong-initiative-ministerial/.
26. "Treasury Sanctions the Zhao Wei Transnational Criminal Organization," U.S. Department of the Treasury, news release, January 30, 2018, https://home.treasury.gov/news/press-releases/sm0272.

provide an initial $14 million, was intended to support anti-crime efforts backed by Australia.

On the sidelines of the ASEAN summits in Bangkok in August 2019, Pompeo said Washington would hold an Indo-Pacific conference aimed at strengthening governance of transboundary rivers, including bolstering support for "a transparent, rules-based approach" to the Mekong.

Pompeo added that the United States would roll out initiatives and more funding to help Mekong nations in the infrastructure, energy, and digital sectors at a business forum at the time of the East Asia Summit as well as an ASEAN leaders summit in Bangkok in November. In the end, neither Trump, nor Vice President Mike Pence, nor Pompeo attended the summit, and since Congress had not approved the needed spending measures, Pompeo's earlier Mekong pledges were left dangling in limbo.

In August, the U.S. secretary announced that Washington, in cooperation with South Korea would fund a new project that would use satellite imagery to assess patterns of flooding and drought on the Mekong.

Pompeo also said he supported Thailand's ACMECS scheme under which Bangkok plans to set up a regional infrastructure fund with its Mekong neighbors.[27] The goal is to provide these countries an alternative to turning to China for financing. In addition to receiving contributions from supporting countries like the United States, the fund will also raise funds for projects through stock and bond markets. One project touted by the Thais is a regional power grid that could, for example, send surplus power from Laos to a power-hungry area such as central Vietnam.

The initiatives Pompeo announced for U.S. support for the Mekong were a good start, but the $44 million he pledged was only a drop in the bucket compared to the $400 million China pledged just for assistance for small and medium-sized enterprises along the river in 2017, not to mention the billions of dollars China is lending Laos and Cambodia for dam construction. For Washington to be taken seriously in Southeast Asia as a possible balance to China, senior U.S. leaders will need to attend regional meeting regularly and Washington will need to find vehicles through which to kick in substantially more funding.

27. Pompeo, "Opening Remarks at the Lower Mekong Initiative Ministerial."

There are at least two other Mekong issues on which the international community, including the United States, should try to help: First, it should explore ways to mitigate the threat of the dams that China has supported in Laos and Cambodia and will build or finance in the future on two of the most economically vibrant areas in the lower Mekong: the Tonle Sap in Cambodia and the Mekong Delta in southern Vietnam. Would it be possible to allow more water through the dams during the dry season, more silt to flow especially during the rainy season, and ease the movement of fish, particularly during times the fish migrate for spawning?

Second, schemes must be devised to support Laos in finding alternatives to hydropower dams, particularly as Thailand is less interested in buying hydropower as its population becomes more concerned about environmental challenges. One suggestion is that Laos could make up much of the lost income through solar and wind farms.

South China Sea

The South China Sea saw a new level of tension unfold in 2019 between China and two Southeast Asia claimants over the exploration and exploitation of oil and gas reserves. In May, a large Chinese coast guard ship began challenging vessels contracted by Malaysia to service a drilling rig exploring for hydrocarbons off the coast of Sarawak State. The Chinese vessel's maneuvers continued over the next two weeks as it sought to harass Malaysia's drilling operations before finally returning to its port in China's Hainan Province.

But by June 16, the same ship began operating in the waters off Vietnam's southern coast, where vessels contracted by Vietnam were drilling an offshore well. When the rig refused to stop its work, China sent in another ship to begin conducting its own survey activities off the coast of Vietnam, ignoring the fact that it was in an area over which international laws give Vietnam undeniable rights. Vietnam responded by sending its own coast guard ships to protect its rig and track the Chinese survey vessel. The showdown created a potentially dangerous situation in which an accident could occur that could lead to a military altercation.

During this standoff, the U.S. State Department issued several strong statements condemning China for "continuing interference with Vietnam's longstanding oil and gas activities," saying "it calls into question China's commitment . . . to the peaceful resolution of maritime disputes."[28]

China's goal appeared to be to force Malaysia and Vietnam to end their offshore energy work in the South China Sea even on their own continental shelves. China is convinced the resources within its claimed nine-dash line belong to it. "Beijing until recently saw its position as undermined by other South China Sea littoral states and their offshore energy partnerships with multinationals," says Collin Koh Swee Lean, a South China Sea expert at RSIS in Singapore. "Therefore, China seeks to prevent or forestall other South China Sea littoral states, either unilaterally or with foreign partners, from undertaking such activities," Koh says. "So far we've observed China embarking on a multipronged effort to achieve that."

Trying to stop China from blocking its Southeast Asian neighbors from exploiting the resources on their continental shelves will require some tough diplomatic measures from the United States and its international partners. The South China Sea and East China Sea Sanctions Act introduced in the U.S. Senate in mid-2019 would require, if passed into law, that Washington seize the financial assets based in the United States and deny or revoke U.S. visas for anyone engaged in "actions or policies that threaten the peace, security, or stability" in areas of the South China Sea contested by one or more Southeast Asian countries.[29] (The problem with these sanctions is that China could declare that activities by other claimants are undermining peace, security, and stability in the region, some analysts note.)

The Trump administration routinely preforms freedom of navigation operations (FONOPs) in the South China Sea and China responds by sending planes and sea vessels to warn the U.S. warship to leave. "FONOPs are good but they're not enough," says a Southeast Asian diplomat. "FONOPS don't help change the strategic landscape. They

28. Greg B. Poling and Murray Hiebert, "Stop the Bully in the South China Sea," *Wall Street Journal*, August 28, 2019, https://www.wsj.com/articles/stop-the-bully-in-the-south-china-sea-11567033378?mod=searchresults&page=1&pos=1.

29. South China Sea and East China Sea Sanctions Act of 2019, S.1634, 116th Cong. (2019–2020), https://www.congress.gov/bill/116th-congress/senate-bill/1634/text (accessed September 7, 2019); Owen Churchill, "U.S. Senate Bill Proposes Sanctions for Involvement in 'Illegal' Activities in the South and East China Seas," *South China Morning Post*, May 23, 2019, https://www.scmp.com/news/china/diplomacy/article/3011441/us-senate-bill-proposes-sanctions-involvement-illegal.

don't stop [China's] militarization of its islands." (To be sure, FONOPs do not stop other claimants from expanding their outposts on features they occupy either, which the Chinese believe constitutes militarization.)

"The U.S. needs a more comprehensive approach. The legal aspects are important," the ASEAN official says, urging Washington to put more emphasis on the 2016 arbitral tribunal ruling on the South China Sea, in a case brought by the Philippines, which ruled overwhelmingly against Beijing's claims. He also suggested the United States should ratify the United Nations Convention on the Law of the Sea (UNCLOS) to give Washington more credibility in standing up to Beijing.

Political and Security Cooperation

Security engagement has been one of the robust areas of U.S. engagement with Southeast Asia in recent years. Senior security officials frequently visit the countries facing pressure in the South China Sea, especially Vietnam, the Philippines, and Indonesia.

Under the Maritime Security Initiative, the Pentagon has provided capacity building and patrol vessels to bolster the ability of these countries to respond to China's brazen moves in the South China Sea. Southeast Asian officials on the rim of the disputed sea hope that Washington will continue to provide training and equipment to boost their awareness about what is going on in the South China Sea.

Because Southeast Asian nations remain uncertain about how important the region is under the FOIP strategy, several ASEAN leaders suggest that Trump should invite the group to come visit him for a summit in the United States (similar to what his predecessor did by inviting these officials to Sunnylands, California).

A decade ago, the threat of Southeast Asian countries pivoting increasingly toward the United States was a threat hanging over China's activist policies toward its neighbors. That is not the case in 2019 as the United States is viewed as distracted, inwardly focused, protectionist, and often missing. Regional powers like Japan and India can provide Southeast Asia only a limited hedge without the United States more fully engaged. Washington's distractions no doubt convince Beijing that there is little likelihood that the United States will suddenly appear over the horizon to support its Southeast Asian friends to stand up to China.

To challenge that perception, the Trump administration (and its successors) will have to figure out and articulate what role Southeast Asia will play in U.S. foreign policy calculations and how the region fits into Washington's FOIP strategy. The economic dynamism and strategic location between the Pacific and Indian Oceans warrant Southeast Asia being defined as a key pillar among Washington's international priorities. To support the region as it faces a rising and more assertive China, the United States must remain an actively engaged partner that shows up, brings some resources, and rewrites the perception that it is often unreliable and missing in action.

INDEX

ABOUT THE AUTHOR

Murray Hiebert is a senior associate of the Southeast Asia Program at the Center for Strategic and International Studies (CSIS) in Washington, DC. Earlier, he was a journalist in the China bureau of *The Wall Street Journal* and in Washington for the *Far Eastern Economic Review*. Before that, he was based in Thailand, Vietnam, Malaysia, and Singapore for the *Far Eastern Economic Review*. He is the author of two books on Vietnam, *Chasing the Tigers* and *Vietnam Notebook*.

ABOUT CSIS

The Center for Strategic and International Studies (CSIS) is a bipartisan, nonprofit policy research organization dedicated to advancing practical ideas to address the world's greatest challenges.

Thomas J. Pritzker was named chairman of the CSIS Board of Trustees in 2015, succeeding former U.S. Senator Sam Nunn (D-GA). Founded in 1962, CSIS is led by John J. Hamre, who has served as president and chief executive officer since 2000.

CSIS's purpose is to define the future of national security. We are guided by a distinct set of values—nonpartisanship, independent thought, innovative thinking, cross-disciplinary scholarship, integrity and professionalism, and talent development. CSIS's values work in concert toward the goal of making real-world impact.

CSIS scholars bring their policy expertise, judgment, and robust networks to their research, analysis, and recommendations. We organize conferences, publish, lecture, and make media appearances that aim to increase the knowledge, awareness, and salience of policy issues with relevant stakeholders and the interested public.

CSIS has impact when our research helps to inform the decision-making of key policymakers and the thinking of key influencers. We work toward a vision of a safer and more prosperous world.

CSIS is ranked the number one think tank in the United States by the University of Pennsylvania's annual think tank report.

CSIS does not take specific policy positions; accordingly, all views expressed herein should be understood to be solely those of the author(s).

CPSIA information can be obtained
at www.ICGtesting.com
Printed in the USA
LVHW111320061020
668096LV00001B/1